The Equity Risk Premium ◢

Essays and Explorations

William N. Goetzmann

Roger G. Ibbotson

Yale School of Management

OXFORD
UNIVERSITY PRESS

2006

OXFORD

UNIVERSITY PRESS

Oxford University Press, Inc., publishes works that further
Oxford University's objective of excellence
in research, scholarship, and education.

Oxford   New York
Auckland   Cape Town   Dar es Salaam   Hong Kong   Karachi
Kuala Lumpur   Madrid   Melbourne   Mexico City   Nairobi
New Delhi   Shanghai   Taipei   Toronto

With offices in
Argentina   Austria   Brazil   Chile   Czech Republic   France   Greece
Guatemala   Hungary   Italy   Japan   Poland   Portugal   Singapore
South Korea   Switzerland   Thailand   Turkey   Ukraine   Vietnam

Published by Oxford University Press, Inc.
198 Madison Avenue, New York, New York 10016
www.oup.com

Oxford is a registered trademark of Oxford University Press

Library of Congress Cataloging-in-Publication Data

Goetzmann, William N.
    The equity risk premium : essays and explorations / William N. Goetzmann
  and Roger G. Ibbotson.
      p. cm.
  Includes bibliographical references and index.
  ISBN-13 978-0-19-514814-5
  ISBN 0-19-514814-2
  1. Stocks. 2. Risk. 3. Investments. I. Ibbotson, Roger G. II. Title.
  HG4661.G64 2004
  332.63′22—dc22

                               2004050076

9 8 7 6 5 4 3 2 1

Printed in the United States of America
on acid-free paper

To Zoë and Mariko with love. To my coauthors in these various essays, with great thanks.

W.N.G.

To my family with love, including my wife, Jody L. Sindelar, who is also a Yale economics professor; and my children, Tyler and Timothy, who both have an interest in finance. To my firm, Ibbotson Associates, and my universities, Yale School of Management and the University of Chicago—thanks for the inspiration, data, research environment, and encouragement throughout the last quarter century.

R.G.I.

Contents

Contributors *ix*

Introduction: Opening Remarks and Motivation *3*

Part I   *The Lessons of History*

1   History and the Equity Risk Premium   *25*

2   Stocks, Bonds, Bills, and Inflation: Year-by-Year Historical
Returns (1926–1974)   *41*

3   A New Historical Database for the NYSE 1815 to 1925:
Performance and Predictability   *73*

4   The United States Market Wealth Portfolio   *107*

5   World Wealth: U.S. and Foreign Market Values
and Returns   *138*

Part II   *Demand, Supply, and Building Block Forecasting Methods*

6   How to Forecast Long-Run Asset Returns   *175*

7   The Demand for Capital Market Returns: A New
Equilibrium Theory   *184*

8   The Supply of Capital Market Returns   *201*

9   Building the Future from the Past   *212*

10   Long-Run Stock Returns: Participating in the
Real Economy   *214*

Part III   *Simulating and Forecasting*

11   Stocks, Bonds, Bills, and Inflation: Simulations of the
Future (1976–2000)   *237*

12   Predictions of the Past and Forecasts for the Future:
1976–2025   *266*

13   Short-Horizon Inputs and Long-Horizon Portfolio Choice   *270*

Part IV   *Survivorship and Selection Bias*

14   Survival   *283*

15   Survivorship Bias in Performance Studies   *307*

16   Global Stock Markets in the 20th Century   *335*

17   Re-Emerging Markets   *365*

Part V   *Predicting Variations*

18   The Dow Theory: William Peter Hamilton's Track
Record Reconsidered   *407*

19   Patterns in Three Centuries of Stock Market Prices   *431*

20   Bootstrapping Tests of Long-Term Stock Market Efficiency   *454*

21   Testing the Predictive Power of Dividend Yields   *473*

22   A Longer Look at Dividend Yields   *494*

23   Does Asset Allocation Policy Explain 40, 90, or 100 Percent of Performance?   *521*

Suggested Readings   *535*
Index   *539*

Contributors

Stephen J. Brown
David S. Loeb Professor of Finance
New York University

Peng Chen
Chief Investment Officer
Ibbotson Associates

Jeffrey J. Diermeier
President & CEO
CFA Institute

Franklin R. Edwards
Arthur F. Burns Professor of Free and Competitive Enterprise
Columbia University

Carol L. Fall

Philippe Jorion
Professor of Finance
University of California, Irvine

Paul D. Kaplan
Director of Research
Morningstar, Inc.

Alok Kumar
Assistant Professor of Finance
Notre Dame University

Kathryn S. Love

Liang Peng
Assistant Professor of Finance
University of Cincinnati

Stephen A. Ross
Franco Modigliani Professor of Finance and Economics
MIT

Laurence B. Siegel
Director of Investment Policy Research
Ford Foundation

Rex A. Sinquefield
Co-Chairman
Dimensional Fund Advisors

These essays have been revised slightly for inclusion in this volume. The authors gratefully acknowledge the editors and publishers of the journals and books in which the original essays appeared.

"History and the Equity Risk Premium," also appearing in *Handbook of Investments: Equity Risk Premium,* North-Holland, 2006.

"Stocks, Bonds, Bills and Inflation: Year-by-Year Historical Returns (1926–1974)," originally appeared in *Journal of Business,* January 1976, pp. 11–47. Reprinted with kind permission from the University of Chicago Press.

"A New Historical Database for the NYSE 1815 to 1925: Performance and Predictability," originally appeared in *The Journal of Financial Markets,* March 2001. Reprinted with kind permission from Elsevier Science.

"The United States Market Wealth Portfolio," originally appeared in *Journal of Portfolio Management,* Fall 1979. Reprinted with kind permission from Institutional Investor.

"World Wealth: U.S. and Foreign Market Values and Returns," originally appeared in *Journal of Portfolio Management,* Fall 1985. Reprinted with kind permission from Institutional Investor.

"How to Forecast Long Run Asset Returns," originally appeared in *Investment Management Review,* September/October 1988.

"The Demand for Capital Market Returns: A New Equilibrium Theory," copyright 1984, Association for Investment Management and Research. Reproduced and republished from the *Financial Analysts Journal.* Reprinted with kind permission from the Association for Investment Management and Research.

"The Supply of Capital Market Returns," copyright 1984, Association for Investment Management and Research. Reproduced and republished from the *Financial Analysts Journal.* Reprinted with kind permission from the Association for Investment Management and Research.

"Building the Future from the Past," originally published in *TIAA/CREF Investment Forum,* June 2002, Vol. 6, No. 2. Reprinted with kind permission from TIAA/CREF.

"Long-Run Stock Returns: Participating in the Real Economy," copyright 2003, Association for Investment Management and Research. Reproduced and republished from the *Financial Analysts Journal.* Reprinted with kind permission from the Association for Investment Management and Research.

"Stocks, Bonds, Bills, and Inflation: Simulations of the Future (1976–2000)," originally appeared in *Journal of Business,* January 1976, Vol. 49, No. 1, pp. 11–47. Reprinted with kind permission from the University of Chicago Press.

"Predictions of the Past and Forecasts of the Future." Originally published by Ibbotson Associates, 1999. Reprinted with kind permission of Ibbotson Associates.

"Short-Horizon Inputs and Long-Horizon Choice," originally appeared in *Journal of Portfolio Management,* Summer 1994, Vol. 20, No. 4, pp. 76–81. Reprinted with kind permission from Institutional Investor.

"Survival" originally appeared in *Journal of Finance,* July 1995, Vol. 50, No. 3, pp. 853–73. Reprinted with kind permission from Blackwell Publishers.

"Survivorship Bias in Performance Studies," originally appeared in *Review of Financial Studies,* 1992, Vol. 5, No. 4, pp. 553–80. Reprinted with kind permission from Oxford University Press.

"Global Stock Markets in the Twentieth Century," originally appeared in *Journal of Finance,* June 1999, Vol. 54, No. 3, pp. 953–80. Reprinted with kind permission from Blackwell Publishers.

"Re-emerging Markets," originally appeared in the *Journal of Financial and Quantitative Analysis,* March 1999, pp. 1–32. Reprinted with kind permission from the University of Washington.

"The Dow Theory: William Peter Hamilton's Track Record Reconsidered," originally published in the *Journal of Finance,* August 1998. Reprinted with kind permission from Blackwell Publishers.

"Patterns in Three Centuries of Stock Market Prices," originally published in the *Journal of Business,* April 1993, Vol. 66, No. 2, pp. 249–70. Reprinted with kind permission from the University of Chicago Press.

"Bootstrapping Test of Long-Term Stock Market Efficiency," adapted from Yale School of Management Working Paper, 1991.

"Testing the Predictive Power of Dividend Yields," originally published in the *Journal of Finance,* June 1993, Vol. 48, No. 2, pp. 663–79. Reprinted with kind permission from Blackwell Publishers.

"A Longer Look at Dividend Yields," originally published in the *Journal of Business,* October 1995, Vol. 68, No. 4, pp. 483–508. Reprinted with kind permission from the University of Chicago Press.

"Does Asset Allocation Policy Explain 40%, 90%, or 100% of Performance?", copyright 2000, Association for Investment Management and Research. Reproduced and republished from *Financial Analysts Journal,* with kind permission from the Association for Investment Management and Research.

The Equity Risk Premium

The equity risk premium is commonly viewed as the extra return needed to induce investors to risk their money in the stock market, rather than opting for the safe haven of government bonds. It is simple theory based on common sense. Economic risk-taking must be rewarded, or else no rational person would prefer a gamble over a sure thing. Although reasonable people may disagree about whether equity investing is a gamble and whether government securities are a sure thing, the principle of the equity premium is the main reason to invest in the stock market.

The movement toward equity investing is among the most significant trends of the past two or three decades in the United States, driven in large measure by the empirical analysis of the equity risk premium. Long before the fever of high-tech investing attracted speculators in record numbers to their trading screens in search of overnight profits, individuals and institutions had been shifting increasingly toward equities throughout the 1980s and 1990s. Perhaps some of this reallocation was motivated directly or indirectly by studies in this book. The analysis of the historical equity premium in the United States in articles such as Ibbotson and Sinquefield (1976) made it clear to academia and to the investing public that, over the long term, equities yielded considerably higher returns than bonds.

Events of the last few years have now raised public doubt about the equity premium. Although equity investment is predicated on reward for risk, few investors were psychologically prepared for the dramatic downdraft in the markets that occurred at the beginning of the new century. The current situation has even led popular economic forecasters to suggest that the equity premium may be dead for the foreseeable future, predicting that bonds will beat stocks over the next 10 years. We do not agree with this pessimistic assessment. We believe the analysis in this volume is as relevant today as it was at the height of the Internet craze. Just as the numbers at that time were telling those who would listen that there is no free lunch in the market and that annual returns of 20% per year were the exception rather than the rule, now they are telling us that the probability of a negative equity premium of the next decade is a relatively small one, despite the current soul-searching of Wall Street. Recall, for example, how the fever of enthusiasm about the possibilities of the Internet led to media speculation about the existence of a "New Economy." Now discussion has abruptly flipped to whether the equity risk premium is shrinking—or even has disappeared. From a historical perspective, neither extreme is justified. In the parlance of "behavioral finance," they are *both* based on the "representativeness" heuristic—the belief that recent or immediate experience can tell us more about the world than the longer view.

Now, more than ever, it is important to take a comprehensive, dispassionate look at what we know about the long-term behavior of the stock market. The current volume brings together a number of research studies that the two of us have conducted over the past 30 years or so. These studies, performed in close association with a number of other researchers and coauthors, were designed to increase our understanding of the equity risk premium; to answer such questions as how large it is, whether it varies through time, whether it can be predicted, whether it holds true for markets outside the United States, how it relates to inflation, how to use the premium for market risk assessment, how the survival of markets affects our premium measurement, and a host of other essentially practical investment questions.

◣ History as a Guide

Nearly all of these studies are based on historical data or take a historical perspective. Throughout both of our careers in financial economics we have found that history teaches vital lessons. The historical perspective expands the analyst's horizon far beyond the immediate, overcoming the emotional heuristics that inevitably govern our discussion of current events. Studying and using long-term data imposes an intellectual discipline that even the authors of this book must struggle at times to maintain when concerns about current events seem to direct us otherwise.

The current fears and doubts about the equity premium make it all the more important to review and reinterpret what we have learned from our empirical studies. History gives us a crucial context for interpretation of recent events. It allows us to take the measure of recent booms and busts with the yardstick of past capital markets, and to assess the rational probabilities of either one's becoming permanent. It is ironic that 30 years ago, when the earliest of the studies in this volume first appeared, the equity premium over the preceding decade was near zero. Then as now, academic analysis leaned against the wind, extrapolating from a historical experience that looked wildly optimistic in view of recent investment outcomes. Yet look what happened. The 1976 Ibbotson and Sinquefield study turned out to be a slight underestimate of the relative performance of stocks over bonds, even taking into consideration the poor experience of the last few years.

The most basic message of this book is that history matters. This remains as true today as it did 30 years ago. However, as researchers, we have continued to learn a great deal about how to use financial history to answer research questions. For example, some of the most exciting developments in this volume are the various computer-intensive techniques used for simulating historical capital market returns. One approach, called "boostrapping," uses actual history to create "pseudo-histories"—events in time that never happened, but that nevertheless allow us to assess the probability of their occurrence in the future. It is the econometric analogue to the new "virtual history" school of research pioneered by Oxford historian Niall Ferguson. We share with the virtual historians the conviction that the single, historical path we have encountered in the U.S. capital markets over the centuries cannot be fully understood without considering what other outcomes might have been possible.

Another key historical theme extending though many of the articles in this volume is that "vanished" financial history has as much to teach us as recorded financial history. Although both of us began our careers collecting and analyzing U.S. stock market data, we both came to suspect that the United States may not be entirely representative of the expected future performance of equity investing. After all, the United States is the winner in the contest of global capital markets, but only, perhaps, by virtue of the fact that two world wars went our way, and that Marxist revolutions deprived the world of two potentially dynamic emerging markets in the early 20th century. The only way to explore this issue is to collect more data; however, records from the losing markets of the last century are harder to come by. Yet once collected, the information has the potential to reveal what can go wrong with a market, as well as to present a more realistic picture of risk. Ignoring the alternative market paths can obviously affect the assessment of the equity risk premium. How to adjust for this survival effect has become an interesting current research question in the field. Our approach, as we show in this volume, continues to be "financial archaeology." At the International Center for Finance at the Yale School of Management, we maintain an active program of sifting through the archives of historical capital markets to bring them into the research light for comparison to the data from the ex post success stories. This archival research has provided data for several of the research papers in this volume.

Can history help forecast shifts in the equity premium? That engaging question is yet another variation on the role historical data play in equity premium studies, and is the topic of a number of the essays in this volume. At a fundamental level, it comes down to the question of whether history repeats itself in a predictable manner. Is there deep structure to the market, and can our statistical techniques uncover it? If it exists, could it help investors avoid crashes and exploit booms? We present what we have learned about using history to predict the premium's ebb and flow, and discuss the mixed evidence on this question.

◣ Compilation of Articles

This book is a compilation of published articles, most of which appeared previously in academic journals. They were written originally for an academic audience, but they are also accessible to the more general reader interested in the financial markets. The preparation of this volume has given us a chance to further reflect on the research and to tie earlier results together in a way that is meaningful to the question of the equity premium. We have added considerable new commentary and in some cases updated the empirical results to include recent experience. We have also sought to include new insights from some of our professional colleagues, and to relate these to our own research results. The equity premium continues to be a hot topic for research, and a number of academic researchers have contributed significantly to this field. We wish to express our appreciation to them for their willingness to share their insights, data, and analyses with us through the years. It is particularly rewarding to find that the academic debate on the equity premium has been as collegial and professional as it has been passionate. With very few exceptions, academic disagreements have been conducted in a positive spirit of common concern. Although we may sometimes disagree with one another in financial economics, we maintain high respect for our colleagues' research and intentions. Perhaps this is what has kept the field so productive and facilitated research that has meaning beyond the academy.

We owe an unusual level of gratitude to our coauthors. As you will see, virtually all the articles in this book were written in association with other scholars, whose efforts in many cases far exceeded our own. This book is as much their work as it is ours, and the ideas and insights for the articles have been shared property from the very beginning. In particular, many of Will Goetzmann's articles are joint work with Stephen A. Ross, Stephen J. Brown, and Philippe Jorion, and they grew out of constant conversations, computer programs, and manuscripts exchanged between Yale, MIT, NYU, and UC Irvine over the years. Joint work published in this volume with Alok Kumar, Liang Peng, and Franklin Edwards was also deeply rewarding. Roger Ibbotson's coauthors include the initial work with Rex Sinquefield, several works with Laurence B. Siegel, and current work with Peng Chen. Other coauthors include Jeffrey J. Diermeier, Paul D. Kaplan, Carol Fall, and Kathryn S. Love. Their contributions are deeply appreciated. Roger owes special thanks to Jim Licato, Mike Barad, and many others at Ibbotson Associates for assisting in making so much updated information available. Both of us particularly appreciate the efforts of Eli Levy, Tanisha Bolt, Felicia Ballard, and Mary Ann Nelson for facilitating the production of this book. We would also like to thank Faith Middleton, the host of Connecticut Public Radio's *The Smart Investor.* Our conversations with Faith and the callers to the program over the years convinced us that the material in this volume remains important to investors seeking answers to the fundamental question of how to save for the future.

The volume is divided into five sections. Part I, "The Lessons of History," presents the essential argument of the book—that the historical information about capital markets is a crucial foundation for estimating the equity premium. Part II, "Demand, Supply, and Building Block Forecasting Methods," explores the fundamental economic drivers of the equity premium, and also puts historical measures to use in estimating the expected returns for securities and asset classes. In Part III, "Simulating and Forecasting," we show how bootstrapping and simulation procedures can be used to create realistic assessments of future capital market outcomes. Part IV, "Survivorship and Selection Bias," focuses on the crucial question of whether the measures of the equity premium are biased by a focus on winners. Finally, Part V examines the evidence for the predictability of the equity premium. We hope the reader will enjoy the voyage through our research on this important topic and will find the results useful.

▶ Major Concepts and Roadmap Through the Book

The "equity risk premium" is the title and topic of this book. Yet the term is used in many different contexts and with varying definitions. In this opening section, we define some of the terms, clarify a few of the concepts, and link the basic themes that extend through the collection of articles comprising this book.

What Is the Equity Risk Premium?

Let us start with a definition: The *equity risk premium* is the expected return of the stock market minus the expected return of a riskless bond. This seems straightforward enough, but it needs more precision to put it into practice. What definition of the stock market is appropriate? What riskless bond should we use? Do we measure the arithmetic difference between stock and bond expected returns or the difference of the geometric returns? Over what horizon is our expectation? Although we will provide measures of the equity risk premium that incorporate answers to these questions, there is no one answer, but only answers that seem more appropriate in certain contexts.

One of the areas of great confusion is in the term "expected" equity risk premium. We do not usually specify "expected," as it is implied by the definition. However, we will often measure "realized" equity risk premiums, usually as an indication of what might be "expected" in the future. Since an equity risk premium is expected, it is by its very nature usually unobservable. An important number that is never observed is ripe for varying opinions and fascinating discussions. The concept is at a level of abstraction, despite the steady stream of "realized" equity risk premiums that we do observe, over various markets, time periods, geographic locations, and so on.

Why Is the Equity Risk Premium So Important?

Since stocks are much riskier than bonds, the equity risk premium has to be high enough to induce risk-averse investors to invest in stocks. Some investors have to hold equities, and the equity risk premium is the premium that they can expect to earn. However, by its nature this equity risk premium is not guaranteed, for it is only an expectation or average. It is the fact that realizations are so volatile that leads to the premium in the first place. This high volatility also makes the equity risk premium very difficult to estimate or predict.

The equity risk premium is also important since it is at the very core of so much financial theory. The equity risk premium can be used in three quite different theoretical contexts. First, from the investor's point of view, it is the expected excess return of equities over bonds. Second, from the corporation's point of view, it figures into the cost of equity capital and consequently into the firm's weighted average cost of capital. Third, from the valuation point of view, it figures into the discount rate that is used in calculations of present value. The equity risk premium is the same from all three perspectives, except for some potential market imperfection adjustments, such as taxes and transactions costs.

What Is the Investment Horizon of Our Expectations?

Although we could, in principle, choose any investment horizon, the nature of the equity risk premium leads us into choosing a *long-term* horizon. This is because we view the equity risk premium in equilibrium, and not as a statement about whether stocks are overvalued or undervalued at any particular time. If we take the assumption of efficient markets, then we want to know what excess return is expected when the market is "fairly" valued.

The assumption of current fair valuation with long-term expectations is, itself, an arena of some controversy. Some analysts want to assume that the market today is misvalued, and then include its correction over a relatively short interval. Although some of these forecasts may have some predictive power, we would like to classify them as "market timing" rather than as estimates of the equity risk premium. Our estimate of equity risk premium always assumes fair pricing and the long-run expected return of stocks in excess of bonds.

What Can History Tell Us About Capital Market Returns?

Much of our work uses historical realized equity risk premiums to estimate the expected equity risk premium. To use this method, we require a long historical period. This is because even if the equity risk premium is constant and stationary, the estimation error declines only with the square root of time. This will be discussed in more detail in the next section; however, a useful example is that, if we assume that realizations of the equity risk premium are drawn from independent, identical distributions (i.i.d.) with an annualized standard deviation of 20%, then 16 years, 25 years, 64 years, and 100 years would give standard errors of estimation of 5.0%, 4.0%, 2.5%, and 2.0%. Since arithmetic average equity risk premium realizations are likely to be in the single digits, the estimation error is likely to be a high proportion of the estimate. This can be mitigated only by choosing long time periods. However, the underlying stationarity of the return series (especially the mean) can be questioned. In other words, are distant returns likely to be as informative as more recent returns? Does the evolution of history render the concept of an equilibrium risk premium less meaningful?

A whole section of this book—Part I, "The Lessons of History"—provides a set of our historical measures. After the Goetzmann and Ibbotson (2006) historical overview, it starts with the original Ibbotson and Sinquefield (1976) article, covering stocks, bonds, bills, and inflation over the period 1926–1974. This article provided one of the first empirical estimates of the historical equity risk premium, as well as risk premium estimates for the bond horizon (interest rate) risk premium, the default risk premium, and the real interest rate.

Goetzmann, Ibbotson, and Peng (2001) put together a database of all NYSE individual stock data back to 1815. The Ibbotson and Fall (1979) article expands the coverage to the entire U.S. market-wealth portfolio, and the Ibbotson, Siegel, and Love (1985) article expands the coverage to the global market, with returns that include stocks, bonds, and other assets. These articles allow us to examine realized risk premiums across a broad variety of markets and very long time periods.

How Is the Equity Risk Premium Used in Forecasting Returns?

The equity risk premium is one component of the expected return on stocks. Underlying this is the expected return on bonds, which are themselves composed of several expected components: inflation, real interest rates, and horizon or interest rate risk premiums. Fortunately, the riskless bond expected return is, for the most part, observable in the bond's yield. Yet we may care at times about the components, since we may want to estimate not just the stock return in excess of the bond yield, but the stock return in either nominal or real (inflation-adjusted) terms. Usually we can forecast the stock market by simply adding (more accurately, by geometrically adding) the equity risk premium to the riskless bond yield.

The initial Ibbotson and Siegel (1988) article in Part II, "Demand, Supply, and Building-Block Forecasting Methods," explains the building block method of forecasting returns. The building block method is commonly used with historical inputs, but it does not need to be. The method is completely general, and merely consists of adding up the different types of risk premia. It is the simplest of all methods, and is usually compatible with the primary ways to estimate the equity risk premium.

Is the Expected Return Set by the Interaction Between the Demand for and Supply of Risk Capital?

From the demand perspective, the risk premium is based upon investors' demand to be compensated with expected returns for taking on the extra risk and other undesirable attributes of some securities (e.g., common stocks) relative to riskless bonds. The supply perspective looks to what the underlying economy and corporations can supply in the way of expected returns. Both perspectives are relevant, and both may provide separate ways of estimating risk premia.

The Ibbotson, Siegel, and Diermeier (1984) article provides an equilibrium framework across multiple asset classes, taking into account investors' demand. This includes risk aversion, as well as other aversions to taxes, transaction costs, and so on. This study takes the approach of estimating the risk premium from the supply perspective. It analyzes how much the economy has produced, and then assumes constant factor shares for stocks and bonds, allowing for inflows and outflows to our capital markets.

The supply approach argues that the stock market participates in the overall economy. In an early article, Diermeier, Ibbotson, and Siegel (1984) use GDP growth to estimate the stock market, assuming it maintains a constant share of the economy. By looking at the historical U.S. economic growth, with particular emphasis on the earnings growth, Ibbotson and Chen (2003) are able to forecast future earnings growth. Historical earnings growth is a low estimate of future growth because of declining dividend payout ratios, and the current, high price-earnings (PE) ratio. After adjusting for both effects, and adding the current dividend yield, the supply approach gives an equity risk premium estimate that is 1.25% per year lower than the equity risk premium estimated by the historical, realized equity risk premiums.

There are four primary ways that one might estimate the future equity risk premium:

1. Historical equity risk premiums.
2. The equity risk premiums demanded by the investor.
3. The equity risk premiums supplied by corporations and the economy.
4. The consensus equity risk premium estimate of investors.

This book emphasizes the first three approaches, but we discuss all estimation methods.

How Can We Use Realized Equity Risk Premia to Forecast Returns?

Part III, "Simulating and Forecasting," starts off with the Ibbotson and Sinquefield simulations done in 1976, forecasting markets from 1976 to 2000. The simulations are based upon the historical risk premia from the earlier 50-year period. These risk premia are randomly drawn, but in vectors, to preserve their cross-correlations. Risk premia are then forecast for equities (the equity risk premium), bonds (horizon and default risk premia), and real interest rates.

Since the Ibbotson and Sinquefield forecasts have now been realized, a short recent article by Ibbotson (1999) examines the accuracy of the forecast. In general, stock returns were somewhat underestimated, but were still relatively close to the mean 25-year forecast.

The Ibbotson and Sinquefield simulations rely on yearly data. The article by Goetzmann and Edwards (1994) examines the extent to which yearly inputs cause problems in making long-term portfolio choices. The potential difficulties arise from the impact of serial correlation on the measurement of long-term risk.

Does Past History Contain a Survival Bias?

We usually assume constant premiums so that longer historical data give us more accurate equity risk premium estimates. But what if the past data are biased in some way relative to the future? These biases would be called a *selection bias*, meaning that there is something atypical about the returns in the selected historical period or sample.

A potentially extreme form of selection bias is *survivorship bias*. This bias results from the fact that our observations tend to come from surviving markets. The markets that did survive tend to be the markets with higher historical returns. The markets that did not survive in some cases end up with a negative 100% return, or in other cases, with just a lot of missing data. Many markets did not survive World War II, communism, or other causes, and even when they did survive, the equity claims were restructured.

Since much of our historical risk premiums come from the United States, the selection or survivorship bias would seem to be present. The United States can be thought of as the winning country, and not necessarily representative of other markets, or even of the expectation of the future for the U.S. capital markets. In Part IV, "Survivorship and the Selection Bias," we include two articles, coauthored with Stephen Brown and Stephen A. Ross, showing how survivorship can affect performance studies. The historical equity risk premium is a form of this performance, so that these papers have a direct bearing on our equity risk premium estimates. "Survival," by Brown, Goetzmann, and Ross (1995), demonstrates that surviving markets have higher returns, especially during their earlier periods, conditional on their survival. "Survivorship Bias in Performance Studies," by Brown, Goetzmann, Ibbotson, and Ross (1992), shows that winning markets, stocks, and investment managers can have the appearance of predictability, merely because they have survived. Both of these articles show how survivorship bias can make realized returns appear to be higher than they actually were.

At the end of this section we include two articles that Goetzmann coauthored with Philippe Jorion. The first, "Global Stock Markets in the 20th Century," compiles returns across 39 markets starting in the 1920s. This is perhaps the most extensive long-term data set covering so many markets, but by its very nature it includes some "holes" with missing data. The final Goetzmann and Jorion (1999) article analyzes these results by focusing on reemerging markets. The very fact that a market has reemerged is likely to be associated with high performance. Therefore, the history of a reemerging market is atypical, and contains a selection bias, which is tested in the context of survivorship models. These two papers together provide a good indication of the level of survivorship bias that might be found in the historical data that we collected in this book.

Does the Equity Risk Premium Vary, or Can We Time the Market?

Conceptually, the equity risk premium does not have to be a constant. Fundamentally, the equity risk premium is the price of risk, and it would be set by supply-and-demand conditions. The amount of risk available on the stock market is not likely to be constant, because of continual issuances and repurchases of stock, changes in leverage, changes in underlying business, and even changes in the covariances of individual stocks with each other.

The demand for risk might often change as well. Aggregate investor behavior might be sensitive to changing wealth, past returns, changing incentive structures, and so on. It might even depend upon the age and life-cycle structures of the population, as argued by Bakshi and Chen (1994; see "Suggested Reading" for reference). Early attempts to measure risk were made by assuming static utility functions. But these demand theories may not have been robust enough to capture the dynamic and behavioral aspects of real investing.

In most of our book we view the equity risk premium in a long-term context. In Part V, "Predicting Variations," we also consider the possibility of shorter-term timing of the market. A changing estimate of the excess return of stocks over bonds has either of two interpretations. First, it may be that the equity risk premium is continually dynamic, that at each instant it is another number, with the market still being efficient. The other interpretation is that the market is often inefficient, so the expected return differential is merely reflective of a movement toward fair valuation from over- or undervaluation.

It is not necessary for us to distinguish these two perspectives to be able to search for equity risk premium return variations. Goetzmann and Jorion have two articles (1993, 1995) on using dividend yields to predict returns, and generally their results are disparaging of the predictability hypothesis. Goetzmann (1993) looks further for patterns in three centuries of London and NYSE exchange data. He finds some evidence of both persistence and mean reversion by looking at such a long sample period. Goetzmann, Brown, and Kumar (1998) are also able to document that the Dow Theory seems to have some predictive power. In a methodological article, Goetzmann (1991) shows how bootstrapping tests can improve tests of market efficiency.

Ibbotson and Kaplan (2000) show that the volatility of realized equity risk premiums is the most important factor in explaining asset allocation results. Time series returns of balanced mutual funds and pension funds reveal that although more than 90% of the variation in returns is explained by the asset mix, almost 80% of the variation over time can be explained purely by the stock market. Ibbotson and Kaplan also show that asset allocation policy explains 40%, 90%, or 100% of performance, depending on how the question is asked.

Although these sections address many of the basic questions concerning the equity premium that people have asked us about, the studies in this volume will undoubtedly raise more questions in the minds of readers. Indeed, in preparing this volume, simply reviewing these articles has motivated further research questions for the authors; at times, we stopped production and addressed the questions directly and included the results in the volume. Others will have to wait for later analysis. Academic research on the equity premium is an ongoing project involving researchers from all around the world. In some sense, it is the fundamental question of the rewards to capitalism. Without corporate capitalism, there would be no equity sector—and no spread between government and private financing. As the world moves forward with this great, collective experiment in privatization we call capitalism—sometimes the hero and sometimes the villain in world history—we may look back happily at rates of return as an indication of its economic success. However, investors are constantly wondering what the future of capitalism will hold. As world events shake the markets, anxiety about our institutional future translates into anxiety about the premium itself. This great uncertainty, shared by all equity investors around the globe, is reason enough for us, and many other researchers and analysts, to have devoted years of research to this topic. History is a rich fabric of people, institutions, stories, and text. Out of this fabric, we have pulled a few threads mostly gathered from financial records—composed mostly of numbers—and subjected them to statistical analysis. Although our analysis in this volume takes financial history out of its broader political and economic contexts, readers should recognize that these factors are always there. And sometimes, as we hope to show in this volume, numbers themselves tell a fascinating story.

The Lessons of History

Virtually all discussion of the equity risk premium begins with the historical experience of the U.S. stock market. The broad lesson from U.S. capital market history is a comforting one. Stocks have consistently outperformed bonds and other fixed income assets, while crashes have been followed by recoveries. However, an important question is whether past U.S. history is representative of the future. The 20th century was the American Century, a period in which the U.S. economy and its stock market grew to the biggest in the world. Was this the luck of winning a few key wars, or was it the result of a special formula for success—perhaps the right legal code and regulatory environment, a common language, and the geographical benefits of relative isolation? Both answers may contain a grain of truth. In this section, we focus on the historical performance of the U.S. capital markets and their role in the world portfolio. In particular, our analysis documents the statistical measurement of the U.S. equity premium over the past two centuries. If the conditions that made the U.S. a great investment over this time period continue to prevail, then history is an indispensable guide to measuring the equity premium in the future. If not . . . well, we explore that dark possibility in a later section.

▲ Defining the Realized Equity Premium

The simplest definition of the realized equity risk premium is the realized annual growth rate (geometric rate of total return) of the risky asset, in excess of that of the safe asset. To calculate the equity risk premium, one must identify an investable risky asset and an investable riskless asset. In the U.S., we commonly take a value-weighted portfolio of the largest stocks traded in the U.S. markets as the risky asset and either U.S. Treasury Bills or U.S. Treasury Bonds as the riskless asset—assuming that the probability of default by the U.S. Government is zero. We can the compound the realized returns (or yields for the riskless asset) to calculate an index. The annualized growth rate for each is expressed as:

$$r_G = \left[\frac{V_n}{V_0}\right]^{\frac{1}{n}} - 1,$$

where V_n is the value of the index at time, n, of the growth of V_0 invested in the asset at time 0. The equity premium is typically constructed by compounding the monthly risky returns in excess of the return to the riskless asset. Define the equity risk premium at time t as $ERP_t = (1 + R_{stocks,\,t})/(1 + R_{T\text{-Bills},\,t}) - 1$. Then the equity risk premium can be constructed by compounding the monthly premia and annualizing the result:

$$r_G = \left[\prod_{t=1}^{n} (1 + ERP_t) \right]^{\frac{1}{n}} - 1.$$

Logic suggests that the required return to investing in a risky asset should be higher than the required return to investing in a safe asset—but by how much? One approach to answering this question is to use the historical financial record. In doing so, we rely on the presumption that today's investors expect roughly what yesterday's investors received.

Statistical theory suggests that under certain assumptions, realized equity risk premia may give quire reliable estimates of the expected risk premium. If we assume that the equity premium is constant through time, so that the spread between the realized stock return and the realized safe asset return is uncorrelated from one year to the next, then the longer the time period of observation, the less is the uncertainty about its value. The standard error of the estimate of the mean of an independent and identically distributed random variable decreases with the square root of the time period of observation. Thus 100 years of observations shrinks the standard error by a factor of ten. The annual standard deviation of the equity premium is roughly 20%, so the standard error of the mean estimated over a century, assuming the equity premium is stationary, and that the observations are independent through time, is approximately 2%. This provides some level of confidence about the magnitude of historical mean returns, but still leaves some uncertainty about the actual premium one should assume for future investing.

▲ Historical Evidence on the Equity Risk Premium

The second article in this section (chapter 2) is adapted from a paper published by Roger Ibbotson and Rex Sinquefield in 1976 in the *Journal of Business*. The study lays out the basic problems of measuring investor returns over almost a 50 year time span—from 1926 to 1974. Ibbotson and Sinquefield estimated the risk, return, and correlations to five basic investment series in the United States: Common Stocks, U.S. Treasury Bonds, U.S. Corporate Bonds, U.S. Treasury Bills, and Inflation. Among the challenges they faced were how to include dividends as well as share price growth in the calculation of total investor returns, and how to calculate the performance of a realistic, investable portfolio strategy that could be replicated by an individual or a mutual fund. The authors solved this latter problem by constructing a value-weighted portfolio based on the Standard & Poors (S&P) 500 index. The Ibbotson and Sinquefield numbers showed this passive, value-weighted strategy for investing in the U.S. stock market to be a remarkably attractive portfolio. It returned 8.5% annual geometric growth rate over the period 1926 through 1974, 6.1% in excess of the return on U.S. Treasury Bills over the same time period.

These returns are updated for the period 1926 through 2006 in table 1. The updated equity return over the 80 year period is geometrically 6.6% in excess of the U.S. Treasury Bill return.

A graph of a dollar invested in the different asset classes forcefully shows the importance of the equity premium to investors. A dollar invested in U.S. large stocks in December 1925, grew to $2,658 by December 2005, assuming free dividend reinvestment and no taxes and transaction costs. Compare this to the $18 that a 100% investment in T-Bills would have earned over the same period, or the $71 terminal value earned by government bonds. The performance graph (fig. 1) also suggests a reason for the dramatic equity performance. The stock investment line is a lot less smooth than the investment line for bonds and bills. The riskiness of stocks is nowhere more in evidence than in the first few years of the sample period—in the late 1920s and the Great Depression—an erratic period of high volatility—brief booms, crashes, and recoveries.

In the 1976–2005 period after the Ibbotson and Sinquefield study, how did stock and bonds perform? Common stocks returned 12.7%, while long-term U.S. Treasury Bonds and Bills returned 9.5% and 6.0%, respectively. All

Table 1
Summary Statistics for the Period 1/1926 through 12/2005

	Geometric Mean (%)	Arithmetic Mean (%)	Annual STD (%)
S&P 500	10.4	12.3	20.2
U.S. LT Corp Bonds	5.9	6.2	8.5
U.S. LT Gvt Bonds	5.5	5.8	9.2
U.S. 30 Day T-Bills	3.7	3.8	3.1
U.S. Inflation	3.0	3.1	4.3
Long-horizon equity risk premium (Stocks minus long-term government bond yield returns)	4.7	6.2	
Short-horizon equity risk premium (Stocks minus U.S. Treasury bill returns)	6.4	8.4	

Source: Stock, Bonds, Bills and Inflation 2006 Yearbook, Ibbotson Associates. Used with permission. All rights reserved.

Note: Table reports annualized total return for each asset in percentage terms, following the methodology of Ibbotson and Sinquefield (1976) (chapter 2).

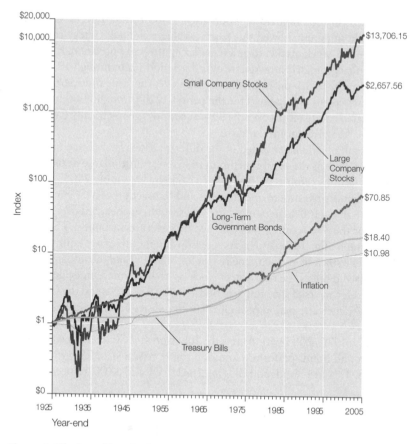

Figure 1. The Long-Term Performance of the U.S. Capital Markets
Source: Stock, Bonds, Bills and Inflation 2006 Yearbook, Ibbotson Associates. All rights reserved. Used with permission.

markets performed better than the previous 50 year period, but the realized equity risk premia remained generally consistent with their historical levels.

Interestingly enough, even before the boom years of the 1980s and 1990s, the historical spread of U.S. stock returns over Treasury Bills was so high that it puzzled economists. Classical models of investor behavior and attitudes toward risk suggest that investors should demand far less compensation for assuming equity risk. The term "equity premium puzzle" was coined by Mehra and Prescott (1985), who pointed out that the most popular utility models used by economists would only justify a risk premium on the order of 1/2% per year. In the past 15 years, attempts to explain this mismatch between utility theory and historical evidence has generated some of the most creative work in economics and finance—scholars have proposed an astounding array of behavioral models to help explain why the premium is as high as it is. By last count, the Mehra and Prescott paper had more than 400 citations in academic journals, and to date, there is no commonly accepted solution to the puzzle posed by the simple spread in the U.S. between stock and T-Bill returns. Nevertheless, many potential explanations have been proposed that are consistent with the high realized equity risk premiums.

▲ Impact on Investing and Asset Allocation

Although historical measures of the risk premium have generated considerable fascinating research, the greatest impact of the Ibbotson and Sinquefield capital market statistics has been on practice. The article's message to investors at the time was simple—a straightforward, passive investment strategy in U.S. equities, followed over the long term, yields remarkably attractive results. Vanguard launched its flagship S&P 500 Index Trust in 1976, and index investing has grown dramatically since then. Indeed, in the year 2000, the Vanguard Market Index Trust finally became the largest equity mutual fund in the United States—eclipsing Fidelity Magellan's actively managed fund. But whether investing actively or passively, investors have learned as per Ibbotson and Kaplan (2000) (chapter 23) that an asset allocation including stocks explains a large part of a portfolio's return.

The demand for historical statistics about the U.S. capital markets has also grown over the past 25 years. Means, standard deviations, and correlations are necessary inputs to the Markowitz mean-variance model of portfolio choice. The mean-variance framework for asset allocation is now widely used by institutional investors, and is becoming available to individual investors who use professional investment advisors. Under independence and stationary assumptions, the best estimate of the inputs to the mean-variance model are the long-term historical measures. Since 1977, Roger Ibbotson's firm, Ibbotson Associates—which he founded in response to the demand for stocks, bonds, bills, and inflation time-series data reported in the article—has calculated and supplied these data to both the private sector and to academia, as well as providing asset allocation advice and software. This demand can be used a a measure of the success of quantitatively based asset allocation strategies in general.

Figure 2 shows the cumulated growth of the U.S. equity premium from 1926, compared to the investment in stocks and T-Bills. It is of interest to note that the publication of the Ibbotson-Sinquefield study occurred after nearly a 10-year period in capital market history when the equity premium was, on average, zero. From 1961 to 1982, the excess return of stocks over U.S. Treasury Bills was negligible. The historical experience of the U.S. equity market appears to divide cleanly into a pre-war Depression, a post-war boom, followed by a flattening of equity performance, and finally ending with the 1980s and 1990s boom. However, dividing history into these apparent subperiods masks the basic positive trend of the equity premium—a trend that, in fact, extrapolated well from the first 50 years of the period to the most recent 25 years.

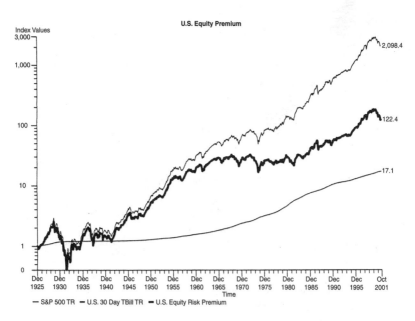

Figure 2. Cumulated Growth of the U.S. Equity Premium from 1926, Compared to Investment in Stocks and T-Bills

◣ *The Very Long Term Perspective*

If gathering and reporting 80 years of U.S. capital market returns has helped investors make investment decisions, why not go further back in time? That is the motivation for the last article in this section, adapted from our paper written with Liang Peng, "A New Historical Database for the NYSE 1815 to 1925: Performance and Predictability," published in 2001 (chapter 3). It represents the culmination of more than a decade of hand-collecting individual stock data from New York City financial periodicals through the 19th and 20th centuries. Many other authors studied the long-term performance of the U.S. capital markets. Alfred Cowles (1938) collected U.S. stock data from 1871 to the mid-1930s to estimate equity returns. Fisher and Lorie (1965, 1968, 1977), Ibbotson and Brinson (1987, 1993), Wilson and Jones (1987, 2002), Shiller (1989, 2000), Schwert (1990), Siegel (1992, 1998), and Goetzmann (1993) all measured long-run U.S. equity performance by assembling, and in many cases correcting, indices from the work of previous researchers. However, prior to our work, not since Cowles' work has there been a comprehensive analysis of the major U.S. equity market based on information from primary sources at the individual security level.

In this study, we use security data to develop measures of the equity premium over the very long term. We found that the total returns for U.S. stocks

Large Company Stocks

Summary Statistics of Annual Returns

	Geometric Mean (%)	Arithmetic Mean (%)	Annual STD (%)
From 1825 to 1925			
Total Return	7.3	8.4	16.3
Income Return	5.9	5.9	1.9
Capital Appreciation	1.3	2.5	16.1
From 1926 to 2005			
Total Return	10.4	12.3	20.2
Income Return	4.2	4.2	1.5
Capital Appreciation	5.9	7.8	19.5
From 1825 to 2005			
Total Return	8.6	10.1	18.2
Income Return	5.1	5.2	1.9
Capital Appreciation	3.3	4.9	17.8

were actually somewhat less in the pre-SBBI period from 1825 to 1925, 7.3% as opposed to 10.4% from 1926 to 2005.

What was the equity premium in the early years? This is a difficult question to answer for two reasons. The first is that the U.S. Government did not regularly issue Treasury Bills over this period. However, more importantly, even if it did, we would be hard-pressed to consider them riskless securities for much of the early 19th century. A more reasonable benchmark might be a consumer price index, which was essentially flat over the 19th century for the United States. This point is an important one to consider when calculating the equity premium for markets other than the United States. The theory of the equity premium is based on the difference between a risky and a riskless asset. It provides little guidance on the relative difference between two uncorrelated risky assets.

▶ The Cross-Sectional Perspective

Quite apart from the important issue of the relative long-term benefits of stock investing over bonds, the equity premium has long been important as a tool for quantifying differences in the expected return to individual securities and individual portfolios. The Sharpe-Lintner-Mossin Capital Asset Pricing Model (CAPM) implies that the expected return to a security or a portfolio with constant security weights can be expressed as:

(1) $E(R_i) = R_f + \beta_i E(R_m - R_f).$

In other words, the expected return of the individual security or portfolio, i, is a simple linear function of the risk premium $R_m - R_f$, where R_f is the return to the riskless asset, and β_i is the covariance of R_m and R_i, scaled by the variance of R_m. This and related multi-factor models, such as Ross' (1976) Arbitrage Pricing Theory (APT), have been widely used to estimate the discount rate for future cash flows, and to evaluate systematic risk-adjusted managerial performance in the corporate and investment sectors. Unlike the APT, the CAPM model makes a distinctive claim about the return of the market, R_m. It must be the return on the market wealth portfolio. The model is an equilibrium argument that includes all assets in the economy. In practice, the risk premium has often been taken to be that of the S&P 500, and the β_i estimated by regression of the past time-series of security, i, returns on S&P 500 returns. Richard Roll (1978) pointed out that the market wealth portfolio means the full market portfolio—that the metonymy of using top U.S. equities is invalid. It leads to an incorrect estimation of expected returns and invalid risk-adjustment of manager performance. The empirical solution to this problem is difficult—construct a time-series of returns to the world wealth portfolio—including liquid assets such as stocks and bonds, as well as less liquid assets such as real estate.

The articles in this section by Ibbotson and Fall (chapter 4), and Ibbotson, Siegel, and Love (chapter 5) attempt to do exactly that. The first aggregates U.S. capital market data and includes real estate as a major factor. The second extends this approach to estimating the world wealth portfolio. This approach necessitated the assembly of values and returns for a range of international markets—20 in all—and a range of asset classes, including cash, bonds, real estate, precious metals, and equities from 1960 to 1984. The result was a measure of the rate of return to the world wealth portfolio of 8.39%, with cash earning 6.38%. The nost striking thing about the evidence in the paper is the contrast to the experience of the world markets since 1984, which we present in boxes as updates to the two articles. In particular the 1970s were lean ones for the United States. Domestic stocks underperformed international bonds—indeed they all underperformed cash! Real estate and precious metals were the real winners in the full 25 year period. Strangely enough, these two asset classes are now hot performers again, after being dominated by the stock market boom decades of the 1980s and 1990s. These articles may cause some to reconsider their allocations for the future.

◤ Summary

Much of the analysis in this section of the book is based on the value of history as a guide to measurement. In short, we take the long-term view. This is not always easy to do. Investors are constantly aware of current events, and always curious how these will affect the returns on their portfolios. News media and investment analysts are motivated by a need to identify change or alert the public to economic turning points—whether it is the New Economy or a new war. Nevertheless, the statistics about the stock market in this section tell a simple, powerful story. For investors holding for the long term, equities provide an attractive rate of return. A striking feature of the historical analysis of the U.S. equity premium over the past 80 years—indeed over the past 190 years—is its reliability. Stocks performed well, whether America was in the Federalist Era or the Computer Age. The premium was positive in periods when the market paid high dividends or low dividends. Although there have been extended periods when the equity premium was flat—most notable the 20 years from 1962 to 1981, the recovery of the market suggests that the basic theory of the equity risk premium is correct—that investors demanded and received higher returns for taking a risk on equities as opposed to safe investments over the long term.

1   William N. Goetzmann and Roger G. Ibbotson

History and the Equity Risk Premium

▲ *Abstract*

We summarize some of our own past findings and place them in the context of the historical development of the idea of the equity risk premium and its empirical measurement by financial economists. In particular, we focus on how the theory of compensation for investment risk developed in the 20th century in tandem with the empirical analysis of historical investment performance. Finally, we update our study of the historical performance of the New York Stock Exchange over the period 1792 to the present, and include a measure of the U.S. equity risk premium over more than two centuries. This last section is based upon indices constructed from individual stock and dividend data collected over a decade of research at the Yale School of Management, and contributions of other scholars.

▲ *Introduction*

The equity premium puzzle posed in Mehra and Prescott (1985) was, in part, motivated by historical evidence on the return of U.S. stocks in excess of the riskless rate. Much of our own research has focused on estimating the equity risk premium using long-term historical data, and examining how historical accident may relate to the classic puzzle. While the equity premium is a fascinating topic for scholarship, it is also one of the most important economic topics in modern finance. The equity risk premium is widely used to forecast the growth of investment portfolios over the long term. It is also used as an input to the cost of capital in project choice, and employed as a factor in the expected rate of return to stocks. Given its prevalence in practice and its importance to academic thought, it is interesting to discover that the calculation of the equity risk premium is a fairly new phenomenon. Reliable data to estimate the historical premium of stocks over bonds were only collected in the mid-20th century, and precise econometric estimates of the equity premium only came after the development of the theory that uses it as a central input—the Capital Asset Pricing Model, or CAPM.

*This is a draft of a chapter intended for a collection of essays on the equity risk premium edited by Rajneesh Mehra. It summarizes our past research related to the equity premium, and places it in historical context. We thank professor Mehra for the opportunity to contribute, and for his feedback on the research.

The chapter in part is intended to review our own contributions to the literature on the equity risk premium. Working both separately and together on a series of empirical research studies conducted with colleagues through the years, we have looked at the equity risk premium from a few different perspectives. First, research by Roger Ibbotson and Rex Sinquefield provided some of the first accurate calculations of the annual rate of return on U.S. asset classes over long investment horizons with specific measures of the equity and other risk premiums. These calculations have come into widespread academic and industrial use as inputs to research and investment decision-making through numerous works that Ibbotson has produced. Second, Will Goetzmann and co-authors Stephen Brown and Stephen Ross proposed and examined the hypothesis that the equity premium estimated from U.S. financial data alone is subject to a bias due to analysis of a winning market rather than losing ones. Third, both of us together with our co-author Liang Peng have constructed one of the most complete long-term databases of U.S. financial returns yet developed and have used it to study the variations in the equity risk premium through nearly 200 years. Finally, both of us have worked on other related concepts, including the predictability of the equity premium, alternate ways of measuring the equity risk premium and on other applications of the concept. This chapter will summarize this past work and place it in the historical context of the evolution of the concept of the equity premium.

The chapter is structured as follows. We first review the historical development of the idea of the equity risk premium in financial economics as the theory of compensation for investment risk developed in tandem with the empirical analysis of historical investment performance. Next we summarize some of our past findings about the historical equity risk premium and present further analysis on potential survival biases. Finally, we update our analysis of the historical performance of the New York Stock Exchange over the period from 1792 to the present, and include a measure of the U.S. equity risk premium over more than two centuries. This last section is based upon indices constructed from individual stock and dividend data collected over a decade of research at the Yale School of Management.

▲ Historical Conception and Measurement of the Equity Risk Premium

One of the earliest and most succinct expressions of the concept of the equity risk premium came from John Stuart Mill in his 1848 classic *Principles of Political Economy.* Writing about a farmer considering investment in the land, Mill argues that

> . . . he will probably be willing to expend capital on it (for an immediate return) in any manner which will afford him a surplus profit, however small, beyond the value of the risk, and the interest which he must pay for the capital if borrowed, or can get for it elsewhere if it is his own.[1]

Mill thus separates profit into three parts: first, the interest that must be paid for the capital borrowed, determined in terms of the alternative opportunity cost of money. This is equivalent to the riskless rate. The second component is the value of the risk associated with the investment. This is equivalent to the equity risk premium. Mill's third component is a surplus profit, no matter how small, in modern parlance, the "alpha"—a portion of compensation expected to be small in a competitive market.

Despite Mill's early formulation of the idea, the concept of equity profit as compensation for risk did not develop quickly. Economists at the turn of the century tended to focus instead on the apparent paradox of profit and perfect competition rather than risk and return. Columbia University Professor John Bates Clark, for example, asserted that returns in excess of the riskless rate were due to monopolistic advantage, rather than compensation for insurable risk. In his view, innovation led to a comparative advantage, which was in turn rewarded by excess return.[2]

Chicago economist Frank Knight responded to Clark's formulation by asserting the importance of risk. In his famous 1921 work *Risk, Uncertainty and Profit*, he noted the lack of useful models of risk and return in economic research. Knight reviewed the role of risk in the economic theory of profit up to the 1920s and took exception to the lack of distinction in previous analyses between quantifiable and unquantifiable risk—the latter he termed uncertainty, but both of which he asserted should command an investment premium. Knight's philosophical treatise did little, however, to clarify how the different roles of risk and uncertainty would affect prices and business ventures in a practical manner, and he was completely silent on the issue of how one might quantify the equity risk premium.

As theorists debated the role of risk in the expected return to investment, empirical researchers in the early 20th century began to collect historical performance data from the markets. The earliest attempts to construct stock price indices were motivated by the need for a "barometer" of current market trends, or as an indicator of fluctuating macroeconomic conditions. Charles Henry Dow's famous index of 30 stocks was not originally intended as a measure of long-term investment performance, but rather as a daily measure of the market. A number of macroeconomists began to create stock price indexes in the early 20th century. Mitchell (1910, 1916), Persons (1916, 1919), and Cole and Frickey (1928) are among the number of scholars who collected U.S equity prices and constructed indices as a means to study the interaction between economic cycles and the financial markets. Likewise, Smith and Horne (1934) and Bowley, Schwartz, and Smith (1931) built similar indices for Great Britain. None of them addressed the obvious question—at least from our modern perspective — of long-term investment returns.[3]

Edgar Lawrence Smith's 1924 book *Common Stocks as Long Term Investments* is the first significant attempt to advocate equity investing as a means to achieve higher investment returns. Smith collected price and dividend data for U.S. stocks over the period 1837 to 1923 and computed a total return index, which he compared to a fixed rate of interest over the corresponding period. He also collected historical price and dividend data for stocks and corporate bonds over the period 1866 through 1923 from the Boston and New York Stock Exchanges. He formed stock and bond investment portfolios of ten securities each as the basis for simulating investor performance over four different time periods. He studied the relative appreciation returns and income returns from both asset classes, and documented fairly convincingly that over a variety of subperiods, equities yielded higher income than bonds and also provided significant capital appreciation.

Smith simulated the performance of these portfolios in a number of ways. The simplest was to treat the income and capital appreciation returns from the stock and bond portfolios separately and show that stocks nearly always dominated in both measures. He came close to developing a total return measure for the equity premium by the mechanical process of taking the income return each year from stocks and "paying" out of it the amount generated by the bond portfolio and then reinvesting the residual back into shares. The relative growth of the stock portfolio through this procedure can be interpreted as a measure of the equity premium—at least with respect to corporate bonds.

Smith's book was not only widely read by investors but also closely studied by scholars. It was immediately cited by Yale's Irving Fisher as an argument for investing in a diversified portfolio of equities over bonds.[4] Based on Smith's findings, Fisher theorized that the trend toward investment in diversified portfolios of common stock had actually changed the equity premium in the 1920s. His views on the factors influencing the equity risk premium are worth quoting at length.

> Studies of various writers, especially Edgar Smith and Kenneth Van Strum have shown that in the long run stocks yield more than bonds. Economists have pointed out that the safety of bonds is largely illusory since every bondholder runs the risk of a fall in the purchasing power of money and this risk does not attach to the same degree to common stock, while the risks that do attach to them may be reduced, or insured against, by diversification . . .
>
> It is in this way that investment trusts and investment council tend to diminish the risk to the common stock investor. This new movement has created a new demand for such stocks and raised their prices, at the same time it has tended to decrease the demand for, and to lower the price of, bonds.[5]

Smith's empirical approach to measuring the relative performance of the two asset classes was widely imitated in later studies. In 1937, Brown University Professor Chelcie Bowland published a synthesis of research following Smith's book and showed how the common stock investment strategy performed through the worst years of the depression.[6] Bowland concluded on considerable empirical evidence that the theory of common stock investment survived the crash. An interesting feature of the studies cited in Bowland's book is that none of them produced what we now think of as a measure of the equity premium—that is, the difference in total return between a portfolio of equities and the riskless rate over the same period.

The most carefully crafted early empirical analysis of the long-term performance of the stock market was *Common Stock Indices,* by Alfred Cowles III, published in 1938. This ambitious study, undertaken before the advent of computers, but assisted by the invention of Holerith cards, collected individual stock prices (actually monthly highs and lows by stock) and dividends from 1872 to 1937 for stocks on the NYSE. Its stated goal was to "portray the average experience of those investing in this class of security in the United States from 1871 to 1937."[7]

Two important features of the Cowles study were that he collected data on virtually all of the stocks on the New York Stock Exchange, and that he capital-weighted them, a procedure that allowed the index to simulate a passive buy and hold investment strategy. The one serious limitation of the Cowles study is that it relied on the average of high and low prices during the month as a proxy for end-of-month stock prices. This had a smoothing effect on the returns, downward biasing the volatility, and muddying up any econometric analysis of the data.[8] Oddly enough, given such widespread interest in Edgar Smith's earlier study, the Cowles analysis was silent on the relative performance of stocks and bonds.

The first book to explicitly define, model, and estimate an equity risk premium was John Burr Williams' *The Theory of Investment Value,* also published in 1938. According to Williams "The customary way to find the value of a risky security has always been to add a 'premium for risk.'"[9] He provides a table of "Interest Rates, Past Present and Future," which takes the riskless rate as the long-term government bond rate of 4% and the expected return to "Good stocks" as 5 1/2%.[10] Williams' estimated the forward equity premium from a dividend discount model, and he was careful to explain that historical (i.e., past) estimates provide a good forecast of the future, even when they deviate from present conditions.

In sum, by the end of the 1930s, economists had developed a clear conception of the equity risk premium, a means to measure rates of return on investments, and had collected historical data extending back through American financial history for several decades. The first empirical estimate of the equity premium by Smith is generally regarded as a major factor in the rush by retail investors into the stock market in the 1920s, and Irving Fisher is often taken to task for his theory that stock prices increased to new levels in the 1920s as a result of a decreasing equity risk premium. Alfred Cowles created the first relatively accurate long-term index of total return to investing in common stocks, and J. B. Williams provided the first numeric estimate of the forward-looking equity risk premium. Their work provided a valuable foundation for the next generation of financial research.

The next major attempt to empirically quantify the equity returns was undertaken at the University of Chicago. Beginning in 1960, CRSP, the Chicago

Center for Research on Security Prices, headed by economists Lawrence Fisher and James H. Lorie, systematically began to collect stock prices and dividends from U.S. capital market history. Fisher and Lorie published the results of their study of returns to U.S. stocks in 1964, as "Rates of Return on Investments in Common Stocks"[11] and in 1977 as a volume including returns to U.S. government securities as well.[12] Like Cowles, they based their analysis of individual share prices and reinvestment of dividends of U.S. stocks.

The theoretical developments in financial economics in the 1950s and 1960s made these empirical estimates of rates of return particularly interesting. In 1952, Harry Markowitz published his famous model of portfolio selection, which explicitly linked investment return and risk. Markowitz proposed taking as inputs to his model the historical means, variances, and covariances of individual securities, although he regarded this as a method that could be improved upon with better forecasting tools. Yale economist James Tobin is credited with adding an important feature to the Markowitz model: a non-zero riskless rate, leading to an explicit expression for a risk premium.

The Markowitz model, as it is now applied, identifies an optimal portfolio of assets in expected return and standard deviation space by the point of tangency formed by a ray extending from the expected return of the riskless (zero standard deviation) asset to the continuous frontier of portfolios providing the highest return for each level of standard deviation. The difference between the return of the riskless asset and the expected return of the tangency portfolio in this model is the equity risk premium.[13] In the Markowitz framework, the size of the equity risk premium is an empirical question. Later scholars took a theoretical approach to its estimation.

The Sharpe-Lintner-Mossin Capital Asset Pricing Model (CAPM) was independently developed in the 1960s in part as a means to identify the optimal portfolio of risky assets in the Markowitz framework. As such, the CAPM takes an analytical approach to the equity risk premium. The theory endogenizes asset prices as a function of the risk aversion of the representative investor and the variance-covariance structure of the universe of assets. The shape of the representative investor's utility function, parameterized by a coefficient of risk aversion for the market as a whole, is central to identification of the equity premium.

In the framework of the CAPM, if the form of the utility function and the coefficient of risk aversion are both known, then knowledge of the variance-covariance of the universe of assets (or the variance of the portfolio of risky assets) is sufficient to identify the spread between risky and riskless asset portfolios.

An important feature of the Markowitz model and the CAPM is that they provide a theoretical foundation for estimating the magnitude of the equity risk premium directly from investor preferences. It was not until Mehra and Prescott (1985), however, that anyone attempted to compare the equity premium implied by preferences with the empirical measures provided by historical returns.

▶ *Stocks, Bonds, Bills, and Inflation*

In 1976, Ibbotson and Sinquefield published "Stocks, Bonds, Bills and Inflation: Year-by-Year Historical Returns (1926–1974)." The stock market returns were calculated as total returns from the S&P 500 index, which up to this time did not include dividends. The authors also used CRSP government bond data to include U.S. Treasury bond and bill indexes. They also included a corporate bond index constructed from bond yields, as well as inflation rates. Besides displaying total returns across all yearly hold periods, the paper was unique in that it explicitly measured historical risk premiums, not only for equities, but also including the horizon (maturity) premium, the default premium, and real interest rate. Results were presented in real (inflation adjusted) terms as well. In Ibbotson Associates Yearbooks, they later added the small stock premium, the value premium, as well as various other data. These historical premiums came to be used in practice and theory as the risk premium input into the CAPM model, as well as for other models.

Later in 1976, Ibbotson and Sinquefield showed how historical data could be used to simulate the probability distributions of future returns. They started with the then current yield curve with its implicit forward interest rate structure. They added the various historical premiums using bootstrapping methods that retained the correlation structure among the asset classes. They used a historical equity risk premium, which was measured during the previous half century to be 6.3% geometrically relative to U.S. Treasury Bills, but a lesser number relative to longer-term bonds, which contained horizon risk premiums.

Interestingly, 1976 was also the year that Vanguard launched its market index trust, a passive, value-weighted portfolio of large-cap U.S. stocks designed to match the performance of the S&P 500. The excellent excess performance of stocks from 1926 to 1974 reported in Ibbotson and Sinquefield may have helped build demand for a passive portfolio that sought to capture these historical returns. Just as the empirical study by Edgar Lawrence Smith demonstrated to investors in the 1920s the superiority of stocks over bonds and motivated a move toward equities, indexation made a lot of sense to investors in the 1970s when they had 5 decades of historical performance upon which to base their expectations for the future.

An important historical note is that the decade of the 1970s was one of the worst periods in U.S. capital market history for stocks. The crash of 1973–74, the experience of double digit inflation, and the erosion of capital was fresh in the public imagination in 1976. Equity returns had not exceeded debt returns over nearly the preceding decade. Thus the historical equity premium appeared to most as a wildly optimistic forecast of the future expected return of stocks over T-bills. In fact it was not—the equity risk premium since 1976 has nearly matched the estimate made at the time.

There are several ways one might estimate an expected risk premium used for forecasting. One way is to extrapolate historical risk premiums as Ibbotson and Sinquefield did. Another is to use investor demand models based upon investor risk aversion, as Mehra and Precott did. In Ibbotson, Siegel, and Diermeier (1984), demand is shown to be impacted not only by systematic risk, but also by liquidity, taxation, and idiosyncratic risk. A third way is to look at the type of returns that the corporate sector supplies. Diermeier, Ibbotson, and Siegel (1984) and then later Ibbotson and Chen (2003), use this supply approach. They extrapolate the cash flows and earnings growth generated by companies themselves. These forecasts tend to give somewhat lower forecasts than historical risk premia, primarily because part of the total returns of the stock market have come from price–earnings ratio expansion. This expansion is not predicated to continue on indefinitely, and should logically be removed from the expected risk premium.

▲ History as Written by the Winners?

A major conceptual problem with equating the ex post historical realization of the equity premium with its ex ante expectation is that history could simply have turned out better than people expected. Recall that in 1938, J. B. Williams calculated the market forecast of the equity risk premium as a mere 1 1/2%. He might have been shocked to see the realized premium over the following 5 decades exceed his forecast by a multiple of four. A more subtle problem is that historical records of successful markets tend to get preserved, but it is difficult to dig up the records of failed markets. To study these issues, Brown, Goetzmann, and Ross (1997) built a model of stock market performance that examined the ex post historical return conditional upon survival. Their analytical results showed that when a market is confronted with the continuous possibility of failure (modeled statistically as an absorbing lower bound) the ex post realized growth can be substantially higher than the unconditional mean. The fact that the U.S. survived two world wars and periods of global political unrest that caused other major markets to fail would suggest that the historical mean return of the U.S. market is an overestimate of its expectation.

It is important to point out that this view of the equity risk premium is quite different than the critique of the equity premium puzzle posed by economist Thomas Reitz. Reitz (1988) theorized that a high ex ante equity premium could be justified by a fear of a huge crash. An equity premium of 6% would thus reflect the potential for an event which may not have been realized in America's financial history but that nevertheless was a possibility in people's minds. One limitation of the Reitz critique is that it conflicts with historical expectations of stock returns—most notably the J. B. William's forward-looking premium in 1938 of 1 1/2%. The survivorship story, on the other hand, is entirely consistent with low historical expectations of the future, although it would be unlikely to reduce the equity risk premium to such a low number.

In order to estimate the potential scale of the survival bias, and to look for empirical evidence that the U.S. market was an unusual performer in the global economy, Jorion and Goetzmann (1999) collected capital appreciation and inflation data for a large sample of the world's equity markets from 1921 forward. They found that the U.S. was the top performer out of 39 markets, in terms of real capital appreciation of stocks. Studying this effect subsequently with a smaller but richer sample, Dimson, Marsh, and Staunton (2002) collect total real returns for twelve countries over the entire century and found that the U.S. was in the top quartile of performers in real terms— inched out by Sweden and Australia over the first couple of decades of the century.[14] The Jorion and Goetzmann GDP-weighted index of the 44 non-U.S. equity markets had an arithmetic real return of 3.84% per year, compared to the U.S. value of 5.48%, suggesting a survival bias on the order of 1.5% per annum. The geometric return values were closer (roughly 90 basis points) because the world market index was less volatile over the period due to diversification. Thus the work found evidence that the equity premium estimate is affected by survival issues, however the magnitude is insufficient to explain away the equity premium puzzle.

◣ The Equity Premium Over the Very Long Term

One of the major issues with statistical estimation of the realized equity risk premium is that a very long time series of stationary returns is required to achieve a high degree of confidence in the estimate. The longer the data series, the more accurate the equity risk premium calculation, as long as the fundamental expectations have remained the same. In order to estimate the U.S. equity premium using total returns over the longest possible time period we have collected the most complete dataset of U.S. stock prices and dividends assembled to date.[15] Working with our colleague Liang Peng, we gathered individual security data from U.S. financial periodicals on a monthly basis, beginning with the official list of the New York Stock Exchange in 1815, and collected available dividends from 1825 to 1872. Among other things, this direct data collection enabled us to collect month ending prices, avoiding the Cowles data problem of averaging high and low prices for the month. It also allowed us to avoid the heterogeneity problems of Ibbotson and Brinson (1987), Schwert (1990), Goetzmann (1993), and Siegel (1998), all of whom had to rely upon chained indices constructed by earlier researchers.[16]

Recently, Sylla, Wilson, and Wright completed the collection of weekly NYSE stock prices over the late 18th and early 19th centuries. They generously shared this data with us, and from it we are able to construct a complete index of capital appreciation returns for the New York Stock Exchange from 1792 (its inception) to the present. In this chapter, using the combined databases of Sylla, and Goetzmann, Ibbotson, and Peng (2000), as well as annual bond yield data from Homer and Sylla's (1991) *The History of Interest Rates,* we are able to estimate an equity premium for the New York Stock Exchange over its pre-1925 history.

Capital appreciation returns in this study are based on a price-weighted index of all stocks trading in the year, using the last price observation in the year. Income returns from 1825 to 1871 are constructed in two ways and then averaged. The first method is to sum all the dividends paid in that year and divide by the prices of all firms from the previous year. This probably underestimates the income return because some actual dividend payments may not be in the data set. The second method focuses solely on the income return of firms that paid regular dividends and for which prices were collected—this likely overestimates returns because some stocks may not have paid any dividends. It is important to note that no previous researchers collected actual dividend data on U.S. stocks before 1872. All analyses before our own was based upon econometric methods to fill in income returns. Thus, although our two methodologies sometimes diverge, they are at least based upon empirical observation. However, like previous analysts, in order to estimate the pre-1825 dividends, we employ a linear forecasting model using next year's dividend and this year's capital appreciation as forecasting variables.[17] Our dividend returns from 1872 to 1925 were taken from Cowles (1938).

The most problematic variable in our study is the riskless rate. In 1792, the United States was an emerging market and U.S. securities were considered far from riskless. Homer and Sylla report yields on U.S. government and U.S. municipal debt in the 18th and 19th centuries. For long stretches of time the yields on municipals were less than yields of treasuries, and this difference was not due to tax treatment. We took the minimum yield of the two series' each year as a measure of a (nearly) riskless rate and the pre-1798 data was set to the 1798 value. Of course yields are not returns when the debt is not held to maturity. Thus using them to capture the riskless rate ignores the capital appreciation component of bond returns. Returns to shorter maturity instruments are available for periods of U.S. financial history before 1926. Mehra and Prescottt (1985) used commercial paper rates reported in the earlier edition of Sylla and Homer back to 1883. We report these in our analysis as well. Homer (1963) notes that these are quite volatile in the early years, perhaps reflecting the lack of an organized money market.[18] Commercial paper rates from 1830 to 1857 are from the Boston money market, and afterwards from the New York market. We econometrically estimated commercial paper rates from 1792 to 1834 by projecting them on bond yields.[19] Other types of short term rates in the early 19th century are dubious due to regulation of interest rates. Inflation data is taken from Ibbotson and Brinson (1987).

Table 1.1 presents the results of the analysis for the period 1792 to 1925. Note that the arithmetic equity premium measured by the spread over bonds is about 3.8% and the geometric spread is 2.7%. A major issue, however is that the interest rate series we have constructed is not riskless. Comparing the returns instead to inflation indicates an arithmetic real return of about 7%. The bond returns would appear to be anomalous with respect to expectations, not the equity returns.

Table 1.1
Summary Statistics for New York Stock Exchange Total Returns, U.S. Bond Yields, Call Money Rates, and Inflation, 1792–1925

	Arithmetic Return (%)	Geometric Return (%)	Standard Deviation (%)
Stocks TR	7.93	6.99	14.64
Cap Ap	1.91		
Income	6.01		
Bonds	4.17	4.16	4.17
Comm. paper	7.62	7.57	3.22
Inflation	0.85	0.61	7.11

The low capital appreciation returns to stocks prompted us to test the hypothesis that for much of U.S. financial history investors expected their equity returns to come in the form of dividend payouts rather than capital appreciation. We found that that vast majority of stock in our sample traded around par value, implying an expectation of payout. If this was strictly the case, it would allow the ex ante measurement of the equity risk premium through financial history. Unfortunately we cannot verify that expected returns carried no anticipated long-term price growth. The 1.91% appreciation we document in Table 1.1 exceeds the realized inflation over the period, and thus may have been ex ante expected. On the other hand, in our paper we show that through most of U.S. capital market history, dividend yields were higher than bond yields, suggesting that differential income flow was a major part of the compensation for equity risk during the early period.

Table 1.2 presents summary statistics for the major U.S. asset classes over the period 1926 through 2005. The arithmetic average return to common stocks over the second period is 400 basis points per year higher than in the first. In real terms, however, this differential is slightly less dramatic: 7.1% to 9.2%.

Table 1.2
Summary Statistics for Total Returns in U.S. Stocks, Bonds, Bills and Inflation, 1926–2005

	Arithmetic Return (%)	Geometric Return (%)	Standard Deviation (%)
Stocks TR	12.3	10.4	20.2
Cap Ap	7.85		
Income	4.27		
LT govt. bonds	5.8	5.5	9.2
T-Bills	3.8	3.7	3.1
Inflation	3.1	3.0	4.3

Source: Stocks, Bonds, Bills and Inflation, 2006 Yearbook, Ibbotson Associates, Chicago.

◣ Conclusion

The concept of the equity risk premium is fundamental to modern financial theory and a basic building block in most forecasting models of long-term expected investment returns. A review of the economic literature after the turn of the 19th century suggests that the concept of the equity risk premium was not clearly formulated until the late 1930s. While the notion of return as a premium for risk above and beyond the pure time value of money dates at least to the work of John Stuart Mill, the basic technique of calculating the total return to investing in equities versus debt developed relatively slowly, with the key insight provided by Edgar Smith and Alfred Cowles—a calculation of investment return in equities requires regular reinvestment of income through the purchase of shares.

The historical development of the concept and measurement of the equity risk premium provides the context for our own research contributions. The first Ibbotson and Sinquefield study represented a culmination of research on the basic building blocks of expected returns for different asset classes. The notion of building up expected returns from blocks of risk premia was viewed by J. B. Williams as a natural approach, however it is surprising how long it took for the basic empirical calculus of risk and return to come into use. The Ibbotson and Sinquefield numbers as reported in 1976 were striking evidence that common stock investment, so avidly proposed by Smith and Fisher 5 decades earlier, was in fact a wise course of action to take. A new generation of investors in the 1970s used these numbers as a guide to expectations of future returns to equity investment, and 25 years later they were not disappointed. History proved an accurate forecast.

The sheer magnitude of the equity premium in U.S. capital markets over the 20th century has caused both scholars and practitioners to ask whether these returns were simply an accident of history or evidence of a different kind of attitude toward risk than seems justified by theoretical models. The importance of Mehra and Prescott (1985) is that they pointed out the apparent contradiction between the U.S. market experience and academic models of human behavior.

A part of our own inquiry into the equity premium puzzle has been the question of whether the history we examine is an unusual path—one unlikely to be realized in the future. Most Americans who lived through a significant portion of the 20th century count themselves fortunate compared to large sectors of the global populace who suffered a catastrophic loss of savings as a result of the political tumult of two world wars and widespread redistribution of wealth. In light of America's political and economic success in the 20th century, it is not surprising to find that its markets dominated as well. A test of this "survivor" story in our research finds some empirical support, but does not fully explain the high equity risk premium enjoyed through U.S. capital market history.

The survival hypothesis suggests that the American experience may not be the best example on which to base future expectations—then again, maybe it is for those who plan to continue investing in the U.S. capital markets. Perhaps the positive American experience was actually due to our particular configuration of laws, political system, cultural mixture, and practical orientation.

A longer look at the American financial experience affords a chance to test this proposition. Although the 20th century may be the American Century, the 19th century was not. Europe's financial markets were dominant through the First World War. American finance was parochial and limited. One important qualification to this, however, was the comparative freedom of American equity markets. Britain severely limited the issuance of corporate shares until the mid-19th century, and full corporate access to the capital markets did not exist until the British Companies Acts of the 1860s. By that time, American equity markets had been operating in New York, Philadelphia and Boston for many decades. Indeed the U.S. might have been the best market to study the early development of unfettered capitalism in the early 19th century.

What do we find when we look at the 19th century numbers? First, the measurement of the equity risk premium in the U.S. before 1925 is nearly impossible due largely to the fact that there was no meaningful riskless rate as a benchmark. Had the Capital Asset Pricing Model been transported back from the 1960s to the 1860s, the challenge would have been to determine R_f, not R_m. When we look at the premium of stocks over inflation, however, we find that the real rate of equity returns in the first 125 years of its history pretty nearly resembles the real rate of equity returns in the last 80 years. Through that trajectory of time, the U.S. went from being an emerging market to a capital importer to a capital exporter. Given what would seem to be major regime changes in the U.S. economy, it is extraordinary to find such stability in the rate of return on investment capital. Is that stability due to a "country factor" in modern asset pricing terminology? This will have to await further tests using data from global capital market history.

Our research together and separately has focused to a large degree on measurement and interpretation of history. Despite decades of research on early capital markets, however, much remains to be done. Our understanding of the historical experience of investors is relatively limited once we step beyond a few well-studied markets. Basic information about investor returns is lacking and may never be recovered. Nevertheless, efforts to quantify the equity risk premium are well rewarded by insights into both the stability and dynamics of long-term investment performance.

◤ References

Bowland, C., 1937, *The Common Stock Theory of Investment,* The Ronald Press Company, New York.

Bowley, A. L., G. L. Schwartz, and K. C. Smith, 1931, *A New Index of Securities,* London and Cambridge Economic Service, London.

Clark, J. B., 1892, "Insurance and Business Profit," *Quarterly Journal of Economics,* 7(1), 40–54.

Cole, A. C. and E. Frickey, 1928, "The Course of Stock Prices, 1825–66," *Review of Economic Statistics*, 10(3), 117–39.

Cowles, A., 1938, "Common Stock Indices," *Cowles Commission for Research in Economics*, Monograph number 3, Principia Press, Bloomington.

Cowles, A., 1960, "A Revision of Previous Conclusions Regarding Stock Price Behavior," *Econometrica*, 28(4), 909–915.

Diermeier, J., R. Ibbotson, and L. B. Siegel, 1984, "The Supply for Capital Market Returns," *Financial Analysts Journal*, 40(2).

Dimson, E., P. Marsh, and M. Staunton, 2002, *Triumph of the Optimists: 101 Years of Global Investment Returns*, Princeton University Press.

Fisher, I., 1925, "Stocks vs. Bonds," *American Review of Reviews*, July.

Fisher, I., 1930, *The Theory of Interest*, The Macmillan Company, New York, 220–21.

Fisher, L., and J. Fisher, 1964, "Rates of Return on Investments in Common Stocks," *Journal of Business*, 37, 1–21.

Frickey, 1919, "An Index of Industrial Stock Prices," *Review of Economics Statistics*, 3(8), 264–77.

Goetzmann, W., 1993, "Patterns in 3 Centuries of Stock-Market Prices," *Journal of Business*, 66(2), 249–70.

Goetzmann, W., R. G. Ibbotson, and L. Peng, 2000, "A New Historical Database for the NYSE 1815 to 1925: Performance and Predictability," *Journal of Financial Markets*, 4(1), 1–32

Hautcoeur, P.-C., and M. Petit-Końiczyk, 2005, "The Development of the Paris Bourse in the Interwar Period," Working Paper, Université Paris I (Matisse) and DELTA.

Hawley, F. B.,1893, "The Risk Theory of Profit," *Quarterly Journal of Economics*, 7(4) 459–79.

Homer, S., 1963, *A History of Interest Rates*, Rutgers University, New Brunswick.

Homer, S., and R. Sylla, 1991, *A History of Interest Rates*, Third Edition, Rutgers University, New Brunswick.

Ibbotson, R. G., and G. P. Brinson, 1987, *Investment Markets*, McGraw-Hill.

Ibbotson, R. G., and P. Chen, 2003, "Long-Run Stock Returns: Participating in the Real Economy," *Financial Analysts Journal*, 59(1).

Ibbotson, R. G., J. Diermeier, and L. B. Siegel, 1984, "The Demand for Capital Market Returns: A New Equilibrium Theory," *Financial Analysts Journal*, 59(1).

Ibbotson, R. G., and R. A. Sinquefield, 1976, "Stocks, Bonds, Bills, and Inflation: Year-by-Year Historical Returns (1926–1974)," *Journal of Business*, 49(1), 11–47.

Ibbotson, R. G., and R. A. Sinquefield, 1976, "Stocks, Bonds, Bills and Inflation: Simulations of the Future 1976–2000," *Journal of Business*, 49(3).

Jorion, P., and W. N. Goetzmann, 1999, "Global Stock Markets in the Twentieth Century," *Journal of Finance*, 54(3), 953–80.

Knight, F., 1921, *Risk, Uncertainty and Profit*, Hart, Shaftner, and Marx, New York.

Markowitz, H., 1952, "Portfolio Selection," *Journal of Finance*, 7(1).

Mehra, R., and E. Prescott, 1985, "The Equity Premium Puzzle," *Journal of Monetary Economics*, 34(4).

Mill, J. S., 1848, *The Principles of Political Economy*, Longmans, Green, and Co., London.

Mill, J. S., 1874, "Essays on Some Unsettled Questions of Political Economy," *History of Economic Thought Books*, McMaster University Archive for the History of Economic Thought, edition 2, number mill1874.

Mitchell, W. C., 1910, "The Prices of American Stocks: 1890–1909," *Journal of Political Economy*, 18(5), 345–80.

Mitchell, W. C., 1915, *The Making and Using of Index Numbers,* Bulletin of the U.S. Bureau of Labor Statistics, 173; 2e édition Bulletin 284.

Mitchell, W. C., 1916, "A Critique of Index Numbers of the Price of Stocks," *Journal of Political Economy,* 24(7), 625–93.

Persons, W. M., 1916, "Construction of a Barometer Based upon Annual Data," *American Economic Review,* 6(4), 739–69.

Reitz, T., 1988, "The Equity Premium: A Solution?" *Journal of Monetary Economics,* 22(1), 133–36.

Schwert, W., 1990, "Indexes of US Stock Prices from 1802 to 1987," *Journal of Business,* 63, 399–426

Siegel, J. J., 1998, *Stocks for the Long Run,* 2nd Edition, McGraw-Hill.

Smith, E. L., 1924, *Common Stocks as Long Term Investments,*

Smith, K. C., and G. F. Horne, 1934, *An Index Number of Securities,* London and Cambridge Economic Service, London.

Williams, J. B., 1938, *The Theory of Investment Value,* Harvard University Press, Cambridge.

Wilson, J., and C. P. Jones, 2002, "An Analysis of the S&P 500 Index and Cowles's Extensions: Price Indexes and Stock Returns 1870–1999," *Journal of Business,* 75(3).

◣ Notes

1. Book 2, Chapter 16, *The Principles of Political Economy,* 1848. See also J. S. Mill, *Essays on Some Unsettled Questions of Political Economy. Essay IV: On Profits, And Interest.* "The profits of stock are the surplus which remains to the capitalist after replacing his capital: and the ratio which that surplus bears to the capital itself, is the rate of profit. The gross profits from capital, the gains returned to those who supply the funds for production, must suffice for these three purposes. They must afford a sufficient equivalent for abstinence, indemnity for risk, and remuneration for the labour and skill required for superintendence." It is somewhat unclear whether he is referring only to a return that covers a probability of expected loss instead of the equity risk premium's increase of expected return to cover systematic risk.

2. J. B. Clark, "Insurance and Business Profit," *Quarterly Journal of Economics,* 7, no. 1 (1892): 40–54. See a response to Clark by Fredrick B. Hawley, "The Risk Theory of Profit," *Quarterly Journal of Economics,* 7, no. 4 (1893): 459–79.

3. For an excellent discussion of the development of early equity indices, see Hautcoeur, Pierre-Cyrille, and Muriel Petit-Kończyk (2005). For a complete list of indices developed before Cowles (1938), see Cowles' own discussion and notes in his volume.

4. Irving Fisher, 1925, "Stocks vs. Bonds," *American Review of Reviews,* July issue.

5. Irving Fisher, *The Theory of Interest* (New York: Macmillan, 1930, 220–21).

6. Chelcie Bowland, *The Common Stock Theory of Investment* (New York: The Ronald Press, 1937).

7. Alfred Cowles, "Common Stock Indices," *Cowles Commission for Research in Economics,* Monograph number 3 (Bloomington, In.: Principia Press, 1938, 2).

8. Alfred Cowles, "A Revision of Previous Conclusions Regarding Stock Price Behavior," *Econometrica,* 28, no. 4 (1960): 909–15.

9. John Burr Williams, *The Theory of Investment Value* (Cambridge, Mass.: Harvard University Press, 1938, 67). Of interest to those interested in financial history is that Williams solves algebraically for the discount rate on the common stock of a firm as a function of the discount rate for the all-equity firm and the firm debt—preceding Modigliani and

Miller in arguing that "The investment value of an enterprise . . . in no way depends upon what the company's capitalization is" (p. 72).

10. Ibid., p. 387.

11. Lawrence Fisher and James H. Lorie, "Rates of Return on Investments in Common Stocks," *Journal of Business,* 37 (1964): 1–21, covered the period 1926–60, which in 1968 they updated through 1965.

12. L. Fisher and J. H. Lorie, "A Half Century of Returns on Stocks and Bonds," University of Chicago Graduate School of Business.

13. The Markowitz framework is a single-period model. As such, the arithmetic return and the geometric return are the same.

14. Elroy Dimson, Paul Marsh and Mike Staunton, *The Millenium Book: A Century of Investment Returns* (ABN-AMRO and London Business School, 2000, 55).

15. William Goetzmann, Roger G. Ibbotson, and Liang Peng, "A New Historical Database for the NYSE 1815 to 1925: Performance and Predictability," *Journal of Financial Markets,* 4, no. 1 (2000): 1–32.

16. · The NYSE database is available for download on the website of the International Center for Finance at the Yale School of Management at www.icf.yale.edu.

17. The R-square of this model was .17, suggesting it has some power.

18. Homer, p. 317.

19. The regression yielded and R-square of 22% with a *t*-statistic of 5.

2 Roger G. Ibbotson and Rex A. Sinquefield

Stocks, Bonds, Bills, and Inflation: Year-by-Year Historical Returns (1926–1974)

▶ *Overview*

Our Ibbotson and Sinquefield article presents almost 50 years of historical total returns on the major asset classes in the United States. The study became the standard for most rate of return studies, and starting in 1983 became updated every year in Stock, Bonds, Bills and Inflation *(SBBI) Yearbooks, published early each year by Ibbotson Associates, in Chicago.*

The study was forward thinking in many respects:

(1) The accuracy of the numbers were carefully documented.

(2) The included asset classes covered a broad spectrum of investing.

(3) The returns reported were "total returns" instead of price returns, which were more conventional at the time.

(4) Returns were compounded, annualized, with arithmetic means, and standard deviations reported.

(5) The results were easily conveyed through one of the earliest uses of "return triangles."

(6) The results were broken into components which included equity, horizon, and default risk premiums, as well as inflation-adjusted real returns for each asset class.

The study includes returns from the 1926–1974 period. Toward the end of the article we present some of the updated results, obtained from Ibbotson Associates.

▶ *Introduction*

In 1964, Lawrence Fisher and James H. Lorie published in this journal their classic study, "Rates of Return on Investments in Common Stocks."[1] In 1968, they extended their study to include all yearly holding period returns from 1926 to 1965.[2] These two articles prompted a widespread interest in the long-run behavior of stock market returns. Motivated by their example, we present in this paper year-by-year *historical* rates of return for five major classes of assets in the United States. In a companion paper forthcoming in this journal,[3] we show how to use the historical data in simulating *future* return distributions for the same five asset classes.

The five asset classes included in this study are (1) common stocks, (2) long-term U.S. government bonds, (3) long-term corporate bonds, (4) U.S. Treasury bills, and (5) consumer goods (inflation). For each asset we present total rates of return which reflect dividend or interest income as well as capital gains or losses.

In addition to the five basic series listed above, we present seven derived series. These derived series represent the component parts of asset returns. They include real (inflation-adjusted) returns for the first four basic series. They also include a series measuring the net return from investing in common stocks rather than bills, the net return from investing in long-term government bonds rather than bills, and the net return from investing in long-term corporate bonds rather than long-term government bonds.

In the second section, we describe the data and computations used for the five basic series. In the third section, we present the rates of return for all yearly holding periods from 1926 to 1974 followed by an index of cumulative wealth relatives for each of the five basic series. In the fourth section, we describe the computation of the derived series, again presenting annual rates of return and an index of cumulative wealth relatives for each of these series. In the fifth section, we give a convenient summary table as well as some highlights of the results.

The Center for Research in Security Prices

The Center for Research in Security Prices (CRSP) at the University of Chicago was founded in 1960 through a grant by Merrill Lynch and provides monthly data on NYSE stock prices, dividends, capitalizations, and returns. CRSP also includes daily returns starting in mid 1962 on other markets, later including NASDAQ. In addition, CRSP includes government bonds and other databases. These raw databases have been instrumental in precipitating huge quantities of empirical research in U.S. capital markets.

The earlier Fisher and Lorie rate of return studies were based upon the CRSP data, and indeed James H. Lorie and Lawrence Fisher were the founders of CRSP and set up the original NYSE monthly databases. The Ibbotson and Sinquefield common stocks were based upon Standard and Poor's data, so that it is reasonable to compare the differences between Fisher and Lorie with Ibbotson and Sinquefield.

Ibbotson and Sinquefield use CRSP data in constructing the U.S. Government Bond and U.S. Treasury Bill series. Roger Ibbotson was Executive Director at CRSP from 1979 to 1984.

◣ Basic Historical Series

We initially construct the five basic return series covering common stocks, long-term government and corporate bonds, Treasury bills, and inflation. Annual returns for each asset are formed by compounding monthly returns. In all cases, returns are formed assuming no taxes or transactions costs.

Common Stocks

Our common stock total return index is based upon the Standard and Poor's (S&P) Composite Index.[4] We use this index because it is a readily available, carefully constructed, market value weighted benchmark of common stock performance. By market value weighted, we mean that the weight of each stock in the index equals its price times the number of shares outstanding. Currently the S&P Composite includes 500 of the largest stocks (in terms of stock market value) in the United States; prior to March 1957 it consisted of 90 of the largest stocks. To the extent that the stocks included in the S&P Composite Index represent the market value of stocks in the United States, the weighting scheme allows the returns of the index to correspond to the aggregate stock market returns in the U.S. economy.

Although Standard and Poor's reports its Composite Index exclusive of dividends, it also reports a quarterly dividend series. Except for the most recent years (since 1968) the dividend series is available only in the form of four-quarter moving totals. However, given four separate dividends for any one year, it is possible to unravel the moving totals into separate quarterly dividends for all the years prior to 1968.[5] Monthly dividends are then formed by proportioning the quarterly dividends into the 3 months of the quarter according to recently observed proportions.[6]

Designating common stocks as m, we form monthly returns by

$$R_{m,t} = (P_{m,t} + D_{m,t})/P_{m,t-1} - 1, \qquad (1)$$

where $R_{m,t}$ is the common stock total return during month t; $P_{m,t}$ is the value of the S&P Composite Index at the end of month t; and $D_{m,t}$ is the estimated dividends received during month t and reinvested at the end of month t.

Since there will inevitably be comparisons between our results and those of the Fisher and Lorie studies,[7] some differences in methodology should be noted. Their studies measured annual returns (calculated like ours from monthly returns) of an *equally* weighted portfolio of all New York Stock Exchange (NYSE) common stocks. Thus, their weighting scheme measures the performance of an investor who chose stocks through simple random selection. Ours measures the return to an investor who "bought the market" in the sense that the stocks included in the S&P Composite Index represent most of the value of the U.S. publicly traded stocks.

Another difference between our results and the results of Fisher and Lorie is that they measure returns from a buy and hold strategy, while our portfolio weighting scheme is continuously updated. This allows them to measure the returns on 40 separate portfolios, one starting each year from 1926 to 1965. For example, their 1926–65 period return (compounded annually) is the return on a portfolio equally weighted as of January 1926 and held (not reweighted except by market movements and dividend reinvestments) throughout the entire period. In comparison, our 1926–65 period return (compounded annually) is the return on a portfolio that is market weighted each month throughout the entire period. Our procedure only approximates a buy and hold strategy since our weighting scheme takes into account increases and decreases in the amount of a company's stock outstanding as well as any changes in the stocks included in the S&P Composite Index. An advantage of their buy and hold procedure is that they can present return series for various tax rates with and without commissions. An advantage of our procedure is that our returns can easily be interpreted since they always reflect a market weighted portfolio.

Long-Term U.S. Government Bonds

To measure the total returns of long-term U.S. government bonds, we construct a bond portfolio using the bond data obtained from the U.S. Government Bond File at the Center for Research in Security Prices (CRSP).[8] Our objective is to maintain a 20-year-term bond portfolio whose returns do not reflect potential tax benefits, impaired negotiability, or special redemption or call privileges. We follow with a brief description of the types of bonds included and excluded from the portfolio.[9]

Prior to March 1941, the income from almost all U.S. government bonds was exempt from "normal" income taxes. However, some of the bonds were subject to the surtax. Since surtax rates were far higher than normal tax rates for large investors, the returns (yields) of the bonds subject to the surtax are not lowered to reflect substantial tax advantages. Therefore, we choose to include in our index only those bonds subject to the surtax during the period 1926–March 1941. Our bond returns are somewhat analogous to our stock returns during most of this period since cash dividends were also exempt from normal income taxes until 1936. The income on all bonds issued subsequent to March 1941 is subject to federal income taxation.

The large size and large number of investors associated with government issues usually ensures high marketability. As direct obligations of the U.S. government, default risk is virtually nonexistent. Consequently, government bonds usually are ideal collateral. However, some 2¼ and 2½ percent bonds issued during the 1940s were restricted until 1953 from bank portfolios, substantially reducing their collateral value. Since returns from bank ineligible bonds are inflated to compensate for their impaired negotiability, these bonds are excluded from the index.

Many government bonds (commonly known as "flower" bonds) have a redemption feature which allows the investor to redeem his bonds at par (plus accrued interest) in payment of federal estate taxes. Some bonds must be owned by the decedent for a 6-month period prior to his death, while other bonds need be owned only at the time of death. Since part of the return on these bonds is the capital gain from early redemption, the return exclusive of the redemption is lower in general than the return on other bonds not possessing the redemption feature. We therefore seek to avoid using flower bonds in the index. During the many periods when we must use flower bonds, we indirectly avoid their effects on returns. In general, the users of the redemption feature have short time horizons so that they are more interested in low bond prices (relative to par) than high bond yields. By including only those flower bonds with high yields and prices relative to other existing flower bonds, we effectively restrict the index to bonds whose redemption features are seldom exercised while they are in the index.

Finally, our index must take into account that most long-term government bonds were callable by the U.S. Treasury after a designated first call date. For callable bonds, it is unclear whether the life of the bond should be measured by the first call or the maturity date. We attempt to reduce the problem by avoiding bonds with early first call dates relative to their maturity dates. We then attempt to hold a 20-year-life portfolio with the life arbitrarily measured as the simple average of the maturity and first call dates minus the holding period date.[10]

The above-mentioned constraints severely limit the bonds eligible for inclusion in our index. The problem is that the U.S. government bonds available at any one time usually have somewhat homogeneous characteristics. We can either build a multibond index (say, by linearly combining bond lives to satisfy our 20-year term objective), or select the one bond which best fits our criteria. We choose to form a one-bond portfolio since there are some periods when only one bond reasonably fits our criteria. However, the lack of diversification in a one-bond portfolio is not a serious defect. Since we assume no default risk, one fairly priced bond adequately reflects the return of other bonds with similar characteristics (maturity date, first call date, coupon, tax, etc.).

Appendix 2 lists the actual bonds held in the portfolio. Over the sample period, the average term to maturity is 23.2 years while the average term to first call is 18.2 years, giving an average life of 20.7 years. While, on average, we come close to maintaining a 20-year life, the maturities range from 18.2 to 30.7 years and the first call ranges from 9.4 to 25.7 years.

Monthly returns on government bonds are formed according to

$$R_{g,t} = (P_{g,t} + D_{g,t})/P_{g,t-1} - 1, \tag{2}$$

where $R_{g,t}$ is the long-term government bond total return during month t; $P_{g,t}$ is the average between the bid and ask flat price (includes accrued interest) of the bond at the end of month t; and $D_{g,t}$ is the coupon payment received during month t and invested at the end of month t.

Long-Term Corporate Bonds

Since most large corporate bond transactions take place over the counter, the natural source of data is a major dealer. Salomon Brothers has already constructed the High Grade Long-Term Corporate Bond Index.[11] We use this monthly index from its beginning in 1969 through 1974. For the period 1946–68 we backdate the Salomon Brothers' Index using Salomon Brothers' monthly data and similar methodology. For the period 1926–45 we use the Standard and Poor's monthly High-Grade Corporate Composite Bond Index,[12] assuming a 4 percent coupon and a 20-year maturity.

The purpose of the Salomon Brothers' Index is to approximate the total returns that would be earned by holding the entire high-grade long-term corporate bond market. The relevant market is defined as all industrial and utility issues which were originally publicly offered with a maturity of 1985 or longer, a Moody rating of Aaa or Aa, and an outstanding par amount of at least $25 million.

The Salomon Brothers' Index is constructed by computing a weighted average of the returns from 17 representative bonds. The yields of these bonds are identical with 17 Salomon Brothers' corporate bond monthly yield series listed as industrial or utility by coupon range.[13] Each of the 17 representative bonds is assigned a maturity, a coupon, and a weight by determining the market weighted average maturity and coupon in each coupon range and the weight of each coupon range in the market. Monthly prices and total returns are then computed for each bond given its yield, coupon, and maturity date. The index is formed as a cumulative wealth relative of the weighted average of the 17 bond returns. At the beginning of 1969, the Salomon Brothers' Index had an average maturity of approximately 25 years.

Although the Salomon Brothers' Index is available only from 1969, 8 of their 17 corporate bond yield series were initiated prior to 1969 while one series was initiated as early as 1946. We backdate the index by assuming the mean coupon in the coupon range defined for each of the yield series and a 20-year maturity date. Bond prices are then computed, given the yield, coupon, and maturity date.

Returns for each of the eight yield series are calculated as

$$R_{c,t} = (P_{c,t,19\text{-}11} + D_{c,t})/P_{c,t-1,20} - 1, \tag{3}$$

where $R_{c,t}$ is the monthly bond return for a particular series during month t; $P_{c,t-1,20}$ is the purchase price at the end of month $t-1$ for the yield series bond given a 20-year maturity; $P_{c,t}$,19-11 is the sale price of the yield series bond at the end of month t given at this time 19 years, 11 months to maturity; and $D_{c,t}$ is the coupon received which is one-twelfth the annual coupon given for the bond series.[14] The overall long-term corporate bond return is then calculated as the weighted average of the eight individual bond returns. The weights are shown in Appendix 3.

Since the Salomon Brothers' data start in 1946, it is necessary to link another index for the period 1926–45. We use the monthly yield series represented in Standard and Poor's High-Grade Composite Bond Index, assuming a 4 percent coupon and a 20-year maturity, and calculate bond prices accordingly.[15] Monthly total returns are again formed according to equation (3).

United States Treasury Bills

For the U.S. Treasury Bill Index, we again use the data in the CRSP U.S. Government Bond File. Our objective is to construct an index that includes the shortest-term bills not less than 1 month in maturity. We also want our index to reflect achievable returns. Therefore, rather than compute yields, we measure 1-month holding period returns for a one-bill portfolio.

Although U.S. Treasury bills were initiated as early as 1929, the U.S. Government Bond File does not include any bills until 1931. Prior to that time, we use short-term coupon bonds. The bills are quoted on a discount basis without coupon, and their returns were exempt from all income taxes until March 1941. Thereafter, their returns were subject to normal income taxes as well as any surtaxes.

Beginning in the early 1940s, the yields (returns) on Treasury bills were pegged by the government at low rates. Coupons on new government bond issues were also pegged, but the effect on returns was not as great since a sliding coupon scale was used increasing with maturity. The government pegging ended with the U.S. Treasury–Federal Reserve Accord in March 1951.

The U.S. Government Bond File includes only month-end prices. Although these prices are quoted for same-day delivery during the period 1926–41, they are quoted with deliveries ranging from 2 to 5 days during the period 1942–73. In 1974, the bond quotes are obtained from the *Wall Street Journal*, once again quoted for same-day delivery. Since we wish to follow an achievable investment strategy, we must take these delivery dates into consideration.

We choose to include in the one-bill portfolio the bill having the shortest term without maturing in less than 1 month, after allowing for delivery dates. For example, assume that the bills at the end of calendar month t are quoted for delivery on the second day of calendar month $t + 1$. Then the bill purchased at the end of calendar month $t - 1$ is the shortest-term bill maturing on or after the second day of calendar month $t + 1$. The bill is subsequently sold at the end of calendar month t and delivered 2 days later. Since a new bill is purchased at the end of month t (and delivered 2 days later), this procedure allows us to be continually invested. In the case where the delivery date and the maturity date would be the same, the bond is matured. The yearly average of the days to maturity on monthly purchase dates is shown in Appendix 4.

The monthly total U.S. Treasury bill return during month t, $R_{f,t}$, can be computed directly from the end of the calendar month t discount bill prices, $P_{f,t}$, according to

$$R_{f,t} = P_{f,t}/P_{f,t-1} - 1. \tag{4}$$

Again, the prices used are the average of bid and ask.

Inflation

We utilize the Consumer Price Index (CPI)[16] to measure inflation, which is the rate of change of consumer goods prices. Monthly rates of change are formed by

$$R_{I,t} = V_{I,t} / V_{I,t-1} - 1, \tag{5}$$

where $V_{I,t}$ is the value of the CPI (not seasonally adjusted) measured during month t.

Although we consider the CPI as the best measure of inflation available at the consumer level, there are numerous problems in applying it as a cost-of-living measure. Its official name is the *Consumer Price Index for Urban Wage Earners and Clerical Workers*, and it purports to measure the average "market basket" for this select consumer group rather than for all the consumers in the U.S. economy. Its construction is subject to statistical problems related to the sampling and processing of data. It is also subject to conceptual problems, the most prominent being the handling of commodity quality changes, the changing of people's buying preferences (sometimes caused by the price changes themselves), and the pricing of services rendered by capital goods. In addition, the index is not continuous since it was substantially revised in the years 1940, 1953, and 1964. Numerous minor revisions have also been made from time to time.

Even though we treat $R_{I,t}$ as a measure of the rate of inflation during month t, the way that the Bureau of Labor Statistics measures $V_{I,t}$ causes $R_{I,t}$ to lag behind actual inflation rates. The CPI currently includes about 400 items priced in 56 urban regions weighted by their populations. Thus, the CPI reflects a weighted average of many component indices. While most of the components of the CPI are priced monthly, some are priced quarterly, a few are priced semiannually or annually, and some reflect contractual rent agreements rather than current prices. Even the monthly pricing is not priced as of the end of the calendar month but rather extends throughout the month.

◤ Holding Period Return Matrices for Basic Series

At the end of each month n, we form a cumulative wealth relative index V_n for each of the monthly return series R_t ($t = 1/26, 2/26, \ldots, 12/74$). This index is initialized at $V_{12/25} = 1.0$ and is formed by

$$V_n = \prod_{t=1/26}^{n} (1 + R_t). \tag{6}$$

Annual calendar returns, R_T, are formed by compounding monthly returns or, equivalently, by using year-end index values, V_N, according to

$$R_T = \frac{V_N}{V_{N-1}} - 1. \tag{7}$$

We also compute geometric mean annual returns (the rate of return per annum compounded annually), $R_G^*(T_1, T_2)$, for any calendar holding period beginning with year T_1 and ending with year T_2 according to

$$R_G^*(T_1, T_2) = \left[\prod_{T=T_1}^{T_2} (1 + R_T) \right]^{1/(T_2 - T_1 + 1)} - 1. \tag{8}$$

The geometric mean annual return formed by Equation (8) should not be confused with the arithmetic mean annual return $R_A^*)(T_1, T_2)$ formed by

$$R_A^*(T_1, T_2) = \prod_{T=T_1}^{T_2} R_T / (T_2 - T_1 + 1). \tag{9}$$

In general,

$$R_G^*(T_1, T_2) \leq R_A^*(T_1, T_2), \tag{10}$$

with the equality only holding for constant returns with the difference between the two estimates being positively related to the variance of returns.

Table 2.1 gives the geometric mean annual returns for all calendar yearly holding periods for common stocks. For example, in Table 2.1 the geometric mean annual return for common stocks for the period 1926–74 is 8.5 percent and is found in the matrix in column 1926 and in row 1974.

The year-by-year annual returns, R_T, for common stocks are shown along the diagonals of the matrices in Tables 2.1. The year-end index values of cumulative wealth relatives, V_N, are shown in Table 2.2 for each of the five basic series. Updated results through 2005 are presented in Table 2.3

◣ Derived Series

Seven monthly return series are derived from the five basic series. The first three series include the net return from investing in common stocks rather than bills, the net return from investing in long-term government bonds rather than bills, and the net return from investing in long-term corporate bonds rather than long-term government bonds. We refer to these three series, respectively, as "risk premia," "maturity premia," and "default premia."[17] In addition, we estimate real (inflation-adjusted) return series for common stocks, long-term government and corporate bonds, and Treasury bills. Year-by-year returns, R_T, for each of the derived series are formed by Equation (7) and are listed in Table 2.4. A description of each series follows.

Risk Premia

It is generally accepted in financial theory that capital markets are dominated by risk-averse investors who expect compensation for investing in common

Table 2.1

Common Stocks: Rates of Return for All Yearly Holding Periods From 1926 to 1974 (Percent per Annum Compounded Annually)

To the End Of	From the Beginning Of																
	1926	1927	1928	1929	1930	1931	1932	1933	1934	1935	1936	1937	1938	1939	1940	1941	1942
1926	11.6																
1927	23.9	37.5															
1928	30.1	40.5	43.6														
1929	19.2	21.8	14.7	-8.4													
1930	8.7	7.9	-0.4	-17.1	-24.9												
1931	-2.5	-5.1	-13.5	-27.0	-34.8	-43.3											
1932	-3.3	-5.6	-12.5	-22.7	-26.9	-27.9	-8.2										
1933	2.4	1.2	-3.8	-11.2	-11.9	-7.1	18.9	54.0									
1934	2.0	0.9	-3.5	-9.7	-9.9	-5.7	11.7	23.2	-1.4								
1935	5.9	5.2	1.8	-3.1	-2.2	3.1	19.8	30.9	20.6	47.7							
1936	8.1	7.8	4.9	0.9	2.3	7.7	22.5	31.6	24.9	40.6	33.9						
1937	3.6	3.0	0.0	-3.9	-3.3	0.2	10.2	14.3	5.1	8.7	-6.7	-35.0					
1938	5.5	5.0	2.5	-0.9	-0.0	3.6	13.0	16.9	10.7	13.9	4.5	-7.7	31.1				
1939	5.1	4.6	2.3	-0.8	-0.1	3.2	11.2	14.3	8.7	10.9	3.2	-5.3	14.3	-0.4			
1940	4.0	3.5	1.3	-1.6	-1.0	1.8	8.6	11.0	5.9	7.2	0.5	-6.5	5.6	-5.2	-9.8		
1941	3.0	2.4	0.3	-2.4	-1.9	0.5	6.4	8.2	3.5	4.3	-1.6	-7.5	1.0	-7.4	-10.7	-11.6	
1942	3.9	3.5	1.5	-1.0	-0.4	2.0	7.6	9.4	5.3	6.1	1.2	-3.4	4.6	-1.1	-1.4	3.1	20.3
1943	5.0	4.7	2.9	0.6	1.3	3.7	9.0	10.8	7.2	8.2	4.0	0.4	7.9	3.8	4.9	10.2	23.1
1944	5.0	5.5	3.8	1.7	2.5	4.8	9.8	11.5	8.3	9.3	5.7	2.6	9.5	6.3	7.7	12.5	22.0
1945	7.1	6.9	5.4	3.5	4.3	6.6	11.5	13.2	10.4	11.5	8.4	5.9	12.6	10.1	12.0	17.0	25.4
1946	6.3	6.1	4.7	2.8	3.5	5.6	10.1	11.6	8.8	9.7	6.8	4.4	10.1	7.7	8.9	12.4	17.9
1947	6.3	6.1	4.7	3.0	3.7	5.6	9.8	11.2	8.6	9.4	6.7	4.5	9.6	7.5	8.5	11.4	15.8
1948	6.3	6.1	4.7	3.1	3.8	5.6	9.6	10.8	8.4	9.1	6.6	4.6	9.2	7.3	8.2	10.6	14.2
1949	6.8	6.6	5.3	3.8	4.5	6.3	10.1	11.3	9.0	9.7	7.4	5.6	10.0	8.3	9.2	11.5	14.8
1950	7.7	7.5	5.4	4.9	5.6	7.4	11.1	12.3	10.2	11.0	8.9	7.3	11.5	10.1	11.1	13.4	16.6

Year																
1951	8.3	8.1	7.1	5.7	6.4	8.2	11.7	12.9	11.0	11.7	9.8	8.4	12.4	11.1	12.1	14.3	17.3
1952	8.6	8.5	7.5	6.2	6.9	8.6	12.0	13.2	11.3	12.1	10.3	9.0	12.8	11.6	12.6	14.6	17.4
1953	8.3	8.1	7.2	5.9	6.5	8.2	11.4	12.4	10.7	11.4	9.6	8.3	11.9	10.7	11.5	13.4	15.7
1954	9.6	9.5	8.6	7.4	8.1	9.7	12.9	14.0	12.4	13.1	11.6	10.4	13.9	12.9	13.9	15.8	18.2
1955	10.2	10.2	9.3	8.2	8.9	10.5	13.7	14.7	13.2	13.9	12.5	11.5	14.8	13.91	14.9	16.8	19.1
1956	10.1	10.1	9.2	8.2	8.8	10.4	13.4	14.4	12.9	13.6	12.2	11.2	14.4	13.5	14.4	1.6	18.2
1957	9.4	9.3	8.5	7.4	8.1	9.5	12.3	13.2	11.8	12.4	11.0	10.0	13.0	12.1	12.8	14.3	16.2
1958	10.3	10.2	9.5	8.5	9.1	10.6	13.3	14.3	12.9	13.6	12.3	11.4	14.3	13.5	14.3	15.8	17.6
1959	10.3	10.3	9.5	8.6	9.2	10.6	13.3	14.2	12.9	13.5	12.3	11.4	14.2	13.4	14.1	15.6	17.3
1960	10.0	10.0	9.3	8.3	8.9	10.3	12.8	13.7	12.4	13.0	11.8	10.9	13.5	12.8	13.5	14.8	16.4
1961	10.5	10.4	9.7	8.8	9.4	10.8	13.3	14.1	12.9	13.4	12.3	11.5	14.1	13.4	14.0	15.3	16.9
1962	9.9	9.9	9.2	8.3	8.8	10.1	12.5	13.3	12.1	12.6	11.4	10.7	13.0	12.3	12.9	14.1	15.5
1963	10.2	10.2	9.5	8.7	9.2	10.5	12.8	13.5	12.4	12.9	11.8	11.1	13.4	12.7	13.3	14.5	15.8
1964	10.4	10.4	9.7	8.9	9.4	10.6	12.9	13.6	12.5	13.0	12.0	11.3	13.5	12.9	13.5	14.5	15.8
1965	10.4	10.4	9.8	9.0	9.5	10.7	12.9	13.6	12.5	13.0	12.0	11.3	13.5	12.9	13.4	14.5	15.7
1966	9.9	9.8	9.2	8.4	8.9	10.1	12.2	12.8	11.8	12.2	11.2	10.5	12.6	12.0	12.4	13.4	14.5
1967	10.2	10.2	9.6	8.8	9.3	10.4	12.5	13.1	12.1	12.5	11.6	10.9	12.9	12.4	12.8	13.8	14.9
1968	10.2	10.2	9.6	8.9	9.3	10.4	12.4	13.1	12.1	12.5	11.6	10.9	12.9	12.3	12.8	13.7	14.7
1969	9.8	9.7	9.1	8.4	8.9	9.9	11.8	12.4	11.5	11.8	10.9	10.3	12.1	11.6	12.0	12.8	13.0
1970	9.6	9.6	9.0	8.3	8.7	9.7	11.6	12.2	11.2	11.6	10.7	10.1	11.9	11.3	11.7	12.5	13.5
1971	9.7	9.7	9.1	8.4	8.9	9.9	11.7	12.3	11.3	11.7	10.8	10.2	12.0	11.4	11.8	12.6	13.5
1972	9.9	9.9	9.3	8.7	9.1	10.1	11.9	12.4	11.5	11.9	11.0	10.5	12.1	11.6	12.0	12.8	13.7
1973	9.3	9.3	8.7	8.1	8.5	9.4	11.1	11.7	10.8	11.1	10.3	9.7	11.3	10.8	11.1	11.8	12.7
1974	8.5	8.4	7.8	7.2	7.5	8.4	10.1	10.6	9.7	10.0	9.1	8.5	10.0	9.5	9.8	10.5	11.2

Table 2.1 (*continued*)
Common Stocks: Rates of Return for All Yearly Holding Periods From 1926 to 1974 (Percent per Annum Compounded Annually)

To the End Of	From the Beginning Of															
	1943	1944	1945	1946	1947	1948	1949	1950	1951	1952	1953	1954	1955	1956	1957	1958
1943	25.9															
1944	22.8	19.7														
1945	27.2	27.8	36.4													
1946	17.3	14.5	12.0	−8.1												
1947	14.9	12.3	9.9	−1.4	5.8											
1948	13.2	10.9	8.8	0.9	5.6	5.5										
1949	14.0	12.2	10.7	5.1	9.9	12.0	18.8									
1950	16.1	14.8	14.0	9.9	15.0	18.2	25.1	31.7								
1951	17.0	15.9	15.3	12.2	16.7	19.6	24.7	27.8	24.0							
1952	17.1	16.2	15.7	13.0	17.0	19.4	23.1	24.6	21.1	18.3						
1953	15.3	14.3	13.7	11.2	14.2	15.7	17.9	17.6	13.3	8.3	−1.0					
1954	18.0	17.4	17.1	15.2	18.4	20.4	23.0	23.9	22.0	21.4	22.9	52.6				
1955	19.0	18.5	18.4	16.7	19.8	21.7	24.2	25.2	23.9	23.8	25.7	41.7	31.5			
1956	18.1	17.5	17.3	15.7	18.4	19.9	21.9	22.3	20.8	20.2	20.6	28.8	18.4	6.6		
1957	15.9	15.2	14.9	13.3	15.4	16.4	17.7	17.6	15.7	14.4	13.6	17.5	7.7	−2.5	−10.8	

Year																
1958	17.5	16.9	16.7	15.3	17.5	18.7	20.1	20.2	18.8	18.1	18.1	22.3	15.7	10.9	13.1	43.4
1959	17.1	16.6	16.4	15.1	17.1	18.1	19.3	19.4	18.0	17.3	17.2	20.5	15.0	11.1	12.7	26.7
1960	16.1	15.6	15.3	14.0	15.8	16.6	17.6	17.5	16.2	15.3	14.9	17.4	12.4	8.9	9.5	17.3
1961	16.7	16.2	15.0	14.8	16.5	17.3	18.3	18.3	17.1	16.4	16.2	18.6	14.4	11.7	12.8	19.6
1962	15.3	14.7	14.4	13.3	14.8	15.4	16.1	15.9	14.7	13.9	13.4	15.2	11.2	8.5	8.9	13.3
1963	15.6	15.1	14.9	13.8	15.2	15.8	16.6	16.4	15.3	14.6	14.3	15.9	12.4	10.2	10.8	14.8
1964	15.6	15.2	15.0	13.9	15.3	15.9	16.6	16.4	15.4	14.7	14.4	16.0	12.8	10.9	11.5	15.1
1965	15.5	15.0	14.8	13.8	15.1	15.7	16.3	16.2	15.2	14.6	14.3	15.7	12.8	11.1	11.6	14.7
1966	14.3	13.8	13.6	12.6	13.7	14.2	14.7	14.4	13.4	12.7	12.4	13.4	10.7	9.0	9.2	11.7
1967	14.7	14.2	14.0	13.1	14.2	14.6	15.1	14.9	14.0	13.4	13.1	14.2	11.6	10.1	10.5	12.9
1968	14.5	14.1	13.9	13.0	14.0	14.5	14.9	14.7	13.8	13.3	13.0	14.0	11.6	10.2	10.5	12.7
1969	13.6	13.1	12.9	12.0	13.0	13.3	13.7	13.4	12.5	11.9	11.6	12.4	10.1	8.8	8.9	10.8
1970	13.2	12.8	12.5	11.7	12.6	12.9	13.2	13.0	12.1	11.5	11.1	11.9	9.7	8.4	8.6	10.2
1971	13.3	12.8	12.6	11.8	12.6	12.9	13.3	13.0	12.2	11.6	11.3	12.0	10.0	8.8	8.9	10.5
1972	13.5	13.0	12.8	12.0	12.9	13.2	13.5	13.3	12.5	12.0	11.7	12.4	10.5	9.4	9.5	11.1
1973	12.4	12.0	11.7	10.9	11.7	12.0	12.2	12.0	11.2	10.6	10.3	10.8	9.0	7.9	7.9	9.2
1974	10.9	10.5	10.2	9.4	10.1	10.2	10.4	10.1	9.3	8.7	8.2	8.7	6.9	5.7	5.7	6.7

Table 2.1 (*continued*)
Common Stocks: Rates of Return for All Yearly Holding Periods From 1926 to 1974 (Percent per Annum Compounded Annually)

To the End Of	From the Beginning Of															
	1959	1960	1961	1962	1963	1964	1965	1966	1967	1968	1969	1970	1971	1972	1973	1974
1959	12.0															
1960	6.1	0.5														
1961	12.6	12.9	26.9													
1962	6.8	5.2	7.6	−8.7												
1963	9.8	9.3	12.4	5.9	22.8											
1964	10.9	10.7	13.4	9.3	19.6	16.5										
1965	11.1	11.0	13.2	10.1	17.2	14.5	12.4									
1966	8.2	7.7	9.0	5.7	9.7	5.6	0.6	−10.0								
1967	9.9	9.6	11.0	8.6	12.4	9.9	7.8	5.6	24.0							
1968	10.0	9.8	11.0	8.9	12.2	10.2	8.6	7.4	17.4	11.1						
1969	8.2	7.8	8.7	6.6	9.0	6.8	5.0	3.2	8.0	0.9	−8.4					
1970	7.8	7.5	8.2	6.3	8.3	6.4	4.8	3.4	7.0	1.9	−2.4	3.9				
1971	8.3	8.0	8.7	7.1	9.0	7.4	6.1	5.1	8.4	4.9	2.9	9.0	14.3			
1972	9.0	8.8	9.5	8.1	9.9	8.6	7.7	7.0	10.1	7.5	6.7	12.2	16.6	19.0		
1973	7.3	6.9	7.5	6.0	7.4	6.0	4.9	4.0	6.2	3.5	2.0	4.8	5.1	0.8	−14.7	
1974	4.8	4.3	4.6	3.0	4.1	2.5	1.2	0.1	1.4	−1.5	−3.4	−2.4	−3.9	−9.3	−20.8	−26.4

stocks rather than risk-free assets such as U.S. Treasury bills.[18] The monthly risk premia, $R_{p,t}$, are given by

$$R_{p,t} = \frac{1 + R_{m,t}}{1 + R_{f,t}} - 1 = \frac{R_{m,t} - R_{f,t}}{1 + R_{f,t}}. \tag{11}$$

Equation (11) is presented as the ratio of price relatives. It estimates net returns from investing in common stock, $R_{m,t}$, relative to the returns on bills, $R_{f,t}$. Frequently, risk premia are measured by the simple difference,

$$R'_{p,t} = R_{m,t} - R_{f,t}. \tag{12}$$

Equation (12) estimates net returns from investing in stocks rather than bills relative to beginning of the period dollars. For the small $R_{f,t}$ observed in monthly data, the differences between Equation (11) estimates and Equation (12) estimates are very small.[19]

Maturity Premia

Since U.S. government bonds and bills are not considered subject to default, the net return from investing in bonds rather than bills stems primarily from their differences in maturity. The net returns are often called "liquidity premia," and it has frequently been hypothesized that these returns are positive on average.[20] Since "liquidity" implies marketability rather than the more important bond life characteristic, we relabel this net return "maturity premia" and generate it historically according to

$$R_{L,t} = \frac{1 + R_{g,t}}{1 + R_{f,t}} - 1. \tag{13}$$

From the bond portfolio manager's point of view, $R_{L,t}$ can be thought of as the gains or losses resulting from the decision to hold long-term bonds rather than short-term bonds.

Default Premia

We define the default premia as the net returns from investing in long-term corporate bonds rather than long-term government bonds of equal maturities. We estimate monthly default premia, $R_{d,t}$, according to

$$R_{d,t} = \frac{1 + R_{c,t}}{1 + R_{g,t}} - 1. \tag{14}$$

Since the long-term U.S. government bond series and the long-term corporate bond series have approximately equal maturities, the net rate of return between the two series is primarily related to differences in the probability of coupon or principal default. From the bond portfolio manager's point of view, $R_{d,t}$ is a measure of the gains or losses associated with holding high-quality corporate bonds rather than government bonds.

Table 2.2
Index of Year-End Cumulative Wealth Relatives From 1925 Through 1974

Year	Common Stocks	Long-Term Government Bonds	Long-Term Corporate Bonds	U.S. Treasury Bills	Consumer Price Index
1925	1.000	1.000	1.000	1.000	1.000
1926	1.116	1.078	1.074	1.032	0.985
1927	1.534	1.174	1.154	1.064	0.965
1928	2.203	1.175	1.186	1.106	0.956
1929	2.018	1.215	1.225	1.161	0.958
1930	1.516	1.272	1.323	1.187	0.900
1931	0.859	1.258	1.298	1.195	0.814
1932	0.788	1.470	1.439	1.207	0.731
1933	1.214	1.469	1.588	1.211	0.734
1934	1.196	1.617	1.808	1.213	0.749
1935	1.766	1.698	1.982	1.215	0.772
1936	2.365	1.825	2.116	1.217	0.781
1937	1.537	1.829	2.174	1.220	0.805
1938	2.015	1.930	2.307	1.220	0.783
1939	1.401	2.045	2.398	1.220	0.779
1940	1.811	2.170	2.480	1.220	0.787
1941	1.601	2.190	2.547	1.220	0.863
1942	1.927	2.261	2.614	1.224	0.943
1943	2.426	2.308	2.688	1.223	0.973
1944	2.904	2.374	2.815	1.232	0.993
1945	3.962	2.628	2.930	1.236	1.016
1946	4.377	2.626	2.980	1.241	1.200
1947	3.852	2.557	2.910	1.247	1.308
1948	4.064	2.644	3.031	1.257	1.343
1949	4.828	2.815	3.131	1.266	1.319

Inflation-Adjusted Returns of the Basic Series

The monthly inflation-adjusted returns for the $R_{m,t}$, $R_{g,t}$, $R_{c,t}$, and $R_{f,t}$ series are estimated as

$$R_{mr,t} = \frac{1 + R_{m,t}}{1 + R_{I,t}} - 1, \tag{15}$$

$$R_{gr,t} = \frac{1 + R_{g,t}}{1 + R_{I,t}} - 1, \tag{16}$$

$$R_{cr,t} = \frac{1 + R_{c,t}}{1 + R_{I,t}} - 1, \tag{17}$$

Table 2.2 (continued)
Index of Year-End Cumulative Wealth Relatives From 1925 Through 1974

Year	Common Stocks	Long-Term Government Bonds	Long-Term Corporate Bonds	U.S. Treasury Bills	Consumer Price Index
1950	6.360	2.816	3.197	1.281	1.395
1951	7.887	2.705	3.111	1.300	1.477
1952	9.335	2.737	3.221	1.321	1.490
1953	9.243	2.836	3.330	1.344	1.499
1954	14.107	3.039	3.510	1.355	1.492
1955	18.557	3.000	3.527	1.377	1.498
1956	19.773	2.832	3.286	1.411	1.541
1957	17.639	3.044	3.569	1.455	1.587
1958	25.289	2.859	3.490	1.477	1.615
1959	28.318	2.794	3.456	1.521	1.639
1960	28.449	3.179	3.770	1.561	1.663
1961	36.098	3.210	3.951	1.594	1.675
1962	32.947	3.430	4.265	1.638	1.695
1963	40.451	3.471	4.359	1.689	1.723
1964	47.128	3.594	4.567	1.749	1.745
1965	52.996	3.619	4.546	1.817	1.778
1966	47.671	3.752	4.555	1.902	1.838
1967	59.105	3.408	4.329	1.983	1.894
1968	65.654	3.398	4.441	2.086	1.984
1969	60.119	3.227	4.081	2.223	2.105
1970	62.492	3.616	4.831	2.367	2.220
1971	71.439	4.094	5.363	2.470	2.295
1972	84.992	4.328	5.752	2.565	2.373
1973	72.526	4.566	5.818	2.744	2.581
1974	53.340	4.767	5.640	2.965	2.879

$$R_{fr,t} = \frac{1 + R_{f,t}}{1 + R_{I,t}} - 1, \qquad (18)$$

where the additional subscript r on each of the returns on the left side of Equations (15)–(18) refers to the fact that each series is real (inflation-adjusted).

▲ Historical Highlights

A summary of the annual historical returns for each of the five basic series and the seven derived series is presented in Table 2.5, with partial updates provided by Table 2.6 at the end of this section.[21] Some of the highlights follow.

Table 2.3
Basic Series: Indices of Year-End Cumulative Wealth from 1971 to 2002 (Year-end 1925 = $1.00)

Year	Large Stocks Total Returns	Large Stocks Capital Apprec	Small Stocks Total Returns	Long-Term Corp Bonds Total Returns	Long-Term Government Bonds Total Returns	Long-Term Government Bonds Capital Apprec	Intermediate-Term Government Bonds Total Returns	Intermediate-Term Government Bonds Capital Apprec	U.S. T-Bills Total Returns	Inflation
1971	71.406	8.001	121.423	5.370	3.917	0.844	4.519	1.177	2.490	2.292
1972	84.956	9.252	126.807	5.760	4.140	0.841	4.752	1.168	2.585	2.371
1973	72.500	7.645	87.618	5.825	4.094	0.777	4.971	1.142	2.764	2.579
1974	53.311	5.373	70.142	5.647	4.272	0.750	5.254	1.120	2.986	2.894
1975	73.144	7.068	107.189	6.474	4.665	0.755	5.665	1.121	3.159	3.097
1976	90.584	8.422	168.691	7.681	5.447	0.816	6.394	1.180	3.319	3.246
1977	84.077	7.453	211.500	7.813	5.410	0.752	6.484	1.119	3.489	3.466
1978	89.592	7.532	261.120	7.807	5.346	0.684	6.710	1.069	3.740	3.778
1979	106.113	8.459	374.614	7.481	5.280	0.617	6.985	1.015	4.128	4.281
1980	140.514	10.639	523.992	7.274	5.071	0.530	7.258	0.946	4.592	4.812
1981	133.616	9.605	596.717	7.185	5.166	0.476	7.944	0.903	5.267	5.242
1982	162.223	11.023	763.829	10.242	7.251	0.589	10.256	1.031	5.822	5.445
1983	198.745	12.926	1066.828	10.883	7.298	0.532	11.015	0.997	6.335	5.652
1984	211.199	13.106	995.680	12.718	8.427	0.544	12.560	1.009	6.959	5.875
1985	279.117	16.559	1241.234	16.559	11.037	0.641	15.113	1.100	7.496	6.097
1986	330.671	18.981	1326.275	19.829	13.745	0.737	17.401	1.177	7.958	6.166
1987	347.967	19.366	1202.966	19.766	13.372	0.658	17.906	1.121	8.393	6.438
1988	406.458	21.769	1478.135	21.893	14.665	0.661	18.999	1.096	8.926	6.722
1989	534.455	27.703	1628.590	25.447	17.322	0.718	21.524	1.143	9.673	7.034
1990	517.499	25.886	1277.449	27.173	18.392	0.699	23.618	1.155	10.429	7.464

1991	675.592	32.695	1847.629	32.577	21.942	0.769	27.270	1.240	11.012	7.693
1992	727.412	34.155	2279.039	35.637	23.709	0.772	29.230	1.248	11.398	7.916
1993	800.078	36.565	2757.147	40.336	28.034	0.855	32.516	1.317	11.728	8.133
1994	810.538	36.002	2842.773	38.012	25.856	0.733	30.843	1.170	12.186	8.351
1995	1113.918	48.282	3822.398	48.353	34.044	0.901	36.025	1.283	12.868	8.563
1996	1370.946	58.066	4495.993	49.031	33.727	0.835	36.782	1.233	13.538	8.847
1997	1828.326	76.071	5519.969	55.380	39.074	0.906	39.864	1.257	14.250	8.998
1998	2350.892	96.359	5116.648	61.339	44.178	0.968	43.933	1.316	14.942	9.143
1999	2845.629	115.174	6640.788	56.772	40.218	0.829	43.155	1.223	15.641	9.389
2000	2586.524	103.496	6402.228	64.077	48.856	0.949	43.589	1.296	16.563	9.707
2001	2279.127	89.997	7860.048	70.900	50.662	0.931	52.291	1.338	17.197	9.857
2002	1775.341	68.969	6816.409	82.480	56.699	1.039	59.054	1.453	17.480	10.091
2003	2284.785	87.163	10953.944	86.824	60.564	1.004	60.469	1.446	17.659	10.281
2004	2533.204	95.002	12968.476	94.396	65.717	1.037	61.832	1.431	17.871	10.616
2005	2657.559	97.853	13706.149	99.937	70.852	1.069	62.674	1.394	18.403	10.978

Notes: This table updates the data in Table 2.2. It includes two additional data series (small stocks and intermediate-term government bonds). There are minor changes in some of the index levels from Table 2.6, reflecting some revisions made of the earlier data.

Source: *Stocks, Bonds, Bills and Inflation 2006 Yearbook*, 2006 Ibbotson Associates, Inc. Based on copyrighted works by Ibbotson and Sinquefield. All rights reserved. Used with permission.

Table 2.4
Calendar Year-by-Year Total Rates of Return for Derived Series From the Beginning of 1926 Through 1974 (Returns in Percent per Year)

Year	Risk Premia on Common Stocks	Maturity Premia on Long-Term Gov't Bonds	Default Premia on Long-Term Corp. Bonds	Common Stocks— Inflation Adjusted	Long-Term Gov't Bonds— Inflation Adjusted	Long-Term Corp. Bonds— Inflation Adjusted	U.S. Treasury Bills— Inflation Adjusted
1926	8.2	4.5	−0.4	13.3	9.4	9.0	4.7
1927	33.3	5.6	−1.4	40.4	11.2	9.7	5.3
1928	38.1	−3.7	2.8	45.0	1.1	3.8	5.0
1929	−12.7	−1.5	−0.1	−8.6	3.2	3.1	4.7
1930	−26.6	2.3	3.2	−20.1	11.4	14.9	8.8
1931	−43.7	−1.7	−0.8	−37.4	9.4	8.5	11.3
1932	−9.1	15.7	−5.2	2.3	30.2	23.5	12.6
1933	53.5	−0.4	10.5	53.2	−0.6	9.8	−0.2
1934	−1.6	9.8	3.5	−3.4	7.8	11.6	−1.8
1935	47.5	4.9	4.4	43.4	2.0	6.4	−2.8
1936	33.7	7.3	−0.7	32.3	6.2	5.5	−1.0
1937	−35.2	−0.1	2.5	−37.0	−2.8	−0.3	−2.7
1938	31.1	5.5	0.6	34.9	8.5	9.2	2.9
1939	−30.5	6.0	−1.9	−30.1	6.5	4.5	0.5
1940	29.3	6.1	−2.5	28.0	5.1	2.4	−1.0
1941	−11.6	0.9	1.8	−19.4	−8.0	−6.3	−8.8
1942	20.0	3.0	−0.6	10.1	−5.5	−6.1	−8.3
1943	25.5	1.7	0.7	22.0	−1.1	−0.3	−2.7
1944	19.3	2.5	1.8	17.3	0.7	2.6	−1.7
1945	36.0	10.4	−6.0	33.4	8.3	1.8	−1.9
1946	10.1	−0.5	1.8	−6.5	−15.5	−13.9	−15.1
1947	−12.4	−3.1	0.3	−19.3	−10.7	−10.4	−7.8
1948	4.7	2.6	0.7	2.7	0.7	1.4	−1.8
1949	17.9	5.7	−3.0	21.0	8.4	5.2	2.6

Common Stocks

Some highlights of common stock annual returns are:

1. Over the period 1926–74, stocks returned 8.5 percent per year compounded annually. Excluding dividends, stocks returned 3.5 percent per year. Over the same period, both risk premia and inflation-adjusted stock returns were 6.1 percent per year.

2. Comparing our stock returns with those measured by Fisher and Lorie over the period 1926–65, we find a return of 10.4 percent from holding a market weighted portfolio with weights updated continually, while they find

Table 2.4 (continued)
Calendar Year-by-Year Total Rates of Return for Derived Series From the Beginning of 1926 Through 1974 (Returns in Percent per Year)

Year	Risk Premia on Common Stocks	Maturity Premia on Long-Term Gov't Bonds	Default Premia on Long-Term Corp. Bonds	Common Stocks— Inflation Adjusted	Long-Term Gov't Bonds— Inflation Adjusted	Long-Term Corp. Bond— Inflation Adjusted	U.S. Treasury Bills— Inflation Adjusted
1950	30.2	−1.1	2.1	24.6	−5.4	−3.5	−4.4
1951	22.2	−5.3	1.3	17.1	−9.3	−8.1	−4.2
1952	16.5	−0.4	2.3	17.3	0.3	2.6	0.7
1953	−2.7	1.8	−0.2	−1.6	3.0	2.8	1.2
1954	51.3	6.3	−1.7	53.3	7.7	5.9	1.3
1955	29.5	−2.9	1.8	31.0	−1.7	0.1	1.2
1956	4.0	−7.8	−1.3	3.6	−8.2	−9.4	−0.4
1957	−13.5	4.2	1.1	−13.4	4.3	5.4	0.1
1958	41.2	−7.5	4.1	40.9	−7.7	−3.9	−0.2
1959	8.8	−5.1	1.3	10.3	−3.7	−2.4	1.5
1960	−2.1	10.9	−4.1	−1.0	12.1	7.5	1.1
1961	24.3	−1.1	3.8	26.0	0.3	4.1	1.4
1962	−11.2	4.0	1.0	−9.8	5.6	6.6	1.5
1963	19.1	−1.9	1.0	20.8	−0.5	0.5	1.4
1964	12.5	−0.0	1.2	15.1	2.3	3.5	2.3
1965	8.2	−3.1	−1.2	10.3	−1.2	−2.4	2.0
1966	−14.1	−1.0	−3.4	−33.0	0.3	−3.1	1.4
1967	19.0	−12.8	4.7	20.3	−11.9	−7.8	1.1
1968	5.6	−5.2	2.9	6.1	−4.8	−2.1	0.4
1969	−14.1	−10.9	−3.2	−13.7	−10.5	−13.4	0.5
1970	−2.4	5.3	5.6	−1.5	6.2	12.2	0.9
1971	9.6	8.5	−1.9	10.6	9.5	7.4	1.0
1972	14.6	1.8	1.5	15.0	2.2	3.7	0.4
1973	−20.2	−1.4	−4.2	−21.6	−3.0	−7.0	−1.7
1974	−31.9	−3.4	−7.2	−34.1	−6.4	−13.1	−3.1

a return of 9.3 percent from holding a portfolio that is equally weighted as of January 1926.[22]

3. Over the entire period of study, the arithmetic mean of the annual returns was 10.9 percent for stocks and 8.8 percent for risk premia and inflation-adjusted stock returns. Although stocks outperformed the other assets in the study, their returns were also far more volatile. The standard deviation of common stock annual returns was 22.5 percent, while the returns ranged from 54.0 to −43.3 percent.

4. Stock returns were positive almost two-thirds of the years (32 out of 49 years). The longest period over which a year-end investor in our common

Table 2.5
Basic and Derived Series Historical Highlights (1926–1974)

Series	Annual Geometric Mean Rate of Return	Arithmetic Mean of Annual Returns	Standard Deviation of Annual Returns	Number of Years Returns Are Positive	Number of Years Returns Are Negative	Highest Annual Return (and Year)	Lowest Annual Return (and Year)
Common stocks	8.5%ᵃ	10.9%	22.5%	32	17	54.0% (1933)	−43.3 (1931)
Long-term government bonds	3.2	3.4	5.4	37	12	16.8 (1932)	−9.2 (1967)
Long-term corporate bonds	3.6	3.7	5.1	39	10	18.4 (1970)	−8.1 (1969)
U.S. Treasury bills	2.2	2.3	2.1	48	1	8.0 (1974)	−0.0 (1940)
Consumer Price Index	2.2	2.3	4.8	39	10	18.2 (1946)	−10.3 (1932)
Risk premia on common stocks	6.1	8.8	23.5	31	18	53.5 (1933)	−43.7 (1931)
Maturity premia on long-term government bonds	1.0	1.1	5.6	25	24	15.7 (1932)	−12.8 (1967)
Default premia on long-term corporate bonds	.3	.4	3.2	28	21	10.5 (1933)	−7.2 (1974)
Common stocks— inflation adjusted	6.1	8.8	23.5	31	18	53.3 (1954)	−37.4 (1931)
Long-term government bonds—inflation adjusted	1.0	1.3	8.0	29	20	30.2 (1932)	−15.5 (1946)
Long-term corporate bonds—inflation adjusted	1.4	1.7	7.7	31	18	23.5 (1932)	−13.9 (1946)
U.S. Treasury bills— inflation adjusted	0.1	0.2	4.6	29	20	12.6 (1932)	−15.1 (1946)

ᵃThe annual geometric mean rate of return for capital appreciation exclusive of dividends was 3.5 percent over the entire period.

stock index would have earned a negative return was the 14-year period 1929–42.

5. The 1974 common stock return was −26.4 percent, the third worst yearly return throughout the period and the worst since 1937. The investor who held our common stock index through year-end 1974 would have lost value if he had purchased the index as of any year-end from 1967 on. On the other hand, the purchaser of the index as of any year-end prior to 1967 would be ahead in (nominal) value as of year-end 1974.

6. Five-year annual calendar holding period returns ranged from a high of

Table 2.6
Basic Series: Summary Statistics of Annual Total Returns from 1926 to 2005

Series	Geometric Mean	Arithmetic Mean	Standard Deviation	Distribution
Large Company Stocks	10.4%	12.3%	20.2%	
Small Company Stocks	12.6	17.4	32.9	*
Long-Term Corporate Bonds	5.9	6.2	8.5	
Long-Term Government	5.5	5.8	9.2	
Intermediate-Term Government	5.3	5.5	5.7	
U.S. Treasury Bills	3.7	3.8	3.1	
Inflation	3.0	3.1	4.3	
				−90% 0% 90%

*The 1933 Small Company Stocks Total Return was 142.9 percent.
Note: This table updates Table 2.5.
Source: Stocks, Bonds, Bills and Inflation 2006 Yearbook, 2006 Ibbotson Associates, Inc. Based on copyrighted works by Ibbotson and Sinquefield. All rights reserved. Used with permission.

23.9 percent during the period 1950–54 to a low of −12.5 percent during the period 1928–32. The highest 10-year annual return was 20.1 percent earned from 1949 to 1958, while the lowest 10-year annual return was −0.9 percent earned from 1929 to 1938. For 20-year calendar holding periods, the highest annual return was 16.9 percent earned in the period 1942–61, while the lowest annual return was 3.1 percent earned in the period 1929–48.

Long-Term U.S. Government Bonds

Some highlights of long-term U.S. government annual returns are:

1. Long-term U.S. government bonds returned 3.2 percent per year compounded annually over the period 1926–74. The entire period annual returns for both maturity premia and inflation-adjusted long-term government bonds were 1.0 percent.

2. The arithmetic means of the annual nominal returns, maturity premia, and real returns from long-term government bonds are 3.4 percent, 1.1 percent, and 1.3 percent, respectively. These annual return series are far less

volatile than the common stock series. However, the maturity premia and the real return series are quite volatile relative to their own historical means.

3. Long-term government bond returns were positive 37 out of the 49 years. Their annual returns ranged from 16.8 percent to −9.2 percent.

4. Five-year annual calendar holding period returns for long-term government bonds ranged from a high of 8.1 percent during the period 1970–74 to a low of −2.1 percent during the period 1965–69. The highest 10-year annual return was 5.7 percent earned during 1932–41, while the lowest 10-year annual return was −0.1 percent earned during 1950–59. For 20-year calendar holding periods, the highest annual return was 4.9 percent earned during the period 1926–45, while the lowest annual return was 0.7 percent earned during the period 1950–69.

Long-Term Corporate Bonds

Some highlights of long-term corporate bond annual returns are:

1. Long-term corporate bonds returned 3.6 percent per year compounded annually over the period 1926–74. Default premia returned 0.3 percent, while the inflation-adjusted corporate bond annual return was 1.4 percent.

2. The arithmetic means of the annual nominal returns, default premia, and real returns resulting from long-term corporate bonds are 3.7 percent, 0.4 percent, and 1.7 percent, respectively. The volatility of long-term corporate bonds is similar to that of long-term government bonds. Again, the default premia and the real return series are quite volatile relative to their historical means.

3. Long-term corporate bonds had positive returns in 39 out of the 49 years. Their returns ranged from 18.4 percent to −8.1 percent.

4. Five-year annual calendar holding period returns for long-term corporate bonds ranged from a high of 10.3 percent during the period 1932–36 to a low of −2.2 percent during the period 1965–69. The highest 10-year annual return was 7.1 percent earned during 1926–35, while the lowest 10-year annual return was 1.0 percent earned during 1947–56. For 20-year calendar holding periods, the highest annual return was 5.5 percent earned during the period 1926–45, while the lowest annual return was 1.3 percent earned during the period 1950–69.

U.S. Treasury Bills and Inflation

Some highlights of U.S. Treasury bill annual returns and annual inflation rates are:

1. During the entire period, U.S. Treasury bills returned 2.2 percent compounded annually, a rate which was approximately equal to the rate of inflation.

2. The entire period inflation-adjusted bill return was 0.1 percent. The inflation-adjusted bill return is a measure of the "real rate of interest." Our result of 0.1 percent is substantially different from the 3–4 percent often suggested by the Federal Reserve Bank of St. Louis.[23] Note that we compute the net returns between monthly *total returns* and inflation rates. The St. Louis Federal Reserve Bank measures the difference between observed high-grade long-term corporate bond *yields* and lagged inflation rates. Yields measure promised returns rather than realized returns. The promise extends over the entire *future* life of the bond so that it should not be compared with either current or lagged inflation rates. Another problem with their methodology is that a long-term corporate bond yield incorporates both promised future maturity premia and default premia as well as promised future real interest rates.

3. We can break the 1926–74 period U.S. Treasury bill returns and the inflation rates into five somewhat natural subperiods. During the deflationary period 1926–32, the annual rate of inflation was −4.4 percent while bills returned 2.7 percent annually. During the low inflationary period 1933–41, the annual rate of inflation was 0.9 percent while the annual bill return was a very low 0.1 percent. During the period 1941–51, Treasury bill rates were pegged to return only 0.6 percent while the annual rate of inflation was a high 5.9 percent. Both rates were low during the period 1952–65, with the annual inflation rate being 1.3 percent and the annual bill return being 2.4 percent. Inflation rates and bill returns were generally rising during the last subperiod (1966–74), with the annual inflation rate being 11.5 percent in 1974 and 5.5 percent over the subperiod, while the 1974 bill return was 8.0 percent with a subperiod annual return of 5.4 percent. Thus, even though bill returns and inflation rates were often very related, the entire period real rate of interest of 0.1 percent varied substantially over the subperiods.

4. Five-year annual calendar period returns from holding 1-month bills ranged from a high of 5.9 percent during the period 1970–74 to a low of 0.1 percent during the period 1937–41. The highest 10-year annual return was 5.4 percent earned during 1965–74, while the lowest 10-year annual return was 0.1 percent earned during 1933–42. For 20-year calendar holding periods, the highest annual return was 4.0 percent earned during the period 1955–74, while the lowest annual return was 0.4 percent earned during the period 1931–50.

5. Five-year annual calendar period inflation rates ranged from a high of 6.8 percent during the period 1942–46 to a low of −5.4 percent during the period 1928–32. The highest 10-year annual rate was 5.9 percent during 1941–50, while the lowest 10-year annual rate was −2.6 percent during 1926–35. For 20-year calendar periods, the highest annual rate was 3.8 percent during the period 1941–60, while the lowest annual rate was 0.1 percent during the period 1926–45.

Appendix 1
Comparison of Ibbotson-Sinquefield Common Stock and Long-Term Corporate Bond Annual Returns With Other Studies

	Annual Geometric Mean Rate of Return	Annual Arithmetic Mean Rate of Return	Standard Deviation of Annual Returns	Correlation With Ibbotson-Sinquefield Annual Returns
Common stock return studies compared to Ibbotson-Sinquefield returns, R_m (R_m results over comparable period are in parentheses):				
1. Fisher-Lorie[a]	9.4%	14.0%	32.1%	.924
1926–1965	(10.4%)	(13.0%)	(23.2%)	
2. Fisher-NYSE[b] equal	9.4	13.9	31.7	.922
weighted 1926–1974 (preliminary)	(8.5)	(10.9)	(22.5)	
3. Scholes-NYSE[c] market	8.1	10.4	22.2	.994
weighted 1926–1974 (preliminary)	(8.5)	(10.9)	(22.5)	
4. Scholes-NYSE[c] equal	10.3	15.0	33.6	.896
weighted 1926–1974 (preliminary)	(8.5)	(10.9)	(22.5)	
Long-term corporate bond return study compared to Ibbotson-Sinquefield returns, R_c (R_c results over comparable period are in parentheses):				
5. Fisher-Weil[d]	5.5	5.5	3.6	.882
1926–1945	(5.5)	(5.6)	(3.7)	
6. Fisher-Weil[d]	3.3	3.4	4.1	.884
1926–1969	(3.2)	(3.3)	(4.6)	

[a]The Fisher and Lorie annual returns summarized here are listed in the diagonal of their matrix listed in table 1B, in Fisher and Lorie, 1968, *op. cit.,* pp. 296–97. Note that the 9.4% annual geometric mean rate of return listed here is not their 1926–1965 holding period return of 9.3%, which is the entire period return from holding an equally weighted portfolio as of January 1926.

[b]The Fisher annual returns summarized here are from Lawrence Fisher's preliminary results of equal weighted (reweighted annually) returns presented at the Seminar on the Analysis of Security Prices, CRSP, May 1975.

[c]The Scholes annual returns summarized here are from preliminary results presented by Myron Scholes at the Seminar on the Analysis of Security Prices, CRSP, May 1975.

[d]The Fisher-Weil results summarized here are listed in the diagonal of Table A1 in Fisher and Weil, *op. cit.,* p. 425.

Appendix 2

Holding Periods and Characteristics of Government Bonds Comprising Long-Term Government Bond Index

Coupon (%)	Call-Maturity Date	Income[1] Tax Status	Estate[2] Tax Status	Period Bond Is Held in Index
4.25	10/15/47–52	b	c	1926–1931
3.00	9/15/51–55	b	a	1932–1935
2.875	3/15/55–60	b	a	1936–1941
2.50	9/15/67–72	a	a	1942–1953
3.25	6/15/78–83	a	b	1954–1958
4.00	2/15/80	a	b	1959–1960
4.25	5/15/75–85	a	b	1961–1965
4.25	8/15/87–92	a	b	1966–1972
6.75	2/15/93	a	a	1973–1974

[1] "a" indicates fully taxable; "b" indicates exempt from normal income tax but subject to small surtax.

[2] "a" indicates no estate tax feature; "b" acceptable at par in payment of estate taxes if owned by decedent at time of death; "c" acceptable at par if owned by decedent for 6-month period immediately preceding death.

Appendix 3
Market Weights Assigned to Eight Salomon Brothers Yield Series Used in the Construction of the Long-Term Corporate Bond Index for the Years 1946–1968

Calendar Year	Salomon Brothers Yield Series As Defined by Coupon Ranges								Sum of Weights
	2 3/4–2 7/8	3 1/8–3 3/8	3 5/8–3 7/8	4 1/8–4 3/8	4 5/8–4 7/8	5–5 1/8	5 1/4–5 3/4	5 7/8–6 1/2	
1968	.04	.06	.05	.17	.26	.08	.12	.22	1.00
1967	.05	.08	.05	.19	.30	.09	.14	.10	1.00
1966	.06	.10	.06	.26	.39	.13			1.00
1965	.08	.11	.07	.30	.36	.08			1.00
1964	.09	.12	.08	.33	.29	.09			1.00
1963	.10	.13	.09	.28	.30	.10			1.00
1962	.11	.15	.10	.22	.31	.11			1.00
1961	.13	.17	.11	.15	.32	.12			1.00
1960	.15	.22	.12	.17	.21	.13			1.00
1959	.19	.30	.14	.22	.12	.03			1.00
1958	.21	.34	.16	.20	.09				1.00
1957	.29	.47	.12	.12					1.00
1956	.39	.61							1.00
1955	.42	.58							1.00
1954	.48	.52							1.00
1953	.60	.40							1.00
1952	.71	.29							1.00
1951	.86	.14							1.00
1950	1.00								1.00
1949	1.00								1.00
1948	1.00								1.00
1947	1.00								1.00
1946	1.00								1.00

Notes: Each of the eight coupon ranges corresponds to a corporate yield series presented in *An Analytical Record of Yields and Yield Spreads*, Salomon Brothers, New York (May 1975). Eight bond price series are then computed assuming the mean coupon of each range, and a 20-year maturity. A total return index is then computed for each series assuming no defaults or rating changes. The above table gives the weights applied to the eight total return series in constructing the Long-Term Corporate Bond Index from 1946 through 1968.

The weights in the table are estimated by starting with Salomon Brothers' 1969 market weights and backdating by adjusting for new issues and maturities each calendar year.

Appendix 4

United States Treasury Bill Index: Yearly Average of Days to Maturity on Monthly Dates of Purchase

Calendar Year	Average Days to Maturity	Calendar Year	Average Days to Maturity
1926	90	1951	34
1927	75	1952	33
1928	75	1953	33
1929	75	1954	33
1930	83	1955	33
1931	59	1956	34
1932	46	1957	33
1933	40	1958	32
1934	38	1959	32
1935	50	1960	32
1936	75	1961	32
1937	44	1962	33
1938	34	1963	32
1939	34	1964	33
1940	36	1965	33
1941	34	1966	33
1942	35	1967	33
1943	32	1968	34
1944	33	1969	33
1945	35	1970	32
1946	34	1971	33
1947	34	1972	34
1948	33	1973	35
1949	33	1974	34
1950	33		

Notes: The average of days to maturity is measured from delivery date of purchase to date of maturity. Prior to 1931, the index includes short-term U.S. government obligations instead of Treasury bills. Since these securities had longer maturities, the average days to maturity is substantially longer than 30 days. Prior to 1938, Treasury bills were issued less frequently than in later periods, again resulting in longer average days to maturity.

▲ **Notes**

1. Lawrence Fisher and James H. Lorie, "Rates of Return on Investments in Common Stock," *Journal of Business* 37, no. 1 (January 1964): 1–21.

2. L. Fisher and J. H. Lorie, "Rates of Return on Investments in Common Stock: The Year-by-Year Record, 1926–65," *Journal of Business* 41, no. 3 (July 1968): 291–316.

3. Roger G. Ibbotson and Rex A. Sinquefield, "Stocks, Bonds, Bills and Inflation: Simulations of the Future (1976–2000)," *Journal of Business*, forthcoming.

4. See Standard and Poor's *Trade and Security Statistics, Security Price Index Record* (Orange, Conn.: Standard & Poor's Corp., 1974).

5. Standard and Poor's Corporation constructs four-quarter dividend moving totals $\overline{D}_{m,t}$ for time t according to

$$\overline{D}_{m,t} = \sum_{j=t-3}^{t} D_{m,j}.$$

Given $\overline{D}_{m,t}$ for all t and four successive quarterly dividends, any $D_{m,t}$ can be solved recursively according to

$$D_{m,t} = D_{m,t+4} + \overline{D}_{m,t+3} - \overline{D}_{m,t+4}.$$

When the explicit quarterly dividends were derived two apparently incorrect estimates were observed in the first quarter, 1959, and second quarter, 1949. In each of these years the quarterly distribution of the annual dividend is noticeably different from both the distribution of the immediate subsequent year and from a sampling of firms for the year of the error. Since the errors would become entangled in the subsequent recursive process, we were forced to make corrections. The corrections were made by redistributing the annual dividends quarterly to conform to the subsequent year's quarterly distribution.

6. The proportion of quarterly dividends allocated to each month corresponds to the 1974 monthly income of the American National Bank and Trust Company of Chicago's Multiple Equity Fund, which is an index fund that virtually duplicates the monthly behavior of the S&P Composite Index. During 1974, the average monthly distribution of quarterly dividends was 18 percent, 64 percent, and 18 percent, respectively, for each quarter. These proportions were used throughout the entire study.

7. In addition to the previous Fisher and Lorie works, other common stock indices are currently being constructed at the Center for Research in Security Prices, Graduate School of Business, University of Chicago. Lawrence Fisher has a set of equally weighted indices of NYSE common stocks, again reflecting buy and hold strategies. Myron Scholes has another equally weighted and a market weighted index of NYSE common stocks, both of which are reweighted each month. These indices also cover the period 1926–74. Some comparisons between the preliminary results of their indices and the common stock index presented in this paper are shown in Appendix 1.

8. The U.S. Government Bond File was compiled by Lawrence Fisher and consists of month-end price data on virtually all negotiable direct obligations of the U.S. Treasury for the period 1926–73. We also include 1974 data which are obtained from selected issues of the *Wall Street Journal* (New York: Dow Jones Co.).

9. More detailed descriptions of the U.S. government bond characteristics are available in various *Moody's Municipal and Government Manuals* (New York: Moody's Investor Service).

10. Apart from the issue of whether the bond life is best measured by the maturity or first call date, a more meaningful measure of a bond's life is its "duration," which takes a bond's coupon into account. A higher coupon effectively refunds a bond issue faster than a lower coupon given the same maturity date or call date. Duration is defined by Frederick R. Macaulay, *Some Theoretical Problems Suggested by the Movements of Interest Rates, Bond Yields, and Stock Prices Since 1856* (New York: National Bureau of Economic Research, 1938). Since we can at best only partially achieve the objective of maintaining a stable bond life, the advantages of using the duration measure is small relative to the complexities involved.

11. A description of the index is given by Martin L. Leibowitz and Richard I. Johannesen, Jr., "Introducing the Salomon Brothers' Total Performance Index for the High-

Grade Long-Term Corporate Bond Market," Memorandum to Portfolio Managers (New York: Salomon Bros., November 1973).

12. From 1926 to 1928, this index is based upon the mean of the monthly high-low yields of 45 high-grade bonds. From January 1929 through March 1937, this index is based upon a varying group of AAA bonds priced by their yields as of the first of the month. We lag this series 1 month in order to treat the first of the month prices as end of the previous month prices. Beginning April 1937 through 1945 the monthly index is the arithmetic average of the four or five weekly AAA Industrial, Rail, and Utility Indices. In order not to lose the March 1937 quote, we again lag this series 1 month. Since the index is a weekly average of prices during the month, our lagging it 1 month causes our monthly return estimate to lead actual returns by about 1/2 month.

13. *An Analytical Record of Yields and Yield Spreads* (New York: Salomon Bros., May 1975).

14. The bond returns are upward biased since we assume no defaults or changes in ratings. Although defaults are virtually nonexistent for Aa and Aaa bonds, downward rating changes below Aa cause bonds to be removed from the yield series. Downward rating changes mean higher yields and lower prices and returns. Since lower returns are removed, the remaining returns are overstated.

15. The same bias described in n. 14 applies here. Except for the fact that we use monthly instead of annual data, our methods are similar to the "naive" strategies used by Lawrence Fisher and Roman L. Weil, "Coping With the Risk of Interest-Rate Fluctuations: Returns to Bondholders From Naïve and Optimal Strategies," *Journal of Business* 44, no. 4 (October 1971): 408–31.

16. The CPI is constructed by the U.S. Department of Labor, Bureau of Labor Statistics, Washington, D.C. We use the January 1975 release of index values (1967 base = 100.0). The last backdate of a few index values was November 1974. A complete description of the index is found in Bureau of Labor Statistics, *Handbook of Methods for Surveys and Studies*, BLS Bulletin 1711, rev. (Washington, D.C.: Government Printing Office, 1972). Recent updating procedures are described in Julius Shiskin, "Updating the Consumer Price Index—an Overview," Bureau of Labor Statistics, *Monthly Labor Review* (July 1974).

17. The risk premium, the maturity premium, and the default premium are frequently defined in economic and financial literature as a one-period expected excess rate of return. In hypothesis testing, the various premia are often measured by the arithmetic mean of historical excess rates of return. Since we present historical net returns, our use of the word "premia" refers to period-by-period returns rather than either the historical mean or the expected return.

18. The positive trade-off between risk and return is based upon the capital asset pricing model of William F. Sharpe, "Capital Asset Prices: A Theory of Market Equilibrium Under Conditions of Risk," *Journal of Finance* 19 (September 1964): 425–42; John Lintner, "The Valuation of Risk Assets and the Selection of Risky Investments in Stock Portfolios and Capital Budgets," *Review of Economics and Statistics* 47 (February 1965): 13–37; and Jack L. Treynor, "Toward a Theory of Market Value of Risk Assets" (unpublished manuscript, 1961).

19. Using a binomial expansion, we can express Eq. (11) as: $R_{p,t} = (R_{m,t} - R_{f,t}) - (R_{m,t} - R_{f,t})(R_{f,t}) + (R_{m,t} - R_{f,t})(R_{f,t})^2 - \ldots$. For small $R_{f,t}$, only the first term is important. However, in index construction even small discrepancies matter. Our use of Eq. (11) gives us the 1974 year-end cumulative wealth relative index value of 17.991 versus 17.964 calculated from Eq. (12).

20. For example, see John R. Hicks, *Value and Capital* (Oxford: Clarendon Press, 1946).

21. The monthly returns, R_t, and month-end index of cumulative wealth relatives, V_n, for each of the 12 series described here can be obtained from the Center for Research in Security Prices, Graduate School of Business, University of Chicago, Chicago, Illinois 60637.

22. See Appendix 1 for a more detailed comparison of the series.

23. The Federal Reserve Bank of St. Louis began publishing a monthly series of expected "real" rates on corporate bonds with the study "Strong Total Demand, Rising Interest Rates, and Continued Availability of Credit," *Review* 48 (August 1966): 3, 4. Subsequent graphs and articles have frequently appeared, including William P. Yohe and Denis Karnosky, "Interest Rates and Price Level Changes, 1952–69," *Review* 51 (December 1969): 34–36.

3

William N. Goetzmann, Roger G. Ibbotson, and Liang Peng

A New Historical Database for the NYSE 1815 to 1925: Performance and Predictability

▶ Overview

The performance of the U.S. stock market over the period after 1926 is so compelling that it raises the question of whether the last three-quarters of the 20th century might have been an aberration. To test this possibility, we gathered stock prices and dividends for most of the history of the New York Stock Exchange (NYSE) individual price information for the 110 years before 1926. As a result of this "financial archaeology" we found that U.S. stocks provided a high positive return in the 19th century as well, although the returns were mostly in the form of dividends as opposed to capital appreciation. In other words, the equity risk premium known since 1926 was alive and well in the early history of the U.S. capital markets, albeit slightly lower in magnitude. The raw data had to be hand collected, with many research assistants participating in the process over several years.

The ultimate goal is to link these data with the Center for Research in Security Prices (CRSP) database that begins in 1926. The combined data sets represent almost the total history of the NYSE (which started in 1792). This is the only raw database covering individual U.S. stocks that currently exists over the entire period prior to 1926. All other studies represent spliced-together indices that either existed contemporaneously at the time, or were backdated by earlier researchers.

▶ Abstract

In this paper, we collect individual stock prices for NYSE stocks over the period 1815 to 1925 and individual dividend data over the period 1825 to 1870. We use monthly price and dividend information on more than 600 individual securities over the period to estimate a stock price index and total return series that extends virtually to the beginning of the New York Stock Exchange. We use this data to estimate the power of past returns and divi-

73

dend yields to forecast future long-horizon returns. We find some evidence of predictability in sub-periods but little predictability over the long term. We estimate the time-varying volatility of the U.S. market over the period 1815 to 1925 and find evidence of a leverage effect on risk. This new database will allow future researchers to test a broad range of hypotheses about the U.S. capital markets in a rich, untouched sample

◣ *Introduction*

The University of Chicago Center for Security Prices (CRSP) database of U.S. stock prices is widely used in financial economics to address fundamental questions about the risk and return to equity investment. The CRSP data begin in 1926, shortly before the Great Crash. Prior to the current paper, no broad pre-CRSP database of U.S. security prices has ever been available—with the exception of the data assembled by Alfred Cowles to construct his famous indices of U.S. stock prices from 1871 to 1937. Unfortunately the Cowles data, said to have been one of the earliest uses of Hollerith cards for financial research, were lost.[1]

In this paper, we collect individual stock prices on NYSE stocks over the period 1815 to 1925 and individual dividend data over the period 1825 to 1870. We use monthly price and dividend information on more than 600 individual securities over most of the 19th century and the first quarter of the 20th century to estimate a stock price index and total return series that extends virtually to the beginning of the New York Stock Exchange. Our hope is that this new database will allow future researchers to test a broad range of hypotheses about the U.S. capital markets in a rich, untouched sample. In addition we hope that the long times series we created will lead to a better understanding of how the NYSE evolved from an emerging market at the turn of the 18th century to the largest capital market in the world today. In the current paper, we consider just a few hypotheses of interest; however, we intend to make the data available electronically to other researchers to address interests of their own.

Much recent research has focused on the very long-term performance of equity markets.[2] Studies of markets over the span of the 20th century, and even longer, give some measure of the historical equity premium, and studies of the long-horizon predictability of stock returns by necessity require long time series. For U.S. studies extending back to 1926, high quality United States financial data on individual securities are available from CRSP. For the period 1871 to 1926, researchers are able to use the Cowles (1939) indices, with corrections by Wilson and Jones (1987, 2000). For researchers interested in the dynamics of the U.S. capital markets over earlier decades, it has been necessary to rely upon indices of uneven quality. Goetzmann (1993), Schwert (1990) and Siegel (1992) note many of the problems with U.S. stock indices extending back to 1802. All are spliced from several sources such as Burgess (1932),

Cole and Frickey (1928), the Cleveland Trust Company Indices, Macauley (1938), Matthews (1926) and Cole and Smith (1935). None of these are broad-based, and most of them effectively condition upon the continuity of price records and non-quantifiable features such as representativeness. Even the Cowles indices, despite being carefully constructed in many ways, are based upon the average of high and low stock prices through the month, rather than month-end transactions.

The ultimate goal of our project is to assemble a CRSP-like database for the New York Stock Exchange, over the period prior to 1926, when CRSP begins. This goal is now largely complete for stock prices and partially complete for dividends. In our efforts to create a complete database, we have encountered a number of methodological challenges caused by the infrequent trading of securities and the lack of an official dividend record. Past efforts to create NYSE price indices from primary data for the early period typically relied upon frequently traded securities or securities for which long, unbroken price sequences were available. The selection bias in conditioning on continuity is well known, but not easily addressed econometrically. By collecting all available NYSE data from official records to the mid-19th century, and all available prices in financial periodicals to 1925, we hope to alleviate concerns about selection bias, and to provide a database for widespread future research.

We use these data to address some issues of long-standing interest to empirical research. First, we estimate the stability of long-term measures of risk and return for the U.S. stock market. In particular, we measure the equity premium for the NYSE index over the century preceding CRSP. We find that the risk and return of the U.S. market before 1926 are relatively different from the post-1926 data—the price-weighted NYSE index grew at a geometric monthly average of 0.10% from 1815 to 1925, compared to 0.54% for the S&P from 1926 through 1999. Figure 3.1 shows the capital appreciation index of a dollar invested in the NYSE from 1815; Figure 3.2 shows both the capital appreciation index and the total return index of a dollar invested in the NYSE from 1824. Under certain assumptions about dividend payments detailed below, we calculate total returns using our capital appreciation index to 1871, our dividend series from 1825 to 1870 and Cowles' dividends to 1925.[3]

Next, we examine the predictability of long-horizon returns using both past returns and dividend yields. Using bootstrap methods to estimate standard errors, we find the evidence for predictability using either measure is marginal over the entire span. Finally, we examine the extent to which the volatility of the U.S. market is time-varying, using GARCH estimation. We find that positive shocks and negative shocks have different predictability for future volatility. Specifically, negative shocks tend to introduce more volatility than positive shocks.

The paper is organized as follows. The second section describes the data sources and our collection methods. The third section explains the methodology used for price index estimation. The fourth section summarizes what the data tell us about the risk and return of the NYSE over the long term. The fifth section reports evidence on the long-horizon predictability of returns. The

Figure 3.1. Monthly Capital Appreciation Index, 1/1815–12/1999

sixth section reports evidence on the time variation in volatility. The seventh section concludes.

◣ Data Sources and Collection Methods

Share Prices

We hand-collected all end-of-month equity prices for companies listed on the New York Stock Exchange from three different journals published over the period January, 1815, to December, 1870. From 1871 through 1925, we collected end-of-month prices for NYSE stocks from the major New York newspapers. The *New York Shipping List,* later called the *New York Shipping and Commercial,* is our principal source up to 1855. It was a current price list for a broad range of commodities shipped through the port of New York. It quoted bid and ask prices, as well as transaction prices with share quantity two times per week from 1815 through the mid-1850s, for securities traded on the New York Stock Exchange. During much of this period, the periodical had rights to publish the official price list as established in the resolutions of the New York Stock Exchange Board minutes of November 29, 1817. Apparently, both stocks and bonds were quoted in the *New York Shipping List,* and equity prices and transactions were denominated in shares, while bond prices and transactions were denominated in dollars of face value. In the mid-1850s the official NYS&EB price list designation disappeared from the stock market quotes, and the *New*

From 1824 to 2001

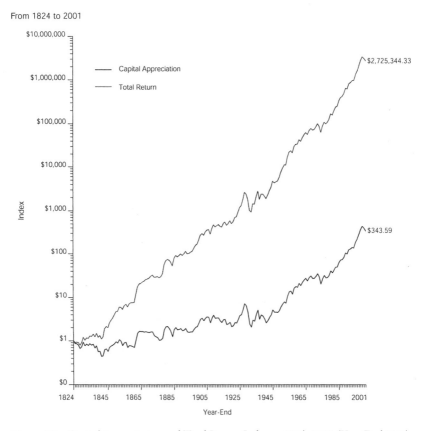

Figure 3.2. Capital Appreciation and Total Return Indexes, 1824–2001 (Year-End 1824 = $1.00)

York Shipping List reported prices for fewer and fewer stocks. Thus, for the period 1855 through 1925, we collected price quotes from the *New York Herald* and the *New York Times*. While neither of these claimed to be the official list for the NYSE, the number of securities quoted by each far exceeded the number quoted by *New York Shipping List*. We hand-collected prices from bound volumes of the *New York Shipping List* in the Yale Beinecke Rare Book Library, and from microfiche copies of the *Herald* and the *Times*. The month-end prices were obtained by searching the end-of-month issues for the last transaction price for each stock that month. When no transaction took place in the last week, the latest bid and ask prices were averaged. In total, we collected at least two prices from 664 companies. From a low number of 8 firms in 1815, the number of firms in the index reached a high point in May 1883 with 114 listed firms. The fact that the number of firms concurrently listed peaked at under 120 while the total number of firms in the database exceeded 600 indicates that, not only did firms appear during the sample period, they also disappeared.

The Old NYSE Research Project

Perhaps the most important thing about this study was the collective effort involved. It took our research team more than a decade of effort to track down individual share prices and dividends, mostly from Yale's Beinecke Rare Book Library. In addition, other scholars interested in the historical development of the NYSE have contributed additions and corrections to our database, filling in gaps and helping to clean the data. Before our work, researchers typically had to rely upon a patchwork of price indices of uneven composition and bias, and upon econometric procedures, as opposed to empirical observation, to estimate dividends. Our Old NYSE research project continues, as we seek to gather price and dividend data for stocks in earlier periods. The current database is available on the World Wide Web site of the International Center for Finance at the Yale School of Management for other researchers to download and use. Our hope is that this rich source of historical information will be used by other scholars and interested analysts to understand the long-term development of the U.S. capital market.

For the period up to the mid-1850s, the *New York Shipping List* regularly and repeatedly listed a set of securities, even when there was no bid, ask or transaction in the period. Apart from the claim to publishing the official NYSE list, this suggests that it represented a fairly comprehensive list of NYSE securities, not simply those stocks that happened to have traded. After the mid-1950s, the coverage of the sources is less clear; however, the securities covered in the *Herald* and the *Times* corresponded closely, suggesting that we obtained a broad, if unofficial, sample in the later years.

There are several categories of equity shares. The first, and the largest, category is common stock. In addition, shares were listed as "old," "new," "preferred" and as scrip. Shares listed as "old" traded concurrently with shares of the same name, and thus we assume that "old" and "new" represent different classes of stock for the same corporation. The new shares are presumably a second issue. Preferred likely meant what it means today. Scrip represented certificates that were not fully paid in subscriptions for shares—convertible into shares at a future date when fully paid-in but receiving no dividends until conversion. All share types are included in our index.

There are a few missing months in our data that create gaps in the analysis. Some of these are institutional. As is well known, the NYSE was closed from July 1914 to December 1914 due to the war. We also have additional gaps. We are missing returns for 1822, part of 1848 and 1849, parts of 1866, all of 1867 and January 1868. We do not know whether the late 1860s missing records are due to the Civil War, but the NYSE was certainly open at that time—among other things, it was the era of heated speculation and stock price manipulation by legendary financiers Gould, Fisk and Drew. We hope further data collection will fill in these missing records. The number of available security records after 1871 was lower than immediately before that year.

This probably does not indicate a decrease in the number of listed securities, only a change in the range of coverage by the financial press.

When possible, companies were categorized by industry. In 1815, the index was about evenly split between banks and insurance companies. By the 1850s, however, banks, transportation firms (primarily canals and railroads) and insurance companies were all about equally common. By the end of the sample period, insurance, bank, mining and utility companies had nearly disappeared from the price lists, so that transport companies and other industrials made up almost all the index.

One interesting feature of the data is that prices for much of the period remained around 100, as can be seen by Figure 3.3. Text discussions of price fluctuations suggest that 100 was the typical par value of shares. Dividends were quoted as a percent of par. We found no reports of stock splits over the period of data, and a single notice of a stock dividend (the railroad Auburn and Syracuse declared a stock dividend of 50% on 10-1-48). Although other such splits were possible, we found no suspicious 50% price drops in the monthly data up to 1848, which might imply a stock split. The distribution of stock prices in the sample is dramatically skewed left with only a tiny fraction of stocks trading above 150% of par value. The mode of the distribution is at $110 with a secondary mode in the $10 to $20 range. The distribution suggests that management maintained an upper bound on stock prices by paying dividends when prices rose. This policy may have something to do with the tax treatment of dividends. For virtually the entire period of this sample, capital gains and dividends were treated equally for tax purposes.

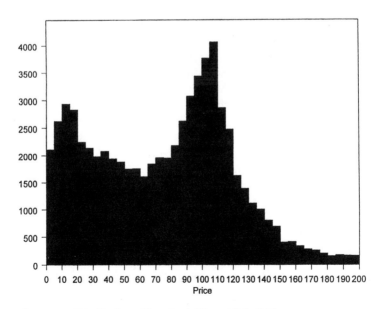

Figure 3.3. Distribution of Raw Stock Prices, 1815–1925

Dividends

We collected dividend data for the period 1825–1870 by identifying the semi-annual dividend announcements for equity securities as reported in the *New York Commercial,* the *Banker's Magazine,* the *New York Times* and the *New York Herald.* Since we do not know whether these journals always reported dividends for all NYSE stocks, we do not know whether exclusions of dividends meant that they were not paid, or whether we failed to find them. We were able to find dividend records for more than 500 stocks in our sample, although the number of stocks for which were have an unbroken series of semi-annual dividend observations is small. We found that most stocks paid dividends semi-annually. Thus, when we found two dividend payments per year, we presumed that the dividend record was complete. In addition, some firms paid extraordinary dividends. These were occasionally identified as a "surplus" dividend, and added to the last regular dividend of the year. Other times it was paid separately. Despite the limitations of our sample, there is no other we are aware of that is as comprehensive. The most widely cited study of 19th century dividends is Anna Schwartz' (1960) survey of dividend payments at multiple-year intervals.

By gathering dividend information on a wide range of companies, we are able to infer something about the total return to equity investors over the period and differences in this return across industries. In addition, we find some interesting features of dividend payouts in the 19th century that make it difficult to generalize occasional dividend observations into a consistent time series. For example, liquidating dividends was not uncommon. The highest dividends in our sample were attributed to "winding up" or "final" dividends, indicating the closure of the company. Many, but not all of these final dividends were paid to "receivers" or "creditors" implying that the company was in receivership. This receivership may not have been due to the failure of the corporation, but merely to the loss of its charter. For instance, a notice in the August 1, 1852, issue of the *New York Commercial* records that "The Trustees of the City Bank (the charter of which has expired . . . have declared a dividend of 10% out of surplus finds, the capital stock having been previously refunded." That same year, the December 1, 1852, issue notes that "Charters for the City and Butchers and Drovers Bank expire. Business to continue under association of the same name." Thus, large occasional dividends recorded in our sources typically represent terminal payments to shareholders. The latter case is particularly troublesome for calculation of statistics of interest, since it implies a dividend yield (i.e., D_t/P_t) of infinity. We found 33 dividend payments noted as a final dividend, or payment to receivers or creditors.

Low Dividend Return Estimate

In order to estimate a lower bound on the income return for each year, we sum all the dividends paid in a given year by firms whose prices were observed in the preceding year, then divide by the sum of the last available in preceding year prices for those firms. From year 1825 to 1870, numbers of firms that have price data for the preceding year range from 28 for year 1849 to 162 for year 1854. On average, there are about 76 firms that have price data for each year. The percentage of them that paid dividends ranges from 21.7% for year 1855 to 52.4% for year 1833. The average of the percentage is 41.2%. Counting only the dividends we found and assuming zero otherwise gives an average of 3.77% income return per year over the period 1825 through 1870—lower than the 1926–1999 average of 4.45%. This almost certainly provides a lower bound on the estimate of the income return for the index since we may not have found all dividends for all firms that pay them. It is about 100 basis points lower than the estimate of income returns in Schwert (1990).

High Dividend Return Estimate

Another approach is to restrict our attention to firms that we know to pay regular dividends,[4] and for which we have price data. Using this approach, we find the dividend yields to be high, by modern standards. Most yields were between 9% and 11% during the period. This was in a period when high quality corporate bond yields average 5% to 7% (see Homer and Sylla, 1992). Even considering the selection bias that may have led us to collect only dividends from high-yield equity securities, this discrepancy between equity yields and bond yields over the course of a decade in our sample period suggests that dividend policy was quite different in the 19th century than it was in the 20th century. The high yields and the fact that many stocks traded near par suggest that most companies paid out a large share of their profits, rather than retaining them. In fact, when we look at the time distribution of dividend changes over this period, we find that dividend decreases were only slightly less common than increases, suggesting that managers may have been less averse to cutting the dividend than they are today. Perhaps in the pre–income tax environment of the 19th century, investors had a preference for income returns, as opposed to capital appreciation. Whether this pattern characterizes the entirety of the 19th century is a question for future research. The implications of the existence of high NYSE dividends for certain stocks suggest that the dividend process has evolved over the past two centuries, and that assumptions based upon projecting current dividend policy into the past may not be correct. This trend is potentially relevant to current research on the U.S. market. Fama and French (1998) document a recent 20-year trend in propensity of stocks not to pay dividends. This recent trend may be part of a two-century evolution in the nature of equities.

▲ Estimation Methodology

A major difficulty with using indices spliced from historical sources is a lack of certainty about the procedures used by researchers to construct indices. Another major potential concern is the effect that bid-ask bounce might have on equal-weighted return indices. Suppose an illiquid stock trades at either $1 or $2 per share. When it goes from $1 to $2 it goes up 100%, while when it goes from $2 to $1, it drops 50%. Equally weighting these returns can induce a substantial upward bias.

Blume and Stambaugh (1983) and Canina et al. (1998) point out the extreme effects that the micro-structure of returns may have on the calculation of long-term means. Even though we are using monthly data, NYSE shares traded much less frequently in the 19th century than they do today, creating a serious potential problem. Indeed, we have calculated an equal-weighted index of returns for our sample, and report it in Appendix 1. It is obvious that the magnitude of the bias is extraordinary.

The procedure we use for calculating our price-weighted index is simple. For each month in our sample, we calculate monthly returns for all stocks that trade in two consecutive periods. We weight these returns by the price at the beginning of the two periods. The return of the price-weighted market index over period t, r_t^m, is defined as

$$r_t^m \equiv \sum_{i=1}^{N} (r_t^i \cdot w_t^i) = \sum_{i=1}^{N} \left(\frac{P_t^i}{P_{t-1}^i} \cdot \frac{P_{t-1}^i}{\sum_{j=1}^{N} P_{t-1}^j} \right) = \frac{\sum_{i=1}^{N} P_t^i}{\sum_{j=1}^{N} P_{t-1}^j}.$$

Here r_t^i represents the return of security i over the period t; w_t^i represents the weight of security i over the period t, which is equal to $P_{t-1}^i / \sum_{j=1}^{N} P_{t-1}^j$ since the index is price-weighted. Notice that return of the price-weighted index closely approximates return to a "buy and hold" portfolio over the period. Buy and hold portfolios are not sensitive to bid-ask bounce bias.

There are many stocks in our data set that do not trade frequently. We compute the returns only when we have two adjacent prices, in a similar manner as CRSP. A common approach to indexing infrequently traded assets is the repeat-sales regression (see, e.g., Bailey et al., 1963; Goetzmann and Spiegel, 1995). Unfortunately, the repeat-sales regression estimates an equal-weighted index. When all securities are infrequently traded, the bid-ask microstructure problems are not serious, but for the NYSE data in this paper, there are enough frequently traded securities that even the repeat-sales regression will be upwardly biased—although not nearly so much as the simple equal-weighted index. We leave it for future researchers to find repeat sales methods that can make use of all of the scattered prices in the index without biasing the results.

As we show below, the price-weighted index corresponds quite closely to the Cowles value-weighted index over the period 1871–1925—and does not suffer from the well-known Working effect (Working, 1960) that induces autocorrelation in monthly returns. This suggests the price-weighted index is likely to be equally reliable over the pre-1870 period. Although there may be superior econometric solutions to the problem, the price-weighted index does a fairly good job.

▶ Results of Index Estimation

Price Indices

Table 3.1 shows summary statistics for the annual capital appreciation return series for the whole period from 1815 to 1999 and breaks out the new data period 1815 to 1870, the Cowles period 1871 to 1925, and the Ibbotson (2000) data (based on Ibbotson and Sinquefield, 1976) from 1926 to 1999. Note that the price-weighted index has an annual geometric capital appreciation return from 1815 through 1870 of 0.84% per year. This is dramatically lower than the 6.62% annual growth experienced by the capital-weighted Ibbotson index of large U.S. stocks over the period 1926 through 1999, and significantly different than the rate of growth in the Cowles period, 1871 to 1925. Note that this is not simply due to using a different methodology, since the price-weighted mean for the Cowles period was only 0.14% per year less than the value estimated by Alfred Cowles. It appears more likely that dividend policies evolved over the 185-year period. In the early era, companies appear to have paid out earnings and kept their stock prices lower. In the modern era, appreciation is accepted as a substitute to dividend payments. Evidence on dividends will be discussed in more detail in the next section.

The summary statistics for the monthly capital appreciation returns are reported in Table 3.2. We compare these to the summary statistics for data supplied by Schwert (1990)—the best pre-Cowles monthly U.S. index constructed to date.[5] Schwert (1990) constructs a series of monthly stock portfolio

---

The Cowles Indices

Prior to the current study, the best data source for NYSE stock was put together by Alfred Cowles. His capital appreciation and total return indices covered the period 1871 through the late 1930s. Since the introduction of the CRSP and Standard and Poor's (S&P) indices, the period for which researchers usually use the Cowles indices is 1871–1925.

Cowles did a careful job of collecting data and constructing his indices. The most major methodological error he made was averaging weekly data each month, to construct the monthly indices, instead of taking the last prices of the month. This downward biases the variance and upward biases serial correlation. Nevertheless, Cowles would be the clear-cut top choice for estimating returns for this period.

Unfortunately, all of Cowles' raw data have been lost, because they were available only on unusable and incomplete sets of Hollerith cards. Only his indices and the descriptions of the methods survive. This article's data set is currently the only one available for looking at raw returns over the Cowles period and the earlier period of the NYSE.

Table 3.1

Annual Summary Statistics for Capital Appreciation, Income and Total Return to the Price-Weighted NYSE Index and Comparison Indices

Date	Series	Geometric Mean (%)	Arithmetic Mean (%)	Standard Deviation (%)	Auto-correlation (%)
Annual NYSE capital appreciation return series					
1815–1925	Price-weighted NYSE	1.24	2.38	15.58	4.36
1825–1925	Price-weighted NYSE	1.34	2.54	16.08	5.35
1815–1870	Price-weighted NYSE	0.84	1.92	15.27	−1.11
1871–1925	Price-weighted NYSE	1.65	2.84	16.01	9.40
1871–1925	Cowles index	1.89	3.14	15.94	−3.0
1926–1999	Ibbotson index	6.62	8.54	19.55	2.19
1815–1999	Price-weighted + Ibbotson	3.36	4.84	17.49	6.14
1825–1999	Price-weighted + Ibbotson	3.54	5.08	17.82	6.34
Annual NYSE income return series					
1825–1925	Low income return + Cowles	4.63	4.64	1.45	73.93
1825–1925	High income return + Cowles	7.09	7.14	3.39	56.68
1825–1870	Low income return	3.77	3.78	1.43	57.92
1825–1870	High income return	9.27	9.34	3.95	29.78
1871–1925	Cowles	5.33	5.34	1.03	77.51
1926–1999	Ibbotson	4.45	4.46	1.39	81.78
1825–1999	Low dividend + Cowles + Ibbotson	4.55	4.56	1.42	77.49
1825–1999	High dividend + Cowles + Ibbotson	5.98	6.02	3.03	67.19
Annual NYSE total return series with low and high dividend income returns and Cowles					
1825–1925	Price-weighted NYSE with low	5.99	7.19	16.37	5.60
1825–1925	Price-weighted NYSE with high	8.50	9.69	16.67	5.99
1825–1870	Price-weighted NYSE with low	4.72	5.97	16.86	2.98
1825–1870	Price-weighted NYSE with high	10.29	11.53	17.41	1.87
1871–1925	Price-weighted NYSE with Cowles div.	7.05	8.18	16.04	7.56
1871–1925	Cowles total return	7.28	8.48	16.07	−4.47
1926–1999	Ibbotson	11.35	13.28	20.14	1.06
1825–1999	Price-weighted low div. + Ibbotson	8.24	9.78	18.26	5.86
1825–1999	Price-weighted high div. + Ibbotson	9.70	11.22	18.26	4.34

Notes: The price-weighted NYSE appreciation series is calculated by compounding the price-weighted monthly NYSE index as described in the text. The Cowles indices are the all-stock indices taken from Cowles (1939). The Ibbotson index is a capital-weighted index of U.S. equities initially constructed by Ibbotson and Sinquefeld and updated by Ibbotson Associates. The low dividend income return series to 1870 is constructed from the sum of all dividends collected in the year for stocks extant in the previous year divided by the sum of the latest available prices for all stocks comprising the index in the preceding year. The high dividend series is the average of the income returns for those stocks reporting dividends in that year. Total returns from 1871 to 1925 are constructed from the price-weighted NYSE and the Cowles income return series.

returns from 1802 to 1925 by splicing monthly data from different sources, such as Cole and Smith (1935), Macaulay (1938), Cowles (1939) and Dow Jones (1972). It includes bank stocks or bank and insurance stocks for 1802 to 1833; bank, insurance and railroad stocks for 1834–1845; railroad stocks only for 1846–1870; the Cowles portfolio for 1871–1885; and the Dow Jones portfolio for 1885–1925. The index is equal-weighted from 1802 to 1862, value-

Table 3.2
Monthly Summary Statistics for the Price-Weighted NYSE Capital Appreciation Index and Comparison Indices

Date	Series	Geometric Mean (%)	Arithmetic Mean (%)	Standard Deviation (%)	Autocorrelation (%)
Monthly NYSE capital appreciation return series					
2/1815–12/1925	Price-weighted	0.1032	0.1858	4.09	−1.88
2/1815–12/1925	Schwert	0.1313	0.2130	4.03	7.38
2/1815–1/1871	Price-weighted	0.0712	0.1592	4.24	−7.76
2/1815–1/1871	Schwert	0.0933	0.1701	3.90	10.02
2/1871–12/1915	Price-weighted	0.1358	0.2128	3.92	5.13
2/1871–12/1925	Schwert	0.1701	0.2568	4.16	4.98
2/1871–12/1915	Cowles	0.1567	0.2094	3.24	28.80

Notes: The price-weighted NYSE appreciation series is calculated by compounding the price-weighted monthly NYSE index as described in the text. The Cowles indices are the all-stock indices taken from Cowles (1939). The Schwert index is described in Schwert (1992) and downloadable from William Schwert's Web site. It is constructed from secondary sources with econometric improvements by Schwert.

weighted from 1863 to 1885, and price-weighted from March 1885 to the end of 1925. In contrast, our price index to 1925 is based on a single database that contains stock prices of more than 600 stocks. It is representative of the range of securities that comprised the NYSE over the period. Also, our index is price-weighted for the whole period from 1815 to 1925. Note that our monthly geometric price-weighted capital appreciation series is slightly lower than the Schwert index over both the pre-Cowles and Cowles periods. This may be due to the difference between price-weighting and equal-weighting.

It is useful to note that our monthly autocorrelation for the price-weighted estimator over the Cowles period is 0.0513, compared to 0.2880 for the Cowles index. This is due to Cowles' use of the average of high and low prices in the month and was first noted by Working (1960). Schwert (1990) econometrically adjusts for the Working effect. Our index requires no adjusting, and appears to have reasonable time-series properties. The Cowles period provides a useful benchmark for evaluating the price-weighted index. Figure 3.4 shows the monthly price-weighted capital appreciation index and the Cowles capital appreciation index over the period 1871 through 1925. Our price-weighted index and the Cowles track fairly closely through the period. In fact, their monthly correlation is 0.95.

Income Returns

Figure 3.5 plots 175 years of annual income returns from 1825 through 1999. Table 3.1 reports the summary statistics. As we note above, there is no way to really tell what percentage of the dividends we found in our search of the

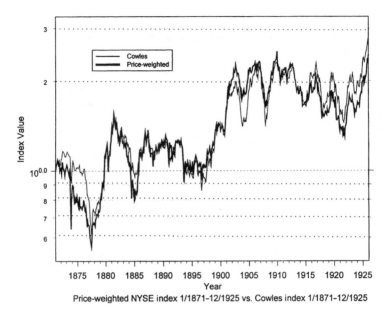

Figure 3.4. Monthly Capital Appreciation Index Comparison

financial press. Thus the figure plots both a high dividend return and a low dividend return series. Table 3.1 provides summary statistics for both. The low income returns from the pre-Cowles period—the period for which we collected dividends—is 3.77% per year—significantly lower than the 5.33% per year over the Cowles period and slightly lower than Schwert's (1990) estimate of 4.40%. When we consider only the dividend paying stocks during that era, however, we estimate much higher income returns—9.27% per year. This higher income return estimate is consistent with the practice of paying out profits to keep stock prices in the early period trading near par values. The true dividend return to a capital-weighted investment in all NYSE stocks is undoubtedly somewhere in between these two extremes.

Total Return

Using the low dividend series we conservatively estimate the lower bound on the total return[5] to a price-weighted investment in the NYSE over the 46-year period from 1825 to 1870 as 4.72% with a standard deviation of 16.86% per year. Using the Cowles income return series we estimate the return from 1871 to 1925 as 7.05% with a 16.04% annual standard deviation. Both of these values are less than the total return to investment in the U.S. market since 1926 of 11.35%. If the high dividend estimate were correct, it would yield a total return in the pre-Cowles period of 10.29%, closer to the post-1926 result, but quite different from the total returns of the Cowles period.

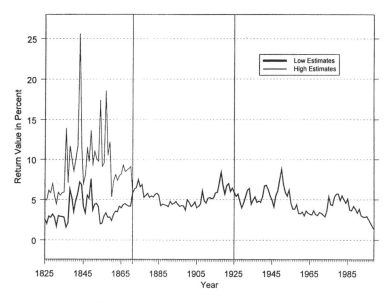

Figure 3.5. Annual NYSE Income Returns in Percent, 1825–1999
Notes: For 1825–1870, low estimates assume zero dividends for missing dividends, high estimates assume missing dividends are at same rate as collected dividend yields. For 1871–1925, both low and high estimates of income returns are equal to the Cowles income returns. For 1926–1999, the Ibbotson and Sinquefield income returns are given.

▶ Forecasting Equity Returns

Much empirical research in financial economics over the past two decades has focused on the potential to forecast time-variation in the equity premium. For example, Fama and French (1988a,b) investigate evidence for mean reversion in stock prices and the forecasting power of dividend yields in the U.S. market since 1926 and find evidence suggesting that the market return can be partially predicted at longer horizons. Scholars since have examined the power of long-horizon statistical tests, the effects of prior beliefs on the tests and the evidence in non-U.S. markets for long-horizon predictability. Although a complete review of the research would take pages, it is fair to say that evidence for mean reversion in U.S. stock prices over the period 1926 to 1999 is marginal—bootstrapping tests under a random walk null, for example, typically cannot reject (cf. Richardson, 1993), although the sign of the reversion coefficient is generally negative. Because tests on short time-series might simply be weak, Goetzmann (1993) extends the analysis to earlier periods in the NYSE and the London Stock Exchange using spliced price series and finds some long-horizon evidence of persistence in the London market, and marginal evidence in U.S. markets. Nevertheless, spliced data are a serious potential problem in that there are regime shifts due to structural changes in index composition and methodologies used by different researchers. The time-series of NYSE returns developed in this paper allows us for the first time to revisit the mean-reversion issue using a time-series of returns to the U.S. market with well-understood properties. In this section, we perform some standard tests of the predictability of long-horizon returns to show what these new data may tell us about long-standing problems in empirical finance.

The predictive power of dividend yields noted by Fama and French (1988b) is compelling; however, the statistical issues involved in testing the forecasting power of yields are subtle. Goetzmann and Jorion (1993, 1995) find that the distribution of the test statistic in the presence of lagged dependent regressors and survivorship is ill behaved. They examine the evidence for the forecasting power of dividend yields in the U.S. and U.K. markets over periods back to 1871 using bootstrap statistics and find the evidence is mixed. While not overwhelmingly strong forecasters in the United States, dividend yields had some forecasting power during sub-periods in the United Kingdom. Campbell and Shiller (1998) argue that the Goetzmann and Jorion simulations are flawed in that they do not build in any reversion of the dividend yield—effectively turning the yield into an unbounded random walk that, when used as a dependent variable in a regression, can be expected to generate odd results. They perform a bootstrap using an autoregressive specification on dividend yields estimated with U.S. annual data from 1871 through 1997. They then add a random-walk stock appreciation series with statistical properties matching those of the real capital appreciation series and transform yields to an artificial total return series. They find that yields at the four-year horizon are significant predictors—in effect, the way the bootstrap is done appears to make a big difference.

Recent work by Welch and Goyal (1999) suggests that the in-sample predictive power of dividend yields is not matched by the power to predict out of sample due to parameter instability. They document the erosion of the ability of yields as predictors in the 1990s. Wolf (2000) takes a different approach. He notes that bootstrapping tests in general are ad hoc in that they eliminate many of the actual time-series characteristics of the data, besides the predictability of yields. He designs a sub-sampling test that largely eliminates this problem and has attractive small-sample properties. Using post-1926 U.S. data, he finds only marginal evidence of the predictability of yields.

In sum, there has been much recent work on the experimental design of statistical tests of the significance of yield regressions, and it is clear that the method of bootstrapping, the time-period of analysis and the analyst's priors all make a difference to inference. With the new dividend data we have collected over the 1825–1870 period, it is actually possible to add a bit more data to the debate.

Mean Reversion

In our first test, we regress annual future long-horizon returns on past long-horizon returns over a number of different intervals. Following Fama and

French (1988a), we use overlapping return observations and thus t-values and R^2 are overstated. We rely upon the bootstrap for corrected significance levels and explanatory power. Table 3.3 reports the results of these regressions, with bold type and stars indicating coefficients lower than the 5th percentile of the bootstrapped distributions.

Using capital appreciation returns only, we find no strong evidence of forecastability over the entire period at horizons of 1 through 10 years, although the coefficients for the 4-year through 7-year horizons are negative, consistent with the mean-reversion hypothesis. Using total returns from 1825 (based upon our low dividend estimates), we find the results slightly stronger. The reversion coefficient at the 6-year horizon is an outlier with respect to the bootstrapped distribution. Likewise, the 2-year reversion coefficient for the period 1871–1825 is unusually low. At the bottom of the table, we report boot-strapped median and 5th percentile values for the whole time period based upon 1,000 bootstrapped simulations. Returns were independently drawn with replacement from the actual 1825–1999 sample. Note the median is slightly negative for all horizons and none of the coefficients in the test cross the 5th percentile. Since small-sample properties of the coefficient distribution are relevant, this bootstrap is useful only for the test over the entire period. Not reported, but used for the sub-period hypothesis tests, are bootstrapped distri-butions using data drawn only from the relevant sub-period.

The sub-period analysis thus tells an interesting story. The 1825–1870 and the 1871–1925 data in fact indicate some evidence of mean reversion at different horizons when compared to the bootstrapped distribution. It is only the 1926 to 1999 period that is weak and this affects inferences drawn over the entire period. There is no reason to presume that parameter values for mean reversion are constant over the various sub-periods. Parameter instability, pointed out by Welch and Goyal, may thus be relevant. There appears to be a strong difference in the pattern of mean-reversion pre- vs. post-1925. Survival may also be relevant to the analysis. Brown, Goetzmann and Ross (1995) find that survival conditioning may affect estimate of mean reversion. Clearly the young NYSE stock market was more subject to the danger of disappearance than the more mature market post-1925.

In sum, the overall mean-reversion evidence is marginal, but it is occa-sionally significant over sub-periods. The fact that it is not consistent over time may simply mean the periodicity of reversion changes, making forecasts for the U.S. market difficult.

Dividend Yields

In Table 3.4, we report the regressions of annual multiple-year-horizon returns on past dividend yields. For the entire period 1825 through 1999, the coeffi-cients are positive for horizons over four years, although not significantly so. Uncorrected t-statistics for sub-periods 1871–1925 and 1926–1999 are of the magnitude of 2 to 4; however, these values are consistent with 95th percentile

Table 3.3

Tests of Long-Term Mean Reversion in Stock Market Returns

Horizon	1	2	3	4	5	6	7	8	9	10
Capital appreciation return 1816–1999, price-weighted series to 1925, Ibbotson to 1999										
Intercept	0.071	0.158	0.239	0.347	0.480	0.587	0.707	0.825	0.892	0.952
t int.	4.415	5.984	6.759	7.235	8.057	8.534	8.691	8.447	8.079	7.934
Coef.	0.064	−0.015	−0.004	−0.043	−0.120	−0.124	−0.115	−0.086	−0.012	0.047
t coef.	0.857	−0.200	−0.052	−0.552	−1.535	−1.588	−1.475	−1.097	−0.154	0.585
r^2	0.004	0.000	0.000	0.002	0.013	0.015	0.013	0.007	0.000	0.002
n	183.000	181.000	179.000	177.000	175.000	173.000	171.000	169.000	167.000	165.000
Total return 1825–1999, price-weighted series to 1925, Ibbotson to 1999, low dividends to 1870, Cowles to 1925										
Intercept	0.116	0.277	0.439	0.639	0.887	1.084	1.254	1.452	1.592	1.771
t int.	6.384	8.680	9.581	9.875	10.680	10.850	10.876	10.305	9.657	9.335
Coef.	0.054	−0.045	−0.054	−0.087	−0.155	−0.141	−0.106	−0.067	0.011	0.059
t coef.	0.706	−0.587	−0.689	−1.111	−1.982	−1.833	−1.462	−0.926	0.148	0.800
r^2	0.003	0.002	0.003	0.007	0.023	0.020	0.013	0.005	0.000	0.004
n	174.000	172.000	170.000	168.000	166.000	164.000	162.000	160.000	158.000	156.000
Total return 1825–1870, price-weighted series, low dividends										
Intercept	0.139	0.357	0.688	1.144	1.833	2.685	3.145	3.440	3.847	4.705
t int.	3.075	4.231	5.220	5.641	7.088	9.731	9.956	7.095	6.132	6.256
Coef.	0.101	0.020	−0.137	−0.268	−0.483	−0.691*	−0.635	−0.465	−0.353	−0.366
t coef.	0.671	0.130	−0.883	−1.672	−3.176	−5.285	−5.355	−3.231	−2.227	−2.189
r^2	0.010	0.000	0.020	0.070	0.224	0.458	0.481	0.265	0.155	0.161
n	45.000	43.000	41.000	39.000	37.000	35.000	33.000	31.000	29.000	27.000
Total return 1871–1925, price-weighted series, Cowles dividends										
Intercept	0.088	0.227	0.324	0.453	0.653	0.677	0.863	1.138	1.336	1.628
t int.	3.499	5.666	6.393	6.823	8.358	7.369	7.991	8.671	9.344	10.587
Coef.	−0.044	−0.347*	−0.312	−0.307	−0.474	−0.299	−0.407	−0.550	−0.583	−0.670

	1	2	3	4	5	6	7	8	9	10
t coef.	-0.317	-2.531	-2.156	-2.046	-3.348	-2.072	-2.790	-3.758	-4.304	-5.153
r^2	0.002	0.114	0.088	0.083	0.203	0.093	0.163	0.271	0.340	0.439
n	54.000	52.000	50.000	48.000	46.000	44.000	42.000	40.000	38.000	36.000
Total return 1926–1999, Ibbotson large stock series										
Intercept	0.129	0.311	0.503	0.715	0.837	0.865	1.039	1.409	1.770	2.466
t int.	4.648	6.398	7.535	7.961	7.409	6.608	6.522	6.849	6.973	8.120
Coef.	0.008	-0.141	-0.229	-0.212	-0.035	0.200	0.243	0.141	0.110	-0.063
t coef.	0.069	-1.171	-1.885	-1.737	-0.274	1.676	2.048	1.112	0.820	-0.469
r^2	0.000	0.019	0.050	0.044	0.001	0.043	0.065	0.021	0.012	0.004
n	74.000	72.000	70.000	68.000	66.000	64.000	62.000	60.000	58.000	56.000
Bootstrapped median for 175-year period										
Intercept	0.120	0.257	0.414	0.595	0.786	1.006	1.257	1.545	1.854	2.226
t int.	6.626	8.109	8.938	9.334	9.598	9.802	9.981	10.117	10.218	10.230
Coef.	0.001	-0.016	-0.028	-0.035	-0.040	-0.051	-0.064	-0.076	-0.074	-0.081
t coef.	0.010	-0.203	-0.375	-0.442	-0.516	-0.650	-0.805	-0.962	-0.941	-1.044
r^2	0.003	0.005	0.006	0.008	0.009	0.011	0.014	0.016	0.018	0.018
n	174.000	172.000	170.000	168.000	166.000	164.000	162.000	160.000	158.000	156.000
Bootstrapped 5% level for 175-year period										
Intercept	0.091	0.189	0.296	0.417	0.549	0.683	0.828	0.982	1.185	1.371
t int.	5.320	6.435	6.897	7.084	7.177	7.215	7.149	7.110	7.014	6.947
Coef.	-0.128	-0.163	-0.195	-0.227	-0.247	-0.269	-0.280	-0.307	-0.321	-0.331
t coef.	-1.690	-2.147	-2.566	-2.922	-3.293	-3.596	-3.695	-4.069	-4.209	-4.347
r^2	0.000	0.000	0.000	0.000	0.000	0.000	0.000	0.000	0.000	0.000
n	174.000	172.000	170.000	168.000	166.000	164.000	162.000	160.000	158.000	156.000

Notes: Each panel reports the results of regressing future multiple-horizon overlapping returns on past multiple-horizon overlapping returns, from 1 to 10 years. Total returns are calculated using the low dividend series and the Cowles dividend series before 1925. Medians and 5th percentiles of a bootstrapped distribution are reported in the final two panels. They are bootstrapped under the null of i.i.d. returns drawn with replacement from the entire time period, under the assumption of stationarity of means.

*Statistically significant at the 10 percent level.

Table 3.4
Tests of Dividend Yield Forecasting Power for Long-Horizon Stock Market Returns

	1	2	3	4	5	6	7	8	9	10
Yield regressions from 1825 to 1999										
Intercept	0.135	0.262	0.508	0.629	0.679	0.891	1.111	1.152	1.430	1.796
t int.	2.933	3.484	5.059	4.483	3.809	4.268	4.336	3.605	3.900	4.462
Coef.	-0.286	0.009	-2.121	-0.898	2.243	1.860	1.995	6.856	6.597	4.792
t coef.	-0.293	0.006	-0.999	-0.304	0.598	0.424	0.372	1.026	0.862	0.571
r^2	0.000	0.000	0.006	0.001	0.002	0.001	0.001	0.006	0.005	0.002
n	174.000	173.000	172.000	171.000	170.000	169.000	168.000	167.000	166.000	165.000
Yield regressions from 1825 to 1870, price-weighted series, low dividends										
Intercept	0.213	0.449	0.833	1.061	1.013	1.182	1.470	1.199	1.245	1.707
t int.	2.109	2.694	3.682	3.223	2.394	2.416	2.442	1.587	1.471	1.942
Coef.	-1.656	-2.911	-7.615	-6.736	2.611	5.966	7.273	25.896	35.510	33.605
t coef.	-0.632	-0.674	-1.299	-0.790	0.238	0.471	0.466	1.324	1.620	1.475
r^2	0.009	0.010	0.037	0.014	0.001	0.005	0.005	0.038	0.056	0.047
n	46.000	46.000	46.000	46.000	46.000	46.000	46.000	46.000	46.000	46.000
Yield regressions from 1871 to 1925										
Intercept	0.012	0.004	0.202	0.145	-0.099	-0.099	-0.191	-0.382	-0.261	-0.130
t int.	0.135	0.026	1.137	0.628	-0.357	-0.321	-0.542	-0.987	-0.660	-0.318
Coef.	1.371	3.335	1.609	4.948	11.850	13.891	17.881	24.037	23.954	23.822
t coef.	0.840	1.310	0.495	1.175	2.344	2.468	2.769	3.394	3.316	3.181
r^2	0.013	0.031	0.005	0.025	0.094	0.103	0.126	0.179	0.172	0.160
n	55.000	55.000	55.000	55.000	55.000	55.000	55.000	55.000	55.000	55.000

Yield regressions from 1926 to 1999

Intercept	0.078	0.094	0.180	0.127	0.161	0.323	0.396	0.428	0.676	0.808
t int.	1.141	0.864	1.288	0.707	0.736	1.259	1.283	1.143	1.505	1.498
Coef.	1.206	4.123	5.399	10.238	13.499	14.348	17.952	23.144	24.325	28.914
t coef.	0.804	1.748	1.794	2.646	2.893	2.631	2.751	2.934	2.585	2.568
r^2	0.009	0.042	0.045	0.093	0.111	0.095	0.104	0.119	0.096	0.096
n	73.000	72.000	71.000	70.000	69.000	68.000	67.000	66.000	65.000	64.000

Bootstrap medians 1,000 iterations using low dividend yield, conditioning upon actual yields

Intercept	0.093	0.198	0.319	0.455	0.600	0.763	0.976	1.191	1.424	1.692
t int.	2.357	3.083	3.552	3.918	4.129	4.244	4.412	4.515	4.552	4.577
Coef.	0.658	1.332	2.054	2.795	3.770	4.670	5.505	6.668	8.342	9.546
t coef.	0.755	0.951	1.083	1.142	1.226	1.245	1.195	1.178	1.214	1.208
r^2	0.005	0.007	0.009	0.010	0.012	0.012	0.013	0.013	0.015	0.015
n	174.000	173.000	172.000	171.000	170.000	169.000	168.000	167.000	166.000	165.000

Bootstrapped 95% level with 1,000 iterations using low dividend yield, conditioning upon actual yields

Intercept	0.160	0.339	0.544	0.788	1.073	1.374	1.747	2.123	2.642	3.240
t int.	4.145	5.259	6.068	6.580	6.954	7.338	7.539	7.699	8.039	8.186
Coef.	2.061	4.010	5.996	8.565	11.905	15.273	19.082	23.399	28.798	35.802
t coef.	2.296	2.885	3.182	3.425	3.728	3.852	3.925	4.058	4.097	4.239
r^2	0.030	0.046	0.056	0.065	0.077	0.082	0.086	0.092	0.093	0.099
n	174.000	173.000	172.000	171.000	170.000	169.000	168.000	167.000	166.000	165.000

Notes: Each panel reports the results of regressing future multiple-horizon overlapping returns dividend yields from one to ten year return horizons. Total returns are calculated using the low dividend series and the Cowles dividend series before 1925. Yields are calculated as the sum of the dividends paid during the year divided by the index price at the end of the year. The bootstrap is performed by fixing the income return series as the historical realized value, drawing total returns with replacement and constructing a dividend yield series consistent with both. Medians and 5th percentiles of the bootstrapped distribution are reported in the final two panels.

bootstrapped values for t-statistics over longer periods. For our bootstraps, we sample appreciation returns by drawing from the distribution with replacement, and reconstruct a dividend yield series and a total return series conditional upon the actual income returns, using the low dividend series. The dividend yield series we create by dividing the actual income return by the bootstrapped appreciation return each period. The total return we construct by summing the actual income return and the bootstrapped appreciation return each period. The median and 95% quantiles of the bootstrapped distribution for the entire time period are reported at the bottom of Table 3.4. Not reported are the sub-period bootstrap distributions, but we use them for our p-values in the table.

None of the coefficients in the full-period regressions exceed the bootstrapped 5% critical values—in fact, they deviate little from the median bootstrapped values. The sub-period evidence is more suggestive of possible forecasting power when uncorrected t-statistics are used. However, the bootstrapped critical 5% values are a high threshold at longer horizons—uncorrected t-values exceeding 3 to 5 are expected 5% of the time. On the other hand, for virtually every sub-period, the coefficients are positive and increasing in the investment horizon as would be predicted by dividend forecasting models. Note that we used only the low dividend series for our analysis. We did not use the high dividend series because of the obvious structural change in the income returns displayed in Fig. 3.4. Thus, our negative results may be in part due to incomplete or uneven dividend data.

◣ *Estimating Time-Varying Volatility*

Our long-term data allow us to investigate additional time-series characteristics of equity returns of interest to research in financial economics. Schwert (1989) analyzes the stock volatility using monthly data from 1857 to 1987. He shows that aggregate financial leverage is correlated with stock return volatility. He also demonstrates that stock return volatility is higher during economic recessions than during expansions. While we do not have information about the capital structure of the market over the early period, we are able to condition upon past returns. Presumably, when stock prices drop, leverage increases in the short term. Using various stochastic volatility models, we investigate the predictability of conditional volatility of the monthly NYSE capital appreciation conditional upon past positive and negative returns from February 1815 to December 1925. We find that higher lagged return shocks and conditional volatility cause higher volatility. At the same time, our results show that negative return shocks cause higher volatility than positive shocks do, which confirms the findings of Schwert (1989).

We obtain the unpredictable part of the capital appreciation returns through a procedure similar to that of Pagan and Schwert (1990) and Engle and Ng (1993). The procedure consists of a month-of-the-year effect adjustment

Table 3.5
Mean Adjustment Regression

Intercept	January	February	March	April	May	June	July	August	September	October	November
					Coefficients of month-of-the-year dummies						
0.027	0.0105	−0.0067	0.0035	0.0025	−0.0015	−0.0079	−0.0010	−0.0015	−0.0032	−0.0016	−0.0008
(0.0041)	(0.0059)	(0.0058)	(0.0058)	(0.0058)	(0.0058)	(0.0058)	(0.0058)	(0.0058)	(0.0058)	(0.0058)	(0.0058)
[0.6648]	[1.7922]	[−1.1695]	[0.5993]	[0.4317]	[−0.2664]	[−1.3765]	[−0.1780]	[−0.2582]	[−0.5490]	[−0.2816]	[−0.1438]

Notes: This table reports the results of an adjustment procedure to remove the month-of-the-year effects from the monthly capital appreciation return of NYSE from February 1815 to December 1925. The procedure is analogous to the one in Pagan and Schwert (1990) and the one in Engle and Ng (1993). First, the monthly return is regressed on 12 month-of-the-year dummies to get the residual u. Then u is regressed on a constant and some lags whose order is determined by Akaike information criterion (AIC). According to AIC, the optimal order of lag is 0. In the table, the numbers in parentheses (.) are the asymptotic standard errors and the numbers in brackets [.] are the t values.

Table 3.6
GARCH Estimation Results

GARCH(1, 1) specification

$$\sigma_t^2 = 0.00119 + 0.25884(\left|\varepsilon_{t-1}\right| - 0.14507\varepsilon_{t-1})^2 - 0.03929\sigma_{t-1}^2$$

(0.00006) (0.003649)   (0.06596)   (0.05164)

[18.94]   [7.09]   [−2.1994]   [−0.7609]

EGARCH(1, 1) specification

$$\ln(\sigma_t^2 = -3.91869 + 0.38592 \cdot \frac{\left|\varepsilon_{t-1}\right| - 0.15383\varepsilon_{t-1}}{\sigma_{t-1}} + 0.44032 \cdot \ln(\sigma_{t-1}^2)$$

(0.47535) (0.04242)   (0.07541)   (0.069334)

[−8.244]   [9.0983]   [−2.039]   [6.3508]

PGARCH(1, 1) specification

$$\sigma_t^{1.937} = 0.00127 + 0.2507(\left|\varepsilon_{t-1}\right| - 0.185\varepsilon_{t-1})^{1.937} + 0.0717\sigma_{t-1}^{1.937}$$

(0.38579) (0.00167)   (0.0363)   (0.06696)   (0.07026)

[5.02]   [0.76]   [6.91]   [−2.76]   [1.02]

TGARCH(1, 1) specification

$$\sigma_t^2 = 0.00122 + 0.19028\varepsilon_{t-1}^2 + 0.1396 \cdot S_{t-1}\varepsilon_{t-1}^2 - 0.04155\sigma_{t-1}^2$$

(0.00006) (0.04561)   (0.06614)   (0.04855)

[20.04]   [4.17]   [2.11]   [−0.86]

Diagnostic test results

$$\sigma_t^2 = 0.00119 + 0.25884(\left|\varepsilon\right|_{t-1} - 0.14507\varepsilon_{t-1})^2 - 0.03929\sigma_{t-1}^2$$

	GARCH(1, 1)	EGARCH(1, 1)	PGARCH(1, 1)	TGARCH(1, 1)
AIC	−4,632.491	−4,615.057	−4,623.691	−4,634.422
BIC	−4,606.765	−4,589.331	−4,592.82	−4,608.696
Jarque-Bera	40,054	53,561	44,784	39,224
Shapiro-Wilk	0.9215	0.912	0.9187	0.922
Ljung-Box(12)[a]	20.13	19.53	20.29	20.09
Ljung-Box(12)[b]	0.4525	0.4514	0.5233	0.4597

and an autoregression that removes the predictable part of the return series. We first regress the monthly returns on month-of-the-year dummies and then use the residuals in an autoregression. We use the residuals from this autoregression as our unpredictable stock returns. It is interesting to notice that there is some evidence of the January effect in our month-of-the-year regression. January has the highest excess return, 1.05%, with a 1.8 t-statistic (corresponding to about 7% p value). The lowest excess return appears in June, −0.79%. The results of the month-of-the-year adjustment are reported in Table 3.5.

Using the unpredictable stock returns, we estimate four different volatility models. They are the standard GARCH, power GARCH (PGARCH), exponential GARCH (EGARCH) and threshold GARCH (TGARCH). The estimation is performed via quasi-maximum likelihood methods using the

Table 3.6 (*continued*)
GARCH Estimation Results

GARCH(1, 2)

$$\sigma_t^2 = 0.00112 + 0.24515(|\varepsilon_{t-1}| - 0.07792\varepsilon_{t-1})^2 - 0.22405\sigma_{t-1}^2 + 0.29598\sigma_{t-2}^2$$

(0.00007)   (0.00316)   (0.04582)   (0.02875)   (0.5588)

[16.35]   [7.77]   [−1.70]   [−7.79]   [5.30]

PGARCH(1, 2)

$$\sigma_t^{2.28994} = 0.00034 + 0.23186(|\varepsilon_{t-1}| - 0.06539\varepsilon_{t-1})^{2.28994} - 0.14113\sigma_{t-1}^{2.28994}$$
$$ + 0.29837\sigma_{t-2}^{2.28994}$$

(0.33031)   (0.00042)   (0.03719)   (0.05012)   (0.04331)   (0.06048)

[6.93]   [0.81]   [5.23]   [−1.30]   [−3.26]   [4.93]

TGARCH(1, 2)

$$\sigma_t^2 = 0.00107 + 0.209\varepsilon_{t-1}^2 + 0.0785 \cdot S_{t-1}\,\varepsilon_{t-1}^2 - 0.2025\sigma_{t-1}^2 - 0.0785\sigma_{t-2}^2$$

(0.00007)   (0.0421)   (0.04644)   (0.03085)   (0.05935)

[14.53]   [4.96]   [1.69]   [−6.56]   [4.79]

Diagnostic test results

	GARCH(1, 2)	PGARCH(1, 2)	TGARCH(1, 2)
AIC	−4,631.306	−4,623.172	−4,629.897
BIC	−4,600.435	−4,587.156	−4,599.026
Jarque-Bera	40,227	45,248	41,595
Shapiro-Wilk	0.9217	0.9188	0.9207
Ljung-Box(12)[c]	20.82	21.36	20.58
Ljung-Box(12)[d]	0.6224	0.6113	0.6039

Notes: This table reports the estimation results of various predictable volatility models for the monthly capital appreciation return of the NYSE from January 1815 to December 1925. Month-of-the-year effects and a predictable component have been removed. The estimation is performed by the method of quasi-maximum likelihood using the BHHH numerical optimization algorithm. In the table, the numbers in parentheses (.) are the asymptotic standard errors and the numbers in brackets [.] are the *t* values.

σ_t^2 is the conditional variance on month *t* and ε_{t-1} is the unpredictable return on month $t-1$.

[a]Test for standardized residuals.

[b]Test for squared standardized residuals.

[c]Test for standardized residuals.

[d]Test for squared standardized residuals.

BHHH numerical optimization algorithm. We include leverage terms in all models to capture possible asymmetric effects of positive and negative returns. For each model, we estimate both (1, 1) and (1, 2) settings. However, the TGARCH (1, 2) estimation does not converge.

In Table 3.6 we report the estimation results. The parameters corresponding to the one-period lagged unpredictable return in all models, the constant term in all models except PGARCH, the leverage term in all (1, 1) models are significant. In sum, our results show that for NYSE monthly capital appreciation from February 1815 to December 1925, higher lagged return shocks and conditional volatility cause higher volatility. These results are also consistent with the hypothesis that negative return shocks cause higher volatility than positive return shocks, which indicates that the so-called "good-news" and "bad-news" asymmetric impacts already existed in the early era of NYSE.

◣ Conclusion

Our data collection efforts over the last 10 years have yielded a comprehensive database of NYSE security prices over nearly the entire history of the stock exchange. While econometricians, including ourselves, have created indices of stock returns over the 19th century, most have conditioned upon availability, or used average of monthly high and low prices. No one has collected dividends for a broad sample of NYSE stocks over the 19th century. Our goal is to construct a CRSP-like database of NYSE stocks for the entire history of the exchange. The current paper reports on the fruits of our efforts thus far. In particular, we construct a price-weighted index for the entire pre-CRSP era of the U.S. stock market from 1815 to 1925. We find that it closely tracks the widely used Cowles index over the 1871 to 1925 period; however, it does not suffer from the well-known bias in the monthly autocorrelation. We believe our index is fairly representative of the behavior of NYSE securities over the early 19th-century indices as well.

Over our entire period (1815–1925), our price-weighted capital appreciation is 1.24% per year, which is substantially lower than the Ibbotson and Sinquefield (1926–1999) capital appreciation of 6.62% annual geometric mean (compounded) return. For the period in which we have dividends (1825–1925) our low income annual return is 4.63%, and our high income annual return is 7.09%. Expressed as total returns, our low dividend price-weighted annualized geometric mean return is 5.99%, and our high dividend price-weighted annualized geometric mean return is 8.50%. This compares to the Ibbotson and Sinquefield (1926–1999) annual income return of 4.45% and the total annual geometric mean return of 11.35%.

Our investigation of the forecastability of long-horizon stock returns using past returns and dividend yields leaves us no closer to rejecting the null of no predictability than researchers were ten years ago. Evidence over sub-periods in the past is tantalizing, but reasonable bootstrap methods fail to clearly reject the hypothesis of no predictability over the entire time period, despite some sub-period evidence.

Our investigation of the conditional volatility of monthly NYSE capital appreciation using various volatility models generally verifies earlier findings in the literature that good news and bad news have different predictability for future volatility. Specifically, all the models except PGARCH find that negative shocks introduce more volatility than positive shocks.

◣ *Appendix 1*

The appendix reports the key annual series used in the paper. The columns are self-explanatory. The method of index construction is described in the text. The total number of securities indicated is the number of different securities that comprised at least part of the monthly price-weighted average returns in the index calculation for that year. Industrial classifications were based upon the company names. Firms were included under Industrials unless otherwise identifiable. These data are available for downloading in spreadsheet format at the website of the International Center for Finance at the Yale School of Management.

Year	Price-Weighted Capital Appreciation	Price-Weighted Appreciation Index	Low Dividend Return	High Dividend Return	Total Return With Low Dividends	Total Return With High Dividends	Equal-Weighted Capital Appreciation Returns	Equal-Weighted Capital Appreciation Return Index	Total Number of Securities in Index	Insurance	Transportation	Banks	Mining	Utility	Industrials and other
1814		1.00						1.00							
1815	-6.65%	0.93					-6.65%	0.93	8	3	0	5	0	0	0
1816	-1.93%	0.92					-1.69%	0.92	8	3	0	5	0	0	0
1817	-19.43%	1.09					19.37%	1.10	8	3	0	5	0	0	0
1818	-3.76%	1.05					23.16%	1.35	13	7	0	6	0	0	0
1819	-8.82%	0.96					-7.45%	1.25	15	9	0	6	0	0	0
1820	9.59%	1.05					10.13%	1.38	15	9	0	6	0	0	0
1821	3.24%	1.09					3.48%	1.42	15	9	0	6	0	1	0
1822	-12.85%	0.95					-6.54%	1.33	6	0	0	0	0	0	0
1823	5.29%	1.00					6.25%	1.41	21	14	0	6	0	1	0
1824	3.70%	1.03					3.92%	1.47	33	22	0	10	0	1	0
1825	-12.99%	0.90	2.53%	5.08%	-10.46%	-7.91%	-13.73%	1.27	32	22	1	9	0	0	0
1826	-1.22%	0.89	2.03%	4.94%	0.81%	3.72%	1.07%	1.28	34	20	1	11	0	1	1
1827	-6.24%	0.83	2.97%	6.18%	-3.28%	-0.06%	-6.86%	1.19	32	19	1	9	0	1	1
1828	-17.95%	0.68	2.82%	5.85%	-15.13%	-12.10%	-21.52%	0.94	29	15	1	10	0	0	3
1829	10.33%	0.75	3.21%	6.99%	13.54%	17.32%	12.10%	1.05	30	18	1	9	0	1	2
1830	27.31%	0.96	2.83%	5.57%	30.14%	32.88%	29.35%	1.36	30	17	1	10	0	0	2
1831	-17.05%	0.80	1.70%	4.44%	-15.35%	-12.60%	-2.55%	1.32	38	17	4	15	0	0	2
1832	8.60%	0.87	3.02%	5.93%	11.62%	14.53%	10.34%	1.46	40	18	4	16	0	0	2
1833	-6.09%	0.81	2.94%	5.54%	-3.16%	-0.55%	-6.56%	1.36	49	22	7	16	0	1	3
1834	8.84%	0.88	2.91%	5.88%	11.75%	14.72%	18.42%	1.61	47	19	6	18	0	1	3
1835	-6.74%	0.82	2.83%	5.93%	-3.91%	-0.81%	-1.60%	1.59	58	23	8	23	0	1	3
1836	4.33%	0.86	1.59%	13.93%	5.92%	18.26%	-5.83%	1.68	46	13	8	22	0	1	3
1837	-18.02%	0.71	2.11%	7.08%	-15.91%	-10.94%	-16.65%	1.40	45	16	7	19	0	1	2
1838	12.20%	0.79	6.27%	11.71%	18.47%	23.91%	-15.09%	1.61	49	18	6	22	0	1	2

Year															
1839	−26.62%	0.58	5.28%	10.01%	−21.34%	−16.61%	−25.59%	1.20	58	21	6	28	0	1	2
1840	3.01%	0.60	3.53%	8.53%	6.54%	11.54%	−17.30%	1.41	56	20	6	27	0	1	2
1841	−23.52%	0.46	4.87%	10.05%	−18.66%	−13.47%	−28.65%	1.00	47	12	7	25	0	1	2
1842	2.34%	0.47	5.77%	11.65%	8.11%	13.99%	−20.38%	1.21	49	16	7	25	0	1	0
1843	39.16%	0.65	7.18%	25.62%	46.34%	64.78%	−72.30%	2.08	47	16	7	22	0	1	1
1844	2.81%	0.67	6.85%	11.74%	9.66%	14.55%	−12.11%	2.34	47	13	8	23	0	1	2
1845	−11.61%	0.59	4.16%	6.97%	−7.46%	−4.64%	−10.93%	2.08	36	8	7	18	0	1	2
1846	23.21%	0.73	3.36%	8.04%	26.57%	31.25%	45.80%	3.03	25	0	8	14	0	1	2
1847	7.65%	0.79	5.55%	11.41%	13.20%	19.06%	23.79%	3.75	29	5	7	13	0	2	2
1848	5.28%	0.83	5.17%	9.72%	10.45%	15.00%	5.34%	3.96	11	1	3	7	0	0	0
1849	7.80%	0.89	7.60%	13.68%	15.40%	21.48%	52.51%	6.03	60	6	28	21	0	1	4
1850	10.48%	0.98	3.73%	9.41%	14.21%	19.89%	18.09%	7.12	72	9	34	22	0	2	5
1851	−5.78%	0.93	4.44%	11.04%	−1.35%	5.26%	−2.26%	6.96	76	7	31	29	3	0	6
1852	18.07%	1.10	4.52%	10.09%	22.59%	28.16%	58.34%	11.02	85	6	33	30	8	0	8
1853	−8.15%	1.01	4.11%	9.77%	−4.03%	1.62%	−13.43%	9.54	120	11	42	36	15	2	14
1854	−20.34%	0.80	1.99%	17.42%	−18.35%	−2.92%	−20.35%	7.60	78	0	32	22	10	3	11
1855	16.26%	0.93	2.09%	9.12%	18.34%	25.38%	15.40%	8.77	73	3	33	23	7	1	6
1856	2.49%	0.95	3.00%	9.57%	5.49%	12.05%	3.50%	9.08	71	4	33	32	5	1	4
1857	−24.22%	0.72	3.39%	18.58%	−20.82%	−5.64%	−12.34%	7.96	81	5	31	33	5	1	6
1858	10.38%	0.80	2.83%	10.53%	13.22%	20.92%	137.91%	18.93	82	2	33	34	4	0	9
1859	−0.62%	0.79	2.86%	12.26%	2.24%	11.64%	−4.44%	18.09	65	1	28	30	2	0	4
1860	−3.93%	0.76	2.41%	5.35%	−1.53%	1.41%	63.93%	29.66	62	1	30	24	4	1	2
1861	−3.73%	0.73	3.21%	7.33%	−0.52%	3.60%	3.49%	30.70	56	2	30	20	3	0	2
1862	49.15%	1.09	3.60%	8.10%	52.75%	57.25%	75.22%	53.78	67	1	34	24	5	0	2
1863	40.95%	1.54	3.52%	7.40%	44.47%	48.35%	60.09%	86.11	82	1	40	24	9	2	6
1864	10.53%	1.71	4.18%	7.97%	14.71%	18.50%	4.94%	90.36	91	1	44	23	17	2	4
1865	−1.33%	1.68	3.97%	8.18%	2.64%	6.85%	8.89%	98.39	82	1	37	20	13	1	10
1866	0.46%	1.69	4.39%	9.31%	4.85%	9.77%	5.73%	104.03	94	0	43	24	10	1	15
1867	−2.61%	1.65	4.50%	8.47%	1.88%	5.86%	−5.37%	98.44	35	1	0	0	0	0	0
1868	1.52%	1.67					4.26%	102.63	75	2	42	19	2	1	10
1869	−2.85%	1.62	4.18%	8.87%	1.33%	6.02%	−0.59%	102.03	106	1	55	29	6	2	12
1870	−1.44%	1.60	4.20%	9.12%	2.77%	7.68%	−0.63%	102.67	103	1	49	31	7	1	14
1871	3.34%	1.65	5.86%	5.86%	9.20%	9.20%	14.65%	117.71	103	1	50	28	9	2	13

(continued)

Year	Price-Weighted Capital Appreciation	Price-Weighted Appreciation Index	Low Dividend Return	High Dividend Return	Total Return With Low Dividends	Total Return With High Dividends	Equal-Weighted Capital Appreciation Returns	Equal-Weighted Capital Appreciation Return Index	Total Number of Securities in Index	Insurance	Transportation	Banks	Mining	Utility	Industrials and other
1872	0.50%	1.06	6.33%	6.33%	6.83%	6.83%	23.08%	144.87	26	0	16	0	2	0	8
1873	−17.70%	1.37	6.51%	6.51%	−11.19%	−11.19%	−23.79%	110.41	33	0	17	0	1	0	15
1874	−5.77%	1.29	7.47%	7.47%	1.70%	1.70%	−10.59%	98.72	31	0	17	0	0	0	12
1875	−4.72%	1.23	6.61%	6.61%	1.89%	1.89%	−16.41%	82.52	36	0	19	0	2	0	15
1876	−13.31%	1.07	6.86%	6.86%	−6.45%	−6.45%	1.55%	81.25	38	0	19	0	2	0	17
1877	1.74%	1.08	5.31%	5.31%	7.05%	7.05%	19.51%	97.10	41	0	24	0	2	0	15
1878	10.50%	1.20	5.54%	5.54%	16.04%	16.04%	24.87%	121.25	48	0	27	0	3	0	18
1879	51.31%	1.81	5.80%	5.80%	57.10%	57.10%	98.27%	240.39	49	0	26	0	3	0	20
1880	19.83%	2.17	5.28%	5.28%	25.12%	25.12%	18.48%	284.81	74	0	24	0	3	0	47
1881	1.88%	2.21	5.48%	5.48%	7.36%	7.36%	10.59%	314.98	67	0	22	0	3	0	42
1882	−9.54%	2.00	5.32%	5.32%	−4.22%	−4.22%	−2.28%	307.81	61	0	22	0	2	0	37
1883	−15.04%	1.70	5.65%	5.65%	−9.39%	−9.39%	−14.67%	262.66	120	0	22	1	2	0	95
1884	−24.28%	1.29	5.81%	5.81%	−18.47%	−18.47%	−24.24%	198.98	116	0	20	1	2	0	93
1885	45.32%	1.87	5.53%	5.53%	50.85%	50.85%	−105.41%	408.72	77	0	14	0	0	0	63
1886	12.46%	2.10	4.23%	4.23%	16.69%	16.69%	−71.82%	702.27	75	0	14	0	0	0	61
1887	−12.13%	1.85	4.43%	4.43%	−7.70%	−7.70%	−10.75%	626.79	68	0	13	0	0	0	55
1888	2.09%	1.89	4.36%	4.36%	6.45%	6.45%	−9.54%	686.62	96	0	19	0	2	0	75
1889	4.49%	1.97	4.28%	4.28%	8.77%	8.77%	−15.33%	791.89	89	0	16	0	2	0	71
1890	−10.72%	1.76	4.14%	4.14%	−6.59%	−6.59%	−1.24%	782.06	91	0	15	0	2	0	74
1891	2.95%	1.81	4.78%	4.78%	7.74%	7.74%	−15.87%	906.18	83	0	15	0	2	0	66
1892	10.35%	2.00	4.44%	4.44%	14.79%	14.79%	−18.64%	1075.08	82	0	15	0	2	0	65
1893	−16.86%	1.66	4.54%	4.54%	−12.33%	−12.33%	−24.23%	814.62	80	0	15	0	2	0	63
1894	−2.82%	1.62	4.76%	4.76%	1.94%	1.94%	−9.16%	889.28	75	0	15	0	2	0	58
1895	2.14%	1.65	4.42%	4.42%	6.56%	6.56%	−26.41%	1124.09	70	0	14	0	2	0	54
1896	0.69%	1.66	4.17%	4.17%	4.86%	4.86%	−7.16%	1204.59	70	0	14	0	2	0	54
1897	14.15%	1.90	4.27%	4.27%	18.41%	18.41%	−22.72%	1478.30	65	0	14	0	2	0	49

1898	12.17%	2.13	4.21%	4.21%	16.38%	16.38%	−37.60%	2034.16	61	0	13	0	2	0	46
1899	4.17%	2.22	3.72%	3.72%	7.89%	7.89%	−10.51%	2247.97	60	0	13	0	2	0	45
1900	17.99%	2.62	4.98%	4.98%	22.97%	22.97%	−31.38%	2953.32	70	0	13	0	2	0	55
1901	24.60%	3.26	4.66%	4.66%	29.26%	29.26%	38.60%	4093.24	75	0	12	0	2	0	61
1902	5.29%	3.43	4.15%	4.15%	9.44%	9.44%	6.42%	4355.86	77	0	11	0	2	0	64
1903	−12.88%	2.99	4.35%	4.35%	−8.53%	−8.53%	−17.93%	3574.82	80	0	10	0	2	0	68
1904	14.94%	3.44	4.72%	4.72%	19.66%	19.66%	−24.42%	4447.64	81	0	13	0	2	0	66
1905	6.67%	3.66	4.00%	4.00%	10.67%	10.67%	7.88%	4797.96	85	0	13	0	2	0	70
1906	−1.09%	3.62	4.19%	4.19%	3.10%	3.10%	−1.23%	4738.98	89	0	12	0	2	0	75
1907	−26.26%	2.67	4.47%	4.47%	−21.79%	−21.79%	−30.64%	3287.01	92	0	12	0	2	0	78
1908	28.47%	3.43	6.09%	6.09%	34.56%	34.56%	49.62%	4917.94	91	0	13	0	2	0	76
1909	18.12%	4.06	4.87%	4.87%	22.99%	22.99%	22.22%	6010.71	90	0	13	0	0	0	75
1910	−15.50%	3.43	4.56%	4.56%	−10.94%	−10.94%	−15.89%	5055.61	88	0	13	0	0	0	75
1911	2.17%	3.50	5.19%	5.19%	7.37%	7.37%	−1.17%	4996.22	90	0	14	0	0	0	76
1912	0.03%	3.50	5.27%	5.27%	5.30%	5.30%	1.26%	5059.00	88	0	14	0	0	0	74
1913	−14.44%	3.00	5.12%	5.12%	−9.32%	−9.32%	−15.68%	4265.65	88	0	13	0	0	0	75
1914	−8.47%	2.74	5.22%	5.22%	−3.25%	−3.25%	−17.88%	3503.14	85	0	14	0	0	0	71
1915	15.88%	3.18	5.85%	5.85%	21.73%	21.73%	46.05%	5116.33	93	0	13	0	0	0	80
1916	1.29%	3.22	5.91%	5.91%	7.19%	7.19%	12.58%	5760.08	95	0	13	0	0	0	82
1917	−23.48%	2.46	7.04%	7.04%	−16.44%	−16.44%	−24.91%	4325.04	88	0	13	0	0	0	75
1918	2.88%	2.53	8.38%	8.38%	11.27%	11.27%	7.41%	4645.40	89	0	13	0	0	0	76
1919	9.38%	2.77	6.71%	6.71%	16.09%	16.09%	16.38%	5406.37	86	0	13	0	0	0	73
1920	−20.74%	2.20	5.72%	5.72%	−15.02%	−15.02%	15.94%	4544.77	90	0	12	0	0	0	78
1921	4.26%	2.29	6.75%	6.75%	11.02%	11.02%	15.13%	5232.28	91	0	13	0	0	0	78
1922	19.74%	2.74	6.98%	6.98%	26.72%	26.72%	32.84%	6950.65	89	0	13	0	0	0	76
1923	−2.13%	2.68	6.04%	6.04%	3.90%	3.90%	7.92%	7501.49	89	0	13	0	0	0	76
1924	19.34%	3.20	6.43%	6.43%	25.77%	25.77%	42.58%	10695.73	87	0	13	0	0	0	74
1925	23.22%	3.95	5.91%	5.91%	29.12%	29.12%	22.31%	13081.57	86	0	13	0	0	0	73

Figure 3.6. Large Company Stocks, 1824–2002 (Year-End 1824 = $1.00)
Notes: For 1825–1925, the capital appreciation series is from this paper. The total return series presented is from the simple average of the high dividend and the low dividend return series. The graph and the data 1926 to the present are from *Stocks, Bonds, Bills and Inflation, 2006 Yearbook,* published by Ibbotson Associates. All rights reserved. Used with permission.

◤ *Notes*

1. See Peter Bernstein, 1992, *Capital Ideas,* p. 31.

2. See, for example, Boudoukh and Richardson (1992), Campbell and Shiller (1988), Fama and French (1988a,b), Fisher and Lorie (1968), Goetzmann (1993), Ibbotson and Brinson (1993), Ibbotson and Sinquefield (1976), Shiller (1989), Schwert (1990), Siegel (1992) and Wilson and Jones (1987). Other uses of long-term stock market indices are legion.

3. For 1825–1925, the capital appreciation series is from this paper. The total return series presented is from the simple average of the high dividend and the low dividend return series. The graph and the data 1926 to the present are from *Stock, Bonds, Bills, and Inflation, 2002 Yearbook,* published by Ibbotson Associates. All rights are reserved. Used with permission.

4. We restrict the sample to firms that have two years of dividend payments (four semi-annual dividends), and for which we have a price observation.

5. Similar long-term series using the same sources are reported in Goetzmann (1993), Ibbotson (1993) and Siegel (1992).

6. We ignore the return of dividend reinvestment by assuming all dividends were paid in December.

◤ *References*

Bailey, M. J., Muth, R., Nourse, H. O., 1963. A regression model for real estate price index construction. *Journal of the American Statistical Association* 58, 933–942.

Bernstein, P., 1992. *Capital ideas.* The Free Press, New York.

Blume, M., Stambaugh, R., 1983. Biases in computed returns: an application to the size effects. *Journal of Financial Economics* 12, 387–404.

Boudoukh, C., Richardson, M., 1992. Stock prices and inflation over the long-term, Working paper, Stern School, NYU.

Brown, S. J., Goetzmann, W. N., Ross, S. A., 1995. Survival. *Journal of Finance* 50, 853–873.

Campbell, J. Y., Shiller, R. J., 1988. The dividend–price ratio and expectations of future dividends and discount factors. *Review of Financial Studies* 1, 195–228.

Campbell, J. Y., Shiller, R. J., 1998. Valuation ratios and the long-run stock market outlook. *Journal of Portfolio Management* 24, 11–26.

Canina, M., Thaler, R., Womack, K., 1998. Caveat compounder: a warning about using the daily CRSP equal-weighted index to compute long-run excess returns. *Journal of Finance* 53, 403–416.

Cole, A. H., Frickey, E., 1928. The course of stock prices, 1825–66. *Review of Economics Statistics* 10, 117–139.

Cole, A. H., Smith, W. B., 1935. Fluctuations in American Business. Harvard University Press, Cambridge, 1790–1860.

Cowles, A., 1939. *Common stock indices.* Principia Press, Bloomington.

Engle, R., Ng, V., 1993. Measuring and testing the impact of news on volatility. *Journal of Finance* 48, 1749–1778.

Fama, E. F., French, K. R., 1988a. Permanent and temporary components of stock prices. *Journal of Political Economy* 96, 246–273.

Fama, E. F., French, K. R., 1988b. Dividend yields and expected stock returns. *Journal of Financial Economics* 22, 3–26.

Fama, E. F., French, K. R., 1998. Disappearing dividends: changing firm characteristics or lower propensity to pay? CRSP working paper no. 509, University of Chicago.

Fisher, L., Lorie, J., 1968. Rates of return on investments in common stocks: the year by year record (1926–1965). *Journal of Business* 41, 408–431.

Goetzmann, W. N., 1993. Patterns in three centuries of stock market prices. *Journal of Business* 66, 249–270.

Goetzmann, W. N., Jorion, P., 1993. Testing the predictive power of dividend yields, *Journal of Finance* 48, July.

Goetzmann, W. N., Jorion, P., 1995. A longer look at dividend yields. *Journal of Business* 68, 483–508.

Goetzmann, W. N., Spiegel, M., 1995. Non-temporal components of residential real estate appreciation. *Review of Economics and Statistics* 77, 199–206.

Homer, S., Sylla, R., 1992. *A history of interest rates.* Rutgers University Press, Rutgers.

Ibbotson, R. G., Brinson, G., 1993. *Global investing.* McGraw Hill, New York.

Ibbotson, R. G., Sinquefield, R., 1976. Stock, bonds, bills and inflation: year-by-year historical returns (1926–1974). *Journal of Business* 49, 11–47.

Ibbotson Associates, 2000. *Stocks, bonds, bills and inflation: 2000 yearbook.* Ibbotson Associates, Chicago.

New York Herald, New York.

New York Shipping List, later, New York Shipping and Commercial, 1815–1926, New York, Day and Turner, Volumes from 1815 in Beineke Rare Book Library, Yale University, New Haven, Connecticut.

New York Times, New York. Microfiche.

Pagan, A., Schwert, W., 1990. Alternative models for conditional stock volatility. *Journal of Econometrics* 45, 267–290.

Richardson, M., 1993. Temporary components of stock prices, a skeptic view. *Journal of Business Economics and Statistics* 11, 199–207.

Schwert, W., 1989. Why does stock market volatility change over time? *Journal of Finance* 44, 1115–1153.

Schwert, W., 1990. Index of U.S. stock prices from 1802 to 1897. *Journal of Business* 63, 399–426.

Shiller, R. J., 1989. *Market volatility.* MIT Press, Cambridge.

Siegel, J. J., 1992. The equity premium: stock and bond returns since 1802. *Financial Analysts Journal* 48, 28–38.

Welch, I., Goyal, A., 1999. Predicting the equity premium, Working paper, University of California at Los Angeles and Yale University.

Wilson, J. W., Jones, C. P., 1987. A comparison of annual common stock returns: 1871–1925 with 1926–85. *Journal of Business* 60, 239–258.

Wilson, J. W., Jones, C. P., 2000. An analysis of the S and P 500 index and Cowles extensions: price indexes and stock returns, 1870–1999, Working paper, University of North Carolina.

Wolf, M., 2000. Stock returns and dividend yields revisited: a new way to look at an old problem. *Journal of Business and Economic Statistics* 18, 18–30.

Working, H., 1960. Note on the correlation of first differences of averages in a random chain. *Econometrica* 28, 916–918.

4   Roger G. Ibbotson and Carol L. Fall

The United States Market Wealth Portfolio: Components of Capital Market Values and Returns, 1947–1978

◣ *Overview*

The U.S. market wealth contains all the primary assets that investors would typically own. These include stocks from the various stock exchanges, corporate, government, and municipal bonds, and both farm and residential real estate. By measuring the size of each market and the returns, Ibbotson and Fall were able to create the first market wealth index, that covered most of the spectrum of assets that investors owned.

A measure of U.S. wealth year-by-year, plus the component returns, is useful for the following reasons:

(1) The market portfolio represents the aggregate investment in the United States
(2) The Capital Asset Pricing Model suggests and assumes that investors actually should hold the market portfolio.
(3) Stocks, bonds, and real estate returns can be compared to each other.
(4) Stocks in the NYSE and OTC markets can be compared.
(5) Fixed income of various maturities and types can be compared:
    a) Preferred Stock
    b) Corporate Bonds
    c) Government Bonds
    d) Municipal Bonds
(6) Farm real estate can be compared to residential real estate.
(7) There are correlations of all series with each other.

Much of the data in this article is difficult to update without a separate study. The returns of most assets are included in Ibbotson Associates EnCorr™ databases, but the capitalizations of most categories are not readily available today. We include some updates later in the article.

Although changes in aggregate market wealth sometimes occur very suddenly (as in the Great Crash of 1929), we can get a better perspective on today's capital market risks by studying more extended periods of time. This study covers the 32-year period 1947–1978. While this interval excludes the Great Crash, it does cover a relatively long period of time that encompasses major changes in aggregate wealth as well as its components.

Our task is to measure the year-by-year aggregate market values and returns of five major categories of capital market securities, including: (1) common stocks; (2) fixed corporate securities; (3) real estate; (4) U.S. Government bonds; and (5) municipal (state and local) bonds. We treat (somewhat loosely) the aggregate sum of all five categories as the "market" portfolio.

Each category of securities includes several components. Common stocks are grouped according to their listing on either the New York Stock Exchange (NYSE), American Stock Exchange (AMEX), or Over-the-Counter (OTC) market. Fixed-income corporate securities include preferred stocks, long-term corporate bonds, intermediate-term corporate bonds, and commercial paper. Real estate includes both farms and residential houses. U.S. Government securities include U.S. Treasury bills, notes, bonds, as well as government agency issues. Municipal bonds are grouped as either short-term or long-term.

The aggregate market values of the categories serve as weights for the components within the major categories and the market portfolio. The returns are then measured and cumulative wealth indices are formed. These results are interpreted through the presentation of a statistical summary. Cross-correlations and regression results are included to measure the interrelationships among the series. Regression results also measure the relation of each return series with respect to inflation. Finally, detailed information is given on the source of the aggregate market value and return data for each series.

◣ *What Is the Market Portfolio?*

The U.S. market wealth portfolio theoretically reflects the entire wealth of the United States, with each sector shown in relation to its pro rata share. Its return is the weighted sum of all the return components to wealth.

Why should we construct such a portfolio? The primary reason is curiosity. We want to know what has happened to aggregate wealth in this country. We want to know the dimensions of the market we invest in, and we want to know the historical returns from alternative investment media as well as the market in aggregate.

In addition, there are some theoretical reasons for studying the market. According to what has come to be known as modern portfolio theory, the market portfolio (not just common stocks) is considered to be perfectly diversified with a capital asset pricing model beta of one. A literal interpretation of the theories as originally formulated would suggest that the market portfolio should represent the ultimate index fund.

We now realize, of course, that no one investor—institutional or individual—would want to hold the market portfolio. Each investor will have his or her own risk preferences, tax considerations, time horizons, and transactions costs. A blatant illustration is that only high tax bracket investors would ever invest in municipal bonds. Other clientele will cluster in other ways, some of them far too subtle to discuss here. Suffice it to say that we wish to construct the market wealth portfolio, not for its eventual purchase, but for the insights it might reveal about the behavior of our capital markets.

Given that we want to construct the market portfolio, what should be included in it? As stated earlier, we have included common stocks, fixed-income corporate securities, real estate, U.S. Government bonds, and municipal bonds. The sharp reader will already have noted that the sum of these securities does not represent the "market." We have left huge categories out of the portfolio, while at the same time we have included categories that are not wealth at all.

Our most important omission is human capital. This is a category that is difficult to measure and even more difficult to buy or sell. Yet, most economists would agree (at least those that would regard humans as "capital") that this is the largest component of national wealth. It is not our only important omission, however. We have also excluded the value and returns from proprietorships, partnerships, and many small corporations. We have excluded personal holdings such as automobiles, cash balances, and numerous other consumer capital goods. We have not only omitted a "large" proportion of wealth, but we also have little idea as to how large the omitted proportion is.

Our inclusions may misrepresent the market even more than our omissions. We have included U.S. Government and municipal debt. But this debt is not backed dollar-for-dollar by assets like parks, buildings, etc. More likely it is backed by claims on a future tax base—in effect, making these future transfer payments, since the governments will be taxing the investors. Other inclusions in our aggregate market series also misrepresent wealth. For example, some corporations own other corporations or other forms of assets, causing double counting.

Admittedly, then, this study does not really measure wealth. But this drawback makes this study no less important. We do measure the aggregate value and returns of the capital market securities that are most marketable and most readily identifiable. These are the securities that make up the opportunity set faced by most investors.

▲ Market Values and Returns

Later in the paper we discuss the sources of the data. For now let us discuss the results.

Table 4.1 presents the aggregate market values of the various series and the total market. As one might have guessed, most of the common stocks in terms of value are listed on the NYSE. Most of the fixed-income securities are classified as long-term corporate bonds. Both farms and residential housing represent huge proportions of the market. U.S. Treasury bonds are declining in importance while Treasury bills and notes as well as agencies are increasing in importance. Almost all municipal debt is longer than one year to maturity. By our measure, the U.S. market portfolio at the beginning of 1978 was $4,184.2 billion.

Table 4.1

Aggregate Value of Capital Market Securities (Billions of Dollars)

Beginning of Year	Common Stocks				Corporate Securities					Corporate Securities Total	Real Estate		
					Fixed Income Corporate Securities								Real Estate Total
					Preferred Stock	Corporate Bonds		Commercial Paper	Total		Farms	Residential Housing	
	NYSE	AMEX	OTC	Total		Long-Term	Intermediate						
1947	60.2	N/A	5.1	65.3	8.3	36.1	15.4	0.3	60.1	125.4	68.5	147.7	216.2
1948	60.7	N/A	5.2	65.9	7.8	36.3	14.6	0.5	59.2	125.1	73.7	174.7	248.4
1949	59.2	N/A	5.0	64.2	7.7	39.8	13.0	0.7	61.2	125.4	76.6	192.3	268.9
1950	68.3	N/A	5.4	73.7	8.0	43.8	11.7	0.8	64.3	138.0	77.6	204.4	282.0
1951	85.7	N/A	6.7	92.4	8.1	44.4	11.5	0.9	64.9	157.3	89.5	228.4	317.9
1952	101.7	N/A	7.4	109.1	7.9	45.5	9.1	1.3	63.8	172.9	98.5	251.0	349.5
1953	112.2	N/A	7.5	119.7	8.2	47.1	8.9	1.7	65.9	185.6	100.1	266.1	366.2
1954	109.3	N/A	7.3	116.6	7.8	46.8	9.2	2.0	65.8	182.4	98.7	278.8	377.5
1955	162.5	N/A	10.7	173.2	8.4	49.1	12.6	2.0	72.1	245.3	102.2	295.1	397.3
1956	200.8	N/A	12.2	213.0	8.0	47.4	14.2	2.1	71.7	284.7	107.5	318.1	425.6
1957	217.3	N/A	13.6	230.9	6.9	43.3	16.7	2.2	69.1	300.0	115.7	336.7	452.4
1958	194.3	N/A	11.2	205.5	6.7	44.0	17.0	2.7	70.4	275.9	121.8	355.4	477.2
1959	276.5	N/A	15.9	292.4	6.9	48.8	15.9	2.8	74.4	366.8	131.1	380.1	511.2
1960	309.3	N/A	16.8	326.1	6.7	47.5	16.0	3.2	73.4	399.5	137.2	406.1	543.3
1961	307.7	N/A	16.4	324.1	6.7	52.3	16.2	4.5	79.7	403.9	138.5	423.3	561.3
1962	388.0	N/A	21.8	409.8	7.3	53.9	17.3	4.7	83.2	493.1	144.5	438.0	582.5
1963	340.0	25.0	18.5	383.5	7.7	55.0	20.8	6.0	89.5	473.0	150.2	454.6	604.8
1964	403.0	27.1	22.4	452.5	7.9	53.8	25.7	6.8	94.2	546.7	158.6	475.4	634.0

Year													
1965	466.1	29.9	27.6	523.6	8.3	52.9	28.5	6.4	96.1	619.7	167.5	496.3	663.8
1966	526.5	32.0	35.9	594.4	9.3	53.4	28.0	9.3	100.0	694.4	179.2	514.3	693.5
1967	470.9	28.5	35.3	534.7	9.7	50.8	28.3	13.6	102.4	637.1	189.1	531.3	720.4
1968	587.5	45.6	54.0	687.1	14.9	49.0	31.8	17.1	112.8	799.9	199.7	574.5	774.2
1969	664.3	59.8	65.3	789.4	24.5	55.3	31.3	21.2	132.1	921.5	209.2	654.3	863.5
1970	600.3	45.3	65.2	710.8	22.6	53.9	30.0	32.6	139.1	849.9	215.8	717.9	933.7
1971	607.8	37.7	56.0	701.5	23.9	64.6	38.7	33.1	160.3	861.8	223.2	754.2	977.4
1972	705.7	45.9	76.6	828.2	27.5	86.5	41.5	32.1	187.6	1015.8	239.6	802.0	1041.6
1973	838.7	55.7	99.6	994.0	27.2	98.3	45.8	34.7	206.5	1200.6	267.3	893.0	1160.3
1974	682.1	37.0	73.7	792.8	23.0	95.1	51.3	41.1	210.5	1003.3	327.8	1023.8	1351.6
1975	481.1	22.2	43.6	546.9	17.8	91.6	54.1	49.0	212.5	759.3	368.5	1140.6	1509.1
1976	652.1	28.9	58.2	739.2	22.0	102.5	67.0	47.1	238.6	977.8	416.9	1262.7	1679.6
1977	915.9	33.9	65.2	915.0	27.8	112.6	73.6	50.8	264.8	1179.8	483.8	1415.8	1899.6
1978	760.8	15.6	72.7	869.1	25.5	123.5	80.7	62.0	291.7	1160.8	525.8	1635.5	2161.8

(continued)

Table 4.1 (continued)
Aggregate Value of Capital Market Securities (Billions of Dollars)

	U.S. Government Securities					Municipal (State & Local) Bonds			Beginning of Year	Market Total Corporate Securities Real Estate U.S. Government Securities Municipal Bonds
	Treasury Issues									
	Bills	Notes	Bonds	Agencies	Total	Short-Term	Long-Term	Total		
1947	17.0	40.9	121.8	1.2	180.9	0.3	14.6	14.9	1947	537.4
1948	15.1	32.8	118.8	1.3	168.0	0.5	15.8	16.3	1948	557.7
1949	12.2	33.0	109.8	1.6	156.6	0.7	17.7	18.4	1949	569.3
1950	12.3	39.3	108.9	1.5	162.0	0.9	20.1	21.0	1950	603.0
1951	13.6	44.8	94.5	1.9	154.8	1.3	23.1	24.4	1951	654.5
1952	18.1	47.0	76.3	2.1	143.5	1.6	25.0	26.6	1952	692.5
1953	21.7	46.4	79.0	2.2	149.3	1.8	28.4	30.2	1953	731.3
1954	19.5	57.8	77.2	2.2	156.7	1.9	32.6	34.5	1954	751.0
1955	19.5	56.6	82.1	2.1	160.3	2.1	38.5	40.6	1955	843.5
1956	22.3	58.0	80.3	3.1	163.7	2.1	43.8	45.9	1956	919.9
1957	25.2	51.8	77.1	3.6	157.7	2.2	47.3	49.5	1957	959.6
1958	25.2	55.5	80.0	5.0	165.7	2.4	51.3	53.7	1958	972.4
1959	29.9	59.4	79.5	5.1	173.9	2.8	56.4	59.2	1959	1111.1
1960	39.6	59.3	78.8	7.3	185.0	3.2	62.3	65.5	1960	1193.3
1961	39.4	68.5	78.5	8.1	194.5	3.5	67.3	70.8	1961	1230.9
1962	43.4	74.8	73.4	8.8	200.4	3.7	72.2	75.9	1962	1351.9
1963	48.3	75.4	77.4	10.4	211.5	3.7	77.5	81.2	1963	1370.5
1964	52.4	67.2	84.6	12.0	216.2	4.1	82.8	86.9	1964	1483.7

1965	56.5	55.2	90.7	12.6	215.0	4.9	88.0	92.9	1965	1591.4
1966	57.7	49.6	98.0	14.7	220.0	5.5	94.8	100.3	1966	1708.2
1967	65.0	52.1	95.8	20.2	233.1	6.2	99.7	105.9	1967	1696.5
1968	68.4	57.4	87.0	20.3	233.1	8.0	105.7	113.7	1968	1920.9
1969	74.8	71.5	79.5	24.1	249.9	8.1	115.1	123.2	1969	2158.1
1970	73.8	77.0	58.3	33.8	242.9	10.9	122.2	133.1	1970	2159.6
1971	87.8	96.3	35.7	43.6	283.4	13.3	131.1	144.4	1971	2267.0
1972	96.9	109.7	48.2	49.5	304.3	15.7	146.1	161.8	1972	2523.5
1973	103.9	120.0	43.5	57.9	325.3	15.8	160.7	176.5	1973	2862.7
1974	107.7	119.7	36.3	77.9	341.6	16.1	175.1	191.2	1974	2887.6
1975	118.3	119.0	30.3	100.2	367.8	18.8	189.6	208.4	1975	2844.6
1976	152.8	159.2	35.8	112.9	460.7	17.1	204.8	221.9	1976	3340.0
1977	161.0	211.2	39.0	131.9	543.1	13.5	223.5	237.0	1977	3859.5
1978	161.1	239.2	44.7	158.5	603.5	18.5	240.1	258.6	1978	4184.2

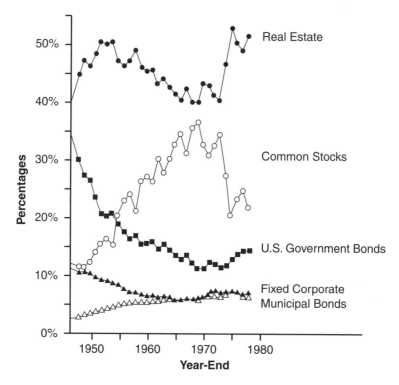

Figure 4.1. Value of Capital Market Security Groups As a Percentage of the Total

Table 4.2 gives us a direct measure of the proportions. Each category is listed each year as a percentage of the overall market. Figure 4.1 is a graph of the major categories of percentages listed in this table. From the figure, we can see immediately that real estate is the largest component of the market. Common stock increased its proportion of the market over most of the period while the fixed corporate security component was reduced. This resulted in a substantial reduction of corporate leverage. The municipal bond component rose during the early part of the period, before leveling off in more recent times. Surprisingly, the U.S. Government debt has dropped in relative wealth terms, almost throughout the period.

Table 4.3 presents the year-by-year total returns for the various components of the market portfolio. Each component is grouped into one of the five major categories. The return of each major category is the market value weighted sum of the returns of its components. The market is the market value weighted sum of all the component returns. The returns themselves are linked (compounded) into cumulative wealth indices. These indices are presented in Table 4.4. Each wealth index is initiated at 1.000 at year-end 1946 and includes reinvestment of all income as well as retention of all capital gains.

Table 4.2
Value of Capital Market Securities As a Percentage of the Totals

	Corporate Securities										Real Estate		
	Common Stocks				Preferred Stock	Fixed Income Corporate Securities				Corporate Securities Total	Farms	Residential Housing	Real Estate Total
						Corporate Bonds		Commercial Paper	Total				
Beginning of Year	NYSE	AMEX	OTC	Total		Long-Term	Intermediate						
1947	11.20%	N/A	0.95%	12.15%	1.55%	6.72%	2.86%	0.06%	11.19%	23.34%	12.74%	27.49%	40.23%
1948	10.88	N/A	0.93	11.81	1.40	6.51	2.62	0.09	10.62	22.43	13.21	31.32	44.53
1949	10.39	N/A	0.88	11.27	1.36	7.00	2.28	0.12	10.76	22.02	13.46	33.78	47.24
1950	11.33	N/A	0.90	12.23	1.32	7.26	1.94	0.13	10.66	22.88	12.87	33.90	46.77
1951	13.09	N/A	1.02	14.12	1.25	6.79	1.76	0.14	9.92	24.04	13.68	34.90	48.58
1952	14.69	N/A	1.07	15.76	1.14	6.57	1.31	0.19	9.21	24.97	14.22	36.25	50.46
1953	15.35	N/A	1.03	16.37	1.12	6.44	1.22	0.23	9.01	25.38	13.68	36.39	50.07
1954	14.55	N/A	0.97	15.52	1.04	6.23	1.23	0.27	8.76	24.28	13.14	37.12	50.26
1955	19.27	N/A	1.27	20.54	0.99	5.82	1.50	0.24	8.54	29.08	12.12	34.98	47.10
1956	21.83	N/A	1.33	23.15	0.87	5.15	1.55	0.23	7.79	30.95	11.69	34.58	46.27
1957	22.65	N/A	1.42	24.06	0.72	4.51	1.74	0.23	7.20	31.27	12.05	35.09	47.14
1958	19.98	N/A	1.15	21.13	0.69	4.52	1.75	0.28	7.24	28.37	12.52	36.55	49.07
1959	24.88	N/A	1.43	26.31	0.62	4.39	1.43	0.25	6.70	33.01	11.80	34.21	46.01
1960	25.92	N/A	1.41	27.32	0.57	3.98	1.34	0.27	6.16	33.48	11.49	34.03	45.53
1961	25.00	N/A	1.33	26.33	0.55	4.25	1.31	0.37	6.48	32.81	11.25	34.39	45.64
1962	28.70	N/A	1.61	30.32	0.54	3.98	1.28	0.35	6.16	36.47	10.69	32.40	43.09
1963	24.81	1.82%	1.35	27.98	0.56	4.01	1.52	0.44	6.53	34.51	10.96	33.17	44.13
1964	27.16	1.83	1.51	30.50	0.53	3.63	1.73	0.46	6.35	36.84	10.69	32.04	42.73
1965	29.29	1.88	1.73	32.90	0.52	3.33	1.79	0.40	6.04	38.94	10.53	31.19	41.71
1966	30.82	1.87	2.10	34.80	0.54	3.13	1.64	0.54	5.85	40.65	10.49	30.11	40.60

(continued)

Table 4.2 (continued)
Value of Capital Market Securities As a Percentage of the Totals

Beginning of Year	Corporate Securities										Real Estate		
	Common Stocks				Preferred Stock	Fixed Income Corporate Securities				Corporate Securities Total	Farms	Residential Housing	Real Estate Total
						Corporate Bonds		Commercial Paper					
	NYSE	AMEX	OTC	Total		Long-Term	Intermediate	Paper	Total				
1967	27.76	1.68	2.08	31.51	0.57	2.99	1.67	0.30	6.03	37.55	11.15	31.32	42.46
1968	30.59	2.37	2.81	35.77	0.77	2.55	1.65	0.89	5.87	41.64	10.40	29.91	40.30
1969	30.78	2.77	3.03	36.58	1.14	2.56	1.44	0.98	6.12	42.70	9.69	30.32	40.01
1970	27.80	2.10	3.02	32.91	1.05	2.50	1.39	1.51	6.44	39.36	9.99	33.24	43.23
1971	26.81	1.66	2.47	30.94	1.05	2.85	1.71	1.46	7.07	38.02	9.84	33.27	43.11
1972	27.97	1.82	3.04	32.82	1.09	3.43	1.64	1.27	7.43	40.25	9.50	31.78	41.28
1973	29.30	1.95	3.48	34.72	0.95	3.45	1.60	1.21	7.22	41.94	9.34	31.19	40.53
1974	23.62	1.28	2.55	27.45	0.80	3.29	1.78	1.42	7.29	34.74	11.35	35.45	46.80
1975	16.91	0.78	1.53	19.22	0.62	3.22	1.90	1.72	7.47	26.69	12.95	40.10	53.05
1976	19.52	0.87	1.74	22.13	0.66	3.07	2.01	1.41	7.14	29.27	12.48	37.81	50.29
1977	21.14	0.88	1.69	23.71	0.72	2.92	1.91	1.32	6.86	30.57	12.54	36.68	49.22
1978	18.18	0.85	1.74	20.77	0.61	2.95	1.93	1.48	6.97	27.74	12.57	39.09	51.65

| | U.S. Government Securities | | | | | Municipal (State & Local) Bonds | | | Beginning of Year | Market Total — Corporate Securities / Real Estate / U.S. Government Securities / Municipal Bonds |
| | Treasury Issues | | | Agencies | Total | Short-Term | Long-Term | Total | | |
	Bills	Notes	Bonds							
1947	3.16%	7.61%	22.67%	0.22%	33.66%	0.06%	2.72%	2.77%	1947	100.00%
1948	2.71	5.88	21.30	0.23	30.12	0.09	2.83	2.92	1948	100.00
1949	2.14	5.80	19.28	0.28	27.51	0.12	3.11	3.23	1949	100.00
1950	2.04	6.51	18.07	0.25	26.87	0.15	3.33	3.48	1950	100.00
1951	2.08	6.85	14.43	0.29	23.65	0.20	3.53	3.73	1951	100.00
1952	2.61	6.79	11.02	0.30	20.72	0.23	3.61	3.84	1952	100.00
1953	2.97	6.35	10.80	0.30	20.42	0.25	3.88	4.13	1953	100.00
1954	2.60	7.69	10.28	0.29	20.86	0.25	4.34	4.59	1954	100.00
1955	2.31	6.71	9.73	0.25	19.00	0.25	4.56	4.81	1955	100.00
1956	2.42	6.30	8.73	0.34	17.80	0.23	4.76	4.99	1956	100.00
1957	2.63	5.39	8.04	0.38	16.43	0.23	4.93	5.16	1957	100.00
1958	2.59	5.71	8.22	0.51	17.07	0.25	5.28	5.52	1958	100.00
1959	2.69	5.35	7.15	0.46	15.65	0.25	5.08	5.33	1959	100.00
1960	3.32	4.97	6.60	0.61	15.50	0.27	5.22	5.49	1960	100.00
1961	3.20	5.57	6.37	0.66	15.80	0.28	5.47	5.75	1961	100.00
1962	3.21	5.53	5.43	0.65	14.82	0.27	5.34	5.61	1962	100.00
1963	3.52	5.50	5.65	0.76	15.43	0.27	5.66	5.93	1963	100.00
1964	3.53	4.53	5.70	0.81	14.57	0.28	5.58	5.86	1964	100.00
1965	3.55	3.47	5.70	0.79	13.51	0.31	5.53	5.84	1965	100.00
1966	3.38	2.90	5.74	0.86	12.88	0.32	5.35	5.87	1966	100.00

(continued)

Table 4.2 (continued)
Value of Capital Market Securities As a Percentage of the Totals

| Beginning of Year | U.S. Government Securities | | | | | Municipal (State & Local) Bonds | | | Market Total — Corporate Securities, Real Estate, U.S. Government Securities, Municipal Bonds |
| | Treasury Issues | | | Agencies | Total | Short-Term | Long-Term | Total | |
	Bills	Notes	Bonds						
1967	3.83	3.07	5.65	1.19	13.74	0.37	5.88	6.24	100.00
1968	3.56	2.99	4.53	1.06	12.13	0.42	5.50	5.92	100.00
1969	3.47	3.31	3.68	1.12	11.58	0.38	5.33	5.71	100.00
1970	3.42	3.56	2.70	1.57	11.25	0.50	5.66	6.16	100.00
1971	3.87	4.25	2.46	1.92	12.50	0.59	5.78	6.37	100.00
1972	3.84	4.35	1.91	1.96	12.06	0.62	5.79	6.41	100.00
1973	3.63	4.19	1.52	2.02	11.36	0.55	5.61	6.17	100.00
1974	3.73	4.15	1.26	2.70	11.83	0.56	6.06	6.62	100.00
1975	4.16	4.18	1.06	3.52	12.93	0.66	6.67	7.33	100.00
1976	4.57	4.77	1.07	3.38	13.79	0.51	6.13	6.64	100.00
1977	4.17	5.47	1.01	3.42	14.07	0.35	5.79	6.14	100.00
1978	3.85	5.72	1.07	3.79	14.42	0.44	5.74	6.18	100.00

Table 4.3
Year-by-Year Total Returns on Capital Market Securities (Percent)

	Corporate Securities										Real Estate		
	Common Stocks				Fixed Income Corporate Securities								
					Preferred Stock	Corporate Bonds		Commercial Paper	Total	Corporate Securities Total			Real Estate Total
Year	NYSE	AMEX	OTC	Total		Long-Term	Intermediate				Farms	Residential Housing	
1947	3.30%	N/A	2.07%	3.20%	−8.33%	−4.64%	−0.01%	1.00%	−3.94%	−0.22%	16.33%	8.22%	10.79%
1948	2.32	N/A	−3.04	1.90	4.56	4.10	8.88	1.34	5.32	3.52	13.13	9.28	10.42
1949	20.21	N/A	16.26	19.90	10.85	8.02	3.79	1.57	7.41	13.80	5.56	1.49	2.65
1950	29.95	N/A	29.22	29.90	0.82	6.90	10.15	1.31	6.67	19.08	21.90	5.75	10.19
1951	20.95	N/A	15.72	20.57	−4.72	−4.00	−1.21	2.10	−3.51	10.63	17.97	11.32	13.19
1952	13.32	N/A	6.52	12.86	11.81	1.37	6.29	2.36	3.39	9.36	7.06	5.30	5.80
1953	0.37	N/A	3.29	0.55	1.96	2.83	2.90	2.54	2.72	1.12	0.98	1.76	3.00
1954	50.53	N/A	50.40	50.52	11.80	−1.20	6.78	1.79	1.55	32.85	7.12	4.30	5.04
1955	25.26	N/A	18.88	24.87	3.97	1.92	1.84	1.80	2.14	18.19	5.97	3.29	3.98
1956	8.62	N/A	15.33	9.00	−13.30	−7.25	−4.69	3.16	−7.11	4.95	7.75	4.13	5.04
1957	−10.70	N/A	−12.16	−10.79	8.87	2.04	2.70	3.79	2.94	−7.62	7.77	6.03	6.47
1958	44.27	N/A	48.34	44.49	1.04	1.31	5.40	2.51	2.32	33.73	12.80	4.05	6.28
1959	12.87	N/A	9.53	12.69	−1.72	−2.44	−1.20	3.67	−1.88	9.73	4.83	3.30	3.84
1960	0.60	N/A	0.99	0.62	11.81	8.01	6.83	4.19	7.94	1.97	4.07	4.33	4.26
1961	27.17	N/A	36.28	27.63	7.12	4.54	4.69	2.87	4.69	23.10	9.10	4.69	5.78
1962	−9.38	N/A	−12.36	−9.54	11.50	6.73	1.59	3.34	5.89	−6.93	8.98	4.20	5.39
1963	21.33	N/A	24.44	21.05	0.32	3.79	2.99	3.34	3.28	17.69	9.79	6.03	6.96
1964	16.29	14.75%	25.87	16.69	6.18	5.19	3.72	4.00	4.79	14.64	7.58	5.13	5.74

(continued)

Table 4.3 (continued)
Year-by-Year Total Returns on Capital Market Securities (Percent)

	Corporate Securities										Real Estate		
	Common Stocks				Fixed Income Corporate Securities									
					Preferred	Corporate Bonds		Commercial		Corporate Securities				Real Estate
Year	NYSE	AMEX	OTC	Total	Stock	Long-Term	Intermediate	Paper	Total	Total	Farms	Residential Housing	Total
1965	13.92	19.47	33.15	15.25	-1.69	-5.19	1.21	4.36	-2.36	12.52	12.64	5.61	7.38
1966	-8.96	-5.86	0.90	-8.20	-7.10	-4.25	-2.75	5.29	-3.21	-7.48	12.23	5.25	7.05
1967	26.96	56.27	56.38	30.46	-7.17	-4.79	-1.21	5.40	-2.67	25.14	10.30	6.29	7.34
1968	12.78	33.18	23.02	14.94	5.44	1.41	3.50	5.98	3.22	13.29	8.71	7.83	8.06
1969	-9.85	-22.51	1.67	-9.86	-8.52	-8.78	-3.36	7.73	-4.81	-9.13	7.24	10.53	9.73
1970	1.40	-16.00	-12.54	-0.99	14.36	15.25	14.15	8.72	13.34	1.36	7.77	11.69	10.78
1971	15.89	21.60	40.65	18.17	6.79	11.83	12.93	5.52	10.04	16.66	11.70	7.69	8.61
1972	17.92	10.08	34.07	18.98	5.67	7.35	8.15	4.47	6.79	16.73	18.34	6.34	9.24
1973	-16.97	-28.25	-22.88	-18.19	-3.69	1.75	2.55	7.64	2.20	-14.69	35.27	6.56	13.17
1974	-26.85	-35.43	-38.50	-28.33	-12.76	-8.48	-2.83	10.34	-3.90	-23.21	19.80	13.21	14.81
1975	37.73	39.56	37.48	37.78	24.24	14.92	17.26	6.97	14.46	31.26	18.52	13.02	14.36
1976	26.27	31.30	15.17	25.59	23.06	17.09	14.41	5.75	14.65	22.92	19.54	7.31	10.35
1977	-4.89	13.16	14.74	-2.82	5.61	2.37	2.65	5.10	3.31	-1.45	11.33	11.38	11.37
1978	7.40	19.35	14.31	8.47	-2.83	-0.14	0.05	7.37	1.27	6.66	17.60	14.22	15.04

| | U.S. Government Securities | | | | | Municipal (State & Local) Bonds | | | | Market Total |
| | Treasury Issues | | | | | | | | | |
Year	Bills	Notes	Bonds	Agencies	Total	Short-Term	Long-Term	Total	Year	Municipal Bonds
1947	0.50%	0.75%	−2.63%	−0.26%	−1.56%	0.75%	−4.48%	−4.37%	1947	3.64%
1948	0.81	1.37	3.40	2.46	2.76	0.80	4.67	4.55	1948	6.39
1949	1.10	1.55	6.45	3.25	4.97	0.80	4.09	3.96	1949	5.79
1950	1.20	0.64	0.06	2.55	0.31	0.60	8.23	7.90	1950	9.49
1951	1.49	0.88	−3.94	0.40	−2.01	0.85	−4.69	−4.39	1951	8.32
1952	1.66	1.74	1.16	2.73	1.44	1.00	−2.00	−1.82	1952	5.49
1953	1.82	3.59	3.63	3.73	3.36	1.70	−0.61	−0.47	1953	2.50
1954	0.86	2.53	7.19	4.22	4.64	0.91	5.93	5.65	1954	11.74
1955	1.57	−0.19	−1.30	−1.18	−0.56	1.00	−0.93	−0.83	1955	7.02
1956	2.46	0.71	−5.59	0.39	−2.15	1.85	−6.60	−6.21	1956	3.17
1957	3.14	6.73	7.45	6.01	6.49	2.27	6.99	6.78	1957	2.09
1958	1.54	0.37	−6.10	2.25	−2.52	2.05	−3.01	−2.78	1958	12.07
1959	2.95	0.65	−2.26	−1.11	−0.34	1.95	−1.59	−1.42	1959	4.85
1960	2.66	10.14	13.78	12.33	10.17	2.91	9.21	8.90	1960	4.67
1961	2.13	2.07	0.97	4.74	1.75	1.57	3.52	3.42	1961	10.69
1962	2.73	5.07	6.89	6.16	5.28	1.71	7.96	7.66	1962	1.00
1963	3.12	2.14	1.21	2.48	2.04	1.78	−3.06	−2.34	1963	9.32

(continued)

Table 4.3 (continued)
Year-by-Year Total Returns on Capital Market Securities (Percent)

| | U.S. Government Securities | | | | | Municipal (State & Local) Bonds | | | Year | Market Total Corporate Securities Real Estate U.S. Government Securities Municipal Bonds |
| | Treasury Issues | | | Agencies | Total | Short-Term | Long-Term | Total | | |
	Bills	Notes	Bonds							
1964	3.54	4.00	3.51	4.59	3.73	2.06	5.98	5.80	1964	8.73
1965	3.93	1.43	0.71	1.03	1.76	2.31	-3.26	-2.97	1965	8.02
1966	4.76	5.02	3.65	4.64	4.32	3.43	0.41	0.58	1966	0.41
1967	4.21	1.79	-9.19	1.74	-2.05	3.12	-4.18	-3.75	1967	12.04
1968	5.21	4.51	-0.26	4.65	2.95	3.19	-1.41	-1.09	1968	9.07
1969	6.58	-0.97	-5.08	0.11	0.09	4.85	-15.69	-14.34	1969	-0.81
1970	6.53	15.13	12.10	15.53	11.84	5.11	18.84	17.72	1970	7.62
1971	4.39	8.20	13.23	8.42	8.04	3.07	14.36	13.32	1971	11.90
1972	3.84	4.23	5.68	4.99	4.46	2.70	4.43	4.26	1972	11.36
1973	6.93	3.85	-1.11	3.76	4.15	4.45	3.88	3.93	1973	-0.10
1974	8.00	6.50	4.35	5.42	6.50	5.28	-14.50	-12.83	1974	-1.21
1975	5.80	8.38	9.19	7.94	7.50	4.34	6.56	6.36	1975	17.40
1976	5.08	11.92	16.75	12.85	10.25	3.09	22.57	21.07	1976	14.73
1977	5.12	2.11	-0.67	2.66	2.94	2.87	7.40	7.14	1977	6.00
1978	7.18	1.90	-1.16	1.22	2.90	4.07	-4.36	-4.22	1978	9.78

Table 4.4

Cumulative Wealth Indices of Capital Market Securities (Year-End 1946 = 1.000)

	Corporate Securities										Real Estate		
	Common Stocks				Preferred Stock	Fixed Income Corporate Securities				Corporate Securities Total	Farms	Residential Housing	Real Estate Total
						Corporate Bonds		Commercial Paper	Total				
Year-End	NYSE	AMEX*	OTC	Total		Long-Term	Intermediate						
1947	1.033	N/A	1.021	1.032	0.917	0.954	1.000	1.010	0.961	0.998	1.163	1.082	1.108
1948	1.057	N/A	0.990	1.052	0.959	0.993	1.089	1.024	1.012	1.033	1.316	1.183	1.223
1949	1.271	N/A	1.151	1.261	1.062	1.072	1.130	1.040	1.087	1.175	1.389	1.200	1.256
1950	1.651	N/A	1.487	1.638	1.071	1.146	1.245	1.053	1.159	1.400	1.693	1.269	1.384
1951	1.997	N/A	1.721	1.975	1.021	1.100	1.230	1.075	1.118	1.548	1.998	1.413	1.566
1952	2.263	N/A	1.833	2.229	1.141	1.116	1.307	1.101	1.156	1.693	2.139	1.488	1.657
1953	2.271	N/A	1.893	2.241	1.164	1.147	1.345	1.129	1.188	1.716	2.160	1.544	1.707
1954	3.419	N/A	2.847	3.373	1.301	1.133	1.436	1.149	1.206	2.280	2.314	1.610	1.793
1955	4.283	N/A	3.385	4.212	1.353	1.155	1.462	1.170	1.232	2.694	2.452	1.663	1.864
1956	4.652	N/A	3.903	4.591	1.173	1.071	1.394	1.207	1.144	2.827	2.642	1.732	1.958
1957	4.154	N/A	3.429	4.096	1.277	1.093	1.431	1.252	1.178	2.612	2.847	1.836	2.085
1958	5.993	N/A	5.086	5.919	1.290	1.108	1.509	1.284	1.205	3.493	3.211	1.911	2.216
1959	6.765	N/A	5.571	6.670	1.268	1.080	1.491	1.331	1.183	3.833	3.366	1.977	2.301
1960	6.806	N/A	5.626	6.711	1.417	1.167	1.592	1.387	1.277	3.908	3.503	2.063	2.399
1961	8.655	N/A	7.667	8.565	1.518	1.220	1.667	1.426	1.337	4.811	3.822	2.160	2.538
1962	7.843	1.000	6.720	7.748	1.693	1.302	1.694	1.474	1.415	4.477	4.166	2.251	2.675
1963	9.517	1.148	8.362	9.379	1.698	1.351	1.744	1.523	1.462	5.269	4.573	2.386	2.861
1964	11.066	1.320	10.525	10.945	1.803	1.422	1.809	1.584	1.532	6.041	4.920	2.509	3.025

(*continued*)

Table 4.4 (continued)
Cumulative Wealth Indices of Capital Market Securities (Year-End 1946 = 1.000)

	Corporate Securities										Real Estate		
	Common Stocks				Preferred Stock	Fixed Income Corporate Securities				Corporate Securities Total			Real Estate Total
						Corporate Bonds		Commercial Paper	Total		Farms	Residential Housing	
Year-End	NYSE	AMEX*	OTC	Total		Long-Term	Intermediate						
1965	12.607	1.578	14.014	12.614	1.773	1.348	1.831	1.653	1.496	6.797	5.542	2.649	3.248
1966	11.477	1.485	14.140	11.580	1.647	1.291	1.781	1.741	1.448	6.289	6.220	2.789	3.478
1967	14.572	2.321	22.113	15.108	1.529	1.229	1.759	1.835	1.409	7.870	6.860	2.964	3.733
1968	16.434	3.091	27.203	17.365	1.612	1.246	1.821	1.944	1.454	8.915	7.458	3.196	4.034
1969	14.815	2.395	27.657	15.653	1.475	1.137	1.760	2.095	1.384	8.101	7.998	3.533	4.426
1970	15.023	2.012	24.189	15.498	1.687	1.310	2.009	2.277	1.569	8.211	8.619	3.946	4.904
1971	17.410	2.446	34.002	28.315	1.801	1.465	2.268	2.403	1.727	9.579	9.628	4.249	5.36
1972	20.530	2.693	45.613	21.791	1.903	1.573	2.453	2.510	1.844	11.182	11.451	4.518	5.818
1973	17.047	1.932	35.177	17.826	1.833	1.600	2.516	2.702	1.884	9.540	15.490	4.815	6.584
1974	12.470	1.248	21.634	12.776	1.599	1.464	2.445	2.982	1.811	7.326	18.557	5.451	7.559
1975	17.175	1.741	29.742	17.603	1.987	1.683	2.866	3.189	2.073	9.616	21.993	6.160	9.645
1976	21.668	2.286	34.254	22.108	2.445	1.971	3.279	3.373	2.377	11.820	26.291	6.611	9.539
1977	20.628	2.587	39.303	21.484	2.582	2.017	3.366	3.545	2.455	11.649	29.270	7.363	10.623
1978	22.155	3.088	44.927	23.303	2.509	2.014	3.368	3.806	2.486	12.425	34.421	8.410	12.221

| | U.S. Government Securities | | | | | Municipal (State & Local) Bonds | | | | Market Total Corporate Securities / Real Estate / U.S. Government Securities / Municipal Bonds |
| | Treasury Issues | | | | | | | | | |
	Bills	Notes	Bonds	Agencies	Total	Short-Term	Long-Term	Total	Year-End	
1947	1.005	1.007	0.974	0.997	0.984	1.007	0.955	0.956	1947	1.036
1948	1.013	1.021	1.007	1.022	1.012	1.016	1.000	1.000	1948	1.103
1949	1.024	1.037	1.072	1.055	1.062	1.024	1.041	1.039	1949	1.167
1950	1.036	1.044	1.072	1.082	1.065	1.030	1.126	1.122	1950	1.277
1951	1.052	1.053	1.030	1.086	1.044	1.039	1.074	1.072	1951	1.384
1952	1.069	1.071	1.042	1.116	1.059	1.049	1.052	1.053	1952	1.460
1953	1.089	1.110	1.080	1.158	1.094	1.067	1.046	1.048	1953	1.496
1954	1.099	1.138	1.157	1.207	1.145	1.077	1.108	1.107	1954	1.672
1955	1.116	1.136	1.142	1.192	1.139	1.087	1.097	1.098	1955	1.789
1956	1.143	1.144	1.078	1.197	1.114	1.107	1.025	1.030	1956	1.846
1957	1.179	1.221	1.159	1.269	1.187	1.133	1.097	1.099	1957	1.884
1958	1.197	1.225	1.088	1.297	1.157	1.156	1.064	1.069	1958	2.112
1959	1.233	1.233	1.064	1.283	1.153	1.178	1.047	1.054	1959	2.214
1960	1.265	1.358	1.210	1.441	1.270	1.213	1.143	1.147	1960	2.317
1961	1.292	1.386	1.222	1.510	1.292	1.232	1.183	1.187	1961	2.565
1962	1.327	1.457	1.306	1.603	1.360	1.253	1.277	1.278	1962	2.591
1963	1.369	1.488	1.322	1.642	1.388	1.275	1.238	1.241	1963	2.832
1964	1.417	1.547	1.368	1.718	1.440	1.301	1.312	1.313	1964	3.080

Table 4.4 (continued)
Cumulative Wealth Indices of Capital Market Securities (Year-End 1946 = 1.000)

| | U.S. Government Securities | | | | | Municipal (State & Local) Bonds | | | | Market Total |
| | Treasury Issues | | | | | | | | | Corporate Securities / Real Estate / U.S. Government Securities / Municipal Bonds |
	Bills	Notes	Bonds	Agencies	Total	Short-Term	Long-Term	Total	Year-End	
1965	1.473	1.569	1.378	1.735	1.465	1.331	1.270	1.274	1965	3.327
1966	1.543	1.648	1.428	1.816	1.529	1.377	1.275	1.282	1966	3.340
1967	1.608	1.678	1.297	1.847	1.497	1.420	1.222	1.233	1967	3.743
1968	1.691	1.753	1.294	1.933	1.541	1.465	1.204	1.220	1968	4.082
1969	1.803	1.736	1.228	1.935	1.543	1.536	1.015	1.045	1969	4.049
1970	1.921	1.999	1.378	2.236	1.725	1.615	1.207	1.230	1970	4.358
1971	2.005	2.163	1.559	2.424	1.864	1.664	1.380	1.394	1971	4.876
1972	2.082	2.254	1.647	2.545	1.947	1.709	1.441	1.454	1972	5.430
1973	2.226	2.341	1.629	2.641	2.028	1.785	1.497	1.511	1973	5.424
1974	2.404	2.493	1.700	2.784	2.160	1.880	1.280	1.317	1974	5.358
1975	2.544	2.702	1.856	3.005	2.322	1.961	1.364	1.401	1975	6.291
1976	2.673	3.025	2.167	3.391	2.560	2.022	1.672	1.696	1976	7.217
1977	2.810	3.088	2.153	3.482	2.635	2.080	1.795	1.817	1977	7.651
1978	3.011	3.147	2.127	3.524	2.712	2.164	1.708	1.740	1978	8.399

*Year-end 1962 = 1.00.

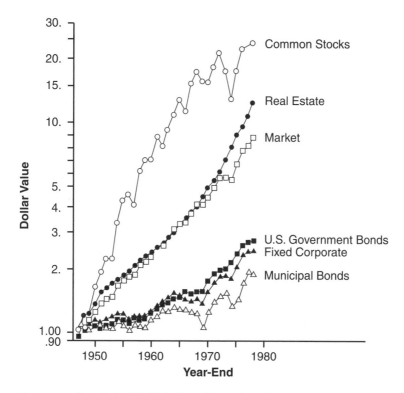

Figure 4.2. Cumulative Wealth Indices of Capital Market Security Groups (Year-End 1946 = $1.00)

Figure 4.2 presents a graphical summary of the results in Table 4.4. The most risky category, common stocks, has the highest return over the period. The real estate series does second best, apparently with little risk or variation. The three fixed-income series have the lowest returns. It is not surprising that municipal bonds do the worst, since they have low yields because of their tax advantages. The fact that governments out-returned corporates is apparently because interest rates rose substantially during the period, while corporates had longer maturities, on average, than governments.

The results presented in Tables 4.3 and 4.4 are summarized statistically in Table 4.5. Common stocks as a group had the highest annual compound (geometric mean) return of 10.34%. The overall winner, however, was the farm component of real estate, with an annual compound return of 11.69%. Farms were also a series that, at least as we measured it, had relatively little variation in returns. Housing also did well for its level of risk.

As for fixed-income securities, no matter what the category—corporate, U.S. Government, or municipal—the shorter term securities tended to out-

Table 4.5
United States Capital Market Total Annual Returns, 1947–1978

	Compound Return	Arithmetic Mean	Standard Deviation
Common stocks			
NYSE	10.16%	11.56%	17.73%
OTC	12.63	14.79	21.79
Total	10.34	11.79	18.02
Fixed-income corporate securities			
Preferred stocks	2.92	3.31	9.20
Long-term corporate bonds	2.21	2.42	6.72
Intermediate corporate bonds	3.87	4.00	5.48
Commercial paper	4.27	4.29	2.37
Total	2.89	3.03	5.53
Corporate securities total	8.19	9.07	13.84
Real estate			
Farms	11.69	11.88	6.79
Residential housing	6.88	6.93	3.28
Total	8.14	8.19	3.53
U.S. government securities			
U.S. Treasury bills	3.51	3.53	2.11
U.S. Treasury notes	3.65	3.73	3.71
U.S. Treasury bonds	2.39	2.56	6.17
Agencies	4.01	4.08	3.92
Total	3.17	3.23	3.78
Municipal (state & local) bonds			
Short-term	2.44	2.45	1.37
Long-term	1.69	2.01	8.20
Total	1.75	2.02	7.62
Market total	6.88	6.97	4.65

return the longer term securities during the rising interest rate postwar period. The Treasury bills and notes each returned (3.51% and 3.65%) an amount almost equal to the inflation rate over the period (3.65%). Generally, though, after extracting this maturity effect, lower quality issues tended to out-return higher quality issues. For example, preferreds had higher returns than long-term corporates, and agencies had higher returns than U.S. Treasury notes.

The market as a whole returned 6.88% compounded annually. There is some evidence to suggest that the five categories of securities provided diversification, since the market annual standard deviation was less than that of three of the five categories. Of course, the large weighting in the high return/low risk real estate investments had a substantial impact on the market portfolio. Table 4.6 partially updates Table 4.5 through 2001.

▰ *The Relationships Among the Series*

We can get a good idea about the interrelationships among the various security returns by looking at the cross-correlation matrix presented in Table 4.7. The various corporate stocks and bonds, real estate investments, and fixed-income securities seem to exhibit high correlation *within* each category. In addition, short-term securities relate positively to other short-term securities and real estate, but negatively to long-term securities and common stock. Both the common stock and the fixed-income components of corporate securities seem to be positively related to municipals.

These results collectively suggest that there may be two factors in the market determining security returns. One may be state-of-the-economy related, as demonstrated in common stocks and default-prone fixed-income securities. The other may be short-term interest rate (inflation) related. We proceed to investigate an overall market factor and an inflation factor.

Table 4.6
U.S. Capital Market Total Annual Returns 1976 to 2001

	Compound Return	Arithmetic Mean	Standard Deviation
Common Stocks			
NYSE	14.36	15.14	13.53
NYSE/AMEX/Nasdaq	14.12	15.10	14.99
Fixed-Income Corporate Securities			
Long-term	9.96	10.54	11.88
Intermediate-term	9.45	9.65	6.86
Commercial Paper	7.41	7.45	3.11
Corporate Total	9.59	9.99	9.72
Real Estate			
Real Estate	12.90	14.17	16.97
U.S. Government Securities			
U.S. Treasury Bills	6.73	6.77	2.79
U.S. Treasury Notes	8.92	9.15	7.23
U.S. Treasury Bonds	9.61	10.33	13.02
Agencies	9.12	9.31	6.54
Government Total	9.14	9.35	7.02
Municipal Bonds			
Long-term	7.07	7.89	13.75

Note: This table is a partial update of Table 4.5.

Source: Common Stocks—Center for Research in Security Prices, University of Chicago; Fixed-Income Corporate Securities—Lehman Brothers & FED Commercial Paper; Real Estate—NAREIT; U.S. Government Securities—Ibbotson Associates & Lehman Brothers; Municipal Bonds—Moodys.

Table 4.8 gives regression results for each of the excess return series regressed upon the excess returns of its own category grouping. Each category's excess returns are then regressed on the market portfolio excess return. The returns are all input as the excess over the riskless rate (Treasury bill) return. Thus, in a market model context, the alpha is a measure of risk-adjusted performance, the beta is a measure of the systematic or market risk, and the R-square is a measure of the percent of the variance that is explained by the market.

The results do not suggest anything particularly unusual about each of the stock exchanges, with the AMEX and the OTC being more risky than the NYSE. Common stocks as a group exhibit a 3.35 beta with a poor −3.29% performance. Meanwhile, corporate fixed maturities also tended to perform poorly, although this is mostly attributable to the long-term corporate bond series. The systematic risk of fixed corporate securities is also somewhat large (0.66), indicating that corporations, leveraged or unleveraged, seem to be related to economy or market risk. This observation is also true of municipals with a beta of 0.73. But it is not true of real estate of U.S. Government bonds whose betas are 0.10 and 0.13.

As we examine other fixed-income securities, it is once again apparent (except in the case of short-term municipals) that the short-term securities outperformed longer term securities. The results also suggest again that the lower quality issues outperformed the higher quality issues.

Finally, we look again at real estate. Both housing and farmland performed extremely well with almost a zero beta relative to the market. Farmland outperformed housing, but the two series were very closely related to one another.

Inflation appears to be the remaining factor that may describe the series. Table 4.9 presents the results of each of the return series regressed against inflation rates. Note that common stocks and longer term fixed-income securities generally have a negative relationship with inflation. Meanwhile, short-term securities and real estate have a positive relationship with inflation.

◤ Sources of Data

The following section is intended to describe the sources of both the market values and the yearly returns for each of the series. The publications cited are included in a reference listing following the text. Here we describe the manner in which we utilized the data from those sources or, in some circumstances, calculated our own estimates.

Common Stocks

NYSE and AMEX yearly market values and returns were obtained from the Center for Research in Security Prices (CRSP) at the University of Chicago.

Table 4.7
Capital Market Security Returns Correlation Matrix

	NYSE	AMEX	OTC	Total Common Stk.	Preferred Stk.	LT Corp. Bond	Int. Corp. Bond	Commercial Paper
NYSE	1.000							
AMEX	0.884	1.00						
OTC	0.876	0.897	1.000					
Total common stk.	0.998	0.911	0.902	1.000				
Preferred stk.	0.371	0.439	0.178	0.356	1.000			
LT corp. bond	0.282	0.313	0.124	0.266	0.863	1.000		
Int. corp. bond	0.422	0.322	0.254	0.405	0.827	0.897	1.000	
Commercial paper	−0.454	−0.576	−0.343	−0.450	−0.067	0.029	0.027	1.000
Total corp. fixed	0.279	0.309	0.120	0.263	0.894	0.986	0.925	0.089
Total corporations	0.982	0.906	0.910	0.987	0.424	0.354	0.473	−0.395
Farms	−0.101	−0.281	−0.144	−0.109	−0.144	0.055	0.146	0.327
Housing	−0.271	−0.206	−0.241	−0.270	−0.068	−0.004	0.121	0.635
Total real estate	−0.227	−0.312	−0.232	−0.231	−0.122	0.017	0.153	0.576
U.S. Treasury bills	−0.459	−0.574	−0.317	−0.450	−0.084	0.019	−0.010	0.980
U.S. Treasury notes	−0.174	−0.037	−0.264	−0.187	0.574	0.669	0.606	0.517
U.S. Treasury bonds	−0.041	−0.005	−0.176	−0.059	0.737	0.754	0.695	0.184
Agencies	−0.073	−0.025	−0.171	−0.088	0.657	0.739	0.682	0.412
Total gov't bonds	−0.229	−0.194	−0.314	−0.244	0.648	0.688	0.611	0.470
Short munic.	−0.439	−0.573	−0.314	−0.435	−0.057	0.048	0.049	0.981
LT munic.	0.201	0.268	0.089	0.191	0.782	0.877	0.789	−0.043
Total munic.	0.192	0.261	0.080	0.182	0.783	0.878	0.789	−0.031
Total market	0.849	0.854	0.803	0.857	0.526	0.530	0.661	−0.116

(continued)

Table 4.7 (continued)
Capital Market Security Returns Correlation Matrix

	Total Corp. Fixed	Total Corporations	Farms	Housing	Total Real Estate	U.S. Treasury Bills	U.S. Treasury Notes	U.S. Treasury Bonds
Total corp. fixed	1.000							
Total corporations	0.352	1.000						
Farms	0.063	-0.126	1.000					
Housing	0.056	-0.258	0.427	1.000				
Total real estate	0.062	-0.233	0.767	0.906	1.000			
U.S. Treasury bills	0.072	-0.393	0.380	0.641	0.604	1.000		
U.S. Treasury notes	0.678	-0.106	0.059	0.254	0.194	0.439	1.000	
U.S. Treasury bonds	0.770	0.004	-0.053	0.029	-0.013	0.131	0.832	1.000
Agencies	0.757	-0.009	0.018	0.157	0.108	0.328	0.962	0.855
Total gov't bonds	0.724	-0.170	0.032	0.203	0.141	0.417	0.911	0.934
Short munic.	0.104	-0.376	0.298	0.600	0.537	0.956	0.524	0.180
LT munic.	0.847	0.257	0.048	-0.107	-0.056	-0.048	0.688	0.762
Total munic.	0.850	0.248	0.053	-0.100	-0.049	-0.036	0.695	0.767
Total market	0.540	0.903	0.090	0.089	0.109	-0.105	0.164	0.192

	Agencies	Total Gov't Bonds	Short Munic.	LT Munic.	Total Munic.	Total Market
Agencies	1.000					
Total gov't bonds	0.910	1.000				
Short munic.	0.431	0.467	1.000			
LT munic.	0.748	0.688	-0.032	1.000		
Total munic.	0.755	0.698	-0.020	1.000	1.000	
Total market	0.221	0.080	-0.117	0.415	0.409	1.000

Table 4.8

Regression Results for Capital Market Returns in Excess of United States Treasury Bill Rates, 1947–1978

Dependent Variable	Independent Variable	Alpha (%)	Alpha T Statistic	Beta	Beta T Statistic	R^2	Std. Dev. of Residuals (%)	1st-Order Auto-Corr. of Residuals
NYSE	Total Com. Stock	-0.10	-0.46	0.98	92.79	0.997	1.13	0.256
AMEX*	Total Com. Stock	0.78	0.28	1.26	8.60	0.841	10.96	0.387
OTC	Total Com. Stock	2.38	1.28	1.07	11.89	0.825	9.59	0.200
Total com. stock	Market	-3.29	-2.23	3.35	14.23	0.871	6.96	0.180
Preferreds	Total Fixed Corp.	0.54	0.77	1.52	12.36	0.836	3.96	0.044
LT corp. bds.	Total Fixed Corp.	-0.51	-2.64	1.20	35.53	0.977	1.08	-0.177
Int. corp. bds.	Total Fixed Corp.	0.95	2.50	0.95	14.29	0.872	2.14	-0.102
Com'l paper	Total Fixed Corp.	0.76	8.17	-0.00	-0.23	0.002	0.53	0.324
Total fixed corp.	Market	-2.76	-2.79	0.66	4.16	0.365	4.67	-0.012
Farms	Total Real Est.	0.74	0.48	1.63	5.82	0.531	4.44	0.226
Housing	Total Real Est.	-0.15	-0.31	0.76	8.74	0.718	1.36	0.174
Total real estate	Market	4.33	7.28	0.10	1.04	0.035	2.81	0.420
T-notes	Total U.S. Gov't.	0.44	1.61	0.87	10.91	0.799	1.54	-0.007
T-bonds	Total U.S. Gov't.	-0.45	-1.81	1.75	24.34	0.952	1.39	-0.157
Agencies	Total U.S. Gov't.	0.84	2.87	0.98	11.45	0.814	1.66	-0.125
Total U.S. gov't	Market	-0.73	-0.99	0.13	1.08	0.037	3.47	-0.096
ST municipal	Total Municipal	-1.03	-6.58	0.03	1.64	0.083	0.87	0.580
LT municipal	Total Municipal	0.01	3.48	1.07	318.44	0.999	0.15	0.173
Total municipal	Market	-4.02	-2.68	0.73	3.04	0.235	7.09	-0.187

*AMEX results cover only the period 1963–1978.

Table 4.9
Capital Market Returns Regressed on Inflation, 1947–1978

Dependent Variable	Independent Variable	Alpha (%)	Alpha T Statistic	Beta	Beta T Statistic	R^2	Std. Dev. of Residuals (%)	1st-Order Auto-Corr. of Residuals
NYSE	Inflation	20.60	4.67	−2.44	−2.69	0.194	16.18	−0.185
AMEX*	"	32.09	2.74	−4.20	−2.13	0.246	23.08	0.171
OTC	"	25.21	4.59	−2.82	−2.49	0.171	20.17	−0.220
Preferreds	"	6.88	2.87	−0.97	−1.95	0.113	8.81	0.126
LT corp. bds.	"	3.77	2.06	−0.36	−0.96	0.030	6.72	0.204
Int. corp. bds.	"	4.50	2.97	−0.13	−0.43	0.006	5.55	0.128
Com'l paper	"	2.56	5.03	0.47	4.48	0.401	1.87	0.558
Total corporations	"	16.38	4.80	−1.97	−2.81	0.208	12.52	−0.196
Farms	"	6.43	4.75	1.47	5.29	0.482	4.97	0.192
Housing	"	3.82	7.32	0.84	7.81	0.671	1.92	0.009
T-bills	"	1.95	4.38	0.43	4.67	0.421	1.63	0.560
T-notes	"	3.00	2.95	0.19	0.91	0.027	3.73	0.021
T-bonds	"	3.36	1.98	−0.21	−0.61	0.012	6.23	0.081
Agencies	"	3.90	3.59	0.05	0.23	0.002	3.98	0.045
ST municipal	"	1.50	4.93	0.26	4.13	0.362	1.11	0.590
LT municipal	"	3.99	1.80	−0.54	−1.18	0.044	8.15	0.035
Market	"	7.86	6.18	−0.24	−0.91	0.027	4.67	−0.078

*AMEX results cover only the period 1963–1978.

Market values on OTC stocks for the years 1976–1978 were found in the *NASDAQ Fact Book*. Market values prior to this time were unavailable from that source, so market values for previous years were calculated by dividing the current year's market value by one plus the previous year's capital gain return. This, in effect, assumes that there are no new issues or delistings, such that the market value will only increase or decrease as a result of the capital gain or loss.

OTC capital gains were calculated from the National Quotation Bureau Industrial Index. The yield on OTC stocks was obtained from Media General over the years 1974–1978 and from the National Quotation Bureau from 1958–1971. In all other years, the OTC yield was calculated as 87% of the yield on NYSE stocks (the average ratio of OTC yields to NYSE yields during the years in which OTC yields were available).

Fixed-Income Corporate Securities

The data on the market value of preferred stocks were measured as the difference between the total value of NYSE common stocks and that of all NYSE stocks. These figures were supplied by the NYSE. The returns on preferreds were estimated by the authors from constructing a small sample of preferred stocks, the year-end prices and dividends of which were obtained from the *Bank and Quotation Record*.

The market values and returns of both series of corporate bonds were obtained from the unpublished Ibbotson corporate bond study. We use Ibbotson's long-term and intermediate-term return series, which are representative of all straight (nonconvertible) corporate bonds in the market. To measure the aggregate market value of the two corporate groupings, we use Ibbotson's summation (at average price) of the total universe of corporate bonds in excess of 15 years to maturity (long-term) and the total universe with less than 15 years to maturity (intermediate-term). We have reason to believe that Ibbotson's summations of raw data may understate the corporate bond market, however. Ibbotson left out convertibles, issues of less than $1 million par, real estate bonds, and a few other categories that may as a group account for a non-negligible proportion of the corporate bond market.

The total value of commercial paper (at par) was obtained from *Flow of Funds Accounts*. Commercial paper rates were obtained from the *Federal Reserve Bulletin*. Returns were calculated under the assumption that six-month commercial paper was purchased and subsequently rolled over at maturity for another six months at the prevailing rates.

Real Estate

The source of all data on farm investments is the United States Department of Agriculture (USDA). The aggregate market value of farmland and buildings is reported in issues of *Balance Sheet of the Farming Sector*. This source also reports imputed rent yields on farm investment after labor and management costs. Capital gain returns are calculated from the USDA price per acre series reported in issues of *Farm Real Estate Market Developments.*

Residential housing aggregate values were estimated by Musgrave in the *Survey of Current Business.* His estimates, unfortunately, do not include the urban land value beneath the structures. Rather than estimate this land value, we leave it out of our analysis. Capital appreciation in residential housing was taken from estimates by Roy Wenzlick and Co. from 1947 to 1952 and from the Consumer Price Index–Home Purchase Index from 1953 to 1978. Rent yields (after depreciation, maintenance, and management costs) were taken from the Sprinkel and Genetski book.

U.S. Government Bonds

The source of the market values and returns on the U.S. Treasury issues is Lawrence Fisher's CRSP U.S. Government bond computer file. The aggregate totals of bills, notes, and bonds were summed (at market) from the file. The returns were also computed from the file. Our Treasury bill and bond return series are the same ones as those reported (and described in detail) in the Ibbotson and Sinquefield book. Our Treasury note return series is the same as the two- to five-year maturity government return series reported (and described in detail) in the unpublished Ibbotson and Vaughan paper.

The market value of agencies was obtained from *Flow of Funds Accounts.* Returns from agencies were calculated under the assumption that a five-year agency bond was purchased at the beginning of the year at par with a coupon rate equal to the prevailing yield for five-year agencies. The bond was sold one year later at the four-year yield. The return was measured as the change in price plus the coupon. We used the yield series from Salomon Brothers, *An Analytical Record of Yields and Yield Spreads,* over the period 1965–1978. Prior to 1965, yield curves were constructed by the authors from prices obtained in the *Bank and Quotation Record.*

Municipal (State and Local) Bonds

The par values of these two series were obtained from *Flow of Funds Accounts.* Unfortunately, neither market values nor average prices were available. Since the average prices of the long-term bonds are likely to be below par during most of the sample period, we are probably overweighting long-term municipals relative to the other categories in this study.

Returns from the short-term series during the years 1953–1978 were obtained from project note yields obtained from the U.S. Department of Housing and Urban development. Before 1953, short-term tax-exempt returns were approximated as the yield which could be obtained from the purchase of a AAA state bond with one year to maturity. These quotes were available in the *Bank and Quotation Record.* The returns on the long-term series were calculated under the assumption that a 20-year municipal bond was purchased at par at the beginning of the year and held until year-end. The beginning and end-of-year yields were based on the Bond Buyer Index. The return reflects the price change plus the assumed coupon.

◣ References

Amex Databook, selected years, American Stock Exchange, Inc., New York.

Balance Sheet of the Farming Sector, selected issues, U.S. Department of Agriculture, Economics, Statistics, and Cooperatives Service, Washington, D.C.

Bank and Quotation Record, 1947–1979, William B. Dana Co., New York.

Banking and Monetary Statistics, selected issues, U.S. Board of Governors of the Federal Reserve System, Washington, D.C.

Daily Bond Buyer, selected issues, The Bond Buyer, New York.

Center for Research in Security Prices (CRSP), (sponsored by Merrill, Lynch, Pierce, Fenner and Smith), Graduate School of Business, University of Chicago.

Farm Real Estate Market Developments, selected issues, U.S. Department of Agriculture; Economics, Statistics, and Cooperatives Service, Washington, D.C.

Federal Reserve Bulletin, selected issues, Board of Governors of the Federal Reserve System.

Fisher, Lawrence. "U.S. Government Bond File," CRSP, University of Chicago.

Fisher, Lawrence and Lorie, James H., *A Half Century of Returns on Stocks and Bonds,* University of Chicago, Graduate School of Business, 1977.

Flow of Funds Accounts: Annual Total Flows and Year-End Assets and Liabilities, selected issues, Board of Governors of the Federal Reserve System, Washington, D.C.

Ibbotson, Roger G., "The Corporate Bond Market: Structure and Returns," unpublished paper, February 1979.

Ibbotson, Roger G. and Sinquefield, Rex A., *Stocks, Bonds, Bills and Inflation: Historical Returns (1926–1978),* Financial Analysts Research Foundation, Charlottesville, Virginia, 1979.

Ibbotson, Roger G. and Vaughan, Richard K., "Estimates of U.S. Government Bond Yield Curves and Returns," unpublished paper in progress.

Media General, Richmond, Virginia.

Musgrave, John C., "Fixed Nonresidential Business and Residential Capital in the United States, 1925–1975," *Survey of Current Business* (April 1976). Updates are provided in the September 1978 issue.

NASDAQ/OTC Market Fact Book, selected years, National Association of Security Dealers, Washington, D.C.

National Quotation Bureau, New York.

New York Stock Exchange Fact Book, selected years, New York Stock Exchange.

The Real Estate Analyst, selected issues, Roy Wenzlick & Co., St. Louis.

Salomon Brothers, *An Analytical Record of Yields and Yield Spreads,* New York.

Sprinkel, Beryl W. and Genetski, Robert J., *Winning with Money,* Dow Jones-Irwin, Homewood, Illinois, 1977.

Stambaugh, Robert F., "Measuring the Market Portfolio and Testing the Capital Asset Pricing Model," unpublished paper, December 1978.

United States Department of Housing and Urban Development, Washington, D.C.

United States Department of Labor, Bureau of Labor Statistics, Washington, D.C.

5 Roger G. Ibbotson, Laurence B. Siegel, and Kathryn S. Love

World Wealth: U.S. and Foreign Market Values and Returns

▲ **Overview**

This article measures the capitalizations and returns of the world wealth portfolio, consisting of U.S. and international stocks and bonds, as well as U.S. real estate, and gold and silver. The data cover the period 1959 through 1984 and come from many sources, which are listed on the last page of the article.

Much of the data presented here are not readily available today, without going back to the original sources. For example, Morgan Stanley Capital International presents detailed country data starting in 1971, but no longer provides the data from the 1960s. A partial update is provided after Table 5.4.

▲ **Abstract**

Stocks, bonds, cash, real estate, and precious metals in 20 industrial countries added up to nearly $30 trillion at the end of 1984, having achieved a compound annual return of 8.39% since 1959.

On two occasions in this journal,[1] we have presented annual aggregate values and total returns for major asset classes in the U.S. and in foreign markets, and we have formed U.S., foreign, and world "market wealth portfolios." The portfolios are composed of five major categories of assets: equities (stocks), bonds, cash equivalents, real estate, and monetary metals (gold and silver). With a quarter century now elapsed since the appearance of accurate foreign equity data, we are newly motivated to examine the aggregate values of and total returns on the components of world wealth.

Why should we want to study the wealth of the world? First, a compendium of aggregate values and returns on investable assets serves the investor's and the researcher's need for data. Second, the concept of a market wealth portfolio is consistent with the principle of diversification that is the cornerstone of modern portfolio theory. Third, we feel compelled by the sheer size of foreign markets, as well as by their increasing importance to the U.S. investor, to regard the world rather than our own country as the appropriate field of view. Finally, we are motivated by curiosity—the need to know the past and current dimensions of the world market in which we invest and to compare historical returns on a broad range of assets.

This article updates the World Market Wealth Portfolio study presented in Ibbotson and Siegel (1983). In addition, we incorporate some updates of the detailed data on U.S. markets first set forth in Ibbotson and Fall (1979).

◤ Construction of the U.S., Foreign, and World Portfolios

This section describes the composition of the various portfolios and the techniques that we used to construct them.

We have collected aggregate values over 1959–1984 and year-by-year returns over 1960–1984 for world equities, bonds, cash, and monetary metals plus real estate in the United States (the returns on foreign real estate being difficult to measure). The analysis covers the capital markets of the United States, Europe, Japan, Hong Kong, Singapore, Canada, Mexico, Australia, and South Africa.

Each category of assets includes several components. The three principal U.S. equity markets—the New York and American stock exchanges and the NASDAQ over-the-counter market—are measured separately; we then aggregate them by market-value weighting to form a U.S. equity total. Foreign stocks are a value-weighted aggregate of returns in nineteen countries, with sub-portfolios representing Europe, Asia, and other non-U.S. markets. U.S. bonds include corporate issues (intermediate and long-term bonds plus preferred stocks) and government issues (Treasury notes, Treasury bonds, and agency issues). Foreign bonds include both domestic corporate and government bonds traded within a country's national capital markets and crossborder bonds traded outside the confines of any one country's markets. Cash includes U.S. issues (Treasury bills, commercial paper, and bankers' acceptances) and those of ten foreign countries. United States real estate is composed of business, residential, and farm components. Foreign real estate is excluded from the study except for a single estimate of market value as of the end of 1984. Monetary metals include the world supply of gold and the non-communist world supply of silver.

The aggregate market values of the categories serve as weights for the purpose of constructing value-weighted portfolios, including the World Market Wealth Portfolio and subsidiary portfolios. We have measured returns and have formed cumulative wealth indices. We present these results in year-by-year form and as summary statistics. We include cross-correlations and regression results to measure the relationships among the series and between the series and inflation. Finally, we provide information on the sources of the market value and return data for each series.

▲ The World Market Wealth Portfolio and Modern Portfolio Theory

As we said earlier, modern portfolio theory provides a theoretical reason for studying a market-value weighted World Market Wealth Portfolio. According to modern portfolio theory, the market portfolio—not just common stocks, and not just in the United States—is considered to be perfectly diversified with a capital asset pricing model (CAPM) beta of 1.0. A literal interpretation of the CAPM on a world basis would suggest that the ideal portfolio should represent each asset class in proportion to its prevalence in the world market— the ultimate index fund.

No individual or institutional investor, of course, would actually want to hold a world index fund. Each investor has his or her own risk preferences, tax considerations, information costs, and time horizons. The most obvious example is that only a high-tax investor would want to hold municipal bonds (which, incidentally, we have excluded from this study because of the effect of their tax-exempt status on returns). Other clienteles would cluster in other ways. Suffice it to say that we wish to construct the World Market Portfolio not for its eventual purchase but for the insights it might reveal about the behavior of our capital markets.

▲ What Should Be Included in a Market Wealth Portfolio

Given that we want to construct a World Market Portfolio and subsidiary portfolios, what should we include in it? As stated earlier, we have included equities, bonds, cash, metals, and U.S. real estate. The astute reader will have already noted that the sum of these securities does not represent the "market." We have excluded huge categories of assets from the portfolio, while at the same time we have included categories that are not wealth at all.

As in our earlier work, the most important omission is human capital, which is probably the largest single component of world wealth. We have also excluded the value of foreign real estate (except as a rough illustrative estimate in Figure 5.1). We have excluded the value and returns from proprietorships and partnerships as well as many small corporations. We have excluded (except in Figure 5.1) personal holdings such as automobiles, cash balances, and various consumer capital goods. We have not only omitted a large proportion of wealth, but we also have little idea as to how large the omitted proportion is.

Our inclusions may misrepresent the market even more than our omissions. We have included U.S. and foreign government debt that is almost certainly not backed dollar-for-dollar by government-owned assets such as parks and bridges. More likely, it is backed by claims on a future tax base. Other inclusions in our portfolio also misrepresent wealth. For example, some corporations own parts of other corporations, causing double counting.

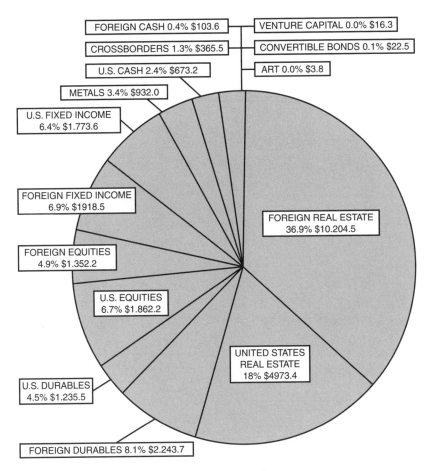

FOREIGN CASH 0.4% $103.6

VENTURE CAPITAL 0.0% $16.3

CROSSBORDERS 1.3% $365.5

CONVERTIBLE BONDS 0.1% $22.5

U.S. CASH 2.4% $673.2

ART 0.0% $3.8

METALS 3.4% $932.0

U.S. FIXED INCOME
6.4% $1.773.6

FOREIGN FIXED INCOME
6.9% $1918.5

FOREIGN EQUITIES
4.9% $1.352.2

U.S. EQUITIES
6.7% $1.862.2

U.S. DURABLES
4.5% $1.235.5

FOREIGN DURABLES 8.1% $2.243.7

FOREIGN REAL ESTATE
36.9% $10.204.5

UNITED STATES
REAL ESTATE
18% $4973.4

Figure 5.1. Total World Wealth: 1984 = $27,681.5 Billion

Therefore, while this study does not really measure the wealth of the world, it nevertheless presents market values and returns for asset classes that make up a large part of that wealth. We measure the values and returns of the capital market securities that are most marketable and most readily identifiable. These are the securities that make up the opportunity set faced by most investors.

▶ Findings: Market Values and Returns

We now present the results, which appear in detail in the tables throughout the article.

Figure 5.1 shows the approximate asset class composition of a broadly defined World Wealth Portfolio as of the end of 1984. We estimate that this

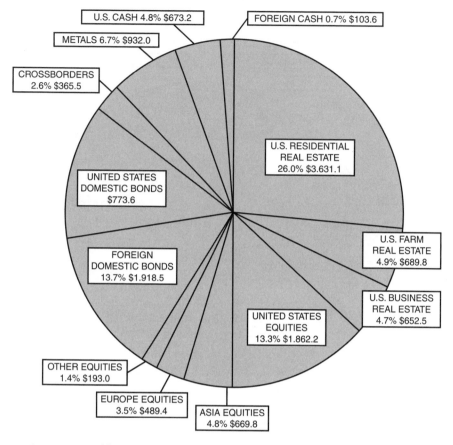

Figure 5.2. World Investable Wealth: 1984 = $13,954.1 Billion

broadly defined portfolio had a value of $27,681.5 billion. Foreign real estate is the largest component of the market, about $10 trillion, or 37% of the total.

Assets residing in foreign countries clearly make up a larger share of wealth than United States assets. Note that only nineteen of the most important foreign industrial countries were used to make these estimates; other countries also hold a substantial share of the world wealth. We see also that automobiles and other consumer durables, excluded in the main body of the study, comprise a substantial portion of world wealth.

In Figure 5.2, we show the distribution as of the end of 1984 of the asset classes included in the World Market Portfolio for which we measure returns. Here we exclude assets that are typically outside the U.S. institutional investor's opportunity set, namely durables, foreign real estate, art, venture capital, and convertible bonds. Of the remaining asset classes, U.S. real estate is the largest. By our measure, the investable World Market Portfolio at the end of

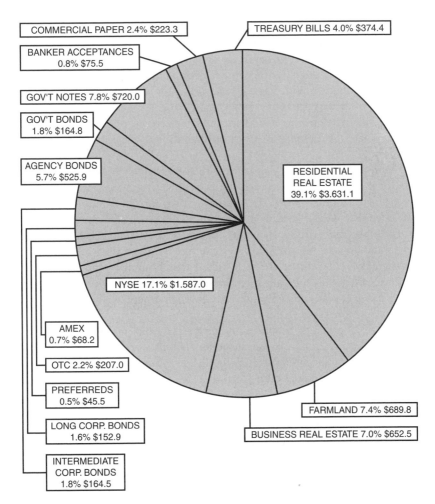

Figure 5.3. U.S. Investable Wealth: 1984 = $9,282.3 Billion

1984 was $13,022.1 billion excluding monetary metals, and $13,954.1 billion including these metals.

Figure 5.3 focuses on the United States. Residential real estate represents almost 40% of investable wealth, but note that most residential real estate, as well as farmland, is held by private (not institutional) investors. The large size of the New York Stock Exchange points out the important role of equities in the U.S. economy; this figure also reflects the importance of government debt (primarily Treasury notes and bills, and agency bonds) relative to corporate debt in the United States.

Table 5.1 shows aggregate market values of the various series and the total market on a year-by-year basis. Figure 5.4 graphically portrays the changing proportions for major categories. There is considerable change in the proportions within the period studied—most dramatically, the sharp 1973–1974 decline in the equity proportion and the 1970s metals boom. The asset proportions at the end of 1984, however, are remarkably similar to those at the end of 1959; moreover, they have the same rank order in both years—real estate is largest, then bonds, equities, metals, and cash. While this consistency may be an artifact of the way the asset class aggregate values are measured, we may also speculate that it represents a fundamental characteristic of the way that society cuts shares of capital—a sort of optimal capital structure for the world economy.

Table 5.2 presents the year-by-year total returns for the various components of the market portfolio, each component being grouped into one of the five major categories. The table includes returns for the U.S., Foreign, and World Market Wealth Portfolios. We also present returns for the world market both with and without monetary metals, since these metals have a large weight and unusual returns; thus, they alter the return on the world portfolio considerably. The returns are then linked (compounded) into cumulative wealth indexes, which are presented in Table 5.3. Each wealth index is initiated at 1.000 at year-end 1959 and includes reinvestment of all income as well as retention of all capital gains.

Figure 5.5 presents a graphic summary of the results in Table 5.3. U.S. real estate had the highest return over the period. Metals, the riskiest category, and equities, having substantial risk, had slightly lower but still generally good performance. Foreign equities outperformed U.S. equities, largely because of the remarkable returns on equities in Japan and other Asian countries. We have almost certainly underestimated the risk of real estate here, due to the lesser marketability of real estate and the various smoothing effects inherent in our measures of annual returns.[2] Cash had returns that tracked the United States inflation rate. U.S. bonds were the worst performer, underperforming cash and, unlike cash, exhibiting appreciable risk. Foreign bonds had generally better results than U.S. bonds.

In Figure 5.6, we focus on returns in the U.S. market. Real estate and equities were the high-performing sectors of the market over the period studied. Cash equivalents and bonds were the low-performing sectors, with bonds underperforming cash as a consequence of generally rising interest rates over the period.

The results presented in Tables 5.2 and 5.3 are summarized statistically in Table 5.4. Looking at specific asset classes, we can see that the biggest winners over the period were Asian equities (with a 15.14% compound annual rate of return), U.S. farm real estate (11.86%), and U.S. over-the-counter equities (11.47%). Metals, which were among the highest returning assets over the 1960–1980 period studied in Ibbotson and Siegel (1983), fell sharply over 1981–1984, so that their returns over the whole period studied here, while above average, were not extraordinary. The least desirable investment was U.S. Treasury bonds. Despite the explosive 1982 bond rally, they earned a compound annual rate of return of only 4.70%. These bonds, along with long-

Table 5.1

Aggregate Value of Capital Market Securities (Billions of Dollars)

Year-End	United States				Equities Europe	Asia	Foreign Other	Total	Equities Total
	NYSE	AMEX	OTC	Total					
1959	309.25	20.13	23.70	353.08	103.00	14.6	23.40	141.03	494.11
1960	307.71	20.97	23.30	351.98	135.08	17.7	27.38	180.16	532.14
1961	388.05	26.37	30.70	445.12	168.40	20.5	32.62	221.52	666.64
1962	337.15	25.02	26.10	388.27	146.56	17.1	31.37	195.03	583.30
1963	401.64	26.68	31.40	459.72	153.86	23.1	34.23	211.19	670.91
1964	462.92	29.46	38.70	531.08	149.88	20.3	41.68	211.86	742.94
1965	523.84	31.12	50.30	605.26	145.08	18.5	40.85	204.43	809.69
1966	469.07	28.10	42.70	539.88	150.81	23.1	38.90	212.81	752.69
1967	585.17	44.94	65.80	695.91	174.89	27.5	42.76	245.15	941.06
1968	662.42	58.10	79.30	799.82	198.97	31.9	51.55	282.42	1,082.24
1969	598.70	43.62	73.30	715.62	196.74	43.8	55.85	296.39	1,012.01
1970	605.26	35.93	63.20	704.40	194.45	50.6	64.17	309.22	1,013.62
1971	705.06	44.37	85.60	835.03	208.52	63.2	63.76	335.48	1,170.51
1972	836.13	53.96	100.30	990.39	269.94	109.2	80.32	459.46	1,449.85
1973	681.10	36.30	69.20	786.60	322.93	171.9	80.25	575.08	1,361.68
1974	479.43	21.47	44.90	545.80	227.24	126.0	62.53	415.77	961.57
1975	648.76	28.60	58.20	735.56	242.06	143.7	66.53	452.29	1,187.85
1976	812.04	33.59	65.20	910.83	233.49	176.9	82.66	493.05	1,403.88
1977	761.57	33.12	72.70	867.39	247.29	195.9	78.66	521.85	1,389.24
1978	790.27	33.80	78.80	902.86	300.54	267.1	92.53	600.17	1,563.03
1979	918.13	54.01	91.70	1,063.84	403.51	310.9	152.72	867.13	1,930.97
1980	1,194.54	72.32	122.40	1,389.26	455.80	418.5	206.30	1,080.60	2,469.86
1981	1,112.84	63.85	124.80	1,301.49	411.40	479.8	184.10	1,075.30	2,376.79
1982	1,294.66	62.57	153.10	1,510.34	407.50	455.3	108.60	1,043.40	2,553.74
1983	1,584.16	80.80	229.30	1,894.26	488.30	573.9	217.90	1,280.10	3,174.36
1984	1,586.98	68.23	206.95	1,862.16	489.40	669.8	193.00	1,352.20	3,214.36

(continued)

Table 5.1 (continued)
Aggregate Value of Capital Market Securities (Billions of Dollars)

| | United States | | | | | | | | Foreign | | | | |
| | Government | | | | Corporate | | | | Domestic | | | | |
Notes	Bonds	Agencies	Total	Med. Term	Long Term	Total	Total	Corp.	Gov't	Cross-borders	Total	Bonds Total
43.29	74.96	7.3	125.55	16.00	47.50	70.20	195.75	121.67	190.16	17.81	329.64	535.39
52.15	76.19	8.1	136.45	16.20	52.30	75.20	211.65	139.99	235.56	18.64	394.19	605.84
71.77	70.79	8.8	151.36	17.30	53.90	78.50	229.86	139.55	251.01	19.79	410.35	640.21
54.16	75.82	10.4	140.38	20.80	55.00	83.50	223.88	136.85	257.59	21.37	415.81	639.69
58.46	82.33	12.0	152.79	25.70	53.80	87.40	240.19	141.49	239.52	22.66	403.67	643.86
52.56	91.73	12.6	156.89	28.50	52.90	89.70	246.59	139.23	234.10	24.00	397.33	643.92
49.78	97.75	14.7	162.22	28.00	53.40	90.70	252.92	135.09	227.40	24.45	386.94	639.86
48.31	93.54	20.2	162.04	28.30	50.80	88.80	250.84	133.06	225.19	24.56	382.81	633.65
51.47	92.76	20.3	164.52	31.80	49.00	95.70	260.22	130.30	232.05	25.48	387.83	648.05
78.51	72.24	24.1	174.85	31.10	55.30	110.90	285.75	128.19	229.97	27.08	385.24	670.99
77.61	57.45	33.8	168.86	30.00	53.90	106.50	275.36	121.64	214.35	27.06	363.05	638.41
100.81	50.90	43.6	195.31	38.70	64.60	127.20	322.51	125.41	233.21	30.34	388.96	711.47
110.67	46.90	49.5	207.07	41.50	86.50	155.50	362.57	163.20	297.70	34.19	495.09	857.66
122.55	40.68	57.9	221.13	45.80	98.80	171.80	392.93	187.98	321.67	39.65	549.30	942.23
123.52	29.72	77.9	231.14	51.30	94.43	168.73	399.87	219.33	358.32	44.43	622.08	1,021.95
121.27	27.68	97.9	246.85	54.10	90.04	161.94	408.79	240.09	403.68	49.08	692.85	1,101.64
162.41	32.32	107.3	302.03	67.00	136.21	203.21	505.24	275.77	448.94	68.75	793.46	1,298.70
207.93	38.07	122.8	368.81	73.60	142.04	243.44	612.25	325.28	574.36	95.08	994.72	1,606.97
232.51	42.81	145.0	420.31	80.70	143.20	249.40	669.71	419.29	771.50	123.92	1,314.71	1,984.42
252.54	54.97	181.7	489.21	78.31	137.14	239.45	728.66	538.19	1,006.25	150.78	1,695.22	2,423.88
267.93	64.80	230.3	563.03	79.59	129.00	233.19	796.22	553.44	1,117.03	171.02	1,841.49	2,637.71
299.38	68.36	273.9	641.64	90.12	121.51	239.04	880.68	615.82	1,305.38	189.59	2,110.79	2,991.47
356.91	76.90	319.4	753.21	98.90	112.21	234.84	988.05	618.76	1,280.32	210.05	2,109.13	3,097.18
492.30	104.54	383.9	980.74	137.92	147.61	319.31	1,300.05	631.06	1,341.60	257.63	2,230.29	3,530.34
574.80	124.00	451.7	1,150.50	143.43	146.00	336.40	1,486.90	653.56	1,473.25	297.34	2,424.15	3,864.08
720.00	164.80	525.9	1,410.70	164.46	152.92	362.86	1,773.56	630.35	1,288.17	365.47	2,283.99	4,057.55

| | Real Estate | | | Cash | | | | | Metals | | | Market Wealth Portfolios | | | |
| | United States | | | United States | | | Foreign | Cash | World | | Metals | | | World Excl. | World Incl. |
Business	Resi-dential	Farm	Total	Treasury Bills	Com-mercial Paper	Total	Total	Total	Gold	Silver	Total	U.S.	Foreign	Metals	Metals
58.8	458.52	137.20	654.52	33.22	3.2	37.62	13.65	51.27	66.96	1.10	68.06	1,240.98	484.32	1,725.20	1,793.36
61.9	476.88	138.50	677.28	32.24	4.5	38.74	13.94	52.68	68.28	1.10	69.38	1,279.64	588.29	1,867.93	1,937.31
66.6	494.04	144.50	705.14	37.14	4.7	44.54	15.16	59.70	69.89	1.24	71.13	1,424.66	647.03	2,071.69	2,142.82
71.4	514.68	150.20	736.28	44.97	6.0	53.67	15.52	69.19	71.16	1.45	72.61	1,402.09	626.36	2,028.45	2,101.06
76.8	527.16	158.60	762.56	49.89	6.8	59.59	16.18	75.77	72.70	1.55	74.25	1,522.06	631.04	2,153.10	2,227.35
82.5	562.44	167.50	812.44	51.81	8.4	63.61	16.86	80.47	74.27	1.55	75.82	1,653.71	626.05	2,279.76	2,355.58
90.6	589.80	179.20	859.60	49.52	9.3	62.22	17.67	79.89	75.88	1.66	77.54	1,780.00	609.04	2,389.04	2,466.58
100.6	635.28	189.10	924.98	56.87	13.6	74.07	18.70	92.77	77.49	1.66	79.15	1,789.77	614.32	2,404.09	2,483.24
109.8	667.68	199.70	977.18	59.00	17.1	80.40	18.03	98.43	79.10	2.65	81.75	2,013.71	651.01	2,664.72	2,746.47
120.6	745.32	209.20	1,075.12	64.60	21.2	90.20	17.73	107.93	90.63	2.52	93.15	2,250.89	685.39	2,936.28	3,029.43
139.9	813.00	215.80	1,168.70	65.52	32.6	103.62	19.94	123.56	97.61	2.33	99.94	2,263.29	679.38	2,942.67	3,042.61
156.1	870.72	223.20	1,250.02	79.40	33.1	119.60	23.08	142.68	87.32	2.45	89.77	2,396.52	721.26	3,117.78	3,207.55
170.4	960.24	239.60	1,370.24	88.97	32.1	128.97	21.17	150.14	100.76	2.09	102.85	2,696.81	851.74	3,548.55	3,651.40
187.8	1,082.64	267.30	1,537.74	97.92	34.7	139.52	26.31	165.83	145.91	2.99	148.90	3,060.58	1,035.07	4,095.65	4,244.55
216.8	1,262.28	327.70	1,806.78	100.53	41.1	150.53	32.16	182.69	247.83	4.73	252.56	3,143.79	1,229.32	4,373.11	4,625.67
267.9	1,422.12	359.80	2,049.82	112.47	49.1	180.07	38.94	219.01	411.07	6.61	417.68	3,184.48	1,147.56	4,332.04	4,749.72
269.8	1,534.68	418.20	2,222.68	150.37	47.7	216.77	47.09	263.87	421.84	6.09	427.93	3,680.25	1,292.84	4,973.09	5,401.02
280.8	1,727.88	496.40	2,505.08	158.87	52.0	233.37	47.69	281.06	332.17	6.48	338.65	4,261.53	1,535.46	5,796.99	6,135.64
318.1	1,959.48	554.60	2,832.18	156.28	63.9	245.88	59.40	305.28	399.08	7.02	406.10	4,615.16	1,895.96	6,511.12	6,917.22
370.8	2,340.60	655.10	3,366.50	155.06	82.2	270.96	80.32	351.28	528.53	8.84	537.37	5,268.98	2,435.71	7,704.69	8,242.06
433.7	2,607.12	763.28	3,804.10	148.80	110.9	305.00	71.90	376.90	851.47	32.47	883.94	5,969.16	2,780.52	8,749.68	9,633.62
496.1	2,862.96	843.66	4,202.72	216.10	121.6	392.40	102.17	494.57	1,654.73	27.13	1,681.86	6,865.06	3,293.56	10,158.62	11,840.48
559.0	3,116.28	843.30	4,518.58	245.00	161.1	475.30	112.15	587.45	1,141.96	15.05	1,157.01	7,283.42	3,296.58	10,580.00	11,737.01
594.0	3,154.92	804.76	4,553.68	311.80	156.2	547.50	105.43	652.93	1,320.83	20.30	1,341.13	7,911.57	3,379.12	11,290.69	12,631.82
603.0	3,318.96	794.03	4,715.99	343.80	175.2	597.30	104.24	701.54	1,119.98	17.48	1,137.46	8,694.45	3,808.49	12,502.94	13,640.40
652.5	3,631.08	689.81	4,973.39	374.40	223.3	673.20	103.58	776.78	919.27	12.72	931.99	9,282.31	3,739.77	13,022.08	13,954.07

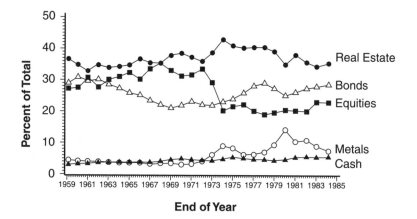

Figure 5.4. World Investable Wealth: Value of Capital Market Securities as a Percentage of the Total

term U.S. corporate bonds, were the only asset classes to return less than the U.S. inflation rate, and were also riskier than any class of cash or real estate (as measured) and the much better performing foreign bond portfolio.

The U.S. market wealth portfolio had positive returns in every year from 1960 to 1984. The year of highest return was 1979 (17.05%) and the lowest was 1973 (0.46%). The foreign market wealth portfolio was much riskier and, over this period, had a lower overall return. The year of highest return was 1978 (23.87%) and the lowest was 1974 (−8.83%).

The World Market Wealth Portfolio, excluding metals, had year-by-year returns ranging from 17.48% in 1975 to −1.35% in 1974. The World Market Wealth Portfolio, including metals, had returns ranging from 21.51% in 1980 to −3.32% in 1981 and had a slightly higher overall return. Thus, reflecting the countercyclical nature of monetary metal returns, the inclusion of metals produced a portfolio with positive total returns in every year except one from 1960 through 1984.

The Relationships Among the Series

We can get a good idea of the interrelationships among the series by looking at the cross-correlation matrix presented in Table 5.5. The various equity, bond, cash, real estate, and metal series exhibit high correlation *within* each category. Although world equities and world bonds have a correlation coefficient of only approximately 0.16, world cash and gold (sometimes considered a form of cash) are substantially correlated. Real estate is uncorrelated with equities and almost uncorrelated with bonds but highly correlated with cash and metals. These higher correlations probably reflect the impoundment of inflation rates into real estate returns and the tendency of hard, or tangible, assets to follow similar trends.

Table 5.2
Year-by-Year Total Returns on Capital Market Securities (Percent)

Year-End	Equities								
	United States				Foreign				Equities Total
	NYSE	AMEX	OTC	Total	Europe	Asia	Other	Total	
1960	0.60	4.16	1.93	0.90	13.65	38.50	-0.69	13.84	4.59
1961	27.17	25.76	35.35	27.63	15.11	-13.03	26.49	14.08	23.04
1962	-9.40	-5.11	-12.44	-9.35	-2.35	4.68	-3.42	-1.86	-6.86
1963	21.41	10.93	23.94	20.90	7.08	8.78	19.19	9.18	16.98
1964	16.36	13.20	26.02	16.84	-2.13	10.93	16.12	2.25	12.25
1965	13.99	15.50	32.90	15.45	3.74	21.39	-1.27	4.45	12.31
1966	-8.87	-7.70	-12.29	-9.10	-5.92	9.04	-3.92	-4.17	-7.85
1967	26.88	51.40	57.47	30.57	18.98	-4.85	22.42	17.02	26.74
1968	12.82	25.94	22.70	14.60	35.05	26.43	27.46	32.76	19.33
1969	-9.82	-27.04	-5.80	-10.67	1.51	34.15	8.26	6.43	-6.21
1970	1.31	-18.14	-12.23	-1.26	-9.04	-4.09	-4.38	-7.43	-3.07
1971	15.81	17.86	37.19	17.83	27.33	48.41	10.91	27.37	20.74
1972	17.77	5.18	20.35	17.36	16.45	134.89	27.80	40.92	24.11
1973	-16.92	-30.09	-28.47	-18.81	-7.78	-24.62	-21.10	-14.11	-17.32
1974	-26.80	-37.61	-32.71	-27.82	-23.34	-19.75	-35.98	-24.03	-26.22
1975	37.72	38.77	33.76	37.44	44.78	23.84	38.51	37.49	37.46
1976	26.26	28.25	29.20	26.57	-7.56	26.17	11.75	6.00	18.74
1977	-4.81	9.80	10.53	-3.18	21.26	13.39	4.61	15.65	3.43
1978	7.39	16.95	15.81	8.46	25.51	51.13	19.79	34.27	18.15
1979	21.82	58.47	31.91	24.07	15.38	-5.57	57.81	12.85	19.33
1980	32.70	30.61	37.38	32.99	14.53	34.09	34.88	25.13	29.46
1981	-4.22	-6.10	-0.01	-3.95	-8.93	12.90	-17.66	-2.14	-3.16
1982	20.72	4.93	21.87	19.98	5.74	-5.67	-1.29	-0.55	10.69
1983	23.00	28.27	22.17	23.09	22.84	24.06	32.85	25.11	23.92
1984	6.88	-5.45	-9.31	4.39	1.67	15.24	-13.76	5.13	4.69

(continued)

Table 5.2 (continued)

Year-by-Year Total Returns on Capital Market Securities (Percent)

	United States Government			United States Corporate			United States Total	Foreign Domestic		Foreign Cross-borders	Foreign Total	Bonds Total
Notes	Bonds	Agencies	Total	Med. Term	Long Term	Total	Total	Corp.	Gov't	Cross-borders	Total	Bonds Total
10.14	13.78	11.04	12.37	6.83	8.01	7.79	10.73	5.83	-0.25	4.66	2.26	5.41
2.07	0.97	2.84	1.50	4.69	4.54	4.96	2.73	6.00	6.49	6.14	6.30	5.05
5.07	6.89	5.79	5.96	1.59	6.73	5.91	5.94	4.44	7.93	7.99	6.74	6.46
2.14	1.21	2.01	1.63	2.99	3.79	3.59	2.36	10.48	4.07	6.03	6.28	4.91
4.00	3.51	5.08	3.82	3.72	5.19	4.75	4.16	5.52	1.71	5.90	3.28	3.61
1.43	0.71	3.65	1.19	1.21	-5.19	-2.81	-0.27	4.82	1.94	1.87	2.95	1.72
5.02	3.65	3.74	4.08	-2.75	-4.25	-4.26	1.09	6.14	4.15	0.48	4.61	3.22
1.79	-9.19	1.62	-4.57	-1.21	-4.79	-3.91	-4.34	3.86	0.23	3.71	1.71	-0.68
4.51	-0.26	4.02	1.76	3.50	1.41	2.69	2.10	5.74	3.74	6.28	4.58	3.58
-0.97	-5.08	-0.82	-2.65	-3.36	-8.78	-7.50	-4.53	2.78	-0.48	-0.08	0.63	-1.57
15.13	12.10	17.62	14.60	14.15	15.25	14.00	14.37	9.02	9.33	5.03	8.91	11.26
8.20	13.23	8.75	9.63	12.93	11.83	11.71	10.45	23.40	21.25	15.70	21.51	16.50
4.23	5.68	5.27	4.81	8.15	7.35	7.12	5.80	9.88	2.78	11.53	5.73	5.76
2.47	-1.11	3.47	2.07	3.19	1.09	1.22	1.70	7.84	5.66	7.78	6.56	4.53
6.50	4.35	12.69	8.31	1.06	-7.61	-5.70	2.40	4.94	3.15	6.34	4.01	3.38
8.38	9.19	6.72	7.81	14.16	17.56	16.60	11.29	11.37	8.10	13.72	9.63	10.25
11.92	16.75	12.58	12.67	14.63	21.03	19.03	15.23	16.74	9.16	17.64	12.53	13.58
2.29	-0.67	2.34	2.00	4.60	2.67	4.09	2.83	30.61	27.15	13.77	27.00	17.80
3.22	-1.16	1.11	2.05	1.65	-0.10	0.39	1.43	20.15	21.37	10.65	19.97	13.71
4.64	-1.22	5.54	4.32	3.35	-4.08	-2.12	2.20	-3.11	1.70	2.85	0.28	0.86
4.55	-3.95	3.55	3.16	5.34	-2.60	-0.31	2.15	7.13	2.71	2.24	4.00	3.44
9.70	1.85	7.65	7.99	8.98	-0.15	3.42	6.75	-1.55	-6.69	-0.54	-4.64	-1.29
23.79	40.35	28.12	27.32	30.02	44.52	38.33	29.93	7.79	10.84	23.49	11.21	17.18
7.52	0.68	7.78	6.89	10.66	8.32	9.20	7.46	4.54	4.19	7.62	4.69	5.71
13.29	15.43	13.88	13.75	14.87	17.66	15.63	14.18	10.16	0.63	10.65	4.43	8.14

Real Estate				Cash					Metals			Market Wealth Portfolios			
United States				United States			Foreign	Cash	World		Metals			World Excl.	World Incl.
Business	Resi-dential	Farm	Total	Treasury Bills	Com-mercial Paper	Total	Total	Total	Gold	Silver	Total	U.S.	Foreign	Metals	Metals
2.49	4.99	4.07	4.57	2.66	3.85	2.79	0.84	2.27	0.00	0.00	0.00	4.44	5.59	4.77	4.58
2.69	5.28	9.10	5.82	2.13	2.97	2.26	-0.33	1.57	0.00	13.19	0.21	11.20	8.53	10.36	10.00
3.29	4.79	8.98	5.51	2.73	3.26	2.81	1.81	2.55	0.00	16.50	0.29	0.85	3.68	1.73	1.69
4.29	6.78	9.79	7.15	3.12	3.55	3.18	3.62	3.28	0.00	7.50	0.15	10.04	7.12	9.14	8.83
2.99	5.83	7.58	5.91	3.54	3.97	3.60	5.40	3.98	0.00	0.00	0.00	8.84	2.99	7.13	6.89
4.09	6.24	12.64	7.34	3.93	4.38	4.00	6.78	4.59	0.00	0.00	0.00	8.68	3.56	7.28	7.04
4.89	5.76	12.23	7.02	4.76	5.55	4.91	5.92	5.13	0.00	0.00	0.00	0.62	1.70	0.90	0.87
6.39	6.83	10.30	7.49	4.21	5.10	4.40	-3.27	2.85	0.00	59.97	1.26	12.67	6.87	11.19	10.87
10.69	8.25	8.71	8.62	5.21	5.90	5.39	6.80	5.64	12.29	-4.85	11.73	9.72	15.25	11.07	11.09
6.09	11.02	7.24	9.73	6.58	7.83	6.92	8.72	7.22	5.60	-7.65	5.24	0.56	3.23	1.18	1.31
9.99	12.16	7.77	11.09	6.53	7.72	6.95	12.90	7.91	-12.29	-9.94	-12.24	7.39	1.90	6.12	5.52
15.49	8.16	11.70	9.71	4.39	5.11	4.62	14.03	6.14	13.19	-14.72	12.43	11.94	23.78	14.68	14.62
9.49	6.73	18.94	9.21	3.84	4.69	4.09	0.80	3.63	42.23	42.45	42.23	11.03	19.46	13.05	13.88
7.39	6.97	35.27	11.94	6.93	8.20	7.30	15.80	8.65	66.90	58.59	66.73	0.46	-2.38	-0.25	2.10
8.09	13.50	19.80	13.99	8.00	10.05	8.67	14.52	9.70	63.29	39.81	62.85	1.80	-8.83	-1.19	2.31
6.60	13.23	18.52	13.29	5.80	6.26	5.98	-2.14	4.53	1.13	-6.83	1.00	16.76	19.33	17.44	16.00
8.55	7.51	19.54	9.90	5.08	5.24	5.12	9.46	5.90	-22.41	6.36	-22.00	13.68	10.13	12.76	10.01
8.67	11.47	11.20	11.10	5.12	5.54	5.26	21.04	7.94	18.36	8.28	18.17	6.54	23.17	10.95	11.35
14.68	14.18	18.18	15.02	7.18	7.94	7.47	18.88	9.69	30.55	25.90	30.47	11.41	23.87	15.04	15.95
14.69	19.01	20.87	18.90	10.38	10.97	10.64	-2.32	7.68	58.83	367.45	63.91	17.05	3.60	12.80	16.13
12.92	14.75	12.63	14.12	11.24	12.66	11.99	15.39	12.63	91.71	-24.78	87.43	15.78	10.88	14.22	20.94
13.46	4.96	2.19	5.41	14.71	15.32	14.98	-1.16	11.65	-32.15	-49.66	-32.43	4.23	-3.71	1.66	-3.18
10.38	11.82	-3.05	8.87	10.54	11.89	11.19	-0.09	9.04	13.94	32.12	14.18	13.86	6.99	11.72	11.96
16.00	7.35	-0.26	7.13	8.80	8.88	8.85	3.10	7.88	-16.50	-17.89	-16.52	10.35	10.94	10.53	7.66
9.99	5.62	-6.65	8.48	9.85	10.10	10.12	-0.64	8.41	-19.19	-28.94	-19.34	8.67	4.53	7.41	5.17

Table 5.3
Cumulative Wealth Indices of Capital Market Securities (Year-End 1959 = 1.00)

Year-End	United States				Equities Foreign				Equities Total
	NYSE	AMEX	OTC	Total	Europe	Asia	Other	Total	
1959	1.000	1.000	1.000	1.000	1.000	1.000	1.000	1.000	1.000
1960	1.006	1.042	1.019	1.009	1.136	1.385	0.993	1.138	1.046
1961	1.279	1.310	1.380	1.288	1.308	1.205	1.256	1.299	1.287
1962	1.159	1.243	1.208	1.167	1.277	1.261	1.213	1.274	1.199
1963	1.407	1.379	1.497	1.411	1.368	1.372	1.446	1.391	1.402
1964	1.637	1.561	1.887	1.649	1.339	1.522	1.679	1.423	1.574
1965	1.867	1.803	2.508	1.904	1.389	1.847	1.658	1.486	1.768
1966	1.702	1.664	2.199	1.730	1.307	2.014	1.593	1.424	1.629
1967	2.158	2.519	3.461	2.259	1.555	1.916	1.950	1.667	2.064
1968	2.435	3.173	4.247	2.589	2.100	2.423	2.485	2.213	2.463
1969	2.196	2.315	4.000	2.313	2.131	3.250	2.691	2.355	2.310
1970	2.225	1.895	3.511	2.284	1.939	3.117	2.573	2.180	2.239
1971	2.576	2.233	4.817	2.691	2.468	4.626	2.853	2.776	2.704
1972	3.034	2.349	5.797	3.158	2.874	10.867	3.646	3.912	3.356
1973	2.520	1.642	4.147	2.564	2.651	8.191	2.877	3.360	2.775
1974	1.845	1.025	2.791	1.851	2.032	6.573	1.842	2.553	2.047
1975	2.541	1.422	3.733	3.544	2.942	8.141	2.551	3.510	2.814
1976	3.208	1.823	4.822	3.220	2.720	10.271	2.851	3.721	3.342
1977	3.054	2.002	5.330	3.118	3.298	11.646	2.982	4.303	3.456
1978	3.280	2.341	6.173	3.381	4.139	17.601	3.572	5.777	4.084
1979	3.994	3.711	8.143	4.195	4.776	16.621	5.637	6.520	4.873
1980	5.301	4.847	11.187	5.579	5.470	22.286	7.604	8.158	6.309
1981	5.078	4.551	11.185	5.359	4.981	25.161	6.261	7.983	6.110
1982	6.130	4.775	13.632	6.430	5.267	23.735	6.181	7.939	6.763
1983	7.540	6.125	16.654	7.915	6.470	29.445	8.211	9.932	8.380
1984	8.058	5.791	15.103	8.262	6.578	33.932	7.081	10.441	8.773

Bonds

| | United States | | | | | | | | Foreign | | | | Bonds |
| | Government | | | | Corporate | | | Total | Domestic | | Cross-borders | Total | Total |
Notes	Bonds	Agencies	Total	Med. Term	Long Term	Total			Corp.	Gov't			
1.000	1.000	1.000	1.000	1.000	1.000	1.000	1.000	1.000	1.000	1.000	1.000	1.000	1.000
1.101	1.138	1.110	1.124	1.068	1.080	1.078	1.107	1.058	0.997	1.047	1.023	1.054	
1.124	1.149	1.142	1.141	1.118	1.129	1.131	1.137	1.122	1.062	1.111	1.087	1.107	
1.181	1.228	1.208	1.209	1.136	1.205	1.198	1.205	1.172	1.146	1.200	1.160	1.179	
1.206	1.243	1.232	1.228	1.170	1.251	1.241	1.234	1.294	1.193	1.272	1.233	1.237	
1.255	1.286	1.295	1.275	1.214	1.316	1.300	1.285	1.366	1.214	1.347	1.274	1.281	
1.273	1.296	1.342	1.290	1.228	1.247	1.264	1.281	1.432	1.237	1.372	1.311	1.303	
1.337	1.343	1.392	1.343	1.195	1.194	1.210	1.295	1.520	1.288	1.379	1.372	1.345	
1.360	1.219	1.415	1.282	1.180	1.137	1.163	1.239	1.578	1.291	1.430	1.395	1.336	
1.422	1.216	1.472	1.304	1.221	1.153	1.194	1.265	1.669	1.340	1.520	1.459	1.384	
1.408	1.155	1.460	1.270	1.180	1.052	1.104	1.208	1.715	1.333	1.519	1.468	1.362	
1.621	1.294	1.717	1.455	1.347	1.212	1.259	1.381	1.870	1.457	1.595	1.599	1.516	
1.754	1.465	1.867	1.595	1.522	1.356	1.406	1.526	2.308	1.767	1.846	1.943	1.766	
1.828	1.549	1.966	1.672	1.646	1.455	1.506	1.614	2.536	1.816	2.058	2.054	1.868	
1.873	1.531	2.034	1.706	1.698	1.471	1.525	1.642	2.734	1.919	2.218	2.189	1.952	
1.995	1.598	2.292	1.848	1.716	1.359	1.438	1.681	2.870	1.980	2.359	2.277	2.018	
2.162	1.745	2.446	1.993	1.959	1.598	1.677	1.871	3.196	2.140	2.683	2.496	2.225	
2.420	2.037	2.754	2.245	2.246	1.934	1.996	2.156	3.731	2.336	3.156	2.809	2.527	
2.476	2.024	2.818	2.290	2.349	1.986	2.077	2.217	4.873	2.971	3.590	3.567	2.977	
2.555	2.000	2.849	2.337	2.388	1.984	2.085	2.249	5.854	3.605	3.973	4.280	3.385	
2.674	1.976	3.007	2.438	2.468	1.903	2.041	2.298	5.672	3.667	4.086	4.292	3.414	
2.795	1.898	3.114	2.515	2.600	1.853	2.035	2.348	6.077	3.766	4.178	4.463	3.531	
3.067	1.933	3.352	2.716	2.833	1.851	2.105	2.506	5.983	3.514	4.155	4.256	3.486	
3.796	2.713	4.295	3.458	3.684	2.675	2.911	3.256	6.449	3.895	5.131	4.733	4.085	
4.082	2.731	4.629	3.696	4.076	2.897	3.179	3.499	6.742	4.059	5.522	4.955	4.318	
4.624	3.153	5.271	4.204	4.682	3.409	3.676	3.995	7.427	4.084	6.110	5.174	4.669	

(continued)

Table 5.3 (continued)
Cumulative Wealth Indices of Capital Market Securities (Year-End 1959 = 1.00)

Real Estate				Cash					Metals			Market Wealth Portfolios			
United States				United States			Foreign	Cash	World		Metals			World Excl.	World Incl.
Business	Residential	Farm	Total	Treasury Bills	Commercial Paper	Total	Total	Total	Gold	Silver	Total	U.S.	Foreign	Metals	Metals
1.000	1.000	1.000	1.000	1.000	1.000	1.000	1.000	1.000	1.000	1.000	1.000	1.000	1.000	1.000	1.000
1.025	1.050	1.041	1.046	1.027	1.038	1.028	1.008	1.023	1.000	1.000	1.000	1.044	1.056	1.048	1.046
1.052	1.105	1.135	1.107	1.048	1.069	1.051	1.005	1.039	1.000	1.132	1.002	1.161	1.146	1.156	1.150
1.087	1.158	1.237	1.168	1.077	1.104	1.081	1.023	1.065	1.000	1.319	1.005	1.171	1.188	1.176	1.170
1.134	1.237	1.359	1.251	1.111	1.143	1.115	1.060	1.100	1.000	1.418	1.006	1.289	1.273	1.284	1.273
1.168	1.309	1.461	1.325	1.150	1.189	1.155	1.118	1.144	1.000	1.418	1.006	1.403	1.311	1.375	1.361
1.215	1.391	1.646	1.422	1.195	1.241	1.201	1.193	1.197	1.000	1.418	1.006	1.525	1.357	1.475	1.457
1.275	1.471	1.848	1.522	1.252	1.310	1.260	1.264	1.258	1.000	1.418	1.006	1.534	1.380	1.489	1.469
1.356	1.571	2.038	1.636	1.305	1.377	1.316	1.223	1.294	1.000	2.268	1.019	1.729	1.475	1.655	1.629
1.501	1.701	2.215	1.777	1.373	1.458	1.387	1.306	1.367	1.123	2.158	1.139	1.896	1.700	1.838	1.810
1.593	1.888	2.376	1.950	1.463	1.572	1.483	1.419	1.466	1.186	1.993	1.198	1.907	1.755	1.860	1.833
1.752	2.118	2.560	2.166	1.559	1.693	1.586	1.603	1.581	1.040	1.795	1.052	2.048	1.788	1.974	1.934
2.023	2.291	2.860	2.377	1.627	1.780	1.659	1.827	1.679	1.177	1.530	1.183	2.293	2.214	2.264	2.217
2.215	2.445	3.402	2.595	1.690	1.863	1.727	1.842	1.739	1.674	2.180	1.682	2.545	2.645	2.559	2.525
2.379	2.615	4.601	2.905	1.807	2.016	1.853	2.133	1.890	2.795	3.457	2.804	2.557	2.582	2.553	2.578
2.571	2.968	5.512	3.312	1.952	2.219	2.013	2.443	2.073	4.563	4.834	4.567	2.603	2.354	2.522	2.637
2.741	3.361	6.533	3.752	2.064	2.358	2.134	2.391	2.167	4.615	4.504	4.613	3.040	2.809	2.962	3.059
2.975	3.613	7.810	4.124	2.169	2.481	2.243	2.617	2.295	3.581	4.790	3.598	3.456	3.093	3.340	3.365
3.233	4.028	8.684	4.581	2.280	2.618	2.361	3.167	2.477	4.238	5.187	4.252	3.682	3.810	3.706	3.747
3.708	4.599	10.263	5.269	2.444	2.826	2.538	3.766	2.727	5.533	6.530	5.547	4.102	4.720	4.263	4.344
4.253	5.473	12.405	6.265	2.698	3.136	2.808	3.678	2.926	8.788	30.524	9.092	4.801	4.889	4.809	5.045
4.802	6.280	13.972	7.150	3.001	3.534	3.144	4.244	3.296	16.847	22.960	17.041	5.559	5.422	5.492	6.102
5.449	6.592	14.278	7.536	3.442	4.075	3.615	4.195	3.680	11.430	11.558	11.514	5.794	5.220	5.584	5.907
6.014	7.371	13.843	8.204	3.805	4.559	4.020	4.192	4.012	13.024	15.271	13.146	6.597	5.585	6.238	6.614
6.976	7.913	13.807	8.790	4.140	4.964	4.376	4.321	4.328	10.875	12.539	10.975	7.280	6.196	6.895	7.120
7.673	8.358	13.717	9.535	4.548	5.466	4.819	4.294	4.692	8.788	8.910	8.852	7.912	6.477	7.405	7.488

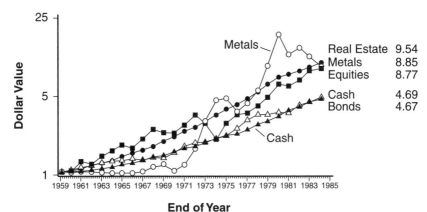

Figure 5.5. Cumulative Wealth Indices of World Capital Market Securities (Year-End 1959 = 1.00)

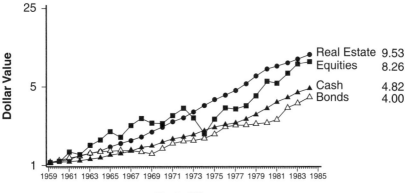

Figure 5.6. Cumulative Wealth Indices of U.S. Capital Market Securities (Year-End 1959 = 1.00)

These results collectively suggest that two factors—economy or market risk and inflation risk—are important in determining security returns. We proceed to investigate these influences by regression analysis.

Table 5.6 gives results for each of the excess return series regressed on the excess return series of the broader category in which the series appears. Each major category's excess return is then regressed on the excess return of the world market, excluding metals. Finally, the excess return of the world market, excluding metals, and the excess returns on metals are regressed on the excess return of the complete world market.

Table 5.4
World Capital Market Total Annual Returns, 1960–1984

	Compound Return	Arithmetic Mean	Standard Deviation		Compound Return	Arithmetic Mean	Standard Deviation
Equities				Cash equivalents			
United States				United States			
NYSE	8.71%	9.99%	16.30%	U.S. Treasury			
AMEX	7.28	9.95	23.49	bills	6.25%	6.29%	3.10%
OTC	11.47	13.88	22.42	Commercial			
United States total	8.81	10.20	16.89	paper	7.03	7.08	3.20
				U.S. Cash total	6.49	6.54	3.22
Foreign							
Europe	7.83	8.94	15.58	Foreign	6.00	6.23	7.10
Asia	15.14	18.42	30.74	Cash total	6.38	6.42	2.92
Other	8.14	10.21	20.88				
Foreign total	9.84	11.02	16.07	Real estate**			
				Business	8.49	8.57	4.16
Equities total	9.08	10.21	15.28	Residential	8.86	8.93	3.77
Bonds				Farms	11.86	12.13	7.88
United States				Real estate total	9.44	9.49	3.45
Corporate							
Intermediate-				Metals			
term	6.37	6.80	7.15	Gold	9.08	12.62	29.87
Long-term	5.03	5.58	11.26	Silver	9.14	20.51	75.34
Corporate				Metals total	9.11	12.63	29.69
total*	5.35	5.75	9.63				
Government				U.S. market wealth			
Treasury notes	6.32	6.44	5.27	portfolio	8.63	8.74	5.06
Treasury bonds	4.70	5.11	9.70				
U.S. agencies	6.88	7.04	6.15	Foreign market			
Government				wealth portfolio	7.76	8.09	8.48
total	5.91	6.10	6.43				
United States total	5.70	5.93	7.16	World market wealth			
				portfolio			
Foreign				Excluding metals	8.34	8.47	5.24
Corporate				Including metals	8.39	8.54	5.80
domestic	8.35	8.58	7.26				
Government				U.S. inflation rate	5.24	5.30	3.60
domestic	5.79	6.04	7.41				
Crossborder	7.51	7.66	5.76				
Foreign total	6.80	7.01	6.88				
Bonds total	6.36	6.50	5.56				

*Including preferred stock.
**United States only.

Table 5.4 (updated)
World Capital Market Total Annual Returns, 1976–2001

	Com-pound Return	Arith-metic Mean	Standard Deviation		Com-pound Return	Arith-metic Mean	Standard Deviation
Equities				Cash equivalents			
United States				United States			
NYSE	14.36	15.14	13.53	Treasury bills	6.73	6.77	2.79
NYSE/AMEX/				Commercial			
Nasdaq	14.12	15.10	14.99	paper	7.41	7.45	3.11
Foreign				Real estate			
Europe	13.31	14.90	20.17	Real estate	12.90	14.17	16.97
World excl.				Metals			
U.S.	11.68	13.45	20.51	Gold	2.65	5.52	29.27
World	12.54	13.60	15.42	Silver	0.42	10.94	74.47
Bonds				U.S. inflation rate			
United States				U.S. inflation			
Corporate				rate	4.55	4.60	3.14
Intermediate-							
term	9.45	9.65	6.86				
Long-term	9.96	10.54	11.88				
Corporate total	9.59	9.99	9.72				
Government							
Treasury notes	8.92	9.15	7.23				
Treasury bonds	9.61	10.33	13.02				
Agencies	9.12	9.31	6.54				
Government							
total	9.14	9.35	7.02				
Government/							
corporate	9.23	9.49	7.75				

Source: Equities (U.S.)—Center for Research in Security Prices, University of Chicago; Equities (Foreign)—Morgan Stanley Capital International; Bonds (U.S. Corporate)—Lehman Brothers; Bonds (U.S. Government)—Ibbotson Associates and Lehman Brothers; Cash (U.S.)—Ibbotson Associates and FED Commercial Paper; Real Estate—NAREIT; Metals—WSJ; U.S. Inflation Rate—Ibbotson Associates.

Excess returns in all cases are defined as the security return minus riskless (U.S. Treasury bill) return. Thus, in a market model context, the beta is a measure of the economy risk of the asset, and the R-square is a measure of the percent of the variance that is explained by the world market. The alpha expresses superior or inferior performance of an asset after adjusting for its beta on the world market.

The results show that world equities were a relatively poor performer, exhibiting a beta of 2.32 and an alpha of −1.14 relative to the total world market. Real estate and metals had positive alphas relative to the world market, while fixed-income securities accompanied equities with a negative alpha. Real estate also had a low beta, regressed on both the U.S. and world portfolios. Cash

Table 5.5
World Capital Market Security Returns Correlation Matrix

	NYSE	AMEX	OTC	U.S. Total Equities	Europe Equities	Asia Equities	Other Equities	Foreign Total Equities	World Equities	U.S. Treasury Notes	U.S. Treasury Bonds	U.S. Agencies	U.S. Total Gov't Bonds
NYSE	1.000												
AMEX	0.851	1.000											
OTC	0.900	0.897	1.000										
U.S. Equities	0.997	0.883	0.929	1.000									
Europe Equities	0.618	0.689	0.651	0.640	1.000								
Asia Equities	0.237	0.123	0.244	0.237	0.391	1.000							
Other Equities	0.792	0.848	0.766	0.807	0.731	0.320	1.000						
Foreign Equities	0.656	0.657	0.666	0.672	0.908	0.695	0.765	1.000					
World Total Equities	-0.955	0.879	0.914	0.964	0.787	0.409	0.853	0.841	1.000				
U.S. Treasury notes	0.105	0.091	-0.117	0.068	-0.159	-0.108	-0.252	-0.192	-0.037	1.000			
U.S. Treasury bonds	0.091	-0.153	-0.094	0.056	-0.130	-0.005	-0.266	-0.165	-0.041	0.904	1.000		
U.S. agencies	0.007	-0.201	-0.187	-0.030	-0.280	-0.178	-0.342	-0.327	-0.156	0.962	0.904	1.000	
U.S. total gov't bonds	0.033	-0.183	-0.189	-0.006	-0.201	-0.067	-0.296	-0.226	-0.105	0.972	0.950	0.964	1.000
U.S. intermediate-term corp. bonds	0.361	0.078	0.132	0.322	0.099	0.045	-0.028	0.072	0.242	0.900	0.865	0.848	0.887
U.S. long-term corp. bonds	0.341	0.058	0.110	0.302	0.095	0.022	-0.033	0.052	0.219	0.858	0.912	0.808	0.859
U.S. total corp. bonds	0.361	0.083	0.132	0.323	0.117	0.033	-0.019	0.075	0.243	0.865	0.902	0.809	0.863
U.S. total bonds	0.206	-0.047	-0.031	0.166	-0.045	-0.007	-0.160	-0.074	0.075	0.954	0.956	0.915	0.967
Foreign domestic corp. bonds	0.044	0.025	0.107	0.050	0.315	0.269	-0.028	0.314	0.156	0.035	0.172	-0.008	0.085
Foreign domestic gov't bonds	0.010	0.078	0.097	0.024	0.345	0.084	0.058	0.255	0.115	0.061	0.190	0.044	0.117
Foreign crossborder bonds	0.270	0.116	0.172	0.255	0.253	0.154	0.017	0.215	0.249	0.560	0.716	0.552	0.607
Foreign total bonds	0.042	0.067	0.112	0.052	0.343	0.153	0.028	0.281	0.144	0.097	0.239	0.072	0.153
World total bonds	0.136	0.035	0.069	0.124	0.248	0.122	-0.041	0.194	0.155	0.511	0.619	0.473	0.561

	U.S. Intermed. Corp. Bonds	U.S. Long Corp. Bonds	U.S. Total Corp. Bonds	U.S. Total Bonds	Foreign Corp. Bonds	Foreign Gov't Bonds	Cross-border Bonds	Foreign Total Bonds	World Total Bonds	Bus. Real Estate	Residential Structures	Farm Real Estate	Total U.S. Real Estate
U.S. business real estate	0.159	0.227	0.138	0.164	0.268	0.218	0.243	0.332	0.233	0.262	0.036	0.179	0.206
U.S. residential real estate	0.123	0.213	0.090	0.125	0.207	-0.080	0.356	0.141	0.133	0.068	-0.039	0.095	0.066
U.S. farm real estate	-0.164	-0.093	-0.223	-0.171	-0.097	-0.003	-0.063	-0.065	-0.139	-0.315	-0.256	-0.273	-0.267
U.S. real estate total	0.054	0.166	0.006	0.054	0.156	-0.033	0.288	0.129	0.083	-0.051	-0.138	-0.024	-0.040
U.S. Treasury bills	-0.055	-0.063	-0.160	-0.070	-0.169	-0.157	-0.101	-0.153	-0.114	0.395	0.111	0.328	0.325
U.S. commercial paper	-0.112	-0.130	-0.210	-0.127	-0.211	-0.176	-0.150	-0.199	-0.174	0.394	0.115	0.348	0.330
U.S. total cash	-0.064	-0.080	-0.170	-0.079	-0.178	-0.159	-0.112	-0.162	-0.125	0.400	0.119	0.340	0.332
Foreign total cash	-0.303	-0.355	-0.289	-0.386	-0.127	0.009	-0.270	-0.107	-0.311	-0.203	-0.183	-0.154	-0.143
World total cash	-0.225	-0.240	-0.284	-0.238	-0.212	-0.115	-0.225	-0.180	-0.242	0.270	0.032	0.237	0.236
Gold	-0.094	-0.024	-0.067	-0.088	0.032	0.046	0.140	0.044	-0.058	-0.277	-0.252	-0.178	-0.206
Silver	0.093	0.374	0.142	0.116	0.052	-0.181	0.410	-0.020	0.070	-0.131	-0.141	-0.064	-0.109
World total metals	-0.093	-0.011	-0.064	-0.086	0.032	0.036	0.152	0.039	-0.058	-0.279	-0.253	-0.177	-0.207
U.S. market wealth portfolio	0.915	0.837	0.831	0.917	0.605	0.209	0.754	0.626	0.886	0.214	0.162	0.139	0.152
Foreign market wealth portfolio	0.493	0.498	0.544	0.510	0.823	0.602	0.556	0.865	0.678	-0.086	0.021	-0.201	-0.083
World market wealth port. (w/o metals)	0.853	0.799	0.814	0.861	0.782	0.406	0.765	0.815	0.914	0.109	0.119	0.007	0.066
World market wealth port. (w/ metals)	0.747	0.723	0.727	0.757	0.706	0.351	0.753	0.732	0.805	-0.010	0.016	-0.059	-0.023
U.S. intermediate-term corp. bonds	1.000												
U.S. long-term corp. bonds	0.941	1.000											
U.S. total corp. bonds	0.960	0.996	1.000										
U.S. total bonds	0.956	0.956	0.962	1.000									

(continued)

Table 5.5 (*continued*)
World Capital Market Security Returns Correlation Matrix

	U.S. Intermed. Corp. Bonds	U.S. Long Corp. Bonds	U.S. Total Corp. Bonds	U.S. Total Bonds	Foreign Corp. Bonds	Foreign Gov't Bonds	Cross-border Bonds	Foreign Total Bonds	World Total Bonds	Bus. Real Estate	Residential Structures	Farm Real Estate	Total U.S. Real Estate
Foreign domestic corp. bonds	0.211	0.263	0.264	0.180	1.000								
Foreign domestic gov't bonds	0.203	0.269	0.266	0.192	0.890	1.000							
Foreign crossborder bonds	0.741	0.814	0.807	0.721	0.626	0.628	1.000						
Foreign total bonds	0.260	0.326	0.323	0.242	0.950	0.985	0.689	1.000					
World total bonds	0.635	0.693	0.692	0.646	0.829	0.860	0.866	0.895	1.000				
U.S. business real estate	0.335	0.107	0.152	0.192	0.165	0.249	0.203	0.228	0.256	1.000			
U.S. residential real estate	0.085	-0.039	-0.030	0.017	0.091	0.293	0.108	0.225	0.191	0.493	1.000		
U.S. farm real estate	-0.252	-0.255	-0.273	-0.274	0.176	0.103	0.049	0.125	-0.013	0.016	0.214	1.000	
U.S. real estate total	-0.004	-0.129	-0.123	-0.082	0.164	0.303	0.123	0.256	0.172	0.518	0.916	0.570	1.000
U.S. Treasury bills	0.336	0.094	0.135	0.244	-0.269	-0.224	-0.060	-0.240	-0.091	0.685	0.428	-0.053	0.389
U.S. commercial paper	0.313	0.070	0.108	0.230	-0.289	-0.232	-0.078	-0.254	-0.108	0.655	0.462	-0.040	0.415
U.S. total cash	0.339	0.096	0.136	0.247	-0.265	-0.217	-0.054	-0.234	-0.085	0.681	0.447	-0.046	0.405
Foreign total cash	-0.091	-0.225	-0.225	-0.192	0.616	0.617	0.101	0.608	0.393	0.231	0.317	0.306	0.399
World total cash	0.222	-0.005	0.029	0.141	0.048	0.080	0.007	0.065	0.106	0.705	0.528	0.096	0.529
Gold	-0.235	-0.316	-0.323	-0.280	0.001	0.107	-0.046	0.062	-0.079	0.219	0.586	0.517	0.684
Silver	-0.150	-0.177	-0.187	-0.153	-0.286	-0.054	-0.076	-0.136	-0.177	0.188	0.532	0.351	0.580
World total metals	-0.239	-0.318	-0.326	-0.282	-0.011	0.104	-0.047	0.056	-0.085	0.220	0.596	0.526	0.696
U.S. market wealth portfolio	0.446	0.367	0.393	0.284	0.153	0.171	0.395	0.191	0.288	0.394	0.422	-0.019	0.371

	U.S. Treasury Bills	U.S. Commercial Paper	U.S. Total Cash	Foreign Total Cash	World Total Cash	Gold	Silver	World Total Metals	U.S. Market Wealth Portfolio	Foreign Market Wealth Portfolio	World Market Wealth Portfolio	World Market Excl. Metals	World Market Incl. Metals
Foreign market wealth portfolio	0.192	0.221	0.236	0.080	0.723	0.687	0.517	0.718	0.603	0.329	0.174	-0.008	0.177
World market wealth port. (w/o metals)	0.390	0.354	0.377	0.231	0.431	0.428	0.504	0.455	0.571	0.407	0.365	-0.014	0.332
World market wealth port. (w/ metals)	0.238	0.193	0.207	0.093	0.380	0.426	0.404	0.429	0.389	0.390	0.552	0.133	0.531

	U.S. Treasury Bills	U.S. Commercial Paper	U.S. Total Cash	Foreign Total Cash	World Total Cash	Gold	Silver	World Total Metals	U.S. Market Wealth Portfolio	Foreign Market Wealth Portfolio	World Market Excl. Metals	World Market Incl. Metals
U.S. Treasury bills	1.000											
U.S. commercial paper	0.990	1.000										
U.S. total cash	0.999	0.995	1.000									
Foreign total cash	-0.008	0.033	0.010	1.000								
World total cash	0.881	0.895	0.891	0.460	1.000							
Gold	0.179	0.256	0.210	0.419	0.366	1.000						
Silver	0.125	0.127	0.123	-0.203	-0.014	0.438	1.000					
World total metals	0.177	0.253	0.207	0.401	0.355	0.999	0.477	1.000				
U.S. market wealth portfolio	0.133	0.088	0.130	-0.233	0.013	0.104	0.291	0.111	1.000			
Foreign market wealth portfolio	-0.254	-0.298	-0.258	0.218	-0.122	0.025	-0.110	0.018	0.533	1.000		
World market wealth port. (w/o metals)	-0.033	-0.083	-0.037	-0.059	-0.053	0.075	0.142	0.077	0.925	0.812	1.000	
World market wealth port. (w/ metals)	-0.014	-0.027	-0.004	0.105	0.046	0.427	0.283	0.427	0.873	0.727	0.924	1.000

Table 5.6

Regression Results for Major Asset Class Returns in Excess of United States Treasury Bill Rates

Dependent Variable	Independent Variable	Alpha (%)	Alpha T-Statistic	Beta	Beta T-Statistic	Adjusted R^2	Standard Deviation of Residuals	1st Order Autocorr. of Residuals
U.S. equities								
NYSE	U.S. equities	−0.06	−0.22	0.96	63.54	0.994	1.32	0.04
AMEX	U.S. equities	−1.10	−0.47	1.22	9.18	0.776	11.54	0.13
OTC	U.S. equities	2.73	1.56	1.24	12.70	0.870	8.51	−0.05
U.S. total equities	World equities	−0.22	−0.23	1.05	17.80	0.929	4.72	−0.05
Europe equities	Foreign equities	−1.57	−1.10	0.89	10.96	0.832	6.85	−0.48
Asia equities	Foreign equities	5.85	1.22	1.32	4.85	0.484	23.00	−0.15
Other equities	Foreign equities	−0.76	−0.26	0.99	5.95	0.589	14.02	−0.06
Foreign equities	World equities	1.19	0.64	0.90	7.90	0.719	9.10	−0.00
World equities	World wealth excl. metals	−1.14	−0.74	2.32	9.98	0.804	7.19	0.26
U.S. corporate bonds	U.S. total bonds	−0.05	−0.10	1.33	18.35	0.933	2.56	−0.28
U.S. government bonds	U.S. total bonds	0.12	0.36	0.84	18.61	0.935	1.60	−0.28
U.S. total bonds	World total bonds	−0.52	−0.47	0.72	4.37	0.430	5.46	0.20
Foreign corporate bonds	Foreign total bonds	1.56	3.31	1.02	17.70	0.929	2.35	−0.08
Foreign government bonds	Foreign total bonds	−1.00	−3.66	1.04	31.37	0.976	1.36	0.08
Crossborder bonds	Foreign total bonds	0.91	1.04	0.64	6.07	0.599	4.33	0.12
Foreign total bonds	World total bonds	0.47	0.77	1.16	12.42	0.865	3.08	0.10
World total bonds	World wealth excl. metals	−1.24	−1.08	0.67	3.82	0.362	5.39	0.17
U.S. cash	World cash	0.25	6.22	0.02	0.66	−0.024	0.20	0.26
Foreign cash	World cash	−0.73	−2.94	5.20	31.13	0.976	1.23	−0.26

World cash	World wealth excl. metals	0.05	0.16	0.04	0.72	−0.021	1.52	0.03
U.S. business real estate	U.S. real estate	1.30	1.65	0.31	1.89	0.097	2.95	0.20
U.S. residential real estate	U.S. real estate	−0.36	−0.87	0.94	10.94	0.832	1.55	0.11
U.S. farm real estate	U.S. real estate	0.44	0.26	1.68	4.84	0.483	6.33	0.18
U.S. real estate	World wealth excl. metals	2.52	3.71	0.31	3.03	0.254	3.20	0.57
U.S. equities	U.S. market wealth	−3.17	−2.10	2.88	11.62	0.848	6.91	0.35
U.S. bonds	U.S. market wealth	−1.34	−0.88	0.40	1.59	0.060	7.00	0.12
U.S. cash	U.S. market wealth	0.28	6.58	−0.01	−1.49	0.048	0.19	0.00
U.S. real estate	U.S. market wealth	2.42	3.35	0.32	2.67	0.203	3.31	0.62
U.S. market wealth	World wealth excl. metals	0.60	1.51	0.85	14.20	0.893	1.86	−0.06
Foreign equities	Foreign market wealth	2.05	1.14	1.50	8.27	0.737	8.80	0.06
Foreign total bonds	Foreign market wealth	−0.48	−0.46	0.67	6.24	0.612	5.21	0.09
Foreign cash	Foreign market wealth	−0.62	−0.41	0.31	2.04	0.116	7.45	0.05
Foreign market wealth	World wealth excl. metals	−1.22	−1.19	1.38	8.87	0.764	4.83	−0.08
World wealth excl. metals	World wealth incl. metals	0.19	0.43	0.88	13.49	0.883	2.16	0.14
Gold	Metals	−0.04	−0.14	1.00	103.02	0.998	1.43	−0.42
Silver	Metals	6.61	0.47	1.20	2.55	0.186	69.07	−0.37
Metals	World wealth incl. metals	2.89	0.48	1.53	1.77	0.082	28.66	0.39

Table 5.7

Capital Market Returns Regressed on U.S. Inflation

Dependent Variable	Independent Variable	Alpha (%)	Alpha T-Statistic	Beta	Beta T-Statistic	Adjusted R^2	Standard Deviation of Residuals	1st Order Autocorr. of Residuals
U.S. equities	U.S. Inflation							
NYSE	"	14.22	2.39	−0.80	−0.86	−0.011	16.73	−0.11
AMEX	"	10.94	1.26	−0.18	−0.14	−0.043	24.48	0.13
OTC	"	20.43	2.51	−1.24	−0.97	−0.002	22.91	−0.07
U.S. total equities	"	14.50	2.35	−0.81	−0.84	−0.012	17.34	−0.09
Europe equities	"	10.76	1.87	−0.34	−0.38	−0.037	16.19	−0.21
Asia equities	"	24.75	2.19	−1.19	−0.68	−0.023	31.73	−0.07
Other equities	"	9.06	1.17	0.22	0.18	−0.042	21.75	−0.04
Foreign equities	"	12.95	2.18	−0.36	−0.39	−0.037	16.70	−0.08
World equities	"	13.75	2.46	−0.67	−0.76	−0.018	15.73	−0.10
U.S. corporate bonds								
U.S. intermediate term	"	7.45	2.82	−0.16	−0.39	−0.037	7.43	0.37
U.S. long term	"	10.42	2.61	−0.91	−1.46	0.046	11.23	0.18
U.S. total corporate bonds	"	9.49	2.75	−0.70	−1.31	0.029	9.69	0.26
U.S. government bonds								
U.S. treasury notes	"	6.72	3.44	−0.05	−0.18	−0.042	5.49	0.15
U.S. treasury bonds	"	8.59	2.46	−0.66	−1.21	0.019	9.81	−0.01
U.S. agencies	"	7.33	3.22	−0.05	−0.15	−0.042	6.40	0.05
U.S. total government bonds	"	6.58	2.76	−0.09	−0.24	−0.041	6.70	0.14
U.S. total bonds	"	7.56	2.88	−0.31	−0.75	−0.018	7.38	0.22

Foreign corporate bonds	"	9.37	3.49	−0.15	−0.35	−0.038	7.55	0.35
Foreign government bonds	"	5.86	2.13	0.03	0.08	−0.043	7.72	0.27
Crossborder bonds	"	8.84	4.18	−0.22	−0.68	−0.023	5.95	0.28
Foreign total bonds	"	7.30	2.86	−0.05	−0.14	−0.043	7.17	0.31
World total bonds	"	7.28	3.55	−0.15	−0.46	−0.034	5.77	0.28
U.S. cash								
U.S. Treasury bills	"	3.11	3.77	0.60	4.66	0.464	2.32	0.74
U.S. commercial paper	"	3.63	4.48	0.65	5.14	0.514	2.28	0.74
U.S. total cash	"	3.18	3.78	0.63	4.83	0.482	2.36	0.75
Foreign cash	"	2.37	0.97	0.73	1.91	0.099	6.88	−0.01
World cash	"	3.05	4.52	0.63	6.02	0.595	1.90	0.39
U.S. business real estate	"	5.08	4.01	0.66	3.33	0.296	3.56	0.44
U.S. residential real estate	"	4.61	5.26	0.81	5.94	0.588	2.47	−0.08
U.S. farm real estate	"	7.18	2.72	0.93	2.26	0.146	7.43	0.46
U.S. real estate	"	5.23	7.53	0.80	7.42	0.693	1.95	0.13
Gold	"	−15.97	−1.90	5.39	4.11	0.398	23.65	0.03
Silver	"	−25.73	−1.01	8.72	2.20	0.138	71.39	−0.19
Metals	"	−15.96	−1.92	5.39	4.15	0.404	23.40	0.06
U.S. market wealth	"	7.88	4.23	0.16	0.56	−0.030	5.24	−0.09
Foreign market wealth	"	9.59	3.07	−0.28	−0.58	−0.028	8.77	0.14
World wealth excl. metals	"	8.32	4.28	0.03	0.09	−0.043	5.47	−0.00
World wealth incl. metals	"	6.71	3.19	0.35	1.06	0.005	5.90	−0.17

had a low alpha and essentially a zero beta. On a beta-adjusted basis, the U.S. market wealth portfolio outperformed the foreign market wealth portfolio.

Inflation appears to be the remaining factor that may describe the series. Table 5.7 presents the results of each of the return series regressed against U.S. inflation rates. A beta of one indicates that nominal returns on the asset fully impound inflation; a zero beta indicates that inflation has no effect on the nominal asset return.

Almost all categories of equities and bonds had negative betas when regressed on inflation; that is, higher inflation rates seemed to hurt returns on these assets and lower inflation rates helped. The beta T-statistics for these assets did not, however, support a statistically significant relationship. Cash and real estate had betas below but near one when regressed on inflation, with high T-statistics indicating that these assets are inflation hedges, although imperfectly so. Metals are extremely responsive to inflation, with a small rise in inflation producing a large rise in metals prices and vice versa.

◣ Notes

1. Ibbotson and Fall (1979); Ibbotson and Siegel (1983).
2. See Ibbotson and Siegel (1984) for a full discussion of the difficulties in measuring the riskiness of real estate returns.

◣ Sources

Capital International Perspective. Geneva, Switzerland: Capital International, S.A., 1959–1984.

CRSP Monthly Stock Returns File. Machine-readable tape published by Center for Research in Security Prices (CRSP) [sponsored by Merrill, Lynch, Pierce, Fenner & Smith], Graduate School of Business, University of Chicago, annual; 1985 and earlier.

Federal Reserve Bulletin. Washington, D.C.: Board of Governors of the Federal Reserve System, January 1960–1984.

Financial Statistics: Part I. Paris: Organization for Economic Cooperation and Development, 1970–1984.

Flow of Funds Accounts. Washington, D.C.: Board of Governors of the Federal Reserve System, selected issues.

Government Finance Statistics Yearbook. Washington, D.C.: International Monetary Fund, 1959–1984.

Ibbotson, Roger G., Richard C. Carr, and Anthony W. Robinson. "International Equity and Bond Returns." *Financial Analysts Journal,* July/August 1982.

Ibbotson, Roger G., and Carol L. Fall. "The U.S. Market Wealth Portfolio." *The Journal of Portfolio Management,* Fall 1979.

Ibbotson, Roger G. and Laurence B. Siegel. "Real Estate Returns: A Comparison With Other Investments." *American Real Estate & Urban Economics Association Journal,* Fall 1984.

————. "The world market wealth portfolio." *The Journal of Portfolio Management,* Winter 1983.

Interest Rates 1960–1974. Paris: Organization for Economic Cooperation and Development, 1975.

The Lehman Brothers Kuhn Loeb Bond Index. New York: Shearson Lehman American Express (formerly Lehman Brothers Kuhn Loeb), 1984.

Moody's Public Utility Manual. New York: Moody's Investors Service, annual; 1985 and earlier.

NASDAQ-OTC Market Factbook. Washington, D.C.: National Association of Securities Dealers, selected issues.

Outlook and Situation Summary: Agricultural Land Values, U.S. Department of Agriculture, Economic Research Service, June 7, 1985.

Stocks, Bonds, Bills, and Inflation: 1985 Yearbook, Ibbotson Associates, Chicago, 1984. (Earlier editions published as Roger G. Ibbotson and Rex A. Sinquefield, *Stocks, Bonds, Bills, and Inflation: The Past and the Future,* 1982; also 1979, 1977 [titles vary]; Financial Analysts Research Foundation, Charlottesville, Va.)

The Wall Street Journal. Dow Jones and Company, New York: selected issues.

Demand, Supply, and Building Block Forecasting Methods

▮▮

The equity premium is not a magic number; it is, in part, a function of the demand and supply of capital in the economy. In equilibrium, it must also be structurally related to the expected returns of other assets. It should be lower than the premium for smaller, riskier equity classes, for instance, but higher than the premium for risk-free long-term bonds. The first article in this section exploits this equilibrium concept to develop a simple but powerful approach to forecasting asset class returns. The method is applied in various forms throughout this book.

Next come four articles that take alternative routes to estimating the equity risk premium. Based on both demand and supply perspectives, the articles differ from the historical approach, relying instead upon economic arguments about the magnitude of the premium. Nevertheless, they depend on the equilibrium logic of the reward for accepting equity risk. These alternative approaches are particularly useful when there are structural changes in the economy and financial markets. For example, when investors prefer capital gains over dividends, the relationship between dividend yields and expected future equity returns will change.

▶ Building Blocks

One widespread application of the equity risk premium is in the estimation of expected rates of return for asset classes and individual assets. The idea is a simple one. In equilibrium, the assets should be priced correctly relative to each other. Thus, the equity premium serves as a benchmark for calculating the expected return, or discount rate, or cost of capital for many different assets. The first article in this section develops a method to combine risk premia to make a forecast of asset class returns. Ibbotson and Siegel (1988) show how the component parts of asset returns—the premia for inflation risk, default risk, horizon risk, and equity risk, when statistically independent of each other, may be simply added up to calculate the expected return. This approach is often called the "building blocks method"—or, in the appraisal literature, the "buildup method." Ibbotson Associates' *Stocks, Bonds, Bills, and Inflation Valuation Edition 2005 Yearbook* devotes a full chapter to the approach, and it is becoming by far the most widely used tool in the appraisal community for determining the discount rate used to discount the cash flows in the valuation of companies.

By simply adding components that can be reliably estimated, the building block method avoids estimation problems that often lead to problematic values for the expected returns to individual securities. In particular, the approach avoids estimation of factors and factor exposures as in the capital asset pricing model (CAPM) or arbitrage pricing theory (APT). It also differs from the classic discounted cash flow (DCF) method, because it sums risk premia, not the growth and income components of expected returns. The components included are as follows:

Cash
    Inflation
    Real riskless rate
Bonds
    Inflation
    Real riskless rate
    Horizon premium
    Default premium
Stocks
    Inflation
    Real riskless rate
    Horizon premium (if base is a long-term yield)
    Equity risk premium
    Small stock premium

The method is flexible. We can add other premia for real estate, for foreign stocks, for lack of marketability, and so forth. Not all of these components have to be treated separately. For example, the observed long-term yield on a government bond might include inflation, the real riskless rate, and the horizon premium. Most of the other methods we now discuss are ways of estimating or interpreting the premia from this building block approach. Thus, this method does not really compete with other approaches to estimating the equity premium, but rather provides a structural framework for assembling the relevant component parts.

◤ *Equity Risk Premium Estimation Methods*

In general, we can classify methods of estimating the equity risk premium into the following four categories:

1. Extrapolating historical risk premia (the "historical approach")
2. Evaluating investors' demand or willingness to take risk (the "demand approach")
3. Extrapolating from history the supply of earnings or cash flows that firms or the economy are likely to produce (the "supply approach")
4. Asking investors to provide their consensus forecasts (the "consensus approach")

The previous section, "The Lessons of History," already discussed the first method. In the historical approach, we collect the historical returns and risk premia, look for predictability, and, usually assuming i.i.d. and constant risk premia, we extrapolate the past into the future.

The consensus method is not really analyzed in this book, as we have not written any articles on the subject. The idea of the method is to survey investors to see what they think the equity risk premium is. The theoretical foundation of this approach is that investors make up the market and thus that their views are important. Whatever investors believe about expected returns should be impounded into the price of stocks, and implicitly into the discount rate at which the expected cash flows are valued.

There are only a few published surveys of investors. The Yale School of Management maintains an investor survey developed by Professor Robert Shiller. This survey has asked investors about their expectations for the stock market for nearly 20 years. Welch (2000, 2001;[1] references are supplied in "Suggested Reading" except where noted otherwise) has a published article and an updated working paper surveying financial economists, who may not be important investors but are likely to be influential. Their arithmetic mean equity risk premium is in line with the Ibbotson and Chen article discussed later. Graham and Harvey (2002) survey corporate chief financial officers (CFOs), and their results are also roughly in line with Ibbotson and Chen. The firm Greenwich Research surveys institutional investors each year, and their estimates of the equity risk premium tend to be substantially lower than these estimates. Other researchers and institutions from time to time have surveyed the expectations of individual investors, and they tend to have higher estimates of expected returns.

Demand Methods

The CAPM and APT model are essentially demand theories. They argue that investors are risk averse and would require a positive equity risk premium to induce them to buy stocks instead of risk free bonds or cash. The CAPM provides an equilibrium for the market portfolio, so that only systematic or market risk is priced. The APT model adds multiple risk factors, but the presumption is that the market participants are averse to each risk category. The models themselves do not, however, provide any direct way of estimating the equity risk premium.

Mehra and Prescott (1985) is the seminal paper on the demand approach. They examine the risk-aversion parameter in investors' utility curves, and suggest that the risk aversion would have to be implausibly high to match the high realized equity risk premia. They call this discrepancy the "equity premium puzzle." The work of Mehra and Prescott precipitated a large body of research, much of it (including their own later work) seeking to reconcile historical equity risk premia with investor risk aversion. Ultimately, the recent behavioral finance literature seems to suggest that investor risk aversion is a rather complicated process, perhaps too complex to be captured by static utility curves.

The Ibbotson, Siegel, and Diermeier article included in this section gives a general framework for considering investors' demand for various assets. In particular, it argues that investors are averse not only to systematic risk, but also to unsystematic risk in various guises, including differential forms of taxation on various assets, transaction costs, information and search costs, and even nonpecuniary benefits of holding various asset classes. All these asset characteristics would go into forming a risk premium for each asset class, and simple models like CAPM and APT are likely to leave out the important pricing criteria, especially as we move away from the large cap stock market. For example, real estate has a relatively low stock market beta, but is more likely to be priced by its tax advantages, lack of marketability, difficulty in forming diversified portfolios, high costs of search and evaluation, and frequent need for the direct management involvement of the investor. The off-the-run bond pricing anomaly is likewise simply explained by this model.

Supply Methods

The basic supply models use dividends, earnings, book values, gross domestic product (GDP) growth, and other economic factors to forecast markets. The simplest supply model is the one-factor Gordon (1962) DCF model. In this analysis, the dividend yield is added to a constant predicted growth in dividends to forecast the expected return. The Equity Risk Premium (ERP) in the DCF model is found simply by subtracting out the riskless rate.

One of the first supply models to look at the GDP in *aggregate* is the Diermeier, Ibbotson, and Siegel (1984) article. It assumes constant factor shares in the economy, so that the capital market remains a constant share of economy before adjusting for capital issuance and interest and dividend payouts. The paper then uses a DCF model to forecast overall capital market returns. The specific risk premia of stocks (the equity risk premium) is not directly forecast. Instead, the returns of firms (stocks plus bonds) are forecast. There has developed a large literature estimating the ERP from the supply-side perspective. This literature includes Shiller (2000), Siegel (1999), Fama and French (2002), Kathari and Shanken (2002), Arnott and Ryan (2001), and Arnott and Bernstein (2002). Much of this literature estimates an ERP that is lower than historical ERP estimates.

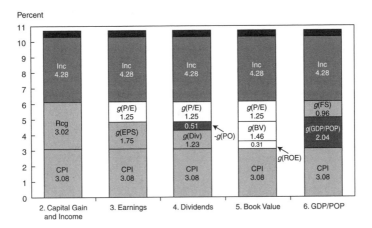

Figure 1. Decomposition of Historical Equity Returns, 1926–2000

Notes: The g(PO) is the growth rate of the dividend payout ratio; g(Div) is the growth rate of the dividend; g(BV) is the growth rate of book value; g(ROE) is the growth rate of return on book equity; g(FS) is the growth rate of equity factor share; and g(GDP/POP) is the growth rate of GDP per capita.

The Ibbotson and Chen (2003) article breaks the stock market realized return into various components. It shows, for example, that historical stock market returns have a direct link to the underlying corporate earning power and the growth of the economy.

Figure 1 shows the basic result. The historical equity premium may be decomposed in a variety of ways—into building blocks based on growth in rates of return on equity, growth in the dividend payout ratio, growth in the book value of equities, or growth in GDP per capita. These equivalencies underscore the fact that the best forecast is one that uses components that can best be forecast or estimated. Components that have grown in the past may not be expected to grow in the future. For example, when Ibbotson and Chen make their forecasts, the historical increase in the PE ratio is removed, giving a forecast that is 1.25% per year lower than if we strictly applied to historical method from Ibbotson and Sinquefield. Nevertheless, the Ibbotson and Chen supply-side forecasts are much closer to the Ibbotson and Sinquefield forecasts than to those of many of the other supply-side writers.

Ibbotson and Chen are able to reconcile the differences between their work and that of the other authors, however. Most other writers mix the current low dividend observed in the stock market (about 1.1%) with historical growth in dividends or earnings. Much of today's low dividend yield reflects the decline in payout ratios, which over the last 75 years have dropped from about 60% to 30%. We know from Miller and Modigliani (1962) that lower payout ratios imply more retention and higher expected earnings growth. This higher expected earnings growth should fully offset the lower payouts. Furthermore, Ibbotson and Chen argue that the current high PE ratios indicate that the market is forecasting higher earnings growth. These factors, taken together, give a stock market equity risk premium that is only 1.25% lower than the historically realized equity risk premium.

6

Roger Ibbotson and Larry Siegel

How to Forecast Long-Run Asset Returns

▶ *Overview*

This article shows how to use components to estimate an expected return for various asset classes, including stocks, bonds, cash, real estate, small stocks, foreign stocks, and foreign bonds. In principle, these components can be used to estimate expected returns on any asset class.

The method is simple and has come to be known as the "buildup method" in the valuation literature. The basis of all buildups is shown in Figure 6.1. The starting point of most analyses is the riskless rate, which includes inflation and real interest rates, and usually the bond horizon premium. This riskless rate is usually observable from the U.S. government bond yield curve.

The valuation community usually uses the buildup to estimate the cost of capital, which is in turn used to discount cash flows to estimate a present value. Included in this article is an updated sample forecast.

Of the many kinds of asset allocation models in use, perhaps the most common is that which uses historical and current data to form long-term equilibrium capital market expectations. These expectations are combined with an analysis of the liabilities of the investor (typically a pension fund). The output consists of policy, or normal, weights for asset classes held or desired to be held by the investor.

This article shows how to use historical and current data to form expectations.

Asset allocation models require as inputs three kinds of data for each asset class:

- expected or forecast return;
- expected standard deviation or returns; and
- expected correlations of returns with the returns on all other asset classes.

This list of required inputs also applies to tactical asset allocation models and other variations on the theme of setting asset class weights. In tactical models, however, the expected return is typically a short-term forecast that differs from the long-run equilibrium return. The forecasts of standard deviation and correlations may also differ from long-run equilibrium in tactical models. This article focuses on the policy or strategic, rather than the tactical, situation.

175

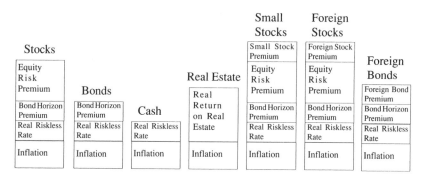

Figure 6.1. The Component Parts of Asset Expected Returns

First, we will focus on estimating, or forecasting, the expected return and standard deviation for the U.S. equity market, the most important asset class for many investors. Later, the forecast method is extended to the other principal asset classes: bonds, cash, real estate, small stocks, and foreign securities. Correlations of asset returns are treated last because they depend on an understanding of all of the asset classes.

The return on an asset may be thought of as the sum of the returns on its component or elemental parts.[1] This makes forecasting much easier. Figure 6.1 shows the components of the total returns on various assets.

The return on the stock market, for example, consists of the *riskless rate* (modeled as the yield on a Treasury bond), plus the equity return in excess of the Treasury yield, or *equity risk premium.* (As shown in Figure 6.1, the riskless rate is itself the sum of components, but it is not necessary to analyze these subparts in forecasting stock returns.) The riskless rate and the equity risk premium behave in very different ways.

The yield on a Treasury bond is observable in the market; you can look it up in the newspaper. This yield is riskless for the investor whose future holding period, or horizon, is equal to the bond's term to maturity.[2] We can take the Treasury yield directly as the forecast of the riskless part of the stock market's return.

The equity risk premium, on the other hand, is practically a random walk.[3] On a yearly basis, equity risk premia—the excess of stock total returns over Treasury bond yields—varied in a range of +50 to −45% in the last 62 years, and may be expected to continue to do so. These wide swings are the source of risk in the stock market; but risk will be treated later. Here, we are forecasting return. A reasonable forecast of next period's equity risk premium is the historical average.

Let us, then, forecast the return on the stock market. The riskless rate in July 1988, as indicated by 20-year Treasury bonds, was 9.0%. The historical

Table 6.1
Buildup Method Cost of Equity Estimate for a Small Company Stock: Current Data,
Updated to Year-End 2002; Sample Forecast

Component	Arithmetic Mean Estimate (%)
Riskless rate	4.8
Equity risk premium	7.0
Size premium	1.5
Cost of equity estimate	13.3

Source: Stocks, Bonds, Bills, and Inflation 2002 Yearbook Valuation Edition, Ibbotson Associates, Chicago, 2003. All rights reserved. Used with permission.

(1926–1987) arithmetic average equity risk premium is 6.8%. The sum of these two components is 15.8%, which is the expected one-year return on the stock market over each of the next 20 years. This compounds to a geometric mean return, or compound annual growth rate, of 13.9%.[4]

In this forecast, we use a 20-year Treasury bond, and the average excess return of stocks over 20-year bonds. This gives a very long-term forecast, roughly corresponding to the typical interval between a pension fund contribution and the associated payout. However, this forecasting method may be adapted to any planning horizon by using a bond with a maturity equal to the horizon desired.

▶ Standard Deviation of Returns

To forecast an asset's risk (the standard deviation of the asset's returns), we project forward the historical standard deviation of the asset's returns, using judgment to pick the relevant historical period. One way to forecast the standard deviation is to use a long historical period. (See Table 6.2.)

For the stock market, the longest period for which reliable data are available is 1926 to the present. The standard deviation of annual returns over this 62-year period is 21.1%. In recent years, annual returns have become more stable, but that does not necessarily justify using a shorter period.

In 1987, for example, the stock market returned 5.2%, a subpar but not unusual performance. The annual number hides the fact that the market soared, then crashed. The standard deviation of monthly returns in 1987, stated in annualized terms, was 29%.

In our view, there is no reason to believe stocks have become less volatile, and consequently no reason to ignore data from the volatile 1920s and 1930s. A sensible forecast of the standard deviation of stock returns is 21%.

The risk of the bond market, unlike that of the stock market, has clearly changed over time. As we will see next, this observation does justify the use of a more restricted period for estimating risk.

Table 6.2
Summary Statistics of Long-Run Asset Total Annual Returns

Asset Class	Time Period	Arith. Mean (%)	Geo. Mean (%)	Standard Dev. (%)
Stocks (S&P 500)	1926–1987	12.0	9.9	21.1
Long-term government bonds	1926–1987	4.6	4.3	8.5
Intermediate government bonds	1926–1987	4.9	4.8	5.5
U.S. Treasury bills	1926–1987	3.5	3.5	3.4
Real estate	1971–1987	12.2	12.1	4.1
Small stocks	1926–1987	17.7	12.1	35.9
Foreign stocks	1960–1987	14.9	13.2	20.1
Foreign bonds	1960–1987	9.1	8.7	10.1
Inflation	1926–1987	3.2	3.0	4.8

Note: Statistics are shown for the longest time period for which data are available. Selected statistics over other periods are provided in the text of this article.
Sources: Stocks, Bonds, Bills, and Inflation 1988 Yearbook, Ibbotson Associates, Chicago, 1988, Institutional Property Consultants, San Diego; Ibbotson Associates' *I/IDEAS.*

▶ Bonds

The expected return on a bond or bond portfolio is closely approximated by its yield to maturity. While the bond expected return has several components, they are all more difficult to forecast than the yield, which is directly observable.

The risk of bonds, or standard deviation of their total returns, has changed dramatically over time. Starting in the late 1960s, and accelerating in the 1970s, bond risk has risen to an unprecedented level. The most volatile period for bonds has been from 1979 to the present. For estimating future year-by-year bond risk, a reasonable forecast is the 20-year historical standard deviation of bond returns, which is 12.5% for long issues and 7.3% for intermediate issues.

Investors with long holding periods will often find the year-by-year standard deviation of bond returns to be inapplicable. For example, an investor who wishes to match a liability 20 years in the future with a corresponding asset will find 20-year, zero-coupon Treasury bonds to be riskless. Cash is risky to such an investor because its yield fluctuates. Thus it is necessary to take the anticipated holding period into account when estimating the riskiness of fixed-income investments.

▶ Cash

The yield on a cash instrument is its expected return over the short life of the instrument. Over longer periods, however, a forecast method is required.

Referring to Figure 6.1, the expected return from rolling over cash in-struments over a long period is equal to the expected return (or yield) on a long-term bond, minus the bond's horizon (maturity) premium. This pre-mium is relatively stable over time and has been estimated at 1.5%.[5] Thus one would subtract 1.5% from the yield on a bond to arrive at the expected return on cash.

The standard deviation of cash returns, like that of bonds, is dependent on the holding period or planning horizon of the investor. Cash returns have no risk over the maturity of the cash instrument being held (presuming free-dom from default, as in a Treasury bill). Over long horizons, cash is risky. The year-by-year historical standard deviation of cash returns over the past 20 years is 2.7%. This measurement reflects the large changes in the levels of short-term interest rates that occurred over 1968 to the present, and should be adjusted downward for the short horizon (say, one-year) investor.

▶ Real Estate

The capital appreciation return on real estate is closely related to inflation, while the income return is relatively constant. Historically, real estate total re-turns have exceeded inflation by about 5.3% per year. Thus, real estate total returns may be forecasted as the anticipated inflation rate plus 5.3%.

Unfortunately, inflation forecasts are not observed in the market. One way to use market information to obtain a long-term inflation forecast is by disaggregating the yield on a long-term bond. Anticipated inflation is modeled as the bond yield, minus the expected real riskless rate (about 1%),[6] minus the bond maturity premium (noted earlier as 1.5%).

The real estate total return forecast, then, is derived from the yield on a long-term bond by adding 2.8%. This latter number is the real (inflation-adjusted) total return on real estate, minus the expected real riskless rate and maturity premium.

The standard deviation of historical real estate total returns is approxi-mately 4%. This number understates the risk of real estate considerably, be-cause the returns are smoothed (made less variable) by the appraisal process used to construct real estate returns. To make the standard deviation compa-rable to that of more liquid assets such as stocks, bonds, and cash, it should be at least doubled.

The justification for this adjustment goes beyond the observation that real estate returns are constructed from smoothed appraisals. Asset allocation in-puts that are intended to characterize long-run capital market equilibrium should be consistent with capital market theory. An asset that has a much higher return than other assets, for its level of risk, should be examined very critically. Such an asset probably has either hidden risks (as we saw for real es-tate), or hidden costs which decrement the expected return. On the other hand, real estate may have high returns for its level of true risk because it is not very liquid, and has high transaction costs, for which the investor expects to be compensated.

◣ Small Stocks

Small capitalization stocks have historically returned more than large stocks. The historical difference, called the small stock premium, had an arithmetic mean of 3.7% over 1926–1987. This compounded to an annual return advantage over large stocks of 2%.[7]

The small stock premium has been highly variable, even turning negative for long periods (including mid 1983 to late 1987). Thus a short-term forecast of the small stock premium should take into account the recent behavior of this premium. However, in forming a long run forecast, it is reasonable to use the historical average. This number is added to the forecasted return on the stock market as a whole.

The standard deviation of small stocks was 35.9% over 1926–1987. This is a reasonable forecast of the future standard deviation of a small stock portfolio.

◣ Foreign Securities

Foreign stocks have exhibited a return premium over U.S. stocks, averaging 4.3% per year. The period examined, 1960–1987, may have been unusually favorable for foreign stocks and it is reasonable to forecast a smaller premium in the future. This premium is added to the forecasted total return on U.S. stocks.

The standard deviation of foreign stocks over 1960–1987 was 20.1%; that is, they were somewhat more risky than U.S. stocks, which had a standard deviation of 16% over the same period. Thus the foreign stock premium may be regarded as a compensation for risk. In the future, foreign stocks may continue to have slightly more risk than U.S. stocks.

Foreign bonds also outperformed those in the U.S., with an average annual premium of 2.3% over U.S. bonds in 1960–1987. As with foreign stocks, a smaller premium is likely to prevail in the future. The standard deviation of foreign bond returns was 10.1%, representing a 10-year portfolio. This was slightly higher than the risk level of 10-year bonds in the U.S., so that risk as well as return can be expected to be higher for foreign bonds.

◣ Nontraditional Assets

Expected returns on nontraditional assets such as venture capital and monetary metals are related to the unusual characteristics of these assets.

For example, gold is a reliable store of value during hyperinflations and wars, and may be regarded as a form of insurance. Like other kinds of insurance, gold probably has a negative expected return after accounting for storage and other costs. Nevertheless, it has a place in some portfolios because it reduces the risk of holding other assets.

The risk of venture capital is difficult to measure but is known to be very high; it should be regarded as an extremely risky equity holding with a commensurately high expected return.

◣ Correlation: Stocks and Bonds

The correlation of two asset returns is a measure of the degree to which the assets move together. Assets with a correlation of one are perfectly correlated: they move in lock step. Assets with a zero correlation have unrelated returns. Assets with negative correlation move opposite one another.

We focus on the correlation between stocks and bonds because these are the asset classes of greatest importance to most investors. The principles applied in forecasting this correlation apply to forecasting other asset-pair correlations as well.

Stocks have had periods of high and low correlation with bonds. Over 1926–1987, the stock-bond correlation was approximately 0.1 (see Table 6.3), but ranged as high as 0.8 (nearly perfect correlation) in parts of the 1980s. Thus the correlation between stocks and bonds is unstable and difficult to forecast.

A possible forecast method is to use a historical period that is shorter than the 62 years for which data are available, but long enough to capture several market cycles. Over the last two decades, for example, the correlation between stocks and bonds was 0.3.

◣ Other Asset Pairs

A similar approach applies to forecasting the correlation of any asset with any other. Fortunately, not all asset relationships have been as turbulent as that between stocks and bonds. For example, the correlation between stocks and cash has remained near zero.

The correlation of stocks in the U.S. with those abroad has followed an interesting pattern. Japanese stocks have always been quite independent of U.S. stocks, but they have only recently come to make up the lion's share of foreign equity capitalization. Other (primarily European) stocks have higher correlations with the U.S. market. Thus as the weight of Japan in foreign stock portfolios has risen, the correlation between U.S. and foreign portfolios has declined. On the other hand, as the Japanese market becomes more integrated into the world economy, the correlation of that market with other important markets such as the U.S. may tend to rise.

Table 6.3
Correlations of Asset Class Total Returns, 1971–1987*

	Stocks	Long-Term Gov't Bonds	Intermediate Gov't Bonds	Treas. Bills	Real Estate	Small Stocks	Foreign Stocks	Foreign Bonds	Inflation
Stocks	1.00								
Long-term gov't bonds	0.37	1.00							
Intermed. gov't bonds	0.36	0.96	1.00						
Treasury bills	-0.06	-0.02	0.23	1.00					
Real estate	0.13	-0.31	-0.19	0.58	1.00				
Small stocks	0.74	0.12	0.14	0.07	0.33	1.00			
Foreign stocks	0.66	0.21	0.07	-0.40	-0.09	0.32	1.00		
Foreign bonds	0.20	0.48	0.28	-0.54	-0.41	0.05	0.64	1.00	
Inflation	-0.32	-0.59	-0.51	0.45	0.50	0.05	-0.51	-0.54	1.00

*The period 1971–1987 is the longest for which annual return data are available for all of the asset classes. The data sources are shown in the notes to Figure 5.2.

Some asset classes, such as real estate, have short historical data series. For these, one should use the longest period for which data are available, so as to pick up at least one, and preferably several, whole market cycles.

▲ Summary

The component return approach provides a simple framework for the estimation of expected (forecasted) returns on assets. Using this approach, the investor can develop forecasts on disparate asset classes in a way that links all the forecasts together and makes the set of forecasts consistent—a prerequisite for use in asset allocation.

Forecasts of standard deviations and correlations are as important as forecasts of return. They determine the risk of the allocated portfolio and the potential gains from diversifying into additional asset classes.

By taking a disciplined approach to forecasting as a starting point, and adding judgement where appropriate, the investor can generate useful asset allocation inputs. In turn, these inputs are used by asset allocation models to create and enhance value over the long run.

▲ Notes

1. See *Stocks, Bonds, Bills, and Inflation 1988 Yearbook,* Ibbotson Associates, Chicago, 1988.

2. The yield is the certain or riskless part of the bond's total return, and is in that sense riskless over any holding period. But most investors are total-return investors, rendering bonds risky unless they are held to maturity. Even investors holding coupon-paying bonds to maturity are subject to some risk (coupon reinvestment risk), but that can be eliminated by holding zero-coupon bonds.

3. To be exact, the cumulative index of equity risk premia follows a random walk. Correspondingly, the equity risk premium return itself is an approximately stationary process with no serial correlation. While there is evidence that the risk premium is in fact nonstationary, that finding is more appropriate to forecasting returns in a tactical setting.

4. This particular application of the component return approach is, as many readers will have discerned, indistinguishable from the Capital Asset Pricing Model (CAPM) with an assumed beta of one. However, the component return approach is more general than the CAPM, as we will see when applying it to other assets.

5. *Stocks, Bonds, Bills, and Inflation 1988 Yearbook,* p. 130.

6. The real riskless rate has fluctuated widely, but averaged less than 1% historically and is only slightly higher (about 1.5%) as of July 1988. Thus, a reasonable forecast of the long-run real riskless rate is 1%.

7. These numbers do not match the simple subtraction of returns in Figure 6.1 because the small stock premium series is constructed as the geometric, not arithmetic, difference of small and large stock returns.

7 Roger G. Ibbotson, Jeffrey J. Diermeier, and Laurence B. Siegel

The Demand for Capital Market Returns: A New Equilibrium Theory

▶ Overview

*The Capital Asset Pricing Model (CAPM) and the Arbitrage Pricing Theory
(APT) model price risk premia that are part of the expected return of an
asset. Since they are equilibrium models and assume fair pricing, they are
used as the discount rate applied to the expected cash flows from an asset,
in determining the asset's present value.*

*But these models price only systematic risk, assuming investors could di-
versify away from nonmarket risks. If the natural holders of an asset would
find it costly or difficult to diversify, nonsystematic risk could also be priced.
Furthermore, many non-risk characteristics of an asset are likely to be priced.
Those include taxation, lack of marketability, information costs, and so on.
Frequently the non-risk characteristics are even more important than the risk
characteristics of an asset.*

*This article presents a demand and supply framework for examining a
wide range of assets, including stocks and bonds, but also real estate, venture capital, private equity, and so on. There is no "formula" presented, but
instead the framework presents how an investor would be relatively averse
to various asset characteristics and how summing demand across all investors gives us the equilibrium price of each asset. The article labels this
a "demand" framework, because in the short run the assets are in fixed
supply, so that the assets are priced according to investors' aggregate
demand for (or aversion to) the various characteristics.*

▶ Abstract

*Investors demand more of an asset, the more desirable the asset's character-
istics. Investors regard these characteristics—risk, taxation, marketability
and information costs, for example—as positive or negative costs, and evaluate expected returns net of these costs. The New Equilibrium Theory integrates all asset characteristics into a unified framework that is applicable to
all types of assets—stocks and bonds, real estate, venture capital, durables
and intangibles. The most important asset characteristic is its price, or expected return. By varying price, any and all assets become desirable enough
for the capital market to clear. Asset characteristics other than price include*

*both risk and non-risk characteristics. The Capital Asset Pricing Model and
Arbitrage Pricing Theory have described the risk characteristics. The non-risk
characteristics are not as well understood. They include taxation, marketability and information costs. For many assets, these non-risk characteristics
affect price, or expected return, even more than the risk characteristics.*

*Investors regard asset characteristics as positive or negative costs, and
investors evaluate expected returns net of these costs. The New Equilibrium
Theory (NET) framework applies to all assets—including stocks and bonds,
real estate, venture capital, durables and intangibles such as human capital—and incorporates all asset characteristics.*

Prices in capital markets are set by the interaction of demand and supply. This
relationship is commonly expressed in terms of the "supply of and demand for
capital." But viewing it from the opposite perspective—that is, in terms of the
demand for and supply of capital market *returns*—has the advantage of focusing our attention on returns as the goods being priced in the marketplace.
This article provides a framework for analyzing the demand for capital market
returns, which we define as the compensation each investor requires for holding assets with various characteristics. A companion article will consider the
supply of returns generated by the productivity of businesses in the real economy, outside the capital market.[1]

The basics of the demand for capital market returns can be explained in
a few sentences. Investors regard each asset as a bundle of characteristics for
which they have various preferences and aversions. Investors translate each
characteristic into a cost, and require compensation in the form of expected returns for bearing these costs. Thus, although all investors are assumed to perceive the same before-cost expected return for any given asset, each has individually determined costs he must pay to hold that asset. On the basis of
perceived expected returns net of these individually determined costs, investors choose to hold differing amounts of each asset. The cost of capital for
an asset is the aggregation of all investors' capital costs on the margin, and represents the market expected return on the asset.

Formal demand-side theories such as the Capital Asset Pricing Model
(CAPM) and Arbitrage Pricing Theory (APT) have prescribed useful mathematical formulations for deriving assets' expected returns.[2] Both these theories, however, assume perfect capital markets in which all costs are due specifically to risk. The CAPM specifies the payoff demanded by investors for
bearing one cost—beta, or market, risk; APT treats multiple risk factors.
Other research has addressed non-risk factors, but in isolation.

Our framework, which we term New Equilibrium Theory (NET), integrates costs arising from all sources—including various risks, as well as taxability, marketability and information costs—and affecting all assets in an investor's opportunity set—stocks, bonds, real estate, human capital, venture
capital, tangibles and intangibles. NET theory does not provide a detailed
analysis of each particular cost, nor does it specify a mathematical asset pric-

ing equation. The NET model is useful, however, in explaining observed investor behavior.

The NET Principle

Investors demand a security (a given set of expected cash flows) for its benefits (expected returns) *net* of investor costs. The market price will be lower, and the expected returns (cost of capital) will be higher, the more "bad" characteristics a security encompasses.

Potential bad characteristics are as follows:

1. Systematic risk factors
   a. Stock market beta
   b. Interest rate risk
   c. Inflation risk
   d. Value versus growth risk
   e. Size risk
2. Residual or unsystematic risk
3. Taxability
4. Lack of marketability
   a. Search and transactions costs
   b. Information costs
   c. Divisibility costs
5. Management or storage costs
6. Nonpecuniary costs or benefits

▲ The New Equilibrium Theory

The objective of the NET framework is to determine the equilibrium cost of capital, r_j, for each asset j in the market, given the characteristics of asset j and the utility functions of all the investors in the market. Conceptually, the cost of capital is the sum of all capital costs at the margin across all holders of all claims on asset j; it is typically expressed as a per year percentage of value. This cost of capital can also be interpreted as an expected return to investors or as a discount rate used in valuation.

Unlike most models in finance, which deal specifically with time and uncertainty, the NET model makes use of the simpler, classical *instantaneous* supply and demand setting. The instantaneous setting incorporates perceived uncertainties, investment horizon, taxation, entry and exit costs, and other factors that affect an investor's perception of an asset's cost, as decrements to the present value of the asset. The instantaneous setting is suitable as long as all costs can be expressed as present values.[3]

The Supply of Assets

Investors view all assets as bundles of characteristics. The NET framework, in its most general form, makes no assertion that there are complete markets for each characteristic. There is not necessarily a separate market for each characteristic, nor any way that an investor could construct his a priori optimum bundle of characteristics, even if there were *shadow* prices for these characteristics. Thus pricing characteristics are translated and aggregated into investor costs at the individual investor level for each asset. It is the asset, rather than each of its characteristics, that is being priced by the market.[4]

NET assumes the existence of a characteristic-free asset, analogous to the risk-free asset in other models, earning the pure time value of money. Investors can invest in, or lend out, unlimited quantities of this asset at the market rate, r_f. Investors are restricted in their borrowing, however, by the inclusion of an investor-specific borrowing cost function, c_{if}, which rises as the amount borrowed increases. Thus investors are divided into lenders and borrowers, with the net quantity of the characteristic-free asset assumed equal to zero in the economy.[5] Borrowing costs are paid to intermediaries to cover their various costs.

Although the NET framework technically allows short selling, the cost of shorting a specific asset is ordinarily too high to make short selling worthwhile. Short selling is thus restricted to the characteristic-free asset, and even this borrowing is limited by increasing costs. The assumption of a characteristic-free return, r_f, provides a homogeneous benchmark for all investors, while the assumption that it is (increasingly) costly to short the characteristic-free asset restricts the market impact of low-wealth investors who might otherwise borrow in infinite quantities.

The Investor Demand for Assets

To focus on the composite market's cost of capital for asset j, we assume that investors have homogeneous expectations concerning r_j, the asset's expected return before investors' costs, as well as r_f, the rate of return on the characteristic-free asset.[6] Our second key assumption is that investors have heterogeneous, or individually determined, costs associated with the holding of asset j. These differing costs are a natural consequence of the fact that investors differ in regard to wealth, risk aversion, access to information, tax bracket and numerous other traits. The individual investor may evaluate an asset's characteristics according to his own classification scheme, and he may measure an asset's characteristics according to his own judgment. Thus each investor will have his own particular utility function, according to which he translates all asset characteristics, including all risks, into costs.[7]

The costs associated with holding each incremental unit of asset j may fall at first because of economies of scale in information, transaction or other costs. At some point, however, the costs of holding additional units of asset j will be-

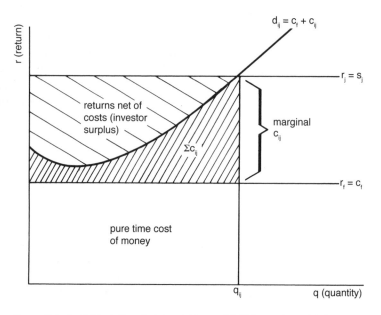

Figure 7.1. Individual: Supply (s_j) and Demand (d_{ij}) for an Asset (j) As Seen by the Individual (i) Given the Homogeneous Before-Cost Expected Return (r_i)

gin to rise. The major cause of this rise is the increasing lack of diversification in the investor's portfolio.

A Graphical Description of NET Equilibrium

Figure 7.1 diagrams the individual's demand and supply equilibrium. The expected return on asset j, viewed homogeneously by all investors, is denoted by the horizontal line r_j. The expected return on the characteristic-free asset is the horizontal line r_f. The latter also represents an opportunity cost curve, c_f, in this context. The cost to investor i of holding asset j will be the sum of this opportunity cost plus all the other costs he associates with holding the asset, c_{ij}.[8] This sum, $c_f + c_{ij}$, equals the individual's demand curve, d_{ij}, which is upward sloping because it is presented in return-quantity space.[9] The investor stops buying the asset when his marginal costs rise to equal the return on asset j, r_j. Thus the before-cost expected return, r_j, serves as the individual supply curve, s_j.

Alternatively, we can view the investor as demanding a return net of his costs, $r_j - c_{ij}$. This return net of costs may also be labeled investor surplus, analogous to the consumer surplus in the classical economic framework. The investor purchases asset j until his return net of costs equals the return on the characteristic-free asset, r_f; that is, he invests in asset j until r_j minus c_{ij} equals r_f.

The individual investor demand curve from Figure 7.1, d_{ij}, is also displayed in Figure 7.2. Here, individual demand curves, d_{ij}, are summed hori-

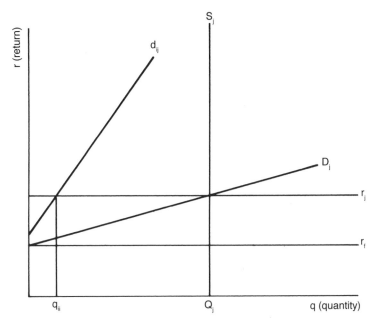

Figure 7.2. Market: Aggregation of Individual Demand Curves (d_{ij}) to Form Market Demand Curve (D_j) and Determine Asset Price and Return (r_j)

zontally to form the aggregate demand curve for security j, D_j. The aggregate supply of shares of security j is perfectly inelastic, and is represented by the vertical line, S_j ($= Q_j$). The intersection of D_j and S_j forms the market return, r_j. This return is the same as the individual supply curve, r_j, shown in Figure 7.1.

Figure 7.3 restates Figure 7.2 in conventional price-quantity (rather than return-quantity) space. In Figure 7.3, both the individual (d_{ij}) and aggregate (D_j) demand curves for asset j are downward sloping. As in Figure 7.2, the supply curve (S_j) for asset j is vertical. The market price (P_j) and individual and aggregate quantities of asset j demanded (q_{ij} and Q_j, respectively) are determined by the intersection of the supply and demand curves.

Figure 7.4 shows what happens when the individual investor is offered the opportunity either to invest in (lend) or to short (borrow) the characteristic-free asset. If he lends, he gets the homogeneous return, r_f, offered to all investors. If he borrows, he pays heterogeneous borrowing costs, c_{if}, and consequently borrows at rate $r_f + c_{if}$, and consequently borrows at rate $r_f + c_{if}$. The individual investor's wealth constraint, and the continuously rising cost functions depicted in Figures 7.1 and 7.4, require that the investor either borrow or lend, which avoids any corner solutions. The investor borrows his optimum quantity of the characteristic-free asset; the cost of borrowing is included in his asset costs in Figure 7.1, so that c_{ij} includes a constant c_{if} for each asset j.[10]

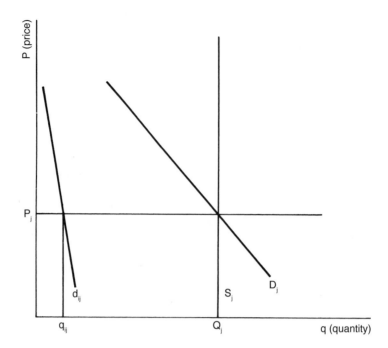

Figure 7.3. Market: Aggregation of Individual Demand Curves, Restated in Price-Quantity Space

Figure 7.5 depicts the aggregate demand curve for the characteristic-free asset, D_f. This aggregate demand curve is the horizontal sum of individual demand curves, d_{if}. The net supply curve for the characteristic-free asset is zero, and is depicted as S_f at a quantity (Q_f) of zero. The characteristic-free asset earns rate r_f in equilibrium, where the demand curve, D_f, intersects with the supply curve, S_f.

Each investor holds a different portfolio, based on his own particular heterogeneous costs. Nevertheless, each investor is relatively diversified, because he has calculated diversifiable risk as one of his costs. By holding a positive, zero or negative position, each investor's marginal cost equals his return for every asset in the market. This means that each investor would change his position in an asset in response to any change in the asset price—i.e., before-cost expected return on the asset—or in response to any change in the aggregate costs he incurs by holding that asset. For a given asset, all investors have equal costs on the margin, constituting the cost of capital for each investor and for the market.[11] Prices are thus set in aggregate by all investors. In sum, both investors and issuers treat the asset characteristics as marginal investor costs that, in the aggregate, sum to the cost of capital.

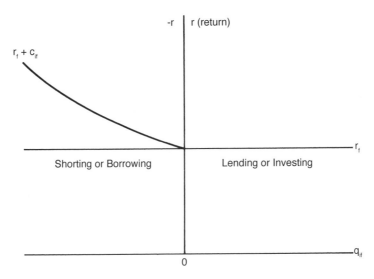

Figure 7.4. Individual: Individual (i) Return on Lending or Borrowing the Characteristic-Free Asset

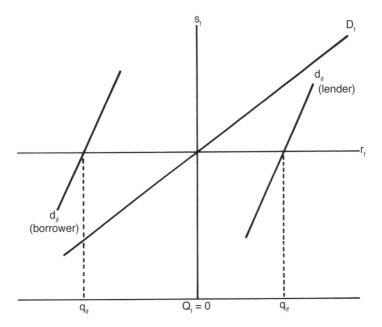

Figure 7.5. Market: Aggregate Demand (D_t) and Supply (S_t) Curves for a Characteristic-Free Asset With Individual Demand Curves (d_{if}) for a Borrower and a Lender

The Role of Financial Intermediaries

The NET framework can readily be expanded to include repackaging opportunities on the part of issuing firms or financial intermediaries. The role of the financial intermediary is to repackage the pricing characteristics so as to reduce investor costs. One way intermediaries accomplish their task is by making the markets for pricing characteristics more complete. By unbundling asset characteristics, for example, they increase the likelihood that those investors with lower costs for a particular characteristic will hold that characteristic in their portfolios. Another way intermediaries reduce investor costs is by optimal bundling of asset characteristics to take advantage of economies of scale.

Investors perceive financial intermediaries as additional asset offerings, whereas issuers perceive them as additional investors. Assuming perfect competition, intermediaries act to maximize aggregate investor surplus by minimizing the sum of *all* investor costs (not just marginal costs) across all assets for all the pricing characteristics.

◤ The Pricing Characteristics of Assets

We have developed a framework in which investors view assets as bundles of characteristics that investors then translate into their own heterogeneous costs. Thus far, these pricing characteristics—those attributes of an asset that affect an investor's ex ante costs—have remained in the background.[12] As the opportunity set of investor assets is worldwide in scope and includes stocks, bonds, real estate, human capital, venture capital, and tangible and intangible goods, we may expect a wide range of pricing characteristics to exist. We delineate below some of the more important pricing characteristics, and suggest informally how they are bundled into familiar assets, how they might be priced, who their investor clienteles are likely to be, and how financial intermediaries might reduce their costs. We consider both risk and non-risk characteristics, the latter including taxation, marketability and miscellaneous pricing factors.

Risk Characteristics

The CAPM states that only one risk pricing characteristic exists—namely, market risk. APT provides for multiple risk pricing characteristics, and treats each risk as orthogonal to all of the others, so that the market payoffs are additive. The NET framework does not directly take sides in this controversy, but does allow for multiple pricing characteristics.[13] We focus here on four of the most intuitive types of risk—beta (market), inflation, real interest rate and residual risk.

Market, or *beta, risk* is the risk that the return of an asset will fluctuate with the market portfolio's return. According to CAPM, beta risk is the only risk that affects expected return. It is assumed that the rational investor will diversify away (at no cost) all other risks. In the NET framework, as noted, each investor translates risks into costs by assigning a price at which he is indifferent between buying and not buying more of the risk.

Inflation risk is the risk that an asset's real value will fluctuate because of unanticipated changes in the inflation rate. This risk is best exemplified by a long-term government bond, which is relatively free of most other pricing characteristics. The bond is a nominal contract, and its yield to maturity consists of three components—the expected inflation rate, the expected real interest rate and the risk premium (if any) associated with inflation and real interest rates. Although the market anticipates all three components over the bond's life, unanticipated changes in current and expected inflation rates cause variations in the bond's real return.

Inflation risk arises when one side explicitly or implicitly contracts in nominal, instead of real, terms. For this pricing characteristic to be nonzero, at least one side must have negative inflation risk costs and be willing to pay the other side to create these risks.[14] The inflation risk premium may be positive for investors in the stock market and for holders of short-term, and possibly long-term, bonds.[15] Other assets likely to contain a nonzero amount of inflation risk include real estate, gold and any other assets whose real returns are correlated (positively or negatively) with unanticipated changes in the inflation rate.

The *real interest rate* is the difference between the instantaneous nominal interest rate (on a characteristic-free bond) and the instantaneous inflation rate. Since real interest rate changes are unanticipated, the investor who rolls over a series of short-term bonds receives an uncertain return in real terms. The investor in long-term bonds can lock in the real rate over the bond's life, but incurs inflation risk in the process. It is, of course, possible to construct a long-term contract in real terms and avoid both inflation and real interest rate risk for any given time horizon. Since these contracts are not commonly seen, we have to presume either that issuers and investors have differing time horizons, or that issuers and/or investors believe that the costs of writing contracts in nominal terms, including the costs of inflation and real interest rate risk, are less than the costs of writing contracts in real terms.[16]

Residual risk is the risk resulting from lack of diversification in a portfolio. Assuming that the risks already described account for an asset's undiversifiable risk, residual risk is the one remaining risk factor. We propose that residual risk, like the other risk factors, may be an ex ante pricing factor.

In CAPM, the rational investor perfectly diversifies so as to eliminate entirely all residual risk. NET assumes that it is costly to diversify. The factors that make perfect diversification either impossible or suboptimal are related to non-risk pricing characteristics. For example, many investors wish to own their residences outright. The large unit size of other real estate investments, along with the high cost of creating divisibility mechanisms such as condominiums and limited partnerships, imposes high costs on investors seeking diversification. Thus most investors do not hold a diversified real estate portfolio—that is, one that is spread over various geographical locations and types of land and structures.

Human capital is subject to even more extreme constraints on diversification. Once acquired, human capital cannot readily be sold, and is usually rented out for wages in the labor market. It follows that one cannot easily buy a portion of another person's human capital in order to diversify within the asset class.

Taxability

Taxability often has a substantial impact on an asset's cost of capital. The taxability characteristic is inherently complex because of the intricacies of the U.S. (and other countries') taxation systems. This complexity consists of (1) the stepwise ("tax bracket") and multiplicative attributes of the tax function; (2) the fact that taxes on a given asset are contingent on the performance (effect on income) of other assets in one's portfolio; (3) the differential treatment of ordinary income and capital gains; (4) special tax laws, such as those allowing depreciation much faster than the useful life of certain assets; and (5) multiple taxing authorities. These attributes cause the tax costs for the same asset to differ across individuals. The general principle is that highly taxable assets are lower priced—i.e., have a higher before-tax expected return—than less highly taxed assets.

For example, municipal bonds, whose coupons are free of U.S. federal income taxes, yield 20 to 50 per cent less than fully taxable corporate bonds of comparable risk. A similar relationship has been suggested for high dividend versus low dividend stocks.[17] Constantinides provides a personal tax equilibrium that includes the timing option for the realization of capital losses and the deferral of capital gains.[18] Most of these and other tax-related theoretical results can be introduced into the general NET framework, because NET does not specify actual investor costs.

Real estate, venture capital, hedging portfolios and leasing arrangements provide special opportunities for financial intermediaries to separate out tax characteristics and repackage them for the appropriate clienteles. After repackaging, many investments may be tax shelters having negative tax rates.[19]

In summary, an asset may generate taxes (positive or negative) on income, expenses or capital appreciation. The investor includes these tax costs in his pricing process. The complexity of the taxation system and the interaction of taxes with other pricing characteristics make it difficult to specify this pricing characteristic. Nevertheless, the magnitude of taxes is sufficiently large that it must be included in any exposition of the NET framework.

Marketability Costs

We group all the entry and exit costs associated with buying or selling an asset into the category of marketability costs. The NET framework is instantaneous, so that it provides no description of how an investor came to hold his particular portfolio or when or how he may rebalance his portfolio. For the NET equilibrium to be descriptive, each investor must reduce the value of his assets by a present value amount to cover these costs.[20] These marketability costs include information, search and transaction, and divisibility costs.

Information costs are the costs that an investor must pay to learn the value of an asset. Since the NET model assumes homogeneous expectations, we have already in some sense assumed these costs away. Nevertheless, we can informally apply the NET model by suggesting that investors must pay some costs to learn what the homogeneous expectations are.[21] In such a world, investors with comparatively lower information costs for a particular asset would tend to own that asset. For example, U.S. investors own stocks and bonds of U.S. corporations in disproportionately large quantities because of the cost of acquiring information across national boundaries. Moreover, assets that are difficult to learn about, such as stocks of small or new companies, should have higher before-cost expected returns than assets that are easier to learn about, such as large company stocks. Finally, information costs tend to favor the large investor, since there are economies of scale in information use.

Search and transaction costs include the costs of looking for the other side of the transaction, as well as the costs of actually closing the transaction. The costs may include the bid-ask spread, the waiting time beyond the investor's desired horizon, the possibility of having to take a price concession, the paperwork and legal costs accompanying a transaction, the cost of advertising or other efforts to locate the other party to the transaction, and the cost of any brokers or agents used to effect the transaction. These costs are treated in search and bargaining theory literature. In the NET framework, these costs are merely estimated by the investor as their present value equivalent costs.

Divisibility costs arise from the large and discrete scale of some investments, such as real estate, venture capital, large-denomination certificates of indebtedness, and certain discrete human capital decisions. Divisibility interacts with many of the other pricing characteristics. Indivisibility's chief burden to investors may be that it forces them to take substantial residual risk. It also causes some investors to hold a suboptimal quantity of a particular investment.[22]

Human capital, once acquired, is often considered nonmarketable as well as indivisible. It can be rented and, to some extent, it can be put up as collateral for loans. When invested in a business, portions of it can sometimes be sold. In the NET framework, we can regard these as high, but not insurmountable, divisibility costs. In some models, an equilibrium is arrived at in which human capital is literally treated as nonmarketable.[23]

One of the principal roles of financial intermediaries is to repackage securities in such a way as to reduce divisibility costs. A saver (small lender) would have great difficulty in finding a borrower with whom to transact and still maintain the liquidity of his savings. By pooling the savings of many persons, a bank can do exactly that. Money market funds reduce the minimum investment amount for cash instruments from $10,000 to very little. Real estate investment trusts and limited partnerships lower the size barrier for investing in large properties from the range of millions of dollars to the range of thousands or less. Each of these mechanisms for reducing divisibility costs is itself costly. For many investors, however, paying the costs of investing through a financial intermediary increases their investor surplus.

Other miscellaneous factors may affect the price of a capital market asset. These include nonpecuniary costs or benefits, all of which we would treat as positive or negative costs. In addition, certain expenses such as management, maintenance and storage costs are best treated as costs of capital, rather than as decrements to cash flow. This is because they differ across investors. Because investors seek to maximize returns net of all costs and benefits, these factors should be included in the set of NET pricing factors.

◤ *Application of the NET Framework*

In NET, we go back to economic basics. We apply the classical supply and demand model to the pricing of assets. Individual investors have homogeneous expected returns but heterogeneous costs associated with multiple risks, various forms of market imperfections and other pricing characteristics. These characteristics are priced at the individual level and treated as present value equivalents in the instantaneous time setting. This simple equilibrium framework cannot provide a pricing equation. It can, however, describe investor portfolios and asset expected returns in broad realistic terms.

Each individual investor maximizes his own investor surplus. He does so by investing in each asset until his own unique costs equal the asset's expected return on the margin. Thus no one holds the market portfolio. Rather, each investor selects his asset holdings according to his comparative cost advantage. Clienteles arise because groups of investors have similar costs.

Assets are treated as bundles of pricing characteristics. The cost of capital for a given asset is the sum of the costs of all its characteristics and is equal to the asset's expected return. Given continuous cost curves, all investors face the same cost on the margin for a given *asset*. However, the cost for each *characteristic* of the asset is not the same for each investor.

Financial intermediaries act to maximize the aggregate sum of investor surplus across all investors by repackaging assets to take advantage of pricing characteristics that are less costly to some investors. They bundle and unbundle characteristics to move toward complete markets and produce investor economies of scale.

The NET framework can readily be adapted to include heterogeneous expectations. In fact, doing so may shed further light on the mechanisms by which investors price assets. We have kept the homogeneous expectation assumption so that we could relate expected returns to the cost of capital.

Table 7.1
The Pricing Characteristics of Assets

Asset	Risks				Taxability*	Marketability			Miscellaneous Factors
	Stock Market Beta	Inflation	Real Interest Rate	Residual Risk Cost*		Information Costs*	Search & Transactions Costs	Divisibility Costs	
Large company stocks	near one	low positive	positive?	near zero	low	low	low	very low	Probably efficiently priced
Small company stocks	varies	low positive	positive?	low	low	high	medium*	very low	
Treasury bonds	near zero	positive	low	near zero	high	low	low	medium*	Efficiently priced
Corporate bonds	low	positive	low	near zero	high	low	low	medium*	
Municipal bonds	near zero	positive	low	low	zero	low	low	medium*	
Treasury bills	zero	zero	high	near zero	high	low	low	high*	
Houses, condos	low	?	?	high	negative	high	high*	very high*	High management costs
Gold	zero or negative	negative?	?	low	low	low	low	very low	No income; portable
Art	low	negative?	?	high	low	very high	very high	very high	Nonpecuniary benefits; no income
Foreign securities	varies	varies	?	varies	low	high	varies	low	
Human capital	high	?	?	very high	very high	high	high*	very high*	Cannot sell, only rent or borrow against

Note: Low, medium, high, etc. refer to positive coefficients unless indicated to be negative.
*Financial intermediaries are likely to be important in reducing these costs.

As a practical matter, it may be useful to make additional assumptions in order to estimate the market cost of capital for an asset. If we assume that there exists a "representative" investor whose cost functions mimic those of all investors in the aggregate, and who perceives all characteristics except tax costs as orthogonal, we can sum the characteristic costs for the representative investor to obtain the after-tax market cost of capital. We may assume that the tax cost, unlike other costs, is multiplicative; thus we divide the after-tax cost of capital by one minus the representative investor's tax rate to arrive at the before-tax cost of capital.

Table 7.1 presents a heuristic summary of selected assets matched with pricing characteristics. The investor must make his own judgments about the quantity of each characteristic embedded in each asset and about the costs he associates with the characteristic. Although NET cannot make these judgments for the investor, NET provides a framework within which an investor can analyze the wide range of assets and characteristics available.

◤ Estimating the Expected Return of an Asset

Table 7.1 provides a rough summary of the relevant characteristics of several asset classes. In general, each risk might carry a risk premium, including the residual risk. Marketability is also delineated by several characteristics. An investor might simply add up return estimates for most of the items in the table. Taxability is more likely to be multiplicative (as one minus a tax rate), with the higher taxed assets having higher expected pretax returns.

Having an idea of all the characteristics of an asset is likely to be more useful in estimating the expected return of an asset, than applying any single model.

NET as it presently stands is a characterization of the way investment practitioners view the world, to some extent explicitly and in large part implicitly or intuitively. NET theory serves to draw all pricing factors into a unified framework. Investors need to know what affects pricing, with or without an algebraic pricing equation. Consideration of all pricing characteristics may be more important to them than a rigorous partial equilibrium treatment of one or a few characteristics. Our hope is that the integrated view of asset characteristics and investor costs presented in this article will be given more explicit consideration by both practitioners and researchers.

◤ Notes

1. Jeffrey J. Diermeier, Roger G. Ibbotson and Laurence B. Siegel, "The Supply of Capital Market Returns," *Financial Analysts Journal,* 1984.

2. William F. Sharpe, "Capital Asset Prices: A Theory of Market Equilibrium Under Conditions of Risk," *Journal of Finance,* September 1974, pp. 425–552; John Lintner,

"The Valuation of Risk Assets and the Selection of Risky Investments in Stock Portfolios and Capital Budgets," *Review of Economics and Statistics,* February 1965, pp. 13–37; and Stephen A. Ross, "The Arbitrage Pricing Theory of Capital Asset Pricing," *Journal of Economic Theory,* December 1976, pp. 341–360.

3. Since there is only one instant of time in the model (the present), the investor is assumed to select his optimal portfolio in a *tâtonnement* process, given the prices (before-cost expected returns) of all the assets in the economy. The *tâtonnement* process is described in Alfred Marshall, *Principles of Economics,* 8th edition (London: Macmillan and Co., 1920). Although the Law of One Price holds for each asset in the economy, other market imperfections are expressed as some of the pricing characteristics.

4. This avoids many aggregation issues presented in John Lintner, "The Aggregation of Investors' Diverse Judgments of Preferences in Purely Competitive Markets," *Journal of Financial and Quantitative Analysis,* November 1969; Mark Rubinstein, "An Aggregation Theorem for Securities Markets," *Journal of Financial Economics,* September 1974; and Sherwin Rosen, "Hedonic Prices and Implicit Markets: Product Differentiation in Pure Competition," *Journal of Political Economy,* January/February 1974.

5. The net quantity of the characteristic-free asset may be assumed to be other than zero without affecting the analysis. For example, an exogenous government may issue this asset in some quantity, similar to the money supply.

6. As we shall see later, the NET model is robust with respect to forming an equilibrium (i.e., a single market price for an asset) given heterogeneous expectations. The concept of cost of capital, however, has very little meaning when related to the diverse expectations of investors. Heterogeneous expectations are better treated in the specific context of information costs and in debating market efficiency, rather than here where we seek to determine an equilibrium cost of capital.

7. To take the most familiar example, that of mapping beta risk into a cost in the CAPM context, each investor's cost function rises as he takes on incremental beta risk. The investor then assigns a price at which he is indifferent between buying and not buying more of the risk. Given complete markets and homogeneous expectations, the market provides one clearing price for beta risk. Each investor buys beta risk until his increasing risk costs equal the market risk payoff. The mildly risk-averse investor has a lower cost for a given amount of beta risk than the highly risk-averse investor, and therefore holds a higher beta portfolio.

8. These costs, c_{ij}, include the borrowing costs, c_{if}, if the investor is a borrower. Borrowing costs are described in Figures 7.4 and 7.5.

9. In Figure 7.1, return is on the vertical axis and quantity on the horizontal axis. Since return is related to the reciprocal of price, supply and demand curves are "upside down" relative to the more familiar price-quantity diagrams. This return-quantity space was made familiar by Merton H. Miller in "Debt and Taxes," *Journal of Finance,* May 1977.

10. In the instantaneous framework presented here, the investor finds his optimum borrowing quantity of the characteristic-free asset and makes his choice of other assets (based on their returns net of perceived costs) simultaneously, using the *tâtonnement* process referred to in note 3.

11. In practice, the utility function that translates characteristics to costs may generate a discontinuous cost curve because of indivisibility of assets or restrictions on short selling. Thus, for many assets, investors will hold only zero or whole number positions. For these assets, there may exist heterogeneous costs on the margin.

12. Although we have noted that NET does not postulate complete markets for these characteristics, which are priced at the individual level, we might have alternatively assumed

that complete markets existed for each pricing characteristic, so that the characteristics could be priced at the market level. The assets would then also be priced at the market level and represented as combinations of characteristics. We deliberately avoid making this assumption, because many of the characteristics we are about to discuss are inseparable, complex, and contradict the complete markets assumption by their very nature.

13. Nai-fu Chen, Richard Roll and Stephen A. Ross, in "Stock Markets, Factors, and the Macroeconomy" (working paper, 1982) have isolated five risk factors—(1) beta risk, (2) the return differential between low and high grade bonds (related to the return differential between small and large capitalization stocks), (3) the return differential between short- and long-term bonds, (4) anticipated inflation, and (5) unanticipated inflation.

14. Jeffrey F. Jaffe, in "Corporate Taxes, Inflation, the Rate of Interest, and the Return to Equity," *Journal of Financial and Quantitative Analysis,* March 1978, shows that inflation risk is not readily separable from taxation costs. Thus it may be impossible to contract totally in real terms.

15. Charles R. Nelson, in "Inflation and Rates of Return on Common Stocks," *Journal of Finance,* May 1976, and Eugene F. Fama and G. William Schwert, in "Asset Returns and Inflation," *Journal of Financial Economics,* November 1977, present results suggesting a positive inflation-risk premium for stocks. J. Huston McColloch, in "An Estimate of the Liquidity Premium," *Journal of Political Economy,* January/February 1975, shows that the inflation-risk premium is positive to bondholders.

16. In high inflation countries such as Brazil and Israel, bonds with price-level-indexed principal have existed for years. The United Kingdom and France now issue them also. Bertrand Jacquillat and Richard Roll, in "French Index-Linked Bonds for U.S. Investors?" *Journal of Portfolio Management,* Spring 1979, have found French price-level-indexed bonds to have high historical returns to a U.S. investor.

17. See Robert H. Litzenberger and Krishna Ramaswamy, "The Effect of Personal Taxes on Dividends on Capital Asset Prices," *Journal of Financial Economics,* June 1979. Both their theory and their empirical results are disputed by Merton Miller and Myron S. Scholes in "Dividends and Taxes," *Journal of Financial Economics,* December 1978.

18. George Constantinides, "Capital Market Equilibrium With Personal Tax," *Econometrica,* May 1983.

19. Merton H. Miller ("Debt and Taxes," op. cit.) shows that the taxation issue cannot be fully analyzed on the investor demand side alone. Corporations (like intermediaries) may react to any pricing characteristic by attempting to offer the types of issues that have the lowest costs in the market.

20. A problem with applying the NET framework to marketability costs is determining the investor's starting portfolio. For example, if the investor holds all cash, then he must pay entry costs on each asset to obtain his optimum portfolio. On the other hand, the investor may already hold his optimum portfolio, so that he has no entry costs.

21. The NET framework cannot directly include results from the variety of information models found in the financial literature. To apply NET here, we have to assert that the investor knows in advance both that he will use the information to buy the appropriate quantity of the asset, and that the purchase of the information is worthwhile.

22. The NET framework as presented in Figure 7.1 uses continuous cost curves, c_{ij}. When divisibility is a problem, cost curves will be discontinuous, and it will no longer be true that the marginal cost of capital of an asset is the same for all investors.

23. See for example, David Mayers, "Non-Marketable Assets and Capital Market Equilibrium Under Uncertainty," in Michael C. Jensen, ed., *Studies in the Theory of Capital Markets* (New York: Praeger Publishing, 1971).

8

Jeffrey J. Diermeier, Roger G. Ibbotson, and Laurence B. Siegel

The Supply of Capital Market Returns

▶ *Overview*

This article presents one of the first supply-side estimates of the aggregate U.S. capital market. This work is based upon the dividend discount model. But unlike most other uses of the model, our estimate of dividend growth is not based upon historical dividend growth. Instead, the estimate is based upon the assumption that the capital market would maintain in aggregate a constant share of gross domestic product (GDP).

In order for the estimate to be correct, it is necessary that it reflect the inflows and outflows into the capital market. The inflows are the net financial new issues, and the outflows are the income generated and paid out of the capital markets.

Note that the 5.4 percent real long-term forecast made here is the aggregate capital market return, not the expected return of any one asset class. Since the bond market has greater net inflows than the stock market, the stock market would have to have higher returns than the bond market to maintain its constant aggregate share of the economy.

Although there is no explicit forecast made of the stock market or equity risk premium in this paper, a real return of the aggregate capital market of somewhat higher than 5.4 percent would be consistent with the realized real return on the stock market of 6.5 percent over the historical period 1926–1983.

▶ *Abstract*

The supply of capital market returns is generated by the productivity of businesses in the real economy. The aggregate of market returns is then divided among various claimants, and is constrained by the amount supplied. GNP measures real economic performance, which determines the supply of returns, and is used in a simple model of the expected return on the aggregate of financial assets.

The supply side model can be used to forecast expected capital market returns. For instance, the real GNP growth rate over the two decades ending in 1982—2.6 percent—may be projected forward and combined with current yield and new issue data to produce a forecast of 5.4 percent per year for real return on the aggregate of financial assets.

The supply model places in perspective the various demand models that dominate thinking about investment returns. For instance, investors should not expect a much greater (or fear a much smaller) return than that provided by businesses in the real economy. Thus investors' expectations should be guided at least in part by the supply of market returns.

In the previous chapter, we posited a New Equilibrium Theory (NET) in which each investor's demand schedule for a given asset is determined by the interaction of that investor's needs and the characteristics of the asset.[1] The cost of capital of an asset is determined as the aggregate of heterogeneous investor costs for holding that asset. These costs include both the cost of assuming various kinds of risk and non-risk costs related to taxes, marketability and information. Like the Capital Asset Pricing Model (CAPM) and Arbitrage Pricing Theory (APT), NET addresses the demand for capital market returns.[2] NET, however, deliberately sacrifices some rigor in order to include both risk and non-risk characteristics in the determination of demand and to describe a wide variety of assets.

This article considers the supply of capital market returns to be the provision of potential future cash flows (or their analogue, investment returns) by businesses. Demand thus reflects investors' desire to receive such cash flows, and their willingness to commit wealth to businesses with that expectation.[3]

Our model of expected investment return uses a supply-side input—namely, macroeconomic performance. This approach rests on the idea that the supply of aggregate returns available for distribution among the various claimants is set by the productivity of businesses. By "aggregate" we mean the weighted sum of returns on stocks, bonds, cash, real estate and other financial instruments. This article suggests a model for the determination of aggregate return only; the relative expected returns on specific assets are determined on the demand side by the NET characteristics of each asset.

◢ A Supply-Side Model of Expected Return

The idea behind a supply-side model of capital market expected returns is that returns are related to the productivity of both capital and labor, each of which gets a share of what is produced. We devise below a means of estimating the aggregate capital market return expectation justified (in this supply view) by a given level of macroeconomic performance. Specifically, we use a macroeconomic input—the rate of change in GNP—as one of the determinants of the aggregate capital market return.

Definitions and Assumptions

Let us posit a closed economy with variables defined as follows, using upper-case letters for macroeconomic variables and lower-case letters for financial market variables:

W = wealth of society including human capital and all other intangibles,

w = aggregate market value of financial or capital market assets (including stocks, bonds, cash equivalents and real estate), and

GNP = Gross National Product of the economy.

Assume that W grows at a constant rate:

G = rate of growth of W.

Assume also that (w/W) is a constant; that is, financial wealth is a fixed proportion of total wealth. This assumption (which we refer to as a constant factor share assumption) combines with the constant growth assumption for W to yield the conclusion that w, too, grows at a constant rate:

g = rate of growth of w.

The above set of definitions and assumptions combines to give us:

$$g = G. \tag{1}$$

Equation (1) merely says that the growth rate of wealth measured in the financial or portfolio accounting discipline, g, should equal the growth rate of wealth measured in the national income and product account discipline, G.

Finally, because W cannot be measured directly, we must posit an additional assumption—namely, that the ratio (GNP/W) is a constant. This assumption enables us to use the growth rate of GNP as the measure of G.

Historical Justification

Figure 8.1 and Tables 8.1 and 8.2 offer some justification for our fairly broad constant growth and constant factor share assumptions.

Figure 8.1 examines the proposition that (w/W) is a constant, using the income shares of capital (financial assets, or w) and labor (the remainder, or $W - w$) as indicators of the underlying aggregate values.[4] These data suggest a relatively constant wealth share for financial assets, with perhaps a slight upward drift for labor and a downward drift for financial assets. One may note that the factor shares of individual components of capital have varied widely, although the total has not; this is to be expected as inflation, taxes and other economic results affect different financial assets differently. A similar breakdown of the labor share into common laborers, factory workers, professionals and high-technology specialists would probably also show varying shares of a relatively constant labor total.

Table 8.1 examines the constant growth assumption for GNP, using decade-by-decade GNP and per capita GNP levels and growth rates stated in both nominal and real (inflation-adjusted) terms.[5] Over the whole period 1889–1982, real

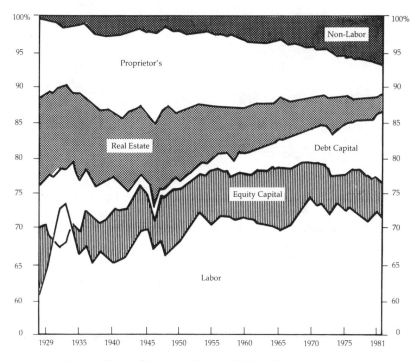

Figure 8.1. Income Shares of Capital and Labor (1929–1981)

GNP grew at a 3.1 percent compound annual rate. The annual GNP growth rate was close to 3 percent in most of the decades of the period; that is, the mean of the series is reasonably constant. Even the depression decade of the 1930s had positive real GNP and real per capita GNP growth.[6] The very fact that any period of negative real GNP growth is officially labeled a recession suggests the extent to which expectations of stable GNP growth are built into our economic system. The historical data thus support a constant growth assumption for GNP, at least within the limited ambitions of this article.

The assumption that g equals G over reasonably long periods is evaluated in Table 8.2. The rate of growth of market capitalization (not returns), g, is measured directly as the nth root of the ratio of the ending to beginning aggregate value of financial assets, where n is the number of years in the period.[7] We measured G as the rate of constant-dollar GNP growth, taken over the same periods as g so that the two could be directly compared. The results show that, despite the use of several strong assumptions and a variety of possible measurement errors, there is a close historical correspondence between g and G for all the periods studied. Of course, since our constant factor share assumption is not literally true, we would not expect a close correspondence between g and G over short (say, yearly) periods.

Table 8.1
Decade GNP and Per Capita GNP Data in Nominal and Real Terms (1889–1982)

Decade	Nominal GNP (Current Dollars) Amount at End of Decade (Billions)	Decade Compound Annual Percentage Change	Real GNP (1982 Dollars) Amount at End of Decade (Billions)	Decade Compound Annual Percentage Change	Per Capita GNP (Current Dollars) Amount at End of Decade	Decade Compound Annual Percentage Change	Per Capita Real GNP (1982 Dollars) Amount at End of Decade	Decade Compound Annual Percentage Change
1889	$12.5		$172.2		$202		$2,783.2	
1890–1899	17.4	3.4%	245.9	3.6%	233	1.4%	3,292.8	1.7%
1900–1909	33.4	6.7	352.1	3.7	369	4.7	3,890.5	1.7
1910–1919	84.2	9.7	464.6	2.8	804	8.1	4,436.9	1.3
1920–1929	103.4	2.1	588.3	2.4	847	0.5	4,818.3	0.8
1930–1939	90.9	−1.3	636.0	0.8	691	−2.0	4,833.6	0.0
1940–1949	258.3	11.0	1,066.8	5.3	1,719	9.5	7,099.3	3.9
1950–1959	487.9	6.6	1,621.1	2.2	2,731	4.7	9,074.3	2.5
1960–1969	944.0	6.8	2,444.8	4.2	4,590	5.3	11,887.6	2.7
1970–1979	2,417.7	9.9	3,075.0	2.3	10,743	8.9	13,663.5	1.4
1980–1982	3,059.3	8.2	3,059.3	−0.2	13,183	7.1	13,183.0	−1.2
Summary Statistics: 1889–1982								
Geometric mean		6.1%		3.1%		4.6%		1.7%
Arithmetic mean		6.5		3.4		5.0		1.9
Standard deviation		8.8		6.5		8.8		6.5
Correlation with:								
Contemporaneous stock return		0.17		0.24		0.17		0.23
Previous year stock return		0.38		0.35		0.37		0.34
Two years' previous stock return		−0.06		−0.11		−0.06		−0.11

Table 8.2
Capital Market Size Growth Rates (g) and GNP Growth Rates (G)

	Compound Annual Rates of Growth in Real (Inflation-Adjusted) Terms			
	1926 to 1982	1947 to 1981	1960 to 1981	1970 to 1981
U.S. capital market aggregate value growth (g)				
Stocks	3.8%	5.2%	1.3%	−1.8%
Bonds and cash equivalents	2.8	0.5	2.3	2.4
Real estate	N/A	4.9	3.8	4.4
Market-value-weighted total	3.5	3.4	2.9	2.4
U.S. gross national product (G)	3.3	3.5	3.2	2.3

▲ A Supply-Based Equation

We can now begin to formulate an expression for r—the supply-based estimate or forecast of aggregate capital market total return, using the following definitions:

r = the total return on the aggregate of financial assets,
d = the income return on the aggregate of financial assets,
a = the capital appreciation return on the aggregate of financial assets, and
n = financial net new issues—i.e., new issues net of maturities, redemptions, bankruptcies, demolition, depreciation, etc.

Two equations relate these variables to each other and to g:

$$r = d + a \tag{2}$$

and

$$n = g - a. \tag{3}$$

Combining Equations (2) and (3), we arrive at:

$$r = d + (g - n), \tag{4}$$

the supply model of expected return. In Equation (4), d represents the income component of expected return and $(g - n)$ the capital appreciation component.[8]

To evaluate Equation (4), we need exogenous estimates of the variables d, g and n. We used current yields observed in the market as the measure of d, the rate of GNP growth (G) as a supply-side substitute for g, and a direct count of new issues as the measure of n.

Table 8.3
Sample Supply-Derived Forecast of Aggregate Real Return on U.S. Financial Assets

Real capital appreciation return:

Real GNP growth forecast (Based on 1963–1982):		2.6%	
Less: Net new issues (Based on 1970–1981):		4.7%	
		−2.1%	−2.1%

Income return:

Asset Class	Current Yields		
	Market Weight	Forecast Yield	Weight × Yield
Stocks	19.4%	4.2%	0.8%
Bonds	15.6	10.7	1.7
Cash eq.	5.3	8.7	0.5
Real est.	59.7	7.5	4.5
Market-value-weighted yield			7.5%

Market-value-weighted yield	7.5%
Forecast real total return on aggregate of stocks, bonds, cash equivalents and real estate:	5.4%

Forecasting the Market

Given best estimates of the future values of the variables G, d and n, Equation (4) can be used to forecast the return on the aggregate of capital market assets.

Table 8.3 illustrates a supply-based forecast based on historical and current data. For G, we used the real value over the 1963–1982 period. We calculated the new issue forecast by averaging the ratios of net new issues to capital stocks over the 1970–1981 period. Simple subtraction yielded a capital appreciation forecast, in real terms, of −2.1 percent.

A negative real capital appreciation forecast is not surprising, because bonds make up a large share of the capital market. Newly issued bonds have a zero nominal expected capital appreciation return, so if inflation is positive, the real capital appreciation return is negative.

We forecast the income return, d, using current market yields.[9] For bonds, we used the current yield (coupon divided by price), not the yield to maturity, which contains the anticipated capital gain or loss over the life of a discount or premium bond. Weighting the yield forecasts by market capitalization, we arrived at an income return forecast of 7.5 percent. Adding this to the forecast real capital appreciation of −2.1 percent gives a forecast total real return of 5.4 percent.

▲ Supply, Demand and Equilibrium Views of Return

We now have a supply and a demand view of the expected returns on assets. The supply view presented here prescribes an aggregate real total return on financial assets but does not suggest how the return will be distributed among the various assets. The demand view presented in our earlier article did not prescribe an aggregate return but suggested that the relative returns on different assets would be determined by the assets' characteristics and investors' preferences for, or aversions to, those characteristics.

Melding the supply and demand views gives us an equilibrium view of return. Historical returns over long periods tend to reveal the equilibrium return, as actual results in the market reflect both the aggregate payoff generated by business activity on the supply side and the relative attractiveness of various assets on the demand side.[10] Thus the use of historical returns to formulate future expectations has support in equilibrium theory.

In addition to this equilibrium view of the market, we now have a supply-side guideline for estimating future real expected aggregate return. Specifically, Table 8.3 suggests 5.4 percent as the supply-governed expected real return. Of course, this number may vary depending upon one's view of future growth or factor shares.

We have propounded an idea we call macroconsistency. Market returns must be governed by the productivity of businesses—i.e., by macroeconomic or supply forces. One must be careful, of course, of interpreting this "governance" too broadly. Inasmuch as supply is affected by demand and forms only half of the equilibrium pricing equation, it would be just as meaningful to say that demand governs. We have emphasized the supply side because it has traditionally been ignored both in the financial context and in the more general context of economic and policy discussion. Given the renewed academic and popular interest in the supply of economic goods, we find it apropos to address supply in the financial context too.

What If Supply Changed?

A supply-demand-equilibrium framework suggests some interesting speculative questions, some of which are sketched out in Table 8.4.[11] This supposes that we live in an economy with $2 trillion of consumption in the current period and a total social wealth of $50 trillion, yielding an income return of 4 percent on society's wealth. In addition, wealth and consumption both grow at 3 percent forever. The cost of capital or rate of total return for society's wealth is thus 7 percent (in real terms, ignoring inflation).

Because of an exogenous occurrence—such as a change in the political system or in the preference for leisure over work—growth stops; i.e., the consumption stream will remain at $2 trillion per year forever. The supply view in isolation suggests that the cost of capital for society's wealth will now be 4 percent. Valuing the $2 trillion perpetuity income stream at 4 percent, we find

Table 8.4
What If Supply Changed: An Illustration

Constant growth model for consumption
  R = cost of capital for the economy
    = (consumption/wealth) + consumption growth rate
Positive growth economy
  R = ($2 trillion/$50 trillion) + 3% growth
    = 4% + 3% = 7%
Zero growth economy
  Supply view: R set by macroeconomic performance
  R = ($2 trillion/$50 trillion) + 0% growth
    = 4% + 0% = 4%
  Demand view: R set by NET characteristics of holding the wealth of the economy
  R = 7% thus
  R = $2 trillion/$28.6 trillion, i.e.,
  Wealth = $28.6 trillion
  Equilibrium view
  R is between 4% and 7%.
  Wealth is between $28.6 trillion and $50 trillion.
    One possibility:
    R = ($2 trillion/$40 trillion) + 0% growth
      = 5% + 0% = 5%

that wealth remains at $50 trillion. The demand view in isolation, on the other hand, suggests that the cost of capital will remain at 7 percent, because the NET characteristics (other than return) of holding society's wealth have not changed. Valuing the $2 trillion perpetuity at 7 percent, wealth will fall to $28.6 trillion.

Which of these two views is correct? We believe that both supply and demand factors set the equilibrium cost of capital, so that the answer will be somewhere in between those suggested by supply and by demand each in isolation. In other words, society's wealth will fall, but not as low as $28.6 trillion, and the cost of capital will fall, but not as low as 4 percent. Table 8.4 illustrates one possible result—wealth of $40 trillion and a cost of capital of 5 percent. Of course, we have no idea what the answer would actually be and hope, in any case, that the scenario is pure fantasy.

Future Work

A supply-side approach to capital market returns offers a potentially useful screen for market forecasts. Doomsday or hypergrowth forecasts ("Dow 300; Dow 3000") clearly defy our supply-side assumptions of constant GNP growth and constant factor share. In general, one should be aware of the implicit assumptions contained in market forecasts and should reject a forecast if its underlying supply assumptions differ from one's own.

Of course, the ultimate goal of the supply and demand approaches is an integrated supply-demand theory of payoffs for asset characteristics, one that can specify expected returns for all assets once their characteristics are known. This result would amount to a prescriptive formula of the kind exemplified by the CAPM and APT, and it is a long way off at best; we do not even know that it is possible. We mention the possibility of a prescriptive formula incorporating both supply and demand in order to stimulate imaginations and to encourage researchers to examine the feasibility of such an undertaking.

◤ Notes

1. Roger G. Ibbotson, Jeffrey J. Diermeier and Laurence B. Siegel, "The Demand for Capital Market Returns: A New Equilibrium Theory," *Financial Analysts Journal,* January/February 1984.

2. The CAPM is developed in William F. Sharpe, "Capital Asset Prices: A Theory of Market Equilibrium Under Conditions of Risk," *Journal of Finance,* September 1964, pp. 425–552 and in John Lintner, "The Valuation of Risk Assets and The Selection of Risky Investments in Stock Portfolios and Capital Budgets," *Review of Economics and Statistics,* February 1965, pp. 13–37. APT is developed in Stephen A. Ross, "The Arbitrage Pricing Theory of Capital Asset Pricing," *Journal of Economic Theory,* December 1976, pp. 341–360.

3. Our usage contrasts with the more widely seen "supply of and demand for capital," in which investors are the suppliers and businesses the demanders. There is no substantive difference between the two; ours is intended to focus on cash flows (or their analogue, investment returns) as the good being priced in the market.

4. We plotted data from U.S. Department of Commerce national income account statistics obtained from DRI-FACS, a service of Data Resources, Inc., Lexington, Mass.

5. Nominal GNP and per capita GNP were obtained from the U.S. Department of Commerce. We converted the nominal series to real terms using the Burgess series from "Editorial," *Review of Economics and Statistics,* February 1934 (original data in W. Randolph Burgess, *Trends of School Costs* [New York: Russell Sage Foundation, 1920]), quoted in *Historical Statistics of the United States,* 1975 edition, page 212, published by the U.S. Department of Commerce, for 1889–1912. To convert from nominal to real terms for 1913–1982, we used the Consumer Price Index (CPI), not seasonally adjusted, with the CPI-U (CPI for All Urban Consumers), not seasonally adjusted, beginning in January 1978.

Correlations with the stock market are based on the value-weighted index of all New York Stock Exchange stocks in Alfred Cowles, *Common Stock Indexes, 1871–1937* (Bloomington, Ind: Principia Press, 1938), adjusted for the reinvestment of dividends, for 1889–1925; and from the value-weighted NYSE total return index constructed by the Center for Research in Security Prices (CRSP), Graduate School of Business, University of Chicago, for 1926–1982.

6. The 1930–1939 compound annual per capita real GNP growth rate reported in Table 8.1—0.0 percent—represents the small positive number 0.032 percent, rounded to one decimal place.

7. We collected aggregate market values of stocks, bonds, cash and real estate for the various starting and ending years shown in Table 8.2 and converted them to constant dollars using the CPI. The sources of the market value data are: Roger G. Ibbotson and

Gary P. Brinson, "World Wealth: The History and Economics of Capital Markets" (Work in progress); Roger G. Ibbotson and Carol L. Fall, "The U.S. Market Wealth Portfolio," *Journal of Portfolio Management,* Fall 1979; and Robert A. Stambaugh, "Missing Assets, Measuring the Market, and Testing the Capital Asset Pricing Model" (Ph.D. dissertation, University of Chicago, 1981).

8. To further an intuitive understanding of the result, it may help to rephrase Equation (4) in the dividend growth model context originally set forth by J. B. Williams in *The Theory of Investment Value* (Cambridge, Mass: Harvard University Press, 1938) and elaborated in Myron J. Gordon and Eli Shapiro, "Capital Equipment Analysis: The Required Rate of Profit," *Management Science,* October 1956, pp. 102–110.

By rearranging Equation (4) as $r = (d - n) + g$, one can separate out $(d - n)$ to represent "net dividends"—i.e., dividends net of new issues, or that part of dividends that does not have to be reinvested in the financial markets in order to sustain constant growth at rate g. In this context, $(d - n)$ is a measure of the consumption flowing from financial markets and g is the rate of growth of $(d - n)$. This concept is consistent with the idea that eventual consumption is the goal of investment.

9. Forecast yields are as of June 30, 1983, and consist of the S&P 500 stock index yield, the Salomon Brothers Inc. long-term high-grade bond index average coupon divided by average price, the 30-day Treasury bill yield, and the authors' estimate of real estate net rental income. Market weights are from Figure 1 of Roger G. Ibbotson and Laurence B. Siegel, "The World Market Wealth Portfolio," *Journal of Portfolio Management,* Winter 1983.

10. See, for example, the returns in Roger G. Ibbotson and Rex A. Sinquefield, *Stocks, Bonds, Bills and Inflation: The Past and the Future* (Charlottesville, Va: Financial Analysts Research Foundation, 1982); Lawrence Fisher and James Lorie, *A Half Century of Returns on Stocks and Bonds* (Chicago: University of Chicago Press, 1977); Cowles, *Common Stock Indexes, 1871–1937,* op. cit.; and Frederick R. Macaulay, *The Movement of Interest Rates, Bond Yields, and Stock Prices in the United States Since 1856* (New York: National Bureau of Economic Research, 1938).

11. This analysis is based on the Williams and Gordon-Shapiro constant growth model, applied to consumption. We have tried to make this example realistic for the United States, at least in the order of magnitude sense. Fifty trillion dollars is a rounded estimate of the U.S. social wealth including human capital and other immeasurables. Since current GNP is about $3.0 trillion, we might suppose that consumption (after extracting savings and the government share) might be in the range of $2 trillion.

9 Roger G. Ibbotson

Building the Future From the Past

▲ *Overview*

This is a short column summarizing the approach Ibbotson and Chen take in the article following the column. The column serves as a good introduction to our latest thinking on the subject of how to estimate the equity risk premium.

Until the last two years, investors had not seen consecutive negative annual stock market returns since the 1970s. In contrast, during the 1980s and 1990s the market produced its best 20-year performance ever. But neither the last two years nor the last two decades are good predictors of the long run.

A forecast usually begins by comparing the expected return on stocks with that of a low-risk asset, such as U.S. government bonds. This difference is called the equity (stock) risk premium, because it is likely to be positive and represents the extra payoff that an investor demands (but does not always get) for investing in something risky (stocks) compared with something nearly risk-free (government bonds). Thus, the bond yield is our starting point, and adding the equity risk premium gives us the expected return on stocks.

Generally, the best way to get a sense of what the future may bring is to look at the past. After all, the past is our primary source of data. But, as you already know from recent market results, the stock market is quite volatile. The only way to get a good representation is to look back over a long period of time, so that the ups and downs of the market tend to cancel out and we get a reasonable average.

The compound average annual nominal rate of return (including inflation) for common stocks was 10.7 percent over the period 1926–2001. This return exceeded long-term U.S. Treasury yields by over 5 percent per year. That difference was the historical equity risk premium—the amount of extra return investors got over the last three-quarters of a century for investing in stocks rather than bonds.

But looking at historical stock returns relative to bond income is not the whole picture. The bull market of the 1980s and 1990s had so much of an impact on stock prices that the price of stocks in the S&P 500 Index is almost 30 times the earnings of the same companies. This contrasts with a price/earnings (P/E) ratio closer to 10 back in the 1970s—and only about 14 over the whole 76 years. This growth in the P/E ratio is not expected to repeat in the future.

Thus, to a certain extent, the stock market has outrun the underlying real earnings power of corporations.

A long-term forecast should not extrapolate the separation of the P/E ratio indefinitely. But today's high P/E ratios are not necessarily going to soon revert to historical levels, because the prices reflect the future outlook of investors—all those people and institutions that hold, buy, or sell stocks. In fact, if today's P/E ratio is higher than in the past, it has to mean one of three things: The price is now unrealistically high, people are willing to accept a much lower expected return for the risk of stocks, or the market is optimistic that the earnings per share growth of corporations will be higher than it was in the past. In fact, I believe in the market's optimism. Earnings per share will grow at faster rates for two reasons. First, corporations are paying out lower dividends and retaining more earnings. These extra retained earnings are reinvested back into firms. If the money is used productively, extra growth can be achieved. Second, investors are rationally willing to pay high prices for current earnings when they think future earnings will grow. The evidence demonstrates that over time investors who buy when the market's P/E ratios are high do just about as well as those who buy when the market's P/E ratios are low.

Stocks are predicted to outperform bonds in the future, but not by further P/E ratio increases. Instead, stocks will tend to participate with the overall U.S. economy and earnings per share growth. My forecast for stocks is somewhat less than 4 percent in excess of long-term bond yields. Applying this premium to recent bond yields gives a long-term forecast of over 9 percent for the stock market. It is high, but lower than the historical stock market return. But, of course, there is no free lunch. The reason stocks are expected to outperform bonds is that they are riskier than bonds. Although stocks belong in most people's portfolios, the smart investor will still want to diversify across different types of stocks, as well as across bonds and other asset classes.

10 Roger G. Ibbotson and Peng Chen

Long-Run Stock Returns: Participating in the Real Economy

◣ *Overview*

The previous Diermeier, Ibbotson, and Siegel paper serves as the inspiration for the supply approach presented here. But, unlike the Diermeier, Ibbotson, and Siegel article, the Ibbotson and Chen paper estimates the equity risk premium directly. The estimate is based upon the actual earnings per share that firms produced over the period 1926 to 2000, as well as the dividends that they paid out. Since all work is done on a "per share" basis, it was not necessary to net out aggregate inflows and outflows from the stock market. It is still important to keep track of the flows on a per share basis though, since any money paid out in dividends becomes part of the total return investors earned over the period.

The earnings growth actually achieved plus the dividends paid out represent the returns investors achieved over the period, except for the change in the P/E ratio. The increase in the P/E ratio over the period (from about 10 times to about 26 times) is considered a one time windfall. Since it is not expected to repeat, the equity growth (1.25 percent per year) is removed from the forecast.

This article reflects our latest current thinking of not only how to estimate the equity risk premium, but also the estimates themselves are all relatively current. Updating the equity risk premium forecast through 2002 using the Ibbotson and Chen method gives us a geometric equity risk premium of 3.41 percent, compared to the equity risk premium of 3.97 percent presented in this article.

In the study reported here, we estimated the forward-looking long-term equity risk premium by extrapolating the way it has participated in the real economy. We decomposed the 1926–2000 historical equity returns into supply factors—inflation, earnings, dividends, the P/E, the dividend-payout ratio, book value, return on equity, and GDP per capita. Key findings are the following. First, the growth in corporate productivity measured by earnings is in line with the growth of overall economic productivity. Second, P/E increases account for only a small portion of the total return of equity. The bulk of the return is attributable to dividend payments and nominal earnings growth (including inflation and real earnings growth). Third, the increase in the equity market relative to economic productivity can be more than fully attributed to the increase in the P/E. Fourth, a secular decline has occurred in the dividend yield and payout ratio, rendering dividend growth alone a poor measure of corporate profitability and future growth. Our forecast of the equity risk premium is only slightly lower than the pure historical return estimate. We estimate the expected long-term equity risk premium (relative to the long-term government bond yield) to be about 6 percentage points arithmetically and 4 percentage points geometrically.

Numerous authors are directing their efforts toward estimating expected returns on stocks incremental to bonds.[1] These equity risk premium studies can be categorized into four groups based on the approaches the authors took. The first group of studies has attempted to derive the equity risk premium from the historical returns of stocks and bonds; an example is Ibbotson and Sinquefield (1976a, 1976b). The second group, which includes our current work, has used fundamental information—such as earnings, dividends, or overall economic productivity—to measure the expected equity risk premium. The third group has adopted demand-side models that derive expected equity returns through the payoff demanded by investors for bearing the risk of equity investments, as in the Ibbotson, Diermeier, and Siegel (1984) demand framework and, especially, in the large body of literature following the seminal work of Mehra and Prescott (1985).[2] The fourth group has relied on opinions of investors and financial professionals garnered from broad surveys.

In the work reported here, we used supply-side models. We first used this type of model in Diermeier, Ibbotson, and Siegel (1984). Numerous other authors have used supply-side models, usually with a focus on the Gordon (1962) constant-dividend-growth model. For example, Siegel (1999) predicted that the equity risk premium will shrink in the future because of low current dividend yields and high equity valuations. Fama and French (2002), studying a longer time period (1872–1999), estimated a historical expected geometric equity risk premium of 2.55 percentage points when they used dividend growth rates and a premium of 4.32 percentage points when they used earnings growth rates.[3] They argued that the increase in the P/E has resulted in a realized equity risk premium that is higher than the ex ante (expected) premium. Campbell and Shiller (2001) forecasted low returns because they believe the current market is overvalued. Arnott and Ryan (2001) argued that the forward-looking equity risk premium is actually negative. This conclusion was based on the low current dividend yield plus their forecast for very low dividend growth. Arnott and Bernstein (2002) argued similarly that the forward-looking equity risk premium is near zero or negative (see also Arnott and Asness 2003).

The survey results generally support somewhat higher equity risk premia. For example, Welch (2000) conducted a survey of 226 academic financial economists about their expectations for the equity risk premium. The survey showed that they forecasted a geometric long-horizon equity risk premium of almost 4 pps.[4] Graham and Harvey (2001) conducted a multiyear survey of chief financial officers of U.S. corporations and found their expected 10-year geometric average equity risk premium to range from 3.9 pps to 4.7 pps.[5]

In this study, we linked historical equity returns with factors commonly used to describe the aggregate equity market and overall economic productivity. Unlike some studies, ours portrays results on a per share basis (per capita in the case of GDP). The factors include inflation, EPS, dividends per share, P/E, the dividend-payout ratio, book value per share, return on equity, and GDP per capita.[6]

We first decomposed historical equity returns into various sets of components based on six methods. Then, we used each method to examine each of the components. Finally, we forecasted the equity risk premium through supply-side models using historical data.

Our long-term forecasts are consistent with the historical supply of U.S. capital market earnings and GDP per capita growth over the 1926–2000 period. In an important distinction from the forecasts of many others, our forecasts assume market efficiency and a constant equity risk premium.[7] Thus, the current high P/E represents the market's forecast of higher earnings growth rates. Furthermore, our forecasts are consistent with Miller and Modigliani (1961) theory, in that dividend-payout ratios do not affect P/Es and high earnings-retention rates (usually associated with low yields) imply higher per share future growth. To the extent that corporate cash is not used for reinvestment, we assumed it to be used to repurchase a company's own shares or, perhaps more frequently, to purchase other companies' shares. Finally, our forecasts treat inflation as a pass-through, so the entire analysis can be done in real terms.

▶ Six Methods for Decomposing Returns

We present six different methods for decomposing historical equity returns. The first two methods (especially Method 1) are based entirely on historical returns. The other four methods are methods of the supply side. We evaluated each method and its components by applying historical data for 1926–2000. The historical equity return and EPS data used in this study were obtained from Wilson and Jones (2002).[8] The average compound annual return for the stock market over the 1926–2000 period was 10.70 percent. The arithmetic annual average return was 12.56 percent, and the standard deviation was 19.67 percent. Because our methods used geometric averages, we focus on the components of the 10.70 percent geometric return. When we present our forecasts, we convert the geometric average returns to arithmetic average returns.

Method 1. Building Blocks

Ibbotson and Sinquefield developed a "building blocks" model to explain equity returns. The three building blocks are inflation, the real risk-free rate, and the equity risk premium. Inflation is represented by changes in the U.S. Consumer Price Index (CPI). The equity risk premium for year t, ERP_t, and the real risk-free rate for year t, RRf_t, are given by, respectively,

$$\text{ERP}_t = \frac{1 + R_t}{1 + \text{Rf}_t} - 1 \tag{1}$$

$$= \frac{R_t - \text{Rf}_t}{1 + \text{Rf}_t}$$

and

$$\text{RRF}_t = \frac{1 + \text{Rf}_t}{1 + \text{CPI}_t} - 1 \tag{2}$$

$$= \frac{\text{Rf}_t - \text{CPI}_t}{1 + \text{CPI}_t},$$

where R_t, the return of the U.S. stock market, represented by the S&P 500 Index, is

$$R_t = (1 + \text{CPI}_t)(1 + \text{RRf}_t)(1 + \text{ERP}_t) - 1 \tag{3}$$

and Rf_t is the return of risk-free assets, represented by the income return of long-term U.S. government bonds.

The compound average for equity return was 10.70 percent for 1926–2000. For the equity risk premium, we can interpret that investors were compensated 5.24 pps a year for investing in common stocks rather than long-term risk-free assets (such as long-term U.S. government bonds). This calculation also shows that roughly half of the total historical equity return has come from the equity risk premium; the other half is from inflation and the long-term real risk-free rate. Average U.S. equity returns from 1926 through 2000 can be reconstructed as follows:[9]

$$\overline{R} = (1 + \overline{\text{CPI}})(1 + \overline{\text{RRf}})(1 + \overline{\text{ERP}}) - 1$$
$$10.70\% = (1 + 3.08\%) \times (1 + 2.05\%) \times (1 + 5.24\%) - 1.$$

The first column in Figure 10.1 shows the decomposition of historical equity returns for 1926–2000 according to the building blocks method.

Method 2. Capital Gain and Income

The equity return, based on the form in which the return is distributed, can be broken into capital gain, cg, and income return, Inc. Income return of common stock is distributed to investors through dividends, whereas capital gain is distributed through price appreciation. Real capital gain, Rcg, can be computed by subtracting inflation from capital gain. The equity return in period t can then be decomposed as follows:

$$R_t = [(1 + \text{CPI}_t)(1 + \text{Rcg}_t) - 1] + \text{Inc}_t + \text{Rinv}_t, \tag{4}$$

where Rinv is reinvestment return.

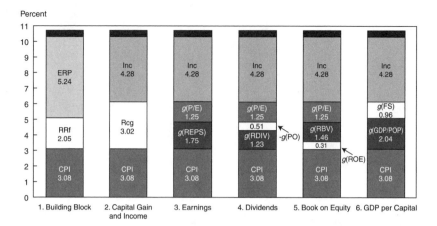

Figure 10.1. Decomposition of Historical Equity Returns by Six Methods, 1926–2000
Notes: The block on the top of each column is the reinvestment return plus the geometric interactions among the components. Including the geometric interactions ensured that the components summed to 10.70 percent in this and subsequent figures. The table that constitutes Appendix 1 gives detailed information on the reinvestment and geometric interaction for all the methods.

The average income return was calculated to be 4.28 percent in the study period, the average capital gain was 6.19 percent, and the average real capital gain was 3.02 percent. The reinvestment return averaged 0.20 percent from 1926 through 2000. For Method 2, the average U.S. equity return for 1926–2000 can thus be computed according to

$$\overline{R} = [(1 + \overline{CPI})(1 + \overline{Rcg}) - 1\,\overline{Inc} + \overline{Rinv}$$
$$10.70\% = [(1 + 3.08\%) \times (1 + 3.02\%) - 1] + 4.28\%$$
$$+ 0.20\%.$$

The second column in Figure 10.1 shows the decomposition of historical equity returns for 1926–2000 according to the capital gain and income method.

Method 3. Earnings

The real-capital-gain portion of the return in the capital gain and income method can be broken into growth in real EPS, g_{REPS}, and growth in P/E, $g_{P/E}$:

$$Rcg_t = \frac{P_t}{P_{t-1}} - 1 \tag{5}$$
$$= \frac{P_t/E_t}{P_{t-1}/E_{t-1}}\left(\frac{E_t}{E_{t-1}}\right) - 1$$
$$= (1 + g_{P/E,t})(1 + g_{REPS,t}) - 1.$$

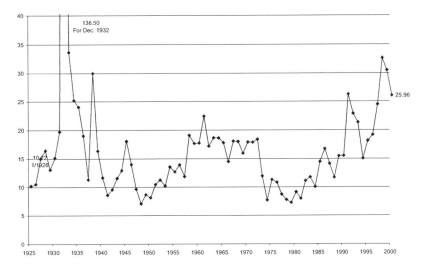

Figure 10.2. P/E, 1926–2000

Therefore, equity's total return can be broken into four components—inflation, growth in real EPS, growth in P/E, and income return:

$$R_t = [(1 + CPI_t)(1 + g_{REPS,t})(1 + g_{P/E,t}) - 1] + Inc_t + Rinv_t. \quad (6)$$

The real earnings of U.S. equity increased 1.75 percent annually between 1926 and 2000. The P/E, as Figure 10.2 illustrates, was 10.22 at the beginning of 1926 and 25.96 at the end of 2000. The highest P/E (136.50 and off the chart in Figure 10.2) was recorded during the Great Depression, in December 1932, when earnings were near zero, and the lowest in the period (7.07) was recorded in 1948. The average year-end P/E was 13.76.[10]

The U.S. equity returns from 1926 and 2000 can be computed according to the earnings method as follows:

$$\overline{R} = [(1 + \overline{CPI})(1 + \overline{g_{REPS}})(1 + \overline{g_{P/E}}) - 1] + \overline{Inc} + \overline{Rinv}$$
$$10.70\% = [(1 + 3.08\%) \times (1 + 1.75\%) \times (1 + 1.25\%) - 1]$$
$$+ 4.28\% + 0.20\%.$$

The third column in Figure 10.1 shows the decomposition of historical equity returns for 1926–2000 according to the earnings method.

Method 4. Dividends

In this method, real dividends, RDiv, equal the real earnings times the dividend-payout ratio, PO, or

$$REPS_t = \frac{RDiv_t}{PO_t}; \quad (7)$$

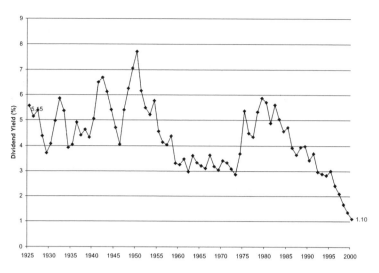

Figure 10.3. Income Return (Dividend Yield), 1926–2000

therefore, the growth rate of earnings can be calculated by the difference between the growth rate of real dividends, g_{RDiv}, and the growth rate of the payout ratio, g_{PO}:

$$(1 + g_{REPS,t}) = \frac{(1 + g_{RDiv,t})}{(1 + g_{PO,t})}. \tag{8}$$

If dividend growth and payout-ratio growth are substituted for the earnings growth in Equation 6, equity total return in period t can be broken into (1) inflation, (2) the growth rate of P/E, (3) the growth rate of the dollar amount of dividends after inflation, (4) the growth rate of the payout ratio, and (5) the dividend yield:

$$R_t = \left[(1 + CPI_t)(1 + g_{P/E,t})\left(\frac{1 + g_{RDiv,t}}{1 + g_{PO,t}}\right) - 1\right] \tag{9}$$

Figure 10.3 shows the annual income return (dividend yield) of U.S. equity for 1926–2000. The dividend yield dropped from 5.15 percent at the beginning of 1926 to only 1.10 percent at the end of 2000. Figure 10.4 shows the year-end dividend-payout ratio for 1926–2000. On average, the dollar amount of dividends after inflation grew 1.23 percent a year, while the dividend-payout ratio decreased 0.51 percent a year. The dividend-payout ratio was 46.68 percent at the beginning of 1926. It had decreased to 31.78 percent at the end of 2000. The highest dividend-payout ratio was recorded in 1932, and the lowest was the 31.78 percent recorded in 2000.

The U.S. equity returns from 1926 through 2000 can be computed in the dividends method according to

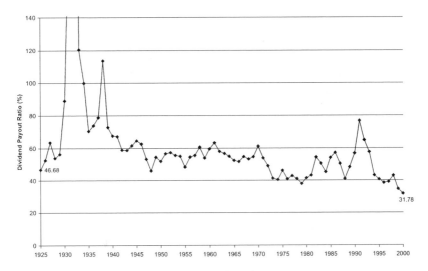

Figure 10.4. Dividend-Payout Ratio, Year-End 1926–2000
Note: The dividend-payout ratio was 190.52 percent in December 1931 and 929.12 percent in December 1932.

$$\overline{R} = \left[(1 + \overline{CPI})(1 + \overline{g_{P/E}}) \left(\frac{1 + \overline{g_{RDiv}}}{1 + \overline{g_{PO}}} \right) - 1 \right] + \overline{Inc} + \overline{Rinv}$$

$$10.70\% = \left[(1 + 3.08\%) \times (1 + 1.25\%) \times \left(\frac{1 + 1.23\%}{1 - 0.51\%} \right) - 1 \right]$$

$$+ \ 4.28\% + 0.20\%.$$

The decomposition of equity return according to the dividends method is given in the fourth column of Figure 10.1.

Method 5. Return on Book Equity

Earnings can be broken into the book value of equity, BV, and return on the book value of equity, ROE:

$$EPS_t = BV_t(ROE_t). \tag{10}$$

The growth rate of earnings can be calculated from the combined growth rates of real book value, g_{RBV}, and of ROE:

$$1 + g_{REPS,t} = (1 + g_{RBV,t})(1 + g_{ROE,t}). \tag{11}$$

In this method, BV growth and ROE growth are substituted for earnings growth in the equity return decomposition, as shown in the fifth column of Figure 10.1. Then, equity's total return in period *t* can be computed by

$$R_t = [(1 + CPI_t)(1 + g_{P/E,t})(1 + g_{RBV,t})(1 + g_{ROE,t}) - 1] \quad (12)$$
$$+ Inc_t + Rinv_t.$$

We estimated that the average growth rate of the book value after inflation was 1.46 percent for 1926–2000.[11] The average ROE growth a year during the same time period was calculated to be 0.31 percent:

$$\overline{R} = [(1 + \overline{CPI})(1 + \overline{g_{P/E}})(1 + \overline{g_{BV}})(1 + \overline{g_{ROE}}) - 1]$$
$$+ \overline{Inc} + \overline{Rinv}$$
$$10.70\% = [(1 + 3.08\%)(1 + 1.25\%)(1 + 1.46\%)(1 + 0.31\%) - 1]$$
$$+ 4.28\% + 0.20\%.$$

Method 6. GDP per Capita

Diermeier et al. proposed a framework to analyze the aggregate supply of financial asset returns. Because we were interested only in the supply model of the equity returns in this study, we developed a slightly different supply model based on the growth of economic productivity. In this method, the market return over the long run is decomposed into (1) inflation, (2) the real growth rate of overall economic productivity (GDP per capita, $g_{GDP/POP}$), (3) the increase in the equity market relative to overall economic productivity (the increase in the factor share of equities in the overall economy, g_{FS}), and (4) dividend yields.[12] This model is expressed by the following equation:

$$R_t = [(1 + CPI_t)(1 + g_{GPD/POP,t})(1 + g_{FS,t}) - 1] + Inc_t + Rinv_t. \quad (13)$$

Figure 10.5 shows the growth of the U.S. stock market, GDP per capita, earnings, and dividends initialized to unity ($1.00) at the end of 1925. The levels of all four factors dropped significantly in the early 1930s. For the whole period, GDP per capita slightly outgrew earnings and dividends, but all four factors grew at approximately the same rate. In other words, overall economic productivity increased slightly faster than corporate earnings or dividends over the past 75 years. Although GDP per capita outgrew earnings and dividends, the overall stock market price grew faster than GDP per capita. The primary reason is that the market P/E increased 2.54 times during the same time period.

Average equity market return can be calculated according to this model as follows:

$$\overline{R} = [(1 + \overline{CPI})(1 + \overline{g_{GDP/POP}})(1 + \overline{g_{FS}}) - 1] + \overline{Inc} + \overline{Rinv}$$
$$10.70\% = [(1 + 3.08\%)(1 + 2.04\%)(1 + 0.96\%) - 1]$$
$$+ 4.28\% + 0.20\%.$$

We calculated the average annual increase in the factor share of the equity market relative to the overall economy to be 0.96 percent. The increase in this factor share is less than the annual increase of the P/E (1.25 percent) over the same time period. This finding suggests that the increase in the equity market share relative to the overall economy can be fully attributed to the increase in its P/E.

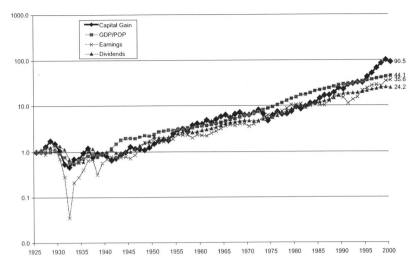

Figure 10.5. Growth of $1 From the Beginning of 1926 Through 2000

The decomposition of historical equity returns by the GDP per capita model is given in the last column of Figure 10.1.

Summary of Equity Returns and Components

The decomposition of the six models into their components can be compared by looking at Figure 10.1. The differences among the five models arise from the different components that represent the capital gain portion of the equity returns.

This analysis produced several important findings. First, as Figure 10.5 shows, the growth in corporate earnings has been in line with the growth of overall economic productivity. Second, P/E increases accounted for only 1.25 pps of the 10.70 percent total equity return. Most of the return has been attributable to dividend payments and nominal earnings growth (including inflation and real earnings growth). Third, the increase in the relative factor share of equity can be fully attributed to the increase in P/E. Overall, economic productivity outgrew both corporate earnings and dividends from 1926 through 2000. Fourth, despite the record earnings growth in the 1990s, the dividend yield and the payout ratio declined sharply, which renders dividends alone a poor measure for corporate profitability and future earnings growth.

▲ Long-Term Forecast of Equity Returns

Supply-side models can be used to forecast the long-term expected equity return. The supply of stock market returns is generated by the productivity of the corporations in the real economy. Over the long run, the equity return should be close to the long-run supply estimate. In other words, investors should not expect a much higher or a much lower return than that produced by the companies in the real economy. Therefore, we believe investors' expectations for long-term equity performance should be based on the supply of equity returns produced by corporations.

The supply of equity returns consists of two main components—current returns in the form of dividends and long-term productivity growth in the form of capital gains. In this section, we focus on two of the supply-side models—the earnings model and the dividends model (Methods 3 and 4).[13] We studied the components of these two models by identifying which components are tied to the supply of equity returns and which components are not. Then, we estimated the long-term, sustainable return based on historical information about these supply components.

Model 3F. Forward-Looking Earnings

According to the earnings model (Equation 6), the historical equity return can be broken into four components—the income return, inflation, the growth in real EPS, and the growth in P/E. Only the first three of these components are historically supplied by companies. The growth in P/E reflects investors' changing predictions of future earnings growth. Although we forecasted that the past supply of corporate growth will continue, we did not forecast any change in investor predictions. Thus, the supply side of equity return, SR, includes only inflation, the growth in real EPS, and income return:[14]

$$SR_t = [(1 + CPI_t)(1 + g_{REPS,t}) - 1] + Inc_t + Rinv_t. \qquad (14)$$

The long-term supply of U.S. equity returns based on the earnings model is 9.37 percent, calculated as follows:

$$\overline{SR} = [(1 + \overline{CPI})(1 + \overline{g_{REPS}}) - 1] + \overline{Inc} + \overline{Rinv}$$
$$9.37\% = [(1 + 3.08\%)(1 + 1.75\%) - 1] + 4.28\% + 0.20\%.$$

The decomposition according to Model 3F is compared with that of Method 3 (based on historical data plus the estimated equity risk premium) in the first two columns of Figure 10.6.

The supply-side equity risk premium, ERP, based on the earnings model is calculated to be 3.97 pps:

$$\overline{ERP} = \frac{(1 + \overline{SR})}{(1 + \overline{CPI})(1 + RRf)} - 1$$
$$= \frac{1 + 9.37\%}{(1 + 3.08\%)(1 + 2.05\%)} - 1$$
$$= 3.97\%.$$

The ERP is taken into account in the third column of Figure 10.6.

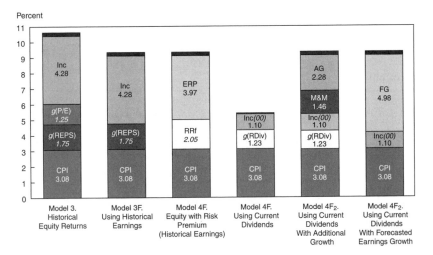

Percent

Figure 10.6. Historical vs. Current Dividend-Yield Forecasts Based on Earnings and Dividends Models

Notes: Inc (00) is the dividend yield in year 2000. FG is the real earnings growth rate, forecasted to be 4.98 percent. Model $4F_2$ corrects Model 4F as follows: add 1.46 pps for M&M consistency and add 2.24 pps for the additional growth, *AG*, implied by the high current market P/E.

Model 4F. Forward-Looking Dividends

The forward-looking dividends model is also referred to as the constant-dividend-growth model (or the Gordon model). In it, the expected equity return equals the dividend yield plus the expected dividend growth rate. The supply of the equity return in the Gordon model includes inflation, the growth in real dividends, and dividend yield.

As is commonly done with the constant-dividend-growth model, we used the current dividend yield of 1.10 percent instead of the historical dividend yield of 4.28 percent. This decision reduced the estimate of the supply of equity returns to 5.44 percent:

$$\overline{SR} = [(1 + \overline{CPI})(1 + \overline{g_{RDiv}}) - 1] + Inc(00) + \overline{Rinv}$$
$$5.54\% = [(1 + 3.08\%)(1 + 1.23\%) - 1] + 1.10\% + 0.20\%,$$

where Inc (00) is the dividend yield in year 2000. The equity risk premium was estimated to be 0.24 pps:

$$\overline{ERP} = \frac{(1 + \overline{SR})}{(1 + \overline{CPI})(1 + \overline{RRf})} - 1$$
$$= \frac{1 + 5.54\%}{(1 + 3.08\%) + (1 + 2.05\%)} - 1$$
$$= 0.24\%.$$

Figure 10.6 allows a comparison of forecasted equity returns including the equity risk premium estimates based on the earnings model and the dividends model. In the next section, we show why we disagree with the dividends model and prefer to use the earnings model to estimate the supply-side equity risk premium.

Differences Between the Earnings Model and the Dividends Model

The earnings model (3F) and the dividends model (4F) differ in essentially two ways. The differences relate to the low current payout ratio and the high current P/E. These two differences are reconciled in what we will call Model $4F_2$ shown in the two right-hand columns of Figure 10.6. First, to reflect growth in productivity, the earnings model uses historical earnings growth whereas the dividend model uses historical dividend growth. Historical dividend growth underestimates historical earnings growth, however, because of the decrease in the payout ratio. Overall, the dividend growth underestimated the increase in earnings productivity by 0.51 pps a year for 1926–2000. Today's low dividend yield also reflects the current payout ratio, which is at a historical low of 31.8 percent (compared with the historical average of 59.2 percent). Applying such a low rate to the future would mean that even more earnings would be retained in the future than in the historical period studied. But had more earnings been retained, the historical earnings growth would have been 0.95 pps a year higher, so (assuming the historical average dividend-payout ratio) the current yield of 1.10 percent would need to be adjusted upward by 0.95 pps.

By using the current dividend-payout ratio in the dividend model, Model 4F creates two errors, both of which violate Miller and Modigliani theory. A company's dividend-payout ratio affects only the form in which shareholders receive their returns (i.e., dividends versus capital gains), not their total returns. The *current* low dividend-payout ratio should not affect our forecast. Companies today probably have such low payout ratios to reduce the tax burden on their investors. Instead of paying dividends, many companies reinvest earnings, buy back shares, or use the cash to purchase other companies.[15] Therefore, the dividend growth model has to be upwardly adjusted by 1.46 pps (0.51 pp plus 0.95 pp) so as not to violate M&M theory.

The second difference between Model 3F and Model 4F is related to the fact that the current P/E (25.96) is much higher than the historical average (13.76). The current yield (1.10 percent) is at a historic low—because of the previously mentioned low payout ratio and because of the high P/E. Even assuming the historical average payout ratio, the current dividend yield would be much lower than its historical average (2.05 percent versus 4.28 percent). This difference is geometrically estimated to be 2.28 pps a year. In Figure 10.6, the additional growth, *AG*, accounts for 2.28 pps of the return; in the last column, the forecasted real earnings growth rate, *FG*, accounts for 4.98 pps. The high P/E could be caused by (1) mispricing, (2) a low required rate of return, and/or (3) a high expected future earnings growth rate. Mispricing as a cause is eliminated by our assumption of market efficiency, and a low required rate of return is eliminated by our assumption of a constant equity risk premium through the past and future periods that we are trying to estimate. Thus, we interpret the high P/E as the market expectation of higher earnings growth; and the following equation is the model for Model $4F_2$, which reconciles the differences between the earnings model and the dividends model:[16]

$$\overline{SR} = [(1 + \overline{CPI})(1 + \overline{g_{RDiv}})(1 - \overline{g_{PO}}) - 1]$$
$$+ \operatorname{Inc}(00) + AY + AG + \overline{Rinv}$$
$$9.67\% = [(1 + 3.08\%)(1 + 1.23\%)(1 + 0.51\%) - 1]$$
$$+ 1.10\% + 0.95\% + 2.58\% + 0.20\%.$$

To summarize, the earnings model and the dividends model have three differences. The first two differences relate to the dividend-payout ratio and are direct violations of M&M. The third difference results from the expectation of higher-than-average earnings growth, which is predicted by the high current P/E. Reconciling these differences reconciles the earnings and dividends models.

Geometric vs. Arithmetic

The estimated equity return (9.37 percent) and equity risk premium (3.97 pps) are geometric averages. The arithmetic average, however, is often used in portfolio optimization. One way to convert the geometric average into an arithmetic average is to assume the returns are independently lognormally distributed over time. Then, the arithmetic average, R_A, and geometric average, R_G, have roughly the following relationship:

$$R_A = R_G + \frac{\sigma^2}{2}, \tag{15}$$

where σ^2 is the variance.

The standard deviation of equity returns is 19.67 percent. Because almost all the variation in equity returns is from the equity risk premium, rather than the risk-free rate, we need to add 1.93 pps to the geometric estimate of the equity risk premium to convert the returns into arithmetic form, so $R_A = R_G + 1.93$ pps. The arithmetic average equity risk premium then becomes 5.90 pps for the earnings model.

To summarize, the long-term supply of equity return is estimated to be 9.37 percent (6.09 percent after inflation), conditional on the historical average risk-free rate. The supply-side equity risk premium is estimated to be 3.97 pps geometrically and 5.90 pps arithmetically.[17]

Appendix 1
Summary Tabulations for Forecasted Equity Return

Method/Model	Sum	Inflation	Real Risk-Free Rate	Equity Risk Premium	Real Capital Gain	g (Real EPS)	g (Real Div)	-g (Payout Ratio)	g(BV)	g(ROE)	g(P/E)	g (Real GDP/POP)	g (FS-GDP/POP)	Income Return	Reinvestment + Interaction	Additional Growth	Forecasted Earnings Growth
A. Historical																	
Method 1	10.70	3.08	2.05	5.24											0.33		
Method 2	10.70	3.08			3.02									4.28	0.32		
Method 3	10.70	3.08				1.75					1.25			4.28	0.34		
Method 4	10.70	3.08					1.23	0.51			1.25			4.28	0.35		
Method 5	10.70	3.08							1.25	0.31	1.25			4.28	0.31		
Method 6	10.70	3.08										2.04	0.96	4.28	0.32		
B. Forecast with historical dividend yield																	
Model 3F	9.37	3.08				1.75								4.28	0.26		
Model 3F (ERP)	9.37	3.08	2.05	3.97										4.28	0.27		
C. Forecast with current dividend yield																	
Model 4F	5.44	3.08				1.23								1.10[a]	0.03		
Model 4F (ERP)	5.44	3.08	2.05	0.24											0.07		
Model 4F₂	9.37	3.08					1.23	0.51						2.05[b]	0.21	2.28	
Model 4F₂ (FG)	9.37	3.08												1.10[a]	0.21		4.98

[a] 2000 dividend yield.
[b] Assuming the historical average dividend-payout ratio, the 2000 dividend yield is adjusted up 0.95 pps.

◤ Conclusions

We adopted a supply-side approach to estimate the forward-looking, long-term, sustainable equity return and equity risk premium. We analyzed historical equity returns by decomposing returns into factors commonly used to describe the aggregate equity market and overall economic productivity—inflation, earnings, dividends, P/E, the dividend-payout ratio, BV, ROE, and GDP per capita. We examined each factor and its relationship to the long-term supply-side framework. We used historical information in our supply-side models to forecast the equity risk premium. A complete tabulation of all the numbers from all models and methods is presented in Appendix 1.

Contrary to several recent studies on the equity risk premium declaring the forward-looking premium to be close to zero or negative, we found the long-term supply of the equity risk premium to be only slightly lower than the straight historical estimate. We estimated the equity risk premium to be 3.97 pps in geometric terms and 5.90 pps on an arithmetic basis. These estimates are about 1.25 pps lower than the historical estimates. The differences between our estimates and the ones provided by several other recent studies result principally from the inappropriate assumptions those authors used, which violate the M&M theorem. Also, our models interpret the current high P/E as the market forecasting high future growth rather than a low discount rate or an overvaluation. Our estimate is in line with both the historical supply measures of public corporations (i.e., earnings) and overall economic productivity (GDP per capita).

The implication of an estimated equity risk premium being far closer to the historical premium than zero or negative is that stocks are expected to outperform bonds over the long run. For long-term investors, such as pension funds and individuals saving for retirement, stocks should continue to be a favored asset class in a diversified portfolio. Because our estimate of the equity risk premium is lower than historical performance, however, some investors should lower their equity allocations and/or increase their savings rate to meet future liabilities.

◤ Notes

1. In our study, we defined the equity risk premium as the difference between the long-run expected return on stocks and the long-term risk-free (U.S. Treasury) yield. (Some other studies, including Ibbotson and Sinquefield [1976a, 1976b] used short-term U.S. T-bills as the risk-free rate.) We did all of our analysis in geometric form, then converted to arithmetic data at the end, so the estimate is expressed in both arithmetic and geometric forms.

2. See also Mehra (2003).

3. Comparing estimates from one study with another is sometimes difficult because of changing points of reference. The equity risk premium estimate can be significantly different simply because the authors used arithmetic versus geometric returns, a long-term risk-free rate versus a short-term risk-free rate, bond income return (yield) versus bond total

return, or long-term strategic forecasting versus short-term market-timing estimates. We provide a detailed discussion of arithmetic versus geometric returns in the section "The Long-Term Forecast."

4. Welch's survey reported a 7 pp equity risk premium measured as the arithmetic difference between equity and T-bill returns. To make an apples-to-apples comparison, we converted the 7 pp number into a geometric equity risk premium relative to the long-term U.S. government bond income return, which produced an estimate of almost 4 pps.

5. For further discussion of approaches to estimating the equity risk premium, see the presentations and discussions at www.aimrpubs.org/ap/home.html from AIMR's *Equity Risk Premium Forum*.

6. Each per share quantity is per share of the S&P 500 portfolio. Hereafter, we will merely refer to each factor without always mentioning "per share"—for example, "dividends" instead of "dividends per share."

7. Many theoretical models suggest that the equity risk premium is dynamic over time. Recent empirical studies (e.g., Goyal and Welch 2001; Ang and Bekaert 2001) found no evidence, however, of long-horizon return predictability by using either earnings or dividend yields. Therefore, instead of trying to build a model for a dynamic equity risk premium, we assumed that the long-term equity risk premium is constant. This assumption provided a benchmark for analysis and discussion.

8. We updated the series with data from Standard and Poor's to include the year 2000.

9. Appendix 1 summarizes all the tabulations we discuss.

10. The average P/E was calculated by reversing the average earnings-to-price ratio for 1926–2000.

11. Book values were calculated from the book-to-market ratios reported in Vuolenteenaho (2000). The aggregate book-to-market ratio was 2.0 in 1928 and 4.1 in 1999. We used the growth rate in book value calculated for 1928–1999 as the proxy for the growth rate for 1926–2000. The average ROE growth rate was calculated from the derived book value and the earnings data.

12. Instead of assuming a constant equity factor share, we examined the historical growth rate of the equity factor share relative to the overall growth of the economy.

13. We did not use Methods 1, 2, and 5 in forecasting because the forecasts of Methods 1 and 2 would be identical to the historical estimate reported in the previous section and because the forecast of Method 5 would require more complete BV and ROE data than we currently have available. We did use Method 6 to forecast future stock returns but found the results to be very similar to those for the earnings model; therefore, we do not report the results here.

14. This model uses historical income return as an input for reasons that are discussed in the section "Differences Between the Earnings Model and the Dividends Model."

15. The current tax code provides incentives for companies to distribute cash through share repurchases rather than through dividends. Green and Hollifield (2001) found that the tax savings through repurchases are on the order of 40–50 percent of the taxes that investors would have paid if dividends were distributed.

16. Contrary to efficient market models, Shiller (2000) and Campbell and Shiller argued that the P/E appears to forecast future stock price change.

17. We could also use the GDP per capita model to estimate the long-term equity risk premium. This model implies long-run stock returns should be in line with the productivity of the overall economy. The equity risk premium estimated by using the GDP per capita model would be slightly higher than the *ERP* estimate from the earnings model because GDP per capita grew slightly faster than corporate earnings in the study period. A similar

approach can be found in Diermeier et al., who proposed using the growth rate of the overall economy as a proxy for the growth rate in aggregate wealth in the long run.

▶ References

Ang, Andrew, and Geert Bekaert. 2001. "Stock Return Predictability: Is It There?" National Bureau of Economic Research (NBER) Working Paper 8207 (April).

Arnott, Robert D., and Clifford S. Asness. 2003. "Surprise! Higher Dividends = Higher Earnings Growth." *Financial Analysts Journal,* vol. 59, no. 1 (January/February): 70–87.

Arnott, Robert D., and Peter L. Bernstein. 2002. "What Risk Premium Is 'Normal'?" *Financial Analysts Journal,* vol. 58, no. 2 (March/April):64–84.

Arnott, Robert D., and Ronald Ryan. 2001. "The Death of the Risk Premium: Consequences of the 1990s." *Journal of Portfolio Management,* vol. 27, no. 3 (Spring): 61–74.

Campbell, John Y., and Robert J. Shiller. 2001. "Valuation Ratios and the Long-Run Stock Market Outlook: An Update." NBER Working Paper No. 8221.

Diermeier, Jeffrey J., Roger G. Ibbotson, and Laurance B. Siegel. 1984. "The Supply for Capital Market Returns." *Financial Analysts Journal,* vol. 40, no. 2 (March/April): 2–8.

Fama, Eugene F., and Kenneth R. French. 2001. "Disappearing Dividends: Changing Firm Characteristics or Lower Propensity to Pay?" *Journal of Financial Economics,* vol. 60, no. 1 (April):3–43.

———. 2002. "The Equity Risk Premium." *Journal of Finance,* vol. 57, no. 2 (April): 637–659.

Gordon, Myron. 1962. *Investment, Financing, and Valuation of the Corporation.* Homewood, IL: Irwin.

Goyal, Amit, and Ivo Welch. 2001. "Predicting the Equity Premium with Dividend Ratios." Working paper. Yale School of Management and UCLA.

Graham, John R., and Campbell R. Harvey. 2001. "Expectations of Equity Risk Premia, Volatility and Asymmetry From a Corporate Finance Perspective." Working paper, Fuqua School of Business, Duke University (August).

Green, Richard C., and Burton Hollifield. 2001. "The Personal-Tax Advantages of Equity." Working paper, Carnegie Mellon University (January).

Ibbotson Associates. 2001. *Stocks, Bonds, Bills, and Inflation: 2001 Yearbook.* Chicago, IL: Ibbotson Associates.

Ibbotson, Roger G., and Rex A. Sinquefield. 1976a. "Stocks, Bonds, Bills, and Inflation: Year-by-Year Historical Returns (1926–1974)." *Journal of Business,* vol. 49, no. 1 (January):11–47.

———. 1976b. "Stocks, Bonds, Bills, and Inflation: Simulations of the Future (1976–2000)." *Journal of Business,* vol. 49, no. 3 (July):313–338.

Ibbotson, Roger G., Jeffrey J. Diermeier, and Laurance B. Siegel. 1984. "The Demand for Capital Market Returns: A New Equilibrium Theory." *Financial Analysts Journal,* vol. 40, no. 1 (January/February):22–33.

Mehra, Rajnish. 2003. "The Equity Premium: Why Is It a Puzzle?" *Financial Analysts Journal,* vol. 59, no. 1 (January/February):54–69.

Mehra, Rajnish, and Edward Prescott. 1985. "The Equity Premium: A Puzzle." *Journal of Monetary Economics,* vol. 15, no. 2 (March):145–161.

Miller, Merton, and Franco Modigliani. 1961. "Dividend Policy, Growth and the Valuation of Shares." *Journal of Business,* vol. 34, no. 4 (October):411–433.

Shiller, Robert J. 2000. *Irrational Exuberance.* Princeton, NJ: Princeton University Press.

Siegel, Jeremy J. 1999. "The Shrinking Equity Risk Premium." *Journal of Portfolio Management,* vol. 26, no. 1 (Fall):10–17.

Vuolenteenaho, Tuomo. 2000. "Understanding the Aggregate Book-to-Market Ratio and Its Implications to Current Equity-Premium Expectations." Working paper, Harvard University.

Welch, Ivo. 2000. "Views of Financial Economists on the Equity Premium and Other Issues." *Journal of Business,* vol. 73, no. 4 (October):501–537.

Wilson, Jack W., and Charles P. Jones. 2002. "An Analysis of the S&P 500 Index and Cowles' Extensions: Price Indexes and Stock Returns, 1870–1999." *Journal of Business,* vol. 75, no. 3 (July):505–535.

Simulating and Forecasting

Finance is fundamentally concerned about the future. Investors make choices today in expectation of future positive returns, but the outcomes are subject to the random fluctuations of the markets. Simulation is a powerful approach to understanding and quantifying investment uncertainty. It allows the researcher to build a model of an asset class or an investment portfolio, and then use the power of the computer to explore the range of future outcomes that the investor could experience. This section begins with an article published by Ibbotson and Sinquefield in 1976 that launched the use of simulations in investment management research and practice. The authors use almost 50 years (1926–1974) of the historical risk premiums measured from their companion article, included in "The Lessons of History" section. The historical data become the basis for forecasting what the next 25 years of the U.S. capital markets—1976–2000—would bring.

The article is one of the first capital market forecasting papers to use Monte Carlo simulations, in which actual historical returns and risk premiums are drawn with replacement from the preceding 50-year period and then used to create "pseudo-histories" of the future paths of the markets. The term "bootstrapping" was coined by Efron (1979; see "Suggested Reading") to describe the general process of random resampling to estimate empirical distributions of sample statistics. However, the Ibbotson and Sinquefield article uses essentially this same technique to characterize the distribution of future wealth levels for investors in U.S. stocks, bonds, and Treasury bills at multiple investment horizons.

The article is particularly important because it develops a structural model as the basis for simulation, and builds expected returns from equilibrium risk premium–based building blocks of the stock and bond markets. To make their forecast, Ibbotson and Sinquefield start with the yield curve, which includes market expectations of inflation, real interest rates, and the maturity (now called horizon or interest rate) premium. The yield curve prices and yields are presumably set by the market consensus, so that the yields embed the market's expectations of inflation, real interest rates, and horizon risk into the forward rates. The historical risk premiums are then added to the yield curve base, to generate expected returns on stocks and bonds. The historical risk premiums, as well as the inflation rate and real interest rate forecast errors, are drawn from the historical sample. Some components are near random, while others, such as real rates and inflation, have intertemporal dependency patterns. Some of the components are highly cross-correlated year by year, and were consequently drawn from vectors together. By breaking the forecast into component parts, they are able to take advantage of the patterns that do exist, while still incorporating the random nature of the historical risk premiums and other data. By providing all results in probability distributions, the forecasts give estimates of both risk and return. The article is also the first to provide long-term forecasts for all the main capital markets. The years since 1976 have put the model to the test.

▲ Comparing Forecasts and Realizations

The Ibbotson and Sinquefield forecasts cover the last quarter of the twentieth century, ending in the year 2000. Given that the 25-year forecast is now itself history, it is interesting to compare the realization with the forecast. The original article forecast the stock market to have an annualized return of 13.0%, compared with the realized return of 15.3%. The forecast return on corporate bonds was 8.2%, the realized return was 9.6%. Both forecasts underestimated the extreme bull markets of the last two decades. This is also true of the over-forecast of inflation of 6.3% per year, compared to its realization of 4.7%. Yet, all three forecasts were given in terms of probability distributions, and the realizations were well within one standard deviation of the forecast mean. Some of the component risk premiums and inflation-adjusted series had bigger forecast errors, but when added together, these tended to offset each other. Some of the actual results from the last 25 years are shown in boxes, so that it is possible for the reader to compare the actual results with those that were forecast.

The short, recent article by Ibbotson (1999) focuses on the Dow Jones Industrial Average. Ibbotson and Sinquefield made many speeches during the 1970s, and one of them in 1974 forecast the Dow to reach 10,000 in 1999. At the time of the forecast, the Dow was at 851. Part of the reason this particular forecast was so accurate was that the base bond yield was at near historical high levels when the forecast was made in 1974. This made the nominal forecast return quite high, in fact substantially higher than the forecasts Ibbotson and Sinquefield later made in the *Journal of Business* published article.

Using the same method, Ibbotson's 1999 article made a forecast for the Dow to hit over 100,000 by 2025. The reason the Dow was predicted to maintain the same rate of growth into the next quarter century, while the base bond yield has dropped, is that the Dow dividend yield has also dropped dramatically. The Dow is of course a capital gain index, so that lower dividend yield means higher capital gains, offsetting predicted lower nominal total returns.

However, given that the stock market has declined since 1999, a current forecast would now be substantially below 100,000.

▶ *What Are Forecasts Used For?*

Forecasts have many different potential uses. Most forecasts are probably used by investors to make timing decisions. Forecasts of very high returns or predicted prices usually imply that the current market is undervalued. Very low returns imply current overvaluation. The implication is that the misvaluation will correct itself in the relatively near term, so that the very high or low return can be realized.

Misvaluation forecasts are very different from the forecasts included in this book. We are usually assuming that the market is fairly priced at the time of the forecast. Sometimes we call this the "efficient markets" assumption. Obviously, for forecasts based upon efficient markets, it is not appropriate to use the forecast as a signal to buy or sell stocks or bonds. In fact, we are interested in making inexact forecasts in the form of probability distributions, since they reflect the risks as well as the returns. The forecasts that we make are long-term, probabilistic, and based upon the assumption of current fair pricing. How does one use this type of forecast?

The most common uses are for long-term planning purposes and in choosing an asset allocation mix. In long-term planning, the investors want to be able to compare their needs with the potential portfolio value at various points in time in the future. Ideally, they want to include their initial portfolios, their savings or cash inflows, their expenditures or cash outflows, and the distributions of their returns. The investors want to be able to interact with their choice of portfolio mixes, across the probability distribution of portfolio returns, taking into account their cash inflows and outflows.

The choice of the portfolio mix is often accomplished using Markowitz optimization software. Optimization requires inputting expected returns, standard deviations, and cross-correlations among the asset classes.

The Goetzmann and Edwards article shows that care must be taken in either simulating long-term returns or in selecting asset allocations based upon annual inputs. The potential problem of autocorrelation over time is that the risk can be underestimated. If an optimized portfolio assumes that returns are i.i.d., when in fact they are autocorrelated, then the potential run of high or low returns causes the risk to persist, rather than tending to cancel out over time. Fortunately, the Ibbotson and Sinquefield article takes explicit account of the autocorrelations inherent in inflation and real rates, in making their forecasts.

The Goetzmann and Edwards article uses vector autoregression (VAR) to capture the temporal dependencies. They show how the optimized portfolios would be modified by taking into account the VAR process. In particular, they show that Treasury bill returns are much more volatile over long-term horizons than their annual volatility would suggest.

11 Roger G. Ibbotson and Rex A. Sinquefield

Stocks, Bonds, Bills, and Inflation: Simulations of the Future (1976–2000)

◤ Overview

In this article, Ibbotson and Sinquefield showed how to use the historical return data from their earlier paper to make long-run forecasts of our capital markets. They used 50 years of stock, bond, and inflation data to make a 25-year forecast through the year 2000.

The forecast method was unique and innovative in several respects:

1. *It was one of the first times that historical data were bootstrapped to form simulations of the future.*
2. *The forecast included all the major asset classes.*
3. *The returns were broken into components so that inflation, real short-term interest rates, equity risk premiums, maturity (horizon or interest rate) risk premiums, and default premiums could be separately and collectively forecast.*
4. *Inflation and real rate expectations were based upon the existing yield curve at the time of the forecast.*
5. *Inflation and real rates were estimated to follow an autoregressive process with only their residuals being randomly drawn.*
6. *Each of the risk premiums were randomly drawn from historical data, but equity and default risk premiums were drawn from the same years, to maintain their historical cross-correlation structure.*
7. *Inflation and real return residuals were drawn during the same years as maturity (horizon or interest rate) risk premiums, to maintain the historical cross-correlation structure.*
8. *The results were portrayed as probability distributions for each asset class.*

Since more than 25 years have transpired, we can now check the results. The updated results are presented in Table 11.8 on page 254.

◤ Introduction

In chapter 2,[1] we presented year-by-year historical returns for common stocks, long-term U.S. government and corporate bonds, U.S. Treasury bills, and consumer goods (inflation) for the period 1926–74. In this article, we present a simulation model to forecast probability distributions of returns for these assets. The model not only makes use of the historical data, but also employs the current U.S. government bond yield curve and integrates the two in a framework of capital market efficiency.

Our forecasting procedure is inherently different from that used by most economists, financial analysts, long-range planners, etc. Whereas they use their expertise in an attempt to "outguess" the market, our purpose is to uncover the market's "consensus" forecast. In an efficient capital market, the consensus forecast removes the opportunity to outguess the market by eliminating over- and underpricing of assets. To the extent that the simulation model portrays the market, its forecast can be thought of as a *benchmark* against which to compare other forecasts.

In the second section we give a brief description of the historical data used in the simulations. In the third section, we present an overview of the entire model. The next two parts of the article provide some justification for our techniques. The fourth section examines the statistical characteristics of the historical data, while the fifth section explains the term structure characteristics of the yield curve. The formal model is presented in the sixth section. The last two parts of the article present the results. The seventh section explains the forecast distributions over the period 1976–2000, while some of the major results are highlighted in the eighth section.

◣ *Description of the Data Series*

The historical total returns used in this article are described in detail in our earlier article. Total returns reflect dividend or interest income as well as capital gains or losses. All the yearly returns are computed from monthly returns. Briefly the series are: $\tilde{R}_m$ = common stock returns derived from Standard and Poor's (S&P's) Composite Index and dividend series;[2] $\tilde{R}_g$ = returns from U.S. government bonds of approximately 20 years to maturity computed from CRSP bond data;[3] $\tilde{R}_c$ = returns from a long-term corporate bond index of approximately 20 years to maturity. The index is based upon Salomon Brothers data from the period 1946–74,[4] and on S&P data from 1926–45;[5] $\tilde{R}_f$ = 30-day U.S. Treasury bill returns computed from the CRSP bond data; $\tilde{R}_I$ = yearly inflation rate measured by the percentage of change in the Consumer Price Index as compiled by the Bureau of Labor Statistics.

In addition to these basic series, $\tilde{R}_m$, $\tilde{R}_g$, $\tilde{R}_c$, $\tilde{R}_f$, and $\tilde{R}_I$, the simulation model employs seven derived series. These series break the basic series into risk and real (inflation adjusted) components. The risk components are:[6]

$$\text{risk premia,} \quad \tilde{R}_p = \frac{1 + \tilde{R}_m}{1 + \tilde{R}_f} - 1 \cong \tilde{R}_m - \tilde{R}_f, \tag{1}$$

$$\text{maturity premia,} \quad \tilde{R}_L = \frac{1 + \tilde{R}_g}{1 + \tilde{R}_f} - 1 \cong \tilde{R}_g - \tilde{R}_f, \tag{2}$$

and default premia, $\bar{R}_d = \dfrac{1 + \bar{R}_c}{1 + \bar{R}_g} - 1 \cong \bar{R}_c - \bar{R}_g.$ (3)

Real returns on Treasury bills (real interest rates) are computed as:

$$\bar{R}_r = \dfrac{1 + \bar{R}_f}{1 + \bar{R}_I} - 1 \cong \bar{R}_f - \bar{R}_I. \qquad (4)$$

Real returns for stocks, $\bar{R}_{mr}$, government bonds, $\bar{R}_{gr}$, and corporate bonds, $\bar{R}_{cr}$, are also computed in the same manner as in (4).

In our simulation model, we use the historical data computed from the ratios in equations (1)–(4). However, later when we recombine components, we will make use of the approximations given by the simple differences also presented in equations (1)–(4).

◣ Overview of the Simulation Model

The model uses two sources of inputs—the historical annual component returns from the period 1926–74 and the government bond yield curve as of December 31, 1975. We attempt to use these inputs in a framework consistent with capital market efficiency. The simulation results are in the form of probability distributions of returns and values.

The term structure of interest rates (the relationship between bond yields and maturities) provides the linkage between the forecasts of the simulation model and the market's ever-changing expectations of inflation and real interest rates. The term structure can be interpreted according to the "pure" version of the expectations hypothesis. The pure version states that the holder of a long-term bond can expect to earn the same rate of return on average as the holder of a series of short-term (say, 1-year) bonds each purchased upon the maturity of the previous bond. We modify the pure version of the theory by allowing the long-term bondholder to be compensated on average by a "maturity" premium[7] for the incremental return volatility he faces each holding period.[8]

We can best explain the term structure of interest rates by introducing the concept of a forward rate. Forward rates are implicit in the bond yield curve since we can think of each bond's yield as the geometric average of period-by-period (e.g., year-by-year) forward interest rates. The set of forward rates inherent in a shorter-term bond yield is a subset of the forward rates inherent in a longer-term bond yield. Thus, we can compute the forward rates as long as we are given the yields and the maturities of the bonds which make up the yield curve. For example, the yield on a 2-year bond is the geometric average of the first and second years' forward rates. Since the first year's forward rate (the spot rate) is directly observable as the yield on a 1-year bond, the second year's forward rate can be solved for directly. Using yields from year-end maturity dates over the 25 forecast years, we compute annual forward rates for each year.

Since forward rates are computed directly from the yield curve, they are market determined. In our model they represent consensus forecasts of 1-year interest rates (after allowing for maturity premiums) year-by-year into the future. Since 1-year nominal interest rate expectations can be broken into 1-year real interest rate, $\bar{R}_r$, and inflation rate, $\bar{R}_I$, expectations, the yield curve constrains the sum of the means of our simulation distribution for these two series.

The five building block components of our model are the yearly $\bar{R}_I$, $\bar{R}_r$, $\bar{R}_p$, $\bar{R}_L$, and $\bar{R}_d$ series. Analysis of the historical behavior of these time series reveals that the first two series ($\bar{R}_I$ and $\bar{R}_r$) exhibit high serial correlation, while the remaining series are relatively uncorrelated through time. We use simple autoregressive processes to explain the behavior of $\bar{R}_I$ and $\bar{R}_r$. The remaining series ($\bar{R}_p$, $\bar{R}_L$, and $\bar{R}_d$) are assumed to follow a random walk; that is, successive returns are assumed to be independent and identically distributed.

The $\bar{R}_r$ probability distribution comes directly from the autoregressive model making use of the historical forecast errors, $\tilde{\varepsilon}_r$. The expected inflation rate is constrained to equal the forward rate (adjusted for the maturity premium) less the real interest rate forecasted by the autoregressive model. The probability distribution of $\bar{R}_I$ is formed by adding the historical forecast errors, $\tilde{\varepsilon}_I$, to the expectation.

From the historical data, it is apparent that some of the component series are cross-correlated. We explicitly assume that $\tilde{\varepsilon}_r$, $\tilde{\varepsilon}_I$, and $\bar{R}_L$ are jointly distributed. We also assume that $\bar{R}_p$ and $\bar{R}_d$ are jointly distributed, and that the two joint distributions are independent of one another. Thus, each simulation drawing consists of selecting $\tilde{\varepsilon}_r$, $\tilde{\varepsilon}_I$, and $\bar{R}_L$ together from the same randomly chosen historical year and then selecting $\bar{R}_p$ and $\bar{R}_d$ together from another randomly chosen historical year.

We have thus far described the process for determining $\bar{R}_I$, $\bar{R}_r$, $\bar{R}_p$, $\bar{R}_L$, and $\bar{R}_d$ for each simulation drawing. This process can be repeated for each forecast year. It is now necessary only to recombine the components to form the remaining seven series. Our model is additive so that each simulation $\bar{R}_f$ is just the sum of $\bar{R}_I$ and $\bar{R}_r$. The $\bar{R}_f$ and $\bar{R}_r$ series are respectively the building blocks for the nominal and real series. We add $\bar{R}_p$ to form common stocks returns, $\bar{R}_m$ and $\bar{R}_{mr}$; we add $\bar{R}_L$ to form long-term government bond returns, $\bar{R}_g$ and $\bar{R}_{gr}$; and we add $\bar{R}_L$ plus $\bar{R}_d$ to form long-term corporate bond returns, $\bar{R}_c$ and $\bar{R}_{cr}$.

◤ Analysis of Historical Data

In this section we describe some of the statistical properties and past research findings that relate both to the historical returns and to our simulation model. Our discussion centers on the behavior of the five building block components of the model, $\bar{R}_p$, $\bar{R}_L$, $\bar{R}_d$, $\bar{R}_I$, and $\bar{R}_r$.

Time Series Behavior

Table 11.1 presents the geometric mean, arithmetic mean, standard deviation, and 12 autocorrelation lags for both the yearly and monthly historical returns over the entire sample period 1926–74. Since the means and standard deviations were described in detail in our previous paper, we focus our attention on the autocorrelations.

Most of the yearly autocorrelations are low (near zero) relative to their standard errors. However, four series ($\bar{R}_f$, $\bar{R}_I$, $\bar{R}_r$, and $\bar{R}_{cr}$) exhibit positive autocorrelations greater than two standard errors away from zero for many early lags. In fact the autocorrelations for the first lag for $\bar{R}_f$, $\bar{R}_I$, and $\bar{R}_r$ are greater than four standard errors away from zero.

Examination of monthly autocorrelations reveals several more series with estimates greater than two standard errors from zero. However, the significance of these estimates is questionable since it is well known that capital market indices measured over short periods (such as monthly) frequently contain spurious autocorrelation. The spurious correlation is caused by the discontinuous trading of some of the securities comprising an index coupled with the tendency for the various securities to be cross-correlated over any given time interval. To illustrate, suppose that an index rose sharply in a given month. Given the cross-correlation, we would expect any unquoted securities to have unreported positive returns. These positive returns would not be reported until a quote appeared in a subsequent month.[9]

We investigate the autocorrelation of $\bar{R}_r$ and $\bar{R}_I$, the components of $\bar{R}_f$. We find that simple autoregressive models describe the two yearly series almost as well as far more complicated models.[10] Our autoregressive results are as follows, with t-statistics in parentheses:[11]

$$\bar{R}_{I,t} = \gamma_{I0} + \gamma_{I}1\bar{R}_{I,t-1} + \bar{\varepsilon}_{I,t}, \tag{5}$$
$$\hat{\gamma}_{I0} = .011, \hat{\gamma}_{I1} = .599, R^2 = .334, \sigma(\bar{\varepsilon}_{I,t}) = .039,$$
$$\quad (1.78) \quad\quad (4.80)$$
$$\text{D-W} = 1.754;$$

$$\bar{R}_{r,t} = \gamma_{r0} + \gamma_{r1}\bar{R}_{r,t-1} + \bar{\varepsilon}_{r,t}, \tag{6}$$
$$\hat{\gamma}_{r0} = -.0015, \hat{\gamma}_{r1} = .623, R^2 = .392, \sigma(\bar{\varepsilon}_{r,t}) = .038,$$
$$\quad (-.279) \quad\quad (5.450)$$
$$\text{D-W} = 1.854.$$

We next turn to the risk components $\bar{R}_p$, $\bar{R}_L$, and $\bar{R}_d$. Table 11.1 reveals that these series are relatively uncorrelated through time for yearly observations. There is some evidence that monthly $\bar{R}_d$ are negatively serially correlated for the first lag. Nevertheless, we assume in our simulation model that successive returns are independent and identically distributed. Our random walk assumption for the three risk premia implies a world where both the unit price of risk (the distribution mean divided by the dispersion) and the level of risk

Table 11.1
Summary Statistics for Historical Returns (1926–1974)

Series	Geometric Mean	Arithmetic Mean	S.D.	Autocorrelation Lag												S.E.
				1	2	3	4	5	6	7	8	9	10	11	12	
A. Yearly Returns																
R_m	.0845	.1086	.2251	.06	-.15	-.07	-.23	-.01	.00	.14	-0.01	.25	.10	-.03	-.08	.14
R_g	.0324	.0337	.0535	-.06	.05	-.04	-.05	-.01	.05	-.14	.14	.12	.07	.17	-.04	.14
R_c	.0359	.0372	.0510	.12	.15	-.10	-.09	-.01	.01	.03	.20	.14	.16	.10	-.17	.14
R_f	.0224	.0226	.0211	.84	.69	.70	.69	.60	.49	.43	.37	.30	.23	.16	.10	.14
R_t	.0218	.0229	.0475	.56	.18	.07	.35	.38	.16	-.02	-.10	-.08	-.17	-.18	-.18	.14
R_p	.0608	.0857	.2277	.09	-.15	-.04	-.19	-.01	.02	.10	.05	.21	.18	-.05	-.09	.14
R_L	.0097	.0113	.0558	.11	.14	.02	.06	.12	.16	-.01	.18	.16	.12	.19	.00	.14
R_d	.0034	.0039	.0315	-.15	-.05	.04	-.06	.07	-.05	-.13	-.01	.19	-.18	.06	-.27	.14
R_r	.0006	.0017	.0457	.66	.34	.20	.38	.37	.19	.03	-.04	-.07	-.17	-.20	-.21	.14
R_{mr}	.0614	.0861	.2285	.07	-.19	-.07	-.18	.04	.06	.07	-.07	.16	.18	-.03	-.10	.14
R_{gr}	.0103	.0134	.0795	.21	.08	-.05	.20	.29	.20	-.03	.06	.08	-.00	.03	-.07	.14
R_{cr}	.0138	.0167	.0770	.39	.22	.06	.24	.35	.21	.03	.08	.05	.04	-.08	-.20	.14
B. Monthly Returns																
R_m	.0068	.0087	.0621	.11	-.02	-.15	.04	.07	-.04	.01	.07	.13	-.01	-.02	-.01	.04
R_g	.0027	.0028	.0154	-.04	.04	-.08	.08	-.03	-.03	-.07	.02	.04	-.06	.04	-.06	.04
R_c	.0029	.0030	.0137	.13	.03	-.09	.05	.03	-.03	-.07	-.05	.08	-.05	.05	.04	.04
R_f	.0018	.0019	.0018	.89	.89	.89	.87	.85	.83	.83	.81	.80	.77	.76	.76	.04
R_t	.0018	.0018	.0062	.51	.35	.33	.34	.26	.23	.28	.28	.23	.22	.25	.26	.04
R_p	.0049	.0068	.0621	.11	-.02	-.15	.05	.07	-.04	.01	.08	.13	.00	-.01	-.01	.04
R_L	.0008	.0009	.0154	-.03	.06	-.06	.10	-.02	-.01	-.05	.03	.06	-.04	.06	-.04	.04
R_d	.0003	.0004	.0130	-.24	-.00	-.07	.05	.03	-.06	-.03	.14	-.11	-.05	-.01	.06	.04
R_r	.0001	.0001	.0062	.52	.35	.34	.35	.28	.24	.30	.30	.26	.24	.28	.30	.04
R_{mr}	.0050	.0069	.0625	.11	-.03	-.15	.05	.08	-.03	.02	.08	.12	-.01	-.03	-.02	.04
R_{gr}	.0009	.0010	.0169	.07	.13	.01	.14	.03	.03	-.01	.08	.07	-.02	.06	.00	.04
R_{cr}	.0011	.0013	.0152	.23	.12	.03	.14	.11	.02	.02	.04	.11	.01	.09	.10	.04

(the dispersion of the distribution) are constant through time. Fama and MacBeth[12] studied the price of risk through time and were unable to reject that it is always positive. Although not specifically tested, their results suggest that the price of risk may not be constant. Officer[13] and others found that volatility of returns and other economic phenomena are not constant. However, changes in volatility and prices of risk are difficult to predict and are therefore ignored in our simulation procedures.

Although we do not make explicit assumptions concerning the behavior of the $\bar{R}_m$, $\bar{R}_g$, $\bar{R}_c$, $\bar{R}_{mr}$, $\bar{R}_{gr}$, and $\bar{R}_{cr}$ series, these series are all formulated from the five component series. Since each series has either an $\bar{R}_r$ component or both an $\bar{R}_r$ and an $\bar{R}_I$ component, we have imputed an autoregressive process into all of them. Examination of Table 11.1 gives little evidence of such autocorrelation. However, the serial effects are small relative to the variation for most of the series. Thus, even though much of the random walk literature involved tests of $\bar{R}_m$, in these tests $\bar{R}_m$ can be thought of as a proxy for $\bar{R}_p$. Although the evidence on bonds is not as extensive as that on stocks, our results indicate that $\bar{R}_L$ and $\bar{R}_d$ are relatively uncorrelated through time. The works of Roll and Nelson are also generally consistent with the random walk assumption for $\bar{R}_L$.[14] We know of no work on the $\bar{R}_d$ series.

Cross-Sectional Relationships

Table 11.2 gives the cross-correlation coefficients for simultaneous observations. These pairwise correlations should be cautiously viewed since frequently one series contains a negative component of another series. Thus, any measurement error in the observed negative component can cause spurious negative correlation even if the true underlying series were independent.

To illustrate this source of spurious negative correlation let us examine one of the pairwise correlations, $\bar{R}_r$ and $\bar{R}_I$. The sample cross-correlation is $-.91$ for the yearly data. If the true underlying inflation rate were

$$\bar{R}'_I = \bar{R}_I + \bar{E}_I \tag{7}$$

and assuming that $\bar{R}_f$ had no measurement error, the true real interest rate would be given by the equation (4) approximation

$$\bar{R}'_r \cong \bar{R}'_f - \bar{R}_I = \bar{R}_f - \bar{R}_I - \bar{E}_I. \tag{8}$$

Then, if the two true series ($\bar{R}'_r$, $\bar{R}'_I$) were pairwise independent, and the measurement errors $\bar{E}_I$ were independent of $\bar{R}'_I$ and $\bar{R}'_r$, it can be shown that the observed correlation would be[15]

$$\text{corr}(\bar{R}_r, \bar{R}_I) = [-\sigma^2(\bar{E}_I)]/[\sigma(\bar{R}_r)\sigma(\bar{R}_I)]. \tag{9}$$

The argument is similar for the other cross-correlations. Thus, any of ($\bar{R}_L$ and $\bar{R}_f$), ($\bar{R}_d$ and $\bar{R}_g$), ($\bar{R}_p$ and $\bar{R}_f$), or ($\bar{R}_d$ and $\bar{R}_L$) can be substituted in equation (9) for ($\bar{R}_r$ and $\bar{R}_I$).

Table 11.2
Sample Cross-Correlations for Historical Returns (1926–1974)

Yearly Cross-Correlation

	R_m	R_g	R_c	R_f	R_l	R_p	R_L	R_d	R_r	R_{mr}	R_{gr}	R_{cr}
R_m	1.00	−0.09	.12	−.24	−.06	.98	.01	.34	−.08	.98	−.05	.09
R_g		1.00	.80	−.02	−.27	−.07	.93	−.38	.27	−.02	.82	.69
R_c			1.00	−.15	−.27	.14	.79	.25	.20	.18	.68	.81
R_f				1.00	.21	−.32	−.38	−.21	.22	−.27	−.14	−.23
R_l					1.00	−.04	−.33	.02	−.91	−.21	−.76	−.78
R_p						1.00	.05	.36	−.13	.98	−.05	.09
R_L							1.00	−.29	.17	.08	.81	.72
R_d								1.00	−.12	.33	−.28	.13
R_r									1.00	.06	.71	.68
R_{mr}										1.00	.09	.22
R_{gr}											1.00	.91
R_{cr}												1.00

Monthly Cross-Correlation

	R_m	R_g	R_c	R_f	R_l	R_p	R_L	R_d	R_r	R_{mr}	R_{gr}	R_{cr}
R_m	1.00	.08	.19	−.06	.00	.99	.09	.10	−.02	.99	.07	.17
R_g		1.00	.60	.02	−.06	.08	.99	−.55	.06	.08	.93	.57
R_c			1.00	−.05	−.04	.19	.61	.33	.02	.19	.56	.91
R_f				1.00	.13	−.08	−.10	−.07	.15	−.07	−.03	−.10
R_l					1.00	.01	−.07	.03	−.96	−.08	−.42	−.44
R_p						1.00	.09	.10	−.04	.99	.07	.17
R_L							1.00	−.54	.05	.09	.93	.58
R_d								1.00	−.05	.10	−.51	.29
R_r									1.00	.06	.41	.41
R_{mr}										1.00	.11	.21
R_{gr}											1.00	.68
R_{cr}												1.00

Table 11.3 gives one-period lagged cross-correlations for each of the 12 series with each of the other series for both yearly and monthly data. It is a difficult table to interpret since it contains the $\tilde{R}_I$ and $\tilde{R}_r$ serial processes, the above mentioned measurement errors, as well as possible evidence of some past market inefficiencies.[16] Given our particular assumptions and our intent to ignore market inefficiencies, we do not investigate these lagged relationships any further.

The cross-correlations for $\tilde{R}_p$, $\tilde{R}_L$, $\tilde{R}_d$, $\tilde{\varepsilon}_I$, and $\tilde{\varepsilon}_r$ are given in Table 11.4. First note the high positive cross-correlation between $\tilde{R}_p$ and $\tilde{R}_d$ (.36 for yearly data). Co-movement of $\tilde{R}_p$ and $\tilde{R}_d$ would be expected using a Black and Scholes[17] options model interpretation. Low stock returns represent decreases in the values of firms and corresponding increases in the probabilities of bond default. This has the effect of increasing corporate bond yields, thus lowering the immediate returns of existing corporate bonds.

Other co-movement of selected series is also apparent from Table 11.4. The high negative correlation between $\tilde{\varepsilon}_I$ and $\tilde{\varepsilon}_r$ $(-.95)$ is at least partly caused by measurement error. Nevertheless, the negative correlation is so substantial that we do not treat these two observations as independent. Also the model explicitly assumes a negative relationship between $\tilde{R}_L$ and $\tilde{\varepsilon}_I$ $(-.25)$, which can be given an economic interpretation. If we use $\tilde{\varepsilon}_I$ as a proxy for unanticipated changes in inflation rates as Fama[18] does, then these higher inflation rates might be reflected in both short- and long-term yields. A rise in long-term yields would lower immediate long-term returns, $\tilde{R}_g$, and maturity premia, $\tilde{R}_L$. This result is substantiated by the $\tilde{R}_I$ and $\tilde{R}_L$ yearly cross-correlation $(-.33)$ in Table 11.3.

◣ Yield Curve Analysis

The previous section presented characteristics of the historical data. We apply the efficient market assumption not only to historical prices but also to the current prices of government bonds comprising the yield curve.

Forward Rates As Revealed Market Expectations

If the government bond market is efficient and if the various term to maturity bonds can be regarded as partial substitutes for one another, then we can make applications of the body of theory pertaining to the term structure of interest rates.

According to the pure expectations hypothesis, long-term bond yields are a geometric average of expected future short-term interest rates. Thus, the holder of a long-term bond would be expected to earn an equal amount on average as the investor who rolled over short-term bonds. We use a version of the expectations hypothesis, incorporating the differences in risk relating to the various terms to maturity of government bonds.

Table 11.3
Sample One-Period Lagged Cross-Correlations for Historical Returns (1926–1974)

First Lag, Cross-Correlation, Yearly

	$R_{m,t-1}$	$R_{g,t-1}$	$R_{c,t-1}$	$R_{f,t-1}$	$R_{l,t-1}$	$R_{p,t-1}$	$R_{L,t-1}$	$R_{d,t-1}$	$R_{r,t-1}$	$R_{mr,t-1}$	$R_{gr,t-1}$	$R_{cr,t-1}$
$R_{m,t}$	.06	.29	.27	−.19	−.01	.07	.33	−.04	−.07	.07	.21	.19
$R_{g,t}$	−.14	−.06	.05	.03	−.15	−.15	−.07	.16	.16	−.13	.04	.11
$R_{c,t}$	−.08	.06	.12	−.02	−.22	−.10	.07	.07	.22	−.06	.18	.22
$R_{f,t}$	.01	−.18	−.22	.84	.15	−.07	−.47	−.06	.20	−.01	−.22	−.25
$R_{l,t}$	.21	.06	−.09	.05	.56	.23	.04	−.22	−.55	.13	−.30	−.40
$R_{p,t}$	.09	.33	.29	−.26	−.08	.09	.40	−.08	−.04	.09	.27	.24
$R_{L,t}$	−.13	.00	.12	−.28	−.19	−.12	.11	.17	.08	−.11	.11	.20
$R_{d,t}$	.07	.21	.11	−.08	−.12	.08	.23	−.15	.09	.10	.23	.16
$R_{r,t}$	−.23	−.12	−.02	.31	−.52	−.28	−.23	.17	.66	−.16	.22	.30
$R_{mr,t}$	.05	.30	.28	−.19	−.17	.04	.35	−.05	.08	.07	.31	.29
$R_{gr,t}$	−.24	−.07	.07	−.02	−.44	−.26	−.06	.21	.44	−.18	.21	.32
$R_{cr,t}$	−.21	.01	.12	−.05	−.50	−.23	.03	.16	.49	−.14	.31	.39

First Lag, Cross-Correlation, Monthly

	$R_{m,t-1}$	$R_{g,t-1}$	$R_{c,t-1}$	$R_{f,t-1}$	$R_{l,t-1}$	$R_{p,t-1}$	$R_{L,t-1}$	$R_{d,t-1}$	$R_{r,t-1}$	$R_{mr,t-1}$	$R_{gr,t-1}$	$R_{cr,t-1}$
$R_{m,t}$	.11	.06	.04	−.08	−.05	.11	.07	−.03	.03	.11	.07	.06
$R_{g,t}$	−.03	−.04	.08	.03	−.04	−.03	−.04	.13	.04	−.03	−.02	.08
$R_{c,t}$	.08	.19	.13	.00	−.04	.09	.19	.08	.04	.09	.19	.13
$R_{f,t}$	−.09	−.02	−.08	.89	.12	−.12	−.12	.06	.13	−.11	−.06	−.12
$R_{l,t}$	.03	−.06	−.08	.12	.51	.03	−.07	−.02	−.48	−.02	−.24	−.28
$R_{p,t}$	.10	.05	.04	−.10	−.03	.11	.07	−.03	.00	.11	.06	.04
$R_{L,t}$	−.02	−.04	.09	−.08	−.05	−.02	−.03	.13	.03	−.01	−.01	.10
$R_{d,t}$	.12	.24	.05	−.03	.00	.12	.25	−.24	−.01	.12	.22	.04
$R_{r,t}$	−.06	.05	.05	.13	−.48	−.07	.04	.00	.52	−.02	.23	.24
$R_{mr,t}$	.10	.06	.04	−.09	−.08	.10	.07	−.03	.05	.11	.08	.07
$R_{gr,t}$	−.04	−.01	.10	−.02	−.22	−.04	−.01	.12	.22	−.02	.07	.18
$R_{cr,t}$	.06	.20	.15	−.05	−.25	.06	.20	−.07	.23	.09	.27	.23

Table 11.4
Sample Cross-Correlations for Historical Returns From Selected Series (1927–1974)
Yearly Returns

	R_p	R_L	R_d	ε_I	ε_r
R_p	1.00	.05	.36	.01	−.11
R_L	...	1.00	−.29	−.25	.13
R_d	...	...	1.00	.10	−.20
ε_I	...	...	...	1.00	−.95
ε_r	...	...	...	...	1.00

We are given a maturity schedule of current market yields Y_N for $N = 1$, 25 years to maturity corresponding to maturity dates 1976–2000. We define forward rates F_n for each year n into the future according to

$$\prod_{n=1}^{N} (1 + F_n)^{1/N} = (1 + Y_N). \tag{10}$$

Given two bond yields with terms to maturity n and $n - 1$, we can solve for each F_n directly by

$$(1 + F_n) = \frac{(1 + Y_n)^n}{(1 + Y_{n-1})^{n-1}}. \tag{11}$$

We assume that each forward rate F_n is comprised of an expected future interest rate n periods ahead $E(\bar{R}_{f,n})$ as well as an expected premium, $E(\bar{L}_n)$, relating to the term to maturity, n. The works of Hicks,[19] Kessel,[20] and others indicate that $E(\bar{L}_n)$ is positive. The work of McCulloch[21] suggests that most of the premium is already observed by the end of the first year into the future. Thus we assume that $E(\bar{L}_n)$ is constant as n increases and estimate it from the 20-year maturity premium $\bar{R}_L$. Making use of our earlier $\bar{R}_L$ random walk assumption, we set $E(\bar{L}_n)$ equal to the historical mean of $\bar{R}_L$, $\hat{E}(\bar{R}_L) = .0113$.

We can approximate the forward rate F_n component form as

$$F_n \cong E(\bar{R}_{f,n}) + \hat{E}(\bar{R}_L). \tag{12}$$

Equation (12) is not exact since F_n is a geometric rate of return whereas both $E(\bar{R}_{f,n})$ and $\hat{E}(\bar{R}_L)$ are arithmetic means for a given period. A geometric mean is less than or equal to an arithmetic mean of a series. The amount of the difference increases with the amount of dispersion for the series. Because $\sigma(\bar{R}_f)$ and $\sigma(\bar{R}_L)$ are small relative to their means, we ignore the difference.[22]

Differences in geometric and arithmetic means also affect the results we obtain from our use of the historical data. Blume[23] shows that for any given sample size forecasts of geometric means decrease as the forecast period n increases. This phenomenon is intensified as the variability of the series increases. This effect occurs in our results as short-term geometric mean forecasts tend to exceed long-term geometric mean forecasts.

Inflation and Real Interest Rate Expectations

We have already separated the nominal interest rate $\bar{R}_f$ into its inflation $\bar{R}_I$ and real interest rate $\bar{R}_r$ components. We can approximate $E(\bar{R}_{f,n})$ by

$$E(\bar{R}_{f,n}) \cong E(\bar{R}_{I,n}) + E(\bar{R}_{r,n}). \tag{13}$$

An exact representation of equation (13) would include second order terms relating to serial correlation, cross-correlation, and variance.[24] These terms have been omitted due to their relatively small magnitudes.

◤ The Formal Simulation Model

In this section we present the step-by-step procedures that are used in forming the simulations. One set of inputs includes the set of year-by-year (1926–74) historical component returns, $\bar{R}_I$, $\bar{R}_r$, $\bar{R}_p$, $\bar{R}_L$, and $\bar{R}_d$, which we define as ϕ_R. The other set of inputs is the year-by-year maturities of the current government bond yield curve which we define as ϕ_Y. Our goal is to develop probability distributions for the five basic series and their seven derived series each year n into the future (1976–2000) according to $f(\bar{R}_{m,n}; \bar{R}_{g,n}; \bar{R}_{c,n}; \bar{R}_{f,n}; \bar{R}_{I,n}; \ldots; \mid \phi_R, \phi_Y)$.

Inputs

The current government bond yield curve can be expressed in terms of a yield each year Y_n as follows: $\phi_Y = (Y_1, Y_2, \ldots, Y_{25})$.

The 1926–74 year-by-year historical returns of the five building block components are listed as follows:

$$\phi_R = \begin{vmatrix} R_{I,1926}; R_{I,1927}; \ldots; R_{I,1974} \\ R_{r,1926}; R_{r,1927}; \ldots; R_{r,1974} \\ R_{p,1926}; R_{p,1927}; \ldots; R_{p,1974} \\ R_{L,1926}; R_{L,1927}; \ldots; R_{L,1974} \\ R_{d,1926}; R_{d,1927}; \ldots; R_{d,1974} \end{vmatrix}$$

The set of inputs also includes $R_{r,1975}$.

$\bar{R}_I$ and $\bar{R}_r$ Regressions

We rewrite regression equations (5) and (6) below:

$$\bar{R}_{I,t} = \gamma_{I0} + \gamma_{I1}\bar{R}_{I,t-1} + \bar{\varepsilon}_{I,t}, \tag{14}$$

$$\bar{R}_{r,t} = \gamma_{r0} + \gamma_{r1}\bar{R}_{r,t-1} + \bar{\varepsilon}_{r,t}. \tag{15}$$

Our model uses the coefficients $\hat{\gamma}_{r0}$, $\hat{\gamma}_{r1}$, $\hat{\gamma}_{I0}$, and $\hat{\gamma}_{I1}$ as well as the regression residuals $\bar{\varepsilon}_I$ and $\bar{\varepsilon}_r$.

Transformation of Inputs

We transform the yields Y_n into forward rates F_n according to equation (11), which we rewrite below:

$$(1 + F_n) = \frac{(1 + Y_n)^n}{(1 + Y_{n-1})^{n-1}}. \tag{16}$$

Accordingly the ϕ_Y vector becomes the ϕ_Y^* vector consisting of $\phi_Y^* = (F_1, F_2, \ldots, F_{25})$.

We transform the return inputs ϕ_R into subsets ϕ_{R1}^* and ϕ_{R2}^* as follows:

$$\phi_{R1}^* = \begin{pmatrix} \varepsilon_{I,1927}; \varepsilon_{I,1928}; \ldots; \varepsilon_{I,1974} \\ \varepsilon_{r,1927}; \varepsilon_{r,1928}; \ldots; \varepsilon_{r,1974} \\ R_{L,1927}; R_{L,1928}; \ldots; R_{L,1974} \end{pmatrix}$$

and

$$\phi_{R2}^* = \begin{pmatrix} R_{p,1926}; R_{p,1927}; \ldots; R_{p,1974} \\ R_{d,1926}; R_{d,1927}; \ldots; R_{d,1974} \end{pmatrix}.$$

The Simulation Drawings

For each year n, there are simulation drawings $k = 1,399$. The kth drawing consists of selecting a column vector (a historical year) chosen at random from the ϕ_{R1}^* and ϕ_{R2}^* input matrices. This procedure assumes that $\tilde{\varepsilon}_{I,n,k}, \tilde{\varepsilon}_{r,n,k}$, and $\tilde{R}_{L,n,k}$ are jointly distributed according to $f(\tilde{\varepsilon}_{I,n,k}, \tilde{\varepsilon}_{r,n,k}, \tilde{R}_{L,n,k} \mid \phi_{R1}^*)$ while $\tilde{R}_{p,n,k}$ and $\tilde{R}_{d,n,k}$ are jointly distributed according to $f(\tilde{R}_{p,n,k}, \tilde{R}_{d,n,k} \mid \phi_{R2}^*)$. The two joint distributions are themselves assumed to be independent of each other, so that the choice of the column (historical year) selected at random from ϕ_{R1}^* is independent of the choice of the column (historical year) selected from ϕ_{R2}^*.

Estimation of $\tilde{R}_I$ and $\tilde{R}_r$ Expectations

We use equations (14) and (15) again to solve for the expected real rate and inflation rate for any period n and for each simulation k according to

$$\hat{E}(\tilde{R}_{r,n,k}) = \hat{\gamma}_{0r} + \hat{\gamma}_{1r} R_{r,n-1,k} \tag{17}$$

where $R_{r,0} = R_{r,1975}$, and

$$\hat{E}(\tilde{R}_{I,n,k}) = \hat{\gamma}_{0I} + \hat{\gamma}_{1I} R_{I,n-1,k} + \delta_n, \tag{18}$$

where δ_n is a constant added to each simulation k in year n. The δ_n constrains the mean of the 399 inflation rate simulations, $\hat{E}(\tilde{R}_{I,n})$, for each year n to be equal to that implied by equations (12) and (13), which we write as

$$\hat{E}(\tilde{R}_{I,n}) = F_n - \hat{E}(\tilde{R}_{r,n}) - \hat{E}(\tilde{R}_L) \tag{19}$$

where F_n comes from ϕ^*_Y, $\hat{E}(\bar{R}_{r,n})$ is the mean of the 399 real interest rate forecasts from equation (17) and $\hat{E}(\bar{R}_L)$ is the historical mean maturity premium.

Summing the Component Simulations

The above procedure gives us $\hat{E}(\bar{R}_{I,n,k})$, $\hat{E}(\bar{R}_{r,n,k})$, $\tilde{\varepsilon}_{I,n,k}$, $\tilde{\varepsilon}_{r,n,k}$, $\bar{R}_{L,n,k}$, $\bar{R}_{p,n,k}$, and $\bar{R}_{d,n,k}$ for each simulation $k = 1,399$. Summing these components gives us the kth simulation for the nth forecast year of the remaining series as follows:[25]

$$\bar{R}_{r,n,k} = \hat{E}(\bar{R}_{r,n,k}) + \tilde{\varepsilon}_{r,n,k}$$
$$\bar{R}_{I,n,k} = \hat{E}(\bar{R}_{I,n,k}) + \tilde{\varepsilon}_{I,n,k}$$
$$\bar{R}_{f,n,k} = \bar{R}_{r,n,k} + \bar{R}_{I,n,k}$$
$$\bar{R}_{m,n,k} = \bar{R}_{f,n,k} + \bar{R}_{p,n,k}$$
$$\bar{R}_{g,n,k} = \bar{R}_{f,n,k} + \bar{R}_{L,n,k}$$
$$\bar{R}_{c,n,k} = \bar{R}_{g,n,k} + \bar{R}_{d,n,k}$$
$$\bar{R}_{mr,n,k} = \bar{R}_{r,n,k} + \bar{R}_{p,n,k}$$
$$\bar{R}_{gr,n,k} = \bar{R}_{r,n,k} + \bar{R}_{L,n,k}$$
$$\bar{R}_{cr,n,k} = \bar{R}_{gr,n,k} + \bar{R}_{d,n,k}.$$

The process is repeated for each forecast year $n = 1, 25$.

▶ Results

The simulation model produces probabilistic forecasts for each of the 12 series for any period in the future through the year 2000. It is necessary only to input the historical data, ϕ_R, the current yield curve, ϕ_Y, and the most recent annual real interest rate.

We choose December 31, 1975, as our current date. Table 11.5 lists the bonds and yields used in constructing the yield curve. The coupons range

Table 11.5
United States Treasury Bonds and Notes Used to Construct the Government Bond Yield Curve as of December 31, 1975

Coupon	Maturity	Yield to Maturity
7 ¼s	1976 December note	6.01
7 ¼s	1977 December note	6.69
8 ⅛s	1978 December note	7.03
7 ½s	1979 December note	7.32
7 ¾s	1981 November note	7.48
6 ⅛s	1986 November bond	7.47
6 ¾s	1993 February bond	7.82
7 ⅞s	1995–2000 February bond	7.96

Table 11.6
Government Bond Yield Curve as of December 31, 1975: Yields to Maturity and Forward Rates

Year-End	Yield to Maturity	Forward Rate	Year-End	Yield to Maturity	Forward Rate
1976	.0601	.0601	1989	.0765	.0843
1977	.0669	.0737	1990	.0770	.0840
1978	.0703	.0771	1991	.0776	.0866
1979	.0732	.0819	1992	.0781	.0861
1980	.0740	.0772	1993	.0784	.0835
1981	.0748	.0788	1994	.0786	.0822
1982	.0748	.0748	1995	.0788	.0826
1983	.0748	.0748	1996	.0790	.0830
1984	.0747	.0739	1997	.0792	.0834
1985	.0747	.0747	1998	.0794	.0838
1986	.0747	.0747	1999	.0796	.0842
1987	.0753	.0819	2000	.0798	.0846
1988	.0759	.0831			

from 6⅛ percent to 8⅛ percent. The list excludes "flower" bonds and all non-callable bonds except the 7⅞ percent bond of February 1995–2000 (callable in 1995, maturing in 2000). Since bonds are not available for each of the 25 year-end dates, we linearly interpolate from adjacent bonds to compute any missing yields. The forward rates are presented in Table 11.6.

Given the kth simulation return of each series, $R_{n,k}$, we form the 12 cumulative wealth relative indices as of the end of period n, $V_{n,k}$. These indices are initialized at December 31, 1975 = 1.00 and are formed by

$$V_{n,k} = V_{n-1,k}(1 + R_{n,k}). \tag{20}$$

We also compute the geometric annualized return $R_{n,k}^G$ for each simulation k across n periods (each beginning with year-end 1975) according to

$$R_{n,k}^G = (V_{n,k})^{1/n} - 1. \tag{21}$$

Table 11.7 lists the probability distribution of 1976 returns for the 12 series. The qth percentile lists the $k/4$th ($k = 1,399$) sorted simulations. Note that the expected return on stocks $\bar{R}_m$ is 14.4 percent. The expected returns on $\bar{R}_g$, $\bar{R}_c$, $\bar{R}_f$, and $\bar{R}_I$ are 7.3 percent, 7.7 percent, 6.1 percent, and 7.3 percent, respectively. Except for rounding errors, these expected returns are sums of the expected returns of their respective components.

Table 11.7 lists the probability distribution of annualized geometric mean returns for all series for the period 1976–2000. The expectations of the probability distributions of geometric means for $\bar{R}_m$, $\bar{R}_g$, $\bar{R}_c$, $\bar{R}_f$, and $\bar{R}_I$ are respectively 13.0 percent, 8.0 percent, 8.2 percent, 6.8 percent, and 6.4 percent. Note that the amount by which returns on stocks exceed returns on other assets appears to

Table 11.7

Simulated Total Return Distributions for the Year 1976: Geometric Average Annual Rates (in %), Selected Percentiles, All Series

Percentile*	$\tilde{R}_m$	$\tilde{R}_g$	$\tilde{R}_c$	$\tilde{R}_f$	$\tilde{R}_l$	$\tilde{R}_p$	$\tilde{R}_L$	$\tilde{R}_d$	$\tilde{R}_r$	$\tilde{R}_{mr}$	$\tilde{R}_{gr}$	$\tilde{R}_{cr}$
5	-26.1	-5.5	-4.5	0.3	-1.7	-34.5	-11.6	-6.0	-9.7	-32.3	-10.7	-11.0
10	-11.1	-1.0	-2.1	1.5	0.4	-15.0	-5.5	-4.4	-6.9	-21.3	-5.8	-7.5
20	-6.7	1.8	1.0	2.9	2.4	-11.6	-3.2	-2.2	-2.8	-12.4	-3.7	-5.0
30	-1.1	3.5	3.7	4.0	4.0	-8.4	-1.4	-1.2	-2.0	-7.3	-2.7	-2.5
40	9.0	5.1	5.5	4.4	5.1	-0.4	-0.4	-0.1	-0.9	-0.7	-1.1	-0.8
50	14.5	6.8	7.2	5.0	6.1	8.5	1.9	0.7	-0.5	7.3	0.9	0.8
60	22.0	8.7	8.8	5.9	7.3	16.7	2.6	1.3	-0.2	13.8	2.6	3.0
70	28.6	10.2	11.5	6.6	8.4	20.1	5.5	1.8	0.0	18.8	3.6	4.5
80	35.8	12.5	13.8	7.6	11.2	29.9	5.9	2.5	1.9	26.0	4.9	5.9
90	45.2	16.5	17.8	11.8	15.6	39.6	8.9	3.8	3.0	36.2	6.2	7.4
95	53.4	22.1	21.9	20.1	21.6	47.5	10.4	6.3	4.3	46.0	6.9	8.7
Mean	14.4	7.3	7.7	6.1	7.3	8.4	1.3	0.4	-1.3	7.0	0.1	0.5
S.D.	23.1	7.5	7.9	4.7	6.8	22.8	6.0	3.4	4.4	22.0	5.1	6.0

*Each series is simulated for $k = 1,399$ for the year. The qth percentile lists the $k/4$th sorted simulation. Even though many of the simulated series are interrelated, each series is sorted independently of the others. Thus, the simulated distribution of any one series conditional upon an observation or the distribution of any other series is not ascertainable from this table. The 1-year forecast simulations are not reported beyond the 5th and 95th percentiles since accurate estimates of the tails cannot be made from our limited historical sample of 49 annual returns.

Table 11.8
Simulated Total Return Distributions for the Period 1976–2000: Geometric Average Annual Rates (in %), Selected Percentiles, All Series

Percentile*	$\tilde{R}_m$	$\tilde{R}_g$	$\tilde{R}_c$	$\tilde{R}_t$	$\tilde{R}_l$	$\tilde{R}_p$	$\tilde{R}_L$	$\tilde{R}_d$	$\tilde{R}_r$	$\tilde{R}_{mr}$	$\tilde{R}_{gr}$	$\tilde{R}_{cr}$
1	2.1	3.1	3.3	2.1	-0.4	-4.6	-1.1	-1.3	-4.8	-5.4	-2.2	-2.5
2	3.2	3.7	3.6	3.1	0.7	-4.3	-1.0	-1.1	-4.4	-3.2	-2.0	-1.9
3	4.3	3.9	4.0	3.3	1.7	-2.8	-0.9	-1.1	-4.1	-2.2	-1.7	-1.7
4	4.9	4.2	4.3	3.4	1.8	-2.1	-0.7	-0.9	-3.8	-1.8	-1.4	-1.6
5	5.2	4.3	4.5	3.5	2.0	-1.8	-0.6	-0.8	-3.4	-1.3	-1.2	-1.5
10	6.9	4.8	5.2	4.1	2.9	0.2	-0.3	-0.6	-2.5	0.1	-0.6	-0.4
20	8.9	6.1	6.1	4.9	4.0	2.5	0.1	-0.3	-1.3	2.7	0.1	0.4
30	10.3	6.6	7.0	5.6	4.7	3.8	0.5	-0.1	-0.7	4.3	0.7	0.9
40	11.8	7.3	7.5	6.2	5.4	4.9	0.9	0.1	-0.2	5.0	1.1	1.4
50	13.1	7.8	8.1	6.7	6.1	5.8	1.1	0.2	0.3	6.2	1.6	1.8
60	14.0	8.4	8.7	7.3	6.9	7.2	1.4	0.5	0.8	7.3	2.0	2.3
70	15.2	9.1	9.4	7.8	7.8	8.6	1.7	0.6	1.2	8.6	2.5	2.8
80	16.9	9.9	10.2	8.6	8.8	10.0	2.0	0.8	1.6	10.0	3.0	3.4
90	19.3	11.0	11.4	9.6	10.2	11.6	2.5	1.2	2.5	12.7	3.5	4.0
95	21.5	12.3	12.7	10.7	11.3	13.6	2.8	1.4	3.1	14.0	4.0	4.4
96	22.1	12.6	13.0	10.9	11.5	13.8	3.0	1.5	3.2	14.5	4.3	4.6
97	23.5	13.0	13.4	11.0	11.8	14.4	3.2	1.5	3.4	15.2	4.5	4.9
98	24.6	13.1	13.9	11.2	12.5	15.5	3.3	1.7	3.5	15.9	4.5	5.2
99	25.0	13.7	14.3	12.1	13.6	16.3	3.5	1.9	4.0	16.9	5.1	5.7
Mean	13.0	8.0	8.2	6.8	6.4	6.0	1.1	0.3	0.1	6.3	1.5	1.8
S.D.	4.9	2.3	2.4	2.1	2.9	4.5	1.1	0.7	1.9	4.6	1.6	1.7

*Each series is simulated for $k = 1,399$ for each year over the period. The qth percentile lists the $k/4$th sorted simulation. Even though many of the simulated series are interrelated, each series is sorted independently of the others. Thus, the simulated distribution of any one series conditional upon an observation or the distribution of any other series is not ascertainable from this table.

Table 11.8 (Actual Results)
Forecast Realizations: Geometric Average Annual Returns

		1976 Forecast		
	1976–2000 Actual	Median	Mean	S.D.
R_m, Common stocks	15.3%	13.1%	13.0%	4.9%
R_g, Long-term gov't bonds	9.6	7.8	8.0	2.3
R_c, Long-term corp. bonds	9.9	8.1	8.2	2.4
R_f, U.S. Treasury bills	6.9	6.7	6.8	2.1
R_I, CPI	4.7	6.1	6.4	2.9

Notes: The bull stock and bond markets of the 1980s and 1990s caused the realizations to out-run the forecasts. However, all realizations were well within one standard deviation forecast error.

The U.S. Treasury bill forecast almost exactly matched the realization. Since all risk premia in this article are measured relative to the Treasury bill rate, the risk premium forecast errors are approximately the same as the above nominal return forecast errors. In fact, the component forecasting approach used in the article starts with the yield curve and forward rates. Thus, all asset class returns are built up from the U.S. Treasury bill forecasts, year by year.

The inflation realization is substantially below the forecast. At the time of the forecast at the beginning of 1976, inflation was very high, resulting in initial negative real short-term interest rates. Although the forward rate term structure relatively accurately forecast the U.S. Treasury bill for the whole 1976–2000 period, the real short-term rate and the inflation rate forecast errors offset each other. Consequently, inflation was overforecast, while short-term real rates were underforecast. This resulted in all the asset class inflation-adjusted forecasts' being substantially under their realizations.

be less for the period 1976–2000 than for the single year 1976 reported in Table 11.7. Since $\tilde{R}_m$ is more variable than other assets, its arithmetic mean exceeds its geometric mean by a greater magnitude than is true for other assets. Note also that in contrast to the arithmetic means reported in Table 11.7, the geometric means of the components shown in Table 11.8 are not strictly additive.

Table 11.9 lists the cumulative wealth relatives for all the series as of the year 2000. Note that all the relatives are positively skewed with the mean wealth always greater than the median. Of all series, common stocks have the highest expected value and variability as of the year 2000. One dollar invested in common stocks at the end of 1975 has an expected value as of the year 2000 of $38.31, a median value of $21.71, and a standard deviation of $61.35. The year 2000 mean cumulative wealth relative value for common stocks is almost five times the mean value for long-term government and corporate bonds.

It should be noted that the simulations for many of the series are interdependent. Nevertheless, for the purposes of presentation, the series in tables 11.7, 11.8, and 11.9 are sorted independently. Thus it is not possible to use these tables to answer such questions as what is the probability that one series will outperform another by a given percentage over some specified period, or what is the probability distribution of returns for a portfolio comprised of two or more asset categories. The first question can be answered only by looking at unsorted simulations. The second question can be answered only by looking at simulations of weighted combinations of assets.

Table 11.9
Simulated Distributions of Cumulative Wealth Relatives for the Period 1976–2000: Selected Percentiles, All Series ($V_{1975} = 1.00$)

Percentile*	$\tilde{V}_m$	$\tilde{V}_g$	$\tilde{V}_c$	$\tilde{V}_f$	$\tilde{V}_l$	$\tilde{V}_p$	$\tilde{V}_L$	$\tilde{V}_d$	$\tilde{V}_r$	$\tilde{V}_{mr}$	$\tilde{V}_{gr}$	$\tilde{V}_{cr}$
1	1.68	2.15	2.25	1.68	0.90	0.31	0.75	0.73	0.29	0.25	0.57	0.53
2	2.20	2.48	2.42	2.15	1.19	0.34	0.78	0.76	0.33	0.44	0.60	0.62
3	2.86	2.60	2.67	2.25	1.52	0.49	0.80	0.77	0.35	0.57	0.65	0.64
4	3.31	2.80	2.86	2.31	1.56	0.58	0.84	0.80	0.38	0.64	0.70	0.67
5	3.55	2.86	3.01	2.36	1.64	0.64	0.87	0.81	0.42	0.71	0.74	0.69
10	5.30	3.23	3.55	2.73	2.04	1.04	0.92	0.86	0.53	1.04	0.87	0.90
20	8.43	4.39	4.39	3.31	2.67	1.87	1.03	0.94	0.73	1.97	1.03	1.10
30	11.60	4.94	5.43	3.90	3.15	2.52	1.13	0.98	0.84	2.86	1.19	1.24
40	16.26	5.82	6.10	4.50	3.72	3.34	1.24	1.02	0.94	3.36	1.31	1.41
50	21.71	6.54	7.01	5.06	4.39	4.14	1.33	1.06	1.09	4.47	1.47	1.57
60	26.46	7.51	8.05	5.82	5.30	5.64	1.42	1.12	1.22	5.83	1.63	1.77
70	34.38	8.82	9.45	6.54	6.54	7.84	1.52	1.17	1.34	7.80	1.87	1.98
80	49.59	10.59	11.34	7.87	8.24	10.73	1.65	1.23	1.47	10.88	2.09	2.28
90	82.42	13.59	14.86	9.89	11.34	15.66	1.84	1.33	1.83	20.08	2.39	2.65
95	130.14	18.18	19.87	12.70	14.53	24.48	2.01	1.40	2.13	26.25	2.66	2.90
96	147.19	19.43	21.23	13.28	15.20	25.56	2.07	1.44	2.22	29.79	2.86	3.06
97	195.74	21.23	23.19	13.59	16.26	28.89	2.17	1.46	2.28	34.51	2.98	3.34
98	244.32	21.71	25.89	14.21	19.00	36.70	2.26	1.52	2.36	39.62	3.03	3.56
99	264.70	24.77	28.26	17.38	24.24	43.75	2.38	1.61	2.65	49.77	3.44	3.95
Mean	38.31	7.81	8.43	5.88	5.81	7.43	1.36	1.09	1.14	8.17	1.57	1.69
S.D.	61.35	4.55	5.30	3.19	4.39	11.92	0.36	0.18	0.50	14.01	0.61	0.71

*Each series is simulated for $k = 1,399$ for each year over the period. The qth percentile lists the $k/4$th sorted simulation. Even though many of the simulated series are interrelated, each series is sorted independently of the others. Thus, the simulated distribution of any one series conditional upon an observation or the distribution of any other series is not ascertainable from this table.

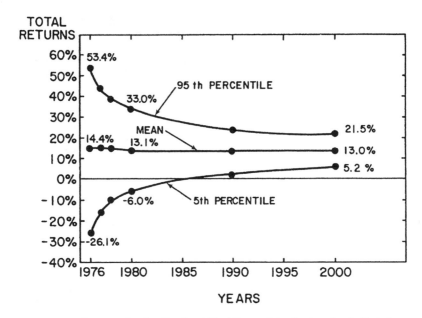

Figure 11.1. Common Stocks: Simulated Total Return Distributions for the Period 1976–2000, Geometric Average Annual Rates

Graphical presentation helps illustrate the changing shape of the simulated distributions over time. Figures 11.1, 11.3, 11.5, and 11.7 present a distribution of annualized geometric mean returns for $\tilde{R}_m$, $\tilde{R}_{mr}$, $\tilde{R}_c$, and $\tilde{R}_I$, respectively. The geometric means are measured over the periods starting with December 31, 1975, and ending with all dates through the year 2000. Figures 11.2, 11.4, 11.6, and 11.8 give logarithmic plots for $\tilde{V}_m$, $\tilde{V}_{mr}$, $\tilde{V}_c$, and $\tilde{V}_I$, respectively. Year-end 1975 is initialized at $1.00. In each plot, historical wealth relatives are given over the period 1950–75[26] along with simulated distributions of wealth relatives for any date within the period 1976–2000.

Figure 11.1 shows the mean, fifth, and ninety-fifth percentiles of the simulated results for $\tilde{R}_m$. The obvious characteristics appear to be symmetry and reduction of uncertainty over time. The narrowing of the distribution results from an averaging effect. Successive period returns are largely, but not totally, independent of one another. Thus, abnormally high and low returns tend to offset each other over time. The slight dependence of returns for all the basic series results from the serial dependence of $\tilde{R}_I$ and $\tilde{R}_r$, both of which enter into all nominal return series. The 1976 forecast mean return for $\tilde{R}_m$, 14.4 percent, exceeds the long-term 1976–2000 mean of 13.0 percent illustrating that short-term geometric mean forecasts tend to exceed long-term geometric mean forecasts.

Unlike the geometric means in Figure 11.1, Figure 11.2 shows that for $\tilde{V}_m$, skewness and uncertainty increase over time. The graph displays the mean,

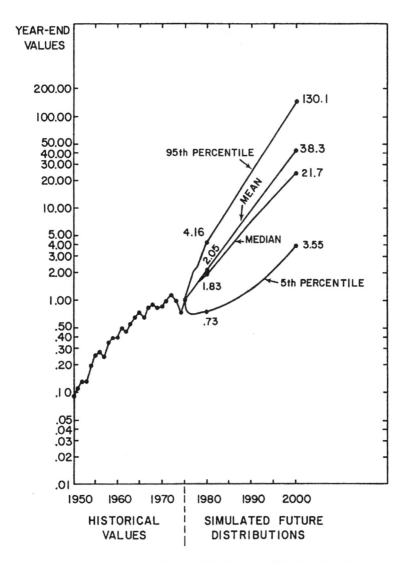

Figure 11.2. Common Stocks: Simulated Distribution of Nominal Cumulative Wealth Relatives for the Period 1976–2000 ($V_{m,1975} = 1.00$)

median, fifth, and ninety-fifth percentiles for the period 1976–2000 with the 1980 and 2000 year-end values written in for convenience. A logarithmic plot actually de-emphasizes the dispersion and skewness of the distribution. By 2000, the mean is nearly double the median, and the ninety-fifth percentile is roughly 37 times the fifth percentile.

It is perhaps surprising that Figures 11.1 and 11.2, which deal with the same simulations over the same period, appear so different. Figure 11.2 may be more revealing than Figure 11.1 in that wealth relatives demonstrate directly

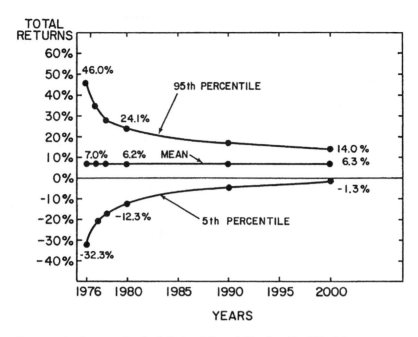

Figure 11.3. Common Stocks, Inflation Adjusted: Simulated Real Total Return Distributions for the Period 1976–2000, Geometric Average Annual Rates

what happens to invested dollars. Similar interpretations apply to Figures 11.3–11.8 which show pairs of graphs for $\bar{R}_{mr}$ and $\tilde{R}_{mr}$, $\bar{R}_c$ and $\tilde{V}_c$, and $\bar{R}_I$ and $\tilde{V}_I$.

The most striking features of Figure 11.3 are the huge dispersion in 1976 real common stock returns along with the nontrivial probability of negative real returns through the year 2000. Figure 11.4 shows that by 2000 real stock wealth relatives exhibit dispersion and skewness similar to that for nominal stock wealth relatives. Figures 11.5 and 11.6 reveal the result that corporate bonds are far less risky than stocks. Nonetheless, there is considerable variation in 1976 corporate bond returns, as well as in wealth relatives for the year 2000. Figure 11.7 demonstrates that the geometric means of inflation rates over long periods do not narrow substantially resulting directly from the high serial correlation in inflation rates. Figure 11.8 shows the relatively wide dispersion of $\tilde{V}_I$ at times in the future.

The forecasts were made as of December 31, 1975, and therefore are technically already out of date. In principle a new set of simulations would be run with each unanticipated change in either the yield curve or the real interest rate. In practice, simulation reruns may not be necessary, since the model is stationary in risk component terms. After making adjustments for any changes in real interest rates, the model is also stationary in real terms.

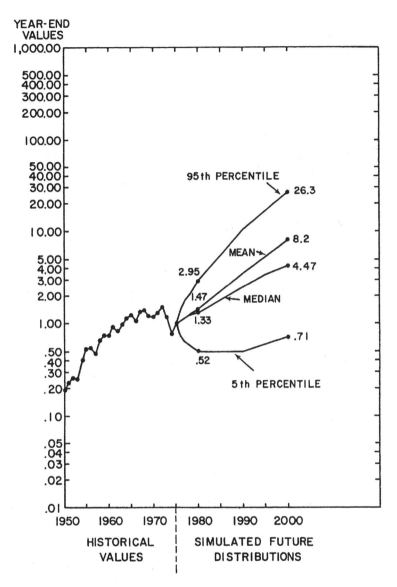

Figure 11.4. Common Stocks, Inflation Adjusted: Simulated Distributions of Real Cumulative Wealth Relatives for the Period 1976–2000 ($V_{mr,1975}$ = 1.00)

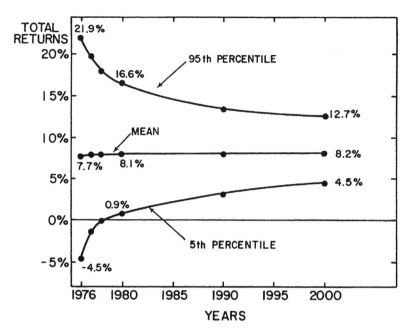

Figure 11.5. Long-Term Corporate Bonds: Simulated Total Return Distributions for the Period 1976–2000, Geometric Average Annual Rates

▰ *Forecast Highlights*

The nominal returns on all assets are forecast to be substantially higher than they have been over the historical period. The higher nominal returns result directly from the high forecast inflation rates which are impounded into all asset returns. The compounded inflation rate is expected to be 6.4 percent per year over the period 1976–2000 compared to the historical compounded inflation rate of only 2.3 percent over the period 1926–75.

The expected compounded return on common stocks for the period 1976–2000 is 13.0 percent per year. However, stocks are risky investments so that actual returns may differ substantially from the expected return. There is a 5 percent probability that returns will exceed 21.5 percent per year and a corresponding 5 percent probability that returns will be less than 5.2 percent per year. Stocks are expected to have a compounded return of 6.3 percent after adjusting for inflation. Despite the high expected inflation adjusted return, there is a 9 percent probability that the nominal stock returns will not be sufficient to offset inflation over the entire forecast period.[27]

The nominal compounded annual returns from maintaining either a 20-year maturity government bond or a 20-year maturity corporate bond port-

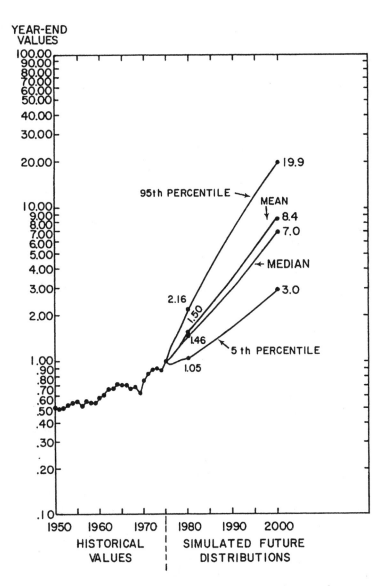

Figure 11.6. Long-Term Corporate Bonds: Simulated Distributions of Nominal Cumulative Wealth Relatives for the Period 1976–2000 ($V_{c,1975}$ = 1.00)

folio are expected to be 8.0 percent and 8.2 percent, respectively, from 1976 to 2000. Maintaining a long-term bond portfolio is less risky than holding stocks. Over a 1-year forecast period corporate bonds have a 5 percent chance of exceeding a 21.9 percent return and a 5 percent chance of falling below a −4.5 percent return. In contrast, 1-year stock returns have a 5 percent chance

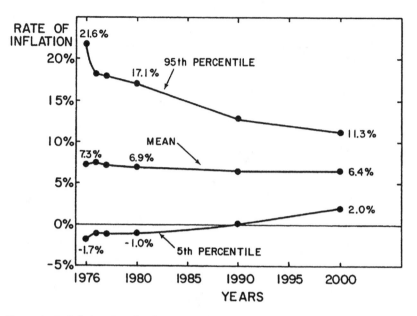

Figure 11.7. Inflation: Simulated Rate Distributions for the Period 1976–2000, Geometric Average Annual Rates

of exceeding a 53.4 percent return and a 5 percent chance of returning less than −26.1 percent. For the entire period 1976–2000, long-term corporate bonds have a 5 percent chance of exceeding 12.7 percent per year and a 5 percent chance of returning less than 4.5 percent per year. The inflation adjusted returns are expected to be 1.5 percent per year for long-term government bonds and 1.8 percent per year for long-term corporate bonds.

The return from rolling over Treasury bills is expected to closely track inflation rates. The nominal compounded Treasury bill return is expected to be 6.8 percent per year, compared to the expected 6.4 percent compounded inflation rate, thus producing a very low inflation adjusted Treasury bill return (real interest rate).

The forecast inflation is not only high but also uncertain. In the next year the expected inflation rate is 7.3 percent with a 7 percent probability of eliminating inflation. Over the period 1976–2000, there is a 5 percent probability that inflation will exceed a compounded rate of 11.3 percent per year and a corresponding 5 percent probability that inflation will be less than a compounded rate of 2.0 percent per year.

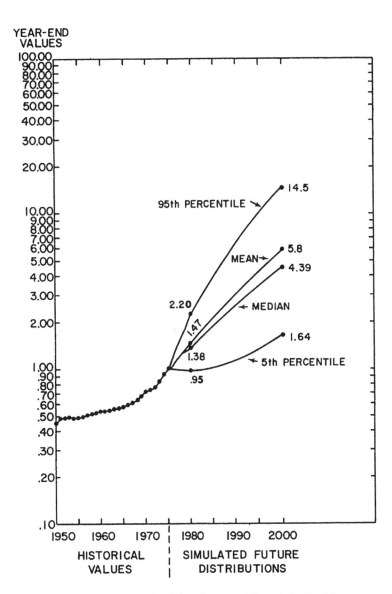

Figure 11.8.   Inflation: Simulated Distributions of Cumulative Wealth Relatives for the Period 1976–2000 ($V_{I,1975} = 1.00$)

◤ Notes

1. Roger G. Ibbotson and Rex A. Sinquefield, "Stocks, Bonds, Bills, and Inflation: Year-by-Year Historical Returns (1926–1974)," *Journal of Business* 49, no. 1 (January 1976): 11–47. A few errors in this historical paper were uncovered after its publication.

2. See Standard and Poor's *Trade and Security Statistics, Security Price Index Record* (Orange, Conn.: Standard & Poor's Corp., 1974).

3. The CRSP U.S. Government Bond File was compiled by Lawrence Fisher.

4. From 1969 to 1974, the Salomon Brothers High-Grade, Long-Term Corporate Bond Index is used. From 1946 to 1968, the Salomon Brothers Index is backdated using Salomon Brothers data and methodology similar to that used by Salomon Brothers. A description of the index is given by Martin Leibowitz and Richard Johannesen, Jr., "Introducing the Salomon Brothers' Total Performance Index for the High-Grade Long-Term Corporate Bond Market," memorandum to portfolio managers (New York: Salomon Bros., November 1973).

5. From 1926 to 1945, a total return index is derived from S&P High-Grade Corporate Bond yields assuming a 4 percent coupon and a 20-year maturity. See *Trade and Security Statistics, Security Price Index Record* (Orange, Conn.: Standard & Poor's Corp., 1974).

6. The ratio form is approximately equal to the difference form. For example, we can use a binomial expansion to express equation (1) as $\tilde{R}_p = (\tilde{R}_m - \tilde{R}_f) - (\tilde{R}_m - \tilde{R}_f)(R_f) + (R_m - R_f)(R_f)^2 - \ldots$. For small R_f, only the first term is important.

7. The "maturity" premium is frequently referred to in the literature as a "liquidity" premium. We purposely avoid the use of the term "liquidity" since it connotes marketability rather than the premium's relationship to the life of the bond.

8. We are implicitly assuming that bondholders are more interested in reducing short-term return volatility than in reducing long-term return volatility.

9. For a discussion of discontinuous trading, see Roger Ibbotson, "Price Performance of Common Stock New Issues," *Journal of Financial Economics* 2, no. 3 (September 1975): 235–72.

10. Eugene Fama uses a similar model to estimate monthly inflation rates in "Short-Term Interest Rates as Predictors of Inflation," *American Economic Review* 65, no. 3 (June 1975): 269–82. Real interest rates are predicted using autoregressive-moving average models by Charles Nelson and G. William Schwert, "On Testing the Hypothesis That the Real Rate of Interest Is Constant," Center for Mathematical Studies in Business and Economics, University of Chicago, Report no. 7522; and by Patrick Hess and James Bicksler, "Capital Asset Prices Versus Time Series Models as Predictors of Inflation," *Journal of Financial Economics* 2, no. 4 (December 1975): 341–60.

11. Analysis of the regression residuals indicates that both processes are heteroscedastic. The data suggest that the variability of $\tilde{\varepsilon}_I$ and $\tilde{\varepsilon}_r$ may be related to the level of interest rates. In addition $\tilde{\varepsilon}_r$ is positively affected by periods of deflation and negatively affected by pegged interest rates. These considerations are ignored in the models presented.

12. Eugene Fama and James MacBeth, "Risk, Return, and Equilibrium: Empirical Tests," *Journal of Political Economy* 81, no. 3 (May/June 1973): 607–36.

13. Robert Officer, "The Variability of the Market Factor of the New York Stock Exchange," *Journal of Business* 46, no. 3 (July 1973): 434–53.

14. See Richard Roll, *The Behavior of Interest Rates* (New York: Basic Books, 1970); and Charles Nelson, *The Term Structure of Interest Rates* (New York: Basic Books, 1972).

15. $\text{Cov}(\tilde{R}_r, \tilde{R}_I) = \text{cov}(R'_I - \tilde{E}_I, \tilde{R}_f - \tilde{R}'_I + \tilde{E}_I)$. Expanding the above and noting that $\text{cov}(\tilde{R}', \tilde{R}'_I) = 0$; $\text{cov}(\tilde{R}'_r \tilde{E}_I) = 0$; and $E(\tilde{E}_I) = 0$, gives $\text{cov}(\tilde{R}_r, \tilde{R}_I) = -\sigma^2(\tilde{E}_I)$; thus, $\text{corr}(\tilde{R}_r, \tilde{R}_I) = -[\sigma^2(\tilde{E}_I)]/[\sigma(\tilde{R}_I)\sigma(\tilde{R}_r)]$.

16. Past market inefficiencies would have occurred if the lagged cross-correlations were significant enough for an investor to profit by trading among asset categories period-by-period. For example, if for any past period the expected returns of a riskier asset were less than that of a less risky asset, it would have profited the risk-averse investor to invest in the less risky asset.

17. Fischer Black and Myron Scholes, "The Pricing of Options and Corporate Liabilities," *Journal of Political Economy* 81, no. 3 (May/June 1973): 637–54.

18. Eugene Fama, "Short-Term Interest Rates as Predictors of Inflation," *American Economic Review* 65, no. 3 (June 1975): 269–82.

19. John Hicks, *Value and Capital* (Oxford: Clarendon Press, 1946).

20. Reuben Kessel, *The Cyclical Behavior of the Term Structure of Interest Rates* (New York: National Bureau of Economic Research, 1965).

21. J. Huston McCulloch, "An Estimate of the Liquidity Premium" (Ph.D. diss., University of Chicago, 1973).

22. Harry Markowitz, in *Portfolio Selection: Efficient Diversification of Investments* (New York: John Wiley & Sons, 1959), pp. 99–102, demonstrates that $E\{\ln[1 + E_G(\bar{R})]\} \cong \ln[1 + E_A(\bar{R})] - 1/2\{\sigma_A^2(\bar{R})/[1 + E_A(\bar{R})]^2\}$, where $E_G(\bar{R})$ is the geometric mean and $E_A(\bar{R})$ is the arithmetic mean of $\bar{R}$. Let $G = 1/2\{\sigma_A^2(\bar{R})/[1 + E_A(\bar{R})]^2\}$ be the bias. In our analysis $\bar{R} = \bar{R}_{fn} + \bar{L}_n \cong \bar{R}_{fn} + \bar{R}_L$ so that $G \cong 1/2\{[\sigma^2(\bar{R}_{fn}) + \sigma^2(\bar{R}_L) + 2\text{ cov}(\bar{R}_{fn}, \bar{R}_L)]/[1 + E(\bar{R}_{fn}) + E(\bar{R}_L)]^2\}$. We can determine from Tables 11.1 and 11.2 that the sample covariance matrix consists of $\sigma^2(\bar{R}_f) = .0004$, $\sigma^2(\bar{R}_L) = .0031$, $\text{cov}(\bar{R}_f, \bar{R}_L) = -.00045$ while all terms in the denominator are positive so that $G < 1/2(.0004 + .0031 - .0009) = .0026$, or less than 0.26 percent return each year. For forecasts shorter than $n = 20$, $\sigma^2(\bar{L}_n) < \sigma^2(\bar{R}_L)$ so that the bias becomes even smaller.

23. Marshall Blume, "Unbiased Estimators of Long-Run Expected Rates of Return," *Journal of the American Statistical Association* 69, no. 347 (September 1974): 634–38.

24. See Stanley Fischer in "The Demand for Index Bonds," *Journal of Political Economy* 83, no. 3 (June 1975): 509–34. He works out relationships for nominal and real interest rates when inflation and asset returns follow a stochastic but stationary process. In our case the mathematics is far more difficult, since $\bar{R}_I$ and $\bar{R}_r$ have already been assumed to follow a first-order autoregressive process.

25. We constrain $\bar{R}_{f n, k} \geq 0$ since negative Treasury bill returns are unlikely. The constraint is put into effect by setting preliminary negative $\bar{R}_{f n, k}$ simulations equal to zero. Offsetting adjustments are then made to the remaining positive $\bar{R}_{f n, k}$ simulations. This procedure maintains the yield curve constraint on the mean of the simulated distribution.

26. The historical wealth relatives were computed using the following preliminary 1975 estimated returns of the five basic series: $R_m = 37.1$ percent, $R_g = 12.0$ percent, $R_c = 14.6$ percent, $R_f = 5.7$ percent, and $R_I = 7.0$ percent.

27. Some of the probabilities cited in this section are obtained from extended versions of Tables 11.7 and 11.8, which are not included in this study due to space limitations.

12 Roger G. Ibbotson

Predictions of the Past and Forecasts for the Future: 1976–2025

▶ Overview

Ibbotson and Sinquefield made only one long-term forecast of the Dow-Jones Industrial Average, and that was in a paper and speech presented at the CRSP conference in May 1974. At the time, interest rates and the yield curve were very high, so that this speech forecast was higher than the later (July 1976) published version of Ibbotson and Sinquefield's article.

In our speech (published as CRSP proceedings), Ibbotson and Sinquefield forecast that the Dow would have a 14.8% return, so that netting out dividends, the Dow was estimated to reach 10,000 in 1999. This turned out to be correct, and what made it all the more remarkable was that the Dow was only at 851 at the time of the forecast at the beginning of 1974. It was also made during the midst of the worst bear market in U.S. stocks since the 1930s Depression.

The following article summarizes the speech and compares the forecast made with the actual results, measured shortly after the Dow first hit 10,000 in 1999.

▶ Glimmer of Hope for Stock Investors

In early 1973, Professor Roger Ibbotson and Rex Sinquefield partnered to research historical returns for common stocks, U.S. government and corporate bonds, U.S. Treasury bills, and inflation. At the time, Professor Ibbotson taught at the University of Chicago Graduate School of Business. Through their research, Ibbotson and Sinquefield hoped to provide an update to the historical performance study done years earlier by Lawrence Fisher and James Lorie,[1] as well as present convincing evidence that common stocks were still appropriate for long-term investors. During the 21-month period between January 1973 and September 1974, investors suffered a 42% drop in the stock market. In order to win over skeptics, Professor Ibbotson believed there needed to be a forecast set in historical terms to convey his prediction that stocks would outperform bonds over long time periods.

To derive the median return forecast for stocks, Professor Ibbotson used a "building block" methodology. The current market estimate of the risk-free rate is derived from the yield curve. Added on top of this is the historical equity

266

risk premium. Together, these two "blocks" provide the expected future return for stocks.

◣ Forecast of Dow 10,000

By May 1974, Professor Ibbotson had collected and analyzed enough data with Sinquefield to present their unpublished conclusions in a speech to the Center for Research in Security Prices (CRSP) at the University of Chicago. During the speech, Professor Ibbotson estimated the future median total return for large company stocks would be 14.8% per year, based on historical data through year-end 1973. The forecast was derived using the unique methodology Ibbotson and Sinquefield had created. Although the 14.8% forecast would fluctuate in the future as the researchers updated the data, the methodology they used to estimate future returns remained the same. In fact, the same forecasting methodology is used today in Ibbotson Associates' *Stocks, Bonds, Bills and Inflation Yearbook,* an annual update of Ibbotson and Sinquefield's original research.

During his speech to CRSP in May 1974, Professor Ibbotson commented to his audience that his forecasted total return of stocks could be applied to the Dow Jones Industrial Average (DJIA) Index. Because the DJIA tracks only the capital appreciation of its inclusive stocks, the 14.8% total return forecast would be an inappropriate measure of the index's growth. By subtracting the dividend return out of the total return, he was able to create a forecast for the capital appreciation return of stocks. The dividend yield on the DJIA was 4.8% at the time; 14.8% (total return) minus 4.8% (dividend yield) equaled 10%. This forecast could then be applied to the DJIA to estimate the growth of the index. At year-end 1973, the DJIA closed at 850.86.

By applying the 10% return to the DJIA year-end 1973 close (and every subsequent year), Ibbotson estimated the DJIA would close over 11,150 by year-end 2000. His forecast for the 1998 year-end DJIA close was less than 50 points away from the actual close that year (9,218 and 9,181, respectively). How close did Ibbotson come to forecasting the recent record close of the Dow at 10,000? Based on his estimates in 1974, he believed the Dow would have hit

Table 12.1
Forecasts From May 1974 Speech to CRSP

Ibbotson's 1974 Forecast Total Return on Stocks	14.8%
Dividend Yield of Large-Cap Stocks	4.8%
Capital Appreciation Forecast Return	10%
DJIA 1973 Year-End Close	850.86
Forecast Return Applied to DJIA 1998 Year-End Close	9,218
Actual DJIA 1998 Year-End Close	9,181
Ibbotson's Forecast for Dow 10,000	November 1999
Actual DJIA Close at 10,000	March 29, 1999

10,000 in November 1999. His prediction was just 8 months shy of the actual record-breaking level hit on March 29 of this year: an amazing proximity considering the forecast was made 25 years in the past.

▲ Stocks, Bonds, Bills, and Inflation

Ibbotson and Sinquefield updated their historical research and formally published "Stocks, Bonds, Bills and Inflation: Year-by-Year Historical Returns (1926–1974)" in the January 1976 issue of the *Journal of Business* of the University of Chicago. The authors also updated their forecasts for the future and published "Stocks, Bonds, Bills and Inflation: Simulations of the Future (1976–2000)" in the July 1976 issue of the *Journal of Business*. The two studies became benchmarks for historical and forecasted investment returns in the finance industry.

Updated with data through year-end 1975, "Simulations of the Future" described Ibbotson and Sinquefield's new estimate that large company stocks would return 13% over time. The actual compound annual return for stocks from 1976 through 1998 was 16.3%. At first glance, the forecast from 1976 may seem far from the actual average. When one considers the investment environment of the time that the forecast was made, a 13% average return on stocks seemed outlandishly high to most investors after suffering through the bear market of the mid-seventies. It is also interesting to note that through 1994, Ibbotson and Sinquefield's 13% forecasted return was actually quite close to the actual compound annual return (stocks had a 13.5% compound annual return from 1976 to 1994). The tremendous performance of large company stocks over the last 4 years significantly increased the average return and pushed the authors' estimate farther away from the actual average.

▲ Forecasts of the Future: 1999–2025

And what does Professor Ibbotson see for the future? Recently, he updated his forecasts from the 1976 study to apply to the next 26 years (through 2025). These predictions use the same methodology as the 1976 forecasts. According to Professor Ibbotson, throughout the period 1999 to 2025 large-cap stocks should produce a median return of approximately 11.6% compared to small-

Table 12.2
Forecasts From "SBBI: Simulations of the Future (1976–2000)"

1976 Forecast for Stock Returns From "SBBI: Simulations of the Future (1976–2000)"	13%
Actual Compound Annual Return of Stocks, 1976–1998	16.3%

Table 12.3
Ibbotson's Forecast for the Future: Stocks, Bonds, Bills, and Inflation (1999–2025)

Forecast Total Return of Small-Cap Stocks	12.5%
Forecast Total Return of Large-Cap Stocks	11.6%
Forecast Total Return of Long-Term Government Bonds	5.4%
Forecast Total Return of Treasury Bills	4.5%
Forecast of Inflation	3.1%

Table 12.4
The Future of the Dow

Ibbotson's Long-Term Forecast Total Return on Stocks	11.6%
Current Dividend Yield of Large-Cap Stocks	1.6%
Capital Appreciation Forecast Return	10%
DJIA 1998 Year-End Closing Level	9,181.43
Ibbotson's Forecast for DJIA 100,000	2,024
Ibbotson's Forecast for DJIA Year-End 2025	120,368

cap stocks, which should have a median return of 12.5%. He believes long-term government bonds should produce a median return of 5.4%, Treasury bills should produce a median return of 4.5%, and inflation should grow at an annual rate of 3.1% over time. Ibbotson and Sinquefield are discussing publishing a full updated version of the original 1976 studies.

◣ Forecast of Dow 100,000

To update his 1974 forecast of the growth of the DJIA, Professor Ibbotson used the same methodology to create a capital appreciation return forecast to apply to the index. Starting with the 11.6% forecast return for large-cap stocks and subtracting the 1998 year-end dividend yield of 1.6%, he estimates a 10% future capital appreciation return for the DJIA. The DJIA closed at 9,181.43 at year-end 1998. Applying a 10% annual return to the DJIA, Professor Ibbotson estimates that the index will reach 100,000 in early 2024, and will reach over 120,000 by year-end 2025. Note that given the poor stock market performance in the early years of the twenty-first century, today's forecast for 2025 would be well below 100,000.

◣ Notes

1. Lawrence Fisher and James Lorie, "Rates of Return on Investments in Common Stocks," *Journal of Business* 37, no. 1 (January 1964).

13 William N. Goetzmann and Franklin R. Edwards

Short-Horizon Inputs and Long-Horizon Portfolio Choice

▶ Overview

The increasing power of the computer has made simulation an extraordinarily valuable tool for investment decision making. A well-designed simulation of capital market returns can give a strikingly realistic view of the range of future outcomes. This article uses simulation to show what happens if an investment manager fails to allow for the long-term trends in stock and bond markets when making an asset allocation using an efficient frontier. Efficient frontiers based on "long-horizon" inputs differ markedly from those based on shorter-horizon inputs. The reason for this is that the statistical inputs—particularly the volatility of the asset classes—change significantly because of the autocorrelation structure of stock, bond, and Treasury bill returns. The simulations tell us that optimizing without correcting for inflation or adjusting to premia over Treasuries can lead to bad portfolio choices.

Despite its well-known limitations, mean-variance optimization is commonly used to make long-term portfolio allocation decisions. See Hakansson (1972, 1974), Jorion (1985, 1986, 1990), Michaud (1989), Broadie (1991), and Best and Grauer (1991), for instance.

In this article we examine the implications of using as Markowitz model inputs the means, standard deviations, and correlations derived from short-term (or short-horizon) asset class returns as opposed to long-term (or long-horizon) asset class returns. More specifically, we simulate long-term returns using a linear model that allows stock, bond, and bill returns to be autocorrelated, and then use these returns to form efficient portfolios.

Our results indicate that for investors with multiple-year investment horizons, summary statistics based upon short-term (annual) returns can be grossly misleading for making asset allocation decisions. In particular, the autocorrelation structure of asset class returns strongly influences both the variance and the interclass correlation of assets, and, as a consequence, changes the composition of the efficient frontier.

Our principal finding, therefore, is that investors with long-term horizons should consider alternative methods of estimating inputs to the mean-variance model when making portfolio decisions.

◣ *Methodology*

The mean-variance framework is a single-period model in which returns are assumed to be normally distributed (see Markowitz [1952]). Under the assumption that asset returns are serially independent, short-term returns (such as annual returns) can be used to estimate the statistical characteristics of long-term returns. That is, the annual variance of the natural log of one plus the annual asset return should be an unbiased estimate of one-tenth the variance of the ten-year log return.[1]

This assumption, however, may not be valid for stock returns (see Fama and French [1988] and Poterba and Summers [1988], for instance). It is certainly not true for bond and Treasury bill returns (see Hakansson [1972]). Indeed, as we show, the latter exhibit an extraordinary level of autocorrelation. Holton (1992) also demonstrates the degree to which long-term volatility may be misjudged by considering the uniformly compounded monthly variance to be representative of long-horizon risk.

Kandel and Stambaugh (1987) show that vector autoregression (VAR) can be used to capture the effect of temporal dependencies in asset returns when making long-horizon forecasts. The VAR is an econometric method that generalizes autoregression to multiple data series: It estimates the lagged relationship of a set of variables (for instance, several asset classes). Campbell and Shiller (1988), Goetzmann and Jorion (1993), Hodrick (1992), and Nelson and Kim (1993), among others, use VAR to simulate distributions of long-horizon asset class returns for the purpose of testing the predictability of stock returns.

In this article, we use the VAR technology instead to simulate long-horizon inputs to the mean-variance model. In a manner similar to Ibbotson and Sinquefield (1976), we use short-term returns to bootstrap empirical distributions of long-horizon asset class returns.

The autocorrelation structures of short-term asset class returns are explicitly incorporated into simulations of long-horizon returns by modeling them using VAR in the following manner:

$$R_t = A'R_{t-1} + \varepsilon_t \tag{1}$$

where R, A, and ε are matrixes. The columns of R are time series observations of log returns to the S&P 500, long-term government bonds, and Treasury bills over the period 1926 through 1991, and the matrix A is the estimate of the VAR coefficients.[2]

The estimated coefficients and the errors, ε, from the VAR are used to generate simulated returns to an investment in each asset class in the manner:

$$R_t^* = \hat{A}'R_{t-1}^* + \hat{\varepsilon}_t^* \tag{2}$$

where $R_0^* = R_0$. In other words, the initial value for the bootstrap is the actual set of log returns for the four series in 1926, and ε_t^* is the bootstrapped error vector, drawn with replacement from the rows of the VAR error matrix.

By drawing the errors as a vector of four, one for each asset series, the contemporaneous covariance structure of the asset classes is preserved. For comparison, we also draw errors from a normal distribution, whose means, variances, and covariances match those of the error matrix ε. This semiparametric approach is used to show the degree to which our results depend upon the deviations of the model errors from normal.[3]

We do not take into consideration here uncertainty about the parameters estimated in the VAR itself. Goetzmann and Jorion (1993) and Jorion (1985) point out that this estimation uncertainty represents an additional element of risk.

We perform this bootstrap procedure 1,000 times, creating 1,000 simulated ten-year return histories. The resulting joint distributions of stock, bond, and bill log returns for the ten-year horizon are then used as inputs to the mean-variance framework, under the constraint that investment weights in each asset class are either zero or positive and add to 100%.

Simulations for Investment Management

The power of simulation in investment management comes largely from the flexibility that it allows. The designer can incorporate a wide variety of assumptions: reversals in stock prices, trends in interest rates, contributions and withdrawals from the portfolio, extreme market crashes, non-normal return distributions, and a host of other real-world considerations that may affect future performance. Interestingly, college endowments have been leaders in the use of simulation tools to model the long-term futures of their portfolios. Commonfund, an investment manager serving primarily college endowments over the past three decades, has long used a simulation program allowing endowment managers to consider the effects of alternate asset allocations on their long-term spending capacities. Yale University has also been in the vanguard of applying simulation tools to model the effects of asset allocation choice on the probability of a significant loss in real purchasing power and on the probability of a serious drop in the value of the portfolio over the long term. The approach of the Yale Investment Office is described in Chief Investment Officer David Swensen's book *Pioneering Portfolio Management.**

*Swensen, David. 2000. *Pioneering Portfolio Management.* New York: Free Press.

◤ Results

Table 13.1 reports the coefficients estimated by the VAR as well as by OLS regression. Stock returns are not well-explained by past values of bonds and bills. Bond returns are explained by past values of T-bill returns, and, conversely, T-bill returns have a significant relationship to bonds.

Table 13.1
VAR Coefficients and OLS Coefficients for Stocks, Bonds, and T-Bills Estimated From the Vector Autoregression

R_t	VAR Coefficients for Lagged Variable R_{t-1}			Regression Coefficients for Lagged Variable R_{t-1}		
	Stocks	Bonds	Bills	Stocks	Bonds	Bills
Stocks	0.023	0.517	−0.063	0.023	0.517	−0.062
				(0.128)	(0.339)	(0.815)
Bonds	−0.028	0.032	0.882	−0.030	0.032	0.905
				(0.047)	(0.123)	(0.296)
Bills	0.013	−0.073	0.963	0.021	−0.072	0.983
				(0.006)	(0.017)	(0.041)

	Tests on Equity Risk Premia and Bond Risk Premia				
	Stocks-Bills	Bonds-Bills	Stocks-Bills	Bonds-Bills	
Stocks-bills	0.00	0.00	0.008	0.601	
			(0.127)	(0.325)	
Bonds-bills	0.00	0.00	−0.056	0.111	
			(0.050)	(0.128)	

Notes: VAR and OLS estimates based upon the times series of log returns to the S&P Index, a portfolio of long-term government bonds, and Treasury bills of six-month maturity. Regression estimates are OLS coefficients and standard errors, using the row value as the dependent variable and the set of column values as the independent design matrix.

When the analysis is performed on the risk premia—that is, upon the stock returns minus the T-bill returns and the bond returns minus the T-bill returns—both the VAR and the regression results show that no relationships exist. Thus, the intertemporal dependencies that exist are clearly due to the time series behavior of T-bill returns.

Table 13.2 reports the means, standard deviations, and correlations of the simulated ten-year log returns and the risk premia, as well as estimates based upon one-year time series returns under the assumption of serial independence. The standard deviations of the Treasury bills are increased significantly by the VAR model: They have nearly the same volatility as do long-term government bonds. (This result is not due to the fact that the riskless asset at the ten-year horizon is a zero-coupon ten-year government bond. The government bond portfolio maintains its long-term duration by rebalancing monthly, so nothing in the portfolio reaches maturity in the tenth year of the simulation.)

The simulations using normal errors yield similar results, indicating that only a small portion of the increased volatility may be attributable to outlying observations, or to deviations of the errors from normality. Further, with respect to the risk premia, the inputs are not affected. Clearly, it is the serial correlation of Treasury yields that is causing the long-horizon inputs to differ from the short-horizon inputs.

Table 13.2

Annualized Statistical Inputs for Stocks, Bonds, and Bills Based Upon VAR Bootstrap of Long-Horizon Returns, VAR Simulation With Normal Errors, and Short-Horizon Summary Statistics for the Period 1926–1991

VAR Bootstrap	Mean	Standard Deviation	Stocks	Bonds	Bills
S&P returns	0.098	0.207	1.00		
Long-term government bonds	0.043	0.061	0.34	1.00	
Treasury bill returns	0.036	0.060	0.19	0.08	1.00
VAR simulation with normal errors			Stocks	Bonds	Bills
S&P returns	0.089	0.186	1.00		
Long-term government bonds	0.048	0.051	0.31	1.00	
Treasury bill returns	0.036	0.056	0.19	0.17	1.00
Summary statistics for annual log returns			Stocks	Bonds	Bills
S&P returns	0.096	0.199	1.00		
Long-term government bonds	0.044	0.077	0.14	1.00	
Treasury bill returns	0.036	0.032	−0.03	0.22	1.00
VAR bootstrap statistics for risk premia			ERP	BRP	
Equity risk premia	0.059	0.210	1.00		
Bond risk premia	0.008	0.082	0.11	1.00	
Summary statistics for annual log risk premia			ERP	BRP	
Equity risk premia	0.060	0.208	1.00		
Bond risk premia	0.008	0.081	0.19	1.00	

Notes: All VAR estimates and summary measures performed on logs of one plus the annual returns. VAR bootstrap procedures are described in Equation (2). For purposes of comparison, annualized returns are calculated by dividing the decade returns by 10. Annualized standard deviations are calculated by multiplying decade standard deviations by the square root of 10. Bootstrap based upon 1,000 simulations.

Equally interesting are the differences in the correlation matrixes. While stocks have a slight negative contemporaneous correlation to T-bills, over the long term, their log returns appear to be slightly positively correlated. This is not surprising, as most pricing models predict that the riskless rate is a component of expected stock returns.[4] On a short-horizon basis, variations in the equity risk premium dominate variations due to the riskless rate, but on a long-horizon basis the riskless component of returns manifests itself. When the riskless return is subtracted out, the correlations are unaffected.

Figures 13.1 and 13.2 show the composition of the efficient frontier using the two different sets of inputs: short-horizon returns and long-horizon returns generated with the bootstrap methodology. Each portfolio on the frontier assumes that the investor rebalances annually to maintain fixed weights over the entire ten-year horizon. One result is that the bootstrapped inputs

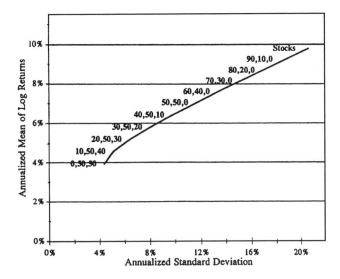

Figure 13.1. Long-Horizon Input Frontier: Stocks, Bonds, Bills

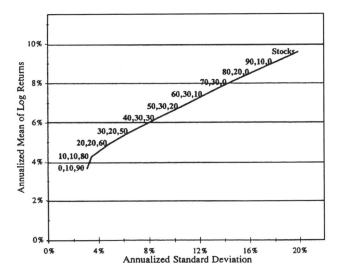

Figure 13.2. Short-Horizon Input Frontier: Stocks, Bonds, Bills

have relatively little impact on the high-risk, high-return portion of the frontier—the location of the all-stock portfolio is virtually unchanged.

The major difference between the two frontiers occurs for the minimum-variance portfolio. Inputs generated by the bootstrap result in a minimum-variance portfolio composed of 50% bonds and 50% bills. In contrast, inputs taken from the time series of short-horizon returns result in a minimum-variance portfolio of 10% bonds and 90% bills. Not only do the bootstrapped inputs increase the minimum achievable risk, but the slightly higher correlation across assets also reduces the curvature of the frontier.

These results must be qualified by the fact that the simulations are conditional upon point estimates of the VAR coefficients, and the assumption of stationarity of all underlying parameters. Further, the period 1926–1991 is chosen for purposes of example, not for purposes of making the best long-horizon forecast of ten-year asset returns. Investors wishing to use this technique should consider further simulations that perturb the underlying parameters: means, standard deviations, correlations, and VAR coefficients.

◣ Conclusion

Simulations of long-horizon returns clearly indicate that mean-variance inputs based upon short-horizon return statistics can lead to incorrect conclusions regarding the composition of the minimum-variance portfolio. This result complements other research regarding the relationship between investment horizons and deviations of returns from a random walk. For instance, Lee (1990) and Butler and Domian (1991) both demonstrate that stocks are more attractive to long-term investors when the time structure of returns is taken into account.

In our research we find that the investment horizon and the temporal structure of returns matter for the opposite end of the efficient frontier as well. The time series behavior of T-bills and bonds dramatically influences the composition of the minimum-variance portfolio and efficient portfolios close to it. In general, Treasury bills are more volatile and are more highly correlated with other assets once their time series behavior is taken into account. As components of long-term returns to stocks and bonds, they also influence the interrelationships among other assets.

The significance of these results for investors depends in large measure upon their portfolio choice criterion. Our results, however, clearly suggest that caution should be exercised when using nominal asset class returns as inputs to the Markowitz model.

In particular, if investors select portfolios on the basis of real expected returns, or on the basis of the mean and variance of the risk premium over Treasury bills, Treasury bills will constitute a major proportion of the minimum-variance portfolio. Similarly, if investors optimize over the mean and variance of the difference between assets and liabilities, the minimum-variance portfolio might be dedicated to assets matching the cash flows of liabilities.

This approach is predicated on the assumption that investors can accurately identify both their investment horizons and the timing of future cash needs. In the absence of such knowledge, there is no riskless asset, and, consequently, the Markowitz model cannot be applied with precision. When investor preferences are expressed over the mean and variance of portfolio wealth for a multiple-period horizon, even though the horizon is uncertain, the time series behavior of returns becomes critical for the prediction of the variances and the correlation matrix to be used as inputs to the Markowitz model.

▲ Notes

1. In discrete time, that is, $\ln(1 + r_t)$, where r is the total annual return for that asset in time t. In fact the ratio of the annual variance to the multiyear variance has been used as a general test of serial dependence by Poterba and Summers (1988) among others.

2. The VAR coefficients are estimated using the S-PLUS statistical package. For a description of the estimation algorithm, see Box and Jenkins (1976). The VAR allows for as many lags as one might want, although we find that the first lag captures virtually all the temporal structure. This is determined by applying the Akaike information criterion (AIC), which chooses the lag k that balances the reduction in error variance achieved by including additional lags against the loss of information as a function of the degrees of freedom.

3. This semiparametric approach also allows for estimating parameters for the VAR and the error matrix using different time periods. This is useful for modeling changing variances as in Hodrick (1992), and for investigating the performance of asset classes for which only a short time period of returns may be obtained.

4. Ibbotson and Sinquefield (1976) break returns into components that include the real rate and the risk premia for stocks and bonds, in order to make their bootstrap consistent with asset pricing models and the assumption that equity risk premia follow random walks.

▲ References

Best, M., and R. Grauer. "On the Sensitivity of Mean-Variance Efficient Portfolios to Changes in Asset Means: Some Analytical and Computational Results." *Review of Financial Studies,* 4 (1991), pp. 315–342.

Box, G. E. P., and G. M. Jenkins. *Time Series Analysis: Forecasting and Control.* Oakland, CA: Holden-Day, 1976.

Broadie, M. "Computing Efficient Frontiers Using Estimated Parameters." Working Paper, Columbia University, 1991.

Butler, K., and D. Domian. "Risk, Diversification and the Investment Horizon." *Journal of Portfolio Management,* Spring 1991, pp. 41–47.

Campbell, J. Y., and R. J. Shiller. "The Dividend-Price Ratio and Expectations of Future Dividends and Discount Factors." *Review of Financial Studies,* 1 (1988), pp. 195–228.

Fama, E. F., and K. R. French. "Permanent and Temporary Components of Stock Prices." *Journal of Political Economy,* 96 (1988), pp. 246–273.

Goetzmann, W., and P. Jorion. "Testing the Predictive Power of Dividend Yields." *Journal of Finance,* 48, 2 (June 1993), pp. 663–679.

Hakansson, N. "Fallacy of the Log-Normal Approximation to Optimal Portfolio Decision-Making Over Many Periods: Comment." *Journal of Financial Economics,* 1 (1974), pp. 95–96.

———. "Mean-Variance Analysis in a Finite World." *Journal of Financial and Quantitative Analysis,* 7, 4 (1972), pp. 1873–1880.

Hodrick, Robert. "Dividend Yields and Expected Stock Returns: Alternative Procedures for Inference and Measurement." *Review of Financial Studies,* 5 (1992), pp. 357–386.

Holton, Glyn A. "Time: The Second Dimension of Risk." *Financial Analysts Journal,* November–December 1992, pp. 38–45.

Ibbotson, R., and R. Sinquefield. "Stocks, Bonds, Bills and Inflation: Simulations of the Future 1976–2000." *Journal of Business,* 49, 1 (1976), pp. 22–33.

Jorion, Philippe. "Bayes-Stein Estimation for Portfolio Analysis." *Journal of Financial and Quantitative Analysis,* September 1986, pp. 279–292.

———. "International Portfolio Diversification With Estimation Risk." *Journal of Business,* July 1985, pp. 259–278.

———. "Portfolio Optimization in Practice: An Application to International Diversification." Working Paper, Columbia University, 1990.

Kandel, S., and R. F. Stambaugh. "On Correlations and Inferences About Mean-Variance Efficiency." *Journal of Financial Economics,* 18 (1987), pp. 61–90.

Lee, Wayne Y. "Diversification and Time: Do Investment Horizons Matter?" *Journal of Portfolio Management,* Spring 1990, pp. 21–32.

Markowitz, H. "Portfolio Selection." *Journal of Finance,* 7, 1 (1952), pp. 77–91.

Michaud, Richard. "The Markowitz Optimization Enigma: Is 'Optimized' Optimal?" *Financial Analysts Journal,* 45, 1 (1989), pp. 11–21.

Nelson, C., and M. Kim. "Predictable Stock Returns: Reality or Statistical Illusion?" *Journal of Finance,* 48 (1993), pp. 641–661.

Poterba, James M., and Lawrence H. Summers. "Mean Reversion in Stock Prices, Evidence and Implications." *Journal of Financial Economics,* 22 (1988), pp. 27–59.

Survivorship and Selection Bias

IV

Almost everything we know about financial markets is due to empirical study of past data. At the same time, the existence of these data is conditioned upon survival, or upon the efforts of researchers to reconstruct the past. Analogous to modern physics, we cannot observe economic data apart from the effects of the observation itself. For example, as we pointed out in the first section of this book, our measures of the equity risk premium are based upon the geometric return of the U.S. stock market over the period 1926 to the present. Indeed, we are fortunate to have nearly 80 years' worth of U.S. capital market data upon which to base this estimate. If not for the efforts of market researchers such as Alfred Cowles (1939), Larry Fisher and James Lorie (1965, 1968, 1977), and Ibbotson and Sinquefield (1976; see Chapter 1 of the present volume) such long-term measures of market return might not even exist. (All references are supplied in "Suggested Reading" unless otherwise noted.)

Yet historical data are both a blessing and a curse. On the one hand, history provides rich information about the behavior of capital markets. On the other hand, we analyze only the data that exist. Unfortunately, more often than not, history is written by the winners. The very fact that quantitative data have survived to be analyzed by the econometrician, or that they are of interest to the current marketplace, may distort the lessons we draw from studying them.

Chapter 14, written jointly with Stephen Brown and Stephen Ross, is entitled "Survival." It is largely an analytical article in which we create a hypothetical stock market that has no equity premium, but does have a survival threshold—that is, the market will disappear if it drifts down more than a certain percentage from its initial value. Our analysis shows that even very simple forms of market survival can bias inferences about the long-term expected return of the market. The higher the conditioning survival threshold, the greater the positive bias in ex post equity returns.

For Chapter 15, we both joined forces with Stephen Brown and Stephen Ross to examine a more subtle survival bias—a bias that potentially affects all cross-sectional studies of winning markets, winning managers, or winning stocks. The study asks, what would happen if you performed simple tests to see whether winners repeat on a sample in which losers drop out? For example, suppose you were to test the conjecture that world markets with the highest equity premiums last year will have high equity premiums next year. Our study highlights the fact that when some markets are riskier than others, picking winners also means you are picking riskier markets. If these markets survive from year to year, they will *appear* to provide consistently higher premiums — but for risky markets, this is a big if. Thus, this article suggests that survival conditioning affects not only the time-series measure of the premium for markets, but also cross-sectional analysis of consistency.

These analytical studies of survival led to a conjecture. Could the well-known equity premium puzzle be attributed in part to the fact that we typically use U.S. data to measure it? To address this question empirically, Philippe Jorion and William Goetzmann collected monthly returns on 39 of the world's equity markets over much of the 20th century. The results surprised us. In Chapter 16 "Global Stock Markets in the Twentieth Century," we show that the United States had the highest uninterrupted real rate of capital appreciation of all countries, at 4.3% annually from 1921 to 1996. For other countries, the median real appreciation rate was 0.8%. The high return premium obtained for U.S. equities therefore appears to be the exception rather than the rule. The real growth rate of a GDP-weighted world equity market over the period, excluding the U.S. market, was 3.39% — nearly 1% per year lower than the growth rate of the U.S. market. While this difference is not big enough to explain the equity premium puzzle, it does suggest that extrapolating past U.S. stock returns to forecast the future equity premium may be too optimistic.

Our analysis in general suggests that conditioning on market survival would have the greatest effect on econometric studies of markets that are in particular danger of disappearance. One clear example is emerging markets. Emerging markets are defined as equity markets in developing countries. They have enjoyed nearly 20 years of popularity with U.S. investors because of their potential for high returns and their low correlation to markets in developed countries. While most emerging markets are regarded by investors as new opportunities, most also have a long history of Western investment — their recent emergence, as often as not, results from their having submerged at some time in the past. Chapter 17, "Re-Emerging Markets," is also coauthored with Philippe Jorion. In it, we explore the implications of using data on a market only since its last emergence — that is, collecting data in an unbroken string as far back as possible and neglecting earlier periods in the market's history.

We show through simulation and through analysis of emerging market histories that statistics about emerging markets may be strongly biased by survivorship and also by a "sorting" bias. A recently emerged market that has existed for a long time is — by the very fact of recent emergence — more likely to be a market with a low expected rate of return. We also verify through simulation that a recently emerged market is likely to have low historical correlation to the market index. This evidence is consistent with the studies by other authors on the distinctive statistical characteristics of emerging markets.

The magnitude of the effects due to analyzing market data only since emergence is striking. Of 11 emerging markets for which we have preemergence data—that is, data from the period before which they are deemed investable by the International Financial Corporation (IFC)—we find preemergence returns to be 1.3% per year, compared to 23.7% per year postemergence. The implication for investors and researchers alike is that preemergence data may tell a very different story about the market. While a natural explanation for the difference between preemergence and postemergence returns may be a fundamental economic shift in the economies of these countries, it would seem prudent to verify such changes in fundamentals before relying solely upon postemergence data for forecasting.

The essence of the survival hypothesis is luck. That is, some economies do well by chance and survive, while others do poorly by chance and fail. However, the reemerging market hypothesis is fundamentally different—it assumes that there are basic differences in the risk and return characteristics of markets and that these characteristics interact differently with the survival conditioning. In short, history records some markets because they are lucky, versus history records some markets because they have higher equity premiums to begin with. Interestingly enough, this second hypothesis has a certain currency in the unlikely field of cosmology. The "many worlds" hypothesis, for example, seeks to explain the oddly precise configuration of universal constants in terms of a survival story. The theory hypothesizes the existence of an infinitum of parallel universes, each with its own configuration of constants, yet only a few with the particular structure that would allow life, and ultimately a conscious observer, to evolve.[1] Assuming that the observed universe describes the entire set of possible physical laws has been called an "anthropic bias," since it fails to take into account that this is the only kind of universe in which a human observer could have evolved. By analogy, the U.S. market could be taken as one of the few "universes" with a particular configuration of risk and return characteristics that would lead an econometrician to study the equity premium puzzle. Heady issues!

The distinction between these two alternative survival stories is actually quite important for investment choice and for international security market regulation. United States investors are confronted with the striking history of the domestic equity premium and the question of whether this was due to a few lucky outcomes or to something special about the U.S. economy that favors equity investors. If it were luck, then it would make sense to more broadly diversify equity investment across a number of the world's countries that face the same ex ante prospects as the United States. On the other hand, if the historical success of the U.S. market were due to the special set of securities laws, business practices, or even the beneficial effects of U.S. geography, then it would make more sense to assume that the U.S. enjoys a structural advantage that—analogous to a set of favorable universal constants—could be expected to continue. The chapters in this section present empirical evidence that both stories may contain a kernel of truth.

◣ Note

1. See Bostrum (2002; cited in full in "Suggested Reading") for a complete review of this hypothesis.

14 Stephen J. Brown, William N. Goetzmann, and Stephen A. Ross

Survival

▲ *Overview*

Much to our surprise, this article has caused a stir in academic and practitioner circles, almost certainly because of a section about the equity premium. The key contribution of the work (from the authors' perspective, at least) is that it analyzes a few basic cases in which the survival of a market or a security might affect econometric analysis. In particular, we show how very simple rules can dramatically bias the measure of the equity risk premium, the measure of the autocorrelation of stock market returns, and the measurement of the significance of corporate events, such as earnings announcements and stock splits. Our analysis of the equity risk premium is the most controversial—we show that if the probability of a market failure is high enough, then a researcher measuring the equity premium ex post, using historical data from only a market that has survived, will overestimate the premium. Although we do not claim that this "solves" the equity premium puzzle, we believe it adds another dimension to consider.

▲ *Abstract*

Empirical analysis of rates of return in finance implicitly condition on the security surviving into the sample. We investigate the implications of such conditioning on the time series of rates of return. In general this conditioning induces a spurious relationship between observed return and total risk for those securities that survive to be included in the sample. This result has immediate implications for the equity premium puzzle. We show how these results apply to other outstanding problems of empirical finance. Long-term autocorrelation studies focus on the statistical relation between successive holding period returns, where the holding period is of possibly extensive duration. If the equity market survives, then we find that average return in the beginning is higher than average return near the end of the time period. For this reason, statistical measures of long-term dependence are typically biased toward the rejection of a random walk. The result also has implications for event studies. There is a strong association between the magnitude of an earnings announcement and the postannouncement performance of the equity. This might be explained in part as an artefact of the stock price performance of firms in financial distress that survive an earnings announce-

ment. The final example considers stock split studies. In this analysis we im-
plicitly exclude securities whose price on announcement is less than the
prior average stock price. We apply our results to this case, and find that the
condition that the security forms part of our positive stock split sample suf-
fices to explain the upward trend in event-related cumulated excess return in
the preannouncement period.

Looking back over the history of the London or the New York stock markets can be extraordinarily comforting to an investor—equities appear to have provided a substantial premium over bonds, and markets appear to have recovered nicely after huge crashes. The tendency of prices and yields to revert toward a mean appears suggestive of a long-term equilibrium in the financial markets. Less comforting is the past history of other major markets: Russia, China, Germany, and Japan. Each of these markets has had one or more major interruptions that prevent their inclusion in long-term studies. This observation suggests that it might be fruitful to consider the possible implications of the most pervasive ex post conditioning in empirical finance: the survival of the return history to be included in the sample.

We derive the distributional properties of stock prices that survive conditioning of this kind. As we would expect, expected returns are biased by this kind of conditioning. The magnitude of this bias is an increasing function of the volatility of returns. The result has immediate implications for the study of equity returns in emerging capital markets. Such markets are characterized by a significant ex ante probability of failure and are quite volatile. We should expect to see a significant equity premium in emerging capital market returns. There are implications for other kinds of studies as well.

Long-term autocorrelation studies focus on the statistical relation between successive holding period returns, where the holding period is of possibly extensive duration. If the equity market survives, then we find that average return in the beginning is higher than average return near the end of the time period. For this reason, statistical measures of long-term dependence are typically biased toward the rejection of a random walk. We find that the direction and magnitude of this bias is sensitive to the choice of return horizon, to the ex ante viability of the exchange in question, and to the criteria for survival. The issue of survival has been noted by researchers who use long-term financial data such as Shiller (1989), and researchers such as Harvey (1994) who use series that are subject to attrition. However, the empirical implications of survival have yet to be specifically addressed. We provide preliminary numerical examples that show how statistics used to detect long-term market patterns are affected.[1]

Event studies typically look at the impact of corporate announcements on security prices after the announcement has been made, and then correlate this impact with the content of the announcement. The object is to discover the speed of market adjustment to this new information. There appears to be a strong association between the magnitude of an earnings announcement and the postannouncement performance of the equity. Firms in financial distress are in effect at-the-money call options, and we would expect the equity to have a higher return than a corresponding all-equity firm. In fact, the average return of firms that survive the announcement will be inversely related to the extent to which the equity represents an in-the-money call option. This will be true for both the announcement period and the postannouncement period. Provided there is cross-sectional dispersion in the extent to which the equity is in-the-money, there will be an induced cross-sectional relationship between average returns in the announcement and in the postannouncement period. Whether this effect is large enough to explain the observed postearnings drift phenomenon depends on a careful reexamination of the empirical evidence.

Event studies sometimes find substantial price increases prior to the public announcement. Many would attribute apparent run-ups in price to market leakages or insider trading activity. In the analysis of positive stock splits, we implicitly exclude securities whose price on announcement is less than the prior average stock price. We apply our results to this case and find that this conditioning suffices to explain the upward trend in event-related security average return in the preannouncement period.

The article is organized as follows. The first section characterizes the properties of the price path, conditional upon surviving a sample selection criterion. The second section studies the implications of this result for the analysis of long-term autocorrelations. The third section analyzes the application of the results to the study of postevent performance subsequent to earnings announcements, whereas the fourth section looks at the run-up in average prices prior to stock splits. The fifth section concludes.

◣ *Properties of Surviving Return Histories*

Virtually all empirical work in finance is conditioned upon the availability of data, but none more so than studies of long-term market behavior. Extending the history of the New York Stock Exchange back in time adds information to researchers about long-term mean, variance, and time-series behavior, but the cost of this information is the potential bias imparted by conditioning upon the survival of the market, or in less extreme cases, the unbroken continuity of transaction prices. As researchers seek to enhance the power of statistical tests by collecting longer and longer market price sequences, accounting for survival becomes a nontrivial problem. Does it comfort investors to know that the world's most successful stock market, a market that survived two world wars and a global depression over the last century, provided a 6 percent equity premium? How meaningful is it to show that markets which bounced back from great crashes in the 1930s and 1970s display ex post evidence of mean reversion?

A survey of the history of the world's equity markets shows that it is not uncommon to have a hiatus in trading that renders the index unsuitable for long-term econometric studies. Since the beginning of organized trading in shares in Holland in the seventeenth century, many stock markets have appeared, but only a few have survived continuously without a break for more than a few decades. For instance, when the New York Stock Exchange began in 1792, it was possible to speculate in shares in the financial markets of Britain, Holland, France, Germany, and Austria. Of these, only the United States and Britain yield continuous historical share price information.[2] Data on German and Austrian markets suffer from a major suspension during World War II, and the hyperinflation in France during this century makes economic return calculation difficult.

Over a more recent horizon, there is historical evidence of at least thirty-six exchanges extant at the beginning of the century.[3] More than half of these suffered at least one major hiatus in trading.[4] Of the survivors, several are still considered emerging markets, suggesting that they have only recently experienced the level of growth that attracts international investors, and in turn induces researchers to gather price data. In fact the very term "emerging markets" admits the possibility that these markets might fail.

Despite historical evidence about the patterns of emergence and disappearance of stock exchanges, correlations across markets make it difficult to estimate the ex ante probability of survival for any given market. Most of the suspensions that prevent long-term econometric studies of investor return were the result of revolutions or major wars. The fact that most of the continuous markets are in former British colonies such as Australia, Canada, India, South Africa, and the United States is almost certainly an accident of political, and perhaps legal, history. Had the outcome of either world war been different, we might currently be studying the long-term behavior of continental European exchanges.

Just as it is difficult to estimate the ex ante probability of market survival, it is also difficult explicitly to model market breaks and suspensions. We have chosen to characterize a market as a stochastic variable, and a break or suspension of trading as an absorbing lower bound. In other words, we assume that market failure or appropriation by the state is likely to be anticipated by falling prices. Other processes are equally reasonable. A hyperinflation prelude to market closure may be characterized by an absorbing upper bound. Revolution may in fact be consequent on sustained excessive rates of return realized by domestic and foreign investors. In the analysis that follows we have taken a few simple rules as illustrative, but by no means definitive, examples of market failure.

Suppose the researcher limits his or her analysis to a price series that has survived a specified period of study. The researcher has observed a time series of prices p_t, which we are assuming is generated on $(0, T)$ by a simple absolute diffusion

$$dp = \mu dt + \sigma dz$$

where μ and σ are parameters and z is a Brownian path.[5] Usually we think of p as the log of asset price.

In a simple example of survival, assume there is a reservation price p below which the stock market ceases to function and securities cease to trade. For purposes of analysis, we start the price level at $p_0 + p$. If the researcher studies only price paths that stay above p on the interval $(0, T)$, what should he or she expect to see? The conditioning event that of interest is

$$A = \{\text{price path is greater than } p \text{ on the interval } [0, T]\}.$$

More generally, the set A defines the set of price paths that survive, where the ex ante probability of survival at date t depends on the level of prices at date t, p_t. Given that event A has occurred, we wish to find the distribution of the path of p_t. The paths in A will be diffusions, and the key to their analysis is the conditional probability that the path belongs to A given that $p_t = p$ at time t:

$$\pi(p, t) = \Pr(A \mid p, t).$$

Ross (1987) introduces the following lemma to describe the properties of the transformed diffusion and shows why π is central to the analysis.[6] The relevant probability concepts may be found in Karlin and Taylor (1975, 1981).

LEMMA 1 (Karlin and Taylor). *Let p follow a diffusion with*

$$dp = \mu dt + \sigma dz$$

where μ and σ are constants. For any set A (with an interior) the process for p conditional on being in A, i.e., p/A, follows a diffusion

$$dp^* = dp \mid A = \mu^* dt + \sigma^* dz$$

with

$$\mu^* = \mu + \sigma^2 \frac{\pi_p}{\pi}$$

and

$$\sigma^* = \sigma$$

where π is the conditional density of A given (p, t).

PROOF. By definition

$$\mu^* = E(\Delta p \mid A, p, t)$$
$$= \int \Delta p f(\Delta p \mid A, p, t) d\Delta p$$

where $f(\Delta p \mid A, p, t)$ is the conditional density of Δp.
    From Bayes' Theorem

$$f(\Delta p \mid A, p, t) = \frac{f(A, \Delta p \mid p, t)}{f(A \mid p, t)}$$

$$= \frac{1}{\pi} f(A, \Delta p \mid p, t).$$

Now, using Bayes' Theorem and the smoothness properties of diffusions,

$$f(A, \Delta p \mid p, t) = f(A \mid p + \Delta p, t + \Delta t) f(\Delta p \mid p, t)$$
$$= [\pi + \pi_p \Delta p + \pi_t \Delta t] f(\Delta p \mid p, t)$$

where we assume that (p, t) is in the interior of A.

Hence

$$\mu^* = E(\Delta p \mid A, p, t)$$
$$= \int \Delta p f(\Delta p \mid A, p, t) d\Delta p$$
$$= \int \Delta p \frac{1}{\pi} [\pi + \pi_p \Delta p + \pi_t \Delta t] f(\Delta p \mid p, t) d\Delta p$$
$$= \mu + \sigma^2 \frac{\pi_p}{\pi}.$$

A similar analysis verifies that $\sigma^* = \sigma$. ■

In our case, A is the set of all paths that survive to period $T > t$, that is, those that do not get absorbed at $\underline{p}$. Define $m(t)$ as

$$m(t) = \inf_{s \in (t, T)} p(s).$$

We use the sets

$$A = \{\text{paths such that } p(t) = p, m(t) > \underline{p}\}.$$

Clearly,

$$\pi(p, t) = \Pr(A(p, t) \mid p(t) = p)$$
$$= \Pr(m(t) > \underline{p}).$$

We will conduct the analysis assuming that the unconditional process has zero drift, that is, $\mu = 0$, although the analysis can be easily extended to cases allowing for a drift term.[7] We use the result from Ingersoll (1987), p. 352, for a Brownian motion with absorbing state at zero

$$\pi(p, t) = \Phi\left[\frac{p - \underline{p}}{\sigma\sqrt{T - t}}\right] - \Phi\left[\frac{-(p - \underline{p})}{\sigma\sqrt{T - t}}\right]$$
$$= 2\Phi\left[\frac{p - \underline{p}}{\sigma\sqrt{T - t}}\right] - 1$$

where $\Phi[\cdot]$ denotes the standard Normal distribution function. Then it follows that

$$\mu^* = \mu + \sigma^2 \frac{\pi_p}{\pi}$$
$$= \frac{2\sigma\varphi[w]}{\sqrt{T - t}\,(2\Phi[w] - 1)}$$

where $\varphi[\cdot]$ is the standard Normal density function and

$$w = \frac{p - \underline{p}}{\sigma \sqrt{T - t}}.$$

With zero drift, the conditional diffusion is then

$$dp^* = \frac{2\sigma\varphi[w]}{\sqrt{T - t}\,(2\Phi[w] - 1)}\, dt + \sigma dz.$$

It follows that even when the underlying process has zero drift, the expected return is positive for all $t < T$. Furthermore, it is easy to show that expected return is an increasing function of the standard deviation parameter σ for all $t < T$.

What does this path look like? The mean Brownian path is represented by the differential equation

$$\frac{dp}{dt} = \frac{2\sigma\varphi[w]}{\sqrt{T - r}\,(2\Phi[w] - 1)}.$$

We can characterize some important properties of this equation, although we cannot solve it directly. Applying L'Hopital's rule and letting T approach infinity, we obtain a simpler expression for the conditional diffusion:

$$dp^* = \frac{\sigma^2}{p - \underline{p}}\, dt + \sigma dz$$

and we can solve for the mean Brownian path directly:

$$\bar{p}_t = \sigma \sqrt{\frac{(p_0 + \underline{p})^2}{\sigma^2} + 2t},$$

which is evidently an increasing concave function of time, with the degree of concavity an increasing function of the volatility parameter σ. This function is given in Figure 14.1 for annual standard deviation 0.2.

This analysis assumes a zero drift process. If we consider the unconditional process to represent excess returns, then the mean Brownian path would correspond to the cumulative average return measure popular in event studies (see Brown and Warner [1980]). In other applications, it is appropriate to consider positive drift processes.

For a nonzero drift μ, it is more difficult to derive the marginal probability

$$\pi(p, t) = \Pr(A(p, t) \mid p(t) = p).$$

We can solve this problem by going directly to $t = \infty$ and searching for a stationary solution. Notice that for $\mu = 0$

$$\pi(p) \equiv \Pr(p(s) \geq \underline{p}, \text{ all } s) = 0,$$

since the price path is certain to hit $\underline{p}$. For $\mu > 0$ the problem is more interesting. The conditioning set A is equivalent to the condition

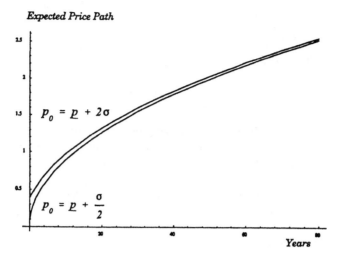

Figure 14.1. The Mean Brownian Path (in Excess of the Minimum Price p) for Annual Standard Deviation $\sigma = 0.2$ for Initial Prices 0.5, and Two Standard Deviations Above $\underline{p}$

$$p(t) = \mu t + \sigma z(t) + p_0 > \underline{p}$$

or $z(t) > [(\underline{p} - p_0)/\sigma] - (\mu/\sigma)t$ for all t. For the process with local drift μ and speed σ we can solve for the marginal probability $\pi(p)$ by employing the (backward) diffusion equation. We want to solve

$$\frac{1}{2}\sigma^2\pi_{pp} + \mu\pi_p = 0$$

subject to a marginal probability of zero at the lower bound $\pi(\underline{p}) = 0$, and a probability approaching unity for an infinite price $\pi(\infty) = 1$. This is easy to solve by conversion to a first order equation. The solution is

$$\pi(p) = 1 - e^{-\frac{2\mu}{\sigma^2}(p-\underline{p})}$$

Hence, the conditional process is

$$dp^* = \left[\mu + \sigma^2\,\frac{\pi_p}{\pi}\right]dt + \sigma dz$$

$$= \left[\mu + \frac{2\mu e^{-\frac{2\mu}{\sigma^2}(p-\underline{p})}}{1 - e^{-\frac{2\mu}{\sigma^2}(p-\underline{p})}}\right]dt + \sigma dz.$$

Note that as μ goes to zero we approach

$$dp^* = \frac{\sigma^2}{p - \underline{p}}dt + \sigma dz$$

as before.

This result suggests that survival will induce a substantial spurious equity premium. Note that the mean return conditional on survival is

$$\mu^* = \mu + \frac{2\mu(1 - \pi(p))}{\pi(p)}$$

where we interpret $\pi(p)$ as the probability that the stock market will survive over the very long term given the current level of prices p.

To take an extreme case, suppose that the true equity premium is in fact zero, with μ equal to the (positive) return on a risk-free security. The observed equity premium is then $\mu^* - \mu$. If the return on a risk-free security is 4 percent, an observed equity premium of 8 percent[8] is consistent with $\pi(p)$ equal to 50 percent. This is perhaps not unreasonable, given the number of stock markets that have survived the past 100 years. If we take a less extreme case, a true equity premium of 4 percent would imply a much higher probability of long-term survival, with $\pi(p)$ equal to 80 percent. This may go at least part of the way to explaining the equity premium puzzle posed by Mehra and Prescott (1985). They observe that the ex post historical premium provided by stocks over bonds is much larger than what can be justified by reasonable specifications of investor risk aversion. We find that, for any positive probability of series survival, the *unconditional* equity premium is lower than would be observed by averaging the differences in *conditional* return series when those series do not have the same variance.[9] Emerging markets provide an example where volatility appears to be associated with substantial equity premia (Harvey [1994]).[10]

Models Versus Historical Evidence

An important question about our analysis is what kind of survival rule might lead to an ex post equity premium as high as we observe in the U.S. market. In one section of our paper, we present a simple example with a survival probability of 50 percent that could lead to an equity premium of 8 percent. There are reasonable grounds for disagreement with our analysis. In recent work, Li and Xu (2002) argue that survival the way we describe it could not explain the magnitude of the equity premium—they part ways with us on the specific definition of the survival probability. While their analysis is sophisticated, the intuition of their claim is simple—when there is a simple, fixed lower bound, a market with a positive expected return will grow away from the bound, and as a result, the probability of disappearance will gradually vanish, rendering the effects of survival biases unimportant in the long term. Their analysis, also based on a fixed lower bound, suggests that the survival bias in the equity premium is only about 1 percent per year. One hundred basis points is a nontrivial bias that may significantly affect investment decision-making, but it is not as high as the 8 percent in our example—which we ourselves characterize as "extreme." The key determining factor, as our article and the Li and Xu article point out, is the distance

(continued)

of the market above an absorbing barrier, expressed in terms of units of standard deviation. A constant barrier, or one growing at a fixed rate, can be fairly easily handled in an analytical framework. However, we have relatively little empirical evidence to guide our modeling of the stochastic properties of the lower bound, and the volatility of the market as it approaches the bound. Collecting historical information about market disappearances should help us estimate a useful functional form—one that could provide tighter bounds on the bias in the equity premium than 1 to 8 percent.

A troublesome but important problem that characterizes the Li and Xu analysis, as well as the extreme equity premium example given in our article, is that the framework taken literally implies that older markets are virtually immune to catastrophe. If Li and Xu are to be believed, a market more than fifty years old has virtually no chance of disappearance—it has grown too far away from its absorbing barrier—maturity has insured it against failure. Alas, this mathematical result is hard to reconcile with empirical evidence. Many of the world's stock markets that failed did so after long and successful histories. Take for example the Russian stock market of 1917. Stocks had been trading on an organized exchange in St. Petersburg from 1836. Indeed, detailed government-collected price information about Russian securities exists from 1876. If we take the Li and Xu analysis as descriptive, the chances that the Russian market could disappear after such a long track record should have been vanishingly small. Similarly, the Shanghai stock exchanges began organized trading in shares in the 1870s—their long market history was probably small comfort to expropriated Chinese capitalists who saw the value of shares in 1949 plummet and finally vanish to practically nothing after 1950. Were these two revolutions simply exogenous events, unrelated to the existence and levels of the capital markets? Unlikely, given the Marxist foundations of both revolutions.

In another recent examination of the survival effects on the equity premium, Basu (2001)* argues that our analysis might in fact be a conservative estimate of the bias in the premium. He notes that the assumption of constant volatility common to our analysis, and that of Li and Xu, is unrealistic for the turbulent period of the 1930s when many markets were in trouble. Allowing for time variation in the survival probability, he finds that the bias in the U.S. equity premium for shorter intervals may have been as much as 14 percent.

*Devraj Basu, "Conditional Diffusions and the Equity Premium," Warwick Business School Working Paper and SSRN, 2001.

◣ Long-Term Dependence

Given that an empirical investigator has observed a price series up to date T that has survived an absorbing barrier and that obeys the conditional diffusion given above, what can we say about long-term dependence? Concavity of the mean Brownian path suggests that long-term holding period returns will be

negatively autocorrelated, as average holding period returns in the initial period will be higher than average returns measured over the entire period, and
average holding period returns in the latter part of the data will be less than the
overall average return.

Analysis of the variance of holding period returns as the holding period
grows longer provides a popular measure of return persistence. Positive autocorrelation in returns implies that annualized variances increase with the holding period for which returns are computed. A decrease in annualized variance
suggests that stock prices exhibit mean reversion properties. In fact, our results
show that annualized variance measures for long-horizon returns will fall to 43
percent of variances estimated using short-horizon data, regardless of the
volatility of returns and distance from the critical reservation price $\underline{p}$.

To analyze the variance of long-horizon returns we consider the distribution of the logarithm of prices p_T at the conclusion of a T-year holding period,
assuming that the return series survives to that point. We again use the result
for a Brownian motion with absorbing state at zero to establish that for price
paths that survive a reservation price of $\underline{p}$, the probability that prices will exceed a level $p_T > \underline{p}$ will be given by

$$\Pr(p > p_T) \equiv P(p_T)$$

$$= 1 - \Phi\left[\frac{-(p_T - \underline{p}) + (p_0 - \underline{p})}{\sigma\sqrt{T}}\right]$$

$$- \Phi\left[\frac{-(p_T - \underline{p}) - (p_0 - \underline{p})}{\sigma\sqrt{T}}\right]$$

$$= \Phi\left[\frac{p_0 - p_T}{\sigma\sqrt{T}}\right] - \Phi\left[\frac{-(p_T + p_0 - 2\underline{p})}{\sigma\sqrt{T}}\right]$$

where $\Phi[\cdot]$ denotes the standard Normal distribution function. Then it follows that the probability density function of p_T given that it survives is

$$f(p_T) \equiv \frac{\dfrac{-\partial P(p_T)}{\partial p_T}}{P(\underline{p})}$$

$$= \frac{\dfrac{1}{\sigma\sqrt{T}}\varphi\left[\dfrac{p_T - p_0}{\sigma\sqrt{T}}\right] - \dfrac{1}{\sigma\sqrt{T}}\varphi\left[\dfrac{p_T + p_0 - 2\underline{p}}{\sigma\sqrt{T}}\right]}{2\Phi\left[\dfrac{p_0 - \underline{p}}{\sigma\sqrt{T}}\right]} - 1.$$

The moment-generating function $\psi_c(\theta)$ of this conditional distribution is

$$\psi_c(\theta) \equiv E[e^{\theta x}]$$

$$= \int_{\underline{p}}^{\infty} e^{\theta x} f(x)\, dx$$

$$
= \frac{\displaystyle\int_{\underline{p}}^{\infty} \frac{1}{\underline{p}\,\sigma\sqrt{T}}\, e^{\theta x - \frac{(x-p_0)^2}{2\sigma^2 T}}\, dx - \int_{\underline{p}}^{\infty} \frac{1}{\underline{p}\,\sigma\sqrt{T}}\, e^{\theta x - \frac{(x-p_0 - 2\underline{p})^2}{\sigma^2 T}}\, dx}{2\Phi[w] - 1}
$$

$$
= \frac{e^{\theta p_0 + \frac{\sigma^2 T}{2}\theta^2}(1 - \Phi[w - \sigma\sqrt{T}\theta]) - e^{\theta(2\underline{p} - p_0) + \frac{\sigma^2 T}{2}\theta^2}(1 - \Phi[-w - \sigma\sqrt{T}\theta])}{2\Phi[w] - 1}
$$

for $w = [p_0 - \underline{p}/\sigma\sqrt{T}]$. By contrast, with no conditioning the terminal price will be distributed as Normal with mean p_0, and the associated moment-generating function will be

$$
\psi_u(\theta) = e^{\theta p_0 + \frac{\sigma^2 T}{2}\theta^2}
$$

with mean $E_u[p_T] = \psi_u'(0) = p_0$ and variance $\mathrm{Var}_u[p_T] = \psi_u''(0) - \psi_u'(0)^2 = \sigma^2 T$. After some simplification, the moments of the conditional distribution are given as

$$
\begin{aligned}
E_c[p_T] &= \psi_c'(0) \\
&= \frac{2\underline{p}\,\Phi[w] - (2\underline{p} - p_0)}{2\Phi[w] - 1}
\end{aligned}
$$

and

$$
\begin{aligned}
\mathrm{Var}_c[p_T] &= \psi_c''(0) - \psi_c'(0)^2 \\
&= \sigma^2 T + (p_0 - \underline{p})^2\left(1 - \frac{1}{(2\Phi[w] - 1)^2} + \frac{2\varphi[w]}{w(2\Phi[w] - 1)}\right).
\end{aligned}
$$

Since it can be shown that the second term in the above expression is negative for all T and for $w > 0$, the conditional variance is always less than the unconditional variance. To determine whether the conditional price displays general mean reverting behavior, or alternatively, a general positive autocorrelation property, we need to know the behavior of the annualized variance

$$
\omega[T] \equiv \frac{1}{T}\mathrm{Var}_c[p_T].
$$

If $\omega[T]$ is falling, this is an indication of mean reversion. A rising $\omega[T]$ indicates positive autocorrelation since the long-run variance exceeds the sum of the short-run variances. This function is given in Figure 14.2 for two assumptions about the initial price. In the first case, we assume the initial price is half a per-period standard deviation above the reservation price. In the second case, we assume the initial price is two standard deviations above the reservation price. In each case, the conditional variance is less than the unconditional variance, and appears to approach an asymptote that is independent of the initial price.

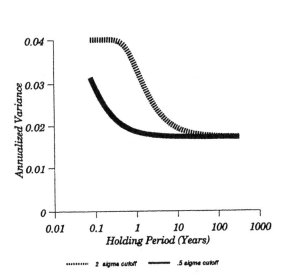

Figure 14.2. Annualized Holding Period Variance ($\omega[T]$ in text) Plotted as a Function of Holding Period T Given Annual Standard Deviation $\sigma = 0.2$ and Initial Prices 0.5, and Two Standard Deviations Above the Reservation Price $\underline{p}$

The limit of $\omega[T]$ as T approaches zero is the unconditional variance σ^2. It can be shown that $\omega[T]$ is everywhere a decreasing function of T and approaches an asymptote as T grows large:

$$\lim_{T \Rightarrow \infty} \omega[T] = \frac{4 - \pi}{2} \sigma^2,$$

which does not depend on how far the initial price p_0 is from the reservation price $\underline{p}$. This result suggests that substantial mean reversion will be evident for any stock return history that has survived, so long as the investigator studies a sufficiently long holding period. This formula indicates that the variance ratio will approach $(4 - \pi)/2$ or 0.429204 regardless of how volatile the market has been or how secure it is from failure.

Of course, empirical studies of long-period return variance ratios (e.g., Lo and MacKinlay [1988] and Poterba and Summers [1988]) do not find numbers this low. The precise value of the variance ratio conditional on survival depends crucially on assumptions that are made about the conditions that define whether or not a particular price path survives. The above results are derived for the special case where returns exhibit zero drift. They can be trivially extended to cases where the lower absorbing barrier rises through time at a rate equal to the positive drift in the sequence of returns. It is difficult to obtain analytic results for the case where the absorbing barrier rises at a rate that differs from the expected return, or where survival depends on

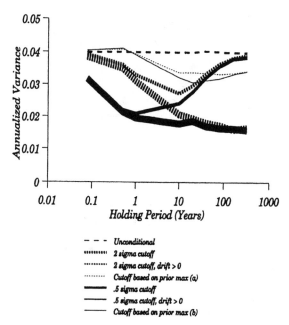

Figure 14.3. Effect of Different Survival Criteria on
Annualized Holding Period Variance
Notes: Simulation results based on 60,000 replications with
annual standard deviation σ = 0.2 and initial prices 0.5
(*solid lines*), and two standard deviations (*dotted lines*) above
the reservation price $\underline{p}$. The *dashed line* gives the
unconditional variance. We consider three cases. In the first
we assume zero drift (corresponding to Figure 13.2). In the
second case, we allow drift to be 10 percent per annum,
with reservation price constant in real terms (2.3 percent
inflation). In the third case, the cutoff is based on price
greater than a fixed value below the prior maximum. In case
(a) the test excludes as many price paths as the zero-drift
case with $p_0 = \underline{p} + 2\sigma$. Case (b) excludes as many price paths
as zero drift with $p_0 = \underline{p} + \sigma/2$.

whether prices are greater than a certain fixed value relative to the previous
maximum price.

   To address these issues, we consider a simple simulation experiment.
Weekly returns are generated from a zero mean Normal distribution with annualized standard deviation equal to 0.20. Holding period returns are computed for 4-week, 26-week, 1-, 10-, 20-, 40-, 80-, 160-, and 320-year holding
periods. The variance of terminal wealth is computed across 60,000 replications of this experiment. As illustrated in Figure 14.3, the variance of terminal
wealth is 0.04 for each holding period. We then consider two cases. In the first
case, we assume the initial price is half an annualized standard deviation above

the reservation price. In the second case, we assume the initial price is two standard deviations above the reservation price. The results closely correspond in numerical value to the theoretical results presented in Figure 14.2.

We then change the experiment to consider a 10 percent annualized expected return. We then assume that the reservation price is constant in real terms, with a 2.3 percent assumed annual rate of inflation. We then consider two examples that correspond to the cases considered above. The variance of terminal wealth for short holding periods corresponds to the zero-drift case. In addition, long holding period variances appear to converge to an asymptote independent of the initial price. This asymptote is the unconditional variance. However, for holding periods less than 100 years, the variance of terminal wealth is significantly below the unconditional variance, implying variance ratios less than one.

In the third experiment, we consider the case where survival depends on the price level's being above a certain fixed value relative to the previous maximum. This corresponds to the case where a market crash precipitates the closure of the market. We again consider two cases. In the first case, we consider the fixed value to be set in such a way as to exclude as many price paths as are excluded with zero drift and an initial price half an annual standard deviation above the reservation price. In the second case, we consider a test as stringent, as where before we assume the initial price is two standard deviations above the reservation price. With an expected return of 10 percent, we obtain results intermediate between those of the first and second experiments reported above. The variance of terminal wealth approaches an asymptote independent of how stringent we make the test for survival. The variance of terminal wealth is everywhere below the unconditional variance.

Each of the three experiments provides results consistent with the view that survival implies that the variance of terminal wealth will be less than the unconditional variance. In other words, the variance ratio will be less than one. The variance ratio appears to converge to a value independent of how stringent we make the test. At least part of the apparent mean reversion in long-period asset returns may be an artifact of survival. To determine how big or small this effect might be, we need additional information relating to the structure of these asset markets and the conditions for their survival.

Another important caveat to these findings is that they apply to the variance of terminal wealth for a potentially long holding period. Empirical work typically examines the time sequence of N period returns, where N is strictly less than the number of time-series observations available to the investigator. In Figure 14.3 each simulated price path starts at the same point, and has an identical a priori probability of survival. When we examine the time sequence of N period returns, the unconditional variance ratio will be greater than $(4 - \pi)/2$, the difference reflecting the variance of the conditional mean return.[11] Simulation evidence (not reported here) confirms that the variance ratio, calculated as in Lo and MacKinlay (1988) with appropriate overlap correction, is less than one but greater than $(4 - \pi)/2$. The same simulation experiment shows that other measures of long-term dependence such as the rescaled range (Mandelbrot [1972]) and long-term autocorrelation measures of the kind employed by Fama and French (1988) are also affected by survival considerations, to a greater or lesser extent. In addition, Goetzmann and Jorion (1995) show how survival similarly affects the distribution of the widely used Dickey-Fuller test for unit roots in time series.

▲ Postearnings Drift

These results find interesting application in the study of cross-sectional cumulated excess return measures (CARs) that are commonly used in the context of event studies (see Brown and Warner [1980]). Ball and Brown (1968) note an upward drift in cumulated excess returns subsequent to a positive earnings announcement surprise. Subsequent work by Foster (1977) and Foster, Olsen, and Shevlin (1984) among others has documented that this drift is related to size of the firm in question. The current state of this literature is summarized in Ball (1992).

The dynamics of the conditional price path have a direct bearing on these results. Firms that are otherwise in financial distress are more likely to survive on a favorable earnings surprise than an unfavorable earnings surprise. In fact the ex ante probability of survival will be an increasing function of the magnitude of this surprise for any given level of financial distress. In a surviving sample, firms working their way out of financial distress will typically have higher earnings announcements and subsequent returns than will other firms whose ex ante probability of survival does not so nearly depend on favorable announcements.[12]

In other words, firms in financial distress are at-the-money call options, and we would expect the equity to have a higher return than a corresponding all-equity firm (Stapleton [1982]).[13] In fact, the average returns of firms that survive the announcement will be inversely related to the extent to which the equity represents an in-the-money call option. This will be true for both the announcement period and the postannouncement period.[14] Provided there is cross-sectional dispersion in the extent to which the equity is in-the-money, there will be an induced cross-sectional relationship between average returns in the announcement and in the postannouncement period. This effect works at the level of the individual security. To the extent that portfolios are formed according to the size of the earnings surprise, this effect will be magnified at the portfolio level (cf. Lo and MacKinlay [1990]).

Event studies typically look at the impact of the earnings announcement on security prices after the announcement has been made, and then correlate this impact with the content of the earnings announcement. These studies typically assume that before the event, the expected change in security prices is zero. Knowing that a quarterly earnings announcement is to be made at some date τ in the future simply adds volatility to the ex ante distribution of stock prices. This increase in volatility reflects the likely magnitude of the earnings announcement, good or bad.

It can be shown (Brown and Ross [1995]) that we can write the security price process as

$$dp = \frac{\sigma^2}{p^- \underline{p}}\, dt + \sigma dz, \quad \text{for } \tau \notin \{\alpha l \mid l = 1, \dots\}$$

$$= \frac{\sigma^2}{p^- \underline{p}}\, dt + \sigma dz + \delta_\tau(p), \quad \text{for } \tau \in \{\alpha l \mid l = 1, \dots\},$$

where the event-related change in price $\delta_\tau(p)$ is a random variable capturing the event-related change in price and $\{\alpha l \mid l = 1, \dots\}$ represents the set of earnings dates separated by a time of α (three months).

We can use this result to determine the relevant distribution of price changes conditional on earnings announcements. Brown and Ross (1995) show that an increase in Δp_τ implies a first-order stochastic increase in $\Delta p_{\tau'}$ for $\tau < \tau'$ in the surviving sample of returns. This result is consistent with empirical results found by Bernard and Thomas (1989, 1990) among others.

◤ Stock Splits

We have chosen to condition upon the price's exceeding the reservation price $\underline{p}$; it may be of interest to condition upon other features of the price path. For instance, Ross (1987) derives the conditional diffusion for the case where the conditioning set A is defined as the set of all price paths on $[0, T]$ that achieve a maximum at point t^*, $0 < t^* < T$. Suppose the empirical investigator observes that the price attains a maximum of m at point t^*, and considers the time series of data up to that point. Ross derives a closed form for the diffusion prior to t^* and shows that the mean Brownian path is increasing at an increasing rate up to t^*. The implication is that the perils of data snooping extend even to preliminary curiosity!

Another interesting example is the case of stock splits studied by Fama et al. (1969). Very rarely does a positive stock split come upon a *decrease* in security prices. If we consider the conditioning set A as the set of all price paths where the price on the event date is greater than the average price measured over the prior period, the cumulative average return statistic measured as the cross-section average of excess returns is in fact the mean Brownian path introduced earlier.

If we assume as before that we observe a time series of prices p_t which is generated on $(0, T)$ according to

$$dp = \mu dt + \sigma dz,$$

we only observe a positive stock split on date T when the current price is at least equal to the geometric average of past prices. For observations prior to T, the conditioning set is then

$$A = \left\{ \text{price path such that } p_T > \frac{\sum_{t=0}^{T} p_t}{T} \right\}$$

we sample the price path on infinitesimal increments, the summation is approximated by the integrated Brownian process

$$w(T) = \int_0^T p_t \, dt$$

and we can represent the conditioning set as

$$A = \left\{ \text{paths such that } p(t) = p, \, p(T) > \frac{w(T)}{T} \right\}.$$

It is a well-known result (e.g., Ross [1983], p. 196) and $p(T)$ and $w(T)$ are bivariate Normal conditional on $p(t)$ and $w(t)$. The quantity

$$e(T) = p(T) - \frac{w(T)}{T}$$

has a conditional Normal distribution with mean

$$E[e(T) \mid p(t), w(t)] = \frac{tp(t) - w(t)}{T} + \mu \frac{T^2 - t^2}{2T} \equiv m(t, p, w)$$

and standard deviation

$$\sqrt{\text{Var}[e(T) \mid p(t), w(t)]} = \sigma \sqrt{\frac{t^3 - T^3}{2T}} \equiv s(t).$$

Hence the marginal probability of set A is given as

$$\pi(p, t) = 1 - \Phi[z],$$
$$z = -\frac{m(t, p, w)}{s(t)}$$

and the mean of the conditional diffusion is given as

$$\mu^* = \mu + \sigma^2 \frac{\pi_p}{\pi}$$
$$= \mu + \sigma^2 \frac{t\varphi[z]}{Ts(t)(1 - \Phi[z])}.$$

The mean Brownian path given as the solution to the differential equations

$$\frac{dp}{dt} = \mu + \sigma^2 \frac{t\varphi[z]}{Ts(t)(1 - \Phi[z])}, \quad t < T,$$
$$= \mu, \quad t \geq T,$$

$$\frac{dw}{dt} = p(t).$$

with initial conditions $p(0) = 0$ and $w(0) = 0$ is particularly interesting, as it represents the cumulative average return statistic (where excess returns are cross-sectionally uncorrelated—as, e.g., where events occur at different points in calendar time). For market model R^2 of 0.15, market return mean of 0.10, and standard deviation of 0.20 (corresponding to Ibbotson [1991]), the mean Brownian path corresponds closely to that reported in Fama et al. (1969) for $T = 2$ years, as shown in Figure 14.4.

We should be careful how we interpret this figure. The fact that the cumulative performance measure is positive on the event date is not an artifact of survival. After all, the experimental design conditions on the price at zero being greater than the average prior price, which is ex post good news. Rather, we should be careful how we interpret the apparent price pattern prior to the event. This point is actually made in the Fama et al. (1969) article, and is also explicit in the work of Mandelkar (1974), who writes in reference to the apparent price run-up prior to merger announcements that the decision to announce a merger at a particular time may not be independent of the pattern of price changes in the period prior to the announcement. Suppose that bad news in the days prior to a planned announcement is sufficient to cause a delay of several days in announcing the acquisition. The present analysis demonstrates that the absence of material bad news prior to the announcement may explain part of the apparent run-up of prices immediately prior to a merger announcement.

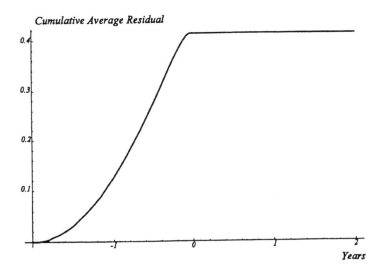

Figure 14.4. Mean Brownian Path for Stock Split Example, for Market Model R^2 of 0.15, Market Return Mean of 0.10, and Standard Deviation of 0.20

◣ Conclusion

Survival is an issue to some extent whenever a researcher chooses to use historical data. We have provided some analysis of the consequences of survival for studies of temporal dependency in long-term stock market returns, event studies, and other applications of empirical finance. The importance of these results is not limited to economics. Mandelbrot and Wallis (1969) identify very long-term dependencies in geophysical records such as river levels and tree rings using the Hurst statistic. They conclude that "the span of statistical interdependence of geophysical data is infinite." They fail, however, to take into account the survival bias in their data.[15] This oversight leads to a tempting conjecture. Given that a series is subject to some form of survival bias, does the probability of false rejection of temporal independence approach one as the period of survival grows to infinity?

These results are not intended to discourage the analysis of historical data. Rather they are intended to describe what researchers should expect to find due to survival alone. Our hope is that this analysis and further extensions of it will help disentangle survival effects from meaningful economic phenomena. Given that all econometricians are, to some extent, prisoners of history, perhaps we should seek to further our understanding of its constraints.

Premium to the Max

Much of our survival research was initially motivated by Stephen Ross' paper "Regression to the Max,"* which describes what might be called the "accidental econometrician"—an analyst who gets interested in testing the significance of an economic event after a large realization occurs. This tendency is familiar to all researchers who seek to understand the world and the events around them. When a large crash occurs, for example, economists are often asked to explain why. The natural thing to do is to use the tools we know—applying regression analysis and hypothesis testing to historical data. Ross' study shows that this will typically bias results in favor of rejecting the null. Conditioning on the max is potentially more powerful a bias than conditioning on survival alone, because the maximum is, by definition, extreme. In Table 14.1, we compare the bias in the equity premium caused by a survival conditioning to the bias caused by focusing on the maximum returning market. We simulate 25,000 independent stock markets over a century of life, 25 at a time, 1,000 times over. Each starts out at an equal size. We assume that the real, lognormal return is zero in each market, the volatility is 20 percent, and a market disappears from the sample if its index ever drops below 50 percent of the initial starting value. We also keep track of the relative capitalization represented by the maximum returning market, assuming reinvestment of dividends in all markets.

The first column of Table 14.1 indicates the percentile out of the 1,000 runs

Table 14.1
Conditioning on Survival and on the Maximum Performer (%)

Percentile	Survived	Average	Surv. Bias	Maximum	Share
0	4	−1.49	0.30	1.33	11.63
5	16	−0.62	0.98	2.46	19.07
25	24	−0.25	1.38	3.29	27.60
50	32	0.02	1.74	3.86	37.00
75	36	0.31	2.09	4.57	50.45
95	48	0.68	2.62	5.85	75.19
100	64	1.61	3.56	8.25	97.37

of pseudo-histories of the capital markets. Zero percent is the lowest value in the simulation, 100 percent is the highest. "Survived" indicates the fraction of markets out of the twenty-five in that run that survived. The mean rate of survival was 32 percent. The median return was close to zero. The highest average return out of 1,000 pseudo-histories was a little more than 160 basis points. "Surv. Bias" reports the percentiles for the bias in the equity premium under the conditions of our simulation. The median was 1.74 percent; however, values exceeding 2 percent were not uncommon. The maximum values are considerably higher. Focusing on the best market out of twenty-five each time results in a median equity premium bias of nearly 4 percent, with values over 5 percent not uncommon. The survival bias and the maximum bias are completely distinct. In fact, they can work in opposite directions. The maximum of the survived series—not reported in the table—is typically somewhat lower because it is a censored sample.

Notice that in these simulations the winning market is also the market that ex post has the largest capitalization—with a median value of about 37 percent, and quite commonly a value close to half of the equity market. Indeed, in this simulation, by focusing attention on the largest equity market, the econometrician is also, by definition, focusing attention on the maximum returning one. Suppose for argument that the world of the twentieth century generally resembled the world we just simulated, and further, that the easiest data to come by were the data generated by vendors in the largest market. The ex ante equity premium might be 3 to 4 percent less than the historical experience.

Of course it is reasonable also to explore the alternative to this hypothesis that the rate of return in the U.S. market is higher than in other markets due to economic fundamentals than have persisted over the century. In addition, this does not explain well the out-of-sample test of the equity premium represented by the Ibbotson and Sinquefield (1976) study included earlier in this volume. Nevertheless, like an observer in a "many worlds" universe, I cannot help but wonder whether our economy, and hence the lessons we draw from our careful econometric analysis, might somehow be largely an accident of history.

*Yale School of Management Working Paper, 1987.

◤ Notes

1. Similar implications follow where the question of interest is the predictive properties of dividend yields for long-term returns (Goetzmann and Jorion [1995]).

2. In fact, the New York and London exchanges were both shut down for a period of months during World War I, creating problems for researchers who use monthly data.

3. A survey of the *GT Guide to World Equity Markets* (O'Connor [1991]) suggests that of the cities that currently have significant exchanges, Amsterdam, Belgrade, Berlin, Bombay, Brussels, Budapest, Buenos Aires, Cairo, Caracas, Copenhagen, Dublin, Frankfort, Geneva, Helsinki, Hong Kong, Istanbul, Johannesburg, Lisbon, London, Madrid, Melbourne, Mexico City, Milan, Montreal, Moscow, New York, Oslo, Prague, Rio de Janeiro, Santiago, Seoul, Stockholm, Tokyo, Vienna, Warsaw, and Wellington all had exchanges in 1901.

4. Amsterdam, Belgrade, Berlin, Brussels, Budapest, Buenos Aires, Cairo, Copenhagen, Frankfort, Hong Kong, Istanbul, Lisbon, Madrid, Mexico City, Moscow, Prague, Rio de Janeiro, Santiago, Seoul, Tokyo, Vienna, and Warsaw all suffered major suspensions in activity due to nationalizations or war.

5. In this and what follows, the relevant material on diffusions and stochastic processes may be found in Karlin and Taylor (1975, 1981). For a discussion of the properties of conditional diffusions see Ross (1987).

6. This result has recently been extended in an obvious way to vector-valued p diffusions by Shui (1995).

7. A trivial extension would be to consider a case where the lower bound K increases with the expected increase in stock price. In this case we would interpret pt as the price in excess of the lower bound. The zero drift results apply. More general results can be obtained using the result cited in Ingersoll (1987, p. 352) for the case of a Brownian motion with drift.

8. In Ibbotson (1991) the average risk-free rate for the period 1926 to 1990 is 3.7 percent, and the average equity premium (stock return minus U.S. Treasury bill return) is 8.4 percent.

9. Rietz (1988) suggests that a small probability of a large "crash" in consumption can justify a large equity premium. The Mehra and Prescott (1988) reply challenges Rietz to identify such catastrophic events, and estimate their probabilities. Our analysis suggests that, when such events are correlated with market closure, they will appear much less frequently in surviving economic histories than their ex ante probabilities would indicate.

10. Harvey (1994) argues that this association is due to an asymmetric response of volatility to price level in emerging markets. The present analysis provides an alternative explanation for this phenomenon. To the extent that investments in emerging markets are like at-the-money call options, we would expect that return increases in the volatility of those markets that survive, and decreases in the extent to which the option is in-the-money ($p_t -$ $\underline{p}$). Notice that the expected price path shown in Figure 14.1 suggests that extending data series back further in time does not necessarily reduce the bias induced by survival. In fact, for fixed lower bounds the bias in average returns is exacerbated.

11. Note that

$$\frac{1}{N}E_0\{r_{\tau+N} - \mu\}^2 = \frac{1}{N}E_0\{r_{\tau+N} - \mu_{\tau+N} \mid p_\tau\}^2 + \frac{1}{N}E_0\{\mu_{\tau+N} \mid p_\tau - \mu\}^2$$

$$\geq \frac{1}{N}E_0\{r_{\tau+N} - \mu_{\tau+N} \mid p_\tau)^2 = \frac{4 - \pi}{2} \sigma^2 \text{ for large } N.$$

12. Note that this skewness argument derived from the option-like characteristics of firms in financial distress (cf. Ball, Kothari, and Shanken [1995]) does not require that any firms actually fail ex post in a finite sample. Therefore, the argument does not really depend on the inclusiveness (or lack thereof) of COMPUSTAT (Chan, Jegadeesh, and Lakonishok [1994]).

13. This assumes that the equity in the corresponding all-equity firm has an expected return greater than the risk-free rate (Cox and Rubinstein [1985], p. 189).

14. Brown and Pope (1995) find that skewness in size-adjusted returns is indeed associated with the postearnings drift phenomenon, and that skewness persists from the announcement to the postannouncement period.

15. Survival bias in this case may be due to disappearances of lakes and rivers, to changing climatic conditions leading to the disappearance of forests, or to the disappearance of the human observer and/or the erasure of the geological record.

◤ References

Ball, Ray, 1992, The earnings-price anomaly, *Journal of Accounting and Economics* 15, 319–345.

———, and P. Brown, 1968, An empirical evaluation of accounting numbers, *Journal of Accounting Research* 6, 159–178.

Ball, R., S. P. Kothari, and J. Shanken, 1995, Problems in measuring portfolio performance: An application to contrarian investment strategies, *Journal of Financial Economics* 37, Forthcoming.

Bernard, V. L., and J. Thomas, 1989, Post-earnings-announcement drift: Delayed price response or risk premium, *Journal of Accounting Research* 27 (Supplement), 1–36.

———, 1990, Evidence that stock prices do not fully reflect the implications of current earnings for future earnings, *Journal of Accounting and Economics* 13, 305–340.

Brown, Stephen J., and Jerold B. Warner, 1980, Measuring security price information, *Journal of Financial Economics* 8, 205–258.

Brown, Stephen J., and Peter Pope, 1995, Post-earnings announcement drift: Market inefficiency or research design biases? Working paper, Stern School of Business, NYU.

Brown, Stephen J., and Stephen Ross, 1995, Survival and post-earnings drift, Working paper, Stern School of Business, NYU.

Chan, Louis K. C., Narisham Jegadeesh, and Josef Lakonishok, 1994, Evaluating the performance of value versus glamour stocks: The impact of selection bias, Working paper, University of Illinois.

Cox, John, and Mark Rubinstein, 1985, *Option Markets* (Prentice Hall, Englewood, N.J.).

Fama, Eugene, Larry Fisher, Michael Jensen, and Richard Roll, 1969, The adjustment of stock price to new information, *International Economics Review* 10, 1–31.

Fama, Eugene, and Kenneth French, 1988, Permanent and temporary components of stock prices, *Journal of Political Economy* 96, 246–273.

Foster, G., 1977, Quarterly accounting data: Time-series properties and predictive-ability results, *The Accounting Review* 52, 1–21.

Foster, G., C. Olsen, and T. Shevlin, 1984, Earnings releases, anomalies, and the behavior of securities returns, *The Accounting Review* 59, 574–603.

Goetzmann, William N., and Phillipe Jorion, 1995, A longer look at dividend yields, *Journal of Business* 68(4), 483–508.

Harvey, Campbell R., 1994, Predictable risk and returns in emerging markets, *Review of Financial Studies* 8(3), 773–816.

Ibbotson, Roger, 1991, *Stocks, Bonds, Bills, and Inflation, 1991 Yearbook* (Ibbotson Associates, Chicago).

Ingersoll, Jonathan Jr., 1987, *Theory of Financial Decision Making* (Rowman and Littlefield, Totowa, N.J.).

Jegadeesh, Narasimhan, 1989, On testing for slowly decaying components in stock prices, Working paper, UCLA.

Karlin, S., and H. M. Taylor, 1975, *A First Course in Stochastic Processes* (Academic Press, New York).

———, 1981, *A Second Course in Stochastic Processes* (Academic Press, New York).

Kendall, M., 1954, A note on the bias in the estimation of the autocorrelation coefficient, *Biometrika* 41, 403–404.

Lo, Andrew, 1991, Long-term memory in stock prices, *Econometrica* 59, 1279–1314.

———, and C. MacKinlay, 1990, Data-snooping biases in tests of financial asset pricing models, *Review of Financial Studies* 3, 431–468.

———, 1988, Stock prices do not follow random walks: Evidence from a simple specification test, *Review of Financial Studies* 1, 41–66.

Mandelbrot, Benoit, 1972, Statistical methodology for non-periodic cycles: From the covariance to R/S analysis, *Annals of Economic and Social Measurement* 1, 259–290.

———, and James R. Wallis, 1969, Some long-run properties of geophysical records, *Water Resources Research* 5, 321–340.

Mandelker, Gershon, 1974, Risk and return: The case of merging firms, *Journal of Financial Economics* 1, 303–335.

Mehra, Rajnish, and Edward C. Prescott, 1985, The equity premium: A puzzle, *Journal of Monetary Economics* 15, 145–161.

———, 1988, The equity premium: A solution? *Journal of Monetary Economics* 22, 133–136.

O'Connor, Selina, 1991, *The GT Guide to the World Equity Markets* (Euromoney Publications, London).

Poterba, James, and Larry Summers, 1988, Mean reversion in stock prices: Evidence and implications, *Journal of Financial Economics* 22, 27–59.

Rietz, Thomas A., 1988, The equity risk premium: A solution, *Journal of Monetary Economics* 22, 117–131.

Ross, Sheldon M., 1983, *Stochastic Processes* (John Wiley & Sons, New York).

Ross, Stephen A., 1987, Regression to the max, Working paper, Yale University.

Shiller, Robert J., 1989, *Market Volatility* (MIT Press, Cambridge, Mass.).

Shui, Bing, 1995, Implications of return survival on event studies and mutual funds, Working paper, Stern School of Business, NYU.

Stapleton, Richard C., 1982, Mergers, debt capacity, and the valuation of corporate loans, in Michael Keenan and Lawrence White, Eds.: *Mergers and Acquisitions* (D. C. Heath, Lexington, Mass.).

15 Stephen J. Brown, William Goetzmann, Roger G. Ibbotson, and Stephen A. Ross

Survivorship Bias in Performance Studies

▶ **Overview**

Some of the most interesting effects of using "survived" data appear in the quest for picking winners—whether it is picking winning markets, winning stocks, or winning investment managers. In this article, we explore the biases that survivorship can induce in the ranking of money managers. When you look only at survived funds or markets, it can appear that winners repeat, even when they do not. A winner last period is more likely to be a winner in the next period simply because of the problem of survival rather than due to inherent skill. The main contribution of the article is in pointing out that the problem of attrition in the analysis of manager performance cannot be ignored. Using historical data without understanding how they came to be included in the data set can lead to incorrect inferences and possibly incorrect investment choice.

▶ **Abstract**

Recent evidence suggests that past mutual fund performance predicts future performance. We analyze the relationship between volatility and returns in a sample that is truncated by survivorship and show that this relationship gives rise to the appearance of predictability. We present some numerical examples to show that this effect can be strong enough to account for the strength of the evidence favoring return predictability.

Past performance does not guarantee future performance. Empirical work from the classic study by Cowles (1933) to work by Jensen (1968) suggests that there is only very limited evidence that professional money managers can outperform the market averages on a risk-adjusted basis. While more recent evidence[1] qualifies this negative conclusion somewhat (Grinblatt and Titman [1989], Ippolito [1988]), there is still no strong evidence that manager performance over and above the market indices can justify the fees managers charge and the commission costs they incur.

The fact that managers as a group perform poorly does not preclude the possibility that particular managers have special skills. Given the high turnover of managers, it is conceivable that the market selects out those managers with skills. Skillful managers are those who succeed and survive. It is this view, fostered by annual mutual fund performance reviews of the type published by

Barrons, Business Week, Consumer Reports, and other publications, that leads to the popular investment strategy of selling shares in mutual funds that under-perform the average manager in any given year, and buying shares in those funds with superior performance. Despite the popular impression that "hot hands" exist among mutual funds, there has been very limited empirical evidence to address this issue.

Past performance is usually a highly significant input into the decision to hire or fire pension fund money managers. However, Kritzman (1983) reports that for fixed-income pension fund money managers retained for at least 10 years, there is no relationship either in returns or in relative rankings between the performance in the first five years and the second five years. In an unpublished portion of the same study, this finding also extended to equity managers. Similar results are found for institutional funds by Dunn and Theisen (1983) and for commodity funds by Elton, Gruber, and Rentzler (1990).[2] In contrast to these findings, Elton and Gruber (1989, p. 602) conclude on the basis of a Securities and Exchange Commission (1971) study that mutual funds which outperform other funds in one period will tend to outperform them in a second. Grinblatt and Titman (1988) suggest that five-year risk-adjusted mutual fund returns do contain some predictive power for subsequent returns. Lehmann and Modest report similar results for the period 1968–1982, but suggest that this finding is sensitive to the method used to compute risk-adjusted performance measures.

On the basis of data for the period 1974–1988 both Hendricks, Patel, and Zeckhauser (1991) and Goetzmann and Ibbotson (1991) obtain far stronger results. The first study is limited to 165 equity funds for the period 1974–1988, while the latter study considers a much larger sample of 728 mutual funds for the period 1976–1988, 258 of which survived for the entire period. The major conclusions of the two studies are similar. Performance persists.[3]

While the experimental designs and data of these studies differ considerably, the generic results may be illustrated on Tables 15.1 and 15.2. The relationship between successive three-year growth equity fund risk-adjusted total returns for the period 1976–1987 is documented in Table 15.1. The 2×2 contingency tables show the frequency with which managers who performed in the top half of all managers (on a Jensen [1968] α risk-adjusted basis) for a given three-year interval also performed in the top half in the subsequent three-year interval. For every period studied, the results are similar. If a manager wins in the first three years, the probability is greater than 50 percent that the manager will win in the second three years. These results are also statistically significant in at least two of the three successive three-year intervals.[4]

Goetzmann and Ibbotson (1991) report contingency tables similar to those given in Table 15.1 for a variety of time periods and performance horizon intervals. The data on which Table 15.1 is based are similar to those of the Hendricks, Patel, and Zeckhauser (1991) study. An alternative approach is to regress second-period Jensen's α's against first-period Jensen's α's. A significantly posi-

Table 15.1

Two-Way Table of Growth Managers Classified by Risk-Adjusted Returns Over Successive Intervals, 1976–1987 (Winners and losers defined relative to performance of median manager)

	1979–1981 winners	1979–1981 losers	
1976–1978 winners	44	19	63
1976–1978 losers	19	44	63
	63	63	126

$$\chi^2 = 19.84 \ (p = .0)$$
$$\chi^2 \text{ (Yates correction)} = 20.40 \ (p = .0)$$
$$\text{Cross-product ratio} = 5.36 \ (p = .0)$$

	1982–1984 winners	1982–1984 losers	
1979–1981 winners	35	33	68
1979–1981 losers	33	35	68
	68	68	136

$$\chi^2 = 0.12 \ (p = .732)$$
$$\chi^2 \text{ (Yates correction)} = 0.12 \ (p = .732)$$
$$\text{Cross-product ratio} = 1.12 \ (p = .432)$$

	1985–1987 winners	1985–1987 losers	
1982–1984 winners	52	25	77
1982–1984 losers	25	52	76
	77	76	153

$$\chi^2 = 18.35 \ (p = .0)$$
$$\chi^2 \text{ (Yates correction)} = 18.74 \ (p = .0)$$
$$\text{Cross-product ratio} = 4.24 \ (p = .0)$$

Notes: This table is derived from total returns on growth equity mutual funds made available by Ibbotson Associates and Morningstar, Inc. Risk-adjustment is the Jensen (1968) α measure relative to total returns on the S&P 500 Index. Each cell represents the number of funds in the sample that share the characteristic defined by the row and the column. For example, the number of funds that were in the top half of mutual funds over the 1976–1978 period and were subsequently also in the top half of mutual funds over the 1979–1981 period may be found in the first row and first column of the upper 2 × 2 table. The χ^2 and χ^2 (Yates correction) refer to standard χ^2 test statistics for independence, where Yates refers to Yates 2 × 2 continuity correction. The cross-product ratio is the ratio of the product of principal diagonal cell counts to the product of the off-diagonal counts. Where (as in this case) the row and column sums are determined ex post the p-value can be inferred from the hypergeometric distribution of the upper left-hand cell count in the 2 × 2 table (Fisher's *exact test*).

Table 15.2

Regression-Based Measures of Persistence in Performance, 1976–1987

Cross-section regression approach[1]

Period January 1976–December 1981:

$$\hat{\alpha}_2 = .0885 + .4134\hat{\alpha}_1$$
$$\quad\;\; (5.38) \quad (6.47)$$
$$R^2 = 2.53; \, n = 126$$

Period January 1979–December 1984:

$$\hat{\alpha}_2 = -.0831 + .0070\hat{\alpha}_1$$
$$\quad\;\; (-3.69) \quad (0.07)$$
$$R^2 = .000; \, n = 134$$

Period January 1982–December 1987:

$$\hat{\alpha}_2 = -.0753 + .3052\hat{\alpha}_1$$
$$\quad\;\; (-6.53) \quad (5.28)$$
$$R^2 = .156; \, n = 153$$

Time-series self-financing portfolio approach[2]

Period January 1977–December 1987:

$$r_{pt} = .0018 - .0078 r_{mt}$$
$$\quad\;\; (2.88) \quad (-.61)$$
$$R^2 = .003; \, n = 132$$

(*t*-values in parentheses)

---

[1]Jensen's α is computed for the sample of funds described in Table 14.1 for each of four three-year subperiods of data starting in 1976–1978. Each panel reports results from the cross-section regression of performance measures on prior performance measures. The first panel gives results from the regression of Jensen's α measures estimated on the basis of data for the period January 1979–December 1981 on similar measures estimated for the period January 1976–December 1978.

[2]This corresponds to the measure employed by Hendricks, Patel, and Zeckhauser (1991) with four quarter evaluation and holding periods. For each year starting in 1976, Jensen's α measures are computed. The deviation of these measures from their mean corresponds to a self-financing portfolio, which is then applied to excess returns on funds measured for the subsequent year. The portfolio is updated at the end of each year. The regression reports results from the time-series regression of the resulting monthly excess returns on market excess returns. The intercept corresponds to a performance measure for this portfolio strategy.

---

tive slope coefficient is evidence of persistence. The result of this exercise is presented in Table 15.2. The results correspond with those reported in Table 15.1. The evidence of persistence is strongest in the first and third subperiods of the data. Hendricks, Patel, and Zeckhauser (1991) suggest computing the returns on a self-financing portfolio strategy, a methodology they attribute to Grinblatt and Titman (1989). The portfolio weights are proportional to the deviation of prior performance measures from the mean performance measure across managers. The performance measure of such a portfolio is a measure of persistence. This measure is computed in Table 15.2. The results are qualitatively similar to ones reported by Hendricks, Patel, and Zeckhauser (1991).

These results of course require careful interpretation. It is tempting to conclude from the type of results reported in Tables 15.1 and 15.2 that "hot hands" exist among mutual fund managers. Actually, the methodologies are silent on whether the persistence relates to positive or negative performance. This is most readily apparent in Table 15.1 when we observe that the row and column sums are specified ex post given the sample of money managers. In other words, given the row and column sums and the "winner-winner" cell count, the "loser-loser" count is simply the residual. Given the "loser-loser" count, the "winner-winner" is the residual. When we measure risk-adjusted performance relative to zero (Table 15.3), we find that persistence can just as easily relate to negative performance as it does to positive performance. Sometimes (1976–1981) good performance is rewarded by subsequent good performance. "Hot hands" are evident. Sometimes (1982–1987) it is the case that bad performance is punished by further bad news. This result is also apparent examining the intercepts of the cross-section regressions reported in Table 15.2. Results reported in Table 15.4 indicate that the persistence of poor performance serves to explain some but not all of the results reported in the previous tables. This table gives regression-based measures of persistence excluding those managers who experienced negative average Jensen's α for the entire period 1976–1987. The results are similar to those reported in Table 15.3. The significance of apparent persistence has fallen. However, both the cross-section and the self-financing portfolio results indicate that there is still statistically significant evidence that performance persists for at least part of the period.

The persistence of negative performance is not surprising. Negative performance can persist where a subset of managers are immune from periodic performance review and where it is difficult to short sell shares of mutual funds.[5] It can be only institutional reasons such as these that allow a fund with sustained poor performance to survive.[6] It is the persistence of positive returns that would be remarkable, if true. The problems of interpretation caused by the ex post definition of winners and losers suggests that the results may also be sensitive to the most obvious source of ex post conditioning: survival.

It is clear that all managers depicted in the 2 × 2 tables have passed the market test, at least for the successive three-year periods. We have no data for the managers who did not survive. If the probability of survival depends on past performance to date, we might expect that the set of managers who survive will have a higher ex post return than those who did not survive. Managers who take on significant risk and lose may also have a low probability of survival. This observation suggests that past performance numbers are biased by survivorship; we see the track records of only those managers who have survived. This does not suggest, however, that performance persists. If anything, it suggests the reverse. If survival depends on cumulative performance, a manager who does well in one period does not have to do so well in the next period in order to survive. Certainly, this survivorship argument cannot explain results suggested by Table 15.1. Moreover, there is a general perception that the survivorship bias effect cannot be very substantial. In a recent study, Grinblatt and Titman (1989) report that the survivorship effect accounts for only about 0.1 to 0.4 percent return per year measured on a risk-adjusted ba-

Table 15.3

Two-Way Table of Growth Managers Classified by Risk-Adjusted Returns Over Successive Intervals, 1976–1987 (Winners and losers defined relative to zero risk-adjusted performance measure)

	1979–1981 winners	1979–1981 losers	
1976–1978 winners	88	11	99
1976–1978 losers	16	11	27
	104	22	126

$$\chi^2 = 12.92 \ (p = .0)$$
$$\chi^2 \ \text{(Yates correction)} = 11.14 \ (p = .001)$$
$$\text{Cross-product ratio} = 5.50$$

	1982–1984 winners	1982–1984 losers	
1979–1981 winners	42	72	114
1979–1981 losers	4	18	22
	46	90	136

$$\chi^2 = 2.87 \ (p = .09)$$
$$\chi^2 \ \text{(Yates correction)} = 3.13 \ (p = .08)$$
$$\text{Cross-product ratio} = 2.62$$

	1985–1987 winners	1985–1987 losers	
1982–1984 winners	20	34	54
1982–1984 losers	15	84	99
	35	118	153

$$\chi^2 = 9.49 \ (p = .002)$$
$$\chi^2 \ \text{(Yates correction)} = 9.15 \ (p = .002)$$
$$\text{Cross-product ratio} = 3.29$$

Notes: This table is derived using the same data as those reported in Table 15.2. Risk-adjustment is the Jensen's α measured relative to total returns on the S&P Index. Winners and losers are defined relative to Jensen's α measure of zero. For example, the number of funds that experienced a positive α over the 1976–1978 period and subsequently experienced a positive α over the 1979–1981 period may be found in the first row and first column of the upper 2 × 2 table. The χ^2 and χ^2 (Yates correction) refer to standard χ^2 test statistics for independence, where Yates refers to Yates 2 × 2 continuity correction. The cross-product ratio is the ratio of the product of principal diagonal cell counts to the product of the off-diagonal counts.

sis before transaction costs and fees. We shall see that the survivorship bias in mean excess returns is small in magnitude relative to a more subtle, yet surprisingly powerful, survival bias that implies persistence in performance.

A manager who takes on a great deal of risk will have a high probability of failure. However, *if* he or she survives, the probability is that this manager took

Table 15.4

Regression-Based Measures of Persistence in Performance, 1976–1987 (Excluding Poor Performers)

Cross-section regression approach[1]

    Period January 1976–December 1981:

$$\hat{\alpha}_2 = .1463 + .2736\hat{\alpha}_1$$
$$\quad\;\; (5.48)\quad (3.13)$$
$$R^2 = .113; \; n = 79$$

    Period January 1979–December 1984:

$$\hat{\alpha}_2 = .0317 - .1815\hat{\alpha}_1$$
$$\quad\;\; (1.04)\quad (-1.55)$$
$$R^2 = .029; \; n = 82$$

    Period January 1982–December 1987:

$$\hat{\alpha}_2 = -.0334 + .0521\hat{\alpha}_1$$
$$\quad (-3.09)\quad (.81)$$
$$R^2 = .008; \; n = 88$$

Time-series self-financing portfolio approach[2]

    Period January 1977–December 1987:

$$r_{pt} = .0008 - .0015 r_{mt}$$
$$\quad\;\; (2.15)\quad (-.20)$$
$$R^2 = .000; \; n = 132$$

(t-values in parentheses)

Notes: This table is intended to show the effect that different standards of performance review might have on measures of persistence in returns. The procedures and data are the same as those presented in Table 15.2, with the exception that managers are excluded whose average value of Jensen's α is negative over the entire period for which data are available.

    [1]Jensen's α is computed for the sample of funds described in Table 15.1 for each of four three-year subperiods of data starting in 1976–1978, excluding those funds that performed poorly over the entire period. Each panel reports results from the cross-section regression of performance measures on prior performance measures.

    [2]This corresponds to the measure employed by Hendricks, Patel, and Zeckhauser (1991) with four quarter evaluation and holding periods, excluding poor performing funds.

a large bet and won. High returns persist. If they did not persist, we would not see this high-risk manager in our sample.[7] Note that this is a total risk effect; risk-adjustment using β or other measure of nonidiosyncratic risk may not fully correct for it. To illustrate this effect, observe in Table 15.3 that the additional 10 firms that come into the database in 1979–1981 are all ex post successful. The average value of residual risk (0.0323) for the new entrants is significantly greater than that of the population of managers (0.0242), with a t-value of 2.02. The new entrants who survived took on more risk and were successful.

    The magnitude of the persistence will depend on the precise way in which survivorship depends on past performance and whether there is any strategic risk management response on the part of surviving money managers.[8] The intent is to show that the apparent persistence of performance documented in

Tables 15.1 and 15.2 is not necessarily any indication of skill among surviving managers.

To the extent that survivorship depends on past returns, ranking managers who survive by realized returns may induce an apparent persistence in performance. Survivorship implies that managers will be selected according to total risk. One way of explaining the Table 15.1 results is to observe that the set of managers studied represents a heterogeneous mix of management styles. Each management style is characterized by a certain vector of risk attributes. By examining the survivors, we are really looking at only those styles that were ex post successful. It may appear that one resolution of this problem is to concentrate on only one defined management style. There are two problems with this approach. In the first instance, we have to be careful to define the style sufficiently broadly that there are more than a few managers represented. In the second instance, we may exacerbate the effect if our definition of manager style is synonymous with taking high total risk positions.

We only observe the performance of managers who survive performance evaluations. The purpose of this article is to examine the extent to which this fact is sufficient to explain the magnitude of persistence we seem to see in the data. In the first section, we examine the relationship between total risk differentials and survivorship-induced persistence in performance. In the second section, we present some numerical results that show that a very small survivorship effect is sufficient to generate a strong and significant appearance of dependence in serial returns. We conclude in the third section.

◤ Relationship Between Volatility and Returns Induced by Survivorship

There are many possible quite complex sample selection rules. We will look at the implications of one class of these rules. Our purpose in this section is to

---

Look-Ahead Bias

The bias we find in this analysis was called "look-ahead bias" by Carhart (1997). In recent work, Carpenter and Lynch (1999) show that multiperiod survival effects, as well as look-ahead biases, can affect the analysis of performance persistence—sometimes in a positive and sometimes in a negative way. In other words, conditioning effects are important, but not always straightforward to sort out. We learn from their work that competing effects can prevail under different rules for when funds survive or disappear.*

*Carhart, Mark M. 1997. "On Persistence in Mutual Fund Performance." *Journal of Finance* 52 (1): 57–82. Carpenter, Jennifer N., and Anthony W. Lynch. 1999. "Survivorship Bias and Attrition Effects in Measures of Performance Persistence." *Journal of Financial Economics* 54 (3): 337–374.

demonstrate that sample survivorship bias is a force that can lead to persistence in performance rankings. For simplicity, assume all distributions are atomless. Our tool is the following lemma.

LEMMA. *Assume*

> (i) *x, y independent random variables,*
> (ii) $\Pr(x \geq 0) = \Pr(y \geq 0) > 0$,
> (iii) $\Pr(x > a) \geq \Pr(y > a)$, $\forall\, a \geq 0$, *with strict inequality for*
>   *some a.*

It follows that

$$\Pr[x > y \mid x,y > 0] > \frac{1}{2}.$$

Before proving the lemma, note that its conditions are satisfied by x and y if they are both normal with mean zero, and if x has a higher variance than y. More generally, for both x and y with mean zero, it is sufficient if x is distributed as λy, where $\lambda > 1$.

PROOF. Let F_x and F_y be the respective cumulative distributions of x and y, and let G_x and G_y be the reverse cumulants

$$G_x \equiv 1 - F_x, \quad G_y \equiv 1 - F_y.$$

Now,

$$
\begin{aligned}
\Pr(x &> y \mid x,y > 0) \\
&= [\Pr(x,y > 0)]^{-1} \Pr(x > y, x > 0, y > 0) \\
&= [G_x(0)\, G_y(0)]^{-1} \int_0^\infty \int_u^\infty dF_x(z)\, dF_y(u) \\
&= [G_x(0)\, G_y(0)]^{-1} \int_0^\infty G_x(u)\, dF_y(u) \\
&\geq [G_x(0)\, G_y(0)]^{-1} \int_0^\infty G_y(u)\, dF_y(u) \\
&= [G_x(0)\, G_y(0)]^{-1} \left\{ -\frac{1}{2} G_y^2(u) \Big|_0^\infty \right\} \\
&= \frac{1}{2} \left[\frac{G_y(0)}{G_x(0)} \right] = \frac{1}{2},
\end{aligned}
$$

with strict inequality if $G_x > G_y$ on some set of positive measure.   ∎

The following corollary establishes that the result generalizes to cases where x and y represent nonzero mean random variates.

COROLLARY 1. *Let ε_x and ε_y satisfy the conditions of the lemma and let*

$$x = f + \varepsilon_x \quad and \quad y = f + \varepsilon_y;$$

then

$$\Pr[x > y \mid \varepsilon_x, \varepsilon_y > 0] > \frac{1}{2}.$$

PROOF. Immediate.   ∎

For the following set of results, let x and y be two random variables drawn from a family of distributions indexed by a spread parameter $\sigma \in [0, \infty)$. The family has the property that

$$G(0 \mid \sigma) = G(0)$$

and $(\forall \, a \geq 0) \, \sigma' > \sigma$ implies that

$$G[a \mid \sigma'] \geq G[a \mid \sigma].$$

COROLLARY 2. *It follows that*

$$\Pr[\sigma_x > \sigma_y \mid x > y; x,y > 0] > \frac{1}{2}.$$

PROOF. From the lemma

$$\Pr[x > y \mid \sigma_x > \sigma_y; x,y > 0] > \frac{1}{2},$$

and, therefore, by initial symmetry and Bayes' theorem,

$$\Pr[\sigma_x > \sigma_y \mid x > y; x,y > 0]$$
$$= \frac{\Pr[x > y \mid \sigma_x > \sigma_y; x,y > 0]\Pr[\sigma_x > \sigma_y \mid x,y > 0]}{\Pr[x > y \mid x,y > 0]}$$
$$> \frac{1}{2}\left(\frac{1/2}{1/2}\right) = \frac{1}{2}.$$ ∎

The next two corollaries verify that if one random variable exceeds another in one observation period, it is likely to do so in other periods.

COROLLARY 3. *Let x and y be independent and (unconditionally) identically distributed with unknown spreads drawn from the family described above. It follows that*

$$\Pr[x_2 > y_2 \mid x_1 > y_1; x_1, y_1, x_2, y_2 > 0] > \frac{1}{2}.$$

PROOF. For notational ease we will omit the ubiquitous conditioning on x_i, $y_i > 0$. From Bayes' theorem,

$$\Pr[x_2 > y_2 \mid x_1 > y_1]$$
$$= \Pr[x_2 > y_2 \mid \sigma_x > \sigma_y, x_1 > y_1] \, \Pr[\sigma_x > \sigma_y \mid x_1 > y_1]$$
$$\quad + \Pr[x_2 > y_2 \mid \sigma_x \leq \sigma_y, x_1 > y_1] \, \Pr[\sigma_x \leq \sigma_y \mid x_1 > y_1]$$
$$= \Pr[x_2 > y_2 \mid \sigma_x > \sigma_y] \, \Pr[\sigma_x > \sigma_y \mid x_1 > y_1]$$
$$\quad + \Pr[x_2 > y_2 \mid \sigma_x \leq \sigma_y] \, \Pr[\sigma_x \leq \sigma_y \mid x_1 > y_1],$$

since σ is sufficient statistic.

By the a priori symmetry of x and y,

$$
\begin{aligned}
1 &= \Pr[x_2 > y_2 \mid \sigma_x \le \sigma_y] + \Pr[x_2 \le y_2 \mid \sigma_x \le \sigma_y] \\
&= \Pr[x_2 > y_2 \mid \sigma_x \le \sigma_y] + \Pr[x_2 \ge y_2 \mid \sigma_x \ge \sigma_y].
\end{aligned}
$$

From the lemma we know that

$$
\Pr[x_2 > y_2 \mid \sigma_x > \sigma_y] \equiv \frac{1}{2} + p, \quad p > 0,
$$

and from Corollary 2 we know that

$$
\Pr[\sigma_x > \sigma_y \mid x_1 > y_1] \equiv \frac{1}{2} + q, \quad q > 0.
$$

Hence,

$$
\begin{aligned}
&\Pr[x_2 > y_2 \mid x_1 > x_1] \\
&= \left(\frac{1}{2} + p\right)\left(\frac{1}{2} + q\right) + \left(1 - \left(\frac{1}{2} + p\right)\right)\left(1 - \left(\frac{1}{2} + q\right)\right) \\
&= \frac{1}{2} + 2pq > \frac{1}{2}. \qquad\blacksquare
\end{aligned}
$$

COROLLARY 4. *The conditions are the same as for Corollary 3 except that the unknown spread parameter is not constant, although ranking by volatility is preserved, that is,*

$$
\sigma_{x_1} > \sigma_{y_1} \Rightarrow \sigma_{x_2} > \sigma_{y_2}.
$$

PROOF. Immediate, given

$$
\Pr[x_2 > y_2 \mid \sigma_{x_2} > \sigma_{y_2}]
$$

$$
= \Pr[x_2 > y_2 \mid \sigma_{x_1} > \sigma_{y_1}] \equiv \frac{1}{2} + p, \quad p > 0. \qquad\blacksquare
$$

This concludes our analytic verification of the relation between volatility and returns in a sample that is truncated by survivorship bias. To say whether this effect is larger or smaller than the natural tendency for regression to the mean depends on the exact sample selection rules.

If the selection rule in a two-period model is $x_1 + x_2 > 0$ (and/or $x_1 > 0$), then we have verified the tendency for one fund to persist in outperforming the other if its volatility is higher. However, with the rule $x_1 + x_2 > 0$, there is another opposing force. In particular, if $x_1 > y_1 > 0$, then x does not have to pass so extreme a hurdle in the next period, and we are likely to have $x_2 < y_2$ if there is no dispersion in volatility across managers (see Appendix 1). We avoided this problem in Corollary 3 by conditioning only on $x_1, y_1 > 0$ and not on $x_1 + x_2 > 0$ and $y_1 + y_2 > 0$. This two-period selection effect would tend to counterbalance the variance-induced apparent persistence of returns. The net effect will depend on assumptions made about the distribution of returns absent the selection effects.

Another mitigating factor would arise if we allow managers to adjust their portfolio policies to adjust risk levels on survival. While the above results require only that the ranking by risk be constant from one period to the next, the extent of the persistence will depend on the way in which survival affects the differences in risk across managers.

It is clear that the magnitude of the persistence in returns will depend on assumptions that are made about the precise nature of survivorship, the distribution of returns across managers, and the way in which portfolio policies of managers evolve through time. In the next section, we shall examine a simple numerical example that demonstrates that very mild survivorship criteria are sufficient to induce strong persistence in performance for a reasonable specification of the distribution of returns across managers.

◤ A Numerical Illustration of the Magnitude of Induced Persistence in Returns

To examine the numerical magnitude of the persistence in performance induced by survivorship, annual returns were generated for a cross section of managers. The moments of the distribution of returns are chosen to match those observed in the data, although it is assumed that manager returns are serially uncorrelated. There is a natural presumption that persistence in observed returns implies that manager returns are predictable. The purpose of this experiment is to provide a reasonable counterexample to this presumption. While there may be many factors that are in fact responsible for the persistence in performance, a simple survivorship argument suffices to explain the magnitude of persistence we observe in the data.

Conditional on systematic risk measure β_i and nonsystematic risk σ_i, annual returns are generated from

$$R_{it} = r_f + \beta_i(R_{mt} - r_f) + \varepsilon_{it},$$

where the annual Treasury bill rate r_f is taken to be 0.07 and the annual equity risk premium is assumed to be normal with mean 0.086 and standard deviation (SD) 0.208 corresponding to the Ibbotson and Sinquefield (1990) numbers for the period 1926–1989. The idiosyncratic term ε_{it} is assumed to be distributed as normal with mean zero and SD σ_{it}.

The managers are defined by their risk measures β_i and σ_i. It is difficult to know what are reasonable values for these parameters. If observed mutual fund data are truncated in possibly complex ways by survivorship, then those data may yield biased measures of the parameters. If, on the other hand, it is held that this truncation is of a second order of importance, then, given this maintained hypothesis, the cross-sectional distribution of the parameters will give some measure of the underlying dispersion of risk. For the purpose of this experiment, it is assumed that β_i is distributed in the cross section of managers as normal with mean 0.95, and SD 0.25 corresponding to the cross-sectional distribution of β observed in the Goetzmann and Ibbotson sample of money managers.[9]

The distribution of nonsystematic risk across managers is functionally dependent on β. Closet index funds with β's close to unity typically have very low values of nonsystematic risk, whereas managers whose β's deviate from the market tend to be less well diversified. This suggests a relationship between nonsystematic risk and β approximated by[10]

$$\sigma_i^2 = k(1 - \beta_i)^2.$$

The value of k chosen in the simulation experiment is 0.05349, which is the value that ensures that the average R^2 across managers is 0.90, given the distribution of β and the assumed variance of the equity risk premium.

The experiment proceeds as follows. For each of 600 managers, a value of β_i is chosen. This defines a measure of nonsystematic risk σ_i given the assumed relationship between the two parameters. Four annual returns are drawn for each manager according to the assumed return generating process. For each of four years, the worst performing managers are eliminated from the group.[11] Four-year returns are computed for each of the managers that survive this sequential cut, and contingency tables corresponding to those of Table 15.1 and regression-based measures of persistence corresponding to Tables 15.2 and 15.4 are calculated.

The results of this experiment will obviously depend on the severity of the cut. In a base case analysis, no managers are cut. In a second scenario, only the bottom 5 percent of managers are cut in each year. In the third and fourth scenarios, the bottom 10 percent and 20 percent of managers are eliminated each year. The entire experiment is then repeated 20,000 times. In this way, we examine not only the expected frequency of persistence as a function of the selection criterion, but also the sampling properties of this persistence.

In our first exercise, we generate results corresponding to Table 15.1. Risk-adjusted performance measures are evaluated for each manager using Jensen's α, and the cumulated risk-adjusted returns are computed for the first two years and second two years. "Winners" and "losers" are defined relative to the risk-adjusted performance of the median manager in each two-year period. This experimental design follows closely the approach adopted by Hendricks, Patel, and Zeckhauser (1991) and Goetzmann and Ibbotson (1991), with the important exception that in constructing risk-adjusted returns, β is assumed known. Thus, we do not consider the possible complications that arise from the necessity to estimate this quantity.

The average values of the frequency of persistence in risk-adjusted return across the replications of this experiment, for different assumed cutoff points, are given in Table 15.5. When there is no truncation by survivorship, there is no apparent persistence of performance. However, when managers are excluded from the sample for performance reasons, there is evidence of apparent persistence in performance. The probability is greater than 50 percent that a manager who wins in the first period will also win in the second. This proba-

Table 15.5
Two-Way Table of Managers Classified by Risk-Adjusted Returns Over Successive Intervals, a Summary of 20,000 Simulations Assuming 0, 5, 10, and 20 Percent Cutoffs

	Second-Period Winners	Second-Period Losers
	No cutoff ($n = 600$)	
First-period winners	150.09	149.51
First-period losers	149.51	150.09

Average χ^2 = 1.04
Average cross-product ratio = 1.014
Average cross-section t-value = $-.004$
Average annual excess return = 0.0%
Average β = 0.950

	Second-Period Winners	Second-Period Losers
	5% cutoff ($n = 494$)	
First-period winners	127.49	119.51
First-period losers	119.51	127.49

Average χ^2 = 1.64
Average cross-product ratio = 1.159
Average cross-section t-value = 2.046
Average annual excess return = 0.44%
Average β = 0.977

bility increases with the extent to which the sample is truncated by survivorship. The effect of truncation is also evident in the increase in the average value of χ^2 and cross-product ratio statistics with the degree to which managers are excluded from the sample for performance reasons. The effect is particularly marked when we regress performance measures in the second two-year period on similar measures computed for the first two-year period. With no cutoff, the mean t-value for the slope coefficient of this regression is zero. However, both the mean and the median t-values are in excess of 2 with just a 5 percent performance cut. This means that on the basis of a cross-section regression of successive α's, we would reject the hypothesis of no persistence at least 50 percent of the time!

The effect of truncation on the distribution of test statistics for dependence is quite marked. In Figure 15.1, we display the boxplots of simulated values of the cross-product ratio for different performance cutoff levels. This solid line within each box represents the median of the empirical distribution of cross-product ratios, whereas the box itself gives the interquartile range. The whiskers above and below each box give the 95th and 5th percentiles, respectively, of the empirical distribution. For comparison purposes, we provide the theoretical distribution implied by the hypergeometric distribution of cell counts implied by independence. When there is no truncation by survivorship, the distribution of this statistic is well specified. However, when mana-

Table 15.5 (*continued*)
Two-Way Table of Managers Classified by Risk-Adjusted Returns Over Successive Intervals, a Summary of 20,000 Simulations Assuming 0, 5, 10, and 20 Percent Cutoffs

	Second-Period Winners	Second-Period Losers
10% cutoff ($n = 398$)		
First-period winners	106.58	92.42
First-period losers	92.42	106.58

Average $\chi^2 = 3.28$
Average cross-product ratio = 1.366
Average cross-section t-value = 3.356
Average annual excess return = 0.61%
Average $\beta = 0.994$

	Second-Period Winners	Second-Period Losers
20% cutoff ($n = 249$)		
First-period winners	71.69	53.31
First-period losers	53.31	70.69

Average $\chi^2 = 7.13$
Average cross-product ratio = 1.919
Average cross-section t-value = 4.679
Average annual excess return = 0.80%
Average $\beta = 1.018$

Notes: For each simulation, manager annual returns are drawn from the market model described in the text, allowing for a dispersion in β and nonsystematic risk in the cross section of managers. In each of the four years, managers who experience returns in the lowest percentile indicated by the cutoff value are excluded from the sample, and this experiment is repeated 20,000 times. Thus, the numbers in the first 2 × 2 table give the average frequency with which the 600 managers fall into the respective classifications. The second panel shows the average frequencies for the 494 managers who survive the performance cut, while the third and fourth panels give corresponding results for 398 and 249 managers. For each simulation, the winners are defined as those managers whose average two-year Jensen's α measure was greater than or equal to that of the median manager in that sample. The average χ^2 refers to the average value of the standard χ^2 test statistic for independence (without Yates' correction) across the simulations, while the average cross-product ratio refers to the average value of the ratio of the product of principal diagonal cell counts to the product of the off-diagonal counts.

gers have to survive a performance cut, there appears to be evidence of short-term dependence in performance. When only 5 percent of managers are cut in each of the first three years, the cross-product ratio is too high relative to its theoretical distribution assuming independence. With a 10 percent performance cutoff each year, three quarters of the time the test statistic lies above the median of its theoretical distribution. Even a small degree of truncation by survivorship will induce an unacceptably high probability of false inference of persistence in performance.

It might be argued that the apparent persistence we observe in these simulation experiments is some artifact of the way in which the test statistics have been computed. After all, the cross-product ratio is not widely used in the

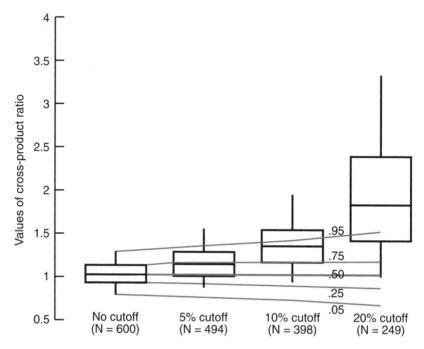

Figure 15.1. Boxplots of 20,000 Simulated Values of the Cross-Product Ratio for Different Performance Cutoff Levels

Notes: The solid line within each box represents the median of the empirical distribution of cross-product ratios, whereas the box itself gives the interquartile range. The whiskers above and below each box give the 95th and 5th percentiles, respectively, of the empirical distribution. The gray lines give the stated fractiles of the theoretical distribution implied by the hypergeometric distribution of cell counts assuming independence.

finance literature. Hendricks, Patel, and Zeckhauser (1991) argue in favor of a t-value statistic based on the returns computed on the basis of a self-financing portfolio strategy where the portfolio weights are proportional to the deviation of performance measures from the average performance measure across managers. The results of this kind of approach are given in Table 15.2, and the simulation results are presented in Figure 15.2. Note that this test statistic is, if anything, more misspecified under a performance cut than is the cross-product ratio. Given that this is true even in the special case where we know precisely the β of the self-financing portfolio, and can compute the theoretical variance of the performance measure, we would expect the performance of the statistic under realistic experimental conditions to be much worse.

It is important to note that truncation by survivorship may imply an apparent persistence in performance without significantly affecting average risk-adjusted returns. As we observed before, Grinblatt and Titman (1989) find that survivorship bias can account for only about 0.1 to 0.4 percent return per year. Table 15.5 shows the average risk-adjusted returns for managers who sur-

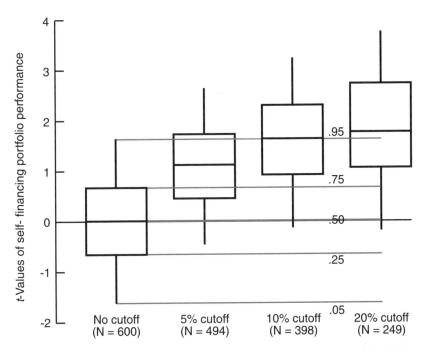

Figure 15.2. Boxplots of *t*-Values Associated With 20,000 Simulated Values of the Self-Financing Portfolio Performance Measure

Notes: The solid line within each box represents the median of the empirical distribution of *t*-values associated with the Jensen's α of the self-financing portfolio strategy described in the text (assuming β known), whereas the box itself gives the interquartile range. The whiskers above and below each box give the 95th and 5th percentiles, respectively, of the empirical distribution. The gray lines give the stated fractiles of the theoretical distribution implied by the null hypothesis of a zero performance measure.

vive the various performance cuts. While there are substantial differences in average risk-adjusted return between managers who did well and poorly in the successive two-year periods, the net effect of survivorship bias on average risk-adjusted returns for all managers in the sample is very small and corresponds to about 0.4 to 0.6 percent per year on a risk-adjusted basis for the 5 to 10 percent cutoff examples. The corresponding number is 0.8 percent for the 20 percent cutoff. These numbers do not differ significantly from those reported by Grinblatt and Titman. It would appear from the results reported in Table 15.5 that truncation of raw returns is compensated for by a corresponding truncation in the cross-sectional distribution of β, leading to no net effect on average risk-adjusted returns.

Of course, it might be said that these results are something of a straw man. After all, the example assumes that manager performance is evaluated on a total return basis. Actually, the apparent persistence in performance is even stronger than that reported in Table 15.5 if managers are terminated for low

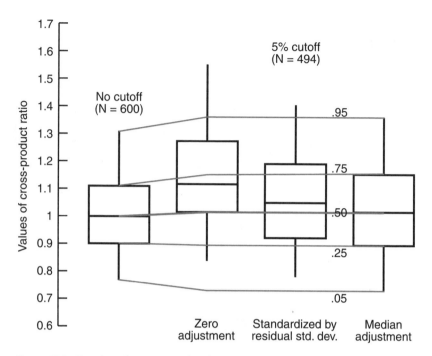

Figure 15.3. Boxplots of 20,000 Simulated Values of the Cross-Product Ratio Showing the Effect of Different Adjustments for Survivorship Bias With a 5-Percent Performance Cutoff

Notes: Zero adjustment refers to the boxplot given in Figure 15.1, where there is a 5 percent performance cutoff. Standardized by the residual standard deviation refers to the cross-product ratio calculated on the basis of defining "winners" and "losers" relative to the median appraisal ratio. Median adjustment corrects the median for the fact that the distribution of appraisal ratios is truncated by survivorship. This correction is described in the text.

α, representing risk-adjusted returns. This result is implied by Corollary 1 above. In this example, what is important is not the dispersion across managers of total risk, but rather the dispersion of residual risk. This suggests that it may be possible to mitigate some of the survival effect by simply standardizing performance measures by the residual standard deviation.[12] In fact, classifying managers into winner and loser categories by α measured in units of residual risk does reduce the apparent persistence in Table 15.5. This reduces the dispersion of measures of persistence but does not eliminate the survivor-induced bias. To eliminate the bias we need to adjust excess returns to account for the fact that the median excess return will be greater than zero by virtue of survivorship.[13] The effect of these separate adjustments on the apparent survivorship effect is illustrated in Figure 15.3.

The numerical example is unrealistic in at least one important respect. In common with the results reported in Table 15.1, it assumes that the excess of

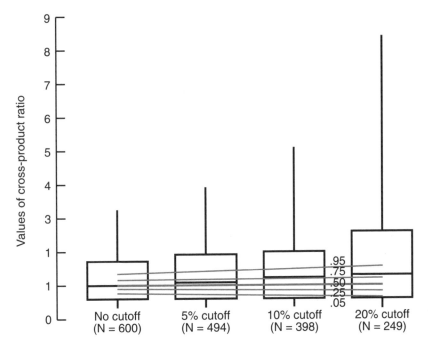

Figure 15.4. Boxplots of 20,000 Simulated Values of the Cross-Product Ratio Showing the Effect of Cross-Correlation in Performance Measures
Notes: This figure corresponds to Figure 15.1, where the cross-correlation of performance measures matches that of the Goetzmann and Ibbotson (1991) sample. The procedure used to induce this level of cross-correlation is described in the text.

returns of managers are cross-sectionally uncorrelated. Of course, there are patterns of performance related to styles of management, and we would expect excess returns to be correlated. In fact, in the sample period covered by Table 15.1, the intra-manager correlation of excess returns can reach as high as .98. This will exacerbate the effect if the pattern of intercorrelation depends on measures of risk. One high-risk manager surviving will increase the chance that other high-risk managers will also survive.

The degree of intercorrelation among managers does indeed appear to be functionally dependent upon β and residual risk.[14] Results of an experiment where the cross-sectional correlation of excess returns corresponds to the Goetzmann and Ibbotson study[15] are presented in Figure 15.4. The cross-correlation effect is sufficiently strong to cause a false inference of persistence even in the absence of a performance cut. Where there are performance cuts, this effect is considerably exacerbated.

Figure 15.4 indicates that the cross-product ratio test statistic is seriously misspecified. To obtain some idea of the order of magnitude, recall that a cross-product ratio of 4 corresponds to a contingency table where the cell counts on the diagonal are twice the off-diagonal terms. With a 5 percent performance cut, apparent dependence of this magnitude will be observed at least 5 percent of the time. It is important to note that the simple cross-section regression approach is also misspecified. The upper 95th percentile of the resulting test statistic, 1.65, is exceeded 32.9 percent of the time with no performance cut. With a 5 percent performance cut, this percentile is exceeded 54.39 percent of the time. The median value of the distribution of t-value statistics is 2.09.

The theoretical distribution assumes the performance measures are uncorrelated in the cross section of managers. Where we induce cross-sectional correlation into the performance measures, with no performance cut the cross-product ratio is unbiased but the variance is far greater than the theoretical distribution would imply. The cross-section regression approach, which imposes far more restrictive assumptions on the process generating sequential returns, is even more seriously affected. One concludes that the combination of dependence in the cross-section distribution of returns with truncation by performance might be sufficient to explain the results reported in Table 15.1.

Where there is cross-sectional dependence, the median adjustment is not well specified, although it does represent an improvement over the unadjusted statistics, as indicated in Figure 15.5. This adjustment assumes the excess re-

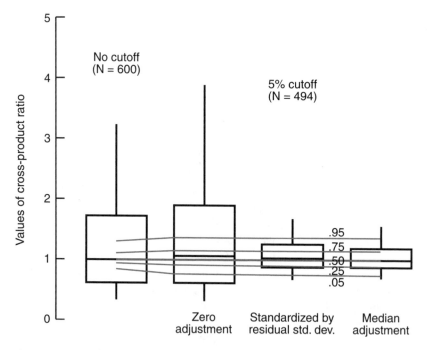

Figure 15.5. Boxplots of 20,000 Simulated Values of the Cross-Product Ratio Showing the Effect of Cross-Correlation on Alternative Adjustments for Survivorship Bias
Notes: This figure corresponds to Figure 15.3, where the cross-correlation of performance measures matches that of the Goetzmann and Ibbotson (1991) sample. The procedure used to induce this level of cross-correlation is described in the text.

turns are independent in the cross section. It is sensitive to violations of this assumption. While it is possible to conceive of an exact adjustment based on the order statistics assuming dependence in manager excess returns, it is interesting to note that the simple residual standard deviation adjustment does at least as well as the median adjustment. This simple measure requires no information about the magnitude of the performance cut. The result suggests the conjecture that the simple prescription of normalizing performance numbers by residual standard deviations may represent a reasonably robust performance statistic.[16]

▶ Conclusion

We show that truncation by survivorship gives rise to an apparent persistence in performance where there is dispersion of risk among money managers. Standard risk-adjustment technology, which adjusts for single-factor β risk, may not suffice to correct for this effect. A numerical example shows that this effect can give rise to a substantial probability that statistical tests based on risk-adjusted return data will give rise to the false inference that there is in fact dependence in security returns.

Our findings in this article are suggestive of implications beyond performance measurement. Where inclusion in a sample depends in part on rate of return, survivorship bias will lead to obvious biases in first and second moments and cross-moments of return, including β. What is not so obvious is that this effect will induce a spurious relationship between volatility and return. This has implications for empirical tests of asset pricing models and in particular for studies of so-called anomalies.[17] It also has implications for studies of post-event performance of firms that survive significant corporate events. Current work examines whether survival bias of the kind reported here may suffice to explain the puzzling post-earnings-drift phenomenon first noted by Ball and Brown (1968) if there is dispersion of residual risk among those firms that survive into the post-earnings sample.[18]

Whether these results suffice to explain the strength of results reported by Goetzmann and Ibbotson (among others) is at this point an open question. We have shown that truncation by survival has a measurable impact on the observed returns of those managers who survive the performance cut. Clearly, the magnitude of the effect will depend on the fraction of managers who in fact survive the performance cut.[19] Furthermore, the numerical example was based on the dispersion of risk measures for managers *who survived*. In addition it is assumed that survival depends on four annual reviews based solely on returns measured over the previous year.

To calibrate the magnitude of the possible bias, we need to know how the characteristics of managers who survive differ from other managers, and the role of past performance in determining which managers survive. Clearly, cumulative performance must have a role in this process. The strength of the apparent persistence evident in Table 15.1 seems to broadly correlate with periods of high volatility in the markets; market conditions may also play a role. As Hendricks, Patel, and Zeckhauser (1991) indicate, in the period 1974–1988, a subset of poorly performing managers appears to be immune from performance review. This factor alone seems to explain most of the apparent persistence in their study. These represent important issues for future research. Until they are resolved, it is difficult to devise a simple adjustment to standard performance measures that will correct for this survivorship bias.

Finally, the simulation results lead to the conjecture that the simple prescription of normalizing performance measures by the residual standard deviation might provide a performance measure that is relatively robust to this source of misspecification. However, there is an important caveat. These experiments assume that the true parameters of the process are known to the investigator. The task of estimating the risk measures in the presence of a potential performance cut and of designing a performance measure that corrects for the resulting apparent persistence in performance is the subject of ongoing research.

◣ Appendix 1

In the text, we demonstrate that with the selection rule conditioning on early performance, there is a tendency for performance to persist. In this section, we show that if the selection rule conditions on overall (two-period) performance, then there is a tendency for performance reversal. The net effect of these two forces must be resolved empirically.

The basic problem we want to consider is

$$\Pr[x_2 > y_2 \mid x_1 > y_1, c],$$

where

$$c = \{x_1 + x_2 > 0, y_1 + y_2 > 0\}.$$

From Bayes' theorem

$$\Pr[x_2 > y_2 \mid x_1 > y_1, c] = \frac{\Pr[x_2 > y_2, x_1 > y_1, c]}{\Pr[x_1 > y_1, c]},$$

and again, by Bayes' theorem,

$$\Pr[x_1 > y_1, c] = \Pr[x_1 > y_1, c] = \Pr[x_1 > y_1 \mid c]\Pr[c].$$

For the purposes of this section we will ignore the possibility of dispersion in the spread parameter and assume x and y have independent and identical distributions. It follows that

$$\Pr[x_1 > y_1 \mid c] = \frac{1}{2}.$$

If we further assume that the distributions are symmetric about the origin, then

$$\Pr[c] = \frac{1}{4}, \quad \Pr[x_1 > y_1, c] = \left(\frac{1}{2}\right)\left(\frac{1}{4}\right) = \frac{1}{8}.$$

We now have the following result.

LEMMA. *Under the above conditions*

$$\Pr[x_2 > y_2 \mid x_1 > y_1, x_1 + x_2 > 0, y_1 + y_2 > 0] < \frac{1}{2}.$$

PROOF.

$$\Pr[x_2 > y_2, x_1 > y_1, c]$$
$$\equiv \Pr[x_2 > y_2, x_1 > y_1, x_1 + x_2 > 0, y_1 + y_2 > 0]$$
$$= \Pr[x_2 > y_2, x_1 > y_1, y_1 + y_2 > 0]$$
$$= \int_{-\infty}^{\infty}\int_{y_1}^{\infty} dF \left\{ \int_{-y_1}^{\infty}\int_{y_2}^{\infty} dF\, dF_{y_2} \right\} dF_{y_1}$$
$$= \int_{-\infty}^{\infty} G(y_1) \int_{-y_1}^{\infty} G(y_2)\, dF_{y_2}\, dF_{y_1}$$
$$= \int_{-\infty}^{\infty} G(y_1) \left\{ -\frac{1}{2} G^2(y_2) \mid_{-y_1}^{\infty} \right\} dF_{y_1}$$
$$= \frac{1}{2}\int_{-\infty}^{\infty} G(y_1)\, G^2(-y_1)\, dF_{y_1}$$
$$= \frac{1}{2}\int_{-\infty}^{\infty} G(y_1)[1 - G(y_1)]^2\, dF_{y_1} \quad (by\ summetry)$$
$$= \frac{1}{2}\left(-\frac{1}{2}G^2 + \frac{2}{3}G^3 - \frac{1}{4}G^4\right)\Big|_{-\infty}^{\infty}$$
$$= \frac{1}{2}\left[\frac{1}{2} - \frac{2}{3} + \frac{1}{4}\right] = \frac{1}{24}.$$

Hence,

$$\Pr[x_2 > y_2 \mid x_1 > y_1, c] = \frac{1/24}{1/8} = \frac{1}{3} < \frac{1}{2}. \qquad\blacksquare$$

This is the tendency for reversal in the absence of any inferences about volatility from returns. It is clear, by continuity, that if we permitted a small disparity in ex post spreads for x and y, this effect would still dominate. However, as the possibility of spreads is increased, the persistence described in the text also increases. In theory and in practice, which effect is dominant depends on both the exact form of the selection rules and the potential dispersion of the spread parameter.

▶ Notes

1. Some of this evidence is controversial in nature. See Elton et al. (1993) for a discussion of the Ippolito findings.

2. The commodity fund result applies to returns on funds. However, Elton, Gruber, and Rentzler (1990) find evidence of persistence in performance of different funds managed by the same general partner. It would be interesting to discover whether dispersion in risk across surviving managers would suffice to explain this result.

3. Note that the Kritzman (1983) and Dunn and Theisen (1983) results apply to pension fund money managers, while the other studies that indicate persistence all refer to mutual funds. Representatives from Frank Russell Company and other pension fund consulting companies indicate that efforts to replicate the mutual fund persistence results using pension fund data have to this date been unsuccessful. Part of the reason for this difference might be that mutual fund returns are measured after fees, while pension fund returns typically are measured before commissions (see note 7).

4. One has to be a little careful interpreting the statistical significance of the χ^2 values. The identification of managers as winners or losers is actually ex post. For this reason, we expect to find the winners-following-winners result at least 50 percent of the time. This ex post conditioning also implies that the standard χ^2 tests (with or without the Yates 2×2 continuity correction) will be misspecified. Fortunately, an alternative statistic, the cross-product ratio (given as the ratio of the product of the principal diagonal cell counts to the product of the off-diagonal counts in the 2×2 table), has well-known statistical properties. Statisticians prefer the cross-product ratio (or measures closely related to it) because it simultaneously provides a test of the hypothesis that the two classifications are independent, as well as giving a measure of the dependence (Bishop et al. [1975, p. 373ff.]). In the present case, row and column sums of each 2×2 contingency table are fixed because of ex post conditioning. Thus, the winner-winner cell count determines all other cell counts, and is distributed as the hypergeometric distribution conditional on row and column counts. Thus, the p-value of the cross-product ratio statistic is given by the sum of hypergeometric probabilities of cell counts at least as great as the observed winner-winner count (Agresti [1990, p. 60]). This is known as Fisher's *exact test*.

5. In fact, Hendricks, Patel, and Zeckhauser provide little reliable evidence of "hot hands." Using either the value-weighted or the equal-weighted CRSP index benchmark, there is no significant persistence of positive performance. The only benchmark for which they find any statistically significant evidence of persistence in positive performance is a self-created benchmark consisting of an equal-weighted average of returns on the mutual funds in their sample.

6. Hendricks, Patel, and Zeckhauser (1991) give the example of the 44 Wall Street funds that survived the period 1975–1988 with a negative annual α of -1.90 (relative to the value-weighted CRSP index) and -4.27 (relative to the equal-weighted CRSP index). One potential explanation for the persistence of negative performance might be that mutual fund data compute returns after fees but before sales and load charges. The negative performance may simply reflect the persistence of high fees.

7. Hendricks, Patel, and Zeckhauser (1991) argue that because fund data are eliminated from their database as the fund ceases to exist or is merged into other funds, their sample is free of survivorship bias effects. However, all funds considered at each evaluation point survived at least until the end of an evaluation period that could extend from one quarter to two years. They are excluded from the analysis *subsequent to* the evaluation period. The numerical example given in the second section of this article matches this ex-

perimental design, and provides a counterexample to a presumption of freedom from survivorship bias effects. The results of such a study would be free of survival bias only if it could be established that the probability of termination or elimination from the sample is unrelated to performance. However, Hendricks, Patel, and Zeckhauser indicate (note 6) that, in fact, funds that go under do quite poorly in the quarter of demise.

8. We show in Appendix 1 that the effect is mitigated somewhat where cumulative performance rather than one-period performance is used as a survival criterion. The analysis of a strategic response is beyond the scope of this article. A possible strategic response is for surviving managers who are subject to the same survival criterion to converge in residual risk characteristics. The results in the next section require only that the ranking of managers by residual risk be constant. This kind of strategic response would also tend to mitigate the effect. This analysis is complicated by the fact that survival criteria are not necessarily the same for all managers.

9. As seen from Table 15.5, a 5 percent performance cut will lead to an increase in the average β of about 5 percent. The increase is due solely to the truncation in the cross-sectional distribution of β. This is an important caveat in interpreting Table 15.5 to imply a calibration of survival measures. There is a more subtle issue here. If there is a performance cut, ordinary least squares will not be appropriate. Beta should be estimated taking account of the fact that the distribution of residuals is truncated by survival. Assuming that the truncation by survival occurs on a quarterly basis, and that the minimum observed return among survivors (relative to the market) defines the point at which the residuals are truncated, it is possible to estimate a truncated regression model for the data described in Table 15.1. The measure of β was not sensitive to truncation; however, the measure of residual risk rose, on average, 2.5 percent. To the extent that our results depend on the distribution of the residual risk across managers, this represents another caveat to the results reported in Table 15.5.

10. This proportional relationship does not only capture the apparent segmentation of mutual funds into closet index funds characterized by a β of unity and a low residual risk, and less well-diversified funds with β's less than or greater than unity. It also matches the empirical regularity that suggests that residual risk is an increasing function of the absolute difference of portfolio β from unity (e.g., Black, Jensen, and Scholes [1972]). This relationship also follows for size-ranked portfolios and managed funds (Connor and Korajczyk [1991], Elton et al. [1993, Table 6]). The constant of proportionality, k, was chosen so that the cross-sectional average R^2 matches the average value of .90 for the Goetzmann and Ibbotson sample. This value also corresponds to the available data. For the 438 money managers for whom Goetzmann and Ibbotson have data for the period 1984–1988, a regression of residual risk on the deviation of β from unity yields the following:

$$\hat{\sigma}_i^2 = .000374 + .00012\,(1 - \hat{\beta}_i) + .005294\,(1 - \hat{\beta}_i)^2,$$
$$\quad\;\;(4.928)\qquad(-3.827)\qquad\quad(13.014)$$
$$R^2 = .360, \quad N = 438$$

(t-values in parentheses). To account for the possibility that this relationship may be an artifact of leptokurtosis in fund manager returns, β and residual risk are estimated on the basis of alternate-month returns (for a discussion of the related issue of skewness-induced correlation of sample mean returns and volatility, see Roll and Ross [1980]). Assuming that the cross-sectional distribution of returns is truncated by the lowest observed return in that month (the survivor), a truncated regression approach applied to the same data yields a coefficient on the squared term of .003552 (t-value 15.325) with intercept and linear terms statistically insignificant. These values expressed on an annualized basis correspond closely to the value for k, 0.05349, used in the simulation experiments.

11. Consistent with Corollary 3, managers are truncated in the final year. Failure to truncate in the final year leads to a small decrease in the apparent persistence of performance in Table 15.5. However, the qualitative conclusions are not affected by this change.

12. This application of the *appraisal ratio*, originally due to Treynor and Black (1972), was suggested to us by William Sharpe. A recent study to examine the properties of this ratio is Lehmann and Modest (1987).

13. If the performance cut occurs at the 10th percentile of the unconditional distribution of manager returns, the median of the truncated distribution will occur at the 55th percentile of the unconditional distribution. To correct for survivorship bias, we first compute the fractile p of the distribution of excess returns for the particular manager that corresponds to the minimum observed return. The quantity q given as the $(1 - (1 - p)/2)$th quantile of the distribution of excess returns is the median excess return induced by survivorship. The median adjustment given in Figure 15.2 is obtained by subtracting q computed for each manager from that manager's annual excess returns. Obviously, this adjustment is highly sensitive to the assumptions made about the distribution of excess returns for each manager, and about the effect of past performance on survival.

14. Two hundred fifty money managers in the Goetzmann and Ibbotson database were ranked according to β. The average β and intracorrelation of performance measures were computed for each of 20 groupings by β. As a purely descriptive measure, the average intracorrelations were related to β as follows:

$$\hat{\rho}_{ij} = .558 - .732(\hat{\beta}_i + \hat{\beta}_j) + 1.216(\hat{\beta}_i \times \hat{\beta}_j),$$
$$(2.04)\ (-2.66)$$
$$R^2 = .3580, \quad N = 190$$

(*t*-values in parentheses). If the true correlation matrix corresponds to this regression equation, it is a simple exercise in matrix algebra to show that the distribution of residual returns is a two-factor structure, with factor loadings and idiosyncratic variances given as analytic functions of the β and β-product terms. This two-factor structure is used to generate Figures 15.3 and 15.4 in the text. As an aside, the same exercise in linear algebra shows that principal components will be an ineffective control for cross-sectional dependence, since the idiosyncratic variances of residual returns will be a quadratic function of β. Using principal components assumes the idiosyncratic variances are constant in the cross section.

As discussed earlier, this result is subject to the important caveat that the residual covariance matrix and β are estimated without regard to the possible effects of survival on the cross-sectional distribution of these parameters and on the distribution of residuals.

15. This uses the two-factor structure described in note 15.

16. To illustrate the likely effects of normalizing performance measures by residual standard deviation, results reported in Table 15.4 were recomputed using this approach. The α and standard deviation measures are estimated using a truncated regression approach, where each month's return is assumed truncated from below by the return of the lowest manager in the group (the survivor). All measures of persistence are now statistically insignificant. The cross-section *t*-value for 1976–1981 falls from 3.13 to 1.77. The *t*-value for the self-financing portfolio approach performance now measures 1.76, whereas before it was 2.16. Two important caveats are in order. The result is sensitive to assumptions made about the way in which past performance influences survival. One could use information on firms that leave the sample to derive an explicit model for survival to construct a more powerful test. This would appear to be a standard application of the censored regression

methodology were it not for the model-specific heteroskedasticity implied (see, e.g., Hurd [1979]). Among other things, such a model would also need to account for cross-sectional correlation of manager performance. The second caveat is that these tests assume manager returns are independent through time. We would not expect such tests to be powerful against an alternative that allows manager returns to be autocorrelated absent the survival effect.

17. Since small firms are less diverse in their activities, we do not find it surprising that the residual risk for such firms is greater than for larger firms. The results of this article would suggest a survival-induced correlation between size and average (risk-adjusted) return.

18. For more discussion on the post-earnings-drift phenomenon, see Foster, Olson, and Shevlin (1984) and Bernard and Thomas (1989, 1990). For a discussion of survival bias effects as they relate to measures of accounting earnings, see Salamon and Smith (1977) and Ball and Watts (1979).

19. Inspecting various annual issues of the Wiesenberger Investment Companies Service *Investment Companies* periodical, we find that for the period 1977–1987 the apparent attrition rate given as the fraction of equity fund managers who simply disappear from coverage, merge, or change their names ranges from 2.6 percent in 1985 to 8.5 percent in 1977, an average attrition rate of 4.8 percent. This average attrition is very close to the 5 percent attrition found by Grinblatt and Titman (1989). However, this number is very much a lower bound on the true attrition rate. To the extent that the number of equity funds increases through time, we should expect that the attrition rate will also increase.

◤ References

Agresti, A., 1990, *Analysis of Ordinal Categorical Data*, Wiley, New York.

Ball, R., and P. Brown, 1968, "An Empirical Examination of Accounting Income Numbers," *Journal of Accounting Research*, 6, 159–178.

Ball, R., and R. Watts, 1979, "Some Additional Evidence on Survival Biases," *Journal of Finance*, 34, 1802–1808.

Bernard, V., and J. Thomas, 1989, "Post–Earnings-Announcement Drift: Delayed Price Response or Risk Premium," *Journal of Accounting Research*, 27, 1–36.

Bernard, V., and J. Thomas, 1990, "Evidence That Stock Prices Do Not Fully Reflect the Implications of Current Earnings for Future Earnings," *Journal of Accounting and Economics*, 13, 305–340.

Bishop, Y., S. Fienberg, and P. Holland, 1975, *Discrete Multivariate Analysis: Theory and Practice*, MIT Press, Cambridge, Mass.

Black, F., M. Jensen, and M. Scholes, 1972, in M. Jensen (ed.), *Studies in the Theory of Capital Markets*, Praeger, New York.

Connor, G., and R. Korajczyk, 1991, "The Attributes, Behavior and Performance of U.S. Mutual Funds," *Review of Quantitative Finance and Accounting*, 1, 5–26.

Cowles, A., 1933, "Can Stock Market Forecasters Forecast?" *Econometrica*, 1, 309–325.

Dunn, P., and R. Theisen, 1983, "How Consistently Do Active Managers Win?" *Journal of Portfolio Management*, 9, 47–50.

Elton, E., and M. Gruber, 1989, *Modern Portfolio Theory and Investment Analysis*, Wiley, New York.

Elton, E., M. Gruber, S. Das, and M. Hlavka, 1993, "Efficiency With Costly Information: A Reinterpretation of Evidence for Managed Portfolios," forthcoming in *Review of Financial Studies,* 6(1), 1–22.

Elton, E., M. Gruber, and J. Rentzler, 1990, "The Performance of Publicly Offered Commodity Funds," *Financial Analysts Journal,* 46, 23–30.

Foster, G., C. Olsen, and T. Shevlin, 1984, "Earnings Releases, Anomalies, and the Behavior of Security Returns," *Accounting Review,* 59, 574–603.

Goetzmann, W., and R. Ibbotson, 1991, "Do Winners Repeat? Patterns in Mutual Fund Behavior," Working Paper, Yale School of Organization and Management.

Grinblatt, M., and S. Titman, 1988, "The Evaluation of Mutual Fund Performance: An Analysis of Monthly Returns," Working Paper 13-86, John E. Anderson Graduate School of Management, University of California at Los Angeles.

Grinblatt, M., and S. Titman, 1989, "Mutual Fund Performance: An Analysis of Quarterly Portfolio Holdings," *Journal of Business,* 62, 393–416.

Hendricks, D., J. Patel, and R. Zeckhauser, 1991, "Hot Hands in Mutual Funds: The Persistence of Performance, 1974–88," Working Paper, John F. Kennedy School of Government, Harvard University.

Hurd, M., 1979, "Estimation in Truncated Samples When There Is Heteroscedasticity," *Journal of Econometrics,* 11, 247–258.

Ibbotson, R., and R. Sinquefield, 1990, *Stocks, Bonds, Bills and Inflation: 1990 Yearbook,* Ibbotson Associates, Chicago.

Ippolito, R., 1989, "Efficiency with Costly Information: A Study of Mutual Fund Performance 1965–1984," *Quarterly Journal of Economics,* 104, 1–23.

Jensen, M., 1968, "The Performance of Mutual Funds in the Period 1945–1964," *Journal of Finance,* 23, 389–416.

Kritzman, M., 1983, "Can Bond Managers Perform Consistently?" *Journal of Portfolio Management,* 9, 54–56.

Lehmann, B., and D. Modest, 1987, "Mutual Fund Performance Evaluation: A Comparison of Benchmarks and Benchmark Comparisons," *Journal of Finance,* 21, 233–265.

Roll, R., and S. Ross, 1980, "An Empirical Investigation of the Arbitrage Pricing Theory," *Journal of Finance,* 35, 1073–1103.

Salamon, G., and E. D. Smith, 1977, "Additional Evidence on the Time Series Properties of Reported Earnings per Share," *Journal of Finance,* 32, 1795–1801.

Treynor, J., and F. Black, 1972, "Portfolio Selection Using Special Information Under the Assumptions of the Diagonal Model With Mean Variance Portfolio Objectives and Without Constraints," in G. P. Szego and K. Shell (eds.), *Mathematical Models in Investment and Finance,* North-Holland, Amsterdam.

16 Philippe Jorion and William N. Goetzmann

Global Stock Markets in the 20th Century

▶ Overview

*The contribution of this article is to present a wide cross section of historical
stock market performance over roughly 80 years of world history. Until recently, studies of the long-term rate of return to the stock market have been
confined only to the U.S. or U.K. markets because of data availability. The
central question to us is whether the U.S. experience is representative of
equity investing around the world through the 20th century. Over the
period we examine, the United States had the highest rate of real appreciation in stock prices in a sample of 39 countries—significantly higher than
the median market and slightly higher than a GDP-weighted index of non-
U.S. markets. Some of the most difficult challenges in this article were trying
to understand what happened to investment markets during crisis periods,
particularly the Second World War, when many markets ceased to function
normally, and legal ownership claims—at least for parts of the population—
ceased to exist. As econometricians, we like to imagine that the economic
environment is roughly stationary—that a stock is a stock whether it trades
in 1941 in Berlin or 2005 in the United States. The experience of the 20th
century cautions us that this is not necessarily true. Major world events, for
which standard econometric models cannot account, are apt to redefine
and realign markets. This work estimates the upward bias of the U.S. equity
market in the neighborhood of 1% per year. It has pushed us, and other researchers, to continue to collect stock market data even further back in time
in a quest for accurate estimation of the global equity premium.* The challenge continues to capture the markets that disappeared, as well as those
that survived.*

▶ Abstract

*Long-term estimates of expected return on equities are typically derived
from U.S. data only. There are reasons to suspect that these estimates are*

---

*See, for example, Dimson, Elroy, Paul Marsh, and Mike Staunton, *The Millenium Book: A Cen-
tury of Investment Returns*, ABN-AMRO, 2000. Using a smaller but longer sample of total returns covering an entire century of stock markets, they find that the United States is in the top quartile, beaten
by Sweden and Australia, once dividends and 20 more years of data are included.

subject to survivorship, as the United States is arguably the most successful capitalist system in the world. We collect a database of capital appreciation indexes for 39 markets going back to the 1920s. For 1921 to 1996, U.S. equities had the highest real return of all countries, at 4.3 percent, versus a median of 0.8 percent for other countries. The high equity premium obtained for U.S. equities appears to be the exception rather than the rule.

In a now-famous article, Mehra and Prescott (1985) argue that standard general equilibrium models cannot explain the size of the risk premium on U.S. equities, which averages about 6 percent over the 1889–1978 period. They show that one would need a very large coefficient of risk aversion, largely in excess of the usual value of 2, to generate such a premium. This unsettling result has sparked a flurry of theoretical research that explores alternative preference structures, including dropping the expected utility assumption and introducing habit formation.[1] Such efforts, however, come at the cost of losing the intuition of standard models.[2]

Rather than searching for preference structures that fit historical data, other explanations focus on the limitations of the data. Rietz (1988) proposes a solution to the puzzle that involves infrequently occurring "crashes." Assuming a crash where output falls by 50 (or 25) percent of its value with a probability of 0.4 percent (or 1.4 percent), Rietz generates ex ante equity premia consistent with those observed in the United States and risk aversion of 5 (or 10).

A related argument is advanced in Brown, Goetzmann, and Ross (1995), who claim that survival of the series imparts a bias to ex post returns. They show that an ex ante equity premium of zero can generate a high ex post positive premium by simply conditioning on the market's surviving an absorbing lower bound over the course of a century.[3] The implication is that risk aversion cannot be inferred from the empirical analysis of historical data whose observation is conditional on survival. Although the Rietz (1988) argument leads to higher ex ante equity premia, the survival argument points to biases in ex post premia.

Unfortunately, these arguments are nearly impossible to sort out based on a century of U.S. equity data. Consider, for instance, a 0.4 percent annual probability of a large crash. We would then expect one crash to occur every 250 years. Even if we observed such a long sample series, our estimate of the crash probability would still be subject to enormous estimation error.

The only solution to this dilemma is to expand the sample by collecting additional cross-sectional data. In this article, we reconstruct real capital appreciation series for equity markets in 39 countries over much of the 20th century. We include not only those markets that survived, but also those markets that experienced both temporary and permanent interruptions. We use this new database to estimate the long-term returns to investing in global markets over the 20th century.

The first part of our analysis treats each market separately. In effect, it takes all stock market histories as draws from one urn. Under these conditions, we show that the process of discarding markets with interruptions creates serious biases in the measurement of expected returns. Such an experiment assumes that all markets have the same statistical characteristics. This framework is valid when markets are segmented due, for instance, to capital controls. The assumption of constraints on such diversification is not unreasonable for the time period under study.

This paper provides the first comprehensive long-run estimates of return on equity capital across a broad range of markets. To date, virtually the only long-run evidence regarding equity rates of return is derived from the United States, for which we have continuous stock price history going back to 1802. We are able to augment the U.S. experience with a wide range of different global equity market histories.

We find striking evidence in support of the survival explanation for the equity risk premium. Over our sample period, the United States has the highest uninterrupted real rate of appreciation, at 4.3 percent annually. For other countries, the median real appreciation rate is approximately 0.8 percent. This strongly suggests that estimates of equity premia obtained solely from the U.S. market are biased upward by survivorship. An alternative line of explanation is that of fundamentally different risk premia. With segmented markets, risk premia are determined by local market conditions. Thus, differing expected returns could be due to different investor expectations about risk or to different risk aversion.

Beyond its potential value for shedding light on the equity premium puzzle, this global database allows a broad investigation into the behavior of equity markets over the very long run. We have been able to construct monthly real and dollar-valued capital appreciation indices for virtually all the equity markets that existed during the 20th century. This enables us to examine markets in crisis and to compare the behavior of losing markets to the behavior of winning markets.

In the second part of the study, we construct a world market appreciation index in order to examine the potential experience of a diversified global investor. This allows us to analyze the benefits of international diversification, comparing return and risk measures across the U.S. and the global portfolios. We estimate the return that such an investor would have earned had it been possible to hold the world market from the early 1920s. Even though one could argue that few investors could have held globally diversified portfolios during these turbulent times, this is still an informative experiment as a guide for future investing.

This paper is organized as follows. The first section motivates the search for differences in return on capital. The second section describes the construction of the global market database. The third section compares the performance of global stock markets and discusses biases affecting the construction of a global stock market index. The fourth section contains some concluding comments.

▲ The Importance of Compound Growth

In September 1626, Pierre Minuit, the Governor of the West India Company, purchased Manhattan Island from the local Indians for the total sum of 60 guilders, or about $24. At first sight, this seems like the deal of the century.

Yet, slight differences in the time value of money over long horizons can result in vastly different conclusions. If one compounds this payment at a 5 percent rate of interest, it would have grown in 1995 to about 1.6 billion in current dollars, which seems expensive for 31 square miles of undeveloped land. Compounding at 3 percent, however, results in a much lower current price of $1.3 million—a thousandfold difference! This story shows that differences in rates of return on capital can lead to drastically different numbers when compounded over long horizons.

Our estimates of the rate of return on equity capital are typically based on a century of U.S. data, which reveals an equity premium of about 6 percent. As shown in this example, however, small differences in rates of return can have momentous implications over the long run. How much faith can we have in this number?

Not much, given the volatility of stock returns. Consider, for instance, a market that grows at a 6 percent annual rate with a standard deviation of 20 percent. The question is, how many years do we require to establish that growth is positive with statistical confidence? Using the standard t-test at the 5 percent level, we require that the statistic

$$t = \frac{\hat{\mu}}{\hat{\sigma}/\sqrt{N}} = \frac{0.06}{0.20/\sqrt{N}} \tag{1}$$

be greater than 2. This requires N to be at least 44 years. In other words, we need approximately half a century of returns to be confident that this 6 percent equity premium is positive. If the expected return is 3 percent instead, we will need more than 178 years of data to establish statistical significance.

Another problem is that we have reasons to suspect that estimates of return on capital from the United States are affected by survival. At the beginning of the century, active stock markets existed in a number of countries, including Russia, France, Germany, Japan, and Argentina. All of these markets have been interrupted for a number of reasons, including political turmoil, war, and hyperinflation. Assuming there was some probability of disruption for the U.S. market, this probability is not reflected in the observed U.S. data. In turn, this will bias our estimates of the equity premium.

As small differences in estimates on equity capital have dramatic implications for long-term growth, we feel it is important to extend our knowledge of equity premia to a large cross-sectional sample of long-term data.

◤ A Global Stock Market Database

The standard data sources on international stock prices are Morgan Stanley Capital International Perspectives (MSCIP) for developed markets and the International Finance Corporation (IFC) for emerging markets. Both are relatively recent.

MSCIP started to construct equity indices in January 1970 for a sample of 19 markets from industrial (developed) countries. These indices are built using a uniform methodology and include income and currency effects. A similar approach was undertaken by the IFC, which in 1980 started to build indices for nine emerging markets, which were expanded to 26 by 1995.

Beyond these databases, unfortunately, there is little systematic information on the long-term performance of global stock markets. The United States is a rare exception, as monthly stock market indices have been constructed by Standard and Poor's and, prior to 1926, by Alfred Cowles (1939), going back into the 1870s.[4]

For the non-U.S. data, we must turn to a variety of sources. The first is the International Monetary Fund (IMF), which publishes monthly stock price indices as reported by the local authorities in its *International Financial Statistics* (IFS) publication. The published indices generally represent monthly averages, as opposed to the end-of-month MSCIP and IFC data, and do not include dividends.[5] The IMF also publishes price indices and exchange rates, which can be used to compute real returns and dollar returns. We use the Wholesale Price Index (WPI) to deflate nominal returns, whenever available. The WPI measure offers a number of advantages, in that the WPI indices generally have longer histories than consumer indices, are less affected by differences in domestic consumption patterns, and are more responsive to monetary disturbances than other inflation measures.[6]

One drawback of this dataset is that it does not allow us to measure directly the equity premium, usually defined as the difference between the total return on stocks minus the Treasury bill rate. Decomposing the total return on stocks (R_S) into capital return (CR_S) and income return (IR_S), and the Treasury bill rate (R_{TB}) into the inflation component and the real rate, we can write

$$\begin{aligned} \text{Equity Premium} &= R_S - R_{TB} \\ &= [CR_S + IR_S] - [\text{Inflation} + \text{Real Rate}] \qquad (2) \\ &= [CR_S - \text{Inflation}] + [IR_S - \text{Real Rate}]. \end{aligned}$$

Our methodology measures the capital return in excess of inflation, which is the first bracketed term. To the extent that cross-sectional variations in the second bracketed term are small, this allows comparisons of equity premia across countries. Some evidence on the quality of this approximation is presented later.

The first IFS publication was issued in 1948. Prior to the IMF, our source is the *Statistical Yearbooks* of the League of Nations (various issues), which include data on the capital appreciation of market indices in the period from

1929 through 1944. This collection effort was bridged by the United Nations' *Monthly Bulletin of Statistics* from 1945 to 1948. Finally, the *International Abstract of Economic Statistics* publications (ICES 1934, 1938) have stock market data going back to 1919.[7]

By connecting data from these sources, we are able to reconstruct histories for a number of stock markets going back to the early 1920s. This is a challenging effort, because of erratic data reporting.[8] The IMF, for example, provides a CD-ROM with data starting in 1957. Unfortunately, this database suffers from sample selection biases, as a number of markets that were followed in the 1960s are not contained in the CD-ROM. Data for these markets have to be collected from the IFS monthly publications. More recent emerging market data, when not available from the IFS publication, are available from the IFC database.

In order to minimize survivorship biases, we follow all markets that were reported by the League of Nations or the IMF at any point during the 1929 to 1970 period. After 1970, a flurry of new markets opened (or reopened). These emerging markets, however, have relatively short histories and are not included in the database as they have been already extensively analyzed. We obtain a total of 39 markets.[9] All in all, this involves a total of approximately 76,000 data points.

Whenever data sources do not overlap, we attempt to link series by comparing annual averages. This is the case for Austria, for instance, whose price history was interrupted by the Anschluss (German annexation) in April 1938. Fortunately, the United Nations' publications provide annual averages from 1946 on and going back to 1935, allowing us to reconstruct a long-term history for Austria, albeit with an eight-year gap during the war.

Initially, we begin by collecting annual data. We find, however, that the monthly data create more precise estimates. In particular, we notice discrepancies between returns using monthly and annual data.[10] We also find that monthly data lead to cleaner linkages between various sources, which is particularly important as we sometimes have to patch series together. Finally, the monthly data allow us to perform event studies centered around specific dates.

Note that, despite all our efforts, this database is still not free from selection biases. The first type of bias occurs when backfilling of an index uses only stocks that are in existence at the end of the sample. In the case of Austria, for instance, even though the stock market has recovered, some companies may have fared badly or disappeared during the war. Therefore, a selection bias is induced if these companies are not included in the index.

The second type of remaining bias is much more serious. The UN-IMF data sources do not allow us to link gaps for six countries. In particular, there appears to be no link between stock market prices of Germany and Japan before and after the war in standard data sources. As these two countries did not fare well during these gaps, we can surmise that omitting the gaps misses important negative information. We attempt to correct for this by turning to other data sources for bridging these gaps.[11]

▶ Empirical Analysis

Performance of Global Stock Markets

We calculate returns using three different numéraires: the local currency, a real price index, and the dollar. Because of wide differences in inflation across time and countries, we primarily focus on WPI-deflated returns. Returns in dollars as a common currency should give similar results over the long run if exchange rates move in line with inflation differentials—that is, if Purchasing Power Parity holds. Differences between real and dollar returns, however, may be induced when exchange rates are pegged by central banks at artificial levels, or when official exchange rates do not reflect the actual rates facing international investors.

Table 16.1 presents geometric returns for 39 markets grouped by regions, compounded annually. These results are striking. Of the sample of 39 countries, real returns are the highest for the United States, at 4.32 percent per annum. There is no country with a higher return over the total period. Therefore, the high U.S. equity premium seems to be the exception rather than the rule.

These results are perhaps better visualized in Figure 16.1, which plots the compound return for each market against its observed "life" since 1921. Longer lives lead to more precise, less volatile estimates of expected returns. Moving to the right of the figure, we observe that the U.S. market has the highest realized return of all markets.

At the bottom of Table 16.1 we show average and median returns for all countries, as well as for a group of countries for which we have data going to the 1920s. The median real returns for all 39 countries is 0.75 percent. By way of contrast, we also analyze countries with continuous histories going back to the 1920s; the median return for this group is also much higher, at 2.35 percent. These results strongly suggest that the 4.3 percent real capital appreciation return for the United States is highly unusual. As it is also one of the few series without any break, this high return could be ascribed to survival.

An alternative explanation is that the United States had a higher level of risk than any other market over the period. In perfectly integrated capital markets, a high equity premium can simply compensate for a high β. Of course, this is a difficult proposition to test directly because survivorship affects not only returns but also capital weights. Ex post, the most successful index will represent the largest share of the market.

Other high returns, however, are obtained in some cases. Over 1921 to 1996, Swedish equities displayed returns quite close to the 4.32 percent obtained in the United States, perhaps not surprisingly as Sweden also avoided major upheavals in this century. Higher returns are observed over more recent periods. For instance, Germany experienced a steep run-up in prices, 6 percent in real terms, over the period 1950 to 1996. But this high return must be offset against mediocre growth up to July 1944; additionally, during the five-year

Table 16.1

Long-Term Performance of Global Equity Markets (Compound Return in Percentage per Annum)

Country	Period	Nominal Return	Real Return	Dollar Return	Inflation
United States	1/21–12/96	6.95	4.32	6.95	2.52
Canada	1/21–12/96	5.78	3.19	5.35	2.51
Austria*	1/25–12/96	5.64	1.62	5.00	3.95
Belgium	1/21–12/96	4.45	−0.26	3.51	4.73
Denmark	1/26–12/96	5.87	1.87	5.19	3.93
Finland	1/31–12/96	10.23	2.07	6.19	7.99
France	1/21–12/96	9.09	0.75	4.29	8.28
Germany*	21–96	4.43	1.91	5.81	2.47
Germany	1/21–7/44	[3.29]	[2.23]	[5.59]	[1.04]
Germany	1/50–12/96	[8.46]	[6.00]	[10.78]	[2.32]
Ireland	1/34–12/96	7.00	1.46	5.14	5.45
Italy	12/28–12/96	10.10	0.15	3.22	9.94
Netherlands	1/21–12/96	3.71	1.55	4.47	2.12
Norway	1/28–12/96	7.13	2.91	6.29	4.10
Portugal*	31–96	6.89	−0.58	3.78	7.51
Portugal	12/30–4/74	[5.21]	[1.16]	[4.96]	[4.00]
Portugal	3/77–12/96	[20.11]	[5.63]	[11.92]	[13.71]
Spain*	1/21–12/96	4.66	−1.82	1.53	6.61
Sweden	1/21–12/96	7.42	4.29	7.00	3.00
Switzerland	1/26–12/96	4.83	3.24	6.84	1.54
United Kingdom	1/21–12/96	6.30	2.35	5.20	3.86
Czechoslovakia	1/21–4/45	4.33	3.79	9.50	0.52
Greece	7/29–9/40	−2.12	−5.50	−8.08	3.58
Hungary	1/25–6/44	6.29	2.80	9.07	3.40
Poland	1/21–6/39	−7.00	−3.97	−4.30	−3.15
Romania	12/37–6/41	−5.36	−28.06	−14.64	31.55
Australia	1/31–12/96	7.06	1.58	6.29	5.39
New Zealand	1/31–12/96	5.69	−0.34	3.63	6.01
Japan*	21–96	7.33	−0.81	1.80	8.21
Japan	1/21–5/44	[1.23]	[−0.34]	[−1.83]	[1.58]
Japan	4/49–12/96	[8.30]	[5.52]	[10.90]	[2.63]

break in our series, German equities fell by 72 percent in real terms. As a result, the long-term growth of the German market is only 1.91 percent when evaluated over most of this century. The story is similar for Japan, where we observe a sharp difference between the postwar return of 5.52 percent and the prewar return of −0.34 percent. During the 1944 to 1949 break, the market fell by 95 percent in real terms.

Other markets that gapped, such as Portugal, Chile, and Peru, also did well recently, but not so well when going back further in time. These are typ-

Table 16.1 (*continued*)
Long-Term Performance of Global Equity Markets (Compound Return in Percentage per Annum)

Country	Period	Nominal Return	Real Return	Dollar Return	Inflation
India	12/39–12/96	5.10	−2.33	0.80	7.60
Pakistan	7/60–12/96	7.79	−1.77	0.59	8.57
Philippines	7/54–12/96	5.95	−3.65	−0.30	9.96
Argentina+	47–65, 75–96	87.48	−4.80	−1.43	96.92
Argentina	9/47–7/65	[−5.78]	[−25.09]	[−23.64]	[25.78]
Argentina	12/75–12/96	[236.29]	[16.71]	[22.43]	[188.15]
Brazil	2/61–12/96	142.34	−0.17	4.68	147.52
Mexico	12/34–12/96	20.13	2.30	6.12	17.43
Chile*	27–96	37.12	2.99	6.38	33.16
Chile	1/27–3/71	[12.98]	[−5.37]	[−4.23]	[19.39]
Chile	1/74–12/96	[64.19]	[15.52]	[20.94]	[42.13]
Colombia	12/36–12/96	10.15	−4.29	−0.88	15.09
Peru*	41–96	45.29	−4.85	3.45	52.68
Peru	3/41–1/53	[2.03]	[−12.36]	[2.03]	[16.41]
Peru	1/57–12/77	[1.53]	[−9.88]	[−7.40]	[12.66]
Peru	12/88–12/96	[340.95]	[30.45]	[50.92]	[232.18]
Uruguay	3/38–11/44	6.70	2.42	10.01	4.19
Venezuela	12/37–12/96	9.67	−2.04	0.78	11.95
Egypt	7/50–9/62	−1.46	−2.84	−1.63	1.42
Israel	1/57–12/96	37.05	3.03	7.21	33.02
South Africa	1/47–12/96	6.13	−1.76	1.48	8.03
All 39 countries					
Mean			−0.47	3.11	
Median			0.75	4.68	
11 countries with continuous histories into the 1920s					
Mean			1.88	5.09	
Median			2.35	5.20	

Notes: The table compares the long-term performance of global equity markets with annually compounded data. The sample period varies across countries and is reported in the second column. Data for subperiods are reported within brackets. Percentage returns are measured in nominal terms in the local currency, in real terms—deflating by the Wholesale Price Index, and translated into U.S. dollars. The last column reports the inflation rate. * indicates a break in the series that has been bridged; + indicates a permanent discontinuity in the series.

ical "reemerging markets," whose recent performance appears to be, on the surface, nothing short of stellar. Our analysis shows that the performance of the same markets has also been mediocre at other times.

Table 16.1 also reports dollar returns. As expected, rankings for this column are very similar to those obtained with real returns.[12] In general, dollar returns for other currencies are slightly closer to U.S. returns than real returns.

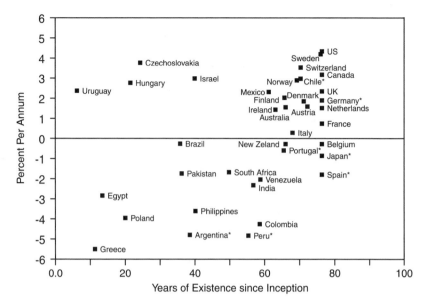

Figure 16.1. Real Returns on Global Stock Markets
Notes: The figure displays average real returns for 39 markets over the period 1921 to 1996. Markets are sorted by years of existence. The graph shows that markets with long histories typically have higher returns. An asterisk indicates that the market suffered a long-term break.

For example, the difference between U.S. equities and the median is 4.32 − 0.75 = 3.57 percent when measured in real terms; the difference is 6.95 − 4.68 = 2.27 percent in dollar terms. This discrepancy reflects the slight depreciation of the dollar, relative to its Purchasing Power Parity value, over the sample period.

In addition to geometric returns, which represent returns to a buy-and-hold strategy, it is also useful to consider arithmetic averages, which give equal weight to each observation interval. Table 16.2 presents conventional measures of annualized average (arithmetic) capital appreciation returns and standard deviations.[13] Data are presented in the local currency, in real terms, and in dollars. The table shows that the 16.2 percent volatility of the U.S. market is not particularly high when compared with other stock markets. Therefore the high return obtained in the United States does not seem to compensate for higher risk as measured by volatility (which would be the appropriate measure of risk under segmented capital markets).

The table also reports the results from standard statistical tests of significance of the real capital appreciation return premium. At the 99 percent level, we can only reject the hypothesis of a zero long-run appreciation return for the United States and Sweden. Over shorter periods, we observe significantly positive returns for Germany and Japan in the postwar period. When averaged with prewar data, however, these returns look less impressive.

Can we really measure an equity premium? This is a tricky question when we turn to international capital markets. The equity risk premium is the expected return to investment in an index of risky assets in excess of the riskless rate. We take it as nearly axiomatic that the U.S. Treasury bill return is a riskless rate; however, this may not have been the case when the United States was a young nation. Nor is it necessarily the case for other countries, whose sovereign debt ratings reflect some probability of default. What, indeed, was the riskless asset through the turmoil of world wars and hyperinflation? How can we define an equity premium without a meaningful riskless asset? For times of crisis, should we use gold, the age-old store of value? Should we use a consumer price index, which captures the fluctuating value of goods that could presumably be used in barter? Should we use the U.S. dollar as the safe haven of investors? We decided to report results for inflation-adjusted returns and dollar-denominated returns, rather than use the short-term interest rates of the countries in the sample. Despite this choice, the question remains whether the concept of a riskless rate is truly meaningful in measuring the equity risk premium in the presence of default risk. There is no good theory to predict the relative expected returns between defaultable bonds and equities. Indeed, as Jeremy Siegel points out in his *Stocks for the Long Run,* there have been episodes when governments have defaulted on their debts, but stock markets have continued to maintain value. If this were common, one might expect the equity risk premium over government treasuries to be negative, rather than positive.

The Effect of Dividend Omission

The previous section has revealed a striking result: long-term returns on the U.S. stock market appear to be greater than those of any other market during this century. One question that arises is whether this result could be due to the omission of dividends. To shed light on this issue, Table 16.3 presents performance numbers for markets for which we have dividend data.

Panel A reports data for the more recent MSCIP indices, which mainly cover industrial countries since 1971. The table displays compound real returns, with and without reinvestment of dividends. The difference due to the omission of dividends is shown in the third column. The fourth column reports the average level of inflation. Presumably, the results in the previous section could simply reflect a bias due to the omission of dividends. For this bias to be effective, other markets must systematically display a higher income component of return than the United States.

Table 16.3 clearly shows that this is not the case. Over the 1970–1995 period, the dividend effect for the United States was 4.14 percent, which is

Table 16.2

Return and Risk of Global Equity Markets (Arithmetic Return in Percentage per Annum)

Country	Period	Nominal Return Average	(Std. Dev.)	Real Return Average	(Std. Dev.)	Dollar Return Average	(Std. Dev.)
United States	1/21–12/96	8.09**	(16.20)	5.48**	(15.84)	8.09**	(16.20)
Canada	1/21–12/96	7.06**	(16.81)	4.54*	(16.65)	6.88**	(18.17)
Austria	1/25–12/96	6.77**	(18.92)	2.32	(19.49)	7.22**	(21.49)
Belgium	1/21–12/96	6.25**	(17.92)	1.49	(18.97)	5.77**	(21.80)
Denmark	1/26–12/96	6.43**	(12.04)	2.65	(12.69)	6.10**	(14.36)
Finland	1/31–12/96	10.74**	(16.56)	3.50	(17.07)	8.18**	(20.49)
France	1/21–12/96	11.19**	(21.57)	3.16	(21.25)	7.76**	(25.50)
Germany (1)	1/21–7/44	10.22	(40.24)	7.62	(34.26)	12.54	(40.49)
Germany (2)	1/50–12/96	9.35**	(15.50)	7.06**	(15.60)	11.75**	(17.19)
Ireland	1/34–12/96	7.88**	(14.85)	2.59	(15.02)	6.43**	(16.73)
Italy	12/28–12/96	12.62**	(26.01)	3.15	(25.66)	3.15	(25.66)
Netherlands	1/21–12/96	4.78**	(15.12)	2.78*	(14.80)	5.85**	(16.50)
Norway	1/28–12/96	8.49**	(17.90)	4.47*	(17.90)	7.97**	(19.33)
Portugal (1)	12/30–4/74	6.50**	(15.15)	2.34	(14.69)	7.40**	(15.03)
Portugal (2)	3/77–12/96	27.08**	(46.38)	14.69	(47.68)	20.42	(47.11)
Spain	1/21–12/96	6.77**	(18.92)	−0.51	(16.00)	2.44	(28.89)
Sweden	1/21–12/96	8.56**	(16.61)	5.60**	(16.65)	8.38**	(17.69)
Switzerland	1/26–12/96	5.83**	(14.79)	4.28*	(14.73)	7.91**	(15.97)
United Kingdom	1/21–12/96	7.25**	(15.43)	3.60*	(15.68)	6.66**	(17.57)
Czechoslovakia	1/21–4/45	5.04*	(12.53)	4.56	(12.84)	10.50**	(17.12)
Greece	7/29–9/40	−0.09	(21.77)	−3.44	(21.61)	−5.31	(25.50)
Hungary	1/25–6/44	9.34	(25.84)	6.20	(26.58)	11.99*	(26.02)
Poland	1/21–6/39	13.60	(71.20)	14.40	(65.69)	16.69	(71.54)
Romania	12/37–6/41	0.14	(33.31)	−27.30	(31.38)	−9.45	(35.06)
Australia	1/31–12/96	7.78**	(13.49)	2.57	(13.94)	7.68**	(18.06)
New Zealand	1/31–12/96	6.20**	(12.12)	0.55	(12.50)	4.98**	(15.97)
Japan (1)	1/21–5/44	2.72	(17.51)	0.89	(15.79)	−0.35	(17.40)
Japan (2)	4/49–12/96	9.79**	(18.78)	7.21**	(18.90)	12.61**	(20.97)

quite close to the group average of 4.25 percent. Therefore, there is no indication that the high return obtained for U.S. equities in Table 16.1 is due to dividend bias. If anything, the bias is in the opposite direction. For example, Japanese equities, which by now constitute the largest market outside the United States, paid an income return of 1.84 percent over the past 25 years, which is much lower than that of U.S. equities.

Panel B of Table 16.3 reports the only long-term data with dividends that we are aware of.[14] To maintain comparability with the original data sources, we use the Consumer Price Index (CPI) to deflate returns, except for Denmark, where the WPI is employed. Including dividends, the United States displays the highest real equity returns since 1921, at 8.22 percent. Britain, another long-term survivor, is a close second; other markets provide returns that are lower by 109 to 334 basis points. Another way to look at the data is to notice

Table 16.2 (*continued*)
Return and Risk of Global Equity Markets (Arithmetic Return in Percentage per Annum)

Country	Period	Nominal Return Average	(Std. Dev.)	Real Return Average	(Std. Dev.)	Dollar Return Average	(Std. Dev.)
India	12/39–12/96	6.18**	(15.53)	−1.07	(16.13)	2.37	(17.46)
Pakistan	7/60–12/96	7.46**	(14.37)	−0.64	(15.23)	2.39	(17.50)
Philippines	7/54–12/96	10.62	(37.35)	1.21	(37.21)	5.30	(38.91)
Argentina (1)	9/47–7/65	−1.13	(31.91)	−23.32**	(32.73)	−18.17	(40.11)
Argentina (2)	12/75–12/96	179.34	(133.55)	49.68	(87.83)	57.85**	(93.68)
Brazil	2/61–12/96	110.69**	(68.22)	12.92	(51.93)	18.45*	(53.44)
Mexico	12/34–12/96	21.97**	(26.79)	5.37	(24.45)	10.46**	(29.09)
Chile (1)	1/27–3/71	14.51**	(22.45)	−3.91	(21.85)	−0.12	(28.64)
Chile (2)	12/73–12/96	57.19**	(40.34)	20.48**	(36.25)	25.94**	(38.59)
Colombia	12/36–12/96	11.66**	(21.56)	−2.32	(21.78)	1.67	(23.39)
Peru (1)	3/41–1/53	3.02	(12.90)	−12.08**	(14.15)	3.39	(16.58)
Peru (2)	1/57–12/77	1.89	(8.62)	−9.94**	(9.08)	−6.61*	(13.66)
Peru (3)	12/88–12/96	200.64**	(118.38)	55.55	(87.98)	71.95*	(87.18)
Uruguay	12/36–11/44	10.55	(28.98)	6.67	(29.66)	13.80	(29.63)
Venezuela	12/37–12/96	12.03**	(24.65)	0.88	(24.84)	4.85	(28.08)
Egypt	7/50–9/62	−0.83	(11.50)	−2.11	(12.54)	−0.19	(17.33)
Israel	1/57–12/96	35.18**	(26.07)	5.68	(22.96)	10.07*	(24.33)
South Africa	1/47–12/96	7.24**	(15.75)	−0.46	(15.89)	3.34	(18.87)

Notes: The table compares average stock returns and their standard deviations. Percentage returns are measured in nominal terms in the local currency, in real terms, deflating by the Wholesale Price Index, and translated into U.S. dollars. The arithmetic average return is obtained from the monthly average multiplied by 12; the standard deviation is annualized by multiplying the monthly volatility by the square root of 12. For series with breaks, (1), (2), and (3) refer to different subperiods.

*, **Significantly different from zero at the 5 and 1 percent levels, respectively.

that the ranking of returns is essentially the same with and without dividends. Therefore, there is no evidence that the performance of U.S. equities is artificially high because of relatively low U.S. dividend payments.

Evidence on the Equity Premium Puzzle

The data we present thus far do not explicitly solve the equity premium puzzle, as theoretically formulated. Strictly speaking, the equity premium puzzle concerns the spread of expected total return on the market portfolio of equities over the return of a riskless security. Siegel (1994) points out that defaults on "riskless" government securities have often occurred in periods of global stress—which of course raises the question of what the riskless asset might actually be and whether the stylized, single-economy, two-asset formulation of the equity premium puzzle is robust.

In the absence of a riskless asset that is immune to the crisis events imagined by Rietz (1988), it seems reasonable to substitute physical storage of goods (i.e.,

Table 16.3
Comparison of Real Returns With and Without Dividends

Country		Compound Return With Dividend (% pa)	Compound Return Without Dividend (% pa)	Difference Due to Dividend	Inflation (% pa)
Panel A: Markets Covered by MSCIP, 1970–1995					
Australia		3.65	−0.71	4.36	6.79
Austria		4.89	2.07	2.82	2.75
Belgium		12.97	4.05	8.92	2.46
Canada		4.34	0.65	3.69	5.78
Denmark		6.54	2.71	3.83	5.62
France		4.45	−0.29	4.74	7.40
Germany		5.52	1.44	4.08	3.09
Italy		−0.26	−2.95	2.69	9.87
Japan		8.59	6.75	1.84	2.18
Netherlands		8.84	3.09	5.74	3.41
Norway		6.03	2.78	3.26	5.90
Spain		2.30	−4.00	6.31	8.40
Sweden		8.79	5.03	3.76	7.42
Switzerland		5.72	3.06	2.66	2.54
United Kingdom		6.39	1.23	5.16	8.35
United States		6.15	2.01	4.14	4.89
Average		5.93	1.68	4.25	5.43
Panel B: Long-Term Markets					
Denmark	1923–95	4.88	0.64	4.24	3.72
Germany	1924–95	4.83	1.21	3.63	2.47
Sweden	1926–95	7.13	3.30	3.83	3.64
Switzerland	1921–95	5.57	2.12	3.45	2.49
United Kingdom	1921–95	8.16	2.99	5.17	3.75
United States	1921–95	8.22	3.38	4.84	2.69
United States	1871–1920	5.43	0.27	5.16	0.59

Notes: The table compares stock returns with and without dividends. Returns are measured in real terms and are annually compounded. The top part reports Morgan Stanley Capital International Perspective (MSCIP) data; the bottom part presents long-term data, obtained from various sources.

inflation rates for T-bill rates). In this case, using real returns as a proxy for the equity premium clearly supports the hypothesis that the ex post observed U.S. premium is higher because the United States was a winner. This evidence, in turn, is consistent with the "survival" hypothesis suggesting that the magnitude of ex post observed equity returns may be higher than their ex ante expectation.

Is there any evidence in the data supporting the Rietz (1988) hypothesis that the ex ante equity premium is as high as supposed? The issue is whether there was some probability of the U.S. market's experiencing a large crash. In fact, this problem is akin to the "peso problem" in the foreign exchange market, where peso forward rates appeared to be biased forecasts of future spot rates over short sample periods, essentially because they account for a nonzero probability of devaluation that is not observed. More generally, peso problems can be interpreted as a failure of the paradigm of rational expectations econometrics, which requires that the ex post distribution of endogenous variables be a good approximation to the ex ante distribution that agents think may happen. The failure may not be that of the economic agent, but that of the econometrician, who only analyzes series with continuous histories. Unusual events with a low probability of occurrence but severe effects on prices, such as wars or nationalizations, are not likely to be well represented in samples and may be totally omitted from survived series.

Our cross-sectional data provide evidence about major market crashes not present in U.S. data. We have, for example, 24 markets for which we have data in 1931. Of these, seven experienced no interruption (the United States, Canada, the United Kingdom, Australia, New Zealand, Sweden, and Switzerland), seven experienced a temporary suspension of trading (less than one year), and the remaining 10 markets suffered long-term closure. Even though these events are not independent, they indicate that market failure is not a remote possibility. Under the assumption that market risks are "priced" individually, rather than under the assumption of integration, the frequency of failure would provide clear justification for a peso problem explanation.

Although it is entirely possible that the magnitude of the observed equity premium is due both to survival bias and to the "pricing" of an infrequently occurring crash, it is difficult to believe that the ex ante premium for the United States should be higher than for other markets. The increased probability of a large crash may explain a higher average equity premium, but if past crash frequency is any indication of future crash probability, then the Rietz (1988) hypothesis would suggest that markets with more interruptions should have higher equity premia. If we believe that the magnitude of the equity premium for each country is related to the ex post historical real appreciation, then the opposite appears to be the case. Absent survival effects, the Rietz hypothesis is inconsistent with cross-sectional differences in historical global equity market returns. In the next section, we investigate the possibility that markets anticipate major crashes.

Table 16.3 provides additional evidence on the equity premium puzzle by comparing the performance of U.S. equities during the recent period with longer term, 1871–1920, Cowles data. The last line in the table shows that the high real capital return obtained since 1921 is much higher than that obtained in the preceding 50 years—3.38 percent during 1921–1995 against 0.27 percent during 1871–1920. Siegel (1992) also points out that the U.S. equity premium is particularly high during this century. Put differently, this large premium seems not only large in a cross-country comparison but also by historical standards. Siegel concludes that "investors in . . . 1872 did not universally

Table 16.4
Analysis of Stock Prices Around Breaks

Country	Break Date	Previous Year Return	Series Restart Date	Subsequent Change	Comment
Hungary	7/31	−0.222	9/32	0.125	Financial crisis, country in default
Germany	7/31	−0.316	4/32	−0.232	Credit crisis
Greece	10/31	−0.099	12/32	−0.581	Financial crisis, drought
Spain	7/36	−0.113	3/40	−0.147	Civil war
Austria	4/38	−0.179	12/46	0.941	Annexation by Germany
Czechoslovakia	10/38	−0.205	1/40	0.015	Cession of land to Germany
Poland	7/39	0.169			Invaded by Germany (Sep 30)
Finland	12/39	−0.192	3/40	−0.101	Invaded by Soviets (Nov 30)
Denmark	4/40	−0.328	6/40	−0.084	Invaded by Germany (Apr 9)
Norway	4/40	−0.274	6/40	−0.154	Invaded by Germany (Apr 11)
Netherlands	5/40	−0.231	9/40	0.105	Invaded by Germany (May 10)
Belgium	5/40	−0.267	12/40	0.850	Invaded by Germany (May 10)
Switzerland	5/40	−0.193	7/40	−0.207	Mobilization
France	6/40	−0.122	4/41	0.824	Invaded by Germany (Jun 14)
Greece	10/40	−0.249	none		Invaded by Germany (Oct 28)
Romania	7/41	−0.396	none		Enters war
Czechoslovakia*	7/43	−0.141	none		War
Japan*	6/44	−0.211	4/49	−0.949+	War
Hungary*	7/44	−0.491	none		War
Belgium*	8/44	0.161	6/45	−0.145	War
Germany*	8/44	−0.013	1/50	−0.838+	Invaded by Allies (Sep 15)
Egypt	10/62	−0.126	none		Arab socialism
Argentina	8/65	−0.692	N/A		Widespread unrest, hyperinflation
Chile	4/71	−0.543	1/74	1.618+	State takes control of economy (Apr 4) Junta reverses policies (Sep 11, 73)
Portugal	4/74	−0.112	3/77	−0.860+	Takeover by leftist junta (Apr 27)

Notes: The table describes the behavior of stock prices measured in real terms around major breaks. It reports the break date, the return in the year previous to the break, the series restart date, and subsequent change, when available. Real returns are in excess of the Wholesale Price Index for the corresponding countries. * indicates that equities were effectively subject to price controls; + indicates that the subsequent change was obtained from alternative data sources.

expect the United States to become the greatest economic power in the next century." If so, returns on U.S. equities this century cannot be viewed as representative of global stock markets.

Disappearance As an Event

To understand how risk premia respond to the probability of major market crashes, we can examine the behavior of markets around interruptions. Sample selection of markets will create a bias if the performance of interrupted markets is systematically poor before the break. By the same token, falling stock

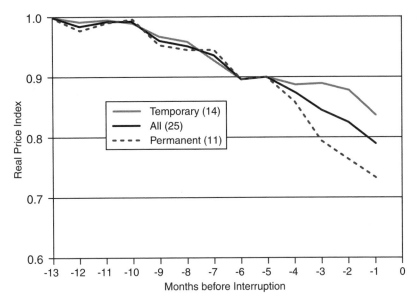

Figure 16.2. Real Stock Prices Before Interruption
Notes: The figure displays the performance of an equally weighted index where real
returns are aligned on the interruption date. The total sample of 25 is further divided into
a sample for which the interruption turns out to be temporary and a sample for which the
interruption is permanent.

prices prior to a market break may be indicative of investor assessment of increasing probability that the market will fail.

To test this hypothesis, we adopt the event-study methodology by constructing an equally weighted index in which real returns are aligned on the
interruption date. We identify a sample of 25 breaks for which the data series
are clearly interrupted. Table 16.4 identifies each of these events. Many are of
a global nature, such as the Second World War, or the depression of the early
1930s. A number of events, however, are country-specific, involving a banking crisis or political turmoil.

Figure 16.2 plots the time-series of the portfolio value, starting one year
before the break. It shows prices falling on average by 21 percent relative to
their peak. The *t*-test based on the standard deviation of monthly changes in
the previous year is −4.95 for this number, which is highly significant. However large, this fall of 21 percent in real terms understates the true loss of value
to equities. During World War II, in particular, prices were kept artificially
high through price controls and do not represent transaction prices as liquidity dried up.[15]

Eventually, reality prevailed. Figure 16.3 compares the performance of
markets sorted by country involvement during the war.[16] As the figure shows,
the advent of the war led to a sharp fall of about 20 percent in the value of equi-

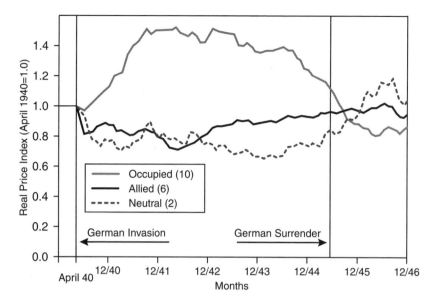

Figure 16.3. Real Stock Prices During World War II
Notes: The figure displays the performance of portfolios of equities measured in real terms during the war. The sample is divided into occupied, Allied, and neutral countries.

ties of Allied countries (including the United States, Canada, the United Kingdom, and Commonwealth countries) for the next two months. A similar fall was suffered by neutral countries (Sweden and Switzerland). The index for occupied countries, in contrast, registered steady gains, which were only wiped out later as stock prices started to reflect transaction prices and as inflation became apparent. Five years later, the index moved below that of Allied countries, as we would have expected. In reality, the index should have been even lower if we had accounted for those markets that disappeared in the process (such as Germany, Hungary, and Czechoslovakia).

Table 16.4 also details the performance around each individual break. All markets suffered a substantial drop before the break, reaching 69 percent for Argentina. One exception is Poland, which experienced a slight price increase, possibly because the series was stopped in July, three months before Poland was invaded, or because the advent of the war was unanticipated. As explained before, the price drops in Germany and occupied Europe are also unusual, for artificial reasons. In all other cases, the event creating the market closure was anticipated.

In 11 of these cases, the UN-IMF equity series are interrupted without restarting later (or there are no continuous series spanning the interruption). These cases include Germany, Japan, Eastern European countries taken over by the Soviet Union, Greece, Egypt, Chile, Argentina, and Portugal. Some of these were the result of a foreign occupation and widespread destruction due to war. In Egypt and Chile, the state took control of the economy. The Buenos Aires Stock Exchange, the oldest in Latin America, virtually disappeared as a result of inflation and interest rate policies in the late 1960s; reportedly, investors lost all interest in the market. These are precisely the situations where we would expect equities to fare most badly.

We have to turn to other data sources to bridge these "permanent" breaks. We find that, over the 1944–1949 break in Japan, equities fell by 95 percent in real terms.[17] For Germany, we find that equities fell by 84 percent in real terms over 1944–1950. Another example is the Portuguese stock market, which closed in April 1974 as a military junta took over the country, reopened in March 1977, then traded intermittently. The stock price series suffered a fall of 86 percent in real terms during the interruption in trading. In contrast, most of the loss for the Chilean stock market occurred before the interruption; the market recovered somewhat over the 1971–1974 break, as the military junta reversed the socialist policies of the Allende government.[18] Furthermore, these numbers probably underestimate the true loss in value by ignoring companies that failed during the interruption, as indices are backfilled from companies quoted before and after the break.

Going back to Figure 16.2, we have separated markets that were temporarily interrupted from those that disappeared, or "died," later. Markets that became extinct dropped by 27 percent the year before the break; markets that subsequently recovered dropped by only 16 percent before the break. To the extent that the event causing the break was anticipated, the market seems to have been able to gauge the gravity of unfolding events. Price declines before breaks are consistent with increasing demand for risk compensation for a catastrophic event.

A Global Stock Index

The global equity data provide a unique opportunity to construct a global equity index—an index that for the first time includes defunct as well as surviving countries and extends back 75 years. Because we have no data on market capitalization going back that far, we assign weights based on Gross Domestic Product (GDP). Annual GDP information is obtained from Mitchell (1992, 1993, 1995) and converted to U.S. dollars using annual averages. At the beginning of each decade, we construct a cross section of national GDPs, which are used to construct initial weights.

To minimize rebalancing, we adopt a portfolio value-weighted approach. Our global indices are therefore similar to market capitalization indices, except that the weights are reset to GDP weights at the beginning of each decade. A value-weighted scheme is more appropriate for measurement of investor returns when survival is an issue. As our analysis in the previous section demonstrates, markets that die tend to have less weight when they do so.

The indices represent the return an investor would have earned had it been possible to hold the market since the 1920s. This is a hypothetical experiment, however, because it would have been difficult to maintain such a

Table 16.5
Relative Importance of Economies (Percentage Weights Based on U.S. Dollar Prices)

Country	GDP Weights			Stock Market Capitalization 1995
	1920	1950	1990	
United States	46.17%	51.52%	30.59%	41.03%
Canada	2.40%	3.16%	3.17%	2.16%
Austria	0.48%	0.47%	0.87%	0.24%
Belgium	0.73%	1.27%	1.09%	0.66%
Denmark	0.55%	0.56%	0.72%	0.37%
Finland	0.17%	0.42%	0.76%	0.26%
France	6.14%	5.19%	6.61%	3.27%
Germany	6.04%	4.19%	8.29%	3.75%
Ireland	0.42%	0.19%	0.24%	0.16%
Italy	1.67%	2.43%	6.07%	1.16%
Netherlands	0.98%	0.89%	1.57%	1.97%
Norway	0.56%	0.38%	0.59%	0.28%
Portugal	0.62%	0.25%	0.33%	0.12%
Spain	2.16%	0.82%	2.72%	0.99%
Sweden	1.22%	1.11%	1.26%	1.14%
Switzerland	0.84%	0.80%	1.25%	2.60%
United Kingdom	10.36%	6.57%	5.41%	8.77%
Czechoslovakia	0.52%	0.31%	0.25%	0.10%
Greece	0.33%	0.39%	0.37%	0.11%
Hungary	0.38%	0.71%	0.18%	0.02%
Poland	1.82%	0.35%	0.03%	
Romania		0.00%	0.21%	

portfolio. Constraints on cross-border capital flows and on liquidation of equity positions were acute during crises—precisely the times when the ability to diversify is most beneficial. In this period, investors were sometimes involuntarily separated from their assets, due to expropriations or nationalizations. As a result, it is not clear whether, for example, a U.S. investor could have continued to hold German or Japanese equities during World War II.

Table 16.5 presents the GDP weights at three points in time: 1920, 1950, and 1990. The table reveals a number of interesting observations. The United States accounts for about one-half of the world's output until the 1950s; the proportion then declines to approximately 30 percent. This decline is due to faster growth in other countries such as Japan and Germany. Japan, in particular, zooms from 4 percent of world GDP to 16 percent over this period, even after dipping below 2 percent after the war.

The GDP-based weights can be compared to stock market capitalization-based weights, which are reported in the last column. We observe that the stock market capitalization percentages of the United States, the United Kingdom, Japan, and South Africa are generally greater than those of other coun-

Table 16.5 (*continued*)
Relative Importance of Economies (Percentage Weights Based on U.S. Dollar Prices)

Country	GDP Weights			Stock Market Capitalization 1995
	1920	1950	1990	
Australia	2.31%	1.07%	1.63%	1.59%
New Zealand	0.15%	0.35%	0.24%	0.21%
Japan	4.06%	1.96%	16.24%	23.19%
India	6.92%	3.54%	1.68%	0.82%
Pakistan		0.67%	0.22%	0.06%
Philippines		0.63%	0.24%	0.38%
Argentina	1.20%	0.90%	0.78%	0.24%
Brazil	0.75%	2.84%	2.66%	0.96%
Mexico	0.66%	0.85%	1.34%	0.59%
Chile	0.19%	0.75%	0.15%	0.48%
Colombia		0.72%	0.22%	0.12%
Peru		0.19%	0.20%	0.08%
Uruguay		0.18%	0.05%	0.00%
Venezuela		0.57%	0.27%	0.02%
Egypt		0.45%	0.31%	0.05%
Israel		0.24%	0.29%	0.24%
South Africa	1.03%	0.65%	0.56%	1.82%
Memorandum:				
GDP (millions)	$198,200	$556.500	$18,049,700	
Market cap (m)				$15,448,900

Notes: The table describes the percentage of each country in the total Gross Domestic Product (GDP) in 1920, 1950, and 1990. The last column shows the percentage weight based on stock market capitalization.

tries. Continental Europe, for example, has a history of relying on bank lending rather than raising funds through capital issues. Overall, however, the GDP weights are roughly of the same order of magnitude as market weights.

Biases can be introduced in the measured performance in a number of ways. The first is backfilling, and the second is due to interruptions. There is not much the researcher can do about backfilling if the series are the only ones available. As for interruptions, the problem is that data before the interruption are commonly ignored. Interruptions can be of two types: temporary closure of an exchange, with the series starting again later, or permanent interruption of these series, with no information about the continuity of prices across the interruption.

We take two approaches to the construction of the global index:

(i) Our "survived markets" index includes all markets since the last interruption, which can be a temporary break or a permanent closure; only markets in existence at the end of the sample are considered. As of De-

Table 16.6
Performance of Global Stock Index: 1921–1996 (Real Returns in Percentage per Annum)

Index	Arithmetic Return	Risk	Monthly Sharpe	Geometric Return	Ending Wealth
U.S. index	5.48	15.83	0.0999	4.32	27.3
Global index					
Survived markets	4.98	12.08	0.1190	4.33	27.3
All markets	4.59	11.05	0.1199	4.04	21.9
Non-U.S. index					
Survived markets	4.52	10.02	0.1301	4.09	22.2
All markets	3.84	9.96	0.1114	3.39	13.1

Notes: The table displays the risk and return of real returns on stock market indices, measured in excess of the Wholesale Price Index inflation. Arithmetic return is obtained from the monthly average multiplied by twelve; risk is monthly volatility multiplied by the square root of twelve; Sharpe ratio is the ratio of monthly average to monthly volatility; geometric return uses annual compounding. Ending wealth reports the final value of $1 invested on December 1920 at the end of the sample. "Survived markets" series includes only markets in our sample in existence in 1996, taken since the last interruption (temporary or permanent). "All markets" series accounts for all markets in the sample, imputing a 75 percent loss in the month the series permanently disappears, or the actual loss spread over the period of the break.

cember 1996, we have a total of 32 markets, of which only 18 had continuous histories to December 1940, for instance.

(ii) Our "all markets" index extends the sample to all markets in existence in our sample, including returns before temporary and permanent closures. As of December 1940, this "comprehensive" series yields 29 markets, adding Austria, Belgium, and France (which suffered a temporary interruption of trading during World War II), Chile, Germany, Japan, Portugal, Uruguay, and three markets that suffered a permanent break during the war: Czechoslovakia, Hungary, and Romania.

We expect the bias to decrease as we move from (i) to (ii). The difficult part, of course, is to estimate market losses during a permanent interruption such as war or nationalization. We have 11 occurrences of permanent breaks (or "deaths") out of our sample of 39 markets. For some of these, such as Germany, Japan, Portugal, we are able to trace the fall in value, which we evenly spread over the time period of the interruption. This smoothing preserves the geometric return, but induces an artificially low volatility and therefore increases the arithmetic return. We should note, however, that the same problem occurs when reported prices are controlled or do not represent transaction data. For the few remaining markets that suffered a permanent interruption, we assume that the market fell by 75 percent the following month.[19]

Table 16.6 presents the performance of the various global stock indices. We focus on performance data first and discuss volatility later. Over the past

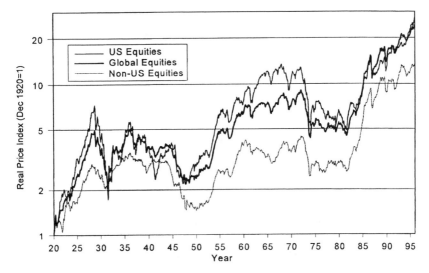

Figure 16.4. A Global Stock Market Index
Notes: The figure displays the performance of the U.S. global, and non-U.S. real capital growth indices. The latter indices are obtained using GDP weights and all existing markets, even if they fail later.

76 years, the U.S. stock market provided an arithmetic capital return of 5.48 percent, measured in real terms. Its geometric growth was 4.32 percent over this period. Figure 16.4 plots the performance of the U.S., global, and non-U.S. real capital growth indices (using the comprehensive series).

The differences in the performance of the global indices point to the importance of accounting for losing markets. The "survived markets" index has a compound return of 4.33 percent; it accounts only for markets in existence in 1996 and examined since their last break. The "all markets" index has a compound return of 4.04 percent; it accounts for all markets and attempts to interpolate returns over major breaks in the series. Going from the first to the second estimate should move us closer to a true, unbiased measure of long-term return.

At first sight, the difference between the long-term performance of the U.S. index and of the global comprehensive index appears to be small, at only 29 basis points. This result may appear puzzling in light of the evidence in Table 16.1 that all non-U.S. markets have lower long-term growth than the United States, often significantly so. One reason for the narrow difference lies in the temporal variation in weights. Consider the Japanese market, for instance. In the first half of the century, the performance of Japanese equities was mediocre. At that time the market carried a weight of less than 4 percent in the global index. In the second half of the century, however, Japanese equities outperformed U.S. equities, precisely at a time when their weight in the index was rising, reaching 16 percent in 1990. Another reason is the large weight in the

Table 16.7

Performance of Global Stock Index: 1921–1996 (Nominal Returns in U.S. Dollars, Percentage per Annum)

Index	Arithmetic Return	Risk	Monthly Sharpe	Geometric Return	Ending Wealth
U.S. index	8.04	16.19	0.1433	6.95	171.2
Global index					
Survived markets	7.98	13.34	0.1728	7.32	222.9
All markets	7.76	12.14	0.1845	7.25	211.2
Non-U.S. index					
Survived markets	7.53	12.17	0.1785	7.00	176.5
All markets	7.28	12.08	0.1740	6.75	146.2

Notes: The table displays the risk and return of dollar returns on stock market indices, translated into U.S. dollars at the official rate. Arithmetic return is obtained from the monthly average multiplied by 12; risk is monthly volatility multiplied by the square root of 12; Sharpe ratio is the ratio of monthly average to monthly volatility; geometric return uses annual compounding. Ending wealth reports the final value of $1 invested in December 1920 at the end of the sample. "Survived markets" series includes only markets in our sample in existence in 1996, taken since the last interruption (temporary or permanent). "All markets" series accounts for all markets in the sample, imputing a 75 percent loss in the month the series permanently disappears, or the actual loss spread over the period of the break.

U.S. market at the beginning of the century. Consider, for example, a $100 investment in global stocks starting in 1921. From the GDP weights in Table 16.5, the amount to allocate to U.S. stocks was $46.17. Over the next 76 years, this amount grew to $1,149, using the 4.32 percent U.S. growth rate. Let us make now an extreme assumption, which is that all of the money invested outside the United States is lost. Using the $1,149-to-$100 ratio, the rate of growth is still 3.26 percent. The large initial size of the U.S. market therefore ensures that the growth on the global index must be within 100 basis points of the U.S. growth number.

The last column in Table 16.6 shows that a difference of 29 basis points can be quite significant over 76 years. Assuming a dollar invested in the U.S. index and in the comprehensive global index, the investments would have grown to 27.3 and 21.9 in real terms, which is a substantial difference.

Table 16.6 also shows that a non-U.S. stock market index, based on our "comprehensive" measure, has grown at the rate of 3.39 percent, which is a full 93 basis points below U.S. equities. If one ignores survivorship issues, however, the return of the non-U.S. index appears to be 4.09 percent. Survival bias therefore induces a difference of 70 basis points in this index, which is quite substantial when accumulated over 76 years.

Table 16.7 presents similar data, measured in nominal U.S. dollars. Over 1921 to 1996, the compound capital return on U.S. equities was 6.95 percent. The return on the global survived index was 7.32 percent; the return on the global comprehensive index was 7.25 percent. Similarly, the average return on the non-U.S. index was 7.00 percent and 6.75 percent. Here the survival bias is on the order of 25 basis points.

As in Table 16.1, we observe that the difference between U.S. and non-U.S. returns is smaller when returns are measured in dollars instead of in real terms. In fact, the return on the unbiased global index is now variation in weights and the real appreciation of most other currencies discussed previously. Also, the return on the value-weighted global index appears not too sensitive to the survivorship issue.

Tables 16.6 and 16.7 also provide estimates of the volatility of the various indices. Using real returns, the volatility of the U.S. index is 15.8 percent. All other indices display lower volatility. For instance, the volatility of the non-U.S. indices is about 10 percent, which is much lower than that of the U.S. market alone, reflecting the fact that the portfolio is spread over a greater number of markets, thus benefiting from imperfect correlations across markets. Next, the risk of our global indices is also driven by correlations. Over the 76 years, the correlation coefficient between returns on the U.S. index and on the comprehensive non-U.S. index is 0.460 in real terms and about the same, 0.452, in dollar terms.[20] As a result of lower volatility for foreign markets and a low correlation coefficient, the risk of the global portfolio is substantially lower than that of U.S. equities. The "comprehensive" global index, for example, displays a volatility of 11.05 percent. Based on these long-term series, the main benefit of going international appears to be risk reduction rather than increased returns.

Taking into account survivorship decreases returns slightly, but also decreases volatility. This is partly due to the (artificial) interpolation of returns when markets are closed, but also because of additional diversification resulting from the inclusion of more markets. We measure the trade-off between risk and return with the Sharpe ratio, defined as average monthly returns divided by their volatility. These are reported in the third columns of Tables 16.6 and 16.7. With real returns, the Sharpe ratio of the global index is 0.1199, which is higher than that of U.S. equities at 0.0999. With dollar returns, the Sharpe ratio of the global indices is about 0.1845, also higher than that of U.S. equities, at 0.1433. These differences, however, are not statistically significant.[21]

Systematic differences in return can be attributed to two classes of explanations. The first is survivorship, an ex post explanation. The second is rational, ex ante, differences in risk profiles. For example, if markets can be viewed as integrated, a higher return for U.S. equities could be explained by the fact that the U.S. market has a higher world β. Indeed, over the 1921–1996 period, U.S. equities had the highest β, with a value of 1.24. A regression of real returns on real betas reveals a correlation of 0.53, which is significantly positive.

Testing this proposition is not straightforward because estimation of β with respect to the world index depends on survival issues as well. Had the outcome of the Second World War been different, for example, the β of the United States on the world index would likely have been different. The regression is also afflicted by data and econometric problems. The variables are

estimated over different periods and thus have quite different sampling variability. Additionally, the betas that include periods of price controls or infrequent trading are not reliable. Thus it seems difficult to disentangle the higher
systematic risk explanation from survivorship to explain the high returns on
U.S. equities.

To understand the momentous implications of differences in long-term
rates of return reported here, consider the following experiment. First, let us
record the current capitalization of non-U.S. equity markets, which was approximately $9,000 billion at the end of 1996. From Table 16.6, these markets
have grown at an average rate of 3.39 percent, which is less than the 4.32 percent growth rate for the United States. Going back to 1921, this implies that
the market capitalization of non-U.S. equities was $9,000 billion divided by
$(1 + 3.39\%)^{76}$, which amounts to $714 billion in current dollars.

Next, assume that all markets have grown at the U.S. rate of growth. The
market value of these equities would then be $714 billion times $(1 + 4.32\%)^{76}$,
which amounts to $17,775 billion. In other words, the opportunity cost of
growing at about 3.4 percent instead of the 4.3 percent U.S. rate is $8,775 bil-
lion in today's dollars. Foreign markets would be double their current size if
they had grown only 1 percent faster than they did. Viewed in this context,
survival biases of 70 basis points recorded in Table 16.6 are quite significant.

▲ Conclusion

"Financial archaeology" involves digging through reams of financial data in
search for answers. Sometimes this involves relying on poor quality data from
which to draw inferences about markets in states of crisis. Even so, these data
provide invaluable information to help understand long-term histories of capital markets. If one relies on historical data as the basis for estimates of long-
term market growth, there is no reason to look at U.S. data only. This is why
our paper paints a broad picture of the performance of global stock markets
over more than 75 years of a turbulent century for financial markets.

The main lesson from our long-term data is that global capital markets
have been systematically subject to dramatic changes over this century. Major
disruptions have afflicted nearly all the markets in our sample, with the exception of a few such as the United States. Markets have been closed or sus-
pended due to financial crises, wars, expropriations, or political upheaval.

No doubt this explains our finding that the 4.3 percent real capital appreciation return on U.S. stocks is rather exceptional, as other markets have
typically had a median return of only 0.8 percent. These results suggest that
the large equity premium obtained in the United States is at least partly the result of conditioning estimates on the best performing market. This conditioning may also create time-variation in expected returns; for instance, we expect markets that have done well to exhibit more mean-reversion than others
because periods of large losses must be followed by periods of upswings.[22]

This line of analysis treats each market separately. Another approach is to track the hypothetical performance of a diversified global investment. Interestingly, we find that the performance of a globally diversified portfolio is much closer to the performance of U.S. equities, averaging 4.0 percent. This is partly because markets with large capitalization at the beginning of the century performed well. This result also reflects the benefits of diversification, which spreads the risk of dramatic events over a large portfolio.

Whether similar disruptions will happen again is an open question. By now, however, it should be clear that if we fail to account for the "losers" as well as the "winners" in global equity markets, we are providing a biased view of history which ignores important information about actual investment risk.

◣ Notes

1. See Epstein and Zin (1991) for nonadditive utility functions and Constantinides (1987) for habit formation. Bansal and Coleman (1996) suggest that liquidity services provided by cash partly explain why returns on cash are so low.

2. Burnside and McCurdy (1992) provide a good review of the equity premium puzzle.

3. A similar argument is advanced by Goetzmann and Jorion (1996). They argue that many so-called "emerging markets" are in fact "reemerging markets" as they have longer histories than commonly believed. Few analysts, however, bother to track the histories of markets that have disappeared.

4. For evidence on long-term U.S. data, see Wilson and Jones (1987), Schwert (1990), Siegel (1992), and Goetzmann and Ibbotson (1994). There is some long-term evidence from the U.K. markets; for instance, see Goetzmann (1993), DeLong and Grossman (1993), and Goetzmann and Jorion (1995). Parsons (1974), Mirowski (1981), and Neal (1987, 1990) provide data on the Amsterdam and London exchanges in the 18th century.

5. Relative to more modern data, the IFS data suffer from two drawbacks: possible noncomparability in the construction of the series and use of monthly average instead of end-month price. The Cowles indices, the standard data source before 1926 for U.S. data, however, have similar drawbacks because prices are measured as the average of high and low values during the month.

6. There are a few instances where we have to use Consumer Price Index data (e.g., post-1947 data for Belgium, France, New Zealand, Peru, and Israel). Because nominal prices in Germany were distorted during the hyperinflation period, we measure nominal prices for 1921–1923 in gold marks.

7. Alfred Cowles, founder of the Cowles Commission for Research in Economics, was apparently the first scholar to document time-series data on global stock markets. We learned of the League of Nations data from the appendix to his 1939 publication which lists periodical sources for stock market data in 20 countries. A recent source of global stock market information which uses the League of Nations data, as well as information from other historical sources, is the Global Financial Markets database collected by Bryan Taylor, which we learned of after submission of this paper for publication. Taylor's database covers similar markets to ours; there are, however, some differences in the data sources and in particular during the breaks. For instance, we find the German stock price data collected by Gielen (1994) to be an excellent source for reconstruction of the German markets during the early part of the 20th century.

8. The measurement of exchange rates also proves quite difficult. The League of Nations, for instance, reports rates in percentage of their 1929 gold parity value, from which current spot rates relative to the dollar have to be reconstructed. Many currencies also changed units or denominations during this century. Around World War II, trading in some currency pairs was either nonexistent or subject to heavy governmental control.

9. The only market we deliberately omit is Lebanon, for which we cannot find inflation data.

10. The difference can be particularly pronounced over short periods when the data are monthly or annual averages. As an illustration, comparing returns on the S&P index total returns series over 1926–1945, we find the annual growth to be 7.2 percent and 6.6 percent, respectively, for monthly and annual data.

11. We have permanent gaps in the series for Chile, Germany, Japan, Peru, Portugal, and Argentina. The gap for Chile is filled using data from publications from the Chilean Central Bank. The gap for Germany is covered using data spliced by Gielen (1994). The gap for Japan is bridged using Bank of Japan (1966) data. The gap for Peru is filled using data received by the Lima stock exchange. To cover the gap for Portugal, we use information from the Portuguese Central Bank. Overall, Argentina is the only remaining country with a permanent break over July 1965 to December 1975, which is the first date for which we have data from the IFC. We have been unable to find data to bridge the gap.

12. Uruguay and Czechoslovakia had higher returns than U.S. equities, but this was over shorter periods during which currencies were subject to controls; hence, these returns are not representative.

13. Since price data are monthly averages, it should be noted that the reported standard deviations are lower than those from using month-end data. Additionally, averaging induces spurious positive autocorrelation in the return series.

14. Data sources are as follows: For the U.S. market, Ibbotson (1995) and prior to that, Cowles (1939); for the United Kingdom, Barclays deZoete Wedd (1993); for Switzerland, Wydler (1989); for Sweden, Frenneberg and Hansson (1992); and for Denmark, Timmerman (1992). All of the data have been updated to 1995 using the MSCIP indices.

15. In Germany, Italy, and German-occupied territories, dealing in shares was subject to strict controls, ranging from taxes on profits and capital gains to the rationing of purchases and to the compulsory declaration of securities holdings. In June 1942, for instance, the sale of German shares became prohibited unless they were first offered to the Reichsbank. The Reichsbank had the option to buy them at December 1941 prices in exchange for bonds that remained in the bank's possession. It is no wonder that this confiscatory system led to a sharp fall in trading activity. There were also rigid price controls in Japan during the war; see for instance Adams and Hoshii (1971). Therefore many of these price indices do not represent market-determined prices.

16. The index for occupied countries includes Belgium, Czechoslovakia, France, Denmark, Finland, Germany, Hungary, Italy, Netherlands, and Norway.

17. The Bank of Japan (1966) estimates that the material damage due to World War II was to reduce national wealth from 253 to 189 billion yen, which is a fall of 64 billion yen (not accounting for human losses), or about $15 billion. For comparison purposes, the market value of equities in 1945 was about 40 billion yen.

18. The market lost 54 percent in the year to April 1971 during the Allende ascent to power, but then increased by 62 percent later, which is only a partial recovery. Assuming a starting value of 100, the market fell to 46, then recovered to 1.62 times 46, or 74, ending with a net loss in value relative to the starting point.

19. The markets affected were Czechoslovakia, Egypt, Greece, Hungary, Poland, and Romania. The 75 percent imputed drop is in line with the fall in value of markets that suffered a severe breakdown. The arbitrariness of the charge is mitigated by the fact that all of these markets are relative small.

20. As for the measurement of volatilities, correlations may be too low because of the smoothing of the series during the breaks. However, the correlation with the survived series is very close, at 0.510 in real terms and 0.520 in dollars. This suggests that the bias is not large.

21. Using the performance tests developed by Jobson and Korkie (1981).

22. Goetzmann and Jorion (1995) also show that survival should induce other effects of interest, such as predictability based on dividend yields.

▲ References

Adams, Thomas, and Iwao Hoshii, 1971, *A Financial History of the New Japan* (Kodansha, Tokyo, Japan).

Bank of Japan, 1966, *A Hundred Years of Statistics of Japanese Economy* (Bank of Japan, Tokyo, Japan).

Bansal, Ravi, and Wilbur Coleman, 1996, A monetary explanation of the equity premium, term premium, and risk-free rate puzzles, *Journal of Political Economy* 104, 1135–1171.

Barclays de Zoete Wedd, 1993, The BZW Equity Gilt Study: Investment in the London Stock Market Since 1918 (Barclays deZoete Wedd, London, United Kingdom).

Brown, Stephen J., William Goetzmann, and Stephen Ross, 1995, Survival, *Journal of Finance* 50, 853–873.

Burnside, Craig, and Thomas McCurdy, 1992, The equity premium puzzle; in Peter Newman, Murray Milgate, and John Eatwell, eds.: *The New Palgrave Dictionary of Money and Finance* (Stockton Press, New York).

Constantinides, George, 1987, Habit formation: A resolution of the equity premium puzzle, *Journal of Political Economy* 98, 519–543.

Cowles, Alfred, 1939, *Common Stock Indices, 1871–1937* (Cowles Commission for Research in Economics, Monograph no. 3, Principia Press, Bloomington, Ind.).

Epstein, Larry, and Stanley Zin, 1991, Substitution, risk aversion and the temporal behaviour of consumption and asset returns: An empirical investigation, *Journal of Political Economy* 99, 263–286.

Frenneberg, Per, and Bjorn Hansson, 1992, Swedish stocks, bonds, bills, and inflation (1919–1990), *Applied Financial Economics* 2, 79–86.

Gielen, Gregor, 1994, *Konnen Aktienkurse Noch Steigen?* (Gabler, Wiesbaden, Germany).

Goetzmann, William N., 1993, Patterns in three centuries of stock market prices, *Journal of Business* 66, 249–270.

Goetzmann, William N., and Roger Ibbotson, 1994, An emerging market, the New York Stock Exchange 1816–1872, *Journal of Business* 68, 483–508.

Goetzmann, William N., and Philippe Jorion, 1995, A longer look at dividend yields, *Journal of Business* 68, 483–508.

Goetzmann, William N., and Philippe Jorion, 1997, Re-emerging markets, (mimeo) University of California at Irvine.

Ibbotson, Roger, 1995, *Stocks, Bonds, Bills, and Inflation: 1995 Yearbook* (Ibbotson Associates, Chicago, Ill.).

International Conference of Economic Services, 1934, *International Abstract of Economic Statistics* (ICES, London, United Kingdom).

International Conference of Economic Services, 1938, *International Abstract of Economic Statistics* (International Statistical Institute, Permanent Office, The Hague, The Netherlands).

International Finance Corporation, 1995, *The IFC Indexes: Methodology, Definitions, and Practices* (International Finance Corporation, Washington, DC).

International Monetary Fund, various issues, *International Financial Statistics* (International Monetary Fund, Washington, D.C.).

Jobson, J. D., and B. Korkie, 1981, Performance hypothesis testing with the Sharpe and Treynor measures, *Journal of Finance* 36, 888–908.

League of Nations, various issues, *Statistical Yearbook* (League of Nations, Geneva, Switzerland).

Mehra, Rajnish, and Edward Prescott, 1985, The equity premium: A puzzle, *Journal of Monetary Economics* 15, 145–161.

Mehra, Rajnish, and Edward Prescott, 1988, The equity premium: A puzzle? *Journal of Monetary Economics* 22, 133–136.

Mirowski, Philip, 1981, The risk (and retreat) of a market: English joint stock shares in the eighteenth century, *Journal of Economic History* 41, 559–577.

Mitchell, Brian, 1992, *International Historical Statistics: Europe, 1750–1988* (Stockton Press, New York).

Mitchell, Brian, 1993, *International Historical Statistics: The Americas, 1750–1988* (Stockton Press, New York).

Neal, Larry, 1987, The integration and efficiency of the London and Amsterdam stock markets in the eighteenth century, *Journal of Economic History* 47, 97–115.

Neal, Larry, 1990, *The Rise of Financial Capitalism: International Capital Markets in the Age of Reason* (Cambridge University Press, Cambridge, Mass.).

Parsons, Brian, 1974, The behavior of prices on the London stock market in the early eighteenth century, Ph.D. dissertation, University of Chicago.

Rietz, Thomas, 1988, The equity premium: A solution. *Journal of Monetary Economics* 22, 117–131.

Schwert, William, 1990, Indexes of U.S. stock prices from 1802 to 1987, *Journal of Business* 63, 399–426.

Siegel, Jeremy, 1992, The equity premium: Stock and bond returns since 1802, *Financial Analysts Journal* 48, 28–38.

Siegel, Jeremy, 1994, *Stocks for the Long Run* (Richard D. Irwin, New York).

Timmerman, Allan, 1992, Changes in Danish stock prices 1914–1990, *Nationalokonomisk Tidsskrift* 130, 473–482.

United Nations, various issues, *Monthly Bulletin of Statistics* (United Nations, New York).

Wilson, Jack, and Charles Jones, 1987, A comparison of annual common stock returns, *Journal of Business* 60, 239–258.

Wydler, Daniel, 1989, Swiss stocks, bonds, and inflation: 1926–1987, *Journal of Portfolio Management* 15, 27–32.

17 William N. Goetzmann and Philippe Jorion

Re-Emerging Markets

▶ Overview

Thanks in large measure to the International Financial Corporation's efforts to identify and gather data on the markets of developing countries, investors over the past 20 years have grown increasingly interested in emerging markets. Suppose we simply defined an emerging market as one that has been continuously "investable" for only a short period of time—that is, it recently emerged. Can we infer anything about its risk and return characteristics? In this article we use a simulation model to argue that recent emergence can potentially reveal a great deal about the statistical properties of a market. In particular, if a market popped up recently, we would expect it to have a low future return, high volatility, and low correlation to the world markets. The importance of this article is that we identify emerging markets as "marginal markets" in the world economy—valuable for diversification, but not obviously attractive for expected return.

▶ Abstract

Recent research shows that emerging markets are distinguished by high returns and low covariances with global market factors. To check whether these results can be attributed to their recent emergence, we simulate a simple, general model of global markets with a realistic survival process. The simulations reveal a number of new effects. We find that pre-emergence returns are systematically lower than post-emergence returns, and that the brevity of a market history is related to the bias in returns as well as to the world beta. These patterns are confirmed by an empirical analysis of emerging and submerged markets.

▶ Introduction

The last 20 years of capital market history have witnessed a dramatic expansion of opportunity for global investors, led primarily by *emerging markets* in Asia, South America, Africa, the Middle East, and Eastern Europe. In many countries, equity markets have grown rapidly from tiny, fledgling markets with little volume and limited international participation to important sources of capital with short but impressive track records of share price appreciation. Although the fundamental shift in the global political environment is undoubtedly a major factor in the growth of emerging markets, consideration of a longer term view is worthwhile.

In this article, we show that markets tend to emerge, submerge, and re-emerge through time. Consider, for instance, the case of Argentina. Even though the Argentinian stock market is usually classified as emerging, it actually dates back to 1872. Since it emerged in 1975, this market has grown at an average compound rate of 27% per annum, measured in dollars. However, collecting data before the market disappeared reveals a less than stellar performance, with a real share price growth of −24% per annum from 1947 to 1965.

We argue that many of today's emerging markets are actually *re-emerging markets*, i.e., were large enough to be included in previous databases, but for one reason or another disappeared from sight. China, Malaysia, India, Egypt, Poland, Romania, Czechoslovakia, Colombia, Uruguay, Chile, Venezuela, and Mexico all had active equity markets in the 1920s. Many of these markets were large enough to attract foreign investors as well as significant enough to have share price indices reported in international publications. For various political, economic, and institutional reasons, investors lost interest in these markets, which then submerged (or disappeared), and re-emerged only recently. Not surprisingly, performance since the last emergence is invariably higher than before emergence. This disparity has serious implications for the performance evaluation of emerging markets.

For example, recent research using short-term, high quality emerging market data collected by the International Finance Corporation (IFC) shows that emerging markets are distinguished by, among other things, high returns and low covariances with global market factors.[1] This is a striking result because of its immediate implications for the international investor. Emerging markets appear to be very attractive investments since they provide very large expected returns, with or without adjusting for systematic risk. Bekaert and Harvey (1995) suggest that the apparent contradiction between low factor loadings and high ex post market returns may be due to the pricing of local factors preceding full emergence and integration into the global market.[2] In other words, a global investor with the ability to diversify idiosyncratic risk may take advantage of higher returns demanded by local, poorly diversified investors. Perhaps this free-lunch hypothesis explains why net private capital flows into emerging countries have reached $240 billion in 1996, a six-fold increase since 1990.[3] A contrasting view is that these stylized empirical facts may be due, in part, to conditioning the data analysis on recent emergence—the key issue addressed in this article.

The potential for certain biases related to emerging markets has already been noted in the literature. In particular, Harvey (1995) observes that high means may be partially due to the practice of backfilling indices. Brown, Goetzmann, and Ross (1995) (BGR, hereafter) provide a general solution for the bias in the mean of a diffusion price path that survives any sample selection criterion as well as an analytical solution for the simple case of survival above an absorbing lower bound. In this model, markets all start at the same time, have the same expected returns, and disappear in a "down and out" process. They show that high ex post means and a convex price pattern are direct consequences of survival.[4]

Unfortunately, there is no analytical result for more complex conditioning processes. We expect markets to start at various points in time, to display different expected returns, to have different risk characteristics, and to be censored after the last emergence. Thus, the current paper explores the effects of using a "last time up" survival process. In particular, we model a price threshold that does not eliminate markets, but instead simply determines how far back historically a time series can be constructed (or is kept) from the present. In other words, we condition upon the ability of the researcher to backfill a continuous series. Because of the lack of analytical solutions, we generate simulations of a global markets model that is quite general. The simulations also provide additional hypotheses which we test with historical data.

Our simulations also show that this type of conditioning induces additional effects of interest. We find that conditioning upon market history, where *history* is defined as the length of time since the market has emerged, should result in a number of empirical regularities. Among other things, the brevity of a market history should be closely related to the bias in annual returns imparted by survivorship, as well as to the low level of covariance with the rest of the markets. These findings are potentially useful for international investors, because *merely knowing that a market has recently emerged* contains information about the future distribution, as well as about its future prospects for survival. Our analysis combines the usual survival effects with new "sorting" effects that are due to inherent differences in expected returns across markets. Given that markets can, in theory, emerge at any point in time, markets that emerge late are more likely to have low true expected returns. Thus, time tends to sort markets by expected returns. These effects interact with each other to create a situation where recently emerged markets have a low unconditional mean.

Second, we provide historical evidence on the extent of survivor conditioning among global markets over the long term. We find that global market data from standard sources are typically characterized by interruptions, reflecting the fact that collecting return data on submerged markets is not an easy matter when investors have lost interest and/or the market has closed. Turning to recent, high quality IFC data, we provide evidence of empirical regularities consistent with the simulations. In particular, we find that returns are greatest and betas low when markets have just emerged. Cumulative returns after emergence display the convex pattern predicted from simulations. Alternatively, these results can be explained by a number of other hypotheses, such as structural changes in emerging economies or price pressures due to the at-

From Colonialization to Globalization

The most striking thing for us to find in the research for this article was the relative age of many of today's emerging markets. We knew of the interrupted 180-year history of the Russian market, and the interrupted 130-year history of the Chinese market, but it was remarkable to learn that many stock markets were founded in countries around the world in the middle and late 19th century—from Southeast Asia to Eastern Europe to South America, capital markets sprung up to trade colonial and domestic market shares, even when an international market for these securities often existed concurrently in London, Brussels, and Paris. The long history of markets in the world puts a different perspective on emerging market investing. The early period of market emergence happened at the apex of European colonial expansion, a process that not only extended European political rule, but also extended European legal codes and financial practices. At its worst, this expansion through the 19th century led to egregious exploitation practiced by such firms as the L'Etat Independent du Congo, which licensed ivory and rubber concessions to companies that mercilessly decimated the native Congo population in their quest for riches. At their best, they provided a framework for preservation of property rights and a climate of capitalism that benefited economic development in the post-colonial era. "Re-emerging" markets have finally begun to reconstitute themselves after the long hiatus of the mid-20th century, but the global framework is vastly different. Colonial empires were loosely affiliated trading networks, often linked by a central money-center financial market. Today's emerging stock markets are, to some extent, an independent apparatus, encouraged but not necessarily supported by the IFC. We may be optimistic about their rebirth, but we should try to understand the political and economic forces that led to their demise in the 20th century, and seek to guard against its happening again. For the analyst interested in estimating the equity premium from these markets, a fundamental question is whether the risk and return characteristics of the markets during the colonial era (or pre–Iron Curtain era) may be taken as representative of the future. Does the very long-term perspective help estimate the future investment characteristics for these markets? We shall have to wait and see.

tention brought by official recognition of a market. The common message, however, is that historical performance will be a poor guide to future returns.

This article is organized as follows. To introduce the issue of survivorship, the second section reviews the literature and presents some evidence from long-term market histories. The third section discusses the process by which markets typically emerge and how this is modeled in our simulations. Results are presented in the fourth section. In the fifth section, we provide performance results for the so-called emerging markets from the last 20 years. The sixth section contains some concluding comments.

Table 17.1
Time Line of Stock Market Founding Dates

The Netherlands	1611	Brazil	1877	The Philippines	1927
Germany	1685	India	1877	Colombia	1929
United Kingdom	1698	Norway	1881	Luxembourg	1929
Austria	1771	South Africa	1887	Malaysia	1929
United States	1792	Egypt	1890	Romania	1929
Ireland	1799	Hong Kong	1890	Israel	1934
Belgium	1801	Chile	1892	Pakistan	1947
Denmark	1808	Greece	1892	Venezuela	1947
Italy	1808	Venezuela	1893	Lebanon	1948
France	1826	Mexico	1894	Taiwan	1953
Switzerland	1850	Yugoslavia	1894	Kenya	1954
Spain	1860	Sri Lanka	1900	Nigeria	1960
Hungary	1864	Portugal	1901	Kuwait	1962
Turkey	1866	Sweden	1901	Thailand	1975
Australia	1871	Singapore	1911		
Czechoslovakia	1871	Finland	1912		
Poland	1871	Indonesia	1912		
Argentina	1872	Korea	1921		
New Zealand	1872	Slovenia	1924		
Canada	1874	Uruguay	1926		

Notes: This table compiles the founding dates of exchanges in cities currently within the borders of the identified countries, in chronological order up to 1975, when standard databases started. Only countries which today have significant equity markets are included in the group, so this sample is subject to selection bias. For instance, it contains no information about Russian exchange(s) and Baltic exchanges. Sources are O'Conner and Smith (1992) and Park and Van Agtmael (1993).

◤ Emergence and Survivorship

Stock Market Histories

In this article, we define an emerging market as a stock market in a developing country that is included in a current major database such as the one maintained by the IFC. In practice, the criterion for inclusion is related to an increase in market capitalization, which must have reached a minimum threshold. The time of emergence is defined as the first date for which an index is computed. This criterion corresponds to the actual performance reporting period for emerging markets. Many of these markets, however, have been around for much longer than is commonly assumed.

Table 17.1 provides a partial list of the founding dates of the world's stock exchanges. It is based upon information in two well-known guides to global stock markets, Park and Van Agtmael (1993) and O'Conner and Smith

(1992). Both of these sources collect information about market histories from currently operating stock exchanges around the world. Because countries without current exchanges are not included, Table 17.1's list of the markets that existed at one time is presumably incomplete.[5] However, even this partial list is interesting because it tells us just how much *we do not know* about equity markets. Of the 40 markets that were founded before the 20th century, only two, the U.S. and the U.K. markets, have been extensively analyzed over long investment horizons. This is not from lack of interest, but from lack of data. While econometricians in the U.S. and the U.K. have compiled reliable price information stretching back into the 19th and 18th centuries, comparable information has only recently become available for other markets such as Germany, France, and Switzerland, albeit with notable gaps due to wars. Even so, this table is informative.

Table 17.1 indicates that *most* of today's stock exchanges have long histories. Many non-European markets began under the aegis of colonial rule, including Hong Kong, India, Pakistan, Sri Lanka, Indonesia, South Africa, Egypt, and Singapore, and have continued with or without interruption to the present. Other markets only recently emerged from communist rule—Hungary, Czechoslovakia, Poland, Romania, and Yugoslavia. Perhaps most surprising is the number of South and Central American countries with long market histories; Argentina, Brazil, Colombia, Uruguay, Mexico, and Venezuela all have had equity markets for more than 60 years.

The League of Nations collected data on the capital appreciation of market indices in the period from 1929 through 1944. This collection effort was continued by the U.N. Using these and other sources, Jorion and Goetzmann (1999) collected a sample of long-term capital appreciation indices for 40 countries with histories from 1921 to 1996.

Interruptions in the series were due to a number of factors, including wars, expropriation, hyperinflation, and political changes. The early price data indicate that hyperinflation closed the Danish and German markets in the early 1920s. While most markets remained open and functional through the Great Depression, WWI caused many of them to shut down in the 1940s. Some Eastern European markets remained open through the war, only to suffer expropriation after 1945. In total, Austria, Belgium, Shanghai, Czechoslovakia, France, Hungary, Japan, Korea, Luxembourg, Malaysia, the Netherlands, Norway, Poland, Portugal, Uruguay, Venezuela, Yugoslavia, and Slovenia all experienced temporary or permanent shutdowns either in the war years, or in occupation following the war. Many of the markets that shut in the mid-century re-emerged after the war or after occupation.

Wars were not the only factors that created discontinuities in the price records. Markets in Egypt, Lebanon, Portugal, and Chile, for instance, were shut down or barred to foreign investors due to political changes largely uncorrelated to outside global trends. Shifting legal factors have changed the attractiveness of markets such as Greece, Turkey, and India to outside investors, and thus caused them to be regarded as emerging markets, despite long histories as capital markets. A turn of political fortunes can make a long forgotten market suddenly of interest to outside investors.

A fair question is whether these events should be considered endogenous or exogenous. Clearly, some of these formerly emerged countries failed to maintain social and political systems that fostered steady industrial growth. While it is not the object of this article to ask why these markets did not prosper in the same way as the U.S. and U.K. markets, it is reasonable to ask whether anything has changed. Have the political and economic forces that caused these markets to submerge been fundamentally altered? Can we expect the next 60 years of capital markets to be different from the last 60 years?

Survivorship Effects

The issue of survivorship in financial markets is starting to attract much deserved attention among financial researchers. Survivorship occurs at various levels, among companies within an exchange, among exchanges within countries, and among countries.

At the level of company selection, Shumway (1997) provides a detailed analysis of what is probably the most comprehensive equity database in the world, the Center for Research in Security Prices (CRSP) database. The CRSP attempts to keep track of all outstanding stocks, even those that disappear. In theory, it does not suffer from survivorship bias. The problem is that the last returns for stocks that disappear for performance reasons are typically omitted because of lack of data. Shumway shows that such delisted firms typically experience returns around -30%. He even recommends setting the delisting return to -100%. This adjustment can have dramatic effects on stock index performance. For small firms (in the NYSE lowest decile), delisting reduces annual returns by 5%; for large firms, there is no effect. Thus, part of the small-firm effect may be due to survivorship.[6]

At the level of exchanges, it is interesting to note that, at some point, the U.S. had more than 250 stock exchanges. While consolidation of stock exchanges is driven by economies of scale, it is fair to surmise that exchanges that fail are not associated with the most successful firms or industries. At the level of countries, we contend in this paper that the selection process for emerging markets also suffers from serious selection biases.

BGR (1995) provide a detailed analysis of the effects of survival conditioning. They specify a model where markets all start at the same time with the logarithm of price p that follows an absolute diffusion process,

$$dp = \mu dt + \sigma dz. \tag{1}$$

BGR show that under any sample selection criterion, the mean return is given by

$$\mu^* = \mu + \sigma^2 \frac{\pi(p)}{\pi}, \tag{2}$$

where $\pi(p)$ is the ex ante probability of surviving the criterion, given the current price level p. The volatility of the survived series, however, is the same as that of the original series,

$$\sigma^* = \sigma. \tag{3}$$

BGR solve analytically for $\pi(p)/\pi$ in the case where markets are eliminated as soon as p falls below a performance threshold $\bar{p}$. For the survived series with an infinite horizon, the mean return is

$$\mu^* = \mu + \frac{2\mu \times \exp\left(\dfrac{-2\mu(p-\bar{p})}{\sigma^2}\right)}{1 - \exp\left(\dfrac{-2\mu(p-\bar{p})}{\sigma^2}\right)} = \mu + \frac{2\mu(1-\pi(p))}{\pi(p)}. \tag{4}$$

Perhaps the most interesting aspect of BGR's result is the positive bias imparted onto the mean. For small μ, this bias tends to $\sigma^2/(p - \bar{p})$. Thus, there is a functional relationship between the bias and the variance of the series. The more volatile markets have, ceteris paribus, a higher probability of failing, and thus have a larger bias in the mean. Ex post, in a world with survival conditioning, risk appears to be priced. Ex ante, of course, these high returns are illusory. This interpretation of emerging market returns is diametrically opposed to the explanation that high returns are due to the pricing of local risk under segmentation. Under the segmentation hypothesis, the first investors who have access to emerging markets reap the benefits of high returns.

Although we learn a lot from the simple BGR framework—particularly about the relationship between risk and conditional returns—analytical results for more complex survival rules such as a last time up emergence at a finite horizon are not easy to obtain. It is difficult, for instance, to adapt the deterministic absorbing barrier framework to the realities of historical market emergences and failures. The BGR solution also assumes that all market returns are independent and identically distributed. With a more general selection process, however, the ratio of probabilities in equation (2) is difficult to solve analytically and explains why we resort to numerical simulations.

Emerging vs. Developed Markets

Are these results consistent with the empirical evidence on emerging markets? Table 17.2 reports performance numbers for the long-term sample of Jorion and Goetzmann (1999). Arithmetic capital appreciation returns are measured in dollar terms, over the longest sample period for which we have continuous data. This includes periods before breaks, but does not cover interruptions for which we could not measure volatility. Note that these data do not include dividends.

Table 17.2
Performance Characteristics of Global Markets

Country	Period (Years)	Dollar Returns		Avg. Return	
		Average	Std. Dev.	Pre-IFC	Post-IFC
Developed					
United States	1920–96	8.1	16.2		
Canada	1920–96	6.9	18.2		
Austria	1924–96	7.2	21.5		
Belgium	1920–96	5.8	21.8		
Denmark	1925–96	6.1	14.4		
Finland	1930–96	8.2	20.5		
France	1920–96	7.8	25.5		
Germany	1920–44, 50–96	12.0	27.3		
Ireland	1933–96	6.4	16.7		
Italy	1928–96	3.2	25.7		
The Netherlands	1920–96	5.9	16.5		
Norway	1927–96	8.0	19.3		
Spain	1920–96	2.4	28.9		
Sweden	1920–96	8.4	17.7		
Switzerland	1925–96	7.9	16.0		
United Kingdom	1920–96	6.7	17.6		
Australia	1930–96	7.7	18.1		
New Zealand	1930–96	5.0	16.0		
Japan	1920–44, 49–96	8.3	19.9		
Average =		6.9	6.9		
Emerging					
Portugal	1930–74, 77–96	11.3	28.8	10.1	18.3
India	1939–96	2.4	17.5	−1.4	8.8
Pakistan	1960–96	2.4	17.5	2.2	2.7
The Philippines	1954–96	5.3	38.9	−7.4	37.6
Argentina	1947–65, 75–96	22.9	74.1	−18.2	57.9
Brazil	1961–96	18.5	53.4	18.0	18.3
Mexico	1934–96	10.5	29.1	4.0	23.0
Chile	1927–71, 73–96	8.8	32.4	1.0	26.7
Colombia	1936–96	1.7	23.4	−2.7	19.2
Peru	1941–52, 57–77, 88–96	11.5	40.4	7.8	28.9
Venezuela	1937–96	4.9	28.1	1.3	18.9
Average =		9.1	34.8	1.3	23.7
All IFC =	1975–96	18.4	41.6		

Notes: The table compares average stock returns and their standard deviations (Std. Dev.) for a group of developed and emerging markets. Monthly returns are computed from capital appreciation indices as collected by Jorion and Goetzmann (1998), measured in U.S. dollars. All data are converted to percent annual numbers. Average for each group is the arithmetic average of performance numbers for the group above. All IFC is average of all IFC markets. Average returns pre- and post-IFC are computed before and after the first IFC date of record.

The table provides two group averages: developed and emerging markets. The sample of 11 emerging markets consists of countries in the long-term database that match the current IFC definition. Developed markets had an average dollar return of 6.9%, with a volatility of 19.8%; emerging markets had an average dollar return of 9.1%, with a volatility of 34.8%. For comparison, the table also reports the capital appreciation performance of all the IFC emerging markets, using the IFC indices since inception, from 1975 to 1996. The average dollar return for them was 18.4%, with a volatility of 41.6%.

These results are striking. We note first that emerging markets have much higher volatility than developed markets. As volatility plays a key role in the sample selection process, the BGR analysis indicates that returns should also be higher. Indeed, they are. Over the last 20 years, IFC markets enjoyed average returns more than three times those of developed markets since the 1920s. Furthermore, the long-term performance of these so-called emerging markets is only 9%, which is half of that in recent history. This number would be even lower if the performance during the breaks were properly accounted for. Our result suggests that survival is an important issue and is why we turn to a stylized model that will be the basis for our simulations.

◣ A Stylized Model

How Markets Emerge

Among the broad range of reasons for market emergence is the common presumption that markets emerge due to some fundamental economic or political shift. We do not develop an explanatory model for global market emergence because the effects are obviously numerous and complex. Rather, we focus on one likely characteristic of emergence—capital appreciation. In our simplified model, markets emerge because the market prices of existing firms increase, or submerge following price drops.[7] Alternatively, prices may be viewed as summary statistics for changing economic and political conditions.

Suppose a number of markets started trading at different times during the past 100 years, each starting with about the same capitalization (without loss of generality), but with differing expected returns. Later, this assumption will be relaxed. In our simple setting, markets with lower expected returns will have lower capitalization in the future than those with higher expected returns, on average. Thus, time will sort markets according to their respective drift processes.

The key feature of our analysis is the assumption that we observe markets only where market capitalization exceeds a barrier, or threshold, *at the end of the sample period*. Figure 17.1 illustrates the model. We define a market as an *emerged* market if it has crossed the barrier from below at least once since $t = 0$, and if the last crossing was from below.

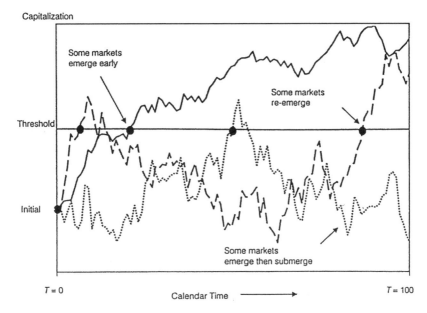

Capitalization

Some markets
emerge early

Threshold

Some markets
re-emerge

Initial

Some markets
emerge then submerge

$T = 0$

Calendar Time ⟶

$T = 100$

Figure 17.1. Emerging . . . or Re-Emerging Markets?

In the BGR setup, markets all start above the barrier but are discarded as soon as they hit the barrier. In the case where the drift is known and the barrier is constant, analytical solutions are available to calculate the bias in the observed mean. In this article, by conditioning upon last time up, we are also implicitly conditioning upon survival since last emergence, and thus, we expect post-emergence biases similar to those found in BGR. The survival bias in BGR, however, is not the whole story.

In our model, the time of emergence contains additional information about the market. When all markets start at the same time, for instance, markets that crossed recently (i.e., later than other markets) are likely to have lower expected returns.

Thus, historical information about when the market began, what its past capitalization was when it started, and what its capitalization was when it last emerged may all be useful inputs to estimating expected returns. Here, the "recentness" of emergence is related to its drift, in contrast to the conditioning process in the BGR analysis, which is "memoryless." In the current analysis, the long-term memory of when and where the process began is crucial.

Model Setup

We now present a simple model that formalizes the above arguments. As Harvey (1995) shows, world markets differ in their systematic as well as unsystematic risk components. Consider a single-factor model excess log return-generating process for the equity market of country k,

$$R_{k,t} = \beta_k R_{m,t} + e_{k,t}, \tag{5}$$

where $E[e_{k,t}] = 0$, $E[R_{m,t}e_{k,t}] = 0$, and $R_{m,t}$ is the excess log return on the global market portfolio at time t. The mean zero term need not be pure noise, but it could be a function of some asset class that has no covariance to the global wealth portfolio, such as gold, or physical assets such as commodities that are known to have nearly zero betas. The log price level of market k at time T can be expressed as $P_{k,T} = P_{k,0} + \Sigma_{t=1}^{T} R_{k,t}$, which converges to $P_{k,0} + TE[R_m]\beta_k$ as T increases. Thus, we expect prices to be distributed according to their beta values—for big enough T, it matters little whether initial capitalizations differ.

Note that under our baseline model, expected returns are driven by exposure to the world market. This setup is akin to a null hypothesis, where no market is mispriced. The only reason to invest in foreign markets is for diversification benefits—markets are perfectly integrated. An opposite view is segmentation, i.e., local factor(s) are priced, perhaps because of barriers to capital flows.[8]

Here we assume that expected returns are driven by outside investors who are able to diversify idiosyncratic risk sufficiently for the standard models to apply. In particular, the prospect of market disappearance for local reasons is not priced, i.e., does not enter expected returns. We will show that, even under our null hypothesis of no mispricing, survivorship creates situations where emerging markets appear attractive for the wrong reasons.

We want to emphasize that it is unlikely that this simple model fully captures the dynamics of emerging markets.[9] Additional factors could be added to the model. Time variation in risk and structural changes could also be incorporated. These additions, however, would obscure the main message from the simulations: a simplistic model can generate, when submitted to selection through survival, complex patterns of biases and time variation in returns.

Simulation Experiment

We simulate emergence among a group of markets as follows.

1. Annual returns for each simulated market are generated by the model in equation (1) in the following.
   a. We simulate 100-year histories of the global market $R_{m,t}$ using i.i.d. normal returns with an annual mean of 10% and an annual standard deviation of 20%, which are typical of stock market data.
   b. We simulate the local factor, $e_{k,t}$, with i.i.d. draws from a normal distribution with a mean of zero and a random standard deviation drawn from a uniform distribution between 10% and 30%.
   c. β_k, the constant loading on the global market index, is drawn randomly from a uniform distribution between zero and two.

2. Markets begin randomly with starting dates drawn from a random uniform distribution over the interval $t = 1$ to $t = 99$. This random starting date is more realistic than usual models where all markets start at a fixed point in time. All markets start at one standard deviation of $R_{k,t}$ below the capitalization threshold.
3. We construct capital appreciation returns for each market, assuming no dividend payments, and cumulate each index from its inception until the last period, to create stock market indices for 100 markets.
4. We censor the markets by dropping those that are below the threshold *at the terminal date.*

This model is quite general. Both beta and residual risk differ to make the model more realistic, as we would expect markets to differ in terms of expected returns and risk. The time of market founding is also random—markets start at any time within the 100-year interval. The important assumptions are that (i) no market is mispriced, (ii) expected returns differ across markets and are constant through time, and (iii) markets are arbitrarily censored if they end up below the threshold.

This procedure is repeated 2,500 times for 100 markets each time, which results in 187,954 simulated price paths of survived series. For each simulation, we save a number of variables, including the year the market began t_1, the year it last emerged t_e, and conditional and unconditional summary statistics; *conditional* statistics are those recorded after the last emergence. Of particular interest to emerging market investors is the difference between the mean annual return of the series *since the time of last emergence* less the expected return of the series, i.e., the true market beta times the global market return realization since emergence. We define this as the bias in the annual mean return,

$$\text{Bias}_k = \left[\frac{1}{T - t_e} \sum_{t=t_e+1}^{T} R_{k,t} \right] - \beta_k \left[\frac{1}{T - t_e} \sum_{t=t_e+1}^{T} R_{m,t} \right], \tag{6}$$

where β_k is the true beta (we found that using the beta estimated over the ex post period led to nearly identical results).

We also wish to examine the relationship between conditional beta and emergence, R^2 and emergence, and finally, the additional information provided by the start date of the series in relation to the emergence date of the series. This last issue is important because it may be possible to develop heuristics for correcting the bias in the mean returns for recently emerged markets. One potentially useful piece of information for this purpose is the length of time that the market has existed. For example, given any two markets that emerged 10 years ago, the market with a longer history should have a lower mean and, therefore, a greater bias than the market with a shorter history. We examine this issue via simulation results.

▶ Simulation Results

Survival Effects

The simulations reveal two effects: survival and sorting effects. Relative to the BGR results, the sorting effects are novel. First, we find that, the more recent the emergence of the market, the higher the bias in the mean return. Figure 17.2 shows the relationship between the bias in the mean and the time of last emergence.

The figure shows quantiles of the distribution of the bias, as defined in equation (6). Notice that for early emergence, that is, for markets that emerged in the early part of our hypothetical century (on the left side of the graph), there is virtually no bias in the distributions—the difference between the sample average annual return and the ex ante return is typically zero. For very recent emergence, i.e., for markets that last emerged only five years ago (on the right side of the graph), the bias is as high as 10% per year, with values more than 20% per year not unusual. Even for markets that emerged a decade ago, we still see a substantial return bias, averaging about 5% annually.

BGR find that survival bias is greater when the price level is near the lower bound. In the context of our simulations, recent emergence implies a proximity to the bound and, thus, a more acute survival bias, since we constructed the sample so that the price never fell below the threshold after emergence. BGR

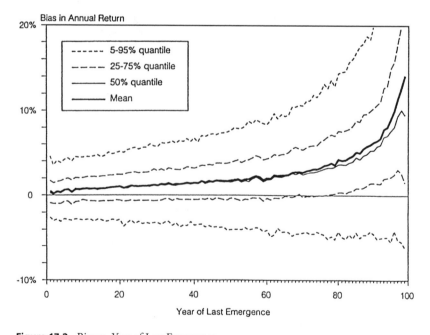

Figure 17.2. Bias vs. Year of Last Emergence

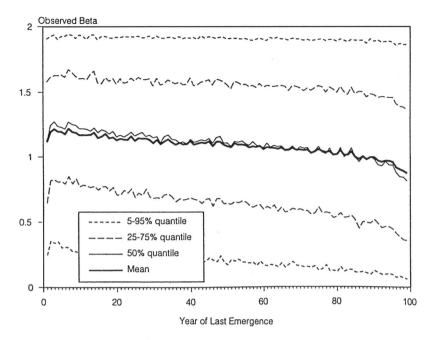

Figure 17.3. Beta vs. Year of Last Emergence

also show that the bias increases in the residual variance of the series. Our regressions confirm that the bias is positively related to the residual risk of the series. In addition, we find that the effect is greatest for recently emerged markets. This provides an interesting possible application. For two markets emerging at the same time, we expect the one with the highest residual variance to have the largest bias. Empirically, this relationship between bias and residual risk may appear as though the local market factor is priced, i.e., that the expected return is positively related to the portion of the variance not correlated to global factors.

Sorting Effects

Our simulations reveal another effect, which differs from the usual survival story. By conditioning on last emergence, we are sorting markets according to their last crossing time through a barrier. Indeed, Figure 17.3 shows the average beta of each market, sorted on the year of last emergence. It shows that recent emergence is negatively correlated with the loading on the global market factor. Markets that emerged near the beginning of the hypothetical century have an average beta of 1.2, while recently emerged markets have much lower average betas, around 0.9. Thus, the period of last emergence is informative about the unconditional expected return of the market—the more recent the last emergence, the lower the beta, and, consequently, the lower the un-

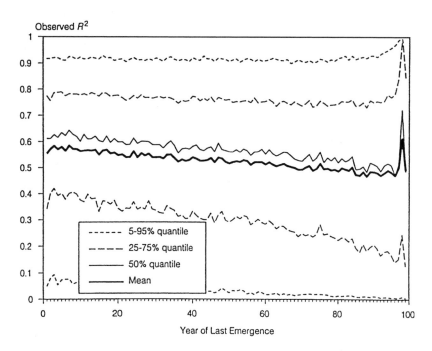

Figure 17.4. R^2 vs. Year of Last Emergence

conditional expected return. This relation between global factor loading and recent emergence accords well with the observation that emerging markets have low betas.

Our simulations reveal a second empirical regularity due to threshold-induced sorting. Figure 17.4 shows the R^2 from the market regression, sorted on period of last emergence. For markets that emerged early, the amount of variance explained by the market is high, about 60%. For markets that only recently emerged, the R^2 is lower than 50%. Thus, by conditioning upon recent emergence, we should expect to find markets with higher ratios of idiosyncratic risk, which corresponds exactly to the observation that emerging markets seem to have low R^2 with respect to worldwide factors. Indeed, emerging markets are often sold to institutional investors on the basis of their substantial diversification benefits. Our analysis suggests that this is a legitimate argument for emerging market investing, as opposed to claims of high alphas.

Recall from Figure 17.1 that last time up conditioning implies that the longer the market history before emergence, the greater the potential bias. The intuition is that markets that remain in the neighborhood of the boundary over time are also likely to be those that emerged and submerged repeatedly. When we condition upon having emerged early in the hypothetical century, we implicitly pick out those markets with positive drift, which, in turn, decreases the probability of being near the barrier for any length of time. This effect provides another possibly useful heuristic for adjusting mean bias for

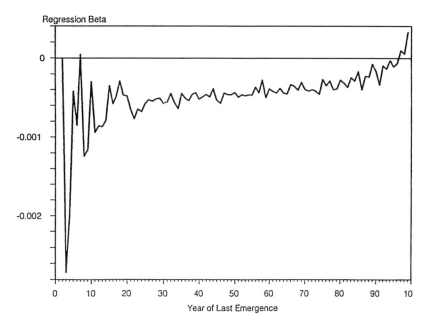

Figure 17.5. Betas of Bias on Start Date

emerging markets. For any two markets that emerged at the same time, the one that began earlier should have the largest bias. The reason for this is that, if a market began a long time previously and still only recently crossed the barrier, it probably has a low beta, whereas a newly formed market that quickly crosses the barrier is likely to have a high beta and, thus, a high expected return.

Figure 17.5 shows precisely this effect. For each period, we select all the markets that last emerged at that time. We regress the bias in the mean upon the starting date for the series. We find the relationship negative for all periods. That is, *the earlier the starting date, the higher is the bias in the mean.* For new markets, the bias is lower. Therefore, the time since last emergence and the time since the market first began may be used to forecast expected returns.

The survival and sorting effects are related. When markets differ in terms of expected returns, sorting effects exacerbate survival effects. In the BGR analysis, for instance, the bias can be shown to be functionally related to the true expected return. Thus, while sorting effects and survival can be considered separately in the simulations, they interact to increase the magnitude of the bias.

Cumulative Average Returns: Emergence as an Event

Another approach to examining the effects of emergence conditioning is to treat the date of emergence as an event and to align the simulations around the event time. Figure 17.6 shows the cumulative and average returns for all mar-

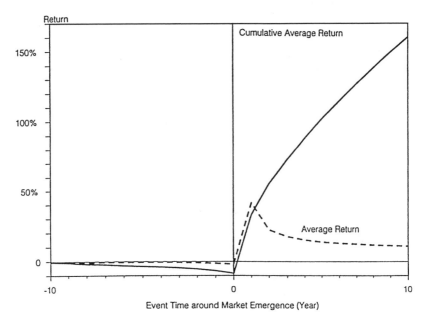

Figure 17.6. Average Returns Around Emergence

kets that last emerged in a given year. The horizontal axis is aligned in event time, as opposed to calendar time, and market emergence is set to year zero. The figure shows a cumulative index of 10 years of returns preceding and following the emergence date.

Notice the strong effect of conditioning upon emergence. Returns are nearly flat before emergence, despite the fact that the average returns in the simulation are positive. Following emergence, cumulative returns follow a positive trajectory, which is slightly convex.

The returns comprising the price path are also shown in Figure 17.6. The difference between pre-emergence and post-emergence returns is dramatic. The low returns preceding emergence result from conditioning upon the market's being below the capitalization threshold. Simply knowing that a market crossed the threshold from below, and remained above until the end of the sample period, helps to differentiate historical returns. Notice also that the largest return is in the year immediately following emergence. This is because year one is the year in which the market is closest to the boundary, thus most likely to fail, and yet has not failed in the subsequent period. As the market climbs away from the boundary, the chances of submerging decrease, and the survival-conditioned return decreases as well. If an econometrician only observes the history of a market since emergence, the simulation suggests that average returns will be greatest just after emergence.

These results are in line with theoretical work by Bossaerts (1996), who analyzes the dynamics of securities prices when investors have rational expectations but incomplete information. He shows that the dynamics of prices can be described when securities have payoffs that can be categorized into two states: an out-of-the-money state, where it pays zero, and an in-the-money state, where the payoff is random. He shows that for securities that end up in-the-money, i.e., that have survived, large returns are associated with low prices. Thus, the slope of the cumulative return line is greater when markets have just emerged.

Implications

The simulations, however stylized, provide some general guidance for investment practice. First, recent emergence by a market has the potential to be a strong conditioning factor that may affect ex post observed return distributions. Some of the effects are due to the fact that recently emerged markets are, by definition, near the lower threshold of capitalization. However, some of the effects are also due to actual differences in long-term expected returns, given differing betas. This sorting also underscores the importance of detecting changing betas for emerging markets. Local or recent changes in expected returns may be sufficient to help a market avoid plunging below the lower threshold. The econometrics of conditional betas would appear to be a crucial step in the analysis of expected returns.

These simulation results have strong implications for applications of mean-variance optimization to emerging market data, as is typically applied to strategic, or long-term, asset allocation. The brevity of emerging market histories induces a well-known uncertainty in the inputs to the mean-variance model, known as estimation risk.[10]

Our work shows that the problem extends beyond input uncertainty to input bias. Recently emerged markets typically have a positive bias in the mean and wider distribution. In a mean-variance framework, the *distribution* of the bias is as important as the average, because extreme values exert a large influence upon the composition of the optimal portfolio. Institutional investors seeking data on emerging markets for use in mean-variance optimization should use recently emerged market data with extreme caution.[11] As the number of emerging markets used in the optimization is increased, the likelihood of overweighing one with an extreme positive bias in the mean increases as well.

Evidence From Long-Term Markets

Later on, we will examine the empirical evidence on emerging markets using recent IFC data. Since these high quality indices, unfortunately, have a rather short history, it is also useful to examine long-term histories of global stock markets.

Using the Jorion-Goetzmann (1999) dataset, all markets were followed continuously from the initial reporting period until 1996, at which time 32 were still included. These authors also compute a global index of stock returns

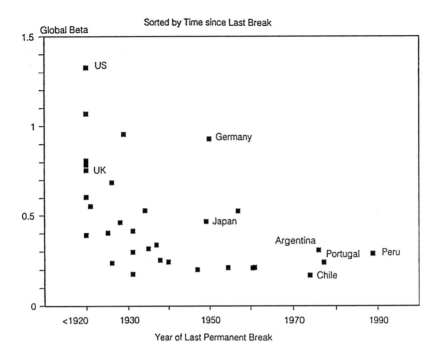

Figure 17.7. Global Beta and Emergence

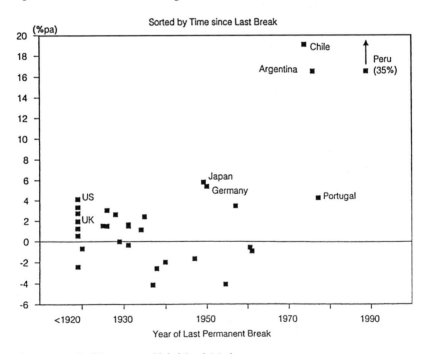

Figure 17.8. Real Returns on Global Stock Markets

weighted by GDP, which will be useful to compute the global beta. For comparison purposes, all series are measured in real terms, using a wholesale price index deflator.

Most of these series have experienced some breaks. Defining emergence as the first observation after the last break, the question is whether observed price patterns are consistent with the simulations. We can use the global stock index to verify a key prediction of the simulation—that the systematic exposure of emerging markets should be less than that of developed markets. Figure 17.7 plots the global beta against time since the last break.

The graph clearly shows a negative pattern, which is consistent with that in Figure 17.4. The U.S. market has the highest beta and also the longest continuous history, going back to the beginning of the sample in 1921. Other markets, such as Peru, Portugal, and Argentina, have had long histories but are only recently re-emerged, with their global betas around only 0.40, suggesting their true expected return is lower than that of other markets.

The other major prediction of the model is the relationship between bias and recent emergence. Figure 17.8 plots the average compound real return for each market against time since the last break and dramatically illustrates the importance of survival conditioning. As expected, markets with shorter histories have greater dispersion, but also much higher returns, while markets with long histories experienced real returns around 2% per annum. More recently emerged markets (with long histories) displayed much higher returns, reaching 35% for Peru. The figure would show even higher performance for recently emerged markets if the IFC data were included.

Figures 17.7 and 17.8 confirm the intuition behind the simulations: Markets with long histories that only recently emerged are likely to have low betas and high returns. The simulations show that such results can be interpreted in terms of conditioning upon recent emergence.

◤ Empirical Analysis of Emerging Markets

One of the obvious problems with evaluating survival issues in emerging markets is that the data may not be readily available before markets are considered to have emerged. Yet a number of empirical regularities should be expected from the simulations. For instance, right after emergence, the bias should be greatest if markets that perform badly do not appear in the sample. This hypothesis is analyzed using a variety of approaches.

Selection of Emerged Markets

The standard data source for emerging stock markets is from the IFC, which is part of the World Bank group. In its laudable quest for promoting private equity investment in less developed countries, the IFC has developed the most comprehensive and consistent database for emerging markets. The database started in December 1980 with nine markets, which were backfilled to December 1975, and has expanded to 25 markets as of December 1995 (Jordan was backfilled to 1978). Other markets are being watched by the IFC, then periodically added to their composite emerging markets index. The IFC collects not only share prices, but also dividend and exchange rate information, allowing construction of a total return index that is consistent across all countries.

The term "emerging stock market" was coined by the IFC in 1981. The IFC defines an emerging stock market as one located in a developing country. Using the World Bank's definition, this includes all countries with a GNP per capita less than $8,625 in 1993. The IFC (1995) states that "although IFC has no predetermined criteria for selecting an emerging market for IFC index coverage, in practice most markets added have had at least 30 to 50 listed companies with market capitalization of U.S. $1 billion or more and annual value traded of U.S. $100 million or more at the start of IFC index coverage." This definition clearly defines a size threshold that markets have to reach before official inclusion in the database.

Backfilling in IFC Indices

In practice, different types of biases are imparted to IFC indices. The first issue relates to the backfilling of IFC indices. The early IFC indices were started in 1980 using companies that were in existence at that time and backfilled to 1975; more recently, the first data points generally predate the decision to include a market by one year or more. Backfilling a market explicitly conditions upon exceeding a threshold as of the decision date. For example, markets that were in existence in 1975 but performed poorly in subsequent years are not included in the database. Therefore, markets that survived the backfilling period are likely to exhibit biases similar to those in the simulations.

Besides the country selection issues, there is the problem of company selection. In 1980, for instance, the IFC indices were constructed using companies that were in existence at that time. As noted by Harvey (1995), the backfilling of the series to December 1975 creates a company-specific bias. We do not address this problem in our simulations.

Survival in IFC Indices

Another issue relates to using long-term market histories. To date, the IFC has never dropped a market from its sample. Does this mean that, absent the backfilling issue, the IFC database is not subject to survival issues? In other words, as long as the IFC keeps following all markets once they enter, would not any potential survival bias be eliminated? The answer is no. The fact that all the IFC markets have survived with continuous return records is not sufficient to prove that there is no survival effect in the series.

Two IFC markets that had near death experiences illustrate this point. Both the Zimbabwean and Nigerian markets became quite small after inclusion in the database. The market value of Zimbabwe began at $450 million in 1980, when it was introduced into the IFC database. It fell to $40 million during the next four years and then increased to $1.5 billion by the end of 1995. The drop in share prices after 1980 can reasonably be attributed to uncertainty regarding the future of the Zimbabwean economy in the early years of the new government. In 1984, there was a real possibility that the equity market would disappear or become so thin that share prices would not be meaningful. Instead, we do observe a continuous series for Zimbabwe because of the successful transition to democratic rule by 1995. However, we completely eliminated from this sample the possibility that the market would not survive this crisis.

A related example is the Nigerian market, which fell to about a fourth of its initial 1984 capitalization of $1.6 billion four years later. The Nigerian market emerged due to soaring oil prices in the early 1980s. The collapse of oil prices in 1986, however, certainly contributed to the subsequent economic crisis. President Babangida addressed the crisis by implementing drastic policy changes. These measures, which included the liberalization of trade and the privatization of agricultural markets, ultimately proved successful, and the market recovered to $1.5 billion in 1995. Again, we have no record of what might have happened to the Nigerian equity market had the adjustment policy not worked.[12]

More generally, the fact that no market was dropped by the IFC does not imply that there is no survival effect. A sample of nine markets over 15 years may not adequately represent the possibility of disappearance. The number of markets and the time span may simply be too low. A lack of sufficient cross-sectional observations of disasters neither proves their non-existence, nor does it prove that the bias imparted by such conditioning is non-existent.

There is further evidence on this point. The IFC also follows stock markets in developing countries that have not yet been included into the official database. One of the largest ones was Kuwait, with $10 billion in market capitalization in the late 1980s. This market was close to making the grade to emerging market. Had Kuwait been included in the IFC indices, the series would no doubt have been interrupted during the 1990 Gulf War. Here, no matter how diligent the IFC researchers were, the interruption in price observations would not have been a matter of choice. Thus, with a larger sample, at least one market would have been dropped during the 1980–1995 period.

Our simulations should not be construed as a critique of the IFC database. In fact, the IFC has demonstrated an awareness of survival biases by following poorly performing markets, even when capitalization dropped sharply. This careful data collection certainly can reduce the magnitude of bias, although, as we have shown, it cannot eliminate it. Whenever a significant probability of market closure exists, any long-term historical series implicitly conditions upon survival. This effect can be demonstrated in the context of the

Table 17.3
Distribution of Stock Market Lives

1929–1995			1953–1995		
Life (Years)	Count	Country	Life (Years)	Count	Country
66	15	Others	42	22	Others
45	1	Mexico	32	1	Peru
44	1	Portugal	21	1	Mexico
42	1	Chile	20	1	Portugal
16	4	Germany, Hungary, Netherlands, Uruguay	18	1	Chile
			9	1	Egypt
			4	2	Argentina, Lebanon
14	1	Romania			
11	1	Greece			
10	3	Austria, Czechoslovakia, Poland			
9	1	Italy			
7	1	Spain			
Total:	29		Total:	29	

Notes: The table describes the distribution of lives or number of years a market has existed without interruption from a fixed starting date. The left column reports the lives of markets that existed in 1929 over the period 1929–1995. The right column starts in 1953.

long-term history of the global markets, rather than from the perspective of an unusually placid 15-year period. Over the long term, how frequent is market closure?

To answer this question, Table 17.3 describes the distribution of lives of stock markets starting at two points in time, 1929 and 1953. These dates correspond to times at which the League of Nations and the U.N. collected a large sample of market indices, which happened to number 29 in both cases (although the markets are not the same). We compute life as the number of remaining years before an interruption in the series of at least one year using the same data sources.

The distributions show that, over long periods, markets do suffer disruptions. Out of 29 markets existing in 1929, 14 did not last until 1995 without major interruptions. Many markets, of course, were either closed or nationalized around WWII. But even more recently, starting in 1953, 7 markets out of 29 did not make it until 1995.

In the long run, it is fair to predict that markets will disappear and reappear. The lack of censored observations over a brief period in the history of global capital markets is not sufficient to prove the absence of survival effects. The question is whether any of the regularities we find in the simulation also appear in recent actual data.

Table 17.4
Emerging Markets Covered by IFC

| Country | IFC Start Date | Capitalization ($ Millions) | | IMF Coverage Start Date |
		Start Date	As of Dec. '95	
Argentina	Dec. 75	83	22,148	
Brazil	Dec. 75	8,469	94,615	
Chile	Dec. 75	180	48,070	Jan. 74
China	Dec. 92	21,369	24,608	
Colombia	Dec. 84	401	8,519	Jan. 57
Greece	Dec. 75	1,677	10,161	
Hungary	Dec. 92	659	796	
India	Dec. 75	527	57,753	Jan. 57
Indonesia	Dec. 89	2,254	27,610	
Jordan	Jan. 78	335	3,484	
Korea	Dec. 75	324	123,648	
Malaysia	Dec. 84	9,523	142,494	
Mexico	Dec. 75	677	60,419	
Nigeria	Dec. 84	1,560	1,537	
Pakistan	Dec. 84	498	6,482	Jul. 60
Peru	Dec. 92	2,081	7,353	Jan. 88
The Philippines	Dec. 84	200	31,965	Jan. 57
Poland	Dec. 92	2,139	1,987	
Portugal	Jan. 86	138	10,932	
Sri Lanka	Dec. 92	1,082	1,249	
Taiwan	Dec. 84	3,532	113,032	
Thailand	Dec. 75	220	94,963	
Turkey	Dec. 86	377	13,782	
Venezuela	Dec. 84	505	2,483	Jan. 57
Zimbabwe	Dec. 75	215	1,517	

Notes: Historical information about the return series calculated for 25 equity markets designated emerging by the IFC. Start Date indicates the month the series begins in the IFC database. Capitalization at Start Date and as of Dec. '95 indicate the IFC index market capitalization in millions of dollars at the start date and at the end of 1995. IMF Coverage Start Date is the date at which IMF data are available for the market.

Performance of Emerged Markets

The IFC dataset has become the standard database for research on emerging markets and provides performance benchmarks for portfolio managers. As a result, the introduction of new markets is watched very closely by portfolio managers, given that it affects the return on their "bogey." We consider the first date at which the IFC compiles a market index as the date of emergence.

Table 17.4 presents start dates and market capitalizations for the markets covered by the IFC. Prior to the IFC, the International Monetary Fund (IMF)

Table 17.5
Risk and Return of IFC Emerging Markets

Country	No. of Months	Returns		Risk			Abnorm.
		Arithm.	Compound	Volat.	β	ρ	α
Argentina	240	61.68	27.14	96.62	−0.07	−0.006	54.95*
Brazil	240	25.36	9.46	57.99	0.35	0.089	15.63
Chile	240	35.34	32.72	37.98	0.12	0.054	27.22*
China	36	1.83	−18.36	76.31	−0.04	−0.007	−1.69
Colombia	132	35.32	35.71	31.25	0.08	0.045	28.75*
Greece	240	8.34	3.00	34.39	0.45	0.191	−2.15
Hungary	36	−2.73	−8.40	36.89	0.80	0.292	−16.67
India	240	16.89	14.11	27.39	−0.03	−0.012	10.03
Indonesia	72	6.88	2.18	31.02	0.19	0.100	1.46
Jordan	215	12.27	11.22	18.12	0.16	0.129	3.70
Korea	240	22.62	19.78	30.80	0.52	0.243	11.65
Malaysia	132	15.73	12.74	26.91	0.73	0.423	2.21
Mexico	240	25.65	15.87	44.15	0.70	0.234	13.20
Nigeria	132	18.44	2.50	53.92	0.30	0.087	9.58
Pakistan	132	16.52	14.60	24.62	0.02	0.012	10.72
Peru	36	35.90	32.72	39.57	0.75	0.252	22.70
The Philippines	132	40.61	40.24	36.66	0.71	0.299	27.41*
Poland	36	81.39	65.14	87.17	1.68	0.265	56.12
Portugal	119	29.66	23.71	43.23	1.06	0.392	14.80
Sri Lanka	36	5.68	0.75	32.08	−0.29	−0.111	4.94
Taiwan	132	31.09	20.93	50.05	0.73	0.227	17.60
Thailand	240	23.62	22.02	26.90	0.34	0.193	13.85*
Turkey	108	38.22	16.72	71.16	0.08	0.017	32.39
Venezuela	132	20.53	8.90	47.88	−0.37	−0.122	19.00
Zimbabwe	240	13.99	8.55	34.21	0.18	0.082	5.48
IFC Composite	132	17.03	15.42	22.76	0.46	0.317	6.42
EW Average	240	24.83	16.56	43.89	0.37	0.155	15.31

Notes: Annualized risk and returns of IFC emerging markets, using the earliest start month (in Table 17.4) until December 1995. The table reports sample size, arithmetic average, compound average, volatility, beta, and correlation with the world market, and alpha from a market model in excess returns. The sample consists of 25 IFC-covered countries plus the IFC Composite Index and an equally-weighted average of all countries. All data are presented in annual terms in percent. Arithmetic returns and abnormal alphas are multiplied by 1,200; compound returns use annual compounding; monthly volatility measures are multiplied by $\sqrt{12} \times 100$.

*Indicates significance at the 5% level.

has also compiled stock index data, which are directly supplied by the central banks or the stock exchanges, and include no dividend data. The table also indicates the first date of record for monthly IMF data when it predated the IFC indices.

So, what is the performance of emerging markets? Table 17.5 displays risk and return characteristics of emerging markets, expressed in percent per annum. For each market, the period covers the inception date until December 1995. The table shows that returns on emerging markets have been very high, using both arithmetic and continuously compounded averages. The return on the equally-weighted index, for instance, was 24.8% per annum, on average, during the last 20 years, which is enormous. These markets, of course, display high volatility, but most of this risk is diversifiable by global investors, since correlations with the world market are generally very low, averaging 0.155. As a result, many of these markets display superior alphas, many of which are statistically significant. Apparently, the combination of these two features, high returns and low correlations with developed markets, makes emerging markets quite appealing. Can these features be attributed to survival?

Expected Returns After Emergence

In the first approach to measuring bias, we track the behavior of IFC indices right after emergence. Returns are measured in U.S. dollars, inclusive of dividends. As some of these markets have experienced hyperinflation, it is essential to measure returns either in a common foreign currency or in real terms, deflating by the local price index. Both approaches should give similar results in situations where purchasing power parity holds, which is likely to be the case in inflationary environments.

HYPOTHESIS 1. *Expected returns will be higher immediately following emergence than later on.*

To test this hypothesis, we adapt the event-study methodology used in the simulation above to the emergence of markets. We construct an equally-weighted index where returns are aligned on the emergence date. The advantage of this portfolio approach is that it fully accounts for cross-correlation between events, which is substantial in this case since 9 markets out of 25 emerge on the same date. Figure 17.9 plots the time series of the emerging portfolio value; this portfolio is compared to that of a benchmark, which is constructed by replacing each market by the Morgan Stanley Capital International World Index.

Figure 17.9 shows that the slope of the line is greater immediately following emergence. This pattern is consistent with the simulation results. The emerging market portfolio also substantially outperforms the benchmark portfolio. The magnitude of the effect is confirmed in Table 17.6, which considers 36-, 48-, and 60-month windows after emergence. The portfolio performance is compared to that over the subsequent window of the same length. The table shows that the performance is significantly greater immediately after emergence. The difference is striking: 15% p.a. using a 60-month window, 29% p.a. with a 48-month window, and 24% p.a. with a 36-month window. These numbers are all statistically significant, as indicated by the *t*-statistics in the table.[13]

Among other explanations and competing theories for the price increase after emergence is the price pressure hypothesis. Official recognition of an

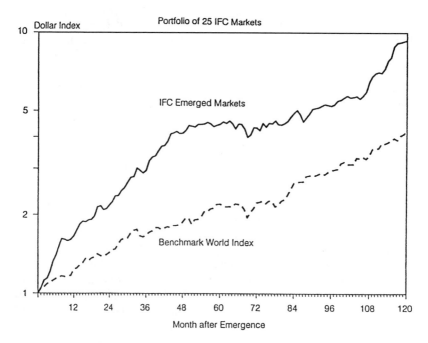

Figure 17.9. Performance After Emergence

emerging market by the IFC could induce purchases by foreign managers, leading to increased prices. These purchases convey no new information about the companies and, therefore, should have no permanent effect on stock prices. In a similar context, Harris and Gurel (1986) report that additions of stocks to the S&P 500 list led to price increases of about 3% during the 1978–1983 period. It is conceivable that, given the thinness of some emerging markets, foreign purchases drive prices by much greater amounts. The price pressure hypothesis, however, should lead to reversals after the initial buying, since the price pressure is temporary; however, reversals are not apparent.

Another explanation is changing economic conditions. Some markets emerge as a result of financial liberalization, which usually coincides with a changing political environment. We would then expect the best investment opportunities to come to the market first, spurring an initial growth that slows down as less profitable investments later appear. On the other hand, emerging markets have been characterized over time by regularly occurring sweeping economic reforms, many of which have been often followed by equally sweeping changes in the opposite direction. One would have to argue that the latest changes are of a permanent nature. Whatever the explanation, it is clear that the long-run performance of markets right after emergence is not sustainable.

Table 17.6
Returns After Emergence

	First Period	Next Period	Difference
60 months			
Mean	30.77	15.74	15.03
Std. Dev.	(10.42)	(11.30)	
t-Stat.			2.19*
48 months			
Mean	36.40	6.92	29.49
Std. Dev.	(10.66)	(10.11)	
t-Stat.			4.01*
36 months			
Mean	37.28	13.41	23.87
Std. Dev.	(10.97)	(10.75)	
t-Stat.			2.69*

Notes: This table reports statistics for returns for 25 IFC-covered markets in two equal-length sequential time periods following market emergence. Emergence is defined as the beginning of the IFC total monthly return series. Data converted to annual measures by multiplying monthly average by 12 and standard deviation by the square root of 12. The *t*-statistic tests the equality of average returns in the first and second subperiods.

*Indicates significance at the 5% level.

Expected Returns Around Emergence

An alternative approach to measuring bias is to recover market information from a completely different source. We take a sample of markets for which equity indices have been collected by the IMF since 1957. These indices are compiled by the local stock exchange and may not be consistent across countries. In addition, they often represent monthly averages, not end-of-month data. Still, comparisons are appropriate as long as the same IMF series is used before and after emergence. Additional data exist for a total of seven markets, which are listed in Table 17.4. The shortest period before emergence is for Peru, for which we have data for only two years.

HYPOTHESIS 2. *Expected returns will be higher after than before emergence.*

To guard against hyperinflation, we measure returns both in dollars and in real terms (deflated by the CPI as provided by the IMF). As before, returns are aggregated into an equally-weighted portfolio of seven markets aligned on the date of emergence. Figure 17.10 displays the time series of cumulative returns. The picture clearly indicates a break in trend, with returns after emergence sharply moving upward. This pattern is also consistent with the simulation results reported from our hypothetical market subject to conditioning upon emergence. In fact, Figure 17.10 is quite similar to Figure 17.6, which aligns simulation returns on the emergence date.

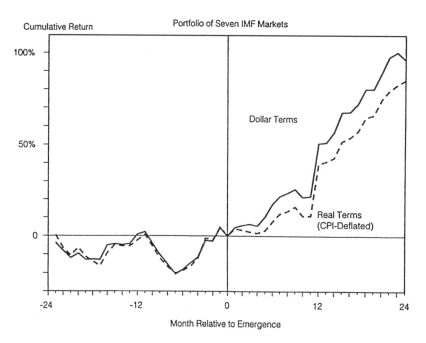

Figure 17.10. Performance Around Emergence

Formal tests of breaks in expected returns are presented in Table 17.7. Both real returns and dollar returns strongly indicate that average returns are higher right after emergence. The difference in real returns, for instance, averages 47% annually. Even with very large standard errors, two years of data are sufficient to bring strong rejections of the null. Again, these results strongly suggest that returns are biased upward once a market is considered emerged.

Expected Returns Before Emergence

A third approach considers markets that have not yet emerged. Besides its official list of emerged markets, the IFC also collects information on a sample of markets that have the potential to emerge. By the end of 1994, the IFC was watching 24 such markets. For these non-emerged markets, the IFC provides annual returns reported by local stock markets, exchange rates, and market capitalization.[14] Therefore, as suggested by the simulations, we find a significant bias due to recent emergence.

Annual returns were collected for this sample of markets varying from 7 in 1985 to 19 in 1994. To compare their performance with those of established emerging markets, we constructed a value-weighted dollar return index that spanned 10 years.[15] This index was compared to the IFC composite index, which is also value weighted. To maintain comparability, both indices include only capital appreciation.

Table 17.7
Returns Around Emergence

	Before Emergence	After Emergence	Difference
Real returns			
Average	−2.09	44.60	46.69
Std. Dev.	16.52	21.27	26.93
t-Stat.	−0.18	2.97	2.45*
Dollar returns			
Average	1.23	50.43	49.20
Std. Dev.	15.00	22.82	27.30
t-Stat.	0.12	3.13	2.55*

Notes: This table reports statistics for returns for seven IMF-covered markets in two-year periods before and after market emergence. Emergence is defined as the beginning of the IFC total monthly return series. Returns are reported for real, CPI-deflated returns, and U.S. dollar-converted returns. Annual returns in percent.

*Indicates significance at the 5% level.

Table 17.8
Returns Before and After Emergence

	Non-Emerged Market Index	Emerged IFC Composite Index	Difference	MSCIP World Index
Annual returns				
Average	12.5	19.1	−6.6	14.0
Std. Dev.	18.1	28.0	40.0	17.0
t-Stat.	2.18	2.16	−0.52	2.61
Compound	11.2	15.7	−4.5	12.7

Notes: This table reports statistics for returns on IFC emerged markets and non-emerged markets. Returns are compared for the MSCIP world index, the IFC composite index, and a value-weighted index of returns on markets that have not yet emerged. Annual returns are measured in dollars, without dividends, over the period 1985–1994.

HYPOTHESIS 3. *Expected returns will be lower before emergence.*

Table 17.8 compares the performance of the two groups of markets, non-emerged and emerged. The table shows that the non-emerged group returned an average of 12.5% over the 10 years, against 19.1% for the emerged index. Using an entirely different dataset, this difference confirms biases in the performance of emerged markets. Emerged markets, on average, return 6.6% more than other markets. For comparison purposes, the table also reports the performance of the MSCIP world index, a value-weighted index of developed markets. Over this period, the average return was 14.0%, which also falls short of the performance of emerged markets. In our model, the 6.6% difference can be attributed either to the fact that non-emerged markets truly have low expected returns (low betas in our model) or to the fact the sample selection process for defining "emerged" creates survivorship biases. Although the volatility of the series is such that the *t*-test is unable to reject equality of mean returns, most portfolio managers would agree that an annual difference of 6.6% over a decade is economically important.

◤ Conclusions

A general model of global markets that allows for differing expected returns and differing correlations to the world market provides the basis for simulations of selection of emerging markets. These simulations show that recently emerged markets have high observed returns. The model also shows that recently emerged countries have low covariances with the global market. These results are striking because they fit the empirical observation that emerging markets appear to have high returns and low correlations with other markets. In our baseline model, which assumes no mispricing of emerging markets, these high returns and low betas are simply due to recent emergence.

The findings of these simulations are confirmed by our empirical analysis, which shows that average returns on markets that have just emerged are temporarily high. The history of emerged markets provides an overly optimistic picture of future investment performance. Therefore, basing investment decisions on the past performance of emerging markets is likely to lead to disappointing results.

Another fruitful line of research would be to examine the predictive power of measures for the probability of market upheaval, such as credit risk ratings or default spreads.[16] Indeed, Erb, Harvey, and Viskanta (1995) find that, cross-sectionally, low credit ratings are associated with high average returns and low betas. As credit rating proxies for the probability of market failure, these results provide additional support for the survivorship story.

A major caveat of our analysis is that it is based upon a stationary model. Economies are never that simple. Global capital markets have been subject to dramatic changes during the 20th century, and many nations with bright economic prospects in the 1920s subsequently failed to reward investors for their high expectations. It seems reasonable to condition expected returns in marginal markets on changing political, legal, and economic environments. It is also important to learn from history. Market contractions, banking failures, and expropriations have occurred in the past, and are likely to occur in the future, even in the absence of a major event such as a world war. If we fail to account for losers as well as winners in the global equity markets, we may be ignoring important information about actual investment risk.

One way to account for losers is to gather additional historical data. Financial economists are accustomed to working with abundant and accurate data, but, unfortunately, data are strongly conditioned upon survival. For instance, we do not as yet have a quality dataset for Argentina's equity market, even though it has existed for more than 100 years. Collecting long series of historical data will allow us to examine the behavior of markets in distress. Instead of blindly projecting returns from short-term historical data, investors should use the information in long-term histories to construct stress testing of portfolios. This parallels the trend in the financial services industry, where methods based on historical risk measures, such as value-at-risk, are widely recognized as unable to capture unusual but highly disruptive events. This is why traditional risk measurement techniques must be complemented by *scenario analysis,* which ideally should rely on long histories of stock markets.

Investors are always hungry for data. This has become especially true for the application of modern portfolio theory to the institutional asset allocation process, which requires quantitative estimates of risk and return. When long-term data series are unavailable for analysis, it has become common practice to use recent data only. The danger is that these data may not be representative of future performance. Although longer data series are of poorer quality, are difficult to obtain, and may reflect various political and economic regimes, they often paint a very different picture of emerging market performance.

◣ Notes

1. See, for example, Bekaert and Harvey (1995), Harvey (1995), and Divecha et al. (1992). More recently, however, Barry et al. (1998) argue that the performance of emerging markets has trailed that of U.S. stocks over longer periods.

2. For prior theoretical and empirical evidence on local pricing, see Stulz (1981) and Errunza and Losq (1985).

3. According to estimates from the World Bank debtor reporting system.

4. In addition, survival induces other spurious relationships. Goetzmann and Jorion (1995), for instance, examine the predictability of stock returns based on dividend yields and find that survivorship biases the results toward finding spurious evidence of predictability. These effects are akin to the peso problem in the foreign exchange market, where forward rates appear to be systematically biased forecasts of future spot rates, essentially because they account for a non-zero probability of devaluation that may not be observed in the test sample period.

5. The actual starting date for France is 1720, but the bourse was closed due to the French Revolution, a time during which capital did not fare well.

6. In a related paper, Stolin (1997) studies the hazard rate of times listed on the London Stock Exchange. He finds probability of disappearance of about 6% per annum, which is quite high.

7. We ignore emergence due strictly to increases in the number of listed firms. A case in point is China, in which the growth of the market has been a function of many new firms' listing. Unless appreciation and issues of new securities are uncorrelated, price appreciation can be treated as an instrument, and the results we obtain are qualitatively valid.

8. There is a long literature on integration vs. segmentation in international capital markets (see, e.g., Jorion and Schwartz [1986] or Stulz [1992]).

9. One further caveat is that the truncations are imposed exogenously. In other words, we assume that the underlying CAPM model is unaffected by re-emergence or disappearance of individual markets. This assumes that the dormant markets are observable to in-

vestors (i.e., for the pricing of global markets) but not to the empirical researcher. This limitation of the model, however, is common for all econometric models of censoring. The exogenous imposition of selection bias imposes even more subtle effects, however. In a global market, we might expect pricing effects on other markets due to the disappearance of markets. A more fundamental model of the global economy with investors, speculators, and a rich specification of the information diffusion process might allow one to investigate this question. Bossaerts (1997) helps identify pricing effects due to updating of beliefs arising from news about market crises.

10. This problem is discussed in Michaud (1989), Jorion (1985) pointed out that the practical application of mean-variance optimization to international diversification is seriously hampered by estimation risk. Stambaugh (1996) provides a framework to analyze investments whose histories differ in length.

11. For instance, Divecha et al. (1992) report that, over the five-year period ending in March 1991, the IFC Index returned 7.1% more than the FT World Index. With a correlation of 0.35 between the two indices, a mean-variance analysis reveals that investing 40% in emerging markets apparently would have increased returns by 4% annually relative to the World Index, with no greater risk.

12. In fact, Nigeria is a country for which the IFC was unable to construct a reliable index of investor return over the period since emergence. In 1993, the IFC started a new series of investable indices that were designed to measure more precisely returns that were available to foreign investors, taking into account legal and practical restrictions. These series were reconstructed to 1988, but omitted Nigeria, which was considered closed to foreign investors. In other words, while the Nigerian market survived its late-1980s crisis and bounced back from the brink of disaster, the return record was not reliable enough to be considered a fair representation of investor returns over the period.

13. We also separated the sample into the initial pre-1980 group and others. In both cases, performance right after emergence is greater than later on, although the effect is most significant for the pre-1980 group.

14. Countries watched by the IFC in 1994 include Bangladesh, Barbados, Botswana, Costa Rica, Ivory Coast, Cyprus, Ecuador, Egypt, Ghana, Honduras, Iran, Jamaica, Kenya, Kuwait, Mauritius, Morocco, Namibia, Oman, Panama, South Africa, Swaziland, Trinidad, Tunisia, and Uruguay. Of those, Costa Rica and Honduras have no stock price index, the series for Uruguay stops in 1991, and the series for Kuwait was interrupted from 1990 to 1993 because of the Gulf War.

15. In the computation of the value-weighted index, we omit South Africa, because its market value would dwarf all others. As of December 1994, the market capitalization was $226 billion, while that of the next largest market is $10 billion.

16. Bailey and Chung (1995), for instance, show that the credit spread on Mexican sovereign bonds has predictive power for expected returns on the local stock market. They hypothesize that credit risk and political risk are positively correlated, which implies that credit spreads proxy for the probability of market upheaval.

▶ References

Bailey, W., and P. Chung. "Exchange Rate Fluctuations, Political Risk and Stock Returns: Some Evidence From an Emerging Market." *Journal of Financial and Quantitative Analysis,* 30 (1995), 541–561.

Barry, C.; J. Peavy; and M. Rodriguez. "Performance Characteristics of Emerging Capital Markets." *Financial Analysts Journal,* 54 (1998), 72–80.

Bekaert, G., and C. Harvey. "Time-Varying World Market Integration." *Journal of Finance,* 50 (1995), 403–444.

Bossaerts, P. "The Dynamics of Equity Prices in Fallible Markets." Working Paper, California Institute of Technology (1997).

———. "Martingale Restrictions on Securities Prices Under Rational Expectations and Consistent Beliefs." Working Paper, California Institute of Technology (1996).

Brown, S. J.; W. N. Goetzmann; and S. A. Ross. "Survival." *Journal of Finance,* 50 (1995), 853–873.

Divecha, A.; J. Drach; and D. Stefek. "Emerging Markets: A Quantitative Perspective." *Journal of Portfolio Management,* 19 (Fall 1992), 41–50.

Erb, C.; C. Harvey; and T. Viskanta. "Country Risk and Global Equity Selection." *Journal of Portfolio Management,* 21 (Winter 1995), 74–83.

Errunza, V., and E. Losq. "International Asset Pricing Under Mild Segmentation: Theory and Tests." *Journal of Finance,* 40 (March 1985), 105–123.

Goetzmann, W., and P. Jorion. "A Longer Look at Dividend Yields." *Journal of Business,* 68 (1995), 483–508.

Harris, L., and E. Gurel. "Price and Volume Effects Associated With Changes in the S&P500 List: New Evidence for the Existence of Price Pressures." *Journal of Finance,* 41 (1986), 815–829.

Harvey, C. "Predictable Risk and Returns in Emerging Markets." *Review of Financial Studies,* 8 (1995), 773–816.

International Finance Corporation. *The IFC Indexes: Methodology, Definitions, and Practices.* Washington, DC: IFC (1995).

Jorion, P. "International Portfolio Diversification With Estimation Risk." *Journal of Business,* 58 (1985), 259–278.

Jorion, P., and W. Goetzmann. "Global Stock Markets in the Twentieth Century." *Journal of Finance,* 54 (1999), 953–980.

Jorion, P., and E. Schwartz. "Integration vs. Segmentation in the Canadian Stock Market." *Journal of Finance,* 41 (1986), 603–616.

Michaud, R. "The Markowitz Optimization Enigma: Is Optimized Optimal?" *Financial Analysts Journal,* 45 (1989), 31–42.

O'Conner, S., and D. Smith. *The G.T. Guide to World Equity Markets.* London: Euromoney Publications (1992).

Park, K., and A. Van Agtmael, eds. *The World's Emerging Stock Markets.* Chicago, IL: Probus (1993).

Shumway, T. "The Delisting Bias in CRSP Data." *Journal of Finance,* 52 (1997), 327–340.

Stambaugh, R. "Analyzing Investments Whose Histories Differ in Length." Working Paper, The Wharton School (1996).

Stolin, D. "UK Share Delisting: A Survival Analysis." Working Paper, London Business School (1997).

Stulz, R. "International Asset Pricing Models: An Integrative Survey." Working Paper, Ohio State Univ. (1992).

———. "On the Effects of Barriers to International Investment." *Journal of Finance,* 36 (Sept. 1981), 923–934.

Predicting Variations

V

Estimating the equity premium over a fixed horizon using long-term historical data is valid only if the equity premium is stationary—that is, if it does not change through time. If the equity premium does evolve over time, then it might be possible to predict it. Indeed, the potential of forecasting the future path of the stock market has captivated investors and their advisors for as long as organized markets have existed. As early as 1908, a market analyst for a popular Wall Street monthly *The Ticker: A Magazine of the Markets, The Investors' Mentor* tried to use fluctuations in the Dow Transportation Index to uncover a pattern of alternating peaks and valleys.[1] Figure 1 was a response to the great panic of 1907—at that time the worst crash in U.S. market history. In solid lines on the chart, the analyst identified roughly 40-month intervals between market peaks. Using this pattern, he (or she, since the analyst is unidentified) predicted a short-term rise in prices, followed by a crash to rival that of 1907. The dotted lines after show the forecast pattern of the market. The analyst called the next peak pretty well—only about three months too soon. However, the dire prediction of a depression in stock prices in 1912 did not materialize. The market did not see a crash of the forecast magnitude for another 18 years.

The possibilities of forecasting the stock market using past patterns of returns, and measures of relative value such as the dividend yield ratio, has been the subject of intense professional and academic research over much of the last century. At heart is the issue of whether the equity premium fluctuates in a predictable manner, using information commonly available to investors. This section of the book is composed of a number of our studies devoted to exploring the possibilities of market forecasting.

Chapter 18 is about the most famous of all stock market forecasting techniques—the Dow Theory. As the above example above shows, the Dow index was used almost since inception as a forecasting tool by analysts. Charles Henry Dow is credited with the Dow Theory, but a man named William Peter Hamilton was the actual Dow forecaster for nearly 30 years. Hamilton served as an editor for the *Wall Street Journal* from 1903 to 1929, and over that period his articles about the course of the market claimed to merely articulate and apply the theory of his predecessor to forecast future market trends. In the

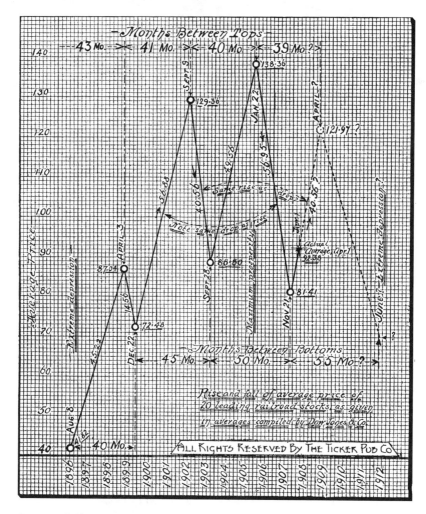

Figure 1. A Chart Record and Forecast

Notes: The analyst who created this chart described it thus: "This chart shows intervals between tops and bottoms on the long swings of the market. According to this method of calculation, the top of the present swing should be reached in April, 1909. The accuracy of the estimate is apparently demonstrated by the fact that on April 1st this year the average prices stood exactly at the point called for by the 39-month interval between the last and the next high point. It may be inferred that prices on the present upswing will not reach the high level of 1906, and that the next extreme depression will occur in 1912. A striking fact is that the last big decline corresponded in extent (within 3/4 per cent.) with the bull market of 1900 to 1902; also that the rise called for in the present upswing should equal in extent the decline in 1903."

same way that the world knows Socrates through the writings of his follower Plato, the world knows the Dow Theory only through the editorials of William Peter Hamilton. Chapter 18 is an attempt to use Hamilton's articles to see if the Dow Theory actually worked. Brown, Goetzmann, and Kumar compared decades of historical return data to the Hamilton forecasts and found that following his predictions would have yielded quite positive risk-adjusted returns—as much as 3% per year over nearly 30 years. What was Dow's secret? To try and answer that question, the article used neural-net techniques to extract the patterns he used in his forecasts. The authors then applied their synthetic Dow theory to the period from 1929 to the modern era. Surprisingly, the model showed some out-of-sample prediction ability at short investment horizons. Alas, this empirical vindication came too late for Hamilton. Academic research from the 1930s until fairly recently has scoffed at the possibility that the market can be forecast by past trends.

Ever since the watershed study by Alfred Cowles (1934; all references supplied in "Suggested Reading" unless noted otherwise) of Hamilton's predictions that virtually defined the concept of an efficient market, the prevailing wisdom in academia had been that the market is inherently unpredictable. But in the last 15 years, empirical research in financial economics has begun to uncover tantalizing evidence that long-term stock market performance might indeed be predictable. For example, in broadly cited research, Fama and French (1988a,b) investigate mean reversion in stock price indices and the forecasting power of dividend yields in the U.S. market from 1926. They find evidence of mean reversion at multiple-year horizons. In particular, a regression of the form $r_{t,t+T} = a + \beta r_{t-T,t} + e_{t,t+T}$, where $r_{t,t+T}$ is the total return or equity premium for the stock market over the horizon of length T is explained by the total return or equity premium over the period of length T immediately preceding it. A negative β suggests that periods of a low premium are followed by periods of a high premium, and vice versa. This is, in fact, a statistical formalization of the pattern that the 1908 analyst identified using graphic methods and shorter time series. Fama and French identified the strongest predictability at the four-year horizon, longer than the roughly two-year horizon estimated by the *Ticker*. Following Fama and French, Poterba and Summers (1988) used variance ratios to confirm mean reversion for a range of different markets. Campbell and Shiller (1998) found evidence that the earnings price ratio also appears to forecasts multiyear market returns. (Complete reference citations are found in "Suggested Reading.")

Although the results of these and other, later studies seem to hold the promise of equity premium predictability, researchers studying the properties of the test statistics for these long-horizon regressions note two major types of measurement problems. The first is sample size. An autocorrelation study of five-year returns has only 16 independent observations when the CRSP or Ibbotson database from 1926 to the present is used. Using overlapping data makes the sample size larger, but introduces its own kind of problems.[2] The second problem has to do with biases introduced in regressions that employ the dividend yield and the earnings price ratio, D_t/P_t and E_t/P_t, to explain future returns, $(P_{t+1} + D_t)/P_t$. Dividing both sides of the regression by a slowly evolving price variable creates problems. In general, this has been termed a "lagged dependent variable" problem. In particular, the distribution of the regression coefficients is skewed right, and ill-behaved.

The solution to the first problem of sample size is simply to collect more data. This is the motive for Chapter 19, "Patterns in Three Centuries of Stock Market Prices." Stock price data for the United Kingdom can be patched together from 1700 to the present, and data for the United States extend back to the late 1700s. The analysis finds some evidence for mean reversion around a time-varying equity premium for the U.K. data, but little evidence of any similar predictability for the U.S. sample. Chapter 20 looks more closely at the U.S. evidence on whether past returns predict future returns at the multiple-horizon level, and uses bootstrapping and simulation methods to understand the small-sample characteristics of the autoregressions, correcting for problems of overlapping observations.

Following the early evidence on dividend yields as predictors, dozens of papers have been written on the predictability of long-horizon stock returns, and the implications for portfolio choice. This is an important issue because the shrinking dividend yield in the U.S. market over the past decade has been taken by many as a prediction of a low or even negative equity premium for the future. The answer to whether these dire predictions make sense depends crucially the reliability of past econometric studies.[3] Chapters 21 and 22 take a close look at the power of dividend yields to forecast stock returns. The Goetzmann and Jorion (1993) article develops methods of testing the dividend yield effect that explicitly account for the problem of the lagged dependent regressor. Essentially, we replicated the null hypothesis that dividends do not predict future returns and then transformed them into yields for purposes of the test. We found that the distribution of the test statistic for dividend yields under the null was dramatically skewed right, biasing the results toward rejection of the null. Our evidence in general contradicts most of the past and current empirical results regarding predictability. In Chapter 22, we (again, Goetzmann and Jorion) collect evidence on U.S. and U.K. dividend yields from 1870 to the present. We find strong evidence that dividend yields forecast U.K. stock returns in the period 1926 to the present; however, the evidence for the entire sample period was near zero. This resulted from an apparently dramatic shift in the statistical relationship between yields and long-horizon returns—it was actually negative from 1871 to 1925. The longer sample for the United States yielded no reliable evidence for the dividend yield effect. Thus, paradoxically, despite positive evidence in the U.K. subsample, we fail to reproduce the effect in the market where it was first discovered.

While the U.K. and U.S. data from 1871 represent long and nearly independent samples for testing predictability, they also owe their existence to the success of the markets. For example, much of the predictive power of U.K. dividend yields is associated with the early 1970s, when share prices plunged but yields did not. Was a bet on U.K. stocks at the nadir of the market a good one? Yes, ex post. Was recovery really a certainty for the London market? We will never know. To what extent are positive results on the predictability of dividend yields due to the survival of the U.K. market? To address this issue econometrically, Goetzmann and Jorion use simulations to evaluate the effects of survival on dividend yield regressions and on tests of yield reversion. Survival makes a difference; the coefficients from regressions based upon survived markets are biased toward rejection of the null. This result is of potential interest to econometricians working on cointegration, or co-movement of economic time-series. We hope that they may eventually find closed-form corrections to the problem.

We are not the only researchers who have failed to verify earlier reports of yields' predicting long-horizon returns. Recent work by statisticians and financial economists suggests that the evidence supporting the use of the dividend yield as a predictor is relatively weak, or at best, varies with the time period over which the studies are conducted. Lanne (2002) develops a method for estimation when the dependent variable follows a near unit root, and finds that financial ratios do not predict long-horizon returns. Wolf (2000) applies subsampling methods to the problem of lagged dependent variables and fails to find evidence that yields predict returns. Ang and Bekaert (2001) look at the evidence for PE ratios and yields in international markets and find no evidence of yields forecasting long-horizon returns. Goyal and Welch (2001) point out that, while dividend yields appear to be significant predictors in the U.S. market prior to 1990, the dividend yield has poor out-of-sample properties, and out-of-sample is what counts in future asset allocation decisions. On the other hand, Lewellan (2004) argues that financial ratios like dividend yields are good predictors in the 1946 to 2000 period when the analyst takes the conditional distribution of the statistic into account.

In Chapter 23, the question is raised as to how important is changing the stock and bond allocation to the overall performance of typical portfolios. Ibbotson and Kaplan analyze a set of pension funds with announced asset allocation policies and a set of balanced mutual funds with average asset allocations. Two studies by Brinson and several coauthors (Brinson, Hood, and Beebower 1986; Brinson, Singer, and Beebower, 1991) had indicated that more than 90% of the variation in time-series returns were due to the portfolios' asset allocation. This is misleading, since 80% of a portfolio's variation in return is simply due to the volatile *realized* equity risk premium. Ibbotson and Kaplan go on to show that two other, more relevant ways of looking at asset allocation decisions have them explaining either 40% or 100% of performance. Certainly the movement of the realized equity risk premiums is the most important result explaining most portfolio performance. But how predictable is the realized equity risk premium?

In sum, the chapters in this section represent a mixed picture of the forecastability of the equity premium. On the one hand, there is evidence that the Dow Theory, long venerated by practitioners and ignored by academia, actually had some forecasting ability for short-horizon out-of-sample returns. On the other hand, the evidence presented in the following chapters, on balance, contradicts widely held academic beliefs regarding the predictability of longer-horizon returns. Although there is some evidence for predictability in subperiods of the data, the overall picture regarding the predictability of the equity premium is not a compelling one.

◣ Notes

1. *The Ticker,* 1908, 2 (2): 55. Published by the Ticker Publishing Company, New York.

2. For a complete analysis of the econometrics of the use of overlapping observations to test predictability, see Richardson and Smith (1991, 1994) and Boudoukh and Smith (1994).

3. For evidence on the dividend yield as a predictor of equity returns and premiums, see Rozeff (1984), Campbell and Shiller (1988), Fama and French (1988a,b), Hodrick (1992), and Kim, Nelson, and Starz (1991).

18 Stephen J. Brown, William N. Goetzmann, and Alok Kumar

The Dow Theory: William Peter Hamilton's Track Record Reconsidered

▲ Overview

This article was one of the most exciting pieces of research that I have ever participated in. It involves the historical clash of two giants in the field of investments, the Dow-Jones Index and the Wall Street Journal *founder Charles Henry Dow, and Alfred Cowles, founder of the Cowles Foundation for Economic Research and the father of the index on which the S&P 500 is now based. That same clash gave rise to the great schism between academic finance and Wall Street practice, between random-walk theorists and technical traders. Our article focuses squarely on the key historical study that gave birth to the random-walk theory—and finds that its conclusion was wrong.*

Alfred Cowles' 1934 test of the Dow Theory apparently provided strong evidence against the ability of Wall Street's most famous chartist to forecast the stock market. We reviewed Cowles' evidence and found that it supported the contrary conclusion. Once the proper adjustments for risk were made, the Dow Theory performed extraordinarily well. We found that following the Wall Street Journal's *timing recommendations from 1902 through 1929, when the Dow Theory articles were published, would have resulted in roughly 3% per year in risk-adjusted excess return.*

Alfred Cowles' test of the Dow Theory apparently provides strong evidence against the ability of Wall Street's most famous chartist, William Peter Hamilton, to forecast the stock market. Cowles' (1934) analysis is a landmark in the development of empirical evidence about the informational efficiency of the market. He claims that market timing based on the Dow Theory results in returns that lag the market. In this article, we review Cowles' evidence and find that it supports the contrary conclusion—the Dow Theory, as applied by Hamilton over the period 1902 to 1929, yields positive risk-adjusted returns. The difference in the results is apparently due to the lack of adjustment for risk. Cowles compares the returns obtained from Hamilton's market timing strategy to a benchmark of a fully invested stock portfolio. In fact, the Hamilton portfolio, as Cowles interprets it, is frequently out of the market. Adjustment for systematic risk appears to vindicate Hamilton as a market timer.

To estimate the risk-adjusted returns that may have been obtained by following the Dow Theory over the Hamilton period, we classify the market forecasts he made in the 255 editorials published in the *Wall Street Journal* during his tenure as editor. Using the riskless rate as a benchmark, we find that Hamilton's ratio of correct to incorrect calls is higher than would be expected by chance. Using total return data for the Cowles index of stock market returns and the S&P index over the 27-year period, we find that the systematic risk of a trading strategy proposed by Cowles based on editorials published in the *Wall Street Journal* is relatively low. We apply market timing measures used to identify skill to the time-series of returns to the Hamilton strategy, and we find significant positive evidence. An event-study analysis of the Dow Industrial Index around Hamilton's editorials shows a significant difference in mean returns over a 40-day period following bull versus bear market calls. The event study also shows that Hamilton's forecasts were based on a momentum strategy. Our finding suggests a plain reason why the Dow Theory remains to this day a popular method for timing the market: During the first three decades of this century it appeared to work. Regardless of whether it has worked since then, this early success established a reputation that has endured for decades.

Although the Dow Theory has outlived most Wall Street analysts and has been taught to generations of undergraduate investment students,[1] it may come as some surprise to learn that the Dow Theory was never written down by Charles Dow. Hamilton claimed to base his market calls on the authority of his eminent predecessor as editor, Charles Dow. It was left to others to infer the nature and content of the Dow Theory from an analysis of his editorials in the *Wall Street Journal* and Hamilton's other writings. Does an analysis of Hamilton's calls justify our belief that there was indeed a coherent theory that we have come to understand as Dow's? To investigate this issue, we develop predictive models for Hamilton's bull and bear market forecasts. A stepwise regression model provides a multivariate linear approximation to the Dow Theory. We also train a neural net on the Hamilton editorials. The results confirm the interpretation of the Dow Theory as a modified momentum strategy. This neural net produces an "automaton," which we then apply to out-of-sample forecasts from the period 1930 to the present. Preliminary results show that the Dow Theory may have continued to work after Hamilton's death.

This paper is organized as follows. The first section provides historical background on the Dow Theory and William Peter Hamilton. The second section describes the empirical test of the Dow Theory published by Alfred Cowles in 1934, and discusses its interpretation in light of current methods of risk adjustment. The third section describes our reanalysis of the Hamilton editorials, the fourth section reports the statistical modeling of Hamilton's editorials, and the fifth section concludes.

▲ *William Peter Hamilton and the Dow Theory*

Most of what we know of the Dow Theory of stock market movements comes not from the founding editor of the *Wall Street Journal,* Charles Henry Dow, but from his successor, William Peter Hamilton, who assumed the editorship of the paper upon Dow's death in 1902. Over the next 27 years until his own death in late 1929, Hamilton wrote a series of editorials in the *Wall Street Journal* and in *Barron's*, discussing and forecasting major trends in the U.S. stock market. Hamilton cited his predecessor Charles Dow's theory of stock market movements as the explicit basis for market predictions. In his 1922 book *The Stock Market Barometer,* Hamilton further explains the basic outlines of the theory. The theory presupposes that the market moves in persistent bull and bear trends. While determination of these trends is hampered by short-term deviations, Hamilton asserts that "charting" past fluctuations in the industrial and transportation indices allows the analyst to identify the primary market movement.

An acute irony, given the current reputation Dow theorists enjoy among financial economists, is that Hamilton's book succinctly articulates and defends the concept we now term informational efficiency of the stock market. According to Hamilton, "The market movement reflects all the real knowledge available. . . ." This assertion is interpreted by a later prominent Dow theorist, Robert Rhea, in 1932, to mean that:

> The Averages Discount Everything: The fluctuations of the daily closing prices of the Dow-Jones rail and industrial averages afford a composite index of all the hopes, disappointments, and knowledge of everyone who knows anything of financial matters, and for that reason the effects of coming events (excluding acts of God) are always properly anticipated in their movement. The average quickly appraise such calamities as fires and earthquakes. (Rhea [1932], p. 12)

How, then, could the theory be consistent with the notion that past market trends are predictive of future price movements? According to Hamilton, ". . . the pragmatic basis for the theory, a working hypothesis, if nothing more, lies in human nature itself. Prosperity will drive men to excess, and repentance for the consequence of those excesses will produce a corresponding depression." In other words, the bull and bear market cycles envisioned by the Dow Theory are due to "the irrational exuberance" of individual investors, which itself appears not to be rationally incorporated into prices. This assertion is one of the three main axioms[2] of the Dow Theory, as interpreted by Hamilton and Rhea.

While the basic outlines of the Dow Theory may be gleaned from Hamilton's book and editorials, Robert Rhea's reduction of the Dow Theory as "theorems"[3] is a useful guide. The main theorem states that the market movements may be decomposed into primary, secondary, and tertiary trends, the most important of which is the primary trend. Primary trends are further classified as bull and bear markets, both of which are characterized by fundamental economic activity as well as market price changes. Bull markets have three stages: "first . . . [is] . . . revival of confidence in the future of business, . . . second is the response of stock prices to the known improvement in corporation earnings, and the third is the period when speculation is rampant and inflation apparent." For primary bear markets, "the first represents the abandonment of the hopes on which the stocks were purchased at inflated prices; the second reflects selling due to decreased business and earnings, and the third is caused by distress selling of sound securities, regardless of their value" (Rhea [1932], p. 13).

The Dow Theory is translated into a guide to market timing by Hamilton by identifying the primary trend through a few key signs. First, a trend must be confirmed by both the industrials and the transportations, but the confirmation need not occur on the same day. In other words, market movements are unreliable unless evidenced across two different market sectors. Second, extended movements sideways, called "lines," presage the emergence of a definite trend. In other words, a big move following a period of quiescence is taken as the beginning of a primary trend in that direction.

These "theorems" are vague enough to admit a variety of statistical interpretations, Hamilton's fellowship in the Royal Statistical Association notwithstanding. Fortunately, we have a specific record of forecasts he made over his lifetime. These forecasts were compiled and published by Robert Rhea in 1932, and published by *Barron's*. Although it is not cited in his references, this source is likely the one used by Alfred Cowles in his analysis of the Dow Theory.

Editorials As Events

Another measure of Hamilton's skill at market timing is to treat each editorial as an event, and examine whether bull market calls are followed by positive market moves and bear market calls are followed by negative market moves. We use event-study methods applied to the daily Dow Industrial Average data to examine the index dynamics around Hamilton's calls.* Figure 18.2 shows the price path for bull, bear, and neutral calls. The paths represent the cumulated sum of the equal-weighted average appreciation return of the Dow Industrial Index over a window of 81 trading days: 40 days before publication date and 40 days following publication of the editorial. Bull calls are followed by a 1.5 percent price increase over the next 40 days on average, and bear calls are followed by 1.74 percent price decrease over the next 40 days. The difference between these two, as measured by a two-tailed t-test allowing for unequal variance, is significant at the 95 percent level (0.034 probability value). The neutral calls have a 0.21 percent return over the next 40 days. The figure also indicates the basis for Hamilton's calls. Bear calls follow steep recent declines in the Dow, and bull calls follow recent positive trends. This is consistent with a theory of market trends. The result is clearly a momentum strategy, in which steep recent declines or advances are taken as signals of future trends in that direction.

*We use the Dow Industrial Index here in place of the Cowles market index because this value-weighted index of U.S. stocks including income return is not available on a daily basis for the period in question.

▶ *Alfred Cowles' Analysis of the Dow Theory*

Alfred Cowles' article "Can Stock Market Forecasters Forecast?" was published in *Econometrica* in 1934, and is widely regarded as a landmark in the development of the efficient market theory. In the article, Cowles tests the Dow Theory by coding each of Hamilton's editorials in the *Wall Street Journal* or *Barron's* as "Bullish," "Bearish," or "Neutral." Cowles then assumes that on a bullish signal an investor places all of his wealth in stocks (50 percent in the stocks comprising the Dow Industrial Index and 50 percent in those comprising the Dow Transportation Index). A bearish signal is taken as a recommendation to short the market and a neutral signal is taken as a recommendation to invest in a riskless asset. Cowles adjusts the Dow Index for splits and dividends and estimated transaction costs to calculate total returns to the Dow timing strategy. For periods when Hamilton is out of the market, Cowles assumes he earns a riskless rate of 5 percent. He then compares this strategy with the alternative of investing 100 percent in the stock market over the same period. He concludes that the Dow Theory would have yielded 12 percent per annum, while an all-stock portfolio would have yielded 15.5 percent per annum. He regards this as prima facie evidence that the Dow Theory does not work.

Despite Cowles' careful work at calculating total returns for the two strategies, he neglects to adjust for differences in relative risk. These differences in fact appear to have been substantial. According to Cowles, "Hamilton was long of stocks 55 per cent, short 16 per cent, and out of the market 29 per cent, out of the 26 years under review." These numbers suggest that the systematic risk of the strategy is very different from 100 percent. Indeed, using the crude approximation for the average beta of $0.55 - 0.16 = 0.39$, it seems that the Dow strategy earned a risk-adjusted return of $0.12 - [0.05 + 0.39(0.155 - 0.05)] = 0.029$. In other words, Cowles' interpretation of Hamilton's strategy seems to earn 290 basis points per year on a risk-adjusted basis.

Cowles also performs a nonparametric analysis of the Hamilton recommendations, reporting the frequency of correct bull and bear market calls. Out of the 255 forecasts, he takes only the changes in recommendations as data. Thus he analyzes 29 bullish forecasts, 23 bearish forecasts, and 38 neutral forecasts. He concludes from this that half the changes in position were profitable, and half were unprofitable. The inescapable conclusion of this analysis is that an investor might have done just as well had he flipped a coin. Or would he? Note that Cowles neglects to consider the efficacy of repeated bull forecasts in a rising market and repeated bear forecasts in a falling market. Any sequence of positive calls confirmed by a rising market would be reduced to a single datum. Given that the Dow Theory is essentially a momentum strategy, this possibility is not remote. Consider an extreme example. Suppose that Hamilton had made 100 forecasts: 49 bull forecasts in a row that proved correct, and then an incorrect bull forecast, then 49 correct bear forecasts in a row, then an incorrect bear forecast. Cowles would have scored this as two correct forecasts and two incorrect forecasts. However, an investor following that advice might have done quite well. The very fact that Cowles analyzes only 90 changes in position out of 255 forecasts in a momentum-based strategy suggests that some significant percentage of the remaining 165 forecasts may have been correct.

Of course, we cannot blame Cowles for not knowing in 1934 how to calculate Jensen's alpha, nor should we have expected him fully to appreciate the subtleties of conditioning in nonparametric tests. Nevertheless, a close look at the Cowles evidence suggests that the Dow Theory, as practiced by William Peter Hamilton, merits reconsideration.

◤ Analysis of the Hamilton Editorials

To evaluate Hamilton as a market timer, we code the 255 Hamilton editorials as bullish, bearish, neutral, or indeterminate. We then collect total return information on the U.S. stock market over that period, and perform parametric and nonparametric tests of trading strategies analogous to those evaluated by Cowles. Finally, we examine the price dynamics of the Dow Industrials around editorial publication dates.

Hamilton's Editorials

Unfortunately, the recommendations in Hamilton's editorials are not always clear. Cowles' solution is to have five subjects score the editorials and then take the majority opinion on each. We use only one subject to score the editorials and find 11 indeterminate cases out of the 255, and eliminate them from the study. We calculate that the portfolio is in stocks 46 percent of the time, in bills 38 percent of the time, and short 16 percent of the time. These percentages are based on the number of months in each asset. When we count the number of bull, bear, or neutral calls, the ratios are much closer to Cowles': long 54 percent, neutral 24 percent, and short 22 percent. Our scoring therefore appears slightly different from the Cowles' analysis, which has the portfolio long more frequently. As we show in the following analysis, it is unlikely that the minor differences in interpretation of the editorials are the basis for the divergence in our results.

Nonparametric Tests

To address the basic question of Hamilton's timing skill, we examine how often the Dow beats the riskless rate over the interval following an editorial, conditional upon a bull or bear call. The interval following the editorial is defined by the day following the editorial to the day of the next Hamilton editorial. Our analysis of the frequency of successful calls differs substantially

Table 18.1
Nonparametric Test of Hamilton's Market Calls

Panel A: Contingency Table Test			
	Market Up	Market Down	Column Sum
Call up	74	56	130
Call down	18	36	54
Row sum	92	92	

Fisher's Exact Test Statistic: 8.74

Panel B: Henriksson-Merton (HM) Nonparametric Test		
Number when $m < rf$	$N1$	92
Number when $m > rf$	$N2$	92
Number of observations	N	184
Number right when $m < rf$	$n1$	36
Number wrong when $m > rf$	$n2$	18
Number of bear calls	n	54
Expected number right when $m < rf$	$E(n1)$	27
Standard deviation of $n1$		2.53
t-test for HM test		3.56

Notes: This table reports the frequency of successful versus unsuccessful bull and bear market calls by William Peter Hamilton in his column in the *Wall Street Journal* and in *Barron's* over the period December 1903 through November 1929. Identification of "Call up" and "Call down" is based on a reading of the editorial to determine Hamilton's assessment of whether the primary movement of the market was up or down. Neutral calls and calls for which the direction could not be assessed from the editorial are omitted. "Market up" and "Market down" refer to whether or not the rate of capital appreciation of the Dow Industrial index (m) exceeds the riskless rate (rf) of 5 percent per annum. We report the t-test for the nonparametric Henriksson-Merton measure of the number of expected correct calls conditional on a bear market. Fisher's Exact Test is a test about the log-odds ratio log[(upup*downdown)/(downup*downdown)]. Under the null, the variance of log odds ratio is 1/upup + 1/downdown + 1/downup + 1/updown (see McCullagh and Nelder [1983], p. 98, for details).

from Cowles. Table 18.1 shows the relationship between market calls and subsequent performance. The proportion of successful "up" calls is greater than failed "up" calls and the proportion of successful "down" calls is much higher than failed "down" calls. In fact, Hamilton appears to have been extremely successful in his bear market calls—he was right twice as often as he was wrong. In total, Hamilton was right 110 times and wrong 74 times, by our count. The neutral scores are not included in this analysis, since they are interpreted as stock returns equaling bill returns. Panel A of the table reports the results of the contingency table analysis. It shows strong evidence of association between Hamilton's calls and subsequent market performance. The Fisher's test[4] is statistically significant at the 1 percent level.

A natural test of the Dow Theory is the nonparametric Henriksson-Merton (HM) test. Developed for tests of timing ability, given a market forecast, the HM test effectively determines whether the manager provided a "put" on the market when it was valuable. The HM test is particularly appropriate in the Hamilton case because it uses the frequency of correct bear market calls as the basis for determining timing success. This is important, because it explicitly conditions on the frequency of down markets—down markets provide the only opportunity for a timer to manifest skill. The HM test gives compelling evidence that Hamilton was particularly effective in bear markets, and thus the proportion of correct bear calls is much higher than would be anticipated by chance. Panel B of the table reports the expected number of correct calls under the null, and HM's parametric approximation to the distribution of this value. The actual number lies more than three standard deviations above the benchmark.

One important issue is the implicit "I told you so" option that Hamilton had. Since we define the interval from editorial to editorial, Hamilton could simply have waited until the market confirmed his previous call, and then written an editorial claiming success. To address this issue, a different trading test is necessary.

Testing a Trading Strategy

Following Cowles, we simulate a trading strategy that moves from long stocks to short stocks to T-bills, depending on the Hamilton editorial. While Cowles apparently uses a 50/50 portfolio mixture of the Dow industrials and the Dow railroads, we use the Cowles market index: a value-weighted index of U.S. stocks, including income return. Since this index ultimately became the basis for the S&P index, we will call it the S&P. This is widely considered the highest-quality monthly return series available, and mimics a passive strategy of holding stocks. As the alternative investment we use the prevailing short-term commercial paper rates. We further assume that the portfolio could only be rebalanced monthly, which allows us to use the monthly Cowles indices. Accordingly, we take the last recommendation that appeared in a month, and then assume that this is used as a guide to rebalancing at the end of the month. As a consequence, we do not pick up intramonth returns to the Hamilton strategy. The advantage is that we avoid any benefits that might have accrued to trading on daily trends and reversals that might have been possible.

Figure 18.1 shows the relative performance of the Hamilton portfolio compared with a portfolio invested entirely in the market over the 27 years. Notice that, for most of the period, the stock market drifts sideways, until a major bull market begins in 1924. The Dow Theory actually beats a full market investment until 1926, at which point the fully invested portfolio advances beyond the timing portfolio. Hamilton's major success occurs in 1907, when he avoids the worst of the panic of that year. He also does well in 1917 and 1920, when the portfolio is out of the market during both bear runs. Overall, the figure shows that the Hamilton portfolio is less volatile than the fully invested strategy.

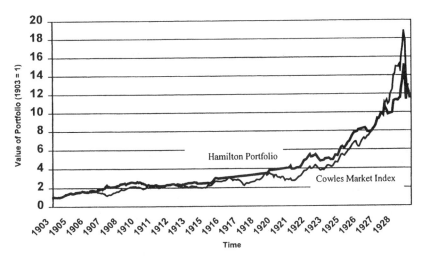

Figure 18.1. Hamilton Portfolio Versus 100% Stocks

Notes: Relative performance of the Hamilton portfolio compared to a portfolio invested entirely in the market over the 27 years. The figure indicates that the Hamilton portfolio was less volatile than the fully invested strategy.

The first column of Table 18.2 reports the results of the simulated investment strategy over the 27-year period. The annual arithmetic return to the Hamilton portfolio is 10.73 percent (10.71 percent geometric), almost indistinguishable from the annual average return obtained by holding the S&P all-stock portfolio, which yields an annual arithmetic average of 10.75 percent (10.38 percent geometric). On a risk-adjusted basis, however, the Hamilton portfolio has a higher Sharpe ratio (0.559 compared with 0.456) and a positive Jensen measure of 4.04 percent—more than 400 basis points per year. This high Jensen measure is due to a beta of 0.326 with respect to the S&P index.

Bootstrapping Tests

The rest of Table 18.2 reports the results of significance tests generated by bootstrapping the Hamilton strategy. The bootstrap is done in two different ways. In Panel A, test statistic distributions are generated by bootstrapping in the space of returns. We generate stock return series by drawing monthly returns with replacement from the S&P total return series over the sample period. Thus, we construct a null hypothesis that Hamilton has no forecasting ability, that the market follows a random walk, and that mean and variance for the market are constant. We report the mean, median, standard deviation, t-test, and extreme simulated values (5th percentile values for standard deviations and 95th percentile values for other statistics). The Hamilton portfolio yields an unusually high annual return compared with the null. The expected

Table 18.2
Summary of Simulated Trading Strategy Based on Hamilton's Editorials

	Panel A. Randomizing Returns: Bootstrap Results						
	Actual Values	Mean	Median	Standard Deviation	t-Test	Percentile Values	Rank
Hamilton beta	0.326	30.58%	30.88%	8.95%	0.220	0.448	0.561
Hamilton annual return	10.73%	5.32%	5.36%	2.10%	2.580	8.8%	0.995
Hamilton std. deviation	10.44%	10.16%	10.15%	0.76%	0.378	8.9%	0.657
Hamilton Sharpe ratio	0.559	0.045	0.043	0.208	2.468	0.401	0.990
Hamilton Jensen alpha	4.04%	−1.28%	−1.29%	2.11%	2.518	2.0%	0.996
S&P annual return	10.75%	11.09%	11.14%	2.39%	−0.140	15%	0.455
S&P std. deviation	12.83%	12.74%	12.68%	0.82%	0.111	11.5%	0.561
S&P Sharpe ratio	.456	.491	.495	.199	−0.175	0.827	0.441
	Panel B. Randomizing Strategies: Bootstrap Results						
Hamilton beta	0.326	30.93%	30.68%	9.98%	0.162	0.468	0.562
Hamilton annual return	10.73%	5.12%	5.07%	1.82%	3.090	8.2%	1.00
Hamilton std. deviation	10.44%	10.25%	10.29%	0.52%	0.369	9.3%	0.619
Hamilton Sharpe ratio	0.559	0.023	0.016	0.178	3.012	0.328	1.00
Hamilton Jensen alpha	4.04%	−1.48%	−1.62%	1.94%	2.844	2.0%	0.997

Notes: Statistics for the trading strategy are reported in column 1. The strategy follows Cowles (1934) and assumes that a short position in the stock market is taken at the end of the month in which a down call is made and that a long position in the market is taken at the end of the month in which an up call is made. Neutral calls are taken as a signal to invest in riskless securities. Randomizing returns bootstrap results are based on 500 outcomes under a null in which market returns are i.i.d. Pseudohistories of total monthly returns for the 27-year period are generated by random draws with replacement from the actual distribution of monthly returns. Randomizing strategies bootstrap results are based on 500 outcomes of a null in which market forecasts are random. Pseudostrategies are generated by drawing with replacement from the actual distribution of Hamilton forecasts with replacement. The median, mean, and standard deviation of bootstrap values are provided, together with a t-test for the significance of the difference between realized and bootstrap values, and percentile values (5th percentile for standard deviation and 95th percentile for other statistics).

return from such a strategy may be approximately 5 percent. The actual return of 9.95 percent ranks above the 99th percentile of the bootstrap distribution. While the standard deviation of the strategy is also low, it appears that the full-investment strategy also results in an unusually low standard deviation.[5] This appears to provide evidence against the random walk assumption of the bootstrap. The Sharpe measure of the Hamilton portfolio exceeds all of the boot-strapped values, and the Jensen measure of the Hamilton portfolio exceeds the 99 percent level. Neither the mean return nor the Sharpe ratio for the all-stock portfolio is unusual, although the low standard deviation puts the Sharpe ratio at the 63 percent level. Note that the standard deviation of the Hamilton Jensen measure is 1.97 percent. This means we cannot reject the joint null hypothesis that the Jensen measure is zero and returns follow a random walk.

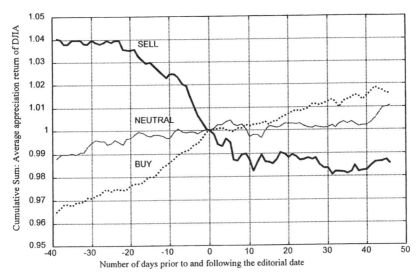

Figure 18.2. Cumulated Value of the Dow Around Editorial Dates
Notes: This figure represents the cumulated sum of the equal-weighted average appreciation return of the Dow Industrial Index over a window of 81 trading days: 40 days before publication date and 40 days following publication of the editorial.

Panel B in Table 18.2 reports the results of a different form of bootstrap. Rather than destroying the time-series structure of stock returns over the period to construct a null, we randomize in the space of strategies, holding the market realization constant. The methodology was pioneered by Cowles himself, in another part of the landmark 1934 article. In order to test whether a sample of investment newsletters has forecasting ability, he simulates a null of random stock selection (using a deck of cards!) and then compares the distribution of actual analyst performance records to those generated under a null that forecasts are simply random. Inability to reject this null leads Cowles to the conclusion that stock market forecasters could not forecast.

We apply this same procedure to Hamilton's forecasts to generate our null. We draw bull, bear, and neutral forecasts with replacement from the actual Hamilton editorial series. We thus generate 500 simulated track records under a null that the editor was, in effect, flipping a coin, properly weighted so as to give the same expected proportions of bull, bear, and neutral forecasts as in the original series. The advantage of this is that we do not break the actual time-series characteristics of the market history itself. Our bootstrap in the space of strategies now conditions upon the true market realization. We do, however, alter the time-series characteristics of Hamilton's calls. Although they no longer forecast future returns by construction, they also bear no relationship to past returns. They are no longer conditioned upon the time-series behavior of the market.

Bootstrapping in the space of strategies yields essentially the same result as bootstrapping in the space of returns. The alpha and Sharpe ratios are in the extreme tails of the bootstrapped distributions. We can clearly reject the null that Hamilton could have done as well by flipping an appropriately weighted coin.

Recovering the Mind of the Dow Theorist

One problem in the modern practice of the Dow Theory is the question of what actually *is* the theory. All we really know about the Dow Theory is contained in the writings of his successor, and these writings do not give us a formal explanation of the philosophy. Rather, they are editorial prophesies on the direction of the market that claim to be based on Dow's theory. They constitute a fascinating but ambiguous text that authors over decades have tried to refine into a consistent, applicable methodology for replicating Hamilton's success. Past researchers interested in testing the Dow Theory have always been challenged to define it first. We took a different approach. We decided to reconstitute the theory using high-tech neural network programs to see if there was any constant pattern to the predictions. For example, were they based on trends or reversal patterns? What time-horizon of market trends did the theory rely on? We "trained" a neural net on Hamilton's predictions to see what patterns they may have been based upon. Our neural net analysis gave us a fascinating array of chart shapes that were apparently latent in the Hamilton editorials. I think of them as ghostly images recovered from a decades-old text that reflect the conceptual patterns—the visual modes of thought—of one of the world's great market timers. The recovery of these past mental forms seems to me a particularly interesting application of neural network technology.

◣ Recovering the Dow Theory

Stepwise Regression

Hamilton's editorials give us a rare opportunity to recover the rules used by a successful Dow theorist. The issue of what exactly is the Dow Theory has challenged market analysts virtually since the beginning of the century. With the series of Hamilton calls, and the technology of modern nonlinear statistical methods, we can attempt to understand the basis for the theory. Was Hamilton simply lucky or did he stick to basic rules? Were these rules consistent with his writings and the writings of others about the Dow Theory? Can these rules help time the market today? To address these questions we develop a linear and a nonlinear model of Hamilton's behavior over the 27-year period. We then see how the rules have performed in the period since Hamilton's death. Table 18.3 reports the results of a stepwise regression for which the standard AIC cri-

Table 18.3
Stepwise Regression of Hamilton's Bear Market Calls

	Value	t-Stat.
(Intercept)	−1.72	−19.94
sixty.day.returns	−14.24	−6.67
sixty.day.returns.tr	−9.72	−6.38
thirty.day.returns	−3.70	−2.70
thirty.day.returns.tr	6.14	3.18
same.sign	0.12	1.30
sixty.day.returns:same.sign	12.19	5.19
sixty.day.returns:thirty.day.returns	−93.76	−6.45
thirty.day.returns:thirty.day.returns.tr	64.39	3.82
sixty.day.returns.tr:thirty.day.returns.tr	−235.84	−6.73
sixty.day.returns:thirty.day.returns.tr	100.69	4.21
sixty.day.returns.tr:thirty.day.returns	110.31	3.64
sixty.day.returns.tr:thirty.day.returns:thirty.day.returns.tr	−951.33	−3.96
sixty.day.returns:thirty.day.returns:thirty.day.returns.tr	345.69	2.73

Notes: This table reports the results of a stepwise regression of Hamilton's bear market calls on a number of variables constructed from the preceding values of Dow Industrial and Dow Transportation indices over the period 1902 through 1929. Industrial Index returns are specified unless the "tr" suffix indicates the transportation index. "Same sign" indicates that the past 30-day returns of the indices have the same sign. Colons indicate interactions among variables.

terion has been used to prune variables. The dependent variable in the regression is a Hamilton bear call. In particular, we use continuous bear calls rather than the handful of bear editorials. The reason for this is our presumption that the failure to make a bull or neutral call is equivalent to a continued forecast of a down market. Of course, this effectively treats each day following a bear call as an independent event for statistical purposes. Nevertheless, we throw away much potentially valuable information that enters the decision to be a bear when we concentrate on editorials alone.

Notice in Table 18.3 that the coefficients confirm the hypothesis that the Dow Theory is a momentum theory. Decreases in the 60-day trends for the Industrials and Transportation indices forecast bear calls. The indicator variable capturing whether the past 30-day returns have been the same sign for the two indices is positive, but not significant. The interaction between this variable and 60-day returns is significant, as are interactions between 60-day and 30-day lagged returns for the two indices. In fact, the significance of these intertemporal interactions strongly suggests a nonlinear response of the decision to call a bear market with respect to past price dynamics. This result is consistent with the conventional wisdom regarding the content of the Dow Theory in general and the axioms set forth in the Rhea (1932) volume in particular.

However, the significance of these nonlinear intertemporal interactions suggests that there may be possible interpretations of the Dow Theory yet to receive attention in the academic or practitioner literature. These potential interpretations are necessarily excluded from the stepwise regression procedure. Recent developments in artificial intelligence–based neural net procedures allow us to search over all possible patterns in the data that could conceivably be input to the theory. These procedures also allow us to construct a Hamilton automaton that can be used to examine the properties of the Dow Theory both during the Hamilton period and after he stopped writing his editorials.

Artificial Intelligence Methods for Detecting Patterns

Artificial intelligence–based procedures have become quite popular among practitioners who seek to identify recurring patterns in time-series data generated in financial markets. The belief is that these patterns reflect the dynamics of the marketplace and that they allow us to predict future market movements. Such patterns generate trading rules. For example, a simple moving average (MA) trading rule states that, when the short-term (usually 1- to 5-day) moving average is greater than the long-term moving average (usually greater than 50 days), a rising market is indicated. The trading rule would then generate a buy signal. Such a trading rule would identify any pattern with a shape similar to the pattern shown in Figure 18.3.

Several studies provide support for the idea that these patterns can predict market movements. In a study by Brock, Lakonishok, and LeBaron (1992), the ability of two simple trading rules to predict the movements of the Dow-Jones Industrial Average (DJIA) is investigated using bootstrapping techniques. Allen and Karjalainen (1995) and Neely, Weller, and Dittmar (1997) use genetic programming to search for optimal trading rules in the foreign exchange market. Our research objectives and the modeling approach are different, though similar in spirit to Brock et al. (1992) and to Neely et al. (1997).

Our goal in this paper is neither to identify a set of optimal trading rules nor to propose an autonomous trading system.[6] Instead, we test whether Hamilton's interpretation of the Dow Theory (based on the 255 editorials he wrote for the *Wall Street Journal*) can predict stock market movements. In more general terms we want to uncover the rules of the Dow Theory (as interpreted by Hamilton) and understand the theory's implications for the efficient market hypothesis.

In contrast to other studies, we have developed a prediction model that operates directly in the domain of patterns. We use the Feature Vector Analysis (FEVA) methodology developed in Kumar and McGee (1996) to forecast the state of Hamilton's recommendation. Feature Vector Analysis is particularly appropriate for modeling Hamilton's decision-making process because it reduces the dynamics of past price series to trend shapes called features. These features amplify the "topological" characteristics of the data set and are typically cited by timers and technical traders as indicators of future market activity. These features include rising trends, falling trends, "head and shoulders," resistance levels, and so on. A recurrent neural net algorithm uses these

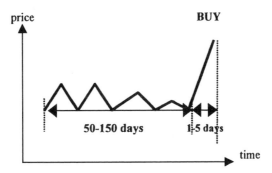

Figure 18.3. An Example (Schematic) of the Type of Pattern a Simple Moving Average (MA) Trading Rule Would Detect

shapes as inputs and, through "training" on the 1902 through 1929 period, identifies a set of characteristic features related to the state of Hamilton's recommendation at any given time. The algorithm then develops a nonlinear function mapping of these features into a recommendation. Clustering of the preprocessed data allows us to identify dominant patterns in the data. In general, interpreting the model identified by the neural net is difficult. However, interpreting the prediction function learned by the neural net is possible. It is the identification of trend shapes through FEVA analysis that distinguishes our methodology from other modeling techniques.

The FEVA methodology used in our study can be extended in an obvious way for identifying "optimal" trading rules. Following the FEVA approach, there is no need to prespecify the trading rules (or rule templates). A search is done directly in the domain of patterns. Such issues are currently being investigated and the results will be reported in subsequent work.

This methodology is closely related to artificial intelligence–based methods such as neural networks (NNs)[7] and evolutionary computation[8] that have been the subject of much recent interest in finance. Neural network algorithms are statistical procedures to fit a reduced functional form to data. They are similar in intent to stepwise regressions in that they try a wide range of model specifications to reduce in-sample residual variation. But unlike stepwise regressions, their specification is not necessarily linear and the model form need not be explicitly specified. In fact, the innovation of NN models is that they offer a parsimonious but flexible nonlinear specification. Campbell, Lo, and MacKinlay (1997) provide a general overview of the applicability of neural net modeling to financial time series prediction problems.[9] Recent applications of neural net methods to financial markets suggest that nonlinear dynamics are potentially important characteristics of markets.

Current research shows that neural net models have the potential to uncover sophisticated nonlinear processes that lead to price changes in financial markets, but they do have limitations. They are simply good tools to fit in sample—indeed, given enough computer time and enough hidden layers, they can fit in sample perfectly.[10] The resulting functions may have no economic interpretation. Unlike the stepwise regression above, it is difficult to check how the rules conform to the general understanding of the Dow Theory. Not only are there no "standard errors" about coefficients, there are no identifiable coefficients, since input data are recombined as intermediate variables in the hidden layers. Finally, as with all curve-fitting, there is no guarantee of out-of-sample performance. Though the neural net can recover sophisticated rules, no such consistent rules may be underlying the observed data. In the case of the Dow Theory, for example, Hamilton's calls may be full of "sound and fury, signifying nothing." The FEVA methodology employed in our work (described in detail in Appendix 1) attempts to eliminate these drawbacks associated with standard NN modeling procedure.

Feature Vectors

To identify the distinct shapes or visual cues that can be used to formulate market timing strategies in the DJIA time series, we classify features according to basic patterns of the DJIA time series. The means of half of the most influential 24 clusters are pictured in Figures 18.4 and 18.5. Each cell represents the daily DJIA trends used to predict a Hamilton call. Figure 18.4 shows the 12 most influential sell signals used by the algorithm. Figure 18.5 shows the 12 most influential buy signals used by the algorithm. Together, they represent the mapping of a visual sign into a recommendation—presumably, Hamilton used the stock-level movements in this way, rather than applying a complex formula estimated with "post-modern" statistical techniques like neural nets.

The sell indicators are what we expect from the linear model. Recent down-trends are signs to sell. We also find, however, that falls from recent peaks are strong sell indicators. One can also find in these patterns classic technical indicators such as "head and shoulders" forms. The buy indicators show forms that differ dramatically: Besides upward slopes, it appears that recovery from recent declines is an indicator to get into the market.

The variety of influential clusters is instructive. Notice that there are not large differences across many of the basic shapes. Could Hamilton have discriminated among these different types? Can we reject the hypothesis that the first, say, five clusters are actually shapes drawn from the same distribution? It is doubtful on both counts. Not only does the clustering stage of our algorithm appear to split cases too finely, it also appears to identify unique cases too often, rather than searching for general rules. Many shapes represent basic forms like positive and negative trends, "U" shapes, and "hump" shapes, but some feature clusters appear noisy or structureless. These must result from overfitting within sample. The structureless clusters are likely to be limited in applications out of sample and their presence in the set is an indication that the model is overfit to some degree. Without training the net on out-of-sample data, however, it is difficult to fine tune the FEVA approach to focus only on general shapes.

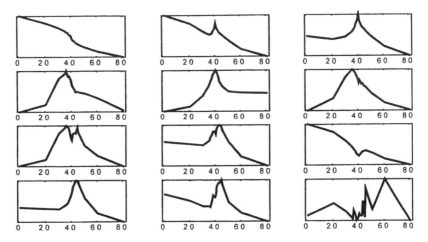

Figure 18.4. Twelve Prominent Sell Indicators

Notes: FEVA plots representing the "structure" of the DJIA time series. We obtain a 100-cluster solution for the enhanced dataset (27,774 × 49 matrix) and select the 12 prominent FEVA sell indicators from the solution. Patterns represent the price path of the DJIA over the 80 days preceding the forecast. The vertical axis is the price and the horizontal axis represents the number of days used to construct the feature vector.

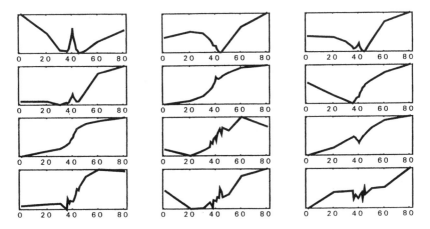

Figure 18.5. Twelve Prominent Buy Indicators

Notes: FEVA plots representing the "structure" of the DJIA time series. We obtain a 100-cluster solution for the enhanced dataset (27,774 × 49 matrix) and select the 12 prominent FEVA buy indicators from the solution. Patterns represent the price path of the DJIA over the 80 days preceding the forecast. The vertical axis is the price and the horizontal axis represents the number of days used to construct the feature vector.

In-Sample Performance

In the 1902 through 1929 period there were 3,599 buy calls, 1,143 sell calls, and 2,912 neutral calls. Compared with this, the NN trained over this interval predicts 4,464 sells, 469 buys, and 2,721 neutrals for the in-sample data. One issue that is not clear from analysis of the Hamilton editorials is why there were long periods over which no forecasts were made. Notice that there are two long neutral periods. Are we to presume that he felt no updating of his previous predictions was necessary, or was he temporarily out of the business of forecasting the market? If the long hiatus in 1917 and 1918 were due to the latter, then the neural net would be training on periods in the sample with no information content. While it might fit these periods well in sample, this would introduce errors in the model.

Out-of-Sample Performance

We have an ideal holdout sample for evaluating whether the Dow Theory (or, more properly, the Hamilton strategy) works to forecast trends in the market. We apply the NN model to predict calls for the period of 15 September 1930 to 1 December 1997, a total of 17,457 trading days. For the out-of-sample data, the NN predicts 10,004 buys, 6,131 sells, and 1,322 neutral calls. Table 18.4 shows the result of a timing strategy based on the Hamilton model.[11] Instead of shorting the market on sell calls we assume the investor holds the riskless asset conditional upon a sell call. We do this under two assumptions. First we assume that the investor can act immediately on the call. This implies that it is possible to buy or sell at the opening stock prices and that these are the same as yesterday's closing prices. This strategy is the "Next Day Hamilton Strategy." As an alternative, we also consider what would happen if the investor could trade only at the close of the day that the forecast comes out. This is the "Second Day Hamilton Strategy." We consider this alternative because on days with big drops, like the 1987 crash, opening prices differ considerably from their previous close. Thus an investor who bought the paper, or saw the signal before the opening of the market, probably cannot take full advantage of the implied signal even absent trading costs or other frictions.

Note that this change makes a big difference. The Next Day Hamilton Strategy has a much higher return than the Second Day Hamilton Strategy. The Second Day Strategy has a return over the entire history almost exactly equal to the buy and hold return, and would be less than that after transactions costs. However, the strategy generates returns with less variance and lower systematic risk. Whether the substantial returns of the Next Day Strategy represent genuine daily persistence, or whether they are simply artifacts of nontrading (which is likely to be more important in the early years of the sample, when volume was lower for all stocks) is a subject for further investigation.

Table 18.4 reports summary statistics for the three strategies over the entire out-of-sample period as well as decade by decade. It is clear that the strat-

Table 18.4
Summary Statistics for Out-of-Sample Performance

Panel A: Whole Period			
	Arithmetic Mean	Geometric Mean	Annual Standard Deviation
DJIA	7.07	5.48	18.30
HamNext	9.97	9.87	11.90
Hamilton2nd	5.91	5.52	12.10

Panel B: Subperiods			
DJIA	Cap App	HamNext	Ham2nd
1930–39	1.477	11.10	2.43
1940–49	3.213	6.04	5.66
1950–59	9.641	9.91	5.27
1960–69	7.712	9.68	6.53
1970–79	0.409	6.74	4.30
1980–89	12.626	11.29	7.01
1990–97	15.442	16.24	10.72

Notes: This table reports the returns for two investment strategies over the period 1 September 1930 through 1 December 1997. DJIA is the capital appreciation returns of the Dow Industrials, without dividends. "HamNext" are the returns to investing at the opening of the day of the out-of-sample Hamilton call generated by the neural net model. A neutral or buy call is taken as a signal to be fully invested in the Dow Jones Industrial Average. A sell call is taken as a signal to be invested in cash, which is assumed to earn no interest. "Hamilton2nd" are the returns to investing at the close-of-the-day prices on the day on which the forecast appears. Arithmetic returns only are reported for the subperiods.

egy works best in periods of sharp market decline. The Second Day Strategy dominates the buy and hold even on an arithmetic return basis in the 1930s, the 1940s, and the 1970s. Even the Next Day Strategy does not dominate the buy and hold in the 1980s. These results indicate that although the Dow Theory appears to have some power to predict returns in the postsample period, normal trading frictions would preclude using the theory to generate large excess returns, particularly in the most recent period. However, it is interesting to note that under the assumption of trading at the close of the editorial day, the results are quite comparable to those obtained during Hamilton's lifetime—returns close to the buy and hold with lower levels of risk. A more precise estimate of trading profits would depend on a realistic estimate of trading costs.[12]

In sum, the results from the application of neural net estimation to William Peter Hamilton's 1902 to 1929 market forecasts suggest that the Dow Theory was more than a random decisionmaking process on the part of one editorialist. Our cluster analysis of the feature vectors used to successfully fit a model of Hamilton's forecasts in sample suggests that he based his decisions on structures that resemble both persistent positive and negative trends, as well as positive and negative reversals. The market forecasts that our neural net algorithm developed appear to have some predictive power out of sample. Lack of reliable daily return data and trading cost data over the period since 1930 prevents us from precisely calculating return earned by following the Hamilton model versus return to the buy and hold strategy. However, it appears that the strategy does reduce portfolio volatility and, depending upon whether immediate execution of a sell signal is possible, it may enhance returns in some periods.

Luck or Skill?

There is a natural survivorship story that could conceivably explain the great success of the Dow Theory. Perhaps there were numerous business periodicals in the early part of the century, each of them making calls about the market. Some were wrong and some were right. Hamilton's famous prediction of a great crash, made in the late summer of 1929, could conceivably have earned the *Wall Street Journal* and the Dow Theory their immortality while the other forecasters ended up in the dustbin of history. In other words, it could have been luck. The real test of the theory would be out of sample, but unfortunately, Hamilton died a few months after the 1929 crash. But, remember, we built a neural net model of his predictions. We were able to run a crude out-of-sample test, beginning in 1929 using this model. Perhaps the results should not have surprised us. Our neural net version of the Dow Theory performed about the same out of sample as in sample. Could investors make money by following the Dow Theory then or now? That, of course, depends on the transactions costs of following the recommendations. Never the less, the statistical success of the Dow Theory suggests that at least some part of the equity risk premium may be forecast with trend information. After all, William Peter Hamilton did it, from 1902 to 1929 and beyond.

◣ Conclusion

A review of the evidence against William Peter Hamilton's timing abilities suggests just the opposite—his application of the Dow Theory appears to have yielded positive risk-adjusted returns over a 27-year period at the beginning of the century. The basis of this track record seems to have been his ability to forecast bull and bear market moves. Whether this means that his interpretation of the Dow Theory is correct, or whether it simply means that Hamilton was one lucky forecaster among many market analysts, is still an open question. Given all of the financial periodicals published at the beginning of the century, it may not be surprising that one turned out to have been correct in calling market moves. Regardless of the issue of luck versus skill, however, it appears that Hamilton followed rules based on observation of recent market trends that are recoverable by nonlinear estimation methods.

The contribution of this paper is not simply to show that Hamilton was a successful market timer. Alfred Cowles' (1934) analysis of the Hamilton record is a watershed study that led to the random-walk hypothesis, and thus played a key role in the development of the efficient market theory. Ever since Cowles' article, "chartists" in general, and Dow theorists in particular, have been regarded by financial economists with skepticism. Our replication of Cowles' analysis yields results contrary to Cowles' conclusions. At the very least, it suggests that more detailed analysis of the Hamilton version of the Dow Theory is warranted. In broader terms it also suggests that the empirical foundations of the efficient market theory may not be as firm as long believed.

◣ *Appendix 1. FEVA Modeling*

Our neural net prediction model employs four distinct methodologies. In the first part, feature vector analysis is used for preprocessing the raw dataset (Kumar and McGee [1996]). Second, a clustering[13] stage identifies feature vector "types." At that point, a recurrent neural network model is employed to build a nonlinear prediction model (Elman [1990]). An evolutionary programming technique is used to select the feature vector size and its components (Fogel [1994]). The main idea in FEVA is to generate a vector of input information as of time t which captures how a data point is "embedded" in its surroundings. It is a snapshot of metric and nonmetric features of the local neighborhood of a given datum. FEVA components can be fundamental metric measures (time, given value of the datum, etc.), derived metric measures (differences, ratios, rates of change, etc.), categorical measures, and non-metric measures (ordinal properties). By introducing these additional attributes for each period, we effectively increase the dimensionality of the dataset, and with increased dimensionality we expect a richer set of features to be identifiable.

The evolutionary feature selection algorithm selects an "enhanced" dataset consisting of 49 features for feature vector analysis, the components of which include various lagged values of the DJIA price level, the DJIA return, and an up/down indicator. All calculations are performed with respect to a time period (focus point) preceding the variable to be predicted. We set this period to 40 days before the call to forecast. Backward lags from the focus point consist of 1, 2, 3, 4, 5, 10, 20, and 40 days, and forward lags of 1, 2, 3, 4, 5, 10, 20, and 40 days are formed. Altogether we use 81 data points for constructing the feature vector. The coded Hamilton editorials, DJIA, and the DJTA form the training set for the NN model (total of 7,735 data points). We lose 81 data points to build feature vectors and are left with a 7,654 × 49 matrix as the training data. The dataset, enhanced by the feature vectors, is used to train a NN: 69-20-3 Elman recurrent neural net model.[14] In an Elman recurrent NN, there are additional time series in the input layer that are simply copies of the values from the hidden layer output. Altogether there are 49 inputs from the dataset and 20 additional series taken by the Elman model from the hidden layer to the input layer, giving a total of 69 inputs in the first layer. The output layer consists of three vectors predicting buy, sell, and neutral calls, each one of them a mutually exclusive binary variable. For example, an output of (1,0,0) is a call to "buy," whereas (0,1,0) is a "sell" signal. The NN is trained for 200 iterations and an SSE of 4,967.87 is obtained. The SSE continues to improve after 200 iterations, but at a very slow rate. So to prevent overfitting, we stop the training after 200 iterations. We find that increasing the number of series in the hidden layer improves the SSE but has an adverse effect on the predictive performance (as expected) of the NN because the network had started to "overlearn."

◣ Notes

1. For a typical (albeit quite excellent) textbook treatment, see Bodie, Kane, and Marcus (1997), pp. 414–417.

2. The other two axioms emphasize the existence of a primary trend in market movements and assert the fact that even though the theory is not infallible, it still is an invaluable aid for making speculations about the market movements.

3. Rhea (1932) proposes 12 theorems but only the relevant ones are discussed in our paper. There is a theorem relating price movements and trading volume: "Bull markets terminate in a period of excessive activity and begin with comparatively light transactions." We do not study price-volume relationships in this article.

4. See McCullagh and Nelder (1983), p. 98, for details of the Fisher's Exact Test.

5. This is consistent with the hypothesis that the market over this period displayed mean-reversion.

6. The results shown in this article must be interpreted with caution. We have not considered transactions costs in our analysis and a successful implementation of our methodology must take these costs into account.

7. Neural net models are generalized, semiparametric, nonlinear function estimators. Smith (1993) is a good introductory book that concentrates on one type of neural networks, namely, feedforward neural networks (one of the most commonly used NNs). The BASIC code for implementing a two-layered network is provided. Wasserman (1993) is an intermediate-level book and provides a good introduction to different flavors of neural networks. Other learning paradigms are also discussed. Hertz, Krogh, and Palmer (1991) provide a clear and concise description of the theoretical foundations of neural networks using a statistical mechanical framework.

8. Evolutionary computation refers to a set of algorithms inspired by the process of natural evolution. These algorithms try to simulate the "survival of the fittest" strategy, a key feature of natural evolution. A "parallel search" is performed in a multidimensional space (problem space) for optimal "good" solutions where the search process is probabilistic but not random. Four methodologies developed independently fall into this class: (1) genetic algorithms (GA), (2) genetic programming (GP), (3) evolutionary programming (EP), and (4) evolutionary strategies (ES). See Mitchell (1996) for an introduction.

9. A collection of papers that investigate the applicability of nonlinear and artificial intelligence–based techniques for time-series prediction tasks appear in Casdagli and Eubank (1992) and Weigend and Gershenfeld (1994).

10. In fact, White (1989) has shown that theoretically a neural net model is capable of representing any nonlinear functional form.

11. However, absent a realistic estimate of transaction costs over this extended interval, the numbers reported in Table 18.4 can best be considered an upper bound on the performance generated by the Dow strategy.

12. In addition, at the present time, we do not have a daily income return series for the Dow that would allow us to exactly calculate returns. To mitigate this, we make the assumption that income is not earned by the riskless asset. Thus, when dividend yields are close to the riskless rate, these effects should be offsetting. Furthermore, the DJIA is a price-weighted index, not value-weighted index, and thus it is not strictly investable without active reweighting. This may also affect the interpretation of the results to the extent that our summary statistics do not represent achievable returns.

13. We use the clustering method developed in Kohonen (1995) for grouping features into a reduced set to examine the structural similarity of the DJIA series.

14. Elman (1990) develops a neural net model that allows the intermediate series—the so-called "hidden layer"—to be used as original inputs. This simply allows for a richer potential nonlinear interaction among series and is well suited for time-series analysis where the objective is to identify spatial and temporal patterns.

▲ References

Allen, Franklin, and Risto Karjalainen, 1998, Using genetic algorithms to find technical trading rules, Rodney L. White Center for Financial Working Papers (Rev. 20-93).

Angeline, Peter, George Sanders, and Jordan Pollack, 1994, An evolutionary algorithm that constructs recurrent neural networks, *IEEE Transactions on Neural Networks* 5, 54–65.

Arthur, Brian, John Holland, Blake LeBaron, Richard Palmer, and P. Tayler, 1997, Asset pricing under exogenous expectations in an artificial stock market; in Brian Arthur, Steven Durlauf, and David Lane, eds.: *The Economy As an Evolving Complex System II,* A Proceedings Volume in the Santa Fe Studies in the Sciences of Complexity (Addison-Wesley Publishing Company, Reading, Mass.).

Bodie, Zvi, Alex Kane, and Alan Marcus, 1997, *Essentials of Investments* (Irwin McGraw Hill, Boston, Mass.).

Brock, William, Josef Lakonishok, and Blake LeBaron, 1992, Simple technical trading rules and stochastic properties of stock returns, *Journal of Finance* 47, 1731–1764.

Campbell, John, Andrew Lo, and Craig MacKinlay, 1997, *The Econometrics of Financial Markets* (Princeton University Press, Princeton, N.J.).

Casdagli, Martin, and Stephen Eubank, 1992, *Nonlinear Modeling and Forecasting,* A Proceedings Volume in the Santa Fe Studies in the Sciences of Complexity (Addison-Wesley Publishing Company, Reading, Mass.).

Cootner, Paul, 1964, *The Random Character of the Stock Market Prices* (MIT Press, Cambridge, Mass.).

Cowles, Alfred, 1934, Can stock market forecasters forecast? *Econometrica* 1, 309–324.

Elman, Jeffrey, 1990, Finding structure in time, *Cognitive Science* 14, 179–211.

Fogel, David, 1994, An introduction to simulated evolutionary optimization, *IEEE Transactions on Neural Networks* 5, 3–14.

Granger, Clive, and Timo Terasvirta, 1992, Experiments in modeling nonlinear relationships between time series, in Martin Casdagli and Stephen Eubank, eds.: *Nonlinear Modeling and Forecasting,* A Proceedings Volume in the Santa Fe Studies in the Sciences of Complexity (Addison-Wesley Publishing Company, Reading, Mass.).

Hamilton, William, 1922, *The Stock Market Barometer: A Study of Its Forecast Value Based on Charles H. Dow's Theory of the Price Movement* (Barron's, New York, N.Y.).

Henricksson, Roy, and Robert Merton, 1981, On market timing and investment performance. II. Statistical procedures for evaluating forecasting skills, *Journal of Business* 54, 513–533.

Hertz, John, Anders Krogh, and Richard Palmer, 1991, *An Introduction to the Theory of Neural Computation* (Addison-Wesley Publishing Company, Reading, Mass.).

Hsieh, David, 1991, Chaos and nonlinear dynamics: Application to financial markets, *Journal of Finance* 46, 1839–1887.

Kohonen, Teuvo, 1995, *Self-Organizing Maps* (Springer Verlag, New York, N.Y.).

Kumar, Alok, and Victor McGee, 1996, FEVA (Feature Vector Analysis): Explicitly looking for structure and forecastability in time series data, *Economic and Financial Computing,* Winter 1996, 165–189.

LeBaron, Blake, 1994, Nonlinear diagnostics and simple trading rules for high-frequency foreign exchange rates, in Andreas Weigend and Neil Gershenfeld, eds.: *Time Series Prediction: Forecasting the Future and Understanding the Past* (Addison-Wesley Publishing Company, Reading, Mass.).

McCullagh, Peter, and John Nelder, 1983, *Generalized Linear Models* (Chapman and Hall, Ltd., Cambridge, England).

Michalewicz, Zbigniew, 1992, *Genetic Algorithms + Data Structure = Evolution Programs* (Springer Verlag, New York, N.Y.).

Mitchell, Melanie, 1996, *An Introduction to Genetic Algorithms* (MIT Press, Cambridge, Mass.).

Neely, Christopher, Paul Weller, and Rob Dittmar, 1997, Is technical analysis in foreign exchange market profitable? A genetic programming approach, *Journal of Financial and Quantitative Analysis* 32, Dec. 1997.

Rhea, Robert, 1932, *The Dow Theory* (Barron's, New York, N.Y.).

Scheinkman, Jose, and Blake LeBaron, 1989, Non-linear dynamics and stock returns, *Journal of Business* 62, 311–337.

Smith, Murray, 1993, *Neural Networks for Statisticians* (Van Nostrand Reinhold, New York, N.Y.).

Wasserman, Philip, 1993, *Advanced Methods in Neural Computing* (Van Nostrand Reinhold, New York, N.Y.).

Weigend, Andreas, and Neil Gershenfeld, 1994, *Time Series Prediction: Forecasting the Future and Understanding the Past* (Addison-Wesley Publishing Company, Reading, Mass.).

Weigend, Andreas, Bernado Huberman, and David Rumelhart, 1992, Predicting sunspots and exchange rates with connectionist networks, in Martin Casdagli and Stephen Eubank, eds.: *Nonlinear Modeling and Forecasting,* A Proceedings Volume in the Santa Fe Studies in the Sciences of Complexity (Addison-Wesley Publishing Company, Reading, Mass.).

White, Halbert, 1989, Connectionist nonparametric regression: Multilayer feedforward networks can learn arbitrary mappings, *Neural Networks* 3, 535–549.

19 William N. Goetzmann

Patterns in Three Centuries of Stock Market Prices

▶ Overview

The key point of this article is that, if you want to look at long-term cyclical patterns in the stock market, you have to get long-term data. Some of the most exciting debates in finance over the last decade have focused on whether there are predictable multiyear fluctuations in the stock market. Of course, the quest for economic cycles in markets precedes even Charles Dow and Nikolai Kondratieff, but data availability is always a fundamental barrier. As Alice Slotsky ([1997] see "Suggested Reading" for full cite) suggests, it may have been the desire to correlate the predictable cycles of astronomical phenomena with the swings in market prices that motivated Seleucid Empire scribes in Babylon to meticulously record monthly prices for six basic commodities, along with planetary positions and river levels from 463 B.C. to 72 B.C. For this article, I had to make do with three centuries of prices taken from the London and New York Stock Exchanges. I found some interesting evidence in the U.K. data for long-term cyclical patterns.

▶ Abstract

This article applies autoregression and rescaled range statistics to very long stock market series to test the hypothesis that long-term temporal dependencies are present in financial data. For the annual capital appreciation returns to the London Stock Exchange, evidence of persistence in raw returns greater than 5 years and of mean reversion in deviations from rolling 20-year averages is found. Similar patterns are observed for the New York Stock Exchange; however, they are not significant at traditional confidence levels.

▶ Introduction

Tests about the temporal behavior of long-horizon stock returns by Fama and French (1988) have suggested the possibility of mean reversion in stock prices and breathed new life into the Dow theory (see Rhea 1932), which claims that the stock market follows an alternating pattern of bull and bear markets. The importance of the Fama and French research lies not in the identification of a particular stochastic model of stock return behavior but in the implication explored by, among others, Poterba and Summers (1988) and Shiller (1989) that financial markets may be subject to temporary "fads" or at least periodically time-varying expected returns. The Fama and French research has motivated several methodological studies of mean reversion tests. Bootstrapping tests by Kim, Nelson, and Startz (1988), Goetzmann (1990), McQueen (1992), and Richardson (in press) have explicitly modeled serial independence of monthly and annual stock returns and have tended to reject mean reversion of long-term stock returns in favor of the more parsimonious random walk model of multiple year stock returns.

Poterba and Summers (1988) observe that the failure to distinguish between low-frequency mean reversion and complete unpredictability of returns lies in the power of the tests used to examine them. For instance, a test of mean reversion in 5-year stock market returns based on the data available from the Center for Research in Security Prices (CRSP) monthly files has only 11 independent observations—hardly enough to draw convincing conclusions about repeated temporal patterns.

This lack of data has led to ingenious attempts to extract more information from the existing series. Fama and French (1988) use overlapping observations rather than temporally independent returns and correct for the lack of independence in the errors by the method proposed by Hansen and Hodrick (1980). They find that 4- and 5-year returns to the equal-weighted New York Stock Exchange (NYSE) over the 1926–87 period are negatively autocorrelated. Richardson and Stock (1989) derive the distribution of the Fama and French regression coefficients and demonstrate that overlapping observations may contain more information than independent observations; however, they cannot reject the random walk model.

Another solution for increasing the power of the test is to collect more data. In tests of long-run price dependency, Poterba and Summers (1988) and Lo (1991) use the annual Cowles (1938) U.S. stock index extending back to 1872. Lo uses the rescaled range (R/S) statistic to test for aperiodic reversals and finds no evidence of them. Poterba and Summers use a variance ratio test and find marginal evidence of mean reversion, although the results are not strong enough to reject the random walk model at traditional confidence levels.

In this article, I extend market history even further back in time. Joint-stock shares have traded in London for 300 years and in New York for 200 years. If cycles of periodicity greater than a year are consistently present in British or American stock prices, one would expect to find them in the longest indices of all. These long series offer an opportunity to identify patterns that shorter time series cannot. For instance, tests of 5-year serial dependence in London and New York stock price indices using the available published data may employ 57 and 39 observations, respectively. In autocorrelation tests of mean reversion and persistence of multiple horizon capital appreciation returns, I apply the bootstrapping methodology to two stock price indices that extend back to the eighteenth century. I perform separate as well as joint significance tests with respect to models that hypothesize long-term periodic behavior. In addition, I measure the R/S statistic proposed by Mandelbrot (1972) and modified by Lo (1991) as a test of long-term dependency in prices. Contrary to the results from tests on the last 120 years of U.S. stock market data, the longer-term perspective suggests that the random walk model does not correctly describe the behavior of U.S. stock prices. I find evidence of long-term structural changes in stock price appreciation. Once these structural changes are incorporated in the tests, I find some evidence of a persistent mean-reverting component in stock market prices of the sort discussed by Fama and French (1988) and Poterba and Summers (1988). Although autocorrelation tests on the long-term NYSE capital appreciation index yield test statistics consistent with mean reversion, the null hypothesis of temporal independence cannot be rejected at traditional confidence levels. The R/S tests, however, provide some evidence that the detrended London Stock Exchange (LSE) and NYSE prices may exhibit long-term memory.

This article is organized as follows: The second section describes the sources of the data and discusses the possible errors and biases in each series. The third section reports the methodology and results of autoregression tests. The fourth section reports the methodology and results of the rescaled range tests. The fifth section concludes.

◣ Data Sources

Shares of the Bank of England were traded on the Royal Exchange in the seventeenth century, and British publications such as John Castaing's *The Course of the Exchange* regularly reported share prices of at least six joint stock companies, beginning in the eighteenth century.[1] According to Mirowski (1981), who compiled an equal-weighted average of British share prices through the eighteenth century, the London market for shares was active and fully functional by 1700, although the frequency of trades and price quotations fluctuated considerably. In this article, I analyze an annual share price index for the LSE compiled from seven different sources, beginning with the Mirowski (1981) index. These sources are reported and described in Table 19.1. Gayer, Rostow, and Schwartz (1953) provide a broad-based index of shares through the first half of the nineteenth century and report the Hayek index that extends the LSE index to 1866. Several economists have constructed indices for periods of the late nineteenth and early twentieth centuries—I use Bowley, Schwartz, and Smith (1931) and Smith and Horne (1934). Two financial periodicals provide index measures of equity price appreciation through the early and middle twentieth century: the *Bankers Magazine* (1915–27) and the *Economist* (to 1970), which prints the *Financial Times Index*. Data on the capital appreciation of the LSE since 1970 are collected by the *Financial Times* in

Table 19.1

Sources of Data for the Construction of the London Share Price Index

Dates	Source	Firms	Types of Firms	Mean	SD	Auto-correlation	Method and Possible Biases
1695–1809	Mirowski 1981	Six or fewer	Banks, insurance, and trading.	.015	.139	−.21	Equal weighted. Selected regularly quoted firms. Infrequent trading and survivorship bias are problems.
1810–50	Gayer, Rostow, and Schwartz 1953	68 entered or exited index	Broad-based. Including banks, insurance, transportation, and mining and utilities.	.008	.092	.29	Value weighted. Selected regularly quoted, representative firms. Some interpolation or smoothing as a result of infrequent trading. Survivorship bias minimal.
1851–66	Hayek Index, in Gayer, Rostow, and Schwartz 1953	Unknown	Unknown.	.017	.094	.00	Unknown.
1867–1914	Smith and Horne 1934	From 25 to 77 companies	Broad-based. Including manufacturing, construction, retail transportation, and communication. No banks or insurance.	.014	.069	.30	Equal weighted. Selected regularly quoted, representative firms. Split correction unclear. Survivorship bias minimal.

Period	Source	Coverage	Description				Notes
1915–27	*Bankers Magazine* 1915–27	More than 200 per year	Virtually all "variable dividend" securities quoted on the exchange.	.011	.089	.00	Equal weighted. Survivorship bias minimal.
1928–29	Bowley, Schwartz, and Smith 1931	92 industrials	Broad-based. Including manufacturing, construction, retail transportation, and banks.	–.034	.135	.00	Value weighted. Selected regularly quoted "important" firms. Survivorship bias minimal.
1930–70	Financial Times Index reported in the *Economist*, 1930–70	30 industrials	"Blue-Chip" index, representing several industries.	.065	.189	.00	Share-price weighted. Selected regularly quoted, "important" firms. Survivorship bias minimal.
1971–89	Financial Times Actuaries Index for 1971–89 (used with permission of Ibbotson Associates, Chicago)	500 industrial companies	Broad-based, representing all industries.	.203	.355	–.37	Value weighted. Survivorship bias minimal.

their *Financial Times Actuaries Index* and by Morgan Stanley Capital International. Both of these are available from Ibbotson Associates, Inc. Because the LSE index is spliced from many sources, it does not necessarily reflect the continuous performance of an investable portfolio through time, although it is probably a fair approximation. The existence of overlapping observations at each splice insures that there is no abrupt change in the composition of the index that could be misinterpreted as an actual return.

Modern analysts are particularly fortunate that earlier researchers over the years have collected and published index data on financial prices. Indeed, Kondratieff developed his 50-year wave theory in part by looking at the quoted yields of British consols and French rentes recorded by the Statistique Générale de la France.* Tables 19.1 and 19.2 show how evidence from previous studies must typically be chained together to achieve a continuous series. Different parts of the indices are constructed with different methodologies and different samples, making it tempting for the researcher to go back and collect his own sample with a uniform methodology. In fact, for the U.S. stock market data, this is precisely what we eventually did. Nevertheless, despite its limitations, the span of the series allows not only an analysis of latent cycles and structures, but also a view of how the markets have reacted to wars, depressions, and crises. Was the crash of 1987 as great as the crash of 1929 or the panic of 1837? These long-term graphs give us a chance to benchmark our own economic experiences with those of our ancestors in the distant past. They also allow us to see whether the process of evolution of capital markets has resulted in fundamental changes to the equity risk premium. The equity series for the United Kingdom extends over the entire history of the industrial revolution. Over that time span the technological factors of production changed radically. In addition, the access of investors to the capital markets changed as well. Investors now are able to diversify their investment portfolios to a much greater extent than 200 years ago. In light of these basic changes in the capital markets, it would seem plausible—even likely—that the equity risk premium would change through time as well. It is somewhat surprising that it has remained as constant as it has through history.

*Kondratieff, Nikolai D. 1935. "The Long Waves in Economic Life." Translated and reprinted in *The Review of Economics and Statistics* 17 (6): 105–115.

Active trading in shares in the United States dates from the end of the eighteenth century (see Table 19.2). The New York Stock Exchange was founded in 1792, and the Foundation for the Study of Cycles (see Ibbotson and Brinson 1987) has compiled an annual stock price series from 1790 to the present that combines a number of other studies.[2] Unfortunately, many of the component series suffer from biases due to smoothing and survivorship. For the period from 1815 to 1859, a broad-based index of the New York Stock Exchange is available from Goetzmann and Ibbotson (1992). It is an equal-

Table 19.2
Sources of Data for the Construction of the NYSE Share Price Index

Dates	Source	Firms	Types of Firms	Mean	SD	Auto-correlation	Method and Possible Biases
1790–1815	Foundation for the Study of Cycles, reprinted in Ibbotson and Brinson 1987	Probably fewer than 20	Banks and insurance.	.076	.256	−.21	Not reported. Possibly spliced from other sources discussed in Schwert (1990).
1816–59	Goetzmann and Ibbotson 1992	20–260	Broad-based. Includes all of the firms listed on the NYSE over the period. For early years, these are principally banks and insurance companies. Later, they include transportation, mining and utilities, and industrials.	.034	.127	.29	Equal-weighted estimate using repeat-sale index construction methodology. May overstate variance and induce negative autocorrelation at 1-year intervals but not longer. May induce some smoothing as well. Survivorship bias minimal.
1860–71	Foundation for the Study of Cycles, reprinted in Ibbotson and Brinson 1987	Fewer than 20	Very narrow. Probably only frequently traded railroads.	.118	.180	.00	Probably based on the Cole and Frickey Index of Railroad Stocks, discussed in Schwert (1990). Extreme survivorship bias.
1872–1925	Cowles 1938; Wilson and Jones 1987	12–351	Broad-based. Including manufacturing, construction, retail, transportation, and communication.	1.03	.161	.30	Value-weighted averages of monthly high and low prices inducing some time averaging. Survivorship bias minimal.
1926–89	S&P Index reported by Ibbotson Associates 1991	90–500	Broad-based. Including manufacturing, construction, retail, transportation, and communication.	.071	.200	.00	Value-weighted average of capital appreciation of industrial shares. Survivorship bias and time averaging are minimal.

weighted annual index of all listed equity shares on the NYSE and is based on the price quotes in the *New York Shipping and Commercial* (see *New York Shipping List* 1815–1926), which provided the official record of NYSE price quotes and representative transactions prices for several decades of the early nineteenth century. It deals with the problem of infrequent trading through the use of the weighted repeat sales method proposed by Case and Shiller (1987) and studied by Goetzmann (1992). For the period from 1860 to 1871, I must again rely on the Foundation for the Study of Cycles index, which is probably composed of the Cole-Frickey (1928) index of railroad shares over this period and is thus not broad based. The index created by Cowles (1938) and adjusted for data errors by Wilson and Jones (1987) begins in 1872 and is constructed using the average of the high and low prices of individual stocks in each month. It is a capital-weighted index that is broad based, but it may be subject to survivorship bias, and, as Working (1960) points out, the averaging procedure introduces monthly smoothing. After 1926, I use the capital appreciation return to the Standard and Poor's index, reported by Ibbotson Associates (1991). For a complete discussion of the limitations and biases in the pre-CRSP U.S. stock return series, the reader is referred to Schwert (1990).

As noted, the problems associated with the spliced long-term appreciation series tend to bias estimates of both the long-term mean and the standard deviation and to a lesser extent the annual autocorrelation. The long-term mean may be upwardly biased due to the selection of frequently traded or surviving securities used to create the indices over the early periods. The standard deviation may fluctuate since the number of stocks in each series also fluctuates — because of the effect of diversification, one would expect the standard deviation of the indices to decline as the number of stocks increases. The direction of the autocorrelation bias at the annual horizon is not clear. While smoothing may be caused by averaging of high and low prices and by infrequent price observations, some annual negative correlation in the NYSE series may be induced by the use of the repeat-sales method. For horizons greater than 1 year, both effects decline in importance; however, the question of dividend yield becomes significant. If total returns are independent, but dividend policy changes slowly through time, then one would observe long-term price dependency. Consequently, in the following tests, I allow for fixed as well as slowly changing mean values. Unfortunately, there is no ready evidence for dividend yields from the early periods covered by the data.[3]

Perhaps more significant than the biases introduced by survivorship, recording methods, data splicing, and dividend policy changes is the fact that the economies of both countries changed profoundly over the course of the last 3 centuries. The LSE series, for instance, documents share prices through the entire industrial revolution, the nation's colonial expansion, and centuries of development in the capital markets. Similarly, the NYSE documents the U.S. equity market over the period of westward expansion, the development of the U.S. rail transportation system, and the evolution of the economy from agrarian to industrial. Such broad historical changes are reflected in the composi-

Table 19.3
Summary Statistics for LSE and NYSE Capital Appreciation Indices

	Arithmetic Mean	Geometric Mean	Standard Deviation	Skewness Log(1 + r)	Kurtosis Log(1 + r)	Auto-correlation
Over the entire length of each series:						
LSE	.031	.021	.157	.013	13.37	−.049
NYSE	.056	.039	.184	−.667	4.60	.017
Over the eighteenth century, through 1800:						
LSE	.014	.005	.144	−1.098	22.166	−.217
NYSE	.076	.066	.150	−.363	1.233	.184
Over the nineteenth century, 1801–1900:						
LSE	.015	.012	.085	−.256	3.263	.266
NYSE	.047	.032	.177	−.343	5.596	.069
Over the twentieth century, 1901–89:						
LSE	.069	.049	.218	.255	6.266	−.065
NYSE	.063	.043	.196	−.886	3.829	−.025

Note. NYSE series for the eighteenth century begins in 1790. Skewness and kurtosis are estimated from the log of one plus the return, which is approximately normal. A Kolmogorov-Smirnov test of normality for each series fails to reject at the 95% confidence level. The probability of rejecting the null that LSE and the NYSE series are distributed log normally is 99.8% and 18.7%, respectively.

tion of both indices as different types of corporations financed growth through the equity markets. Not only would some of these firms have different expected returns, but they would also reflect different kinds of risks. These broad, evolutionary issues present problems in regression tests of mean reversion since the tests assume stationarity of the parameters of the model to be estimated. Thus, by gathering more data I have solved some problems, while introducing others.

Table 19.3 reports summary statistics for the NYSE and the LSE over the entire period for which I have data and also breaks the results down by centuries. These summary figures are interesting in their own right. The long-term annual geometric capital appreciation return of the LSE, based on 290 years of data, is 2.1%. The long-term annual geometric capital appreciation return of the NYSE, based on 197 years of data, is 3.9%. The annual standard deviation of returns to the LSE and NYSE is 15.7% and 18.4%, respectively. The mean return in each country differs significantly over the nineteenth century but not so over the twentieth century. This may reflect the economic return of the underlying assets themselves, or it may reflect international differences in dividend yields. When logged, neither distribution is dramatically skewed, while both are leptokurtotic when compared to normal distribution. Despite the kurtosis, however, a Kolmogorov-Smirnov test rejects normality for the LSE but not the NYSE.[4]

Figure 19.1 plots the LSE and NYSE capital appreciation indices. It is clear that the variance of the LSE is not stable over time; note the high vari-

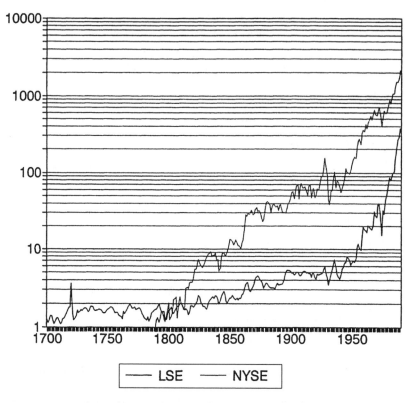

Figure 19.1. London and New York Stock Exchanges Capital Appreciation Indices, 1790–1989
Notes: The dotted line (begins ca. 1800) indicates the annual capital appreciation of the NYSE; the solid line (begins ca. 1700) indicates the annual capital appreciation of the LSE; the *X*-axis indicates the time period from 1790 to 1989; the *Y*-axis indicates the growth of an invested dollar or pound over the period. Sources for both indices are described in the text.

ance periods in the 1720s and in the 1950s through the 1980s, with a long stretch of relative calm in between. The NYSE variance is more stable, although the Great Depression stands out as a period of relatively high volatility, along with occasional dramatic outliers in the first 50 years of the series. Note also that the appreciation rate of the LSE increases dramatically over time. It exhibits practically no increase through the eighteenth century and appears to increase at a lower rate than the NYSE through the nineteenth century and the first half of the twentieth century. After 1950, it appears to increase at a greater rate than the NYSE.

◤ Methodology

Autocorrelation Tests

Following Fama and French (1988), I use an autoregression of multiple year capital appreciation returns to test for long-term serial dependency in stock market prices. Without an ex ante hypothesis regarding the number of years to include in the compound returns, I test the serial dependency of 1–10-year horizon returns. That is,

$$r(t, t + T) = \alpha(T) + \beta(T)r(t - T, t) + e(t, t + T), \tag{1}$$

for $t = 0, T, 2T, \ldots, nT$, where $T = 1, \ldots, 10$.

Unlike Fama and French (1988), I use only nonoverlapping returns, so that I do not need to correct for serial dependency in the residuals;[5] however, I correct for the bias in the autoregression coefficient noted by Kendall (1954) by bootstrapping the autoregression coefficient, under the null hypothesis that successive annual capital appreciation returns to the stock market are independent and identically distributed. The bootstrap is performed by drawing r^*, a bootstrapped pseudohistory of market returns with replacement from the empirical distribution of $r(t)$. The multiple year returns are formed by compounding $r^*(t)$, and the regression test is performed 1,000 times, providing a distribution of regression coefficients, β^*, and R^{2*}:

$$r^*(t, t + T) = \alpha^*(T) + \beta^*(T)r^*(t - T, t) + e^*(t, t + T). \tag{2}$$

The bootstrap not only provides a correction for the autocorrelation bias, but it generates distributions of regression statistics that conform to the null hypothesis that returns are independently and identically distributed (i.i.d.). By comparing the values of β and R^2 to their bootstrapped distributions, I may determine how unusual they are, given a null hypothesis that successive annual returns are independent and identically distributed. In addition, the standard deviation of the bootstrapped distribution of the regression coefficients is a consistent estimate of the coefficient standard error (see Efron 1979) and is used to construct a t-statistic.

Since the dividend yield may have changed over the course of several centuries, I also perform a test that allows for long-term variation in the mean return. Instead of the total capital appreciation, I examine the deviation of the annual capital appreciation return from its 20-year moving average:

$$r^d(t) = r(t) - \frac{1}{20} \sum_{i=t-1}^{t-20} r(i). \tag{3}$$

Because the dividend yields are unknown, I cannot distinguish between long-term changes in expected returns and changing dividend policies. However, for horizons less than 20 years, I can test whether deviations from the long-term mean are reverting or persistent.[6]

As noted earlier, there is no reason to expect that appreciation returns to 3 centuries of stock prices will be homoscedastic. In fact, since the series are spliced from components with varying numbers of securities, I expect the variance of different sections of each index to differ. Consequently, I perform a stratified-variance bootstrap, using the method proposed by Kim, Nelson, and Startz (1988). For both the raw and the demeaned series, I divide the sample into five groups, according to variance, where variance is defined by squared returns. I sample with replacement from each stratum in order to match the approximate temporal pattern of heteroscedasticity present in the sample.[7] As with the boot-strap draws under the assumption that returns are i.i.d., I perform the autocor-relation tests, save the coefficients and R^2s, and then report the empirical quantiles exceeded by the statistics from tests performed on the actual series.

R/S Tests

Autocorrelation tests detect long-term dependency in stock market prices if the dependent behavior is periodic and if the periodicity is consistent over time. Fundamental historical changes may have altered the period of market cycles, however. Mandelbrot (1972) proposes a statistic to measure the degree of long-term dependency, in particular, "nonperiodic cycles." The rescaled range, or R/S statistic, is formed by measuring the range between the maximum and mini-mum distances that the cumulative sum of a stochastic random variable has strayed from its mean and then dividing this by its standard deviation. An un-usually small R/S measure would be consistent with mean reversion, for in-stance, while an unusually large one would be consistent with return persistence.

Mandelbrot (1972) has shown that the R/S statistic is a more general test of long-term dependency in time series than either autocorrelation tests or ex-amination of spectral densities. He points out that, in particular, it is robust to changes in periodicity. Lo (1991) points out that one limitation of the R/S sta-tistic is that it cannot distinguish between short- and long-term dependency, nor is it robust to heteroscedasticity.

Lo (1991) modifies the R/S statistic so that it is more robust to violations in the assumption that returns are i.i.d. The modification consists of replacing the standard deviation with an estimate that explicitly models short-term tem-poral dependency using the autocovariances up to a finite number of lags, weighted by factors proposed by Newey and West (1987):

$$R/S_{Lo} = \frac{1}{\sqrt{T}\hat{\sigma}*} \left[\max_{1 \leq \tau \leq T} \sum_{t=1}^{\tau} (r_t - \bar{r}) - \min_{1 \leq \tau \leq T} \sum_{t=1}^{\tau} (r_t - \bar{r}) \right], \qquad (4)$$

where

$$\hat{\sigma}^{2*} = \hat{\sigma}^2 + 2 \sum_{t=1}^{q} \omega_t(q)\hat{\gamma}_t,$$

$$\omega_t(q) \equiv 1 - \frac{t}{q+1},$$

and

$$\hat{\gamma}_t \equiv \text{the autocovariance operator.}$$

Lo (1991) points out that the uncorrected R/S statistic is sensitive to heteroscedasticity and cannot distinguish the compounded effects of short-horizon patterns from long-term patterns. He derives the distribution of the modified (R/S) statistic, allowing it to be used in a hypothesis test about long-term dependency in stock market returns.[8] While the R/S statistic identifies nonperiodic cycles, it is not free of the choice of return horizon. As with the autocorrelation test, I report the bootstrapped quantile exceeded by the R/S statistic for the raw stock series and the demeaned stock series, under the i.i.d. and stratified variance procedures. In addition, I report the exceeded quantile of the analytically derived distribution of the modified R/S reported in Lo (1991).

Joint Hypothesis Tests

One problem with examining either the autocorrelation coefficient or the R/S statistic for a number of different horizons is that a hypothesis test about the significance of a subset of the coefficients or R/S statistics is misleading. Thus, as in Goetzmann (1989), Richardson and Smith (1991), and Richardson (in press), I perform a joint significance test across all 10 autoregression coefficients. To test that all 10 coefficients are zero, I use the Wald test:

$$W(\overline{\beta}) \equiv T(\overline{\beta}\Omega^{-1}\overline{\beta}) \sim \chi_k^2, \tag{5}$$

where $\overline{\beta}$ denotes the bias-corrected coefficient vector, and the covariance matrix that describes the cross-horizon dependencies is estimated with the bootstrap

$$\hat{\Omega}_{i,j} = \hat{\sigma}^2_{(\overline{\beta}_1^*, \overline{\beta}_j^*)}. \tag{6}$$

The χ^2 distribution is known to be sensitive to deviations from normality in the underlying distribution. Thus the parametric Wald test may be misspecified. Fortunately, the Wald statistic of Equation (5) suggests a nonparametric test as well. A rejection region for the W-statistic based on the distribution of the bootstrapped Wald statistic, W^*, may be identified. In other words, I calculate the Wald statistic for each bootstrapped coefficient vector and use the resulting distribution for hypothesis testing. Thus, while a comparison of the Wald statistic to the χ^2 distribution may cause the null to be rejected as a result of deviations of the coefficient vector from multivariate normality, a comparison to the bootstrapped distribution of the Wald statistic will not since it is based on draws from the empirical coefficient distribution.

As with the autocorrelation test, it is known that the R/S statistic for each horizon is not independent. Thus, it is necessary to perform a joint test of dependency across all 10 lags as before. Lo (1991) demonstrates that the distribution of the R/S statistics is defined by the range of a Brownian bridge process—a distribution that is slightly right-skew and leptokurtotic in comparison to the normal. This biases the Wald test toward rejection; however, as I noted above, a comparison of the Wald statistic to its bootstrapped distribution, rather than the χ^2 distribution, is robust to departures from normality. It may thus be used as a measure of whether R/S statistics for each horizon are jointly unusual.

◣ Results

Tables 19.4 and 19.5 report the autocorrelation and R/S tests for the raw LSE series and the demeaned LSE series, respectively. The bootstrap t-statistic and the bootstrap percentiles derived from the i.i.d. and stratified variance methods are reported for each autoregression coefficient at return horizons from 1 to 10 years.[9] I report bootstrap percentiles for the R/S statistic, as well as Lo's (1991) analytically derived percentiles. In addition, I report the autoregression R^2 with bootstrapped percentiles.

Table 19.4 suggests that returns with horizons greater than 5 years are strongly persistent. The bootstrapped percentiles indicate that the 6-, 8-, 9-, and 10-year coefficients are strongly positive and that the explanatory power of the regression, as measured by R^2, is around 10%–20%. This result may be partially due to the variance structure of the time series, however. Only the 8-year coefficient exceeds the 95th percentile of the stratified variance coefficient distribution. The R/S statistics are unusual at the first three horizons but not at longer intervals. Since they exceed 1 for horizons up to 3 years, they suggest persistence rather than reversion.[10]

Table 19.5 reports the results from the demeaned LSE series. It shows that much of the persistence in raw LSE returns may in fact be due to long-term changes in the mean. Once the 20-year moving average is subtracted, all of the coefficients become negative, and for the 4-, 5-, 6-, and 7-year horizons they are significantly so. In fact, the coefficients display the U-shaped pattern that Fama and French (1988) predict for returns generated by a process having both permanent and temporary components. The evidence from the R/S statistics is less clear. Few are unusual when compared to Lo's analytically derived distribution or to the bootstrapped distributions.

Tables 19.6 and 19.7 report the autocorrelation and R/S tests for the raw NYSE and demeaned NYSE series, respectively. The coefficients for both series are negative at each horizon, although they do not follow the U shape hypothesized by Fama and French (1988). The t-statistics and the bootstrap probability levels suggest that some bias-adjusted coefficients may differ significantly from zero. Table 19.7 reports the results for the demeaned NYSE series. As with the demeaned LSE series, long-horizon returns appear significantly negatively autocorrelated. In addition, the R/S shows evidence of reversion at horizons less than 4 years.

While the statistics about the individual horizons are suggestive of mean-reverting behavior, the joint tests reported in Table 19.8 indicate how unusual

Table 19.4
Autoregression and Rescaled Range Statistics for Multiple-Year Capital Appreciation Returns to the London Stock Exchange Index, 1700–1989

Horizon (Years)	Number of Observations	Coefficient*	R/S Lo Statistic†	R^2†
1	289	−.049	1.953	.002
		$t = 3.26, p = .20, q = .45$	lo = .97, $p = .99, q = .49$	$p = .67, q = .50$
2	144	.093	1.713	.008
		$t = 3.25, p = .91, q = .36$	lo = .90, $p = .99, q = .33$	$p = .79, q = .35$
3	95	−.125	1.764	.011
		$t = 1.15, p = .11, q = .19$	lo = .95, $p = .99, q = .59$	$p = .75, q = .71$
4	71	−.01	1.456	.000
		$t = 1.45, p = .53, q = .52$	lo = .70, $p = .93, q = .32$	$p = .16, q = .05$
5	57	.025	1.318	.000
		$t = 1.72, p = .63, q = .78$	lo = .60, $p = .83, q = .29$	$p = .22, q = .15$
6	47	.543	1.193	.142
		$t = 5.58, p = 1.00, q = .79$	lo = .40, $p = .63, q = .13$	$p = .99, q = .56$
7	40	.052	1.317	.002
		$t = 1.49, p = .71, q = .25$	lo = .60, $p = .90, q = .59$	$p = .29, q = .20$
8	35	1.00	1.106	.227
		$t = 6.54, p = 1.00, q = 1.00$	lo = .30, $p = .45, q = .19$	$p = 1.00, q = .77$
9	31	.681	1.023	.097
		$t = 3.22, p = 1.00, q = .87$	lo = .20, $p = .26, q = .06$	$p = .95, q = .59$
10	28	.929	1.053	.194
		$t = 3.89, p = 1.00, q = .93$	lo = .20, $p = .31, q = .27$	$p = .99, q = .39$

Note. Autoregressions are estimated from the model given in Eq. (1). Lo's rescaled range statistics are heteroscedasticity consistent, after Lo (1991) and are estimated from the model given in Eq. (4). Quantiles for the R/S statistic from Lo (1991) are indicated by "lo." t-statistics are bias corrected using the median values of the bootstrapped distributions and use the standard deviation of the bootstrap coefficient distribution. Probability values p indicate the bootstrap distribution percentile exceeded by the statistic in 1,000 iterations. Probability values q indicate the stratified-variance bootstrap distribution percentile exceeded by the statistic in 1,000 iterations.

*Bootstrap t-statistic and percentiles for i.i.d. and stratified variance draws are also reported.

†Bootstrap percentiles for i.i.d. and stratified variance are also reported.

Table 19.5

Autoregression and Rescaled Range Statistics for Multiple-Year Capital Appreciation Returns to the London Stock Exchange Index, 1700–1989: Corrected for Long-Term Changing Means

Horizon (Years)	Number of Observations	Coefficient*	R/S Lo Statistic†	R^2†
1	269	−.136 $t = 1.06$, $p = .01$, $q = .09$	1.144 lo = .30, $p = .54$, $q = .24$	.02 $p = .98$, $q = .90$
2	134	−.115 $t = .39$, $p = .08$, $q = .00$	.926 lo = .05, $p = .15$, $q = .02$	.01 $p = .82$, $q = .95$
3	89	−.232 $t = 1.46$, $p = .00$, $q = .08$	.943 lo = .10, $p = .16$, $q = .09$	.06 $p = .97$, $q = .91$
4	66	−.372 $t = 3.64$, $p = .00$, $q = .02$	.925 lo = .05, $p = .12$, $q = .01$	.13 $p = 1.00$, $q = .98$
5	53	−.375 $t = 3.25$, $p = .00$, $q = .04$	1.225 lo = .50, $p = .65$, $q = .88$	.13 $p = .99$, $q = .96$
6	44	−.399 $t = .60$, $p = .00$, $q = .02$	1.060 lo = .20, $p = .29$, $q = .47$	.15 $p = .99$, $q = .98$
7	37	−.358 $t = .60$, $p = .01$, $q = .00$	1.217 lo = .50, $p = .60$, $q = .79$	.13 $p = .99$, $q = 1.00$
8	32	−.260 $t = .78$, $p = .06$, $q = .07$	1.368 lo = .70, $p = .86$, $q = .98$	.07 $p = .89$, $q = .90$
9	29	−.183 $t = 1.42$, $p = .15$, $q = .04$	.871 lo = .05, $p = .02$, $q = .08$	.04 $p = .71$, $q = .65$
10	26	−.194 $t = 1.39$, $p = .17$, $q = .04$	.959 lo = .10, $p = .09$, $q = .40$	.04 $p = .67$, $q = .60$

Note. Autoregressions are estimated from the model given in Eq. (1). Rescaled range statistics are estimated from the model given in Eq. (4). Quantiles for the statistic from Lo (1991) are indicated by "lo." t-statistics are heteroscedasticity consistent, after White (1980), and bias corrected using the median values of the bootstrapped distributions. Probability values p indicate the bootstrap distribution percentile exceeded by the statistic in 1,000 iterations. Probability values q indicate the stratified-variance bootstrap distribution percentile exceeded by the statistic in 1,000 iterations.

*Bootstrap t-statistic and percentiles for i.i.d. and stratified variance draws are also reported.

†Bootstrap percentiles for i.i.d. and stratified variance draws are also reported.

Table 19.6

Autoregression and Rescaled Range Statistics for Multiple-Year Capital Appreciation Returns to the New York Stock Exchange Index, 1790–1989

Horizon (Years)	Number of Observations	Coefficient*	R/S Lo Statistic†	R^2†
1	199	.017	1.190	.000
		$t = 4.42$, $p = .63$, $q = .75$	lo $= .40$, $p = .59$, $q = .83$	$p = .19$, $q = .39$
2	99	−.279	1.349	.077
		$t = .57$, $p = .00$, $q = .06$	lo $= .60$, $p = .82$, $q = .95$	$p = .99$, $q = .95$
3	65	−.262	1.358	.068
		$t = 1.93$, $p = .02$, $q = .44$	lo $= .60$, $p = .83$, $q = .87$	$p = .97$, $q = .59$
4	49	−.083	1.372	.007
		$t = 1.97$, $p = .32$, $q = .41$	lo $= .60$, $p = .88$, $q = .91$	$p = .45$, $q = .56$
5	39	−.183	1.431	.031
		$t = 3.13$, $p = .15$, $q = .32$	lo $= .70$, $p = .92$, $q = .55$	$p = .75$, $q = .69$
6	32	−.141	1.246	.019
		$t = .85$, $p = .28$, $q = .51$	lo $= .50$, $p = .69$, $q = .75$	$p = .56$, $q = .49$
7	27	−.202	1.600	.037
		$t = .11$, $p = .18$, $q = .22$	lo $= .80$, $p = .97$, $q = .98$	$p = .70$, $q = .77$
8	24	−.292	1.386	.072
		$t = 1.44$, $p = .08$, $q = .64$	lo $= .70$, $p = .85$, $q = .81$	$p = .84$, $q = .40$
9	21	−.006	1.395	.000
		$t = .97$, $p = .59$, $q = .81$	lo $= .70$, $p = .81$, $q = .68$	$p = .03$, $q = .03$
10	19	−.327	1.201	.082
		$t = 2.87$, $p = .09$, $q = .81$	lo $= .40$, $p = .08$, $q = .49$	$p = .54$, $q = .27$

Note. Autoregressions are estimated from the model given in Eq. (1). Rescaled range statistics are estimated from the model given in Eq. (4). Quantiles from the distribution given in Lo (1991) are indicated as "lo." t-statistics are bias corrected using the median values of the bootstrapped distributions and use the standard deviation of the bootstrap coefficient distribution. Probability values p indicate the bootstrap distribution percentile exceeded by the statistic in 1,000 iterations. Probability values q indicate the stratified-variance bootstrap distribution percentile exceeded by the statistic in 1,000 iterations.

*Bootstrap t-statistic and percentiles for i.i.d. and stratified variance draws are also reported.

†Bootstrap percentiles for i.i.d. and stratified variance draws are also reported.

Table 19.7

Autoregression and Rescaled Range Statistics for Multiple-Year Capital Appreciation Returns to the New York Stock Exchange Index, 1790–1989: Corrected for Long-Term Changing Means

Horizon (Years)	Number of Observations	Coefficient*	R/S Lo Statistic†	R²†
1	179	.063	.710	.004
		$t = .64$, $p = .77$, $q = .62$	lo $= .00$, $p = .23$, $q = .04$	$p = .55$, $q = .63$
2	89	$-.173$	.783	.030
		$t = .09$, $p = .04$, $q = .14$	lo $= .00$, $p = .24$, $q = .04$	$p = .80$, $q = .86$
3	59	$-.230$	.819	.054
		$t = .39$, $p = .05$, $q = .29$	lo $= .03$, $p = .24$, $q = .06$	$p = .81$, $q = .74$
4	44	$-.067$	.970	.005
		$t = 3.43$, $p = .35$, $q = .39$	lo $= .10$, $p = .33$, $q = .04$	$p = .30$, $q = .53$
5	35	$-.167$	1.175	.026
		$t = 3.54$, $p = .20$, $q = .24$	lo $= .40$, $p = .60$, $q = .03$	$p = .57$, $q = .76$
6	29	$-.140$	1.761	.019
		$t = .279$, $p = .27$, $q = .11$	lo $= .95$, $p = .99$, $q = .83$	$p = .46$, $q = .88$
7	24	$-.253$	1.667	.063
		$t = .04$, $p = .13$, $q = .08$	lo $= .90$, $p = .97$, $q = .92$	$p = .71$, $q = .91$
8	21	$-.501$	2.369	.236
		$t = .81$, $p = .00$, $q = .06$	lo $= .99$, $p = .99$, $q = 1.00$	$p = .88$, $q = .95$
9	19	$-.239$	1.515	.050
		$t = 3.57$, $p = .15$, $q = .19$	lo $= .80$, $p = .89$, $q = .94$	$p = .61$, $q = .75$
10	17	$-.567$	.976	.248
		$t = 4.05$, $p = .00$, $q = .03$	lo $= .10$, $p = .29$, $q = .15$	$p = .87$, $q = .97$

Note. Autoregressions are estimated from the model given in Eq. (1). Rescaled range statistics are estimated from the model given in Eq. (4). t-statistics are bias corrected using the median values of the bootstrapped distributions and use the standard deviation of the bootstrap coefficient distribution. Probability values p indicate the bootstrap distribution percentile exceeded by the statistic in 1,000 iterations. Probability values q indicate the stratified-variance bootstrap distribution percentile exceeded by the statistic in 1,000 iterations.

*Bootstrap t-statistic and percentiles for i.i.d. and stratified variance draws are also reported.
†Bootstrap percentiles for i.i.d. and stratified variance draws are also reported.

Table 19.8
Joint Hypothesis Test for 1–10 Horizons Based on the Wald Statistic Described in Equation (5)

	Test Statistic	Quantile	90%	95%	99%
χ^2 distribution			15.99	18.31	23.21
LSE raw capital appreciation series autocorrelation coefficients:					
i.i.d. bootstrap	100.43	1.00	16.76	19.65	29.80
Stratified variance	38.41	1.00	16.20	19.12	26.13
LSE demeaned capital appreciation series autocorrelation coefficients:					
i.i.d. bootstrap	13.20	.79	16.32	19.45	28.07
Stratified variance	16.57	.90	16.02	18.57	24.07
NYSE raw capital appreciation series autocorrelation coefficients:					
i.i.d. bootstrap	14.37	.84	16.99	18.15	24.73
Stratified variance	8.73	.44	16.06	18.13	21.42
NYSE demeaned capital appreciation series autocorrelation coefficients:					
i.i.d. bootstrap	16.11	.90	15.48	18.26	24.09
Stratified variance	7.48	.31	15.97	18.21	23.54
LSE raw capital appreciation series R/S statistics:					
i.i.d. bootstrap	35.08	.98	19.02	23.83	41.18
Stratified variance	6.93	.32	16.90	21.32	28.10
LSE demeaned capital appreciation series R/S statistics:					
i.i.d. bootstrap	34.57	.98	16.22	22.66	57.56
Stratified variance	45.06	1.00	17.84	24.30	38.89
NYSE raw capital appreciation series R/S statistics:					
i.i.d. bootstrap	7.65	.68	14.76	21.65	61.59
Stratified variance	6.20	.34	16.00	19.18	38.47
NYSE demeaned capital appreciation series R/S statistics:					
i.i.d. bootstrap	32.84	.96	16.78	26.39	72.59
Stratified variance	34.73	.98	16.73	22.82	56.47

the pattern of 10 coefficients and R/S range statistics actually may be. The random walk is rejected under both the i.i.d. and the stratified variance procedures for the LSE at the 99% confidence level, using the autoregression coefficient test. The hypothesis that the NYSE autoregression coefficient vector is different from zero cannot be rejected, however. The rejection level of 84% under the i.i.d. sampling scheme is similar to rejection levels found by previous researchers using NYSE data over later periods. The joint tests on autoregression coefficients performed on the deviations from rolling 20-year means fail to reject the null at traditional confidence levels. Thus, while the results are suggestive of mean reversion in both markets, they are not conclusive when autoregression tests are used.

The joint tests on the more general R/S statistics yield slightly stronger results, however. While the joint tests performed on the R/S statistics derived from the raw LSE series and the raw NYSE series are inconclusive, the joint tests performed on the demeaned LSE and NYSE capital appreciation series are both significant at the 95% level. They indicate the likelihood that deviations from the lagged 20-year mean are not temporally independent. Tables 19.5 and 19.7 suggest the reasons for the joint departure from the null. In both tables, the R/S statistics are unusually low over 2–4-year horizons and unusually high over the 8-year horizon, regardless of whether the i.i.d. or the stratified variance bootstrap is used. Thus, the joint rejection does not result from a consistent deviation in one direction but from what appears to be reversion over the short horizons and persistence over the long horizons—even after the 20-year moving average has been removed.

◣ Conclusion

The same tests used in previous research to demonstrate the lack of long-term memory in NYSE stock market prices during the various periods from 1872 to 1987 suggest that long-term memory may exist in LSE stock prices over the period of 1700–1989 and in deviations from 20-year means in both markets. This conclusion is based on autoregression tests as well as on R/S range tests and is robust to techniques designed to preserve the particular temporal pattern of stock market variance. These results may be interpreted as evidence of evolving dividend policies and/or changing expected financial returns that result from the changing composition of the index through the centuries of U.S. and U.K. capital market history. Substituting deviations from the lagged 20-year mean appears to eliminate the evolutionary effects from the LSE series, indicating that the long-term persistent patterns appear to mask a tendency for reversion toward the mean in the LSE and possibly in the NYSE. This behavior is consistent with models of stock returns proposed by Poterba and Summers (1988) and empirically examined by Fama and French (1988). It could be caused by rational time variation in expected returns, as postulated by Conrad and Kaul (1988) and explored by Jacquier and Nanda (1989) or by speculative bubbles of the sort discussed by DeBont and Thaler (1985) and Flood, Hodrick, and Kaplan (1987). Although consistent with all models that hypothesize long-term reversion in asset prices, the tests under discussion in this article, as currently formulated, cannot distinguish among them. Whether the serial dependence in long-term capital appreciation returns may be used to obtain arbitrage profits is another matter entirely. Rhea (1932) and his predecessor, Charles Henry Dow, apparently thought so. A test of market efficiency based on the temporal patterns identified in this article would require a trading test and a measure of the total investor return rather than the capital appreciation component alone, and, in all likelihood, an investor horizon greater than a single lifespan.

▶ *Notes*

1. See Neal (1990) for a discussion of *The Course of the Exchange*. It was published semi-annually, with daily price quotes for major stocks, over the period from 1698 to 1810. These are available in electronic form from Inter-University Consortium for Political and Social Research, P.O. Box 1248, Ann Arbor, MI 48106.

2. See Ibbotson and Brinson (1987). They explain that the index is composed of "an internal index . . . the Cleveland Trust Company Index . . . the Clement-Burgess Index and the Cowles Index" (p. 73). The Cleveland Trust Company Index includes indices compiled from other sources—probably Cole and Frickey (1928), while the Clement Burgess Index is extremely narrow. As Cowles (1938) notes, it is "composed of from four to nine stocks, chiefly leading railroads" (p. 439). This narrow base, which covers periods in the nineteenth century when the NYSE listed over 100 frequently traded stocks, suggests that the index may have been created by using only companies with data extending over the entire period of study, that is, 1854–83. Given this survivorship bias, the Foundation for the Study of Cycles NYSE index from 1790 to the late nineteenth century may be positively biased in the early years.

3. Indirect evidence for the NYSE stocks is implicit in the manner in which stock prices were quoted on the exchange. Prices were quoted with respect to a par value of 100, with prices rarely deviating above 200, and splits were practically nonexistent in the early nineteenth century. This suggests that investors expected earnings to be paid out rather than retained.

4. The probability associated with rejection of the null hypothesis that the series is drawn from a normal distribution is .997 for the LSE and .1872 for the NYSE.

5. Fama and French (1988) employ the Hansen and Hodrick (1980) correction for overlapping returns. Richardson and Smith (1991) have analyzed the behavior of statistics in the presence of overlapping observations and devised appropriate corrections for hypothesis tests involving regression coefficients. Because I am interested in the explanatory power, as measured by R^2 as well as by the significance of the regression coefficients, I have chosen to use nonoverlapping observations.

6. Given the fact that the mean is allowed to vary with time, the term "mean reversion" actually applies only to the deviations from the moving average. Indeed, if the mean were allowed to vary each period, a test of "mean reversion" would be absurd. Thus, the test of deviations from the long-term average should be interpreted as conditional upon the specification in Eq. (3).

7. To the extent that the changing means are components of the squared returns, this will tend to make the bootstrap sample resemble the true sample in general. This weakens the power of the test, and thus I will report bootstrap quantiles generated by the i.i.d. and stratified variance procedures.

8. Green and Fielitz (1977) applied the R/S statistic to examine U.S. stock market behavior but did not formulate an explicit test of long-term market memory.

9. The bootstrap *t*-statistic is formed by dividing the bias-adjusted coefficient vector by the standard deviation of the bootstrapped coefficient samples, in the manner proposed by Efron (1979).

10. The fact that the R/S statistic does not exceed 1 for longer horizons does not imply a contradiction between the autocorrelation test and the R/S test since Lo's (1991) adjustment of the R/S statistic includes multiple lags.

◣ References

Bankers Magazine (London). 1915–27. Available from 1844 to the present.

Bowley, A. L.; Schwartz, G. L.; and Smith, K. C. 1931. *A New Index of Securities.* Special Memorandum no. 33. London: London and Cambridge Economic Service.

Case, Karl, and Shiller, Robert. 1987. Prices of single family homes since 1970: New indexes for four cities. *New England Economic Review* (September/October), pp. 45–56.

Cole, Arthur H., and Frickey, E. 1928. The course of stock prices, 1825–1866. *Review of Economics and Statistics* 10:117–39.

Conrad, Jennifer, and Kaul, G. 1988. Time variation in expected stock returns. *Journal of Business* 61:409–25.

The Course of the Exchange. 1698–1810. London: John Castaing and various publishers.

Cowles, Alfred, III. 1938. *Common Stock Indices, 1871–1937.* Cowles Commission for Research in Economics. Monograph no. 3. Bloomington, Ind.: Principia Press.

DeBondt, Werner, and Thaler, Richard. 1985. Does the stock market overreact? *Journal of Finance* 60:793–805.

Efron, B. 1979. Bootstrap methods: Another look at the jackknife. *Annals of Statistics* 7:1–26.

Fama, E. F., and French, K. R. 1988. Permanent and temporary components of stock prices. *Journal of Political Economy* 96:246–73.

Flood, K. R.; Hodrick, R.; and Kaplan, P. 1987. An evaluation of recent evidence of stock market bubbles. Working Paper no. 1971. Cambridge, Mass.: National Bureau of Economic Research.

Gayer, Arthur; Rostow, W. W., and Schwartz, A. 1953. *The Growth and Fluctuation of the British Economy.* Vol. 1. Oxford: Clarendon Press.

Goetzmann, William N. 1990. Bootstrapping and simulation tests of long-term stock market efficiency. Ph.D. dissertation, Yale University.

Goetzmann, William N. 1992. The accuracy of real estate indices: Repeat sale estimators. *Journal of Real Estate Finance and Economics* 5:5–53.

Goetzmann, William N., and Ibbotson, Roger G. 1992. A broad-based index of New York Stock Exchange prices: 1815–1859. Working paper. New York: Columbia Business School.

Greene, Myron, and Fielitz, Bruce D. 1977. Long term dependence in common stock returns. *Journal of Financial Economics* 4, no. 3:339–49.

Hansen, Lars, and Hodrick, R. J. 1980. Forward exchange rates as optimal predictors of future spot rates: An econometric analysis. *Journal of Political Economy* 88:829–1054.

Ibbotson Associates. 1991. *Stocks, Bonds, Bills and Inflation: 1990 Yearbook.* Chicago: Ibbotson Associates, Inc.

Ibbotson, Roger G., and Brinson, Gary. 1987. *Investment Markets.* Englewood Cliffs, N.J.: McGraw-Hill.

Jacquier, Eric, and Nanda, V. 1989. Cyclicality of stock returns and the mean reversion puzzle. Working paper. Los Angeles: University of Southern California.

Kendall, M. 1954. A note on the bias in the estimation of autocorrelation. *Biometrika* 41:403–4.

Kim, Myung Jig; Nelson, C. R.; and Startz, R. 1988. Mean reversion in stock prices? Mimeographed. Seattle: University of Washington.

Lo, A. 1991. Long term memory in stock prices. *Econometrica* 59:1279–1314.

Mandelbrot, B. 1972. Statistical methodology for non-periodic cycles: From the covariance to R/S analysis. *Annals of Economic and Social Measurement* 1:259–90.

McQueen, Grant. 1992. Long-horizon mean-reverting stock prices revisited. *Journal of Financial and Quantitative Analysis* 27, no. 1 (March): 1–18.

Mirowski, Phillip. 1981. The rise (and retreat) of a market: English joint stock shares in the eighteenth century. *Journal of Economic History* 41, no. 3:559–77.

Neal, Larry. 1990. *The Rise of Financial Capitalism.* Cambridge: Cambridge University Press.

Newey, W., and West, K. 1987. A simple positive definite heteroscedasticity and autocorrelation consistent covariance matrix. *Econometrica* 55:703–5.

New York Shipping List, later *New York Shipping and Commercial.* 1815–1926. New York: Day & Turner. Volumes from 1816 in Beineke Rare Book Library, Yale University, New Haven, Conn.

Poterba, James M., and Summers, Lawrence H. 1988. Mean reversion in stock prices, evidence and implications. *Journal of Financial Economics* 22:27–59.

Rhea, Robert. 1932. *The Dow Theory.* New York: Barron's.

Richardson, Matthew. 1993. Temporary components of stock prices: A skeptic's view. *Journal of Business Economics and Statistics* 11:199–207.

Richardson, Matthew, and Smith, Tom. 1991. Tests of financial models in the presence of overlapping observations. *Review of Financial Studies* 4, no. 2:227–54.

Richardson, Matthew, and Stock, James. 1989. Drawing inferences for statistics based on multiyear asset returns. Unpublished manuscript. Philadelphia: University of Pennsylvania. Wharton School.

Schwert, William. 1990. Indexes of U.S. stock prices from 1802 to 1897. *Journal of Business* 63, no. 3:399–426.

Shiller, Robert. 1989. *Market Volatility.* Cambridge, Mass.: MIT Press.

Shiller, Robert J., and Perron, P. 1985. Testing the random walk hypothesis: Power versus frequency of observation. *Economics Letters* 18:381–86.

Smith, K. C., and Horne, G. F. 1934. *An Index Number of Securities, 1867–1914.* Special Memorandum no. 37. London: London and Cambridge Economic Service.

White, Halbert. 1980. A heteroskedasticity-consistent covariance matrix estimator and a direct test for heteroskedasticity. *Econometrica* 48:817–38.

Wilson, Jack, and Jones, C. P. 1987. A comparison of annual common stock returns: 1871–1925 with 1926–85. *Journal of Business* 60:239–58.

Working, H. 1960. A note on the correlation on first differences of averages in random chains. *Econometrica* 28 (October): 916–18.

20 William N. Goetzmann

Bootstrapping Tests of Long-Term Stock Market Efficiency

◤ Overview

The major contribution of this article is methodological. It develops a way that researchers can use a randomization procedure—bootstrapping—to test for time-series structure in a return series, particularly multiple-year cycles. At the time this article was written, a number of other researchers were also working out how to extract the most information econometrically from limited time-series data.* Many of us were excited about applying then-novel bootstrapping methods developed in statistics to the problems of financial econometrics. A particular challenge was how to deal with the fact that autocorrelation could conceivably be identified at a number of intervals—if you look over enough return horizons, perhaps one is likely to appear significant, if only by chance.

In this study, we use the bootstrap to examine the behavior of the coefficients in autoregressions of the equal-weighted New York Stock Exchange (NYSE) long-term returns. Both Fama and French (1988a) and Lo and MacKinlay (1988a) observe that the evidence for time dependency of returns is strongest for smaller capitalized stocks. Both find that the random walk may be rejected for the equal-weighted indices but not necessarily for the value-weighted indices. We report the results of overlapping and nonoverlapping return autoregressions for equal-weighted NYSE returns drawn from the Center for Research in Security Prices (CRSP) files, as well as for several other, longer historical stock return and price series that represent the behavior of the U.S. stock market. Based upon these studies, we propose a test of the random-walk hypothesis that uses the joint distribution of the set of autoregression coefficients derived from autoregressions on different return horizons, and also a simple test of the random walk that compares the bootstrapped sample standard deviations to the sample standard deviations of multiple-horizon returns.

This article is adapted from "Bootstrapping and Simulation Tests of Long-Term Patterns in Stock Market Behavior," Ph.D. diss., Yale University, 1991.

*For example, see Richardson and Smith's excellent analysis of the use of overlapping horizon return data to test for long-term autocorrelation. Richardson, Matthew, and Tom Smith, 1991, "Tests of Financial Models in the Presence of Overlapping Observations." *Review of Financial Studies* 4:227–254.

The results of these tests fail to convincingly reject the random-walk model for NYSE equal-weighted returns from 1926 to 1985 with horizons in excess of one year. Longer stock return series yield mixed results.

▶ Background

Many alternatives to the random-walk model of stock prices have been considered. Poterba and Summers (1988b) and Fama and French (1988b) model stock prices in related fashion as the sum of temporary and stationary components and white noise. That is,

$$P(t) = q(t) + z(t).$$

The first term, $q(t)$, is the permanent component: a random walk with drift p and noise $v(t)$.

$$q(t) = q(t-1) + p + v(t)$$

The second term, $z(t)$, is the temporary component. This is generally modeled as an AR(1) process. The autocorrelation in the temporary component causes prices to be mean reverting, and implies that the variance of long-horizon returns will be less than the variance of long-horizon returns would be if prices followed a random walk. Several authors, including Shiller and Perron (1985) and Summers (1986), have remarked on the difficulty of distinguishing the behavior of prices driven by mean reversion or a related "long-term memory" model from the behavior of prices driven by a random walk. Poterba and Summers (1988) suggest that traditional confidence levels should be adjusted to increase the penalty for Type II error in tests of the random-walk hypothesis. They use the variance ratio to reject the random walk.

Since mean reversion also implies that autoregression coefficients for long-horizon returns will be negative, Fama and French (1988a) focus on regression statistics as potential evidence of mean reversion. They use Hansen and Hodrick–corrected t-statistics (see Hansen and Hodrick, 1980) from individual autoregression coefficients of increasingly longer return horizons to likewise reject the random walk, observing that the particular shape—first decreasing, then increasing—suggests the existence of a temporary component.

In contrast, Lo and MacKinlay (1988b) find their own rejection of the random walk inconsistent with the long-term mean-reversion model. They observe that weekly NYSE equal-weighted returns display significant positive serial correlation. Conrad and Kaul (1988) show that this apparent positive weekly autocorrelation of the stock market is consistent with time-varying expected returns. Lo (1988) further disputes the evidence for long-term dependency in stock prices by using tests designed to identify nonperiodic reversals in time series.

In the following tests, we examine the evidence for long-term mean reversion, using the autoregression methodology that tests for serial dependence in multiple-year returns. We compare the use of overlapping return observations to the use of nonoverlapping observations in efficiency tests, and find significant differences in the outcomes of the two test methods.

◣ Tests Using Overlapping Returns

For purposes of comparison to Fama and French (1988b), we follow their test procedures for the equal-weighted NYSE monthly returns index. We perform autoregressions on the chained monthly series of 1-, 2-, 3-, 4-, 5-, 6-, 7-, 8-, 9-, and 10-year return horizons, using CRSP data from 1926 through 1985. These take the form

$$r(t, t + T) - a(T) + P(T)r(t - T, t) + e(t, t + T),$$

where $r(t, t + T)$ is the log price relative of the equal-weighted CRSP NYSE index assuming reinvestment of dividends, and T is the return horizon (in months). Thus, the autoregression of 10-year returns, for instance, uses 480 observations rather than the 5 we would have if we chose to perform regressions on nonoverlapping return intervals. The hypothesis test based upon these autoregressions is fairly straightforward: If the price process has a temporary component, the slopes of the regressions of $r(t, t + T)$ on $r(t - T, t)$ will be negative. We thus may regress $r(t, t + T)$ on $r(t - T, t)$ and perform a single-tailed hypothesis test to determine whether the coefficient is significantly less than zero.

Table 20.1 reports the estimated coefficients and their associated R-squared values. Note that the three-, four- and five-year coefficients are lower than the others, as well as yielding the highest R-squared—the largest being the 5-year value, at 34%! There are a number of other issues that make the autoregression test difficult to perform and interpret. First, the overlapping return series itself lacks serial independence. Since $r(t + 1, t + T + 1)$ and $r(t, t + T)$ overlap, they are correlated; as a result, the errors in the regression are correlated. The larger T is, the greater the correlation. Alternatively, testing the hypothesis with independent returns requires using only every Tth observation, thereby greatly reducing the sample size. Hansen and Hodrick (1980) develop a "corrected" standard error that presumably accounts for the autocorrelation of the chained series.

Another problem is that of small sample bias in the autocorrelation coefficients, noted by Marriot and Pope (1954) and Kendall (1954), who show that differing sample estimates of the mean in the measurement of autocorrelation induce a negative bias in the coefficient. Fama and French (1988b) perform simulations of autoregressions with random data drawn from the normal distribution to correct for this negative bias. We find that the bootstrap procedure below yields similar results.

Implicit in parametric tests of efficiency in general and tests of mean reversion using regression methods in particular is the assumption that the test

Table 20.1
Coefficients and R^2 for the Equal-Weighted NYSE Market Portfolio 1926–1985
Regression

$$r(t, t + T) = \alpha(T) + \beta(T)r(t - T, t) + e(t, t + T)$$

Return Horizon, in Months (T)	Coefficient $\beta(T)$[a]	R^2
12	−.03	.00
24	−.20	.04
36	−.35	.14
48	−.46	.34
60	−.47	.34
72	−.31	.15
84	−.14	.03
96	−.22	.06
108	−.23	.05
120	−.22	.05

[a]No correction has been made for the negative bias in the autocorrelation coefficient induced by estimation of means from small samples (see Marriot and Pope 1954; Kendall 1954).

statistics are distributed according to a known function. This issue is difficult to address without simulation procedures. A benefit of the bootstrap is that it provides a means to investigate the validity of the distributional assumptions. As we will show below, the bootstrapped distributions of coefficients differ significantly from the normal and the Student's t, suggesting that t-tests of hypotheses about these distributions are flawed.

Of greater importance is the fact that the noise component of the stock price also makes the mean-reversion hypothesis difficult to test using autoregressions. Fama and French (1988b) show that the relative magnitude of the variance of the white noise with respect to the variance of the temporary component differs according to the return estimation interval. Consequently, for large enough T, $P(T)$ approaches zero. Thus, according to Fama and French (1988b), if mean reversion is a significant component of the stock price, the mean-reversion model predicts that as T increases $P(T)$ will start near zero, approach but not fall below −.5, and then increase to zero.

This important consequence of the mean-reversion model means that the power of the test increases, then decreases as the estimation interval increases. As Summers (1986) has observed, this is a problem endemic to tests of long-term mean reversion in the stock market. Perhaps the most important issue in the autoregression test using overlapping returns is that the coefficients for successive return horizons are highly correlated. Consequently, our tests for each horizon are not independent. To see this, consider the fact that the vector of 10 regression coefficients is drawn from a joint distribution in which the elements are positively correlated. Consequently, even under the null hypothesis, when an unusually low value for the four-year coefficient occurs, an unusually low value for the five-year coefficient is very likely to occur. Thus we cannot infer that, if 2 or 3 of the 10 coefficients are significant, then their joint occurrence is unusual. Once the decision has been made to examine 10 different interval lengths, the test should properly be formulated as a joint hypothesis about all 10 coefficients. In the fifth section we perform this joint significance test. In light of the statistical problems, great and small, associated with autoregression tests using overlapping data, the bootstrap presents itself as a useful approach.

▲ Bootstrapping the Coefficients

In the absence of information about the true distribution of the autoregression coefficients, we estimate the distribution with an extension of the bootstrap method proposed by Efron (1979). We use the following procedure:

1. A random sample of length 720 is chosen with replacement from the 720 monthly NYSE equal-weighted index returns (1926–85). We add 1 to the returns and take the natural log to form log price ratios.
2. From each sample we create 10 vectors of overlapping returns corresponding to 10 different interval lengths from 12 to 120 months.
3. Autoregressions of $r^*(t, t + T)$ on $r^*(t - T, t)$ are performed, and the coefficients and R-squares are saved.

This process is performed 10,000 times, yielding 10,000 independent observations of the 10-dimensional coefficient vector. The resulting 10,000 observations are then used to approximate the joint distribution under the null hypothesis.

This approach has several advantages. First, the 10,000 samples represent a "control" group formed from the same data distribution used to perform the autoregressions. We construct the null by assuming that the monthly returns are independent and identically distributed (i.i.d.). Thus the resulting coefficients have an intuitively meaningful interpretation. Second, the bootstrap is a nonparametric procedure that does not require the coefficient distributions to conform to theory. In fact, we will soon see that the autoregression coefficients are almost certainly not drawn from marginal Student's t or normal distributions. Third, and perhaps most useful for our purposes, the bootstrap implicitly models features of the coefficient distributions that are only partially susceptible to analysis and control through methods such as the Hansen and Hodrick (1980) correction. Any bias introduced by the process of summing monthly returns to create long-horizon returns is automatically accounted for. We do not need to understand the idiosyncrasies of the data, or the problems induced by overlapping observations; we need only consistently reproduce them.

Whether the 10,000 bootstrap samples are enough depends upon what kind of test will be performed. But the accuracy appears to decline dramatically as the dimensionality of the parameter space increases (see Efron and Tibshirani, 1986). We will propose an approximate method to deal with this problem.

Results of the Bootstrap

Table 20.2 reports the bootstrapped means, medians, and standard deviations for the 10 different return horizons. Note the increasing negative bias of the coefficients as the return horizon increases. In the 5- to 10-year range, the bias is typically the same order of magnitude as the corrected coefficients reported in Table 20.1. The difference between the mean and the median of the bootstrapped coefficient distribution indicates that the distribution is not symmetric. The bootstrapped distribution is skewed left. This asymmetry may slightly bias a single-tailed *t*-test toward rejection, when the mean value of the distribution is used as a correction.

The bootstrap procedure provides the data to perform a direct nonparametric test, rather than a Hansen-Hodrick corrected *t*-test. Table 20.3 reports the autoregression coefficients, together with the relevant quantiles of the marginal distributions of the bootstrapped coefficients. The final column reports the fractile of each distribution. We find that the equal-weighted NYSE return series produces two coefficients significant at the 90% level and one coefficient significant at the 95% level. These accord well with the results reported by Fama and French for similar tests on the real return series. Kim, Nelson, and Startz (1988) performed analogous bootstrapping and randomization proce-

Table 20.2
Bootstrapped Means, Medians, and Standard Errors From the Regression
$$r(t, t + T) = \alpha(T) + \beta(T)r(t - T, t) + e(t, t + T)$$

	Bootstrapped Values[a]		
T	Means	Medians	Std. Errors
12	−.02	−.02	.10
24	−.04	−.04	.15
36	−.07	−.07	.18
48	−.09	−.10	.20
60	−.12	−.13	.23
72	−.15	−.16	.25
84	−.18	−.19	.26
96	−.21	−.23	.28
108	−.24	−.26	.30
120	−.28	−.30	.32

[a]The bootstrapped values are generated by the ordinary least squares (OLS) regression $r^*(t, t + T) = \alpha^*(T) + \beta^*(T)r^*(t - T, t) + e^*(t, t + T)$, where $r^*(t)$ is drawn with replacement from the observed distribution of the CRSP equal-weighted NYSE returns from 1926 to 1985. The bootstrap procedure is repeated 10,000 times.

Table 20.3

**Regression Coefficients, Quantiles of the Bootstrapped Distributions, and Fractiles
Represented by the Coefficients**

$$r(t, t + T) = \alpha(T) + \beta(T)r(t - T, t) + e(t, t + T)$$

Horizon, in Months (T)	Coef. $\beta(T)$	Percentile			Fractile
		10%	5%	1%	
12	−.03	−.15	−.19	−.26	.46
24	−.20	−.23	−.29	−.38	.15
36	−.35	**−.30***	−.36	−.47	.06
48	−.46	−.36	**−.42***	−.54	.03
60	−.47	**−.41***	−.48	−.60	.06
72	−.31	−.46	−.54	−.67	.26
84	−.14	−.52	−.60	−.74	.57
96	−.23	−.57	−.65	−.81	.51
108	−.23	−.61	−.70	−.88	.55
120	−.22	−.66	−.75	−.96	.60

Notes: Percentile and fractile values are reported from the bootstrapped distribution generated by the OLS regression $r^*(t, t + T) = \alpha^*(T) + \beta^*(T)r^*(t - T, t) + e^*(t, t + T)$, where $r^*(t)$ is drawn with replacement from the observed distribution of the CRSP equal-weighted NYSE returns from 1926 to 1985. The bootstrap procedure repeated is 10,000 times.
*Significance at 10% level.

dures on real, value-weighted NYSE returns and observed standard errors for the coefficients similar to ours; however, they performed a bias-corrected t-test rather than using the empirical distribution function.

◤ A Joint Hypothesis Test

An examination of the marginal distributions of the bootstrapped autoregression coefficients is instructive but is not a direct test of the mean-reversion hypothesis. As we mentioned above, that test should properly focus on the question of whether the autoregression coefficients represent an unusual pattern in the context of their joint distribution. The difference is that, by simply reporting results for several different time horizons, we are implicitly looking for the maximum t-statistic in the group. This biases the test toward rejection. A joint test corrects for this implicit bias.

If the bootstrapped vectors $P^*(r^*)$ were distributed multivariate normally, and the variance-covariance matrix were known, we could use the χ^2 distribution to perform a joint test of the null on the 10-dimensional autoregression coefficient vector—call it $fi(r)$. That is:

if $\beta(r)$ is distributed multivariate normal MVN(m, Σ)

then

$y = \Sigma^{-.5} * [\beta(r) - m]$ and

$y \sim MVN (0, I)$

and $y'y \sim \chi^2$.

Under the assumption that a sample of 10,000 is sufficient to identify Σ and m with certainty, unusual values of $y'y$ would lie in the tails of the $\chi^2(10)$ distribution, and hypothesis tests about the magnitude of $y'y$ could be performed accordingly.

Table 20.4 reports the results of a Kolmogorov-Smirnov test for normality on each of the marginal distributions. Interestingly, normality is rejected for intervals over 48 months. The bootstrapped distributions for the longer intervals have fatter tails than normal. Thus we cannot assume that the distribution of the norm of the y vector is $\chi^2 (n)$. The bootstrapped distributions, however, allow us to perform an analogous test in the absence of normality. For each bootstrapped vector of 10 coefficients, we form a test statistic in the following manner:

$$\hat{\Sigma} = \frac{1}{N-1} \sum_{1}^{N} (\beta_k^* - \beta^*)(\beta_k^* - \beta^*)$$

and

$$\beta^* = \frac{1}{N} \sum_{1}^{N} \beta_k^*$$

Table 20.4
Kolmogorov-Smirnov Test for Normality of the Distributions of the Bootstrapped Regression Coefficients Generated by the Model
$$r^*(t, t + T) = \alpha^*(T) + \beta^*(T)r^*(t - T, t) + e^*(t, t + T)$$

Horizon, in Months (T)	Confidence Level for Rejection of Normality
12	.0005
24	.5038
36	.5346
48	.9505
60	.9864
72	.9971
84	.9969
96	.9996
108	.9997
120	.9999

Notes: The value of $r^*(t)$ is drawn with replacement from the observed distribution of the CRSP equal-weighted NYSE log returns from 1926 to 1985. The bootstrap procedure is repeated 10,000 times.

Table 20.5

Chi-Squared and Related Test of the Joint Significance of the Autoregression Coefficients Generated by the OLS Regression

$$r(t, t + T) = \alpha(T) + \beta(T)r(t - T, t) + e(t, t + T)$$

for $T = 12, 24, 36, 48, 60, 72, 84, 96, 108, 120$

Test statistic $(Y' Y)$[a]	16.29
χ^2 (8) 95% confidence level	18.31
Probability value (assuming MVN[b])	.91
Bootstrapped 95% confidence level[c]	22.83
Probability value	.87

[a] Y is formed as $Y = \Sigma^{-.5} * [B(r) - m]$; $B(r)$ is the vector of estimated coefficients; m is the vector of bootstrapped coefficient means; and Σ is the variance-covariance matrix of the coefficients estimated by the bootstrap.

[b] Assuming that $B(r) \sim MVN(m, \Sigma_n)$, $Y \sim \chi^2 (n)$.

[c] The bootstrapped confidence level is the 95th percentile of the distribution generated by $Y^* = \Sigma^{-.5} * [B^*(r^*) - m]$, where the bootstrap is performed 10,000 times and $r^*(t)$ is drawn with replacement from the observed distribution of the CRSP equal-weighted NYSE returns from 1926 to 1985.

where β^* is a bootstrapped vector of coefficients, and Σ is the variance-covariance matrix estimated from the 10,000 joint observations of coefficients, that is,

$$y^* = \hat{\Sigma}^{-1/2} (\beta^* - m).$$

Even if the distribution of $y^{*\prime}y^*$ is not $\chi^2(10)$, we may observe the bootstrapped quantile values as before, when we were interested in the marginal distributions. The results of this test, as well as a χ^2 test under the assumption of multivariate normality, are reported in Table 20.5.

We find that the assumption of normality makes some difference in the results of the test. Table 20.5 shows that the test statistic approaches the 91% confidence interval under the assumption of normality, while it lies at the 87% level when that assumption is relaxed. In both cases, however, the result suggests that, given the autoregression coefficient vector for the equal-weighted NYSE index from 1926 through 1985, we cannot reject the null hypothesis of a random walk at the traditional 95% confidence level. Whether one chooses a lower confidence level for the test is another issue.

Since the bootstrap methodology essentially derives the joint distribution under the null hypothesis there are other ways to evaluate the potential significance of the coefficients. We report several of these. First consider the chances of observing one unusually negative coefficient out of 10. To test this, we calculate the distribution of the minimum over T of $\beta^*(T, r^*)$. The minimum over $\beta^*(T, r^*)$ proves to be in no way unusual: More than 36% of the distribution of the bootstrap minimum falls below the minimum of the test coefficients ($-.47$). Thus, the chances of observing at least one very negative co-

Table 20.6

Nonparametric Tests of the Autoregression Coefficient Vector Using the Bootstrapped Distribution

Condition	Percent of Cases
Minimum over T of $B^*(T, r^*) <$ minimum of $B(T, r)$	.36[a]
Average of B_1^* and B_{10}^* exceeded B_4^*	.44[b]
Maximum of $B^*(T, r^*) > 0$	.26[c]

Note: Percentage is expressed as the number of cases satisfying the criterion out of 10,000 bootstrapped observations.

[a] $B^*(T, r^*)$ represents the bootstrapped coefficient vector. The minimum over T selects the lowest of the eight values in the vector. In more than 3,600 cases this value was below the minimum of $B(T, r)$, the Fama-French coefficient vector.

[b] B_i^* represents the ith element of the bootstrapped coefficient vector.

[c] The maximum selects the largest coefficient of the eight values in the bootstrapped vector.

efficient in 10 appears to be about 36%. Next, we examine the chances of observing the case in which the average of the 1-year and 10-year coefficients exceeds the 4-year coefficient. We find that this occurs 44% of the time. Finally, we can consider the chances of observing the case in which all of the coefficients are negative. This occurs 26% of the time. The results of these three tests are reported in Table 20.6.

Considering that the random-walk model is probably an overly restrictive model of stock price movements, the fact that we cannot clearly reject it suggests that weak form efficiency for long-horizon returns is still a valid hypothesis. In a later section, we test to see whether the 1926 to 1985 regression coefficients are unusual when compared to regression coefficients derived from 1872 to 1925 data.

◤ *Nonoverlapping Interval Tests*

Since nonoverlapping returns represent independent observations, the errors in autoregression tests performed on them are presumed to be uncorrelated. This is an appealing feature because it eliminates one major potential source of bias in the test: the spurious structure imposed by the serial correlation of the returns. It also means that the R-squared may be interpreted as a measure of explanatory power. As before, we utilize monthly return data, which are sampled more finely than the return interval, to model the null hypothesis. This provides a much richer set of possible price histories conforming to the null hypothesis than if we had confined ourselves to data sampled at the same intervals as the return horizon. To see this, consider the bootstrap test of decade returns that does not use data sampled more finely than the return inter-

Table 20.7

Nonoverlapping Return Regression Coefficients, Bootstrapped t-Statistics, Quantiles of the Bootstrapped Distributions, and Fractiles Represented by the Coefficients

$$r(t, t + T) = \alpha(T) + \beta(T)r(t - T, t) + e(t, t + T)$$

Horizon, in Months (T)	Coef. $\beta(T)$	Percentile			Fractile
		10th	5th	1st	
12	−.13	−.18	−.22	−.30	.87
24	−.19	−.25	−.31	−.42	.19
36	−.38	−.31	−**.38***	−.52	.05
48	−.20	−.37	−.45	−.61	.28
60	−.49	−**.42***	−.52	−.68	.06
72	−.23	−.47	−.57	−.80	.33
84	−.42	−.55	−.68	−1.01	.19
96	−.19	−.60	−.74	−1.16	.47
108	−.00	−.69	−.85	−1.55	.68
120	−.89	−.70	−**.86***	1.76	.04

Notes: Percentile and fractile values are reported from the bootstrapped distribution generated by the OLS regression $r^*(t, t + T) = \alpha^*(T) + \beta^*(T)r^*(t - T, t) + e^*(t, t + T)$, where $r^*(t)$ is drawn with replacement from the observed distribution of the CRSP equal-weighted NYSE returns from 1926 to 1985. Returns are nonoverlapping. The bootstrap procedure is repeated 10,000 times.
*Significance at 10% level.

vals. The sample distribution would consist of six realizations, over which the bootstrap would randomize again and again. Schenker (1985) points out that when the underlying sample is small, the bootstrap performs poorly. This is because the empirical distribution function, while it rapidly approaches true distribution function, may significantly depart from it in small sample. Thus the bootstrap estimate of the function remains a poor one, no matter how many bootstrap samples are taken. In contrast, bootstrapping the monthly returns selects from an empirical distribution function defined by more than 700 observations. It thus provides a much broader range of realizations under the null, and satisfies the conditions for an accurate bootstrap estimate of the distribution function.

As before, we bootstrap the distributions of the autoregression coefficients for return intervals ranging from 1- to 10-year lengths. We compound these monthly and immediately reinvest dividends.

Table 20.7 reports the autoregression coefficients, critical values of the marginal bootstrapped distributions, and the fractile represented by each coefficient. Notice that the three- and five-year coefficients are similar to the coefficients for overlapping returns; however, there is less apparent correlation from one return horizon to the next. This is most likely due to the fact that the dramatic reversal of the market during the 1930s makes the autoregression of nonoverlapping returns quite sensitive to when the series begins. For instance, the three-year interval just happens to nicely divide the period 1926–28 from

Table 20.8
Chi-Squared and Related Test of the Joint Significance of the Autoregression Coefficients Generated by the Nonoverlapping OLS Regression

$$r(t, t + T) = \alpha(T) + \beta(T)r(t - T, t) + e(t, t + T)$$
$$\text{for } T = 12, 24, 36, 48, 60, 72, 84, 96, 108, 120$$

Test statistic $(Y'Y)$[a]	8.51
χ^2 (10) 95% confidence level	18.31
Probability value (assuming MVN[b])	.42
Bootstrapped 95% confidence level[c]	21.65
Probability value	.62

[a] Y is formed as $Y = \Sigma^{-.5} * [B(r) - m]$; $B(r)$ is the vector of estimated coefficients; m is the vector of bootstrapped coefficient means; and Σ is the variance-covariance matrix of the coefficients estimated by the bootstrap.

[b] Assuming that $B(r) \sim \text{MVN}(m, \Sigma_n)$, $Y \sim \chi^2 (n)$.

[c] The bootstrapped confidence level is the 95th percentile of the distribution generated by $Y^* = \Sigma^{-.5} * [B^*(r^*) - m]$, where the bootstrap is performed 10,000 times, and $r^*(t)$ is drawn with replacement from the observed distribution of the CRSP equal-weighted NYSE returns from 1926 to 1985.

the period 1929–31. This means that a positive return of about 90% is followed by a negative return of about 81%. Other temporal divisions do not create such dramatic negative autocorrelations. Thus, one benefit of using overlapping data is that it corrects for the sensitivity to the starting date of the series.

The nonoverlapping autoregression tests yield roughly the same number of significantly negative coefficients as do the overlapping tests. The test of their joint significance is reported in Table 20.8. It likewise fails to reject at conventional confidence levels. The probability values of the test statistic lie in the 40% to 60% range.

Table 20.9 reports the sample R-squares for the nonoverlapping autoregression tests, together with the relevant bootstrapped fractiles, and the quantiles represented by the estimated statistics. Notice that the median R-squared values range from near 1% for the 1-year horizon to over 9% for the 10-year horizon. In fact, about 1 out of 10 times the 10-year test results in a 50% R-squared. Given these biases, we find that only one R-squared value exceeds the 95% quantile, and the average of their fractiles lies below 70%.

Table 20.10 is closely related to the variance ratio tests of Lo and MacKinlay (1988a), Kim, Nelson, and Startz (1988), Jacquier and Nanda (1989), Poterba and Summers (1988), and Fama and French (1987). It compares the sample standard deviation of the actual long-horizon return series to the sample standard deviation of the same return horizon generated under the null hypothesis. One advantage to this method is that we need not make the usual assumption that the N-year return variance is well estimated as N times the annual variance (see Poterba and Summers), nor must we correct for finite sample bias inherent in the estimation procedure (see Kim, Nelson, and Startz, Poterba and Summers, and Jacquier and Nanda). In addition, we are

Table 20.9

Regression R^2 Bootstrapped Quantiles of the Bootstrapped Distributions and Fractiles Represented by the R^2 Values

$$r(t, t + T) = \alpha(T) + \beta(T)r(t - T, t) + e(t, t + T)$$

Horizon, in Months (T)	$R^2(T)$	Percentile			Fractile
		50th	90th	95th	
12	.014	.006	.042	.059	.678
24	.037	.014	.084	.119	.720
36	.149	.020	**.122***	.172	.933
48	.041	.028	.162	.227	.582
60	.327	.036	.208	**.286***	.966
72	.150	.043	.257	.344	.791
84	.275	.060	.328	.443	.862
96	.048	.076	.390	.518	.409
108	.000	.093	.486	.623	.056
120	.464	.092	.497	.627	.883

Notes: Percentile and fractile values are reported from the bootstrapped distribution generated by the OLS regression $r^*(t, t + T) = \alpha^*(T) + \beta^*(T)r^*(t - T, t) + e^*(t, t + T)$, where $r^*(t)$ is drawn with replacement from the observed distribution of the CRSP equal-weighted NYSE returns from 1926 to 1985. Returns are nonoverlapping. The bootstrap procedure is repeated 10,000 times.
*Significance at 10% level.

Table 20.10

Standard Deviation of Return Series, Compared to that of the Bootstrapped Distributions and Fractiles Represented by the Standard Deviation Values, As Well As the Values Implied by the Random-Walk Model

$$r(t, t + T) = \alpha(T) + \beta(T)r(t - T, t) + e(t, t + T)$$

Horizon, in Months (T)	Std. Dev. (T)	Percentile			Fractile
		50th	25th	10th	
12	.280	.107	.086	.070	.955
24	.403	.293	.212	.158	.860
36	.513	.464	.369	.268	.611
48	.433	.664	.487	.375	.164
60	.511	.990	.587	.433	.165
72	.6831	.479	.676	.481	.254
84	.9122	.015	.747	.500	.323
96	.5862	.814	.805	.520	.132
108	.4223	.777	.880	**.534***	.069
120	.5725	.424	.949	.563	.103

Notes: Percentile and fractile values are reported from the bootstrapped distribution generated by the OLS regression $r^*(t, t + T) = \alpha^*(T) + \beta^*(T)r^*(t - T, t) + e^*(t, t + T)$, where $r^*(t)$ is drawn with replacement from the observed distribution of the CRSP equal-weighted NYSE returns from 1926 to 1985. Returns are nonoverlapping. The bootstrap procedure is repeated 10,000 times.
*Significance at 10% level.

performing something slightly more general than a test of the random walk. We are considering whether the actual, realized return series is less variable than under the null. This could be true, even if the N-year variance were not well approximated by N times the annual variance. As we show in Table 20.10, the average fractile represented by the sample variance is greater than 35%, with a single observation below the 10% threshold. This accords well with the results reported by Kim, Nelson, and Startz as well as those reported by Jacquier and Nanda. In sum, we find it difficult to reject the null of serial monthly independence using bootstrap methods to perform variance-based tests.

◤ Longer Time Series and a Look at History

What do the regressions reveal when we extend the sample period into the 19th century? We would expect additional observations to increase the power of the test, albeit only slightly. In addition, a longer series may help to determine whether market behavior during a brief subperiod causes the appearance of mean reversion. We examine four additional stock indices: The Dow-Jones monthly index from 1885 to 1988, the Cole and Frickey Monthly Rail Index combined with the Dow from 1834 to 1988, and the Cowles Monthly Common Stock Index combined with the SBBI Index including dividends from 1871 to 1987.

All of these series have certain drawbacks that have been discussed in the literature. All are monthly series. The Dow is a narrow index that suffers from changing relative stock weights and sensitivity to the selection of stocks it comprises. Consequently, any periodicity in the pattern of stock splits of the companies composing the Dow may well be reflected in the time series of returns. Perhaps most significant is the fact that it captures only capital appreciation returns; thus, particularly over the long term, it measures something fundamentally different than the other indices do. While the Cowles index measures total return weighted by market capitalization, Wilson and Jones (1987) recently found apparent data errors in the index—notwithstanding Alfred Cowles' (1938) pioneering use of the computer to manage his data. Although they corrected some errors, others may have gone undetected. In addition, the infrequency of stock price quotations necessitated Cowles' use of monthly average rather than observed end-of-month prices. The Cole and Frickey (1928) index extends monthly capital appreciation returns back to 1834; however, the authors were highly selective in their choice of stocks. Railroad shares make up most of the series, and stocks that showed "little, or erratic movement" were omitted. Although railroad stocks were dominant for most of the middle of the 19th century in the NYSE, a large sector of the market, most notably bank and insurance companies, was excluded. Thus, the series suffers from selection bias. Despite their best efforts, some of the stocks that Cole and Frickey did include in their index traded rather infrequently. Thus, the monthly observations of stock prices for the different companies are likely to have been

Table 20.11

Autoregressions of Log-Term Stock Market Returns Using Overlapping Series

Return Horizon (Years)	Overlapping Interval Series									
	1	2	3	4	5	6	7	8	9	10
NYSE 1926–85	−.03	−.20	−.35	−.46*	−.47	−.31	−.14	−.23	−.23	−.22
	(.46)	(.15)	(.06)	(.03)	(.06)	(.26)	(.57)	(.51)	(.55)	(.60)
NYSE 1834–1988	.04	−.09	−.22*	−.35**	−.40**	−.32*	−.28	−.33	−.33	−.29
	(.80)	(.22)	(.04)	(.01)	(.00)	(.04)	(.10)	(.09)	(.09)	(.17)
Dow 1885–1988	−.02	−.15	−.21*	−.23	−.33*	−.41**	−.47**	−.31	−.19	−.20
	(.45)	(.09)	(.05)	(.06)	(.03)	(.01)	(.00)	(.12)	(.38)	(.35)
Cowles 1871–1986	−.06	−.20*	−.21*	−.18	−.24	−.28*	−.27	−.06	−.00	−.01
	(.29)	(.03)	(.04)	(.09)	(.06)	(.05)	(.09)	(.53)	(.69)	(.72)

Note: Fractiles in parentheses below each coefficient are based on 1,000 bootstrapped values.
*Significance at 10% level.   **Significance at 5% level.

observed on different days. This "nontrading" effect may induce positive monthly autocorrelation in the return series. Finally, the Cole and Frickey index suffers from rounding errors that are apparent when it is plotted.

One can easily imagine how the various problems in these long-term monthly series might induce spurious time structure in the return data, or cause the existing time structure to be overlooked. Nonetheless, both the Dow and the Cowles indices may be regarded as reasonably reliable descriptions of investment in common stock over the last 103 and 117 years, respectively.

The monthly indices allow us to perform both overlapping and nonoverlapping interval autoregressions. Significance tests on the individual coefficients are based on bootstrapped distributions of 1,000 replications. As before, we form a test of the null based on the joint distribution of the coefficients. Table 20.11 reports the autoregression coefficients for the overlapping historical series, and Table 20.12 reports the autoregression coefficients for the nonoverlapping historical series. In both cases we report the bias-corrected t-statistic based upon the bootstrapped coefficient standard errors.

Tables 20.11 and 20.12 show that several of the coefficient patterns are roughly U-shaped as predicted by Fama and French (1988b). The significance levels of the coefficients accord well with the results from the later subperiod. Note in Table 20.11, for instance, that all of the significant negative coefficients are in the two- to seven-year range. The Cole-Frickey index (NYSE 1834–1988) and the Dow index both yield four coefficients that are significant at the 5% level.

In Table 20.12 we also note several significantly negative coefficients. This suggests that the use of nonoverlapping data does not greatly weaken the marginal tests of the coefficients. The U-shaped pattern is less evident than in the previous table, however.

We report the joint test of the coefficients for each of the series in Table 20.13. It includes both the bootstrapped quantile levels of the test statistics as

Table 20.12
Autoregressions of Log-Term Stock Market Returns Using Nonoverlapping Series

Return Horizon (Years)	Non-overlapping Interval Series									
	1	2	3	4	5	6	7	8	9	10
NYSE 1926–1985	−.13	−.19	−.38*	−.20	−.49	−.23	−.42	−.19	−.00	.089
	(.87)	(.19)	(.05)	(.28)	(.06)	(.33)	(.19)	(.47)	(.68)	(.04)
NYSE 1834–1988	.07	−.24*	−.33*	−.20	−.43**	−.26	−.43*	−.62**	−.62**	−.10
	(.83)	(.02)	(.02)	(.16)	(.01)	(.15)	(.03)	(.00)	(.01)	(.46)
Dow 1885–1988	.10	−.01	−.39*	−.57**	−.26	−.48*	.05	−.06	−.33	−.32
	(.89)	(.54)	(.02)	(.00)	(.18)	(.05)	(.70)	(.57)	(.24)	(.25)
Cowles 1871–1986	.01	−.05	−.11	−.24	.04	−.00	−.22	−.08	.18	.06
	(.55)	(.40)	(.31)	(.93)	(.66)	(.58)	(.87)	(.49)	(.82)	(.71)

Note: Fractiles in parentheses below are based on 1,000 bootstrapped values.
*Significance at 10% level.   **Significance at 5% level.

Table 20.13
Joint Tests of the Hypothesis That Autoregression Coefficients for Different Return-Interval Lengths Are Unusual

Overlapping Series	$y'y^a$	χ^2 Values		Bootstrap Values[b]	
		.95 Level	P-Value	.95 Level	P-Value
NYSE 1926–85	16.3	18.3	.91	22.83	.87
NYSE 1834–1988	30.9	18.3	**.99**	19.55	**.99**
Dow 1885–1988	14.6	18.3	.85	17.15	.91
Cowles 1871–1986	23.2	18.3	**.99**	25.21	**.98***

Nonoverlapping Series	$y'y^a$	χ^2 Values		Bootstrap Values	
		.95 Level	P-Value	.95 Level	P-Value
NYSE 1926–85	8.5	18.3	.42	21.65	.62
NYSE 1834–1988	20.0	18.3	**.97***	18.80	**.97***
Dow 1885–1988	21.9	18.3	**.98***	19.58	**.97***
Cowles 1871–1986	07.7	18.3	.35	18.69	.37

[a]The value of y is formed as $y = \Sigma^{-.5} * [B(r) - m]$, where $B(r)$ is the vector of estimated coefficients; m is the vector of bootstrapped coefficient means, and Σ is the variance-covariance matrix of the coefficients estimated by the bootstrap.
[b]Assuming that $B(r) \sim MVN(m, \Sigma_n)$, $y \sim \chi^2(n)$.
[c]The bootstrapped confidence level is the 95th percentile of the distribution generated by $Y* = \Sigma^{-.5} * [B^*(r^*) - m]$, where the bootstrap is performed 1,000 times and $r^*(t)$ is drawn with replacement from the observed distribution of the return series.
*Significance at 10% level.   **Significance at 5% level.

well as the levels under the assumption that they are drawn from the χ^2 distribution. Although we used only 1,000 bootstrap iterations, the theoretical and empirical distributions are quite close. Note in Table 20.13 that we rejected the null at the 95% confidence level for the overlapping autoregressions on the Dow-Jones and Cowles indices. We also reject the null for the nonoverlapping regressions on the Dow-Jones and Cole-Frickey indices. Thus, we can reject the null in about half the series examined, while the other half are marginal or inconclusive.

▲ Long-Term Mean Reversion?

The Cowles data also allow us to perform an out-of-sample test of the coefficients derived from the 1926–87 autoregressions on stock market data from the 54 years preceding the CRSP series. Table 20.14 reports the results of the autocorrelation tests using overlapping long-horizon returns over the period 1872–1925. As with the previous tests, the coefficients tend to be negative, although in no cases do the coefficients lie below the 95% threshold. The χ^2 and the χ^2-like tests fail to reject the null hypothesis of a random walk. In Table 20.15, we use the bootstrapped standard errors from the 1872–1925 autoregressions to see whether the 1926–85 autoregression coefficients are unusual with respect to those from the earlier period. Although no single horizon reveals a significant difference between the earlier and later periods, a χ^2 test re-

Table 20.14
Autoregression Test on Cowles Series Over the Period 1872–1925 Using Overlapping Total Returns

Horizon	Coefficient	50%	95%	99%
12	−.065	−.013	−.200	−.277
24	−.255	−.032	−.295	−.390
36	−.279	−.077	−.354	−.464
48	−.345	−.099	−.426	−.534
60	−.457	−.135	−.503	−.620
72	−.358	−.164	−.555	−.674
84	−.419	−.202	−.617	−.788
96	−.499	−.245	−.686	−.835
108	−.593	−.277	−.730	−1.006
120	−.681	−.312	−.800	−1.085

χ^2 Test Across All 10 Return Horizons				
Test Statistic		Quantile	90%	95%	99%

Test Statistic		Quantile	90%	95%	99%
χ^2	11.85	.705	15.99	18.31	23.27
χ^2-like	11.85	.775	17.75	21.30	41.26

Table 20.15
Test of Similarity Between Cowles 1871–1925 Coefficients and Equal-Weighted NYSE 1926–1987 Coefficients

Horizon	Bootstrapped *t*-Statistic
12	.343
24	−.653
36	.446
48	.333
60	−.039
72	.026
84	−1.31
96	−1.02
108	−1.44
120	−1.62

χ^2 Test of Similarity Across All 10 Horizons					
Test Statistic		Quantile	90%	95%	99%
χ^2	69.94	1.00	15.99	18.31	23.27
χ^2-like	69.94	.997	17.54	21.30	41.26

Notes: The *t*-test for horizon T is formed as $(\beta_{T1872-1925} - \beta_{T1926-1987})/\sigma_{T1872-1925}$, where $\sigma_{T1872-1925}$ is the standard deviation of the bootstrapped distribution of the coefficient.
The χ^2 test statistic is formed as $Y'Y$, where $Y = \Sigma^{-.5} * (\beta_{T1872-1925} - \beta_{T1926-1987})$ and $\Sigma^{-.5}$ is formed as before from the bootstrapped distribution of coefficients.

jects the hypothesis that the vector of coefficients is drawn from the same distribution.

◢ Conclusion

Although we have performed a number of tests, we have not tested to determine whether the stock market is efficient, nor have we tested to see whether the market exhibits time-varying expected returns. What we have shown, however, is that when autoregression procedures are used to examine the temporal behavior of stock returns, particularly long-term stock returns, the results may be misleading. We show that for the equal-weighted NYSE series from 1926 to 1987 it is difficult for the autoregression test to reject that prices follow a random walk. By extension, it is also difficult for the tests to reject the whole class of return-generating models in which successive observations are independent.

▲ References

Cole, Arthur H., and E. Frickey. 1928. The course of stock prices, 1825–1866. *Review of Economics and Statistics* 10:117–139.

Conrad, Jennifer, and Gautam Kaul. 1988. Time variation in expected returns. *Journal of Business* 61:409–425.

Cowles, Alfred. 1938. *Common stock indices 1871–1937*. Bloomington, Ind.

Efron, B. 1979. Bootstrap methods: Another look at the jackknife. *Annals of Statistics* 7:1–26.

Efron, B., and R. Tibshirani. 1986. Bootstrap methods for standard errors, confidence intervals, and other measures of statistical accuracy. *Statistical Science* 1:54–77.

Fama, Eugene F., and K. French. 1987. Forecasting returns on corporate bonds and common stocks. Working paper no. 4-88, John E. Anderson Graduate School of Management at UCLA.

———. 1988a. Dividend yields and expected stock returns. *Journal of Financial Economics* 22:3–25.

———. 1988b. Permanent and temporary components of stock prices. *Journal of Political Economy* 96:246–273.

Hansen, Lars, and R. J. Hodrick. 1980. Forward exchange rates as optimal predictors of future spot rates: An econometric analysis. *Journal of Political Economy* 88:829–1054.

Jacquier, Eric, and Vikram Nanda. 1989. Cyclicality of stock returns and the mean reversion puzzle. Mimeograph. School of Business Administration, University of Southern California.

Kendall, Maurice G. 1954. A note on bias in the estimation of autocorrelation. *Biometrika* 41:403–404.

Kim, Myung Jig, C. R. Nelson, and R. Startz. 1988. Mean reversion in stock prices? Mimeograph. University of Washington.

Lo, Andrew. 1988. Long-term memory in stock market prices. Unpublished ms., Department of Finance, Wharton School, University of Pennsylvania.

Lo, A., and C. MacKinlay. 1988a. Long-term memory in stock prices. Mimeograph. Wharton School, University of Pennsylvania.

———. 1988b. Stock market prices do not follow random walks: Evidence from a simple specification test. *Review of Financial Studies* 1:41–65.

Marriot, F. H. C., and J. Pope. 1954. Bias in the estimation of autocorrelations. *Biometrika* 41:390–402.

Poterba, James M., and Lawrence H. Summers. 1988. Mean reversion in stock prices: Evidence and implications. *Journal of Financial Economics* 22:27–59.

Schenker, Nathaniel. 1985. Qualms about bootstrap confidence intervals. *Journal of the American Statistical Association* 80:360–361.

Shiller, Robert J., and P. Perron. 1985. Testing the random walk hypothesis: Power versus frequency of observation. *Economics Letters* 18:381–386.

Summers, Lawrence H. 1986. Does the stock market rationally reflect fundamental values? *Journal of Finance* 41:591–601.

Wilson, Jack, and C. P. Jones. 1987. A comparison of annual common stock returns: 1871–1925 with 1926–85. *Journal of Business* 60:239–258.

21

William N. Goetzmann and Philippe Jorion

Testing the Predictive Power of Dividend Yields

Overview

Do low dividend yields forecast a stock market decline? Does this commonly used financial ratio indicate whether stocks are over- or undervalued? This apparently simple question has been widely debated for financial economists for more than 10 years, and subjected to a battery of tests. In particular, a number of top research teams have found evidence that yields do *predict returns. These include Michael Rozeff (1984), Eugene Fama and Kenneth French (1988a,b), John Campbell and Robert Shiller (1988), and Robert Hodrick (1992) (all cited in full in "Suggested Reading"). On the other hand, we come to the opposite conclusion. What might explain the differences in research outcomes?*

A key issue in crafting an empirical test of the predictability of dividend yields is to recognize the fact that dividing a dividend by the stock price on one side of the regression and using a lagged value of that same stock price on the other side of the regression can cause test statistics to behave quite poorly—so poorly, in fact, that standard t-*statistics are quite misleading. In this paper, Philippe Jorion and I develop a procedure that builds this dependent price structure into a simulation. Using U.S. data from 1926, we find the evidence on dividend yields as a predictor to be marginal, not quite strong enough to reject the null hypothesis at standard confidence levels.*

Abstract

This article reexamines the ability of dividend yields to predict long-horizon stock returns. We use the bootstrap methodology, as well as simulations, to examine the distribution of test statistics under the null hypothesis of no forecasting ability. These experiments are constructed so as to maintain the dynamics of regressions with lagged dependent variables over long horizons. We find that the empirically observed statistics are well within the 95% bounds of their simulated distributions. Overall there is no strong statistical evidence indicating that dividend yields can be used to forecast stock returns.

A number of recent studies appear to provide empirical support for the traditional use of the dividend-price ratio as a measure of expected stock returns.

Rozeff (1984), for instance, finds that the ratio of the dividend yield to the short-term interest rate explains a significant fraction of movements in annual stock returns. Fama and French (1988) use a regression framework to show that the dividend yield predicts a significant proportion of multiple year returns to the NYSE index. They further observe that the explanatory power of the dividend yield increases in the time horizon of the returns; over 4-year horizons, R^2's range from a low of 19% to an astonishingly high value of 64%. Similar results are reported by Flood, Hodrick, and Kaplan (1987) and Campbell and Shiller (1988).

The apparent predictability of market returns from past values of dividend yields is regarded by Rozeff (1984) as support for the rejection of the random walk model of stock prices, and by Fama and French (1988) as support for the cyclical behavior of expected returns. Flood, Hodrick, and Kaplan (1987) interpret their results as support for time-varying expected returns to stocks. The direct, and somewhat disturbing, implication of most of these studies is that significant components of long-term stock returns may be predictable using combinations of past returns and macroeconomic variables.

There are a number of reasons, however, why these results should be regarded with caution. Given the persistent patterns of dividend payments, movements in dividend yields are essentially dominated by movements in prices. Therefore, the forecasting regressions suffer from biases due to the fact that the right-hand-side variables are correlated with lagged dependent variables, instead of being predetermined as assumed in standard statistical models. In addition, the usual GMM corrections to the standard errors are valid only asymptotically, and there is some question as to whether "asymptotic" should be measured in terms of years, decades, or even centuries, especially for long-horizon forecasts.

Nelson and Kim (1992), in an independent study, analyze these biases in simulations of a VAR system under the null hypothesis of no predictability of returns. Using returns sampled annually, they report that the simulated distribution of t-statistics is displaced upward, but they still find some evidence of predictability at conventional significance levels. Hodrick (1992), making full use of the information available in monthly data, extensively simulates a VAR model applied to long-horizon returns, and also finds evidence of predictability in stock returns.

While the VAR model addresses the endogeneity of the predictor, it does not fully account for biases due to the fact that the regressor behaves like a lagged dependent variable. Our research illustrates a case where this problem still biases tests toward rejection of the null. We use the bootstrap methodology, as developed by Efron (1979), to model the distributions of regression statistics under the null hypothesis that stock returns are independently and identically distributed, and are not related to past dividends. Our approach differs from previous VAR simulations in that we explicitly incorporate the lagged price relation between returns and dividend yields. We find that this explicit specification of the null makes a substantial difference in hypothesis tests of the significance of the dividend yield regression.

In bootstrapped regressions of 1- to 4-year returns to the S&P stock return index on the preceding dividend yield, we fail to reject the null hypothesis that future returns are unrelated to past dividend yields at conventional significance levels. In addition, we find that the observed explanatory power of the model, as measured by the coefficient of determination, is only marginally significant when compared to bootstrapped distributions of R^2's; OLS t-statistics over 18 and R^2 over 38% for all multiple year horizons are not unusual. Overall, when we explicitly model the null hypothesis as a random walk, we find that the observed regressions of returns on past dividend yields provide only marginal statistical evidence against the random walk model.

This article is organized as follows. The basic dividend yield regressions are presented in the first section. The second section describes the modeling of the null hypothesis in a numerical analysis framework. The bootstrapping tests and results are presented in the third section. Finally, the last section contains some concluding observations.

◣ Dividend Yields

Dividend yields have long been used to evaluate the expected return to investment in common stocks. If the stock price represents a claim to the future stream of dividends, the price can be exactly determined assuming constantly growing dividends and a known discount rate. This is the model variously attributed to Williams (1938) or Gordon and Shapiro (1956). Campbell and Shiller (1988) more recently refer to this model as the "dividend-ratio" model in the absence of uncertainty:

$$P_t = \sum_{i=1}^{\infty} D_t(1 + g)^i/(1 + r)^i = \frac{D_{t+1}}{r - g}, \tag{1}$$

where P is the stock price, D is the dividend, r is the discount rate, and g is the constant growth rate of dividends. In the certainty model, the discount rate is the expected return on the stock. Although the model is not directly applicable to the case in which growth rates and discount rates vary through time, the model suggests that dividend yields should capture variations in expected stock returns.

If long-term market returns are predicted by the dividend yield, the following regression should produce a significant coefficient and a non-trivial R^2:

$$R_{t,t+T} = \alpha_T + \beta_T Y_t + \varepsilon_{t,t+T} \tag{2}$$

where $R_{t,t+T}$ is the compound total stock return from month t to month $t + T$, and Y_t is the ratio D_t/P_t, the annual dividend up to time t divided by the stock price as of time t.

The null hypothesis is that there is no relation between $R_{t,t} + T$ and Y_t, i.e., that $\beta_T = 0$. Following Fama and French (1988), we perform all tests using

Table 21.1
Long-Horizon Dividend Yield Regressions

Horizon (Months)	Beta	t-Statistic			R^2
		OLS	GMM	NW	
Period: 1927–1990					
1	0.386	2.80	1.21	1.21	0.010
12	5.108	9.97	2.95	3.17	0.116
24	9.071	12.73	5.32	5.38	0.179
36	12.939	15.38	5.97	4.77	0.244
48	21.392	21.42	7.37	7.30	0.390
Period: 1927–1958					
1	0.415	1.89	0.85	0.85	0.009
12	5.846	6.97	2.53	2.61	0.116
24	10.778	8.97	5.70	4.64	0.183
36	16.167	11.30	5.16	3.74	0.269
48	28.987	18.06	11.20	7.05	0.493
Period: 1959–1990					
1	0.668	2.76	2.42	2.42	0.020
12	8.757	11.04	4.03	4.46	0.247
24	14.401	14.29	3.65	4.32	0.363
36	19.740	17.15	4.56	4.90	0.459
48	27.911	20.26	4.68	5.19	0.551

Notes: $R_{t,t+T} = \alpha_T + \beta_T Y_t + \varepsilon_{t,t+T}$ where $R_{t,t+T}$ is defined as the total stock return from time t to time $t + T$, and $Y_t = D_t/P_t$ is the annual dividend yield measured as of time t. The t-statistics presented are: t(OLS), from the classical OLS regression, t(GMM), which adjusts for heteroskedasticity and the moving average process induced by the overlapping observations (using the sample autocovariances), and t(NW), which in addition uses the Newey and West adjustment to ensure that the variance-covariance matrix of estimated coefficients is positive definite.

overlapping observations. As is well known, this procedure results in more powerful tests but induces a moving average process in the errors, which invalidates the usual OLS standard errors.[1] The standard error corrections are computed using the method proposed by Hansen and Hodrick (1980), in which the autocovariances are estimated from the data, with a modification due to White (1980) and Hansen (1982) that allows for conditional heteroskedasticity. These will be referred to as "Generalized Method of Moments" estimators. There are situations, however, where the variance-covariance matrix of the estimated coefficients is not positive definite. Therefore, standard errors are also reported using a correction due to Newey and West (1987) that ensures that the matrix is positive definite.[2]

To investigate the predictive power of dividend yields, we use data on the S&P 500 index over the period 1927 through 1990. Monthly total and income returns were used to construct a price series P, exclusive of dividends, from which monthly dividend payments were inferred. Because of seasonalities in monthly dividends, an annual dividend series D was computed by reinvesting the dividends at the monthly riskless rate. A price series P^R was also computed from the total returns R, assuming reinvestment of dividends; this series represents the value of a fund invested in the S&P 500 stocks with reinvested dividends. Appendix 1 contains a complete description of the data.

Table 21.1 presents long-horizon forecasts for returns on the S&P index over the period 1927 to 1990, and two subperiods of equal length, 1927 to 1958 and 1959 to 1990. Over the total 64-year period, the results seem to suggest strong predictive ability for dividend yields. The slope coefficients increase from 0.39 to 21.39 when the horizon lengthens from 1 month to 4 years.[3] The OLS t-statistic also increases uniformly with the horizon, up to 21.42; since the R^2 is a simple transformation of the OLS t-statistic, it increases to 39%, which appears to be substantial. These OLS t-statistics and R^2's, however, are seriously biased upward because of overlapping observations. This is apparent from the much lower values of the GMM and Newey and West (NW) t-statistics, which are 7.37 and 7.30 at the 4-year horizon. These values, however, still indicate predictability.

The lower panels of the table reports estimates for the two subperiods. A similar pattern emerges: high values of β increasing with maturity up to 29.0 and 27.9, and high R^2's, going up to 49% and 55% in the two respective subperiods. The fact that the predictive power is consistently stronger over shorter sample periods to some extent suggests that the small-sample bias may be enhancing the apparent significance of the results.

◢ Testing Predictive Power

In fact, dividend yield regressions are similar to regressions on a lagged dependent variable, which suffer from well-known biases. To illustrate this, assume as before that dividends grow at a constant rate g. For illustration purposes, it is slightly more convenient to use continuously compounded returns, and the series with reinvested dividends. Dividends then grow as $\ln D_t^R = \ln D_0^R + gt$, and regression (2) becomes:

$$\ln(P_{t+T}^T/P_t^R) = \alpha + \beta \ln D_t^R - \beta \ln P_t^R + \varepsilon_{t,t+T} \qquad (3)$$
$$= \alpha' + \beta(-\ln P_t^R) + \gamma t + \varepsilon_{t,t+T}.$$

In this setup, all of the economic time variation in the dividend yield derives from the time variation in the price level.

Equation (3) suffers from the classical bias due to the fact that a right-hand-side variable is a lagged dependent variable. When $T = 1$, Kendall (1973), for instance, shows that the OLS estimate, although consistent, is centered at values less than zero in finite samples, even when the slope is truly zero. Dickey and Fuller (1979) tabulate by simulations new values for the OLS *t*-statistic under the null. The downward bias is shown to be substantial in small samples, and is of the order of $(-4/n)$, where n is the sample size.

In overlapping regressions, however, it is harder to predict the extent of the bias for the slope coefficient. While the GMM corrections to the standard errors are valid asymptotically, even with 64 years of data, there are only 16 truly independent observations in the case of 4-year overlapping returns. Econometric theory offers little guidance as to whether 16 observations qualify for asymptotic status. For these reasons, it seems prudent to investigate the small-sample characteristics of these regressions by numerical analysis.

The Bootstrap

The bootstrap was proposed by Efron (1979) as a nonparametric randomization technique that draws from the observed distribution of the data to model the distribution of a test statistic of interest. For example, suppose $X = (X_1 \ldots X_n)$ are i.i.d. random variables drawn from the unknown distribution F. Define θ as some parameter of the population, and $\hat{\theta}(X)$ as an estimator of θ. Let $\hat{F}$ be the sample distribution, from the observed X_i, that assigns a mass $1/n$ to each X_i. The bootstrap estimates the distribution of $\hat{\theta}(F)$ by the sampling distribution $\hat{\theta}(\hat{F})$. This procedure is carried out by the following steps:

1. From the observed $(X_1 \ldots X_n)$, compute the test statistic $\hat{\theta}(X)$.
2. Draw a bootstrap sample $(X_1^* \ldots X_n^*)$, with replacement, from the empirically observed distribution $\hat{F}$.
3. Calculate $\hat{\theta}^* = \hat{\theta}(X^*)$ from the pseudodata.
4. Repeat steps 2 and 3 K times, obtaining $\hat{\theta}_k^*$, $k = 1, \ldots, K$.

The empirical distribution of $(\hat{\theta}_k^* - \hat{\theta})$ can be used to approximate the distribution of $(\hat{\theta} - \theta)$. The asymptotic properties of the bootstrap for commonly used statistics such as the mean, median, variance, and distribution quantiles have been studied by Bickel and Freedman (1981) and Freedman (1981). Freedman (1981) demonstrates the validity of the bootstrap for the regression model, showing that, under the assumptions of predetermined variables and i.i.d. errors, the distribution of the coefficients converges to the normal. As we shall see, the bootstrapped distributions of coefficients may converge to a nonnormal distribution when these conditions are violated.

The bootstrap approach, it should be noted, has limitations. For small sample sizes, the bootstrapped distribution $\hat{\theta}(\hat{F})$ may be a poor approximation to $\hat{\theta}(F)$. Schenker (1985), for instance, shows a simple example where the bootstrapped distribution of standard errors would lead the researcher to underestimate the size of confidence intervals. For sufficiently large sample sizes, however, an important advantage of the bootstrap is that it allows the researcher to control for the presence of potentially biasing factors such as the use of overlapping return intervals, the lagged correlation between independent and dependent regression variables, and other idiosyncrasies in the distribution of the returns or in the error structure.

Bootstrapping Dividend Yields

We adapt the bootstrapping methodology to the dividend yield problem by considering the following model. We want to specify a temporal relationship between returns, dividends, and prices that is analogous to their historical pattern. In particular, price levels—the denominator in the yield term—are dependent upon the capital appreciation return history to that point, and dividends are highly autocorrelated. To capture this relationship in the bootstrap model, we randomly sample total returns $R*$ from their true distribution, subtract off the contemporaneous income return R_I^* to create a pseudo-capital-appreciation-return series R_X^*. We compound these to calculate a pseudo-price-level series, $P*$, which in turn is used to create a pseudo-dividend-yield, $Y*$, where $Y_t^* = D_t/P_t^*$ in which D_t are the actual annual dividend flows, and $P*$ is the simulated price series.

Because total returns have been randomized, there is no relationship between returns and dividends. At the same time, the dividend series exhibits the high degree of persistence actually observed. Therefore, this setup introduces the possibility of autocorrelated errors in the regression, and potential bias in the estimated coefficients. This is a desired feature of the model, since it remains consistent with the null hypothesis.

Thus, our bootstrap procedure is the following:

1. Form the empirical distribution of monthly total stock returns and their associated income returns from the observed vectors of S&P returns.
2. Draw 718 of these observations ($R_1^* \ldots R_{718}^*$ with replacement.
3. Compute the relevant statistics:
   a. Form $P*$ from $R_X^* = R* - R_I^*$ as described above. Use this to form $Y* = D/P*$.
   b. Construct multiple horizon return vectors R_T^* for overlapping T-year returns.
   c. Perform the regressions of future returns on dividend yields, for each horizon T, and save the resulting coefficients β_T^*, the R_T^{2*} and the t-statistics t_T^*.
4. Repeat steps 2 through 3 five thousand times.

▲ Empirical Results

Table 21.2 reports the relevant quantiles, means, and standard deviations of the bootstrapped distributions of regression coefficients, t-statistics, and R^2's under the null hypothesis. The mean of the coefficient distribution increases uniformly in the return horizon, from 0.15 to 9.59, and the median of the coefficient differs increasingly from the mean, indicating right-skewed distributions. The extent of the skewness is apparent from Figures 21.1 and 21.2, which present histograms of the bootstrapped betas over 1-month and 4-year horizons.[4] The critical value at the 5% level for the 4-year slope coefficient is

Table 21.2
Bootstrap on Total Returns: 1927 to 1990

Statistic	Fractiles of Statistics							Mean	Std. Dev.	Observed Statistic	Empirical p-Value
	0.010	0.050	0.100	0.500	0.900	0.950	0.990				
1-month											
β	−0.071	−0.020	0.003	0.106	0.374	0.484	0.767	0.154	0.173	0.386	0.0920
t(OLS)	−0.885	−0.298	0.073	1.284	2.436	2.753	3.453	1.270	0.928	2.795	0.0464
t(GMM)	−0.936	−0.312	0.077	1.287	2.384	2.712	3.292	1.257	0.904	1.208	0.5358
t(NW)	−0.936	−0.312	0.077	1.287	2.384	2.712	3.292	1.257	0.904	1.208	0.5358
R^2	0.00000	0.00003	0.00012	0.00217	0.00771	0.00981	0.01533	0.003	0.003	0.010	0.0466
12-month											
β	−0.972	−0.280	0.022	1.329	4.847	6.391	9.968	1.972	2.200	5.108	0.0878
t(OLS)	−2.926	−0.995	0.117	4.298	8.613	9.816	12.220	4.373	3.311	9.969	0.0462
t(GMM)	−1.031	−0.344	0.040	1.369	2.749	3.188	4.182	1.398	1.092	2.948	0.0740
t(NW)	−1.207	−0.411	0.049	1.628	3.271	3.707	4.752	1.653	1.269	3.167	0.1146
R^2	0.00001	0.00029	0.00120	0.02431	0.08948	0.11317	0.16513	0.037	0.038	0.116	0.0462
24-month											
β	−2.190	−0.0642	0.044	2.936	10.520	13.468	20.894	4.222	4.661	9.071	0.1348
t(OLS)	−3.768	−1.341	0.171	5.904	12.497	14.348	18.006	6.167	4.813	12.730	0.0932
t(GMM)	−1.074	−0.342	0.046	1.466	3.157	3.861	5.715	1.587	1.425	5.319	0.0140
t(NW)	−1.233	−0.414	0.053	1.710	3.539	4.226	5.746	1.785	1.435	5.379	0.0138
R^2	0.00002	0.00054	0.00210	0.04531	0.17368	0.21696	0.30380	0.069	0.073	0.179	0.0932

36-month

β	−3.793	−1.102	0.026	4.776	16.482	21.567	32.303	6.745	7.417	12.939	0.1620
t(OLS)	−4.542	−1.585	0.138	7.069	15.489	18.061	22.920	7.508	6.050	15.375	0.1034
t(GMM)	−1.165	−0.388	0.022	1.555	3.644	4.659	7.178	1.679	3.643	5.972	0.0214
t(NW)	−1.292	−0.435	0.038	1.779	3.890	4.794	6.824	1.917	1.634	4.773	0.0514
R^2	0.00003	0.00077	0.00281	0.06459	0.24710	0.30854	0.41814	0.098	0.102	0.244	0.1034

48-month

β	−6.426	−1.564	0.050	6.872	23.174	30.018	46.231	9.589	10.546	21.391	0.1166
t(OLS)	−5.349	−1.734	0.134	7.945	18.068	21.157	27.167	8.636	7.123	21.419	0.0460
t(GMM)	−1.246	−0.406	0.030	1.632	4.149	5.492	9.333	1.972	2.579	7.367	0.0222
t(NW)	−1.349	−0.456	0.034	1.822	4.235	5.283	8.107	2.045	1.849	7.300	0.0158
R^2	0.00005	0.00093	0.00354	0.08115	0.31226	0.38369	0.50653	0.124	0.127	0.390	0.0460

Notes: The bootstrap uses 5,000 replications, resampled from the actual distribution of total returns, under the null hypothesis of no linear relationship between returns and dividend yields. The table reports the distribution of β, t-statistics, and R^2 from dividend yield regressions. The last two columns report the actual statistics observed over the 1927 to 1990 sample, as well as the empirical p-value, which is the proportion of times the observed statistic was exceeded under the null.

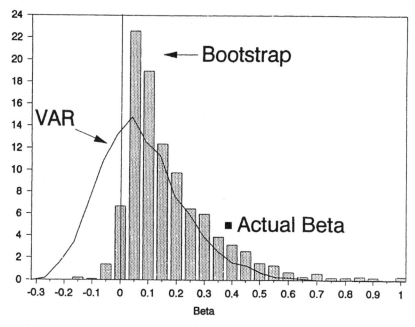

Figure 21.1. Distribution of Beta: 1-Month Horizon
Notes: Distribution of slope coefficient from 1-month horizon dividend yield regression under the null. The histogram describes the bootstrap distribution, and the solid line describes the VAR distribution. The actual beta measured over 1927 to 1990 is also reported.

Testing the Tests

A considerable amount of research into testing the predictive power of dividend yields has occurred since we wrote this paper. Recently, some progress has been made on the methodology itself. Michael Wolf (2000), for example, develops a robust structure for estimation, based upon current sub-sampling methods in statistics. Wolf's work is particularly interesting because it addresses a legitimate concern about our analysis raised by John Campbell. The idea is that, by constructing a dividend yield that is tied-in to the price process, we have introduced a regressor with a unit root—or near unit root—which is troublesome by design. What is nice about Wolf's sub-sampling methods (also called "moving blocks bootstrap" because it draws blocks from the sample rather than single period observations). It thus avoids the problem by preserving the particular time-series characteristics of the original series, allowing for very near unit root processes as regressors. Despite taking a very different tack to the study of the predictive power of dividend yields, Wolf concludes, as we do, that the evidence of forecastability is weak, at least, given the limits of the U.S. data we have available to us.

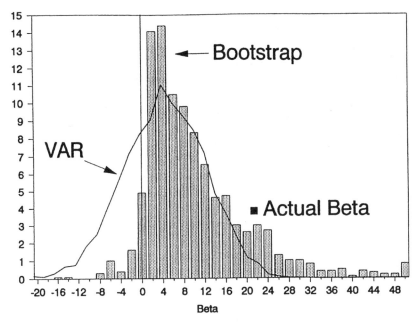

Figure 21.2. Distribution of Beta: 4-Year Horizon
Notes: Distribution of slope coefficient from 4-year horizon dividend yield regression under the null. The histogram describes the bootstrap distribution, and the solid line describes the VAR distribution. The actual beta measured over 1927 to 1986 is also reported.

30.02, which is very high. Notice that the overlap is not the cause of the skewness; skewness occurs at the 1-month horizon as well as at the 4-year horizon.

The table also shows that all t-statistics increase in the time horizon. As other researchers have noted, the OLS t-statistics are grossly misleading since they fail to correct for the autocorrelated errors induced by the use of overlapping returns, as well as for the bias in the slope coefficient. At the 4-year horizon, OLS t-statistics above 21.16 are observed in 5% of all experiments. What is more worrisome, however, is the fact that the corrected GMM and NW t-statistics also appear to be seriously biased upward. At 4-year horizons, GMM t-statistics above 5.49 are observed in 5% of the sample.[5] The mean of the R^2's also increases uniformly in the return horizon, from near zero to a mean value of 12% for 4-year forecasts. The 5% critical level for the 4-year R^2 is above 38%.

The right-hand-side columns in Table 21.2 report the observed statistics from the actual regressions of returns on lagged dividend yield. Note that, while the slope coefficients all exceed the median values for their bootstrapped distributions, none exceeds the relevant 95% fractile. Thus, it is difficult to conclude that the regression statistics differ significantly from those obtained under the null hypothesis as specified, using conventional significance levels. While some of the t-statistics and the R^2 barely exceed the 95% fractiles, these statistics may not be directly applicable in view of the asymmetry in the distribution of slope coefficients.

As noted in Richardson and Smith (1991) and Goetzmann (1990), it is insufficient to examine the coefficients separately. Following Hodrick (1992), we assess joint significance of all five slope coefficients by formulating a statistic similar to the Hotelling T^2: $\hat{\beta}V(\hat{\beta}*)^{-1}\hat{\beta}$, where $V(\hat{\beta}*)$ is the covariance matrix of all 5,000 jointly bootstrapped betas. The observed statistic of 11.40, compared to its bootstrapped distribution, is exceeded in 9.5% of the experiments, which again indicates that the slope coefficients are only marginally significant.

Table 21.3 presents the results of the bootstrap applied to the two subperiods, 1927 to 1958 and 1959 to 1990. The empirical p-values of the actual 4-year slope coefficients are 0.130 and 0.317 in the two respective samples. Therefore, there is little statistical evidence that the slope coefficients are different from what could be expected under the null of no forecasting ability for dividend yields.

While the previous analysis is distribution free, it may be of some interest to investigate the sensitivity of the results to the distributional assumptions. Therefore, the numerical analysis was also performed using total returns $R*$ drawn from a normal distribution with mean and variance equal to those of the original sample.[6] Table 21.4 reports summary statistics for the simulation under normally distributed returns.

The table is substantially in agreement with the results in Table 21.2; none of the slope coefficients is significant at the 5% level. The empirical p-values, however, are systematically lower than those reported from the bootstrap. For instance, the 4-year p-value is 0.0878, instead of 0.1166 previously; the 1-month p-value is 0.0628, instead of 0.0920 previously. Differences appear to be due to the fact that there are fewer extreme observations in the tails of the normal distribution than actually observed over the sample; the bootstrap more accurately reflects the actual distribution of stock returns. In spite of these slight differences, the general conclusions are not affected by the distributional assumptions behind the returns simulations.

To understand why these results are so different from traditional regressions, consider another bootstrap experiment where the right-hand-side variables are exogenous. In this setup, the independent variables are taken to be the actual dividend yield $Y = D/P$, and monthly returns are randomized to generate the dependent variables and multiple horizon returns. The middle panel in Table 21.4 reports information on the bootstrapped statistics in this traditional regression framework. The table shows that the bootstrapped GMM t-statistics correspond much more closely to their expected distribution than in Table 21.2. For instance, the empirical one-tailed 5% level for the GMM t-statistic at the 4-year horizon is 2.13, which is close to what was expected from traditional regression theory. Using the empirical distributions in Table 21.4 would lead to the misleading conclusion that all of the multiyear statistics are strongly significant. This further indicates the need to specify a framework allowing the right-hand-side variables to be endogenous.

As Nelson and Kim (1993) and Hodrick (1992) point out, the issue of endogeneity could be analyzed by modelling a first-order VAR process,

$$Z_{t+1} = AZ_t + u_{t+1} \tag{4}$$

where the columns of Z represent monthly stock returns and dividend yields. In order to simulate Z_{t+1} under the null, we set the slope coefficients in the return equation equal to zero. Then we bootstrap the sample distribution of errors.[7]

This procedure has two desirable features: it models the dividend yield as a highly autocorrelated series, with a first-order autocorrelation of 0.96, and also as an endogenous variable, with a contemporaneous correlation with returns of -0.90. The bootstrapped distributions are summarized in the right-hand-side panel of Table 21.4. The VAR approach corrects for the small-sample bias due to the use of an endogenous variable, as well as for biases in the t-statistics, but only indirectly models the serial dependence resulting from the lagged price effect in dividend yield regressions.

As a result, the distributions of slope coefficients appear much closer to normal than under the bootstrap. The curves labelled "VAR" in Figures 21.1 and 21.2 clearly show that the VAR model only partially capture the skewness in slope coefficients. In terms of inference, Table 21.2 might indicate predictability in dividend yields: for all horizons, the empirical p-value for the observed coefficient is below 5%. Our results suggest that these rejections may be misleading, because they do not explicitly incorporate the dynamics of regressions with lagged dependent variables.

The results of the dividend yield regressions, for which the price process is endogenous, bear a close resemblance to the well-known simulations performed by Granger and Newbold (1974) and further analyzed by Phillips (1986). Granger and Newbold regressed two independent random walks, and found rejection of the null the rule, rather than the exception. Indeed, their paper has frequently been cited as justification for the need to use differenced price series in econometric studies (see Plosser and Schwert [1978], for example). These results may help us understand the spuriously high R^2's obtained in the preceding tests. The greater the overlap in the return series, the more closely the return series resembles a price level series, rather than a return series. Although each successive return may be independent (in fact, the bootstrapped returns are independent by construction), the series comprised of a rolling sum of returns is not. Likewise, dividends also resemble random walks. It would thus not be surprising to find that the combination of these two series in a regression could result in spurious conclusions regarding both significance and explanatory power.

To present another perspective on the results, Table 21.5 reports estimates of Equation (3), which explains returns by the logarithm of the lagged price plus a time trend. As shown before, this specification assumes that dividends grow at a constant rate. Table 21.5 shows that the R^2's obtained in this specification range from 1.1% for a 1-month horizon to 64% for a 4-year horizon. These values, as well as t-statistics, are typically higher than those found for the equivalent dividend yield regressions. Figure 21.3 compares the 4-year returns with fitted values

Table 21.3
Bootstrap on Total Returns: Actual Distribution (Monthly Data: Subperiods)

	Period: 1927–1958				Period: 1959–1990			
	Bootstrap Betas		Observed	Empirical	Bootstrap Betas		Observed	Empirical
Statistic	Mean	Std. Dev.	Statistic	p-Value	Mean	Std. Dev.	Statistic	p-Value
1-month								
β	0.247	0.271	0.415	0.195	0.380	0.352	0.668	0.160
t(OLS)	1.219	0.933	1.888	0.239	1.411	0.843	2.761	0.044
t(GMM)	1.195	0.899	0.855	0.658	1.425	0.849	2.424	0.122
t(NW)	1.195	0.899	0.855	0.658	1.425	0.849	2.424	0.122
R^2	0.00606	0.00680	0.00924	0.239	0.00698	0.00636	0.01956	0.044
12-month								
β	3.030	3.436	5.846	0.158	4.768	4.148	8.757	0.137
t(OLS)	4.152	3.542	6.972	0.201	4.982	2.972	11.041	0.022
t(GMM)	1.424	1.244	2.530	0.170	1.686	1.079	4.028	0.021
t(NW)	1.644	1.405	2.614	0.224	1.976	1.236	4.456	0.024
R^2	0.06750	0.07369	0.11586	0.201	0.07783	0.06669	0.24733	0.022
24-month								
β	6.278	7.450	10.778	0.202	10.063	8.381	14.401	0.243
t(OLS)	5.838	5.305	8.970	0.265	7.170	4.479	14.291	0.057
t(GMM)	1.806	1.991	5.700	0.025	2.095	1.572	3.651	0.126
t(NW)	1.883	1.776	4.642	0.058	2.287	1.581	4.322	0.101
R^2	0.12186	0.13017	0.18311	0.265	0.14600	0.11933	0.36259	0.057

36-month

β	9.757	12.150	16.167	0.205	15.657	12.758	19.740	0.309
t(OLS)	7.089	6.762	11.302	0.248	8.845	5.799	17.154	0.081
t(GMM)	1.772	7.805	5.163	0.111	2.337	6.092	4.562	0.145
t(NW)	2.142	2.151	3.740	0.185	2.609	1.952	4.904	0.105
R^2	0.16414	0.17266	0.26908	0.249	0.20485	0.15875	0.45889	0.081

48-month

β	13.462	17.845	28.987	0.130	21.882	17.763	27.911	0.317
t(OLS)	8.153	8.138	18.061	0.126	10.353	7.051	20.258	0.082
t(GMM)	2.605	7.862	11.204	0.040	2.459	10.371	4.677	0.218
t(NW)	2.445	2.695	7.049	0.055	2.976	2.388	5.188	0.149
R^2	0.19912	0.20547	0.49333	0.126	0.25728	0.19112	0.55056	0.082

Notes: The bootstrap uses 1000 replications. The "Observed Statistic" column reports the actual statistic over the subsample. The empirical p-value is the proportion of times the observed statistic was exceeded under the null.

Table 21.4
Alternative Models (Monthly Data: 1927 to 1990)

Statistic	Observed Statistic	Simulations: Normal Distribution Bootstr. Betas Mean	Std. Dev.	Empirical p-Value	Bootstrap: Fixed Yield Bootstr. Betas Mean	Std. Dev.	Empirical p-Value	Bootstrap: VAR Bootstr. Betas Mean	Std. Dev.	Empirical p-Value
1-month										
β	0.386	0.135	0.141	0.0628	0.003	0.145	0.0062	0.064	0.149	0.0322
t(OLS)	2.796	1.307	0.856	0.0356	0.018	0.992	0.0034	0.338	0.986	0.0068
t(GMM)	1.208	1.321	0.867	0.5628	0.017	1.003	0.1164	0.340	0.992	0.1908
t(NW)	1.208	1.321	0.867	0.5628	0.017	1.003	0.1164	0.340	0.992	0.1908
R^2	0.0101	0.003	0.003	0.0356	0.0013	0.0019	0.0056	0.0014	0.0020	0.0070
12-month										
β	5.108	1.738	1.856	0.0588	0.025	1.821	0.0052	0.779	1.792	0.0166
t(OLS)	9.969	4.500	3.103	0.0386	0.052	3.259	0.0026	1.202	3.191	0.0036
t(GMM)	2.948	1.447	1.039	0.0686	0.001	1.159	0.0088	0.434	1.117	0.0192
t(NW)	3.167	1.710	1.208	0.1064	-0.002	1.346	0.0116	0.496	1.291	0.0250
R^2	0.1163	0.037	0.036	0.0386	0.0135	0.0189	0.0030	0.0147	0.0204	0.0038
24-month										
β	9.071	3.722	4.006	0.0940	0.022	3.834	0.0114	1.610	3.647	0.0264
t(OLS)	12.730	6.320	4.553	0.0822	0.038	4.324	0.0024	1.729	4.228	0.0066
t(GMM)	5.319	1.618	1.286	0.0104	-0.010	1.245	0.0010	0.559	1.287	0.0022
t(NW)	5.379	1.836	1.383	0.0134	-0.021	1.391	0.0012	0.583	1.375	0.0018
R^2	0.1791	0.070	0.068	0.0822	0.0235	0.0312	0.0028	0.0259	0.0349	0.0072

36-month										
β	12.939	5.959	6.477	0.1230	0.023	6.074	0.0200	2.539	5.584	0.0338
t(OLS)	15.375	7.691	5.746	0.0908	0.027	4.969	0.0020	2.156	4.821	0.0046
t(GMM)	5.972	1.754	2.586	0.0172	−0.022	1.296	0.0004	0.616	3.505	0.0052
t(NW)	4.774	1.955	1.564	0.0442	−0.030	1.405	0.0016	0.669	1.438	0.0060
R^2	0.2444	0.099	0.097	0.0908	0.0309	0.0396	0.0020	0.0344	0.0451	0.0050
48-month										
β	21.392	8.534	9.363	0.0878	0.002	8.668	0.0092	3.606	7.621	0.0068
t(OLS)	21.419	8.842	6.787	0.0402	0.006	5.422	0.0000	2.526	5.152	0.0002
t(GMM)	7.367	1.958	2.483	0.0142	−0.030	1.332	0.0000	0.382	7.412	0.0084
t(NW)	7.300	2.067	1.764	0.0110	−0.033	1.404	0.000	0.755	1.482	0.0006
R^2	0.3895	0.126	0.122	0.0402	0.0368	0.0459	0.0000	0.0405	0.0522	0.0002

Notes: Five thousand replications. Alternative models are: (1) a simulation assuming normally distributed returns, modelling the dependence between returns, prices, and yields; (2) a bootstrap experiment assuming predetermined yields, and (3) a bootstrap experiment based on a VAR model that allows for endogenous yields. For each model, the mean and standard deviation of the statistic are reported, as well as the empirical p-value, which is the proportion of times the observed statistic, reported in the second column, was exceeded under the null.

Table 21.5
Long-Horizon Regressions on Lagged Prices and a Time Trend

Horizon		t-Statistic			t-Statistic		
(Months)	Beta	OLS	GMM	Gamma	OLS	GMM	R^2
Period: 1927–1990							
1	0.0164	2.83	2.22	0.0001	2.90	2.34	0.011
12	0.2217	11.04	2.23	0.0011	11.37	1.96	0.147
24	0.4461	17.60	2.77	0.0022	18.44	2.53	0.315
36	0.6418	25.69	6.28	0.0033	27.38	7.17	0.507
48	0.7973	33.25	7.04	0.0041	35.94	9.08	0.643
Period: 1927–1958							
1	0.0145	1.63	1.30	0.0001	1.97	1.96	0.011
12	0.2289	7.14	1.90	0.0011	7.41	1.41	0.155
24	0.4966	11.71	2.56	0.0023	12.46	1.96	0.351
36	0.7186	16.84	4.69	0.0036	20.21	6.93	0.584
48	0.8731	21.82	4.52	0.0046	29.04	9.35	0.749
Period: 1959–1990							
1	0.0210	2.01	1.55	0.0001	2.19	1.93	0.012
12	0.2383	6.77	2.88	0.0012	7.72	3.27	0.012
24	0.3336	7.36	3.03	0.0017	9.41	3.55	0.207
36	0.3612	7.24	3.18	0.0020	10.67	3.47	0.280
48	0.3915	6.27	3.28	0.0024	11.02	3.69	0.342

Notes: $\ln(P_{t,t+T}/P_t) = \alpha_T + \beta_T(-\ln P_t) + \gamma T^t + \varepsilon_{t,t+T}$ where $\ln(P_{t,t+T}/P_t)$ is the continuously compounded total stock return from time t to time $t + T$, P_t is the price as of time t, t is a time trend. The t-statistics presented are: t(OLS), from the usual OLS regression, t(GMM), which adjusts for heteroskedasticity and the moving average process induced by the overlapping observations.

of dividend yield and price regressions. Apparently, the regression on lagged prices fits the returns even better than the regression on dividend yield. These results imply that the economic time variation in the ratio of dividends to past prices may be due primarily to the time variation in the price series, and that long-term forecasting ability has little to do with variation in dividends.

◤ Conclusions

Regression tests of long-horizon returns on dividend yields have previously been interpreted as providing strong evidence of predictability in stock returns. These studies, however, have failed to recognize the serious biases arising from regressions on lagged dependent variables. To illustrate how inference may be affected, we have used bootstrapping techniques, and have modelled the null hypothesis that returns conform to a random walk while at the same time preserving the actual patterns of dividends.

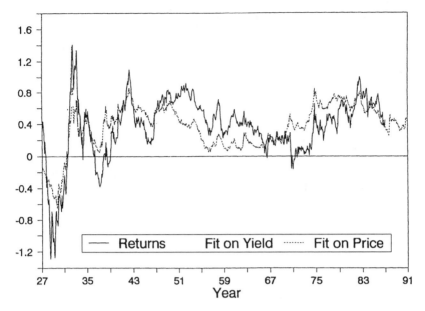

Figure 21.3. Comparison of 4-Year Returns and Fitted Values Using Yields and Using Lagged Prices
Note: Total 4-year returns are compared with the fitted values from regressions of returns on yields and on lagged prices plus a time trend.

The results of our tests show that, in a simple setting with no linear relationship between future returns and the dividend-price ratio, the OLS procedure, even with standard errors corrected for overlapping data, will often yield results that suggest otherwise. Indeed the coefficients, t-statistics, and R^2's from such regressions are shown to be misleading in the sense that, even when generated by data conforming to the null hypothesis, they yield what might normally be interpreted as strongly significant results. The biases are much stronger than previously thought. As an example, consider the GMM t-statistics for 4-year returns measured over 64 years of monthly data. In a conventional setting, the 5% upper tail critical value is 2.1; using a VAR approach, this value increases to 3.9; our approach yields a value of 5.5.

Our findings argue for a different formulation of such tests, and caution against drawing inferences from usual regression statistics without a thorough understanding of their underlying distributions. The implications of these results extend far beyond tests of the predictive power of dividend yields. Time series studies of returns conditioned upon any ratio involving price levels are also susceptible to the biases reported here. While GMM adjustments and VAR simulations clearly help to adjust for overlaps and small-sample biases, this study shows that in some situations they may not be adequate for the purposes of hypothesis testing.

▲ Appendix 1. Data Construction

The data series were constructed as follows: monthly total, capital, and income returns on the S&P 500 index were obtained from Ibbotson Associates. These are defined, respectively, as

$$R_{t,t+1} = R^X_{t,t+1} + R^I_{t,t+1} = (P_{t+1} - P_t)/P_t + d_{t+1}/P_t,$$

where P_t is a price series that excludes the reinvestment of dividends. Setting P_0 at 100, we recursively compute P_t, as well as the monthly dividend d_t, from these series.

A monthly annualized dividend series was computed from compounding 12 monthly dividends at the 1-month Treasury bill rate r_t:

$$D_t = d_t + (1 + r_t)d_{t-1} + (1 + r_t)(1 + r_{t-1})d_{t-2} + \ldots$$

Annual dividend yield is then defined as $Y_t = D_t/P_t$.

For the simulation using total returns, we computed a "total" price that represents the value of a fund mimicking the index with monthly reinvestment of dividends, as $R_{t,t+1} = (P^R_{t+1} - P^R_t)/P^R_t$, with $P^R_0 = 100$. The actual income on such a fund is computed recursively from $R^I_{t,t+1} = d^R_{t+1}/P^R_t$ and D^R is computed from d^R as explained above.

▲ Notes

1. See for instance Richardson and Smith (1991).

2. The covariances were weighted up to the number of overlaps.

3. Part of this increase is explained by the fact that the variance of the dependent variable increases over longer horizons. In line with most previous research, we have chosen not to adjust returns for the length of the horizon.

4. Similar results are found in empirical tests of the random walk assumption for real exchange rates, which involve regressions on lagged dependent variables. See for instance Abuaf and Jorion (1990).

5. There were a few instances where the GMM covariance matrix was not invertible (five cases at 3-year horizons, one at 4-year); the frequencies reported are out of the total number of cases for which GMM t-statistics could be calculated.

6. Because a pair of total and income returns is not available in this setup, the dividend yield D^R is constructed from the total price series P^R, as explained in Appendix 1. The simulation first generates total returns R^*, from which the pseudoseries P^{R*} is obtained and combined with the actual annual dividend series D^R, to form a pseudo-dividend-yield $Y^* = D^R/P^{R*}$.

7. Nelson and Kim (1993) randomize on the observed errors, while Hodrick (1992) generates the errors from a multivariate distribution following a GARCH process.

▲ References

Abuaf, N., and P. Jorion, 1990, Purchasing power parity in the long run, *Journal of Finance* 45, 157–174.

Bickel, P., and D. Freedman, 1981, Some asymptotic theory for the bootstrap, *Annals of Statistics* 9, 1196–1271.

Campbell, J., and R. Shiller, 1988, The dividend price ratio and expectations of future dividends and discount factors, *Review of Financial Studies* 1, 195–228.

Dickey, D., and W. Fuller, 1979, Distribution of estimators for autoregressive time series with a unit root, *Journal of the American Statistical Association* 74, 427–431.

Efron, B., 1979, Bootstrap methods: Another look at the jackknife, *Annals of Statistics* 7, 1–26.

Fama, E., and K. French, 1988, Dividend yields and expected stock returns, *Journal of Financial Economics* 22, 3–25.

Flood, K., J. Hodrick, and P. Kaplan, 1987, An evaluation of recent evidence on stock market bubbles, Working Paper 1971, National Bureau of Economic Research, Cambridge, Mass.

Freedman, D., 1981, Bootstrapping regression models, *Annals of Statistics* 9, 1218–1228.

Goetzmann, W., 1990, Bootstrapping and simulation tests of long-term patterns in stock market behavior, Ph.D. thesis, Yale University.

Gordon, M., and E. Shapiro, 1956, Capital equilibrium analysis: The required rate of profit, *Management Science* 3, 102–110.

Granger, C. J. W., and P. Newbold, 1974, Spurious regressions in econometrics, *Journal of Econometrics* 2, 111–120.

Hansen, L., 1982, Large sample properties of generalized method of moments estimators, *Econometrica* 50, 1029–1054.

—— and R. Hodrick, 1980, Forward exchange rates as optimal predictors of future spot rates, *Journal of Political Economy* 88, 829–853.

Hodrick, R., 1992, Dividend yields and expected stock returns: Alternative procedures for inference and measurement, *Review of Financial Studies* 5, 357–386.

Kendall, M. G., 1973, *Time-Series* (Griffin, London).

Nelson, C., and M. Kim, 1993, Predictable stock returns: The role of small sample bias, *Journal of Finance* 48, 641–661.

Newey, W., and K. West, 1987, A simple, positive definite, heteroskedasticity and autocorrelation consistent covariance matrix, *Econometrica* 55, 703–708.

Phillips, P., 1986, Understanding spurious regressions in econometrics, *Journal of Econometrics* 33, 311–340.

Plosser, C. I., and W. Schwert, 1978, Money income and sunspots: Measuring economic relationships and the effects of differencing, *Journal of Monetary Economics* 4, 637–660.

Richardson, M., and T. Smith, 1991, Tests of financial models in the presence of overlapping observations, *Review of Financial Studies* 4, 227–254.

Rozeff, M., 1984, Dividend yields are equity risk premiums, *Journal of Portfolio Management* 11, 68–75.

Schenker, N., 1985, Qualms about bootstrap confidence intervals, *Journal of the American Statistical Association* 80, 360–361.

White, H., 1980, A heteroskedasticity-consistent covariance matrix estimator and a direct test for heteroskedasticity, *Econometrica* 48, 817–838.

Williams, J. B., 1938, *The Theory of Investment Value* (Harvard University Press, Cambridge, Mass.).

Wolf, M., 2000, Stock returns and dividend yields revisited: A new way to look at an old problem, *Journal of Business Economics and Statistics*, 80, 18–30.

22 William N. Goetzmann and Philippe Jorion

A Longer Look at Dividend Yields

◤ *Overview*

This article brings the research on survivorship together with research on predicting the stock market. A key argument of the article is that studies of long-term prediction can and should take into account the fact that a market has survived. Survival looks like a rebound, ex post. If stock market crises were always followed by rebounds, then markets would have the wonderful feature of reversing themselves after bad times, and of rising after large increases in dividend yields. Alas, history is not so kind. As a result, researchers have to account for the "bounce" when they look at countries such as the United States and the United Kingdom and also have to try to figure out what to do with the gaps and interruptions of other stock markets from other countries, should they decide to use them.

◤ *Abstract*

This article reexamines the evidence on the ability of dividend yields to predict long-horizon stock returns. We use two new series beginning in 1871, a monthly series for the United States, and an annual series for the United Kingdom. Conditional on survival over the entire 122 years, dividend yields display only marginal ability to predict stock market returns in either country. We also argue that tests over long periods may be affected by survivorship. Simulations show that regression statistics based on a sample drawn solely from surviving markets can be seriously biased toward finding predictability.

There is by now a substantial body of empirical work in finance which suggests that the returns on a variety of financial assets can be forecast. In particular, a number of researchers, including Rozeff (1984), Campbell and Shiller (1988a, 1988b), Fama and French (1988), Fuller and Kling (1990), and Hodrick (1992), consider multiple-year return horizons and find that dividend yields are positively correlated with future stock returns. Because of the low power of statistical tests used to identify predictability in long-horizon returns, these studies are perforce based on the longest time series of financial data available.

The use of long-term data, however, raises a crucial issue. The ex post observed structural relationship between dividends and prices is clearly conditioned on the survival of the asset series. This conditioning may have non-

494

trivial effects on inferences about the behavior of dividend yields. For instance, when we look back over the history of the world's financial markets, we should expect the dividend yields for stock markets that existed for long uninterrupted periods of time to display mean reversion. As we show below, this mean reversion in dividend yields will manifest itself in return forecastability.

While long price and dividend series are available for today's major markets, such as the United States and the United Kingdom, few data are available for the Japanese and German markets before suspension of trading in the 1940s or for the Russian market before the major hiatus in capitalism. In this article, we explore the implications of relying solely on survived series, or series with continuous price and dividend records, for drawing inferences about dividend yield regressions. Our simulations of the effects of survivorship on dividend yield regressions and on tests of cointegration suggest that the distribution of test statistics under the null hypothesis becomes more leptokurtic and can lead to more frequent false rejection.

Survivorship is not the whole story with dividend yield tests, however. We also show that predictability in dividend growth tends to obscure the explanatory ability of dividend yields. This bias, in the direction opposite to the previous one, suggests that researchers investigating the forecasting power of dividend yields should attempt to incorporate forecasts of dividend growth.

We perform dividend yield tests on two new historical series. The first is a monthly series of returns and dividend yields for the New York Stock Exchange (NYSE), which is based on the Cowles (1939) monthly data and begins in 1872. The second is an annual U.K. stock exchange return and yield series that begins in 1872. To account for regression biases, we report empirical marginal significance levels using a "fixed dividends" procedure and a VAR (vector autoregression) with stochastic prices and dividends.

We find that the monthly NYSE data provide only marginal evidence of the predictability of long-horizon returns via dividend yields. This is consistent with previous analyses over the more recent historical era.[1] We find similar results for the U.K. data, with the exception of the subperiod from 1926 to 1992. In the modern era, the U.K. market displays strong evidence of predictability. A closer look at the data indicates that most of the effect is due to the extraordinary crash and rebound of the early 1970s, that is, the continuity of the U.K. market index during a period of global social and economic upheaval. The question of whether yields predict stock returns in the United Kingdom may ultimately rest on the chances of market closure at that critical juncture. Had the market closed, and remained shut for an appreciable length of time, we might not be using it to study dividend yields.

Survivorship effects on the dividend yield regressions are akin to the "peso problem" in the foreign exchange market, where forward rates appear to be systematically biased forecasts of future spot rates. This is because forward rates account for a nonzero probability of devaluation that may not be observed in the test sample period. More generally, peso problems can be interpreted as a failure of the paradigm of rational expectations econometrics, which requires that the ex post distribution of endogenous variables be a good approximation to the ex ante distribution that agents think may happen. The failure may not be that of the economic agent, but that of the econometrician, who only analyzes series with continuous histories. Unusual events with a low probability of occurrence but severe effects on prices, such as wars or nationalizations, are not likely to be well represented in samples and may be totally omitted from survived series. The implication is that the power of yields to forecast returns is strongly conditioned on survival.

The article is organized as follows. The first section is a review of the literature. The second section models the dividend yield regressions and survivorship effects. The third section describes the construction of the long-term stock market series. The fourth section reports the results of the dividend yield regressions. The fifth section presents the results of the survivorship simulations, and the sixth section concludes.

◤ Literature Review

Over the past decade, a number of researchers have explored the time-series behavior of dividend yields. Several studies provide support for the use of the dividend-price ratio as a measure of expected stock returns. Rozeff (1984) showed that dividend yields forecast equity risk premia, as would be predicted by a deterministic dividend discount model. For example, if the stock price represents a claim to the future stream of dividends, the price can be exactly determined assuming constantly growing dividends and a known discount rate. Under the Gordon growth model,

$$P_t = \sum_{i=1}^{\infty} D_t(1 + g)^i/(1 + r)^i = \frac{D_{t+1}}{r - g},$$

where P is the stock price, D is the dividend, r is the discount rate, and g is the constant growth rate of dividends.[2] In the certainty model, the discount rate is the expected return on the stock. Although the model is not directly applicable to the case in which growth rates and discount rates vary through time, the model suggests that dividend yields should capture variations in expected stock returns.

Campbell and Shiller (1988a, 1988b) develop a stochastic approximation to the dividend discount model and estimate the model in a VAR framework. Fama and French (1988) provide the strongest evidence in support of the dividend yield effect by using overlapping multiple-year horizon returns. They observe that the explanatory power of the dividend yield increases in the time horizon of the returns; over 4-year horizons, R^2s reach an astonishing high value of 64%. Fuller and Kling (1990) use dividend yield regressions to simulate out-of-sample trading rules and find that the dividend yield effect allows for profitable, although somewhat erratic, trading strategies.

Several recent studies, however, have demonstrated that tests involving long-horizon returns present econometric difficulties. For the most part, these

Figure 22.1 illustrates the tricks that history can play on financial researchers. Each line traces the *t*-values of the dividend yield regression through time, calculated using only backward-looking data to 1926. Note that the predictability of next year's return with the dividend yield was insignificant at traditional confidence levels until 1977. The *t*-values for all other horizons are higher than 2 because we have not corrected for the problem of overlapping observations. Thus they are considerably overstated. Nevertheless, the time trends are important. From the mid-1950s to the mid-1970s the significance levels of all dividend yield regressions were generally low. Few researchers running these regressions with these data would have concluded that the market could be forecast with past data. Evidence in favor of predictability increased through the 1980s, and coincided nicely with the publication of positive results. In the 1990s the *t*-values dropped precipitously. The message from this figure is that reasonable researchers might strongly disagree about the empirical evidence for dividend yield predictability simply because the time interval of study differs. Indeed, this figure might tell yet a different story if data through the 2000s were available. If our tests were in fact able to capture a fundamental, unchanging, and permanent phenomenon underlying the valuation of capital market prices, we would like to see this chart settle down, as more data would decrease the uncertainty about parameter estimation.

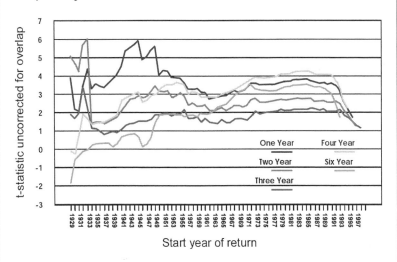

Figure 22.1. *T*-Values of Dividend Yield Regressions: Overlapping Multiple-Horizon Returns Using Data Available Up to Each Year

studies have emphasized the bias toward rejection of the null. In particular, the usual corrections to the standard errors are valid only asymptotically, and there is some question as to whether "asymptotic" should be measured in terms of years, decades, or even centuries, especially for long-horizon forecasts.[3] Another problem, pointed out by Stambaugh (1986), is that the explanatory variable, the dividend yield, is not properly exogenous, but rather contains a price level that also appears in the regressand. Finally, Fama and French (1988) point out an "errors-in-variables" problem due to the fact that yields contain forecasts of future returns and dividend growth. This may bias downward the regression coefficient in the dividend yield regression.

Some of these issues are addressed in recent research. Hodrick (1992), for instance, examines the implications for hypothesis testing of using different specifications of the forecasting equation. Nelson and Kim (1993) analyze small-sample biases in simulations of a VAR system for returns and yields, under the null hypothesis of no predictability of returns. Using U.S. returns sampled annually, they report that the simulated distributions of t-statistics are displaced upward, but they still find some evidence of predictability at conventional significance levels. In the case of the dividend yield regression, however, price levels appear in both the regressor and the regressand. From the work of Dickey and Fuller (1976) and Stambaugh (1986), we know that regressions on lagged dependent variables lead to biased coefficient estimates. To address this problem, Goetzmann and Jorion (1993) use a bootstrapping approach where they fix the history of dividends to their historical values, then bootstrap the returns series, from which they reconstruct a pseudo-dividend yield. They report only marginal evidence of predictability. Finally, papers by Fama (1990) and Kothari and Shanken (1992) suggest that the errors-in-variables problem is a potentially major one, since a significant percentage of return variance may be explained by changes in the growth rate of future dividends.

▲ *Dividend Yield Regressions*

The regressions performed by Fama and French (1988) capture the basic dividend yield forecasting effect. They regress multiple-year stock returns on the preceding period dividend yield. If long-term market returns are predictable, the following regression should produce a significant coefficient:

$$R_{t,t+T} = \alpha_T + \beta_T Y_t + \varepsilon_{t,t+T}, \tag{2}$$

where $R_{t,t+T}$ is the compound total stock return from month t to month $t + T$, and Y_t is the ratio D_t/P_t, the annual dividend up to time t divided by the stock price as of time t. The null hypothesis is that there is no relation between $R_{t,t+T}$ and Y_t, that is, that $\beta_T = 0$.

Survivorship complicates this regression. Suppose the observation of $R_{t,t+T}$ is conditional on exceeding a threshold, which in turn is correlated to Y_t. For instance, when Y_t goes to 1 or zero, the market disappears. This correlation is known to result in biased estimates of β_T. Heckman (1977) suggests modeling this conditioning factor in the context of a limited dependent variable framework. For example, he shows that under certain circumstances, the bias in the regression coefficient can be mitigated by including an additional variable, λ, that measures the inverse of the odds ratio of the dependent variable exceeding the threshold. That is, the regression

$$R_{t,t+T} = \alpha + \beta_T Y_t + \gamma \lambda_t + \varepsilon_{t,t+T}, \tag{3}$$

produces consistent estimates of β_T.

The problem with the dividend yield regressions is measuring λ. Estimation of market disappearance requires a sample of markets that failed as well as markets that survived. Even with information about missing markets, however, accurately modeling survival may be impossible. Instruments to capture "political risk" may prove useful, but they are not easily constructed. Our approach to the problem is to simulate market disappearance based on a few simple rules. While this does not necessarily allow us to estimate the unconditional distribution of β_T, it indicates the possible magnitude of survivorship effects.

Following Fama and French (1988), we perform all tests using overlapping observations. As is well known, this procedure results in more powerful tests but induces a moving average process in the errors, which invalidates the usual ordinary least squares standard errors.[4] The standard error corrections are computed using the method proposed by Hansen and Hodrick (1980), in which the autocovariances are estimated from the data, with a modification due to White (1980) and Hansen (1982) that allows for conditional heteroscedasticity. These will be referred to as "Hansen-White" (HW) estimators. Our simulations will be based on bootstrapping and randomization procedures described in Hodrick (1992) and Goetzmann and Jorion (1993). Because these methods are used to generate the simulated distributions of regression statistics under the null, they are described in detail below.

A Fixed Dividend Approach

The fixed dividend approach explicitly conditions on the actual dividend series and proceeds as follows:

1. Form the empirical distribution of total stock returns and their associated income returns from the observed vectors of returns.
2. Draw T observations $(R_1^* \ldots R_T^*)$, with replacement, where T is the sample size.
3. Compute the relevant statistics, as follows:
   a. Form a pseudo-capital-appreciation series P^* from the sampled appreciation series; use this to form $Y^* = D/P^*$, where D is the actual dividend series.
   b. Construct multiple-horizon-return vectors R_T^*, for overlapping T-year returns.

    c. Perform the regressions of future returns on dividend yields, for each horizon *T,* and save the resulting coefficients β_T^*, the R_T^{2*}, and the *t*-statistics t_T^*.
4. Repeat steps 2 and 3 one thousand times. Empirical *p*-values are calculated from the number of times that the observed test statistics are exceeded for all the replications.

The advantages of this procedure are threefold: first, by using the actual realization of the dividend series, we preserve its time-series characteristics—including possibly complex temporal relations between past and future dividend changes. This is useful, since we would like the bootstrapped yields to include forecasts of future dividend changes. In addition, by using the actual distribution of returns, we preserve the marginal distribution of returns, which typically has fatter tails than a normal distribution. The fixed dividend bootstrap also explicitly models the lagged dependent variable relationship caused by the fact that prices appear in both the left- and right-hand sides of the equation.

    Implicit in this procedure is a model of the temporal behavior of stock returns and of the pattern of income and capital appreciation components. We are assuming that the stock market follows a random walk, that is, capital appreciation returns are independently and identically distributed through time. Further, we are assuming that the income return history is prespecified—there is no temporal relationship between dividend and prices, *as specified under the null hypothesis.* Thus, neither past returns, nor past dividends, nor any combination of the two should predict future capital appreciation returns.

    One potential criticism of the analysis based on the bootstrap is that we fail to allow for a long-run relationship between dividends and prices, which can have the effect of placing a unit root on the dividend yield.[5] Because of the low power of unit root tests, however, it is often difficult to reject the hypothesis that yields follow an integrated process; as a result, researchers can take different stands on the stationarity of dividend yields, without being disproved by the data. In addition, as Campbell and Perron (1991, p. 163) point out in their survey, "It may be better to use integrated asymptotic theory for near-integrated stationary models." The reason for this is that dividend yields appear to be near-integrated and that models that assume stationarity, such as the VAR-using yields, rely on estimates of the persistence parameter that are severely biased downward.[6] The behavior of the test statistics, however, may be better approximated by a bootstrap experiment that assumes a unit autocorrelation than by an experiment that relies on biased parameter values. Finally, the sample autocorrelation coefficient may be biased because of survivorship, an interesting issue that will be discussed in a later section.

A VAR Approach

An alternative approach to the bootstrap as implemented here is to model stochastic prices and dividends in a VAR framework. Hodrick (1992) employs a

VAR to estimate the predictive power of dividend yields. The methodology accounts for the contemporaneous relationship between prices and dividends, but does not force yields to be stationary.

The VAR is specified in terms of relative price changes and dividend changes:

$$Z_{t+1} \equiv \begin{pmatrix} R_{t+1} \\ d_{t+1} \end{pmatrix} = \begin{pmatrix} a_{10} \\ a_{20} \end{pmatrix} + \begin{pmatrix} a_{11} & a_{22} \\ a_{21} & a_{22} \end{pmatrix} \begin{pmatrix} R_t \\ d_t \end{pmatrix} + \begin{pmatrix} u_{1t} \\ u_{2t} \end{pmatrix}, \tag{4}$$

where d_t is the relative change in dividend from $t - 1$ to t. We simulate Z_t under the null by setting the slope coefficients in the return equation (a_{11}, a_{12}) to zero and then drawing errors from a bivariate distribution with errors u_t bootstrapped from the data.[7]

Note that in these simulations, the dividend process is highly predictable; typically, the coefficient a_{22} is large and significant, reflecting the autocorrelation in dividend growth. In addition to allowing past dividend changes to predict future dividend changes, the VAR also allows past returns to impact dividends.[8] This is useful because Kothari and Shanken (1992) find that future dividend changes explain movements in current returns. Thus, while expected returns are held constant, dividend growth is allowed to vary through time. The implications of this predictability are explored in a later section.

Using two different approaches, fixed dividend and VAR, allows us to assess whether the results are robust to the simulation procedure. We report in all tables the empirical marginal significance levels from both approaches.

◣ Stock Return Data

While U.S. stock price indices are available back to 1802,[9] reliable dividend information is available only from 1871 to the present. For the pre-1926 period, we obtained the Cowles (1939) monthly U.S. stock price index, which consists of a total return series, as well as a price appreciation series. As noted by Wilson and Jones (1987), there are occasional errors in the series, which sometimes imply negative income returns, which clearly cannot be. Given that the income series is relatively smooth, comparing price and total returns allowed us to correct the time series. Monthly total and income returns were used to construct a price series, exclusive of dividends, from which monthly dividend payments were inferred.

For the post-1926 period, we used the income and capital appreciation returns to the Standard and Poor's (S&P) Index provided by Ibbotson Associates. Because of seasonalities in monthly dividends, an annualized dividend series D was computed by cumulating the income payments, before 1926, and reinvesting the dividends at the monthly riskless rate, after 1926. Price levels were taken from the consumer price index series provided by Ibbotson Associates; prior to 1926, prices are measured by the wholesale price index series reported in Warren and Pearson (1933).

We obtain U.K. data from several sources. Following Shiller (1989), De Long and Grossman (1993), and Goetzmann (1993), we used the pre-1918 December share price index of industrials for the years 1870–1914 reported by Smith and Horne (1934) and the London and Cambridge Economic Service Annual Price Index from 1915 through 1917. We used the yield series created by De Long and Grossman (1993) for the period 1870–1917. From 1918 to 1992, the selected stock index is the Barclays-DeZoete-Wett December price index, provided with and without dividend. Nominal returns were adjusted to real returns using the December Retail Price Index.

Tables 22.1 and 22.2 present a detailed breakdown of total stock market returns in the United States and the United Kingdom, based on annual data over the last 121 years. We first consider arithmetic averaging of simple annual returns. Over 1872–1992, U.S. equities returned 10.6% per annum, using arithmetic averaging of simple returns, of which 5.5% was due to capital return. We divided the total period into a "Cowles" subperiod, covering 1872–1926, as well as the more usual S&P 1927–92 subperiod. Over the former period, U.S. equities returned 8.5% versus 12.4% over the latter period. When expressed in real terms, U.S. equities returned 8.6% per annum over the total period, and also about the same amount over the two subperiods. Next, the Compound column refers to annually compounded returns. Under

Table 22.1
Return and Risk for United States Equities, 1872–1992

| Period | Arithmetic | | | Compound | |
	Income Return	Capital Return	Total Return	Total Return	Inflation
Nominal:					
1872–1992	4.98	5.46	10.60	8.89	2.10
	(1.32)	(18.25)	(18.93)		(7.41)
1872–1926	5.36	3.12	8.49	7.84	.64
	(1.22)	(15.83)	(16.45)		(9.54)
1927–92	4.67	7.41	12.37	9.33	3.31
	(1.32)	(19.83)	(20.61)		(4.64)
Real:					
1872–1992	...	3.58	8.64	6.94	...
		(17.97)	(18.69)		
1982–1926	...	2.88	8.23	7.66	...
		(15.21)	(15.86)		
1927–92	...	4.16	8.97	5.89	...
		(19.96)	(20.75)		

Note. Averages and standard deviations for annual data are expressed as percentages. Averages are expressed as arithmetic and compound. Data are measured in nominal and real terms. Risk, or standard deviation, is in parentheses.

Table 22.2
Return and Risk for United Kingdom Equities, 1872–1992

Period	Arithmetic			Compound Total Return	Inflation
	Income Return	Capital Return	Total Return		
Nominal:					
1872–1992	6.99	6.10	13.09	11.41	3.03
	(2.33)	(20.27)	(20.63)		(8.18)
1872–1926	9.04	2.68	11.72	11.51	0.32
	(1.40)	(11.36)	(11.01)		(8.32)
1927–92	5.28	8.94	14.23	11.23	5.28
	(1.39)	(25.06)	(26.00)		(7.33)
Real:					
1872–1992	. . .	3.52	10.37	8.48	. . .
		(19.90)	(20.47)		
1872–1926	. . .	3.20	12.26	11.65	. . .
		(16.01)	(16.14)		
1927–92	. . .	3.78	8.80	5.83	. . .
		(22.63)	(23.37)		

Note. Averages and standard deviations for annual data are expressed as percentages. Averages are expressed as arithmetic and compound. Data are measured in nominal and real terms. Risk, or standard deviation, is in parentheses.

this measure, real returns grew at the rate of 6.9% over the whole sample period.

It is interesting to notice that a much higher proportion of returns came from dividend payments in the first subperiod, 5.4% out of 8.5% versus 4.7% out of 12.4% after 1926. In the first 50 years of our sample, stocks paid high yields and were much more stable investments than later. Over this period, the industrial composition of the index changed substantially, from mostly utilities and railroads to a more heterogeneous mix.[10]

From Table 22.2, we see that U.K. equities returned an average of 13.1% per annum, or 10.4% in real terms. As before, we note that a much higher proportion of total return came from dividends in the first subperiod, 9.0% out of 11.7%, against 5.3% out of 14.2% in the second subperiod. The variability of total returns was also much higher in the second subperiod, at 26.0% versus only 11.0% in the first subperiod. This higher variability substantially lowered geometric returns in the second period; in addition, higher inflation reduced compound real returns from 11.7% to 5.8% after 1926. Again, the British evidence indicates that before 1926, equities paid a higher proportion of total returns as dividends and satisfied investors with lower total returns.

Figure 22.2 displays the increase in wealth for U.S. and U.K. equity investors, expressed in real terms. One dollar or one pound invested in 1870 would have grown to $360,547 or £2,361,372, respectively. All of the differ-

Dividend Yields

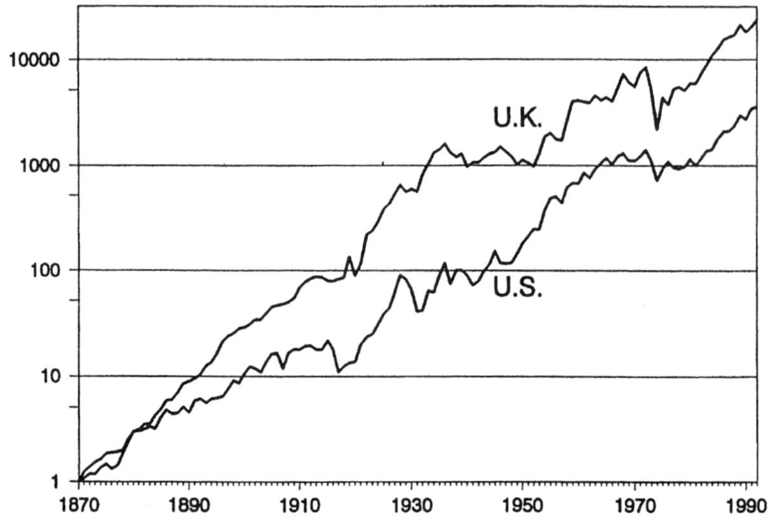

Figure 22.2. The U.S. and U.K. Equity Index: 1870–1992
Note: Real returns are presented with dividends reinvested.

ence, however, occurred in the first 50 years of the sample; after 1926, returns in both countries grew at the same 5.9% rate. The graph also shows that the volatility of returns substantially increased after the 1920s.

Yield Regressions

Empirical Evidence

Table 22.3 presents long-horizon forecasts for nominal returns on the U.S. stock market over the period 1872–1992 and over two subperiods. The first, 1872–1926, corresponds to the Cowles data, and the second, 1927–92, to the S&P data. Overall, there is little evidence of predictive ability for dividend yields. The slope coefficients increase with maturity,[11] and they appear to be marginally significant, with an HW t-statistic value of 3.03 at the 4-year horizon. We report the empirical probability levels for the observed slope coefficient in the last columns. They show that none of the slope coefficients is significantly different from zero—typical bootstrapped p-values are around 0.20 and VAR p-values are around 0.10. Thus, despite the fact that we extended monthly data by about 50 years, our results support the findings of previous research—using the empirical distribution, the dividend yield effect is marginal when traditional rejection levels are used. These results differ from the conclusions of Campbell and Shiller (1989), who report uncorrected p-values

Table 22.3
Yield Regressions: United States Nominal Returns
$R_{t,t+T} = \alpha_T + \beta_T Y_t + \varepsilon_{t,t+T}$

Horizon (Months)	Beta	t-Statistic		R^2	p-Value: Beta	
		OLS	HW		Fixed Dividend	VAR
Period: 1872–1992						
1	.159	1.79	.81	.002	.231	.159
12	3.130	8.63	2.27	.038	.145	.071
24	5.868	11.06	3.38	.051	.175	.090
36	7.897	11.70	2.77	.048	.213	.126
48	14.043	16.54	3.03	.083	.183	.092
Cowles period: 1872–1926						
1	−.142	−1.41	−1.23	.003	1.000	.999
12	.847	1.68	.55	.003	.471	.437
24	2.458	3.22	.96	.011	.390	.332
36	1.763	1.94	.54	.003	.630	.566
48	4.036	3.67	.98	.011	.457	.437
Standard & Poor's period: 1927–92						
1	.373	2.76	1.19	.009	.096	.108
12	4.986	9.92	2.89	.086	.077	.108
24	8.861	12.70	5.22	.107	.115	.162
36	12.527	15.11	5.79	.119	.157	.200
48	20.712	21.01	7.03	.178	.106	.159

Note. In the regression, $R_{t,t+T}$ is defined as the total stock return from time t to time $t + T$, and $Y_t = D_t/P_t$ is the annual dividend yield measured as of time t. The t-statistics presented are t(OLS), from the classical ordinary least squares (OLS) regression, and t(HW), which adjusts for heteroscedasticity and the moving average process induced by the overlapping observations (using the sample autocovariances). Empirical p-value is obtained from the simulation experiments as the proportion of times the observed beta coefficient was exceeded under the null hypothesis of no predictability. Under the fixed dividend approach, dividends are taken from their historical values, and capital returns are bootstrapped from the actual return series; under the vector autoregression (VAR), prices and dividends follow a joint stochastic process with innovations bootstrapped from the actual series. HW = Hansen-White.

of around 1%–3% for 3-year horizon regressions, and is due to the bootstrap/VAR corrections.

During the 1927–92 period, which corresponds to most other studies, the empirical p-values are around 0.10. It is interesting to note that the evidence for the Cowles period 1871–1926 is much weaker than for the former period. Slope coefficients, while similar in sign, are systematically lower than in the former period, and empirical p-values are higher.[12] In practical terms, were an analyst such as Alfred Cowles to use the 162 months of pre-1927 data to develop a forecasting model of stock returns, he would have been too conservative in calling market moves.

Table 22.4
Yield Regressions: United States Real Returns
$R_{t,t+T} = \alpha_T + \beta_T Y_t + \varepsilon_{t,t+T}$

Horizon (Months)	Beta	t-Statistic		R^2	p-Value: Beta	
		OLS	HW		Fixed Dividend	VAR
Period: 1872–1992						
1	.264	2.95	1.35	.006	.176	.070
12	4.278	11.76	2.90	.074	.135	.035
24	7.447	14.40	4.00	.093	.160	.055
36	10.648	16.66	4.79	.107	.188	.068
48	17.965	23.00	5.15	.170	.160	.049
Cowles period: 1872–1926						
1	.010	.10	.08	.000	1.000	.781
12	2.522	4.74	1.42	.027	.295	.107
24	4.938	6.42	1.57	.043	.231	.117
36	7.287	8.02	2.36	.056	.219	.135
48	12.711	11.61	3.43	.102	.100	.075
Standard & Poor's period: 1927–92						
1	.431	3.17	1.38	.012	.080	.080
12	5.540	11.02	3.06	.117	.065	.078
24	9.260	13.50	5.75	.147	.105	.130
36	12.640	16.15	5.66	.177	.164	.174
48	20.403	22.70	5.19	.271	.112	.143

Note. In the regression, $R_{t,t+T}$ is defined as the total stock return from time t to time $t + T$, and $Y_t = D_t/P_t$ is the annual dividend yield measured as of time t. The t-statistics presented are t(OLS), from the classical ordinary least squares (OLS) regression, and t(HW), which adjusts for heteroscedasticity and the moving average process induced by the overlapping observations (using the sample autocovariances). Empirical p-value is obtained from the simulation experiments as the proportion of times the observed beta coefficient was exceeded under the null hypothesis of no predictability. Under the fixed dividend approach, dividends are taken from their historical values, and capital returns are bootstrapped from the actual return series; under the vector autoregression (VAR), prices and dividends follow a joint stochastic process with innovations bootstrapped from the actual series. HW = Hansen-White.

Table 22.4 presents regression results for returns deflated by the price index. The results are generally similar to those obtained using nominal data. While the slope coefficients are generally higher than in Table 22.3, the evidence for predictability is marginal using the bootstrapped marginal significance levels. Thus, despite the fact that we used monthly data over 121 years, our results show that there is little predictive content in U.S. dividend yields.

Table 22.5 presents regression results for nominal annual British stock market data from 1871 to 1992. Over the total sample period, there is no evidence of predictability. Slope coefficients are very low, and the HW t-statistics are generally around unity. The regressions, however, look very different across

Table 22.5
Yield Regressions: United Kingdom Nominal Returns

$R_{t,t+T} = \alpha_T + \beta_T Y_t + \varepsilon_{t,t+T}$

Horizon (Years)	Beta	t-Statistic OLS	t-Statistic HW	R^2	p-Value: Beta Fixed Dividend	p-Value: Beta VAR
Period: 1871–1992						
1	1.196	1.61	1.19	.021	.191	.058
2	1.505	1.43	1.09	.017	.324	.185
3	2.464	1.67	.94	.023	.332	.185
4	2.994	1.65	.87	.023	.380	.233
5	3.600	1.66	.86	.023	.427	.267
First period: 1871–1926						
1	−.934	−1.14	−.81	.023	1.000	.992
2	−1.329	−.95	−.63	.017	.996	.964
3	−3.581	−1.85	−1.44	.061	1.000	.999
4	−3.187	−1.15	−1.18	.025	.993	.968
5	−2.325	−.72	−.68	.010	.951	.868
Second period: 1927–92						
1	13.198	6.54	3.98	.405	.016	.008
2	18.586	6.80	7.22	.427	.045	.022
3	31.558	10.03	12.38	.623	.033	.019
4	37.631	9.99	13.76	.624	.062	.030
5	45.077	10.26	12.34	.641	.081	.044

Note. In the regression, $R_{t,t+T}$ is defined as the total stock return from time t to time $t + T$, and $Y_t = D_t/P_t$ is the annual dividend yield measured as of time t. The t-statistics presented are t(OLS), from the classical ordinary least squares (OLS) regression, and t(HW), which adjusts for heteroscedasticity and the moving average process induced by the overlapping observations (using the sample autocovariances). Empirical p-value is obtained from the simulation experiments as the proportion of times the observed beta coefficient was exceeded under the null hypothesis of no predictability. Under the fixed dividend approach, dividends are taken from their historical values, and capital returns are bootstrapped from the actual return series; under the vector autoregression (VAR), prices and dividends follow a joint stochastic process with innovations bootstrapped from the actual series. HW = Hansen-White.

the sample periods. In the first 55 years, the coefficients are negative, and the empirical probability levels indicate that they are unusually so. In the second subperiod, there appears to be strong evidence of predictability. The HW t-statistics climb from 3.98 for the 1-year horizon to 12.34 for the 5-year horizon. The empirical p-values of the slope coefficients are generally below 5%.

Clearly, there was a dramatic shift in the relationship between past dividends and stock returns between the two subperiods. The existence of such a major regime switch suggests that the dividend yield effect may be highly conditioned on the period of estimation. De Long and Grossman (1993) suggest that U.K. investors in the pre–World War I era suffered from an "irrational"

Table 22.6
Yield Regressions: United Kingdom Real Returns
$R_{t,t+T} = \alpha_T + \beta_T Y_t + \varepsilon_{t,t+T}$

Horizon (Years)	Beta	t-Statistic		R^2	p-Value: Beta	
		OLS	HW		Fixed Dividend	VAR
Period: 1871–1992						
1	1.777	2.44	2.26	.038	.063	.028
2	2.996	2.77	2.10	.041	.100	.030
3	4.321	3.14	1.95	.045	.121	.040
4	5.876	3.43	1.98	.048	.135	.051
5	7.689	3.69	2.01	.052	.149	.057
First period: 1871–1926						
1	−1.081	−.89	−.76	.009	.999	.990
2	−1.400	−.70	−.61	.004	.987	.971
3	−5.105	−2.01	−2.17	.027	.999	.999
4	−5.996	−1.55	−2.31	.017	.993	.996
5	−6.101	−1.17	−1.38	.010	.991	.984
Second period: 1927–92						
1	10.474	5.41	5.71	.280	.006	.002
2	14.191	4.99	3.66	.228	.027	.015
3	22.613	6.84	5.05	.321	.026	.012
4	25.664	6.80	4.82	.290	.052	.021
5	28.476	6.49	3.36	.253	.075	.036

Note. In the regression, $R_{t,t+T}$ is defined as the total stock return from time t to time $t + T$, and $Y_t = D_t/P_t$ is the annual dividend yield measured as of time t. The t-statistics presented are t(OLS), from the classical ordinary least squares (OLS) regression, and t(HW), which adjusts for heteroscedasticity and the moving average process induced by the overlapping observations (using the sample autocovariances). Empirical p-value is obtained from the simulation experiments as the proportion of times the observed beta coefficient was exceeded under the null hypothesis of no predictability. Under the fixed dividends approach, dividends are taken from their historical values, and capital returns are bootstrapped from the actual return series; under the vector autoregression (VAR), prices and dividends follow a joint stochastic process with innovations bootstrapped from the actual series. HW = Hansen-White.

fear of equities that forced yields high and made the market drop in subsequent periods. While we have no behavioral evidence on this hypothesis, it is clear that there was a structural break around this time. This switch suggests that it might be profitable for econometricians to look for underlying causes for dividend movements.

Table 22.6 presents results for U.K. returns expressed in real terms. Estimates are similar to those in nominal terms. Over the entire span, there is little evidence of predictability, but the second period regressions provide support for predictability.

Biases Due to Dividend Growth

Fama and French (1988) point out an additional source of bias in regression (2) that may obscure the forecasting power of yields. In the original present-value model, Equation (1) implies that the yield captures expectations about dividend growth as well as expected returns. When expected dividend growth is stochastic, the dividend yield is a noisy proxy for expected returns. This errors-in-variables problem biases β_T downward.

Kothari and Shanken (1992), in a study of the sources of variance in stock returns, find that inclusion of additional variables to (2) reduces the downward bias. As instruments for changes in expected dividend growth $E_{t+T}[d_{t+i}] - E_t[d_{t+i}]$, they use future stock returns $R_{t+i,t+T+i}$, and they use future dividend growth rates d_{t+i} as regressors. When these *forward* variables are included, the regression R^2 sharply increases to about 70% for annual nonoverlapping data, and the coefficient on dividend yields likewise increases—suggesting an errors-in-variables problem. Fama (1990) also finds a substantial increase in R^2 when using *future* industrial production.

This suggests that the explanatory power of dividend yields might be improved by adding suitable variables to the regression. To analyze the extent of this bias, Table 22.7 presents regressions on the dividend yield, current and future values of dividend growth, and future market returns. As an illustration, we use a 1-year, nonoverlapping horizon, with U.S. nominal returns measured over 1872–1989.

Without other variables, the β coefficient on the yield is 0.032, which is marginally significant. Adding other variables such as future dividends and returns increases β from 0.032 to 0.063, which is highly significant, even accounting for econometric biases. Similar results are obtained across subperiods, and for the British data, which are reported in the bottom half of the table.

This confirms the view that using variables that proxy for dividend growth exposes the information in yields about expected returns. This approach, however, uses future variables and does not directly address the issue of the *forecasting* ability of dividend yields in univariate regressions conditional on past and present information. Perhaps other predictive variables might be used to signal future changes in dividend growth. In such a case, dividend yields might then prove useful for forecasting purposes.

Predictable dividend growth may also present a problem in simulations that do not allow for predictability. In our experiments, however, the VAR and fixed dividend setups already allow for predictability in dividends. The VAR assumes an AR(1) process for dividend growth and dependence on past returns; the fixed dividend approach, in contrast, uses the actual dividend process, which may be more complicated than an AR(1), but which is nonetheless highly predictable.

One way to assess the impact of the bias in the regression coefficient is to force the dividend growth to be unpredictable. This can be done easily in the

Table 22.7
Impact of Dividend Growth: Nominal 1-Year Returns

$$R_{t,t+1} = \alpha + \beta Y_t + \gamma_0 d_{t,t+1} + \sum_{i=1}^{3} \gamma_i d_{t+i,t+1+i} + \sum_{i=1}^{3} \delta_i R_{t+i,t+1+i} + \varepsilon_{t,t+1}$$

R^2	Constant	Y_t	Coefficients							
			$d_{t,t+1}$	$d_{t+1,t+2}$	$d_{t+2,t+3}$	$d_{t+3,t+4}$	$R_{t+1,t+2}$	$R_{t+2,t+3}$	$R_{t+3,t+4}$
U.S. returns: 1872–1989										
.045	-.054	.032	...	...	...	...	...	...	...
	(.071)	(.014)							
.460	-.147	.044	.817	...	...	...	...	...	...
	(.054)	(.010)	(.087)						
.487	-.144	.049	.804	-.122	-.125	-.033	...	...	...
	(.054)	(.011)	(.089)	(.072)	(.070)	(.072)			
.491	-.155	.043	.835	...	...	...	-.061	.185	.106
	(.056)	(.011)	(.087)				(.088)	(.087)	(.087)
.583	-.202	.063	.832	-.205	-.340	-.192	.133	.455	.229
	(.054)	(.011)	(.083)	(.093)	(.083)	(.088)	(.112)	(.103)	(.109)
U.K. returns: 1872–1989										
.020	.051	.012	...	...	...	...	...	...	...
	(.055)	(.008)							
.045	-.005	.018	.315	...	...	...	...	...	...
	(.064)	(.008)	(.182)						
.080	.041	.018	.321	-.135	-.142	-.067	...	...	...
	(.068)	(.008)	(.182)	(.092)	(.091)	(.092)			
.266	-.158	.033	.368	...	...	...	.826	.263	.085
	(.065)	(.008)	(.162)				(.151)	(.150)	(.150)
.397	-.141	.040	.422	-.346	-.300	-.115	.900	.561	.383
	(.061)	(.008)	(.150)	(.086)	(.084)	(.077)	(.140)	(.154)	(.153)

Note. In the regression, $R_{t,t+1}$ is defined as the total stock return from time t to time $t + 1$, $Y_t = D_t/P_t$ is the annual dividend yield measured as of time t, and $d_{t,t+1}$ is the relative change in dividend from time t to time $t + 1$. Ordinary least squares standard deviations are in parentheses.

VAR setup by setting the (a_{21}, a_{22}) coefficients in the dividend equation to zero. The distribution of slope coefficients is then slightly displaced upward. Thus, predictable dividend growth obscures the explanatory power of yields by biasing the slope coefficient toward zero. In our experiments, however, the bias is rather small, with a displacement in the median slope coefficient of about 5%.

◤ Survivorship Bias

Empirical Evidence

Apparently, the dividend yield effect has been strong in the United Kingdom since 1927. To assess the robustness of this result, Figure 22.3 plots the total return over 1 year against the dividend yield; each data point is represented by the corresponding year. As the figure dramatically shows, 1975 was an extreme outlier that must have pulled up the regression line.[13]

This does not necessarily mean that this effect is economically meaningless, however. If the dividend yield can forecast a market rebound in times of extreme economic distress, then it clearly has value to risk-averse investors. By any measure, 1974 was a period of severe economic distress. The stock market fell by 53%, and as a result, dividend yields went up from 4.4% to 11.8%. The following year, the stock market recovered to its previous level (an increase of

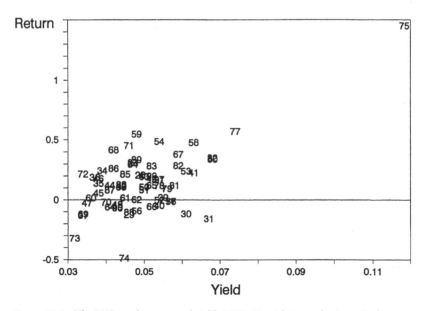

Figure 22.3. The U.K. stock return and yield: 1927–92, with 1-year horizon. Each number represents the year in which a 1-year return is associated with the yield.

136%), and yields dropped to 5.7%.[14] Because the high yield was associated with a high subsequent return, the year 1975 was a major contributor to high slope coefficients.

It is not always easy to identify the financial effects of social and political phenomena. There is little doubt, however, that the early 1970s were a period of global social unrest and political upheaval. The oil crisis and the Arab-Israeli war led to global concerns about energy and the stability of the international banking system. The Labour government in the United Kingdom was in turmoil.[15] While the British and U.S. markets successfully weathered the storms of the 1970s, other countries such as Portugal did not. The Lisbon equity market, functioning since 1910, was shut down by the Salazar government. Hindsight makes it easy to dismiss the likelihood of more radical changes in Britain during the 1970s, but the last 200 years of European history should temper such skepticism.

Investors who knew that the U.K. market would survive these years would have made a fortune by buying when yields were over 11%. Does this mean that the extreme drop of 53% in 1974 was market overreaction, or are we simply exercising perfect hindsight?

From Figure 22.3, the dynamics of a dividend yield series that has survived appear to be stationary: after 1974, yields revert to a normal level. While we might expect yields to be bounded above and below by economic forces under normal financial conditions, we also expect markets to encounter conditions that are *not* normal over long histories. For instance, when yields are formed by trailing dividends, they may go to infinity when industries are nationalized or in times of destruction due to wars. Alternatively, yields may go to zero in times of hyperinflation, when nominal prices soar.

Survivorship Simulations

In order to assess more precisely the impact of survivorship, consider the following experiment. We wish to simulate a situation where stock markets disappear and where dividend yield regressions are run only on data with continuous histories. This requires modeling the stochastic behavior of prices and dividends, as well as specifying a model for market disappearance. One problem is that we cannot simply use distribution parameters estimated from existing series, since these markets never disappeared. Instead, simulation parameters must be adjusted to reflect the possibility of disappearance. That is, we wish to choose reasonable values for unconditional return distribution parameters. There are only a few choices for conditioning rules that allow the estimation of unconditional parameters. Brown, Goetzmann, and Ross (in press) show how the problem is similar to a situation where a diffusion process hits an absorbing barrier at the origin. In this simple circumstance, the probability of eventual absorption is $e^{-2x_0\bar{r}/\sigma^2}$, where $\bar{r}$ is the mean of the process, σ is the volatility, and x_0 is the initial value. Given a probability, a fixed floor, and estimates of conditional parameters, we can choose sets of unconditional parameters to satisfy this equation.

The choice of the disappearance probability is a difficult one. Of the dozen or more active equity exchanges that existed in 1871, two of the four largest stock markets, Germany and Japan, were subject to extreme shocks and effectively disappeared during a war. For purposes of illustration, we therefore consider a probability of disappearance of 50%.

Assume now that the volatility of returns is 25% per annum and that a market disappears when it loses 75% of the real value at the beginning of the sample. Setting the probability equal to 50%, and $x_0 = 0.75$, we solve for $\bar{r}$ and find an expected capital appreciation of $\bar{r} = 2.9\%$ per annum in real terms. This number appears reasonable; it is lower than the 3.58% and 3.52% real capital appreciation observed in the United States and Britain over 1872–1992, which are conditioned on survival.

The bootstrap is then modified as follows. We use the U.K. data, expressed in real terms, over 1871–1992. The capital appreciation returns are modified so that their mean is 2.9%, instead of the historical average. We then bootstrap and reconstruct the series as before and keep track of the cumulative real price index series. When it falls below 25% of the initial value in 1871, the series is deemed to have "disappeared." The regressions can then be recorded for two samples, the "total sample" and the "survived sample."

Alternatively, we also implemented a truncation method based on a "variable floor." The previous procedure is somewhat conservative given the long-term capital appreciation of stock prices. Ideally, the lower bound, or floor, should grow over time. We therefore also specify a variable floor initially set at 25% of the initial value and which grows in line with the expected real price appreciation series.

Table 22.8 reports bootstrap results with survivorship. We find that the mean real capital appreciation of the full sample is 2.9%, and that of the "fixed floor" survived sample is 3.6%, which is in line with historical numbers.[16] The mean return of the survived variable floor series is 5.1%, slightly higher than expected. For comparison purposes, the right panel also presents results when the expected return of the real capital appreciation series is set at 1.9%. This leads to lower values in the mean of the survived series and to lower survival rates. The question is whether focusing on survivors biases the result of the regression.

Figure 22.4 compares the empirical distribution of the 1-year horizon beta for the survived fixed floor sample with that of the total sample. Clearly, the slope coefficients in the survived sample are upward biased; the median is 0.47, versus 0.24 for the total sample. Whereas researchers are really sampling from the survived sample, they use the total sample distribution to draw inference. Table 22.8 shows that, in the case of the 1-year regression, the empirical p-value of the slope coefficient is 0.072, against 0.050 when ignoring the survivorship issue. With a variable floor, the empirical p-value is 0.143.

Table 22.8
Effect of Survivorship: United Kingdom Real Returns, 1872–1992

	Expected Return = 2.9%			Expected Return = 1.9%		
	Total Sample	Survived Fixed Floor	Survived Variable Floor	Total Sample	Survived Fixed Floor	Survived Variable Floor
Return:						
Mean	.029	.036	.051	.019	.030	.041
SD	.198	.198	.201	.198	.198	.201
Survival rate (in %)	. . .	69.2	20.3	. . .	52.4	19.8
Empirical p-values:						
β_1	.050	.072	.143	.031	.059	.143
β_2	.084	.121	.227	.053	.100	.243
β_3	.104	.150	.278	.067	.128	.297
β_4	.114	.165	.300	.075	.142	.318
β_5	.124	.179	.316	.079	.151	.333
$t(\rho)$	.103	.147	.381	.049	.091	.220
Upper 97.5% fractile:						
β_1	1.77	1.95	2.63	1.44	1.89	2.57
β_2	3.79	4.28	5.62	3.06	3.97	5.40
β_3	6.04	6.83	9.16	4.95	6.50	8.40
β_4	8.84	9.92	12.38	7.05	9.38	12.00
β_5	11.94	13.19	17.17	9.58	12.65	16.08
$t(\rho)$	4.34	4.78	7.03	3.49	4.01	5.27

Note. Simulations of dividend yield predictive power regressions and dividend yield mean-reversion regressions $R_{t,t+T} = \alpha_T + \beta_T Y_t + \varepsilon_{t,t+T}$; $Y_{t+1} = \mu + \rho Y_t + \eta_{t+1}$, where $R_{t,t+T}$ is defined as the total stock return from time t to time $t + T$, and $Y_t = D_t/P_t$ is the dividend yield. A series is deemed to not survive when, over 121 years, the value of the capital index falls below (i) a fixed floor of 25% of the initial value, or (ii) a variable floor initially set at 25% of the initial value and growing at the rate of appreciation in capital returns. Survival rate is the proportion of experiments where the series did not hit the floor. Empirical p-value is obtained from the bootstrap experiment as the proportion of times the observed beta coefficient was exceeded under the null hypothesis of no predictability. The table should be interpreted as follows: researchers use the "total sample" to draw inference, when they are really sampling from a "survived" distribution.

Alternatively, the 97.5% upper fractile shifts from 1.77 to 1.95 to 2.63 when we increase the incidence of truncation. This experiment shows that survivorship can bias inference toward more frequent rejection than warranted for dividend yield regressions. In addition, the biases seem to grow with the length of the horizon; differences in p-values are systematically higher for 5-year betas than for 1-year betas.

It is also instructive to consider whether tests of mean reversion in dividend yields are affected by survivorship. These tests typically use regressions of the type

$$Y_{t+1} = \mu + \rho Y_t + \eta_t + 1 \tag{5}$$

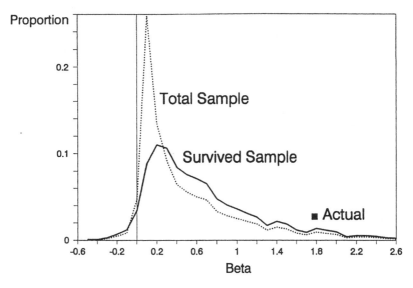

Figure 22.4. Distribution of Beta: 1-Year Horizon, With 5,000 Replications for U.K. 1871–1992 Sample

and report the *t*-statistic for the hypothesis that $\rho = 1$, $t(\hat{\rho}) = (1 - \hat{\rho})/s(\hat{\rho})$, which is compared to critical values reported by Dickey and Fuller. Low values of $\hat{\rho}$, away from unity, suggest that yields may be stationary. As Table 22.8 shows, we find that the distribution of $t(\rho)$ is displaced upward for the survived sample, with the 97.5% fractile, for example, going from 4.34 to 4.78 to 7.03 when we increase the incidence of truncation. Survived series appear to be more mean reverting than otherwise. Therefore, conventional applications of stationarity tests may be misleading, because they are predicated on a theoretical distribution that includes all experiments, whereas we observe markets only with continuous histories. These results are certainly discouraging, since tests of unit root have notoriously low power and tend to reject only when using very long time series. Our results show that, unfortunately, using long time series is not a remedy but instead can seriously bias inference when survivorship is an issue.

The results of the simulations, however, should be taken with caution. In fact, the extent of the bias depends on underlying parameters unknown to the researcher. In this case, we are still using the bootstrapped returns of a series that has a continuous history; other markets may have disappeared after very large declines, which are seldom recorded. Ideally, one would want to compare a broad cross section of markets with and without continuous price histories. Unfortunately, we analyze markets only with continuous histories or that have performed well in the past.

The Changing Significance of the Dividend Yield

As we expand our horizons to look at the long-term performance of the stock market, we must worry about larger structural issues and shifts. In the long term, many factors are no longer constant. Political events, wars, structural changes in the economy, even the role and relevance of the capital market itself may shift over time. Most econometric models, on the other hand, rely on a fixed structure. The most unexpected thing we found in our analysis of the U.K. data is that the relationship between dividends and future returns reversed sign between the period before and after 1927. Yields forecast returns in the earlier period of U.K. capital market histories, but high yields predicted low returns, not high returns. This suggests that the role of dividends may have evolved through time in the United Kingdom in ways we do not clearly understand. At the very least, it suggests that we cannot take the historical statistical estimates of the return-yield relationship as a reliable guide for future investing. This point is made quite nicely in research by Amit Goyal and Ivo Welch (1999), who examine the out-of-sample predictive power of dividend yields using U.S. data. The effect is marginal out of sample, and clearly depends on the time period the study is performed over. Indeed yields have a hard time adding more information than simply the long-term historical average equity premium, when using data looking only backward.

◣ Conclusions

Previous tests of the predictive power of dividend yields have led to mixed conclusions, in part because of statistical biases due to the econometric procedure. In addition, however, there is a more subtle form of bias, which is that induced by "data mining." The latter can be dealt with by examining new data sets, such as other countries or longer time series.

This article extends the analysis of dividend yield regressions in two directions. First, we use a long U.K. data series. Second, we use monthly U.S. data going back to 1871. Because of the additional data points, which now cover 121 years, we would expect much stronger rejections of the hypothesis of no predictability than reported before. To address regression biases, we report empirical marginal significance levels using a fixed dividend procedure and a VAR with stochastic prices and dividends. We find largely similar results across the two procedures.

For both the U.S. and U.K. data, we find little evidence of predictability over the whole sample period. When considering different sample periods, however, we find that the predictability results: (a) do not extend to pre-1926 U.S. data, (b) are very strong for post-1926 U.K. data, and (c) are perverse (significant but with negative coefficients) for pre-1926 U.K. data. These breaks in predictability are similar to the shifts in mean reversion identified by Kim,

Nelson, and Startz (1991) and are difficult to explain. Perhaps these results are related to the stability of returns pre-1926 reported earlier in the article. If returns are stable, then dividend yields will be stable, and there is not much to predict, and not much to predict with. Post-1926, returns become more variable, and dividend yields become more useful predictors.

Alternatively, the predictability results could be explained in terms of survivorship. In particular, the evidence of predictability for post-1926 U.K. data appears to be largely driven by an "outlier"—1974—when there was a real possibility that capitalism would disappear in Britain. But as we know, the stock market survived, and Britain is one of the few countries for which we have a continuous record going back more than 100 years. Over long horizons, survivorship inevitably arises as an important issue, akin to peso problems in the foreign exchange market.

Similar problems plague the analysis of emerging stock markets, which have recently attracted the attention of investors because of their recent stellar performance. Few analysts, however, emphasize the disappearance of many of the Latin American markets, for instance, at the beginning of the century. In addition, the markets that have not been doing well seldom draw attention and may not be included in standard databases. As a result, the reported performance numbers for emerging markets most likely overstate the true potential for returns.

This article offers simulation evidence that survivorship tends to bias inference in favor of finding that dividend yields help predict long-horizon returns. We also show that tests of unit roots in dividend yields are affected by focusing on series with continuous histories.

A word of caution, however, is in order. The simulations presented in this article only consider univariate regressions of stock returns on dividend yields. Given that dividend yields also contain forecasts of dividend growth, they are a noisy proxy for expected stock returns. Therefore, if analysts have some ability to forecast expected dividend growth, these forecasts should be included in the forecasting regression, in which case dividend yields might be useful predictors of stock returns.

Overall, the economic significance of predictability hinges on whether there was a positive probability of disruption in the U.K. equity price series. If the chances of a market's disappearing are truly zero, then the predictability we found in recent U.K. data is consistent with the market overreaction hypothesis. Otherwise, the predictability of future returns based on dividend yields may be overstated.

◣ Notes

1. See, e.g., Nelson and Kim (1993) or Goetzmann and Jorion (1993).
2. Actually, *D* should represent all cash flows to investors. This has important implications for tests of excess volatility. Given that dividend series are so smooth, prices are typi-

cally found to be excessively variable in comparison with "rational" present values. However, Ackert and Smith (1993) show that rationality cannot be rejected when taking into account not only dividends but also share repurchases and takeover distributions.

3. See also Boudoukh and Richardson (1994).

4. See, e.g., Hansen and Hodrick (1980), Richardson and Smith (1991), and Boudoukh and Richardson (1994).

5. We thank John Campbell for this observation.

6. As an example, assume that the true autocorrelation coefficient for yields is $\rho = 0.99$. In small samples, the estimated coefficient will be downward biased, by a factor of $(1 + 3\rho)/T$, to, say, 0.97; this number will be typically taken as the underlying parameter for VAR simulations.

7. An earlier version of the article reports similar results with bivariate normal errors sampled with the empirically observed covariance matrix. There were slightly more occurrences of rejections using normal errors than bootstrapped errors, because there are more outliers than expected under a normal distribution.

8. For instance, for the 1927–92 period for nominal U.S. data, we find $a_{22} = 0.177$, with a t-statistic of 5.1, and $a_{21} = 0.011$, with a t-statistic of 1.0.

9. See Schwert (1990) and Siegel (1992).

10. Structural changes in dividend yields might obscure their forecasting ability. To assess the impact of nonstationarity, we also estimated regressions where yields are replaced by their deviation relative to a 10-year moving average. The results were essentially unchanged.

11. Part of this increase is explained by the fact that the variance of the dependent variable increases over longer horizons. In line with most previous research, we have chosen not to adjust returns for the length of the horizon.

12. In Table 22.3, we note that the empirical p-values for the 1-month regression for the Cowles period are very high, implying that there were few, if any, instances of the bootstrap where a coefficient lower than -0.142 was obtained in the simulations. This can be traced to the fact that Cowles measured prices as the average of high and low during the month instead of month-end values. As Schwert (1990) has noted, this method induces spurious positive autocorrelation in the return series. Indeed, we find a first-order autoregression coefficient of 0.29 for the Cowles period and only 0.09 for the latter period, both with standard errors around 0.05. Because our simulations are constructed under the null hypothesis of no autocorrelation (no predictability), the observed slope coefficient appears to fall outside our empirical distribution. We found, however, that the observed coefficient is not unusual in simulations with autocorrelated returns. At longer horizons, the p-values are virtually unchanged. Thus the 1-month results should be interpreted with caution.

13. To confirm that this year is an outlier, we computed measures of leverage and influence for this observation, as defined in Belsley, Kuh, and Welsh (1980). These measure the effect of one observation on the parameters of a linear regression. "Leverage" measures the potential influence of one observation and depends on the quantity $h_t = x_t(X'X)^{-1}x_t'$, where x_t refers to the vector of regressors at time t. For the 1-year regression, the leverage of year 1975 is 0.033, six times the lowest leverage value, which suggests a large impact on the regression coefficients. "Influence" is defined by the quantity $e_t h_t/(1 - h_t)$, where e_t is the residual at time t, and measures how omitting the tth observation from the regression affects the fitted value or residual for that observation. For the 1-year regression, the influence of year 1975 is 0.055, which is again much higher than for any other observation. These regression diagnostics therefore show that results in the latter subperiod have been unduly affected by events in 1975.

14. Note that stock price movements in the United States were much less extreme, with a drop of 28% in 1974 and a recovery of 36% in 1975.

15. Britain had the highest inflation rate of any industrial country and faced severe labor trouble. In its March 9, 1974, issue, the *Economist* stated that "Britain faces the most precarious crisis in its peacetime history."

16. The probability of surviving is 69%, higher than the assumed 50% because the sample is finite and also because of differences in the return distribution.

◣ References

Ackert, L. F., and Smith, B. F. 1993. Stock price volatility, ordinary dividends, and other cash flows to shareholders. *Journal of Finance* 48 (September): 1147–60.

Belsley, D.; Kuh, E.; and Welsh, R. E. 1980. *Regression Diagnostics*. New York: Wiley & Sons.

Boudoukh, J., and Richardson, M. 1994. The statistics of long-horizon regressions revisited. *Mathematical Finance* 2:103–19.

Brown, S.; Goetzmann, W.; and Ross, S. 1995. Survival. *Journal of Finance* 50 (July): 853–73.

Campbell, J., and Perron, P. 1991. Pitfalls and opportunities: What economists should know about unit roots. *NBER Macroeconomics Annual* 6:141–201.

Campbell, J., and Shiller, R. 1988a. The dividend price ratio and expectations of future dividends and discount factors. *Review of Financial Studies* 1:195–228.

Campbell, J., and Shiller, R. 1988b. Stock prices, earnings and expected dividends. *Journal of Finance* 43 (July): 661–76.

Campbell, J., and Shiller, R. 1989. The dividend ratio model and small sample bias: A Monte-Carlo study. *Economic Letters* 29:325–31.

Cowles, A. 1939. *Common Stock Indices, 1871–1937*. Cowles Commission for Research in Economics Monograph no. 3. Bloomington, Ind.: Principia Press.

De Long, J. J., and Grossman, R. 1993. Excess volatility on the London stock market, 1870–1990. Working paper. Cambridge, Mass.: Harvard University, Business School.

Dickey, D., and Fuller, W. 1979. Distribution of estimators for autoregressive time series with a unit root. *Journal of American Statistical Association* 74:427–31.

Economist. 1974. The old firm. *Economist* 250 (March 9): 11–12.

Fama, E. 1990. Stock returns, expected returns, and real activity. *Journal of Finance* 45 (September): 1089–1108.

Fama, E., and French, K. 1988. Dividend yields and expected stock returns. *Journal of Financial Economics* 22 (October): 3–25.

Fuller, R., and Kling, J. 1990. Is the stock market predictable? *Journal of Portfolio Management* 16 (Summer): 28–36.

Goetzmann, W. 1993. Patterns in three centuries of stock market prices. *Journal of Business* 66 (April): 249–70.

Goetzmann, W., and Jorion, P. 1993. Testing the predictive power of dividend yields. *Journal of Finance* 47 (June): 663–79.

Goyal, A., and Welch, I. 1999. Predicting the equity premium with dividend ratios. Working paper. Yale School of Management.

Hansen, L. 1982. Large sample properties of generalized method of moments estimators. *Econometrica* 50:1029–54.

Hansen, L., and Hodrick, R. 1980. Forward exchange rates as optimal predictors of future spot rates. *Journal of Political Economy* 88:829–53.

Heckman, J. 1977. Sample selection bias as specification error. *Econometrica* 47:153–62.

Hodrick, R. 1992. Dividend yields and expected stock returns: Alternative procedures for inference and measurement. *Review of Financial Studies* 5:357–86.

Ingersoll, J. 1987. *Theory of Financial Decision Making.* Totowa, N.J.: Rowman & Littlefield.

Kim, M.; Nelson, C.; and Startz, R. 1991. Mean reversion in stock prices: A reappraisal of the empirical evidence. *Review of Economic Studies* 58:515–28.

Kothari, S., and Shanken, J. 1992. Stock return variation and expected dividends: A time-series and cross-sectional analysis. *Journal of Financial Economics* 31 (April): 177–210.

Nelson, C., and Kim, M. 1993. Predictable stock returns: Reality or statistical illusion? *Journal of Finance* 48 (June): 641–61.

Richardson, M., and Smith, T. 1991. Tests of financial models in the presence of overlapping observations. *Review of Financial Studies* 4:227–54.

Rozeff, M. 1984. Dividend yields are equity risk premiums. *Journal of Portfolio Management* 11 (Fall): 68–75.

Schwert, W. 1990. Indices of U.S. stock prices from 1802 to 1897. *Journal of Business* 63 (July): 399–426.

Shiller, R. J. 1989. Comovements in stock prices and comovements in dividends. *Journal of Finance* 44 (July): 719–29.

Siegel, J. 1992. The equity premium: Stock and bond returns since 1802. *Financial Analysts Journal* 48 (January): 28–38.

Smith, K. C., and Horne, G. F. 1934. *An Index Number of Securities, 1867–1914.* Special Memorandum no. 37. London: London and Cambridge Economic Service.

Stambaugh, R. 1986. Biases in regressions with lagged stochastic regressors. Working Paper no. 156. Chicago: University of Chicago, Graduate School of Business.

Warren, G., and Pearson, F. 1933. *Prices.* New York: Wiley.

White, H. 1980. A heteroskedasticity-consistent covariance matrix estimator and direct tests for heteroskedasticity. *Econometrica* 48:817–38.

Wilson, J., and Jones, C. 1987. A comparison of annual common stock returns. *Journal of Business* 60 (April): 239–58.

23 Roger G. Ibbotson and Paul D. Kaplan

Does Asset Allocation Policy Explain 40, 90, or 100 Percent of Performance?

Disagreement over the importance of asset allocation policy stems from asking different questions. We used balanced mutual fund and pension fund data to answer the three relevant questions. We found that about 90 percent of the variability in returns of a typical fund across time is explained by policy, about 40 percent of the variation of returns among funds is explained by policy, and on average about 100 percent of the return level is explained by the policy return level.

Does asset allocation policy explain 40 percent, 90 percent, or 100 percent of performance? The answer depends on how the question is asked and what an analyst is trying to explain. According to well-known studies by Brinson and colleagues, more than 90 percent of the variability in a typical plan sponsor's performance over time is the result of asset allocation policy. So, if one is trying to explain the variability of returns *over time,* asset allocation is very important.

Unfortunately, the Brinson et al. studies are often misinterpreted and the results applied to questions that the studies never intended to answer. For example, an analyst might want to know how important asset allocation is in explaining the variation in performance *among funds.* Because the Brinson studies did not address this question, the analyst can neither look to them to find the answer nor fault them for not answering it correctly. A different study is required.

Finally, an analyst might want to know what percentage of the *level* of a typical fund's return is ascribable to asset allocation policy. Again, the Brinson studies do not address this question. A different study is needed.

Thus, three distinct questions remain about the importance of asset allocation:

1. How much of the variability of returns *across time* is explained by the policy (the question Brinson et al. asked)? In other words, how much of the fund's ups and downs do its policy benchmarks explain?
2. How much of the variation in returns *among funds* is explained by differences in policy? In other words, how much of the difference between two funds' performance is a result of their policy difference?
3. What portion of the *return level* is explained by policy return? In other words, what is the ratio of the policy benchmark return to the fund's actual return?

Much of the recent controversy about the importance of asset allocation stems from treating the answer that Brinson et al. provided to Question 1 as an answer to Questions 2 and 3.

The purpose of our study was to ask and answer all three questions. To do this, we examined 10 years of monthly returns to 94 U.S. balanced mutual funds and 5 years of quarterly returns to 58 pension funds. We performed a different analysis for each question.

▲ Framework

Our data consisted of the total return for each fund for each period of time (a month or a quarter). The first step in our analysis was to decompose each total return, TR, into two components, policy return and active return, as follows:

$$TR_{i,t} = (1 + PR_{i,t})(1 + AR_{i,t}) - 1,$$

where

$TR_{i,t}$ = total return of fund i in period t
$PR_{i,t}$ = policy return of fund i in period t
$AR_{i,t}$ = active return of fund i in period t

Policy return is the part of the total return that comes from the asset allocation policy. Active return is the remainder. Active return is the remainder. Active return depends on both the manager's ability to actively over- or underweight asset classes and securities relative to the policy and on the magnitude and timing of those bets.

The asset allocation policy of each fund can be represented as a set of asset-class weights that sum to 1. For the pension funds in this study, these weights were known in advance. For the mutual funds, the policy weights were determined by return-based style analysis, which is described in the "Data" section. The policy return of the fund over a given period of time can be computed from the policy weights and returns on asset-class benchmarks as follows:

$$PR_{i,t} = w1_i R1_t + w2_i R2_t + \ldots + wk_i Rk_t - c,$$

where

$w1_i, w2_i, \ldots, wk_i$ = policy weights of fund i
$R1_t, R2_t, \ldots, Rk_t$ = returns on the asset classes in period t
c = approximate cost of replicating the policy mix through indexed mutual funds, as a percentage of assets

Thus, in addition to fund returns, we needed policy weights for each fund and total returns on asset-class benchmarks. Given the total returns to the funds and the estimated policy returns of the funds, we solved for the active returns.

Universal Misunderstanding

From the marketing materials of mutual fund companies and financial planning firms to the mouths of academics and financial representatives, there is a universal misunderstanding of the relationship between asset allocation and performance. The specific claims vary, but financial professionals generally assert that asset allocation is the most important determinant of returns, accounting for more than 90 percent of performance.

This assertion stems from studies by Brinson et al. (Brinson, Hood, and Beebower 1986; Brinson, Singer, and Beebower 1991), which state, ". . . investment policy dominates investment strategy (market timing and security selection), explaining on average 93.6 percent of the variation in total plan return." This conclusion has caused a great deal of confusion in both the academic and financial communities. In fact, a survey by Nuttall and Nuttall (1998; see Table 23.1) demonstrates that out of 50 writers who quoted Brinson, only one quoted him correctly. Approximately 37 writers misinterpreted Brinson's work as an answer to the question, "What percent of total return is explained by asset allocation policy?" and five writers misconstrued the Brinson conclusion as an answer to the question, "What is the impact of choosing one asset allocation over another?"

Brinson's conclusion has been universally misinterpreted and it's time to set the record straight. This paper clarifies the Brinson studies, detail criticisms of the studies, explains the link between asset allocation and investment returns, and explores the implications for individual investors.

Table 23.1
Nuttall & Nuttall Survey Results

Percent of writers who misinterpret the Brinson work as an answer to the relationship between asset allocation and return level	75%
For example: "One study suggests that more than 91 percent of a portfolio's return is attributable to its mix of asset classes. In this study, individual stock selection and market timing together accounted for less than seven percent of a diversified portfolio's return."—Vanguard Group	
Percent of writers who misinterpret the Brinson work as an answer to the impact of choosing one asset allocation policy over another	10%
For example: "A widely cited study of pension plan managers shows that 91.5 percent of the difference between one portfolio's performance and another's is explained by asset allocation."—Fidelity Investments	
Other misquotations	13%
Percent of writers who accurately quoted Brinson (only one correct interpretation)	2%

Criticism of the Brinson Studies

According to the well-known studies by Brinson et al., more than 90 percent of the *variability* of a portfolio's performance over time is due to asset allocation. Brinson is measuring the relationship between the movement of a portfolio and the movement of the overall market. He finds that more than 90 percent of the movement of one's portfolio from quarter to quarter is due to market movement of the asset classes in which the portfolio is invested.

As mentioned above, these findings have been largely misinterpreted. They have also been criticized.

Hensel, Ezra, and Ilkiw (1991) argue that the Brinson results are not informative because bull and bear markets explain most of the variation in returns. In other words, "a rising tide raises all boats." William Jahnke (1997), however, asserts that the Brinson results are irrelevant because Brinson does not ask the right question. Jahnke believes that a more appropriate question would be one that probes the difference in returns between funds. Stevens, Surz, and Wimer (1999) also argue that Brinson is asking the wrong question, but they feel the most relevant question pertains to the relationship between asset allocation and returns, not volatility. (See Table 23.2 for a summary of these opinions.)

Table 23.2
The Asset Allocation Debate

Hensel, Ezra, and Ilkiw: Brinson result not informative since bull and bear markets explain about 80% of the variation.

Jahnke: Brinson studies irrelevant. Need to compare return differences between funds.

Stevens, Surz, and Wimer: Brinson studies should have asked how much of the return level comes from asset allocation.

In our time-series analysis, we used the period-by-period returns. In our cross-sectional analysis, we used the compound annual rates of return over the period of analysis. For each fund, we computed the compound annual total return over the entire period as follows:

$$TR_i = \sqrt[N]{(1 + TR_{i,1})(1 + TR_{i,2}) \ldots (1 + TR_{i,T})} - 1,$$

where

TR_i = compound annual total return on fund i over the entire period of analysis

$TR_{i,t}$ = total return of fund i in period t

T = number of period returns

N = length of the entire period of analysis, in years

Similarly, we computed the compound annual policy return over the entire period as follows:

$$PR_i = N\sqrt{(1 + PR_{i,1})(1 + PR_{i,2}) \ldots (1 + PR_{i,T})} - 1,$$

where PR_i is the compound annual policy return on fund i over the entire period of analysis and $PR_{i,t}$ is the policy return to fund i in period t.

▶ Data

For the mutual fund portion of this study, we used 10 years of monthly returns for 94 U.S. balanced funds. The 94 funds represent all of the balanced funds in the Morningstar universe that had at least 10 years of data ending March 31, 1998. Policy weights for each fund were estimated by performing return-based style analysis over the entire 120-month period.[1] Table 23.3 shows the asset-class benchmarks used and the average fund exposure to each asset class.

In calculating the policy returns for each fund, we assumed that the cost of replicating the policy mix through index mutual funds would be 2 basis points a month (approximately 25 bps annually).

Stevens, Surz, and Wimer (1999) provided the same type of analysis on quarterly returns of 58 pension funds over the five-year 1993–97 period.[2] We used the *actual* policy weights and asset-class benchmarks of the pension funds, however, rather than estimated policy weights and the same asset-class benchmarks for all funds. In each quarter, the policy weights were known in

Table 23.3
Asset Classes and Benchmarks for Balanced Mutual Funds

Asset Class	Benchmark	Average Allocation
Large-cap U.S. stocks	CRSP 1–2 portfolio[a]	37.4%
Small-cap U.S. stocks	CRSP 6–8 portfolio[a]	12.2
Non-U.S. stocks	MSCI Europe/Australasia/Far East Index	2.1
U.S. bonds	Lehman Brothers Aggregate Bond Index	35.2
Cash	30-day U.S. T-bills[b]	13.2

[a]Constructed by CRSP. CRSP excludes unit investment trusts, closed-end funds, real estate investment trusts, Americus trusts, foreign stocks, and American Depositary Receipts from the portfolios. CRSP uses only NYSE firms to determine the size breakpoints for the portfolios. Specifically, CRSP ranks all eligible NYSE stocks by company size (market value of outstanding equity) and then splits them into 10 equally populated groups, or deciles. The largest companies are in Decile 1, and the smallest are in Decile 10. The capitalization for the largest company in each decile serves as the breakpoint for that decile. Breakpoints are rebalanced on the last day of trading in March, June, September, and December. CRSP then assigns NYSE and Amex/Nasdaq companies to the portfolios according to the decile breakpoints. Monthly portfolio returns are market-cap-weighted averages of the individual returns within each of the 10 portfolios. The 1–2 portfolio is the combination of Deciles 1 and 2, and the 6–8 portfolio is the combination of Deciles 6, 7, and 8.

[b]Ibbotson Associates (1998).

advance of the realized returns.[3] We report the pension fund results together with our analysis of the mutual fund returns in the next section.

▲ Questions and Answers

Now consider the original three questions posed by the study: How much of the variability of return across time is explained by asset allocation policy, how much of the variation among funds is explained by the policy, and what portion of the return level is explained by policy return?

Question #1: Variability Across Time

The Brinson et al. studies from 1986 and 1991 answered the question of how much of the variability of fund returns is explained by the variability of policy returns. They calculated the result by regressing each fund's total returns ($TR_{i,t}$ in our notation) against its policy returns ($PR_{i,t}$), reporting the R^2 value for each fund in the study, then examining the average, median, and distribution of these results.

Figure 23.1 illustrates the meaning of the time-series R^2 with the use of a single fund from our sample. In this example, we regressed the 120 monthly returns of a particular mutual fund against the corresponding monthly returns

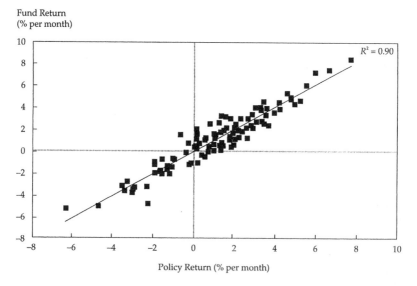

Figure 23.1. Time-Series Regression of Monthly Fund Return Versus Fund Policy Return: One Mutual Fund, April 1988–March 1998
Note: The sample fund's policy allocations among the general asset classes were 52.4 percent U.S. large-cap stocks, 9.8 percent U.S. small-cap stocks, 3.2 percent non-U.S. stocks, 20.9 percent U.S. bonds, and 13.7 percent cash.

Table 23.4
Comparison of Time-Series Regression Studies

Measure	Brinson 1986	Brinson 1991	Mutual Funds	Pension Funds
R^2				
Mean	93.6%	91.5%	81.4%	88.0%
Median	NA	NA	87.6	90.7
Active return[a]				
Mean	−1.10	−0.08	−0.27	−0.44
Median	NA	NA	0.00	0.18

Note: NA = not available.
[a]Active return is expressed as a percentage per year.

of the fund's estimated policy benchmark. Because most of the points cluster around the fitted regression line, the R^2 is quite high. About 90 percent of the variability of the monthly returns of this fund can be explained by the variability of the fund's policy benchmark.

In the first Brinson et al. study (1986), the authors studied quarterly returns over the 1974–83 period for 91 large U.S. pension funds. The average R^2 was 93.6 percent. In the second Brinson et al. study (1991), they studied quarterly returns over the 1978–87 period for 82 large U.S. pension funds. The average R^2 was 91.5 percent. Based on these results, the authors stated that more than 90 percent of the variability of the average fund's return across time is explained by that fund's policy mix.

The Brinson et al. results show that strategic asset allocation explains much of the variability of pension fund returns because plan sponsors select a long-term strategic target and tend to stick to it. If plan sponsors were more active, the R^2s would be lower.

The results from our analysis of both the mutual fund and the pension data are presented in Table 23.4, together with the Brinson et al. results. Our results confirm the Brinson result that approximately 90 percent of the variability of a fund's return across time is explained by the variability of policy returns. The result in our study for the median mutual fund was 87.6 percent, and the result for the median pension fund was 90.7 percent. The mean results in our study were slightly lower (81.4 percent and 88.0 percent, respectively) because they were skewed by the effect of a few outlier funds. These results are consistent with the notion that pension fund managers as a group are less active than balanced mutual fund managers.

Table 23.5 displays the range of outcomes in our study and shows that the mutual funds were more active than the pension funds. The mutual fund at the 5th percentile of R^2 had only 46.9 percent of the variability of returns explained by the variability of returns of the policy, whereas for the fund at the 95th percentile, the R^2 was 94.1 percent. For the pension funds, the R^2s are in the tighter range of 66.2 percent at the 5th percentile and 97.2 percent at the 95th percentile.

Table 23.5
Range of Time-Series Regression R^2 Values

Percentile	Mutual Funds	Pension Funds
5	46.9%	66.2%
25	79.8	94.1
50	87.6	90.7
75	91.4	94.7
95	94.1	97.2

Table 23.6
Explaining a Mutual Fund's Time Series of Returns Using Different Benchmarks

R^2	S&P 500	Average Policy	Fund's Policy
Mean	75.2%	78.8%	81.4%
Median	81.9	85.2	87.6

We next considered that the time-series R^2 may be high simply because funds participate in the capital markets in general and not because they follow a specific asset allocation policy. We explored this idea by regressing each mutual fund's total returns against the total returns to a common benchmark (rather than each against the returns to its own policy benchmark). For common benchmarks, we used the S&P 500 Index and the average of all of the policy benchmarks shown in Table 23.3.

The results are shown in Table 23.6. With the S&P 500 as the benchmark for all funds, the average R^2 was more than 75 percent and the median was nearly 82 percent. With the average policy benchmarks across funds as the benchmark, the average R^2 was nearly 79 percent and the median was more than 85 percent. These results are relatively close to those obtained when we used each specific fund's benchmark. Hence, the high R^2 in the time-series regressions result primarily from the funds' participation in the capital markets in general, not from the specific asset allocation policies of each fund. In other words, the results of the Brinson et al. studies and our results presented in Table 23.4 are a case of a rising tide lifting all boats.

Hensel, Ezra, and Ilkiw (1991) made a similar point in their study of the importance of asset allocation policy. In their framework, a naive portfolio had to be chosen as a baseline in order to evaluate the importance of asset allocation policy. They pointed out that in the Brinson et al. studies, the baseline portfolio was 100 percent in cash. In other words, the Brinson studies were written as if the alternative to selecting an asset allocation policy were to avoid risky assets altogether. When we used a more realistic baseline, such as the average policy benchmark across all funds, we found that the specific policies explain far less than half of the remaining time-series variation of the funds' returns.

10-Year Compound Annual
Fund Return (%)

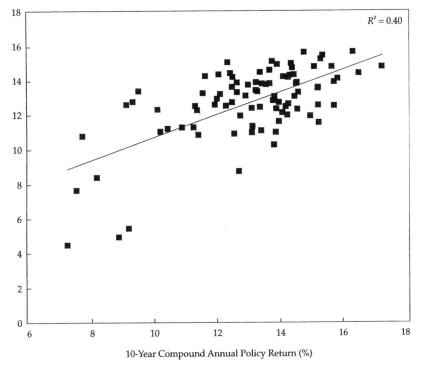

Figure 23.2. Fund Versus Policy: 10-Year Compound Annual Return Across Funds, April 1988–March 1998

Question #2: Variation Among Funds

To answer the question of how much of the variation in returns among funds is explained by policy differences, one must compare funds with each other through the use of cross-sectional analysis. Many people mistakenly thought the Brinson studies answered this question. If all funds were invested passively under the same asset allocation policy, there would be no variation among funds (yet 100 percent of the variability of returns across time of each fund would be attributable to asset allocation policy). If all funds were invested passively but had a wide range of asset allocation policies, however, all of the variation of returns would be attributable to policy.

To answer the question of how much of the variation in returns among funds is explained by policy differences, we compared each fund return with each other fund's return. We carried out a cross-sectional regression of compound annual total returns, TR_i, for the entire period on compound annual policy returns, PR_i, for the entire period. The R^2 statistic of this regression

Table 23.7
Cross-Sectional Distributions of Balanced Mutual Fund Policy Weights

Measure	Large-Cap U.S.Stocks	Small-Cap U.S. Stocks	Non-U.S. Stocks	U.S. Bonds	Cash	Total Equities
Average	37.4%	12.2%	2.1%	35.2%	13.2%	51.6%
Standard deviation	17.0	7.6	2.3	14.4	15.9	16.0
Percentile						
5	1.2	1.1	0.0	12.8	0.0	23.3
25	29.9	7.1	0.0	26.6	1.0	44.5
50	40.2	11.0	1.5	35.2	7.7	54.5
75	48.8	16.5	3.1	45.1	17.5	62.0
95	56.2	24.8	6.4	56.7	47.3	74.1

showed that for the mutual funds studied, 40 percent of the return difference was explained by policy and for the pension fund sample, the result was 35 percent.

Figure 23.2 is the plot of the 10-year compound annual total returns against the 10-year compound annual policy returns for the mutual fund sample. This plot demonstrates visually the relationship between policy and total returns. The mutual fund result shows that, because policy explains only 40 percent of the variation of returns across funds, the remaining 60 percent is explained by other factors, such as asset-class timing, style within asset classes, security selection, and fees. For pension funds, the variation of returns among funds that was not explained by policy was ascribable to the same factors and to manager selection.

The cross-sectional R^2 depended on how much the asset allocation policies of funds differed from one another and on how much the funds engaged in active management. To see how much asset allocation policies differed, we examined the cross-sectional distributions of the style weights. Table 23.7 presents the cross-sectional averages, standard deviations, and various percentiles of the style weights of the mutual funds. The last column presents these statistics for the total style allocation to equity. The large standard deviations and spreads between the percentiles indicate large variations in asset allocation policies among the funds.

Given how diverse the asset allocation policies are among these mutual funds, the relatively low R^2 of 40 percent must be the result of a large degree of active management. To see how the degree of active management can affect the cross-sectional R^2, we calculated the cross-sectional R^2 between the 10-year annual returns of the policy benchmarks and the 10-year annual returns of a set of modified fund returns. Each modified fund return was a weighted average of the actual fund return with the return on the policy benchmark so that the degree of active management was adjusted as follows:

$$TR^*_{i,t} = xTR_{i,t} + (1-x)PR_{i,t},$$

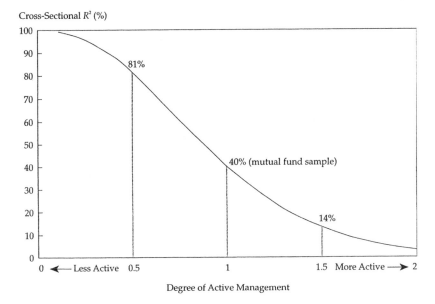

Figure 23.3. Degree of Active Management Versus Cross-Sectional R^2, April 1988– March 1998

where the value of x sets the level of active management. Setting x equal to 1 gives the sample result. Setting x less than 1 reduces the level of active management below what the funds actually did. Setting x greater than 1 shorts the benchmark and takes a levered position in the fund, thus increasing the level of active management beyond what the funds actually did.

The compound annual return of modified fund returns, TR_i^*, was calculated the same way as the compound annual return of actual fund returns (i.e., as the geometric mean of the modified annual returns).

Figure 23.3 shows the cross-sectional R^2 from regressing the modified compound annual returns on compound annual policy returns for various values of x. At $x = 1$, the cross-sectional R^2 is our original result, 40 percent. If the funds had been half as active ($x = 0.5$), the R^2 would have been much higher, 81 percent. On the other hand, if the funds had been one-and-a-half times as active ($x = 1.5$), the R^2 would have been only 14 percent. Thus, this approach shows how the degree of active management affects the cross-sectional R^2.

Question #3: Return Level

Many people also mistakenly thought the Brinson et al. studies were answering what portion of the return level is explained by asset allocation policy return, with an answer indicating nearly 90 percent. Brinson and his co-authors were not, however, addressing this question. We can address the

Table 23.8
Percentage of Total Return Level Explained by Policy Return

Study	Average	Median
Brinson 1986	112%	NA
Brinson 1991	101	NA
Mutual funds	104	100%
Pension funds	99	99

Note: NA = not available.

Table 23.9
Range of Percentage of Total Return Level Explained by Policy Return

Percentile	Mutual Funds	Pension Funds
5 (best)	82%	86%
25	94	96
50	100	99
75	112	102
95 (worst)	132	113

question by using the Brinson data and the new data from our pension fund and mutual fund studies. We calculated the percentage of fund return explained by policy return for each fund as the ratio of compound annual policy return, PR_i, divided by the compound annual total return, TR_i. This ratio of compound returns is really simply a performance measure. A fund that stayed exactly at its policy mix and invested passively will have a ratio of 1.0, or 100 percent, whereas a fund that outperformed its policy will have a ratio less than 1.0.

Table 23.8 shows the percentage of fund return explained by policy return for the Brinson studies and the two data sets used in this study. On average, policy accounted for a little more than all of total return. The one exception is the pension fund sample in this study, where the mean result was 99 percent. The pension data did not have any expenses subtracted, however, so if we included external manager fees, pension staff costs, and other expenses, the result would probably be close to 100 percent, meaning that no value was added above the benchmark. On average, the pension funds and balanced mutual funds are not adding value above their policy benchmarks because of a combination of timing, security selection, management fees, and expenses. Moreover, results for both groups here may even be better than expected because the timing component might include some benefit from not rebalancing (letting equities run), which would have helped returns in the sample period's nearly continuous U.S. equity bull market.

The range of percentage of fund return explained by policy return is shown in Table 23.9. The mutual funds have a wider range because they are more willing to make timing and selection bets against the benchmark.

These results were anticipated by Sharpe (1991). He pointed out that because the aggregation of all investors is the market, the average performance before costs of all investors must equal the performance of the market. Because costs do not net out across investors, the average investor must be underperforming the market on a cost-adjusted basis. The implication is that, on average, more than 100 percent of the level of fund return would be expected from policy return. Of course, this outcome is not assured for subsamples of the market, such as balanced mutual funds or pension funds.

In our analysis, a fund's policy return measures the performance of the asset classes in which that fund invests. Therefore, based on Sharpe's thesis, we would predict that, on average, a little more than 100 percent of the level of total return would be the result of policy return.[4] Our results confirm this prediction.

This is not to say that active management is useless. An investor who has the ability to select superior managers before committing funds can earn above-average returns. If, as Goetzmann and Ibbotson (1994) suggested, superior performance and inferior performance persist over time, one need only invest in the funds that have outperformed in the past. Nevertheless, the average return across all funds in the market cannot be greater than the return on the market.

Summary of Results
Measures of Performance

Percent of *variability* of returns across time explained by asset allocation policy	90%
Percent of variation *between* funds explained by differences in asset allocation policy	40%
Percent of return *amount* explained by asset allocation policy	100%

◤ Conclusion

We sought to answer the question: What part of fund performance is explained by asset allocation policy? If we think of this issue as a multiple-choice question with "40 percent," "90 percent," "100 percent," and "all of the above" as the choices, our analysis shows that asset allocation explains about 90 percent of the variability of a fund's returns *over time* but it explains only about 40 percent of the variation of returns *among funds.* Furthermore, on average across funds, asset allocation policy explains a little more than 100 percent of the *level* of returns. So, because the question can be interpreted in any or all of these ways, the answer is "all of the above."

▲ Notes

1. Return-based style analysis was first proposed by Sharpe (1992). See Lucas (1998) for a detailed discussion.

2. The results are reported in Stevens, Surz, and Wimer, together with the mutual fund results reported here.

3. The average allocations among the general asset classes used in the pension fund study were 43.7 percent U.S. stocks, 38.0 percent U.S. bonds, 5.0 percent cash, and 13.3 percent other asset classes.

4. We have taken out the cost of indexing from the policy return, so the average underperformance of the fund is less than what Sharpe's analysis would suggest.

▲ References

Brinson, Gary P., L. Randolph Hood, and Gilbert L. Beebower. 1986. "Determinants of Portfolio Performance." *Financial Analysts Journal*, vol. 42, no. 4 (July/August): 39–48.

Brinson, Gary P., Brian D. Singer, and Gilbert L. Beebower. 1991. "Determinants of Portfolio Performance II: An Update." *Financial Analysts Journal*, vol. 47, no. 3 (May/June):40–48.

Goetzmann, William N., and Roger G. Ibbotson. 1994. "Do Winners Repeat?" *Journal of Portfolio Management*, vol. 20, no. 2 (Winter):9–18.

Hensel, Chris R., D. Don Ezra, and John H. Ilkiw. 1991. "The Importance of the Asset Allocation Decision." *Financial Analysts Journal*, vol. 47, no. 4 (July/August): 65–72.

Ibbotson Associates. 1998. *Stocks, Bonds, Bills, and Inflation, 1998 Yearbook*. Chicago, IL: Ibbotson Associates.

Ibbotson, Roger G., and Paul D. Kaplan. 2000a. "Does Asset Allocation Policy Explain 40, 90, or 100 Percent of Performance?" *Financial Analysts Journal* (January/February).

———. 2000b. "Does Asset Allocation Policy Explain 40, 90, or 100 Percent of Performance?: Authors' Response." *Financial Analysts Journal* (May/June).

Jahnke, William W. 1997. "The Asset Allocation Hoax." *Journal of Financial Planning*, vol. 10, no. 1 (February):109–113.

Lucas, Lori. 1998. "Analyzing Manager Style." In *Pension Investment Handbook, 1998 Supplement*. Edited by Mark W. Riepe and Scott L. Lummer. New York: Panel Publishers.

Nuttall, Jennifer A., and John Nuttall. 1998. "Asset Allocation Claims—Truth or Fiction?" Unpublished paper.

Sharpe, William F. 1991. "The Arithmetic of Active Management." *Financial Analysts Journal*, vol. 47, no. 1 (January/February):7–9.

———. 1992. "Asset Allocation: Management Style and Performance Measurement." *Journal of Portfolio Management*, vol. 18, no. 2 (Winter):7–19.

Surz, Ronald J., Dale H. Stevens, and Mark E. Wimer. 1999. "The Importance of Investment Policy." *Journal of Investing*, vol. 8, no. 4 (Winter):80–85.

Ang, Andrew, and Geert Bekaert. 2001. Stock return predictability: Is it there? Columbia University and NBER Working Paper.

Arnott, Robert D., and Peter L. Bernstein. 2002. What risk premium is "Normal"? *Financial Analyst Journal* 58 (2): 64–84.

Arnott, Robert D., and Ronald Ryan. 2001. The death of the risk premium: Consequences of the 1990s. *Journal of Portfolio Management* 27 (3): 61–74.

Bakski, Gurdip S., and Zhiwu Chen. 1994. Baby boom, population aging, and capital markets. *Journal of Business* 67 (2): 165–202.

Basu, Devraj. 2001. Conditional diffusions and the equity premium. Working paper. Warwick Business School and SSRN.

Bostrum, Nicholas. 2002. *Anthropic bias: Observation selection effects in science and philosophy.* New York: Routledge.

Boudoukh, Jacob, Matthew Richardson, and Thomas Smith. 1993. Is the ex-ante risk premium always positive? A new approach to testing conditional asset pricing models. *Journal of Financial Economics* 34 (3): 387–408.

Brinson, Gary P., L. Randolph Hood, and Gilbert L. Beebower. 1986. Determinants of portfolio performance. *Financial Analysts Journal* 42 (4): 39–48.

Brinson, Gary P., Brian D. Singer, and Gilbert L. Beebower. 1991. Determinants of portfolio performance II: An update. *Financial Analysts Journal* 47 (3): 40–48.

Campbell, J. Y., and Shiller, R. J. 1988. The dividend-price ratio and expectations of future dividends and discount factors. *Review of Financial Studies* 1:195–228.

———. 1998. Valuation ratios and the long-run stock market outlook. *Journal of Portfolio Management* 24:11–26.

Carhart, Mark M. 1997. On persistence in mutual fund performance. *Journal of Finance* 52 (1): 57–82.

Carhart, Mark M., Jennifer N. Carpenter, and Anthony W. Lynch. 1999. Survivorship bias and attrition effects in measures of performance persistence. *Journal of Financial Economics* 54 (3): 337–374.

Coleman, Thomas S., Lawrence Fisher, and Roger G. Ibbotson. 1993. *Historical U.S. Treasury yield curves.* Moody's Investors Service and Ibbotson Associates.

Constantinides, George. 2002. Rational asset prices. *Journal of Finance,* forthcoming.

Cowles, A. 1934. Can stock market forecasters forecast? *Econometrica* 1:309–324.

———. 1938. Common stock indices, 1871–1937. Cowles Commission for Research in Economics Monograph no. 3. Bloomington, Ind.: Principia Press.

———. 1939. *Common stock prices.* Bloomington, Ind.: Principia Press.

Dimson, Elroy, Paul R. Marsh, and Michael Staunton. 2002. *Triumph of the optimists: 101 years of global investment returns.* Princeton, N.J.: Princeton University Press.

Efron, B. 1979. Bootstrap methods: Another look at the jackknife. *Annals of Statistics* 7:1–26.

Fama, E. F., and K. R. French. 1988a. Dividend yields and expected stock returns. *Journal of Financial Economics* 22:3–26.

———. 1988b. Permanent and temporary components of stock prices. *Journal of Political Economy* 96:246–273.

———. 2002. The equity risk premium. *Journal of Finance* 57 (2): 637–659.

Ferguson, Niall. 1999. *Virtual history: Alternatives and counterfactuals*. New York: Basic Books.

Fisher, L., and J. Lorie. 1964. Rates of return on investments in common stocks. *Journal of Business* 37 (January): 1–21.

———. 1968. Rates of return on investments in common stocks: The year by year record (1926–1965). *Journal of Business* 41:408–431.

———. 1977. *A half century of returns on stocks and bonds: Rates of return on investments in stocks and on U.S. Treasury securities, 1926–1976*. Chicago: University of Chicago Graduate School of Business.

Gordon, Myron. 1962. *The investment financing and valuation of the corporation*. Homewood, Ill.: Irwin.

Goyal, Amit, and Ivo Welch. 2001. Predicting the equity premium with dividend ratios. Working paper. Yale School of Management and UCLA.

Graham, John R., and Campbell R. Harvey. 2001. Expectations of equity risk premia, volatility and asymmetry from a corporate finance perspective. Working paper. Fuqua School of Business and Duke University, August 3.

Hodrick, Robert. 1992. Dividend yields and expected stock returns: Alternative procedures for inference and measurement. *Review of Financial Studies* 5:357–386.

Ibbotson, R. G., and Gary P. Brinson. 1987. *Investment markets*. Englewood Cliffs, N.J.: McGraw-Hill.

———. 1993. *Global investing*. New York: McGraw-Hill.

Kim, M., C. Nelson, and R. Startz. 1991. Mean reversion in stock prices: A reappraisal of the empirical evidence. *Review of Economic Studies* 58:515–528.

Lanne, Markku. 2002. Testing the predictability of stock returns. *Review of Economics and Statistics* 84 (3): 407–415.

Lewellan, Jonathan. 2004. Predicting Returns with Financial Ratios. *Journal of Financial Economics* 74:209–35.

Li, Haitao, and Yuewu Xu. 1999. Can survival bias explain the "equity premium puzzle"? Working paper. Cornell University, Johnson Graduate School of Management.

Mehra, Rajnish, ed. 2002. *Handbook of investments: The equity risk premium*. North Holland Elsevier.

Mehra, Rajnish, and Edward C. Prescott. 1985. The equity premium: A puzzle. *Journal of Monetary Economics* 15:145–161.

Miller, Merton, and Franco Modigliani. 1961. Dividend policy, growth and the valuation of shares. *Journal of Business* 34 (4): 411–433.

Poterba, James M., and Lawrence H. Summers. 1988. Mean reversion in stock prices: evidence and implications. *Journal of Financial Economics* 22:27–59.

Richardson, M., and T. Smith. 1991. Tests of financial models in the presence of overlapping observations. *Review of Financial Studies* 4:224–254.

Roll, Richard. 1978. Ambiguity when performance is measured by the securities market line. *Journal of Finance* 33 (4): 1051–1069.

Ross, Stephen. 1987. Regression to the max. Working paper. Yale School of Management.

Rozeff, M. 1984. Dividend yields are equity risk premiums. *Journal of Portfolio Management* 11:68–75.

Schwert, W. 1989. Why does stock market volatility change over time? *Journal of Finance* 44:1115–1153.

Shiller, R. J. 1989. *Stock market volatility*. Cambridge: MIT Press.

———. 2000. *Irrational exuberance*. Princeton, N.J.: Princeton University Press.

Shiller, Robert J., and John Y. Campbell. 1988. Stock prices, earnings and expected dividends. *Journal of Finance* 43 (3): 661–676.

Siegel, Jeremy J. 1992. *Stocks for the long run: A guide to selecting markets for long-term growth.* New York: McGraw-Hill.

———. 1998. *Stocks for the long run* (2nd ed.) New York: McGraw-Hill.

———. 1999. The shrinking equity premium: Historical facts and future forecasts. *Journal of Portfolio Management* 26 (1): 10–16.

Slotsky, Alice Louise. 1997. *The bourse of Babylon: Market quotations in the astronomical diaries of Babylonia.* Bethesda, Md.: CDL Press.

Swensen, David. 2000. *Pioneering portfolio management.* New York: Free Press.

Welch, I. 2000. View of financial economists on the equity premium and other issues. *Journal of Business* 73 (4): 501–537.

Welch, I., and A. Goyal. 1999. Predicting the equity premium. Working paper. UCLA and Yale University.

Wilson, Jack W., and Charles P. Jones. 1987. A comparison of annual stock returns: 1871–1925 with 1926–85. *Journal of Business* 60 (2): 239–258.

———. 2002. An analysis of the S&P 500 index and Cowles's extensions: Price indices and stock returns, 1870–1999. *Journal of Business* 75 (3): 505–534.

Wolf, M. 2000. Stock returns and dividend yields revisited: A new way to look at an old problem. *Journal of Business and Economic Statistics* 18:18–30.

Asset categories pertain to U.S. if not otherwise specified.

Akaike information criterion (AIC), 277 n. 2
American Stock Exchange (AMEX)
   aggregate value of: (1947–1978), 110–111, 115–116; (1959–1984), 145
   cumulative wealth indices for: (1947–1978), 123–124; (1959–1984), 152
   returns on: (1947–1978), 119–120, 127, 129, 131–132, 134; (1960–1984), 149, 156, 158, 164; (1976–2001), 129, 157; in excess of U.S. T-bill returns (1960–1984), 162
anthropic bias, 281
arbitrage pricing theory (APT) model, 170, 171–172, 184, 185
   vs. CAPM model, 22
   development of, 210 n. 2
   and pricing characteristics, 192
Argentina
   as reemerging market, 366
   beta of, and recency of emergence, 384, 385
   historical market performance, 343, 347, 350, 352, 355, 373, 389, 390
   IFC coverage information, 389
   length of market life, 370
   market founding date, 369
   risk and return characteristics of, 390
art
   pricing characteristics of, 197
   total world value of (1984), 141
artificial intelligence techniques, 420–422. *See also* neural-network techniques
asset allocation
   Brinson studies of, 523–524, 526–528
   importance of in overall portfolio performance, 405 *(see also ch. 23)*
asset allocation models
   inputs required in, 175
   strategic vs. tactical, 175–176 *(see also ch. 6)*
asset allocation policy
   effects of on performance *(see ch. 23)*

asset pairs
   forecasting standard deviation of returns on, 181
assets
   characteristic-free, 186–187
   investor demand for, 187–188
   pricing characteristics of *(see* pricing characteristics)
   supply of, 187
Australia
   historical market performance, 33, 342, 343, 346, 348, 355, 373
   market founding date, 369
Austria
   effects of WWII on market, 340, 350, 370
   historical market performance, 342, 343, 346, 348, 354, 373
   length of market life, 388
   market founding date, 369
autocorrelation
   of long-term holding period returns, 292–294
   problems with using, 235, 454
autocorrelation studies
   long-term, 283, 284
autoregression
   and nonoverlapping returns, 463–464

Babylon, market history, 431
backfilling
   conditioning on, 366–367
backfilling bias, 366, 386
banker acceptances
   total value of in 1984, 142–143
bear markets
   defined, 409–410
   and variation in returns, 524
   See also ch. 18
Belgium
   effects of WWII on market, 350, 370
   historical market performance, 342, 343, 346, 348, 354, 373
   market founding date, 369

beta
    and emerging markets, 367, 377, 379–
        380, 381
    and recency of market emergence, 379–
        380, 381, 383–385
beta (market) risk, 199 n. 7
    defined, 192–193
    on various asset classes, 197
bias
    and backfilling, 355 (see also backfilling
        bias)
    data mining, 516
    due to dividend growth, 509–511
    and market interruptions, 355
    types of in U.S. and U.K. data, 438
    See also specific types of bias
bills. See U.S. Treasury bills
bonds, 9
    as component of world wealth (1959–
        1984), 139, 143–144, 148, 155
    corporate (see corporate bonds)
    correlation with stocks, 181
    duration of, 70 n. 10
    flower (see flower bonds)
    forecasting standard deviation of returns
        on, 178, 181
    historical risk of, 178
    non-U.S (see foreign bonds)
    U.S. government (see U.S. government
        bonds)
bootstrap
    moving blocks, 482
bootstrapping, 31
    defined, 3, 233, 478
    and dividend yields, 479, 500–501
    to test long-term stock market efficiency
        (see ch. 20)
Bowland, Chelcie, 28
Brazil
    historical market performance, 342,
        343, 347, 355, 373, 389, 390
    IFC coverage information, 389
    length of market life, 370
    market founding date, 369
    risk and return characteristics of,
        390
Brownian path, 286, 289, 290, 301
Buenos Aires Stock Exchange, 353. See
    also Argentina

building blocks method, 9, 36, 169–170,
    216–217, 218
    components of, 170
buildup method
    cost of equity estimate (year-end 2001),
        177
bull markets
    defined, 409–410
    and variation in returns, 524
    See also ch. 18
buy indicators, 422–423

Canada
    historical market performance, 342,
        343, 346, 348, 354, 373
    market founding date, 369
capital asset pricing model (CAPM), 21–
    22, 25, 37, 170, 171–172, 184, 185
    development of, 30, 31, 210 n. 2
    and diversification, 193–194
    and pricing characteristics, 192
capital
    income shares of (1929–1981), 204
    supply of/demand for, vs. supply of/de-
        mand for returns, 210 n. 3
capital market
    growth rates (1926–1982), 206
    long-term performance (1925–2001), 18
    returns on (1947–1978), 134
cash (and equivalents)
    aggregate value of: (1959–1984), 147;
        (1984), 141, 142
    as component of world wealth: (1959–
        1984), 138, 143–144, 148, 155
    correlation with other world/U.S. secu-
        rities, 22, 158–161
    cumulative wealth indices for (1959–
        1984), 154
    forecasting standard deviation of returns
        on, 178–179
    non-U.S. (see foreign cash)
    returns on: (1959/60–1984), 151, 156,
        164–165; (1976–2001), 157; in ex-
        cess of U.S. T-bills (1959–1984),
        162–163
    See also under world market wealth port-
        folio, theoretical
Center for Research in Security Prices
    (CRSP), 29–30, 42, 74–75, 371

Chile, 366
  beta of, and recency of emergence,
    384
  historical market performance, 342,
    343, 347, 350, 352–353, 356, 362 n.
    18, 373, 389, 390
  IFC coverage information, 389
  length of market life, 388
  market founding date, 369
  risk and return characteristics of, 390
China, 366
  historical market performance, 389,
    390
  IFC coverage information, 389
  risk and return characteristics of, 390
Colombia, 366
  historical market performance, 342,
    343, 347, 355, 373, 389, 390
  IFC coverage information, 389
  length of market life, 370
  market founding date, 369
  risk and return characteristics of, 390
colonialism, 368, 370
commercial paper, 108
  aggregate value of: (1947–1978), 110–
    111, 115–116; (1959–1984), 147;
    (1984), 143
  correlation with other world/U.S. secu-
    rities, 158–161
  cumulative wealth indices for: (1947–
    1978), 123–124; (1959–1984), 154,
    155
  returns on: (1792–1925), 35; (1947–
    1978), 119–120, 127, 128, 130–132,
    134; (1959/60–1984), 151, 156,
    164–165; (1976–2001), 157; in ex-
    cess of U.S. T-bills (1947–1978), 128,
    133
commodity funds, 308, 330 n. 2
common stock, 108, 109
  aggregate value of: (1947–1978), 110–
    111, 114, 115–116
  cumulative wealth indices for: (1947–
    1978), 123–124, 127
  market value weighted, 43–44
  returns on: (1925/6–1974, *see ch. 2, 11*);
    (1947–1978), 114, 119–120, 127,
    128, 131–132, 134; in excess of U.S.
    T-bills (1926–1974), 49, 55; in excess

of U.S. T-bills (1947–1978), 128,
  133; forecast vs. realized (1976–
  2000), 251, 254, 256–259
Common Stock Indices (Cowles), 29
Common Stocks as Long Term Investments
  (Smith), 27–29
Commonfund, 272
computer simulation. *See* simulation
computer techniques, 4. *See also* artificial
  intelligence techniques; bootstrapping; evolutionary computation; feature vector analysis (FEVA); neural-
  network techniques; simulation
Congo, 368
constant-dividend-growth (Gordon)
  model, 215, 225, 496
consumer goods
  returns on (1926–1974), 42, 48, 56–57,
    62
  total world and U.S. values of (1984),
    141–142
Consumer Price Index (CPI)
  discussed, 71 n. 16
  index of year-end cumulative wealth
    relatives (1925–1974), 56–57
  problems when used as cost-of-living
    measure, 48
  returns on (1926–1974), 62
corporate bonds, 108, 109
  aggregate value of: (1947–1978), 110–
    111, 114, 115–116; (1959–1984),
    146; (1984), 142–143
  correlation with other world/U.S. secu-
    rities, 158–161
  cumulative wealth indices for: (1947–
    1978), 123–124, 127; (1959–1984),
    153
  returns on: (1926–1974; *see ch. 2, 11*);
    (1947–1978), 119–120, 127, 128,
    131–132, 134; (1959/60–1984), 144,
    150, 156, 164–165; (1976–2001),
    148; in excess of government bonds
    (1926–1974), 49, 55, 56–57, 58–59;
    in excess of U.S. T-bills (1947–1978),
    128, 133; in excess of U.S. T-bills
    (1959–1984), 162–163; forecast vs.
    realized (1976–2000), 251, 254, 258,
    260, 261
  studies of, compared, 66

corporate securities, 108, 109
  aggregate value of (1947–1978), 110–
    111, 114, 115–116
  cumulative wealth indices for (1947–
    1978), 123–124
  returns on: (1947–1978), 114, 119–120,
    127, 128, 131–132, 134; (1976–
    2001), 129; in excess of U.S. T-bills
    (1947–1978), 128, 130, 133
Cowles, Alfred, 361 n. 7
  and analysis of Dow Theory, 407–408,
    411–412, 427
  and bootstrapping in the space of strate-
    gies, 418
  Common Stock Indices, 29
Cowles indices, 29, 74, 83, 361 n. 5, 438
  problems with, 29, 34, 75, 85, 467–468
  statistical tests of: (1871–1986), 468–
    470; (1872–1925), 470–471
  in test of Dow Theory, 414–415
crashes
  consideration of in sampling, 336, 349
  See also disappearance events
credit risk
  and political risk, 396, 398 n. 16
cross-product ratio, 330 n. 4
Czechoslovakia, 366
  effects of WWII on market, 350, 370
  historical market performance, 342,
    343, 346, 354
  length of market life, 388
  market founding date, 369

data, historical, 8
  breaks in, 370–371, 385
  demand for, 19
  long-term vs. short-term, 396–397
  for LSE, 433–436 (see also London
    Stock Exchange [LSE])
  for NYSE: (1792–present), 33; (1815–
    1925) (see ch. 3; see also New York
    Stock Exchange [NYSE])
  problems with using, 81–82, 87–88,
    279, 467–468, 496–498, 516; when
    U.S.-only, 280, 338, 360
  and survival bias, 302 (see also survival
    bias)
  vanished vs. recorded, 3–4, 32

world market, 284, 285, 304 nn. 2–4
  (see also stock markets, historical)
default premia, 71 n. 17
  1926–1974, 49, 55 (see also ch. 11)
  See also corporate bonds, returns on, in
    excess of government bonds (1926–
    1974)
delisting
  effects of on returns, 371
demand perspective, 9 (see also forecasting
  methods, demand)
Denmark
  effects of WWII on market, 350
  historical market performance, 342,
    343, 346, 348, 354, 373
  market founding date, 369
disappearance events, 350–353, 356, 361
  n. 3
  and emerging markets, 516–517
  and reemerging markets, 366
  probability of, 513
  simulation of, 512–513
  temporary vs. permanent, 355
discounted flow (DCF) model, 170, 172–
  173
  one-factor Gordon, 172
  See also ch. 8
dividend discount model. See ch. 8
dividend growth
  biasing effect on returns, 509–511
dividend payouts
  ratio (1926–2000), 223
  U.S., relative to other countries', 345–
    347, 348
dividend yields, 475–477
  bootstrapping, 479
  changing significance of, 516
  forecasts of, historical vs. current, 225,
    228
  in forecasting stock returns, 88, 89, 94,
    404–405 (see also ch. 21–22)
  long-term (see ch. 22)
  and monthly NYSE data, 495
  NYSE (1825–1999), 89, 92–93
  predictive power of, 88, 92–93 (see also
    ch. 11)
  recent history of diminishing, 173–174,
    404

regressions, 498–501, 504–511
tests of long-horizon returns on, 490–491
trends in (1825–1870), 80–81
See also forecasting methods, dividends
divisibility costs
defined, 195
on various asset classes, 197
Dow, Charles Henry, 27, 401, 408–409
Dow Jones Index
problems with, 467–468
statistical tests of (1885–1988), 468–470
Dow Jones Industrial Average
forecast of 10,000, 234, 267–268
forecast of 100,000, 234–235, 269
See also ch. 11
Dow Theory, 401–403, 405, 431
ambiguity of, 418
main axioms of, 409, 428 nn. 2–3
See also ch. 18

efficient markets assumption, 235
and Alfred Cowles, 411
Egypt, 366
historical market performance, 342, 343, 347, 350, 352–353, 355
market founding date, 369
emergence. *See* market emergence
emergence events, 381–383
emerging markets, 280–281
biases related to, 366–367
classification of some surviving markets as, 286
covered by IFC, 389
and credit ratings, 396
defined, 280, 365–366, 369
vs. developed markets, 372–374
distinguishing features, 366
empirical analysis of, 385–396
IFC definition of, 386
list of, 373
performance of, 389–391
predictability of, 516–517
and preemergence vs. postemergence data, 281
vs. reemerging markets, 361 n. 3, 366, 375

and return bias vs. year of last emergence, 377–379
risk and return characteristics of, 390–391
selection of, 385–386
and survivorship, 369–374
volatility of, 284
See also market emergence; reemerging markets
equities
Asian, 142, 144, 145, 149, 152, 156, 158–161, 162–163, 164–165
as component of world wealth (1959–1984), 138, 143–144, 148, 155
effect of dividend growth on returns (1872–1989), 509–511
European, 142, 145, 149, 152, 156, 157, 158–161, 162–163, 164–165
regressions on real and nominal returns (1872–1992), 504–508
return and risk for (1872–1992), 502–504
U.S. and foreign: aggregate value of (1959–1984), 145; aggregate value of (1984), 141, 142; correlation with other world/U.S. securities, 158–161; cumulative wealth indices of (1959–1984), 152; returns on (1959–1984), 164–165; returns on (1960–1984), 144, 149, 156; returns on (1976–2001), 157; returns on, in excess of U.S. T-bills (1959–1984), 162–163
equity investing, historical trends in, 3
19th century *(see ch. 3)*
equity premium puzzle, 18, 25, 280, 347–350
critique by Reitz, 32
defined, 347
equity returns
calculated for 1926–2001, 17
components of historical, 224
forecasting, 87–88 *(see also* forecasting methods)
geometric vs. arithmetic estimates of, 227, 229 n. 1, 229–230 n. 3
methods for decomposing historical, 216–223
tests of volatility of, 94–98
See also stock returns

equity risk premium, 215, 229 n. 1
    categories of studies of, 215, 230 n. 3
    defined, 7, 15–16, 212, 345
    difficulty of determining historical, 20–
        21, 25
    dynamic vs. constant, 11, 230 n. 7
    estimating future, 9, 10, 31; methods
        for, 10, 31–32, 230 n. 5 (*see also* fore-
        casting methods)
    expected vs. realized, 7, 17, 18, 32
    formula, 15–16
    geometric vs. arithmetic estimates of,
        227, 229 n. 1, 229–230 n. 3
    on global stock market database, 339–
        340
    historical data on (*see* data, historical)
    historical development of (*see ch. 1*)
    importance of, 7, 21 (*see also ch. 1*)
    and international capital markets, 21, 345
    and long-term investment, 8
    predicting, 401–406
    predictive power of, 88
    vs. riskless rate, 176
    and supply/demand of risk capital, 9–
        10, 11
    survival explanation for, 32, 337 (*see
        also* survivorship)
    variability of, 11–12
    See also risk premium
equity shares, categories of, 78
errors-in-variables problem, 509–511
estimation risk, 383
event studies, 284–285
    analysis of Dow Industrial Index around
        W.P. Hamilton's editorials, 408, 412–
        420
    postearnings drift, 298–299
    stock splits, 299–301
    See also crashes
evolutionary computation, 421, 428 n. 8
expectations hypothesis, 239, 245

feature vector analysis (FEVA), 420–423,
        427–428
financial archaeology, 5, 360
financial intermediaries, role of, 191, 195–
        196
Finland
    effects of WWII on market, 350

historical market performance, 342,
        343, 346, 354, 373
    market founding date, 369
Fisher, Irving, 28, 29
Fisher's *exact test*, 330 n. 4
flower bonds, 44–45, 251
forecasting methods, 169–174
    building blocks model, 169–170 (*see
        also* building blocks method)
    buildup method, 175 (*see also ch. 6*)
    capital gain, 218–219, 222, 228
    consensus, 171
    demand, 171–172, 208–210, 214–215
        (*see also ch. 7–8*)
    dividends, 219–221, 223, 225–226,
        228; vs. earnings, 226–227
    and dividend yields (*see ch. 21*)
    earnings, 218–219, 223, 224, 228
    GDP per capita, 222–223, 228, 230–
        231 n. 17
    historical, 31, 171, 204, 207, 214–215
        (*see also* standard deviation of returns,
        forecasting methods; *and ch. 2–5*)
    income return, 218, 223, 228
    investor surveys, 214–215
    long-term, 223–227 (*see also ch. 10*)
    return on book value of equity, 221–
        222, 228
    simulation, 10, 233–235 (*see also* simu-
        lation)
    supply, 172–174, 202, 206–210, 214–
        215 (*see also ch. 8*)
    See also arbitrage pricing theory (APT)
        model; capital asset pricing model
        (CAPM); discounted flow (DCF)
        model
forecasts
    and long-term data, 494
    of long-term market performance, 401–
        406
    misvaluation, 235
    potential uses of, 235
foreign bonds
    aggregate value of: (1959–1984), 146;
        (1984), 142
    correlation with other world/U.S. secu-
        rities, 158–161
    price-level-indexed in high-inflation
        countries, 200 n. 16

returns on: (1959/60–1984), 150, 156, 162–163, 164–165; (1960–1987), 178; correlations with other asset class returns (1971–1987), 182; in excess of U.S. T-bills, 162–163
U.S. government (*see* government bonds)
See also *under* world market wealth portfolio, theoretical
foreign cash
aggregate value of: (1959–1984), 147; (1984), 141, 142
correlation with other world/U.S. securities, 158–161
cumulative wealth indices for (1959–1984), 154
returns on: (1959–1984), 151, 156, 164–165; in excess of U.S. T-bills (1959–1984), 162–163
foreign stocks
returns on (1960–1987), 178
See also stocks, returns on, components of; stocks, forecasting standard deviation of returns on; *and specific country subentries*
forward rates
computing, 239–240
as revealed market expectations, 245, 247
Foundation for the Study of Cycles, 436, 451 n. 3
France
effects of WWII on market, 350, 370
historical market performance, 342, 343, 346, 348, 354, 373
market founding date, 369, 397 n. 5
free-lunch hypothesis, 366
funds
performance of, and survivorship *(see ch. 15)*
See also *specific kinds of funds*

Germany
beta of, and recency of emergence, 384
effects of WWII on market, 340, 341–342, 344–345, 350, 352, 495
historical market performance, 340, 341–342, 343, 346, 348, 354, 373

length of market life, 388
market founding date, 369
global markets
performance characteristics of, 373
real returns on, 384–385
gold
pricing characteristics of, 197
See also monetary metals
Gordon constant-dividend-growth model, 214–215, 225
Great Panic of 1907, 401, 402
Greece
effects of WWII on market, 350
historical market performance, 342, 343, 346, 352, 354, 389, 390
IFC coverage information, 389
length of market life, 388
market founding date, 369
risk and return characteristics of, 390
gross domestic product (GDP)
aggregate, 172 *(see also ch. 8)*
as weight of relative market performance in global index, 353–355
gross national product (GNP)
decade and per capita data (1889–1982), 203–204, 205
growth rates (1926–1982), 206

Hamilton, William Peter, 401–403 *(see also ch. 18)*
Henriksson-Merton (HM) test, 413–414
holding period, analysis of variance of long-horizon, 292–298
Hong Kong, market founding date, 369
"hot hands," in mutual-fund management, 308, 310–311, 330 n. 5
human capital
constraints on diversification of, 194
and divisibility costs, 195
pricing characteristics of, 197
Hungary
effects of WWII on market, 350, 370
historical market performance, 342, 343, 346, 354, 389, 390
IFC coverage information, 389
length of market life, 388
market founding date, 369
risk and return characteristics of, 390

India, 366
  historical market performance, 342,
    343, 347, 355, 373, 389, 390
  IFC coverage information, 389
  market founding date, 369
  risk and return characteristics of, 390
Indonesia
  historical market performance, 389, 390
  IFC coverage information, 389
  market founding date, 369
  risk and return characteristics of, 390
inflation
  and capital market returns of major
    world/U.S. asset classes, 157, 164–165
  and real estate returns, 179–180
  returns on: (1792–2004), 35; (1926–
    1974), 268; (1926–1987), 178;
    (1960–1984), 156; (1976–2000),
    268; (1976–2001), 157; correlations
    with other asset class returns (1971–
    1987), 182; predicted (1999–2025),
    268–269; simulated (1976–2000, see
    ch. 11)
inflation risk
  defined, 193
  and taxation costs, 200 n. 14
  on various asset classes, 197
information costs
  defined, 195
  on various asset classes, 197
International Finance Corporation (IFC)
  discussed, 339, 340, 368, 386
  emerging markets covered by, 389, 398
    n. 14
  indices: backfilling in, 386; country and
    company selection issues in, 386; to
    date emergence, 389; survival in,
    386–388
International Monetary Fund (IMF), 339,
    340
investors
  ability of to hold foreign equities during
    crises, 354, 362 n. 15, 370
  and beta risk, 199 n. 7
  and demand and supply equilibrium,
    187–192
  demand of for assets, 187–188
  demand of for risk, 12 (see also forecast-
    ing methods, demand)

  and emerging markets, 366, 376, 380,
    389
  expectations of, 35, 196–198, 199 n. 6
  historical experience of (see ch. 1)
  and perceptions of assets, 184–185,
    187
  and perceptions of financial intermedi-
    aries, 192
  role of: in Dow Theory, 409, 411; in
    pre-WWI United Kingdom, 507–
    508
  surveys of, 171 (see also under forecasting
    methods)
  and view of equity risk premium, 7
Ireland
  historical market performance, 342,
    343, 346, 354, 373
  market founding date, 369
Israel
  historical market performance, 342,
    343, 347, 355
  market founding date, 369
Italy
  historical market performance, 342,
    343, 346, 348, 354, 373
  length of market life, 388
  market founding date, 369

Japan
  beta of, and recency of emergence, 384
  effects of WWII on market, 340, 342,
    344–345, 350, 362 n. 17, 370, 495
  historical market performance, 342,
    343, 344–345, 346, 348, 352, 353,
    355, 357, 373
Jordan
  historical market performance, 389, 390
  IFC coverage information, 389
  risk and return characteristics of, 390

Kenya
  market founding date, 369
Kondratieff 50-year wave theory, 436
Korea
  effects of WWII on market, 370
  historical market performance, 389, 390
  IFC coverage information, 389
  market founding date, 369
  risk and return characteristics of, 390

Kuwait
   market founding date, 369
   market history, 387

L'Etat Independent du Congo, 368
labor
   income shares of (1929–1981), 204
lagged dependent variable problem, 404
Lebanon, market founding date, 369
liquidity premium, 55
   vs. maturity premium, 264 n. 7
London Stock Exchange (LSE), 87
   capital appreciation index for: (1700–
      1989), 433–436, 438–440; autore-
      gression and rescaled range statistics,
      444–446, 448–449; summary statis-
      tics, 439
   history of, 433–436
look-ahead bias, 314
Luxembourg
   effects of WWII on market, 370
   market founding date, 369

macroconsistency, 208
Malaysia, 366
   effects of WWII on market, 370
   historical market performance, 389,
      390
   IFC coverage information, 389
   market founding date, 369
   risk and return characteristics of, 390
management styles, 314
many worlds hypothesis, 281
market breaks
   frequency of, 388
market emergence
   average returns around, 381–383
   expected returns before, after, and
      around, 391–396
   preemergence vs. postemergence re-
      turns, 382
   reasons for, 374–375
   recency of: and beta, 379–380, 381; and
      bias, 383–385; and drift, 374–375;
      and R^2, 380; and sur-
      vival bias, 378
   time of, defined, 369
   year of last, conditioning on, 367, 374–
      375, 380

market history
   length of, 367, 377, 383–385 (see also
      under individual countries)
market risk. See beta (market) risk
market simulation. See forecasting meth-
      ods, simulation
market wealth portfolio, U.S. See U.S.
      market wealth portfolio (theoretical)
market wealth portfolio, world. See world
      market wealth portfolio (theoretical)
marketability
   on various asset classes, 198, 197
   costs, 194–195
markets, reemerging. See reemerging mar-
      kets
Markowitz model, 19, 30, 40 n. 13, 270,
      276
Markowitz optimization software, 235
maturity premium, 71 n. 17
   1926–1974, 55, 60–61 (see also ch. 11)
   vs. liquidity premium, 264 n. 7
maximum performer, conditioning on,
      302–303
mean reversion, 88–89, 90–91, 431, 432,
      455–458
   long-term, 470–471
   in stock price indices, 403
   tests of long-term, 455–467
   and white noise in stock prices, 457
mean-variance optimization
   defined, 271
   distribution vs. average of bias in, 383
Mexico, 366
   historical market performance, 342,
      343, 347, 355, 373, 389, 390
   IFC coverage information, 389
   length of market life, 370, 388
   market founding date, 369
   risk and return characteristics of, 390
Mill, John Stuart, 26–27, 39 n. 1
Miller-Modigliani theory, 39–40 n. 9, 216,
      226
modern portfolio theory, 108–109
   and world market wealth portfolio, 140
monetary metals, 181
   as component of world wealth (1959–
      1984), 138, 143–144, 148, 155 (see
      also under world market wealth port-
      folio, theoretical)

monetary metals (*continued*)
correlation with other world/U.S. securities, 158–161
forecasting standard deviation of returns on, 180–181
returns on: (1959–1984), 164–165; in excess of U.S. T-bills (1959–1984), 162–163
money managers, performance of. *See ch. 15*
Morgan Stanley Capital International Perspectives (MSCIP), 339
moving average (MA) trading rule, 420
municipal (state and local) bonds, 108
aggregate value of (1947–1978), 109, 112–113, 114, 117–118
cumulative wealth indices of (1947–1978), 125–126, 127
pricing characteristics of, 197
returns on: (1947–1978), 114, 121–122, 127, 128, 130, 131–132, 134; in excess of U.S. T-bills (1947–1978), 128, 133
mutual funds
and asset allocation policy. *See also ch. 23*
performance of, and asset allocation policy, 523–524
studies of, 405 *(see also ch. 23)*
survivorship of, 307–314, 330 nn. 3, 6, 330–331 n. 7

Netherlands, the
effects of WWII on market, 350, 370
historical market performance, 342, 343, 346, 348, 354, 373
length of market life, 388
market founding date, 369
neural-network techniques, 403, 408, 418, 420–422, 424–426, 427–428, 428 n. 7, 429 nn. 10, 14. *See also* artificial intelligence techniques
new equilibrium theory (NET), 202
model, 184, 185 *(see also ch. 7)*
New York Shipping List, 78
New York Stock Exchange (NYSE) 1815–1999 *(see ch. 3)*
aggregate value of: (1947–1978), 110–111, 115–116; (1959–1984), 145

capital appreciation index for: (1790–1989), 436–440; summary statistics, 439; autoregression and rescaled range statistics, 444–450
cumulative wealth indices for: (1947–1978), 123–124; (1959–1984), 152
history of, 436–438 *(see also ch. 3)*
returns on: (1792–present), 33; (1792–1925), 35; (1947–1978), 114, 119–120, 127, 128, 131–132, 134; (1960–1984), 149, 156; (1976–2001), 129, 157; correlation with other world/U.S. securities, 158–161; in excess of U.S. T-Bills (1960–1984), 162; regressed to inflation, 164
statistical tests of (1834–1988), 456–467, 468–470
tests of similarity to Cowles indices, 470–471
New Zealand
historical market performance, 342, 343, 346, 355, 373
market founding date, 369
Nigeria
historical market performance, 389, 390
IFC coverage information, 389
market founding date, 369
market history, 387, 398 n. 12
risk and return characteristics of, 390
noise, in stock prices, 455, 456, 457
Norway
effects of WWII on market, 350, 370
historical market performance, 342, 343, 346, 348, 354, 373
market founding date, 369

Old NYSE research project, 78. *See also ch. 3*
optimization software, 235
over-the-counter (OTC) stock, 107, 108, 109, 114
aggregate value of: (1947–1978), 110–111, 115–116; (1959–1984), 145; (1984), 142–143
correlation with other world/U.S. securities, 158–161
cumulative wealth indices for: (1947–1978), 123–124; (1959–1984), 152

returns on: (1947–1978), 119–120, 127, 128, 130, 131–132, 134; (1959–1984), 164–165; (1960–1984), 149, 156; in excess of U.S. T-bills (1947–1978), 128, 133; in excess of U.S. T-bills (1959–1984), 162–163

P/E ratio, 212–213
   current vs. historical, 226–227
   expansion of, 32
   on U.S. equity (1926–2000), 219, 220
   See also ch. 10
Pakistan
   historical market performance, 342, 343, 347, 355, 373, 389, 390
   IFC coverage information, 389
   market founding date, 369
   risk and return characteristics of, 390
payout ratios
   current vs. historical, 226–227
pension funds, 308, 330 n. 3
   and asset allocation policy
   studies of, 405
   See also ch. 23
performance
   conditioning on cumulative vs. one-period, 328–329, 331 n. 8
Peru
   beta and recency of emergence, 384, 385
   historical market performance, 342, 347, 355, 373, 389, 390
   IFC coverage information, 389
   risk and return characteristics of, 390
peso problems, 349, 397 n. 4, 495
Philippines, the
   historical market performance, 342, 343, 347, 355, 373, 389, 390
   IFC coverage information, 389
   market founding date, 369
   risk and return characteristics of, 390
Poland, 366
   effects of WWII on market, 350, 352, 370
   historical market performance, 342, 343, 346, 350, 354, 389, 390
   IFC coverage information, 389
   market founding date, 369
   market life of, 388
   risk and return characteristics of, 390

Portugal
   beta of, and recency of emergence, 384, 385
   effects of WWII on market, 370
   historical market performance, 342, 343, 346, 350, 352, 354, 373, 389, 390
   IFC coverage information, 389
   length of market life, 388
   market founding date, 369
   market history, 512
   risk and return characteristics of, 390
postearnings drift, 298–299
preferred stock
   aggregate value of: (1947–1978), 110–111, 115–116; (1984), 142–143
   cumulative wealth indices for (1947–1978), 123–124
   in matrix of U.S. capital market returns (1947–1978), 127, 131–132
   returns on: (1947–1978), 119–120, 128, 133, 134; in excess of U.S. T-bills (1947–1978), 128, 133
price paths, properties of, 286–291
pricing characteristics, 192–196, 197. *See also* marketability, costs; risk characteristics; taxability
Principles of Political Economy (Mill), 26–27, 39 n. 1

R^2
   and recency of market emergence, 377, 379–381
random-walk model
   alternatives to, 455–456
rates of return
   magnitude of effects of, 338, 359–360
real estate, 107, 108
   aggregate value of: (1947–1978), 110–111, 114, 115–116, 123–124; (1959–1984), 147; (1984), 141
   as component of world wealth (1959–1984), 138, 142–143, 148, 155
   correlation with other world/U.S. securities, 158–161
   cumulative wealth indices of: (1947–1978), 123–124, 127; (1959–1984), 154
   forecasting standard deviation of returns on, 179–180

real estate (*continued*)
  foreign, value of in 1984, 141, 142
  houses and condos, pricing characteristics of, 197
  in matrix of U.S. capital market returns (1947–1978), 127, 131–132
  returns on: (1947–1978), 114, 119–120, 127, 128, 131–132, 134; (1959–1984), 164–165; (1960–1984), 151, 156; (1971–1987), 178; correlations with other asset class returns (1971–1987), 182; in excess of U.S. T-bills (1947–1978), 128, 130, 133; in excess of U.S. T-bills (1959–1984), 162–163; and inflation rate, 179
  See also under U.S. market wealth portfolio, theoretical; world market wealth portfolio, theoretical
real interest rate risk
  defined, 193
  on various asset classes, 197
reemerging market hypothesis, 281
reemerging markets, 11
  defined, 366
  and survival bias, 11
  See also Chile; Peru; Portugal; *and ch. 17*
regressions
  problems with long-horizon, 403–404
rescaled range statistic (R/S), 432–433, 442–443
residual risk
  cost of, on various asset classes, 197
  defined, 193–194
returns
  analysis of historical (1926–1974), 240–245
  equilibrium view of, 208–210
  geometric vs. arithmetic, 344
  supply of/demand for *(see ch. 8)*
  and supply of/demand for risk capital, 9–10
  variability of, and asset allocation policy *(see ch. 23)*
  variance ratios of long-term, 293–298
  and volatility, 314–318
Rhea, Robert, 409–410
risk capital, 9–10
risk characteristics, 192–194, 200 n. 13.
  See also specific types of risk

risk premium, 71 n. 17
  1926–1974, 49–55, 60–61 *(see also ch. 11)*
Risk, Uncertainty and Profit (Knight), 27
riskless rate, 175, 176, 177, 345
  as benchmark in testing Dow Theory, 408
  vs. equity risk premium, 176, 177
  historical, difficulty of determining, 34, 37
riskless security, 347
Romania, 366
  effects of WWII on market, 350
  historical market performance, 342, 346, 350
  length of market life, 388
  market founding date, 369
Russia, market history, 495

S&P. *See* Standard and Poor's (S&P)
Salomon Brothers' High Grade Long-Term Corporate Bond Index, 45–46, 70–71 n. 11
samples
  long-term vs. short-term, 467–471
  size of, and test power, 432
  small: attempts to extract more data from, 432; problems with, 403–404
scrip, 78
search and transaction costs
  defined, 195
  on various asset classes, 197
securities
  "bad" characteristics of, 186
  pricing characteristics of, 197
segmentation hypothesis, 372
selection bias, 10, 279–282
  company-level vs. exchange-level, 371
  in construction of global stock market database, 340
  and historical NYSE data, 75
  See also survival bias
sell indicators, 422–423
Shanghai, effects of WWII on market, 370
Sharpe-Lintner-Mossin capital asset pricing model. *See* capital asset pricing model (CAPM)
silver. *See* monetary metals

simulation
    1976–2000 (see ch. 11)
    and college endowments, 272
    of global markets model (see ch. 17)
    for investment management, 272
    of market emergence, 376–385
    and short-horizon vs. long-horizon in-
        puts (see ch. 13)
    of survivorship, 512–516
    of trading strategy, 414–415, 416 (see
        also neural-network techniques)
Singapore, market founding date, 369
Slovenia
    effects of WWII on market, 370
    market founding date, 369
Smart Investor, The, 6
Smith, Edgar Lawrence, 27–29, 31
sorting bias, 280
    and emerging markets, 378, 379–381
South Africa
    historical market performance, 342,
        343, 347, 355
    market capitalization of, 398 n. 15
    market founding date, 369
Spain
    historical market performance, 342,
        343, 346, 348, 350, 354, 373
    length of market life, 388
    market founding date, 369
Sri Lanka
    historical market performance, 389, 390
    IFC coverage information, 389
    market founding date, 369
    risk and return characteristics of, 390
Standard and Poor's (S&P) 500, returns on
    (1926–1987), 178
Standard and Poor's (S&P) Composite In-
    dex
    beta distribution (1927–1990), 479,
        482, 484
    bootstrap on total returns (1927–1990),
        479–481, 484–487
    discussed, 43
    and dividend yields (1927–1990), 475–
        491
    long-horizon dividend yield regressions
        (1927–1990), 476, 479
    summary statistics (1927–1990), 17,
        484, 488–489

standard deviation of returns, forecasting,
    177–183
stocks
    as component of world wealth, 138
    correlation with bonds, 181
    estimated VAR and OLS coefficients on,
        272–273
    forecasting standard deviation of returns
        on, 177, 180, 181
    Japanese, 181
    non-U.S. (see foreign stocks)
    pricing characteristics of, 197
    returns on: (1825–1925), 20, 21;
        (1926–1974), 268; (1926–1987), 178
        (see also ch. 2); (1926–2002), 17, 20;
        (1976–2000), 268; components of,
        176; correlations with other asset
        class returns: (1971–1987), 182;
        (1976–2002), 17; in excess of bonds,
        12; predicted (1999–2025), 268–
        269; with short- vs. long-horizon in-
        put frontiers (see ch. 13); simulations
        of (1976–2000) (see ch. 11)
    small stock premium, 180
    See also common stock; equities; pre-
        ferred stock
stock market indices. See American Stock
        Exchange (AMEX); Cowles indices;
        London Stock Exchange (LSE); New
        York Stock Exchange (NYSE)
stock markets, historical, 284, 285–286,
        291–292, 368, 370
    distribution of market lives, 388
    long-term vs. short-term, 383–385
    time line of founding dates, 369
    See also individual country entries; and
        ch. 16
stock returns
    comparison of studies of, 66, 70 n. 7
    long-run (see ch. 9–10)
    See also equity returns; returns
stock splits, 299–301
supply-side models, 9. See also forecasting
        methods, supply
survival
    conditioning on, 302–303, 331 n. 8, 367
survival bias, 10–11, 285, 511–516
    in Cowles and other historical indexes,
        438

survival bias (*continued*)
  and emerging markets, 371–372, 378–
    379, 381
  and ex post returns, 336, 348
  and historical NYSE data, 89
  in performance studies (*see ch. 15*)
  measured with fixed vs. variable floor,
    513–515
  and reemerging markets, 11
  relationship of to sorting bias, 381
  in U.S. and U.K. data, 404–405
  See also survivorship
survival effect
  in IFC indices, 386–387
survival hypothesis, 36, 281
survival probability, differing views of,
  291–292
survival threshold, 279
survivorship, 279–282, 371
  consequences of, 366–367, 397 n. 4
  and dividend yield regressions, 499
  and emerging markets, 369–374
  as explanation for high U.S. equity risk
    premium, 36, 337, 338
  as explanation of Dow Theory success,
    426
  and long-term stock market predictions,
    494–496
  magnitude of persistence in perfor-
    mance induced by, 318–327
  simulations of, 512–516
  volatility/returns relationship induced
    by, 314–318
  See also disappearance events; *and
    ch. 14–15*
survivorship bias. *See* survival bias
Sweden
  historical market performance, 33, 342–
    343, 346, 348, 354, 373
  market founding date, 369
Switzerland
  effects of WWII on market, 350
  historical market performance, 342,
    343, 346, 348, 354, 373
  market founding date, 369

Taiwan
  historical market performance, 389, 390
  IFC coverage information, 389

  market founding date, 369
  risk and return characteristics of, 390
tâtonnement process, 199 nn. 3, 10
tax code
  and dividend distribution, 230 n. 15
taxability, 194
  on various asset classes, 197, 198
Thailand
  historical market performance, 389, 390
  IFC coverage information, 389
  market founding date, 369
  risk and return characteristics of, 390
Theory of Investment Value, The (Williams),
  29
transaction costs. *See* search and transaction costs
Turkey
  historical market performance, 389, 390
  IFC coverage information, 389
  market founding date, 369
  risk and return characteristics of, 390

U.S. government agency issues, 108
  aggregate value of: (1947–1978), 112–
    113, 117–118; (1959–1984), 146
  correlation with other world/U.S. secu-
    rities, 158–161
  cumulative wealth indices for: (1947–
    1978), 125–126; (1959–1984), 153
  returns on: (1947–1978), 121–122, 127,
    128, 131–132, 134; (1959/60–1984),
    150, 156, 164–165; (1976–2001),
    129, 157; in excess of U.S. T-bills
    (1947–1978), 128, 133
U.S. government bonds
  aggregate value of: (1947–1978), 112–
    113, 114, 127; (1959–1984), 146;
    (1984), 142–143
  correlation with other world/U.S. secu-
    rities, 158–161
  cumulative wealth indices for: (1947–
    1978), 125–126; (1959–1984), 153
  estimated VAR and OLS coefficients on,
    272–273
  index of year-end cumulative wealth rel-
    atives (1925–1974), 56–57
  low default risk of, 44
  in matrix of U.S. capital market returns
    (1947–1978), 131–132

returns on: (1792–2004), 35; (1926–1974, *see ch. 11*); (1926–1987), 178; (1926–2004), 35; (1947–1978), 121–122, 128; (1960–1984), 144, 150, 156; (1976–2000/01), 157, 268; correlations with other asset class returns (1971–1987), 182; (1976–2001), 129; in excess of U.S. T-bills: (1925–1974), 55, 56–57; (1959–1984), 162–163; forecast vs. realized (1976–2000), 251, 254; predicted (1999–2025), 268–269; regressed on U.S. inflation, 164–165; with short- vs. long-horizon input frontiers *(see ch. 13)*

simulations of returns on (1976–2000, *see ch. 11)*

taxation history of, 44

yield curve for, 239–240, 245–247

See also U.S. Treasury bonds

U.S. government notes

  aggregate value of: (1959–1984), 146; (1984), 142–143

  cumulative wealth indices for (1959–1984), 153

  returns on (1960–1984), 150

  See also U.S. Treasury notes

U.S. government securities

  aggregate value of (1947–1978), 112–113, 117–118

  cumulative wealth indices for (1947–1978), 125–126

  returns on: (1947–1978), 121–122, 128; (1976–2001), 129

U.S. market wealth portfolio, theoretical 1947–1978 *(see ch. 4)*

  aggregate value of: (1959–1984), 147; (1984), 141–142; of investable (1984), 142–143

  cumulative wealth indices for (1959–1984), 144, 152–154, 155

  returns on: (1960–1984), 144, 148, 151; (1976–2001), 157; in excess of U.S. T-bills (1959–1984), 162–163

  See also ch. 5

U.S. Treasury bills, 108

  aggregate value of: (1947–1978), 109, 112–113, 117–118; (1959–1984), 147; (1984), 142–143

correlation with other world/U.S. securities, 158–161

cumulative wealth indices for: (1947–1978), 125–126; (1959–1984), 154

estimated VAR and OLS coefficients on, 272–273

index of yearly average of days to maturity (1926–1974), 69

irregularity of issue (1825–1925), 20

pricing characteristics of, 197

returns on: (1926–1974, *see ch. 11*); (1926–1987), 178; (1926–2001), 17; (1926–2004), 35; (1947–1978), 114, 121–122, 127, 128, 130, 131–132, 134; (1959–1984), 164–165; (1960–1984), 151, 156; (1976–2000), 268; (1976–2001), 17, 129, 157; correlations with other asset class returns (1971–1987), 182; forecast vs. realized (1976–2000), 251, 254; predicted (1999–2025), 268–269; with short- vs. long-horizon input frontiers *(see ch. 13)*; simulations of (1976–2000, *see ch. 11)*

U.S. Treasury bonds, 108

  aggregate value of (1947–1978), 112–113, 117–118

  correlation with other world/U.S. securities, 158–161

  cumulative wealth indices for (1947–1978), 125–126

  in matrix of U.S. capital market returns (1947–1978), 127, 131–132

  pricing characteristics of, 197

  returns on: (1947–1978), 121–122, 128, 130, 134; (1959–1984), 164–165; (1960–1984), 144, 156; (1976–2001), 17, 129, 157; in excess of U.S. T-bills (1947–1978), 128, 130, 133

U.S. Treasury issues

  aggregate value of (1947–1978), 112–113, 117–118

  cumulative wealth indices for (1947–1978), 125–126

  returns on: (1947–1978), 121–122; (1976–2001), 129

U.S. Treasury notes, 108

  aggregate value of (1947–1978), 112–113, 117–118

U.S. Treasury notes (*continued*)
  correlation with other world/U.S. securities, 158–161
  cumulative wealth indices for (1947–1978), 125–126
  returns on: (1947–1978), 114, 121–122, 127, 128, 130, 131–132, 134; (1959–1984), 164–165; (1960–1984), 156; (1976–2001), 129, 157; in excess of U.S. T-bills (1947–1978), 128, 133
United Kingdom
  beta of, and recency of emergence, 384
  beta distribution (1871–1992), 513–515
  effect of dividend growth on equity returns (1872–1989), 509–511
  effect of survivorship on real returns (1872–1992), 513–514
  historical market performance, 342, 343, 346, 348, 354, 373
  market founding date, 369
  market history, 432, 433, 495, 511–512, 516 (*see also* London Stock Exchange [LSE], history of)
  market predictability, 495
  regressions on real and nominal equity returns (1871–1992), 507–508
  return and risk for equities (1872–1992), 502–504
  role of dividends in market, 516
  stock return and yield (1927–1992), 511–512
  use of dividend yields in, to forecast returns, 404 (*see also ch. 22*)
United States, 5
  beta of, and length of market history, 383–385
  historical market performance, 32–33, 34, 36, 341–342, 343, 348, 354, 373
  market founding date, 369
  market history, 432, 433, 436 (*see also* New York Stock Exchange [NYSE], history of; *and ch. 1*)
  relative market performance of, 337, 341–342, 345, 354–355, 356–359; and dividend effect, 345–347, 348
Uruguay, 366
  effects of WWII on market, 370

historical market performance, 342, 343, 347, 355
length of market life, 370, 388
market founding date, 369

vector autocorrelation (VAR), 235
  defined, 271
  and dividend yields, 500–501
  and long-horizon forecasts, 271–272
Venezuela, 366
  effects of WWII on market, 370
  historical market performance, 342, 343, 347, 355, 373, 389, 390
  IFC coverage information, 389
  length of market life, 370
  market founding date, 369
  risk and return characteristics of, 390
venture capital
  forecasting standard deviation of returns on, 180–181
  total (world) value of in 1984, 141
volatility
  in emerging vs. developed markets, 374
  and returns, 314–318
  of U.S. vs. theoretical global market, 359

Wholesale Price Index (WPI), discussed, 339
Williams, John Burr, 29, 32, 39–40 n. 9
world equity index, theoretical, 353–360. *See also* world market appreciation index, theoretical
world market appreciation index, theoretical, 337
  constructing, 339–340
  performance of (1921–1996), 356–360
  real stock prices during WWII, 351–352
  relative performance of economies in, 354–355
  time series of portfolio value with respect to market breaks, 351
world market wealth portfolio, theoretical, 138–140
  aggregate value of: (1959–1984), 143–144, 145–147, 148; (1984), 141–142; of investable (1984), 142

bonds, 141, 146, 150, 153, 156, 158–
161, 164–165
cash equivalents, 147, 151, 154, 156,
164–165
components of, 140
constructing, 140–141
cumulative wealth indices of (1959–
1984), 152–154, 155
equities, 141, 142, 144, 145, 149, 152,
156, 157, 164–165
and modern portfolio theory, 140
monetary metals, 141, 142, 144, 147,
151, 154, 156, 157
real estate, 156, 157
returns on: (1960–1984), 144, 148,
149–151, 156; (1976–2001), 157; in
excess of U.S. T-bills (1959–1984),
148, 155, 157, 162–163
security returns correlation matrix, 148,
158–161

See also world equity index, theoretical;
and ch. 5
World War II
effects of on capital markets, 350–353,
362 n. 15, 370. *See also individual
countries,* effects of WWII on market

Yale Investment Office, 272
Yugoslavia
effects of WWII on market, 370
market founding date, 369

Zimbabwe
historical market performance, 389, 390
IFC coverage information, 389
market history, 387
risk and return characteristics of, 390